THE PILLAR NEW TESTAMENT COMMENTARY

General Editor
D. A. CARSON

The Gospel according to MARK

JAMES R. EDWARDS

WILLIAM B. EERDMANS PUBLISHING COMPANY
GRAND RAPIDS, MICHIGAN / CAMBRIDGE, U.K.

APOLLOS
LEICESTER, ENGLAND

© 2002 Wm. B. Eerdmans Publishing Co.
255 Jefferson Ave. S.E., Grand Rapids, Michigan 49503 /
P.O. Box 163, Cambridge CB3 9PU U.K.
All rights reserved

www.eerdmans.com

First published 2002 in the United States of America by
Wm. B. Eerdmans Publishing Co.

and in the United Kingdom by
APOLLOS
38 De Montfort Street, Leicester, England LE1 7GP

Printed in the United States of America

07 06 05 04 03 02   7 6 5 4 3 2 1

Library of Congress Cataloging-in-Publication Data

Edwards, James R.
The Gospel according to Mark / James R. Edwards.
p.   cm.   — (The Pillar New Testament commentary)
Includes bibliographical references and index.
ISBN 0-8028-3734-4 (cloth: alk. paper)
1. Bible. N.T. Mark — Commentaries.
I. Title.   II. Series.

BS2585.3.E39   2002
226.3'07 — dc21
2001040535

British Library Cataloguing in Publication Data

A catalogue record for this book is available from the British Library.

ISBN 0-85111-778-3

Scripture taken from the HOLY BIBLE: NEW INTERNATIONAL VERSION®.
NIV®. Copyright © 1973, 1978, 1984 by International Bible Society. Used by
permission of Zondervan Publishing House.

To my mother,

Mary Eleanor Callison Edwards,

who, in accordance with Hebrews 13:7,

first spoke to me the word of God,

and whose life has been an inspiration to my faith.

Contents

Series Preface

Commentaries have specific aims, and this series is no exception. Designed for pastors and teachers of the Bible, the Pillar commentaries seek above all to make clear the text of Scripture as we have it. The scholars writing these volumes interact with the most important informed contemporary debate, but avoid getting mired in undue technical detail. Their ideal is a blend of rigorous exegesis and exposition, with an eye alert both to biblical theology and the contemporary relevance of the Bible, without confusing the commentary and the sermon.

The rationale for this approach is that the vision of "objective scholarship" (a vain chimera) may actually be profane. God stands over against us; we do not stand in judgment of him. When God speaks to us through his Word, those who profess to know him must respond in an appropriate way, and that is certainly different from a stance in which the scholar projects an image of autonomous distance. Yet this is no surreptitious appeal for uncontrolled subjectivity. The writers of this series aim for an evenhanded openness to the text that is the best kind of "objectivity" of all.

If the text is God's Word, it is appropriate that we respond with reverence, a certain fear, a holy joy, a questing obedience. These values should be reflected in the way Christians write. With these values in place, the Pillar commentaries will be warmly welcomed not only by pastors, teachers, and students, but by general readers as well.

*   *   *   *   *

Good commentaries on the canonical Gospels are particularly difficult to write. The demands are considerable: fine historical sense and theological maturity; working with diverse literary genres; a thorough grasp of both Jewish and Greco-Roman backgrounds; a command of the vast secondary literature without letting that literature dictate the agenda or swamp the reader with endless peripheral details. James Edwards meets these challenges admirably. His commentary reflects a lifetime of study, a quality of judgment that is knowledgeable and sure-footed. To all this he adds a quiet reverence for the text that is both appropriate and edifying. It is a pleasure and an honor to include his commentary in the series.

D. A. CARSON

Author's Preface

The present volume represents a *Lieblingsarbeit* in my scholarly life — a work dear to my heart. This is true not only because of the subject itself but also because of the people to whom it has introduced me. I was first introduced to the academic study of Mark thirty years ago in Professor Eduard Schweizer's New Testament Seminar in Zürich, Switzerland. Schweizer's commentary on Mark had a profound influence on me, and the conversations I enjoyed with Eduard, especially in my frequent visits to his home, remain among the rich memories of my life. When I embarked on Ph.D. studies at Fuller Seminary in the mid-1970s I was fortunate to be able to pursue my studies under another leading Mark scholar, Professor Ralph Martin, whose mastery of both the breadth and details of New Testament scholarship guided me in the completion of my dissertation on the Son of God in the Gospel of Mark. My indebtedness to both these Christian scholars is large and lasting.

For the past twenty years I have taught the Gospel of Mark, first at Jamestown College and now at Whitworth College. In addition, I have taught Mark in seminars for Young Life Institute and Fuller Colorado, as well as in many conferences, lectures, and sermons. The present commentary began to take shape (although in a more modest form) as an aid to my teaching. Although I did not then foresee it, I was fortunate to continue learning about Mark from a different but no less stimulating group of teachers — my students. Over the years I have delighted in the remarkable insights that students and parishioners — some first-semester freshmen and some octogenarians — have contributed to my further understanding of the Gospel of Mark. Along with the sages with whom I have studied, the voices of my many friends in classroom and pew have also shaped this commentary.

I wrote the published form of this commentary at Tyndale House in Cambridge, England, where, from February through August 2000, I spent an eight-month sabbatical generously granted to me by Whitworth College. There the Gospel of Mark again introduced me to a stimulating company of scholars, this time from around the globe. I am grateful to Bruce Winter, Warden of Tyndale House, for permission to pursue my project among the venerable scholars and enviable resources of the library; and to Elizabeth Magba and Kirsty Corrigall, librarians at Tyndale House, who are both long-suffering and skilled at finding misplaced volumes. To David Instone Brewer I am grateful for frequent and generous assistance, especially in computer wizardry. A particular word of thanks is due to Peter Head, who volunteered to read and comment on sections of the manuscript. Two fellow scholars at Tyndale House, George Brunk and Ralph Klein, were more helpful and encouraging to my work than they may have realized. One of the allurements of Tyndale House is morning coffee and afternoon tea with scholars in residence. It was a rare day when the expertise of a scholar, or a bibliographical tip, or an off-hand comment did not expand my understanding of the New Testament and the Gospel of Mark. Among the wider cloud of witnesses to whom I am indebted is D. A. Carson, general editor of the Pillar Series, for his acceptance of me as a walk-on in the series and for his superb scholarly and editorial instincts. I am also grateful to an anonymous donor for a gift that both encouraged and helped finance my sabbatical in Cambridge. The very considerable task of compiling the indexes to this commentary has been ably accomplished by Scott Starbuck, to whom I am sincerely grateful. Finally, I am grateful to the faithful constancy of my wife Jane, who graciously allowed work on this commentary to take precedence over jaunts and journeys in England.

Above all, I am humbly grateful to the Lord for his providence in bringing this commentary to publication in a most remarkable way. Of the scores of New Testament commentary series published today, the Pillar New Testament ideal of first-class exegesis and evangelical warmth is closest to my own aspirations as a scholar of the church.

The format of this commentary follows that of others in the series, with the exception of longer or shorter comments on key terms related to Mark, which I highlight in **bold print**; and of longer excursuses on themes of major importance at designated places in the commentary. In accordance with the purposes of the editors and publishers of the Pillar series, the aim of this volume is to comment on the received text of the Gospel of Mark rather than on hypotheses of its provenance or various schools of its interpretation. The New Testament commentator, especially on the Synoptic Gospels, is heir to a growing number of methodologies of interpretation — some historical, others literary, others philological, others sociological and psychological, and still others political and gender-related. I have sought to employ such methodologies if and when they seemed to me of service in understanding the text of Mark, but I have not endeavored to be an apologist for any of them. My primary objective has been to concentrate on three aspects of the Gospel of Mark that in my judgment are essential to its proper understanding: its *historical* setting and narrative, its *literary* methods, and its *theological* purposes. In discussing these purposes I have endeavored neither to underestimate the intelligence of readers nor to overestimate their knowledge of first-century Palestine, but to expound the Gospel of Mark in such a way that readers may be enabled to see Jesus as God's Son and to follow him as disciples.

JAMES R. EDWARDS

Abbreviations

1 Chr	1 Chronicles
1 Clem.	*1 Clement*
1 Cor	1 Corinthians
1 Enoch	*1 Enoch*
1 Esdr	1 Esdras
1 John	1 John
1 Kgs	1 Kings
1 Macc	1 Maccabees
1 Pet	1 Peter
1QFlor	*Florilegium* of Cave One, Dead Sea Scroll (DSS)
1QM	*War Scroll,* DSS
1QpHab	*Pesher on Habakkuk,* DSS
1QS	*Rule of the Community,* Manual of Discipline, DSS
1QSa	Appendix A *(Rule of the Congregation)* to 1QS, DSS
1 Sam	1 Samuel
1 Thess	1 Thessalonians
1 Tim	1 Timothy
2 Apoc. Bar.	Greek *Apocalypse of Baruch*
2 Apoc. Jas.	*2 Apocalypse of James*
2 Bar.	Syriac *Apocalypse of Baruch*
2 Chr	2 Chronicles
2 Clem.	*2 Clement*
2 Cor	2 Corinthians
2 Esdr	2 Esdras
2 John	2 John
2 Kgs	2 Kings
2 Macc	2 Maccabees

2 Pet	2 Peter
2 Sam	2 Samuel
2 Thess	2 Thessalonians
2 Tim	2 Timothy
3 John	3 John
4 Ezra	4 Ezra
4 Macc	4 Maccabees
4QNah	4QNahum, DSS
4QPrNab	*4Q Prayer of Nabonidus,* DSS
4Q175	*Messianic Anthology,* DSS
11QT	*Temple Scroll,* DSS
AB	Anchor Bible
ABD	*Anchor Bible Dictionary,* 6 vols., ed. D. Freedman
Acts	Acts of the Apostles
Acts John	*Acts of John*
Acts Pet.	*Acts of Peter*
Acts Pil.	*Acts of Pilate*
Acts Thom.	*Acts of Thomas*
Adv. Haer.	Irenaeus, *Against All Heresy*
Ag. Ap.	Josephus, *Against Apion*
AnBib	Analecta biblica
Ann.	Tacitus, *Annals*
Ant.	Josephus, *Antiquities of the Jews*
Ap.	Plato, *Apology*
Ap. Jas.	*Apocryphon of James*
Apoc. Ab.	*Apocalypse of Abraham*
Apoc. Elijah	*Apocalypse of Elijah*
Apoc. Pet.	*Apocalypse of Peter*
Apol.	Justin Martyr, *First Apology*
Aram.	Aramaic
art.	article
Asc. Isa.	*Ascension of Isaiah*
AsiaJournTheol	*Asian Journal of Theology*
As. Mos.	*Assumption of Moses*
ASNU	Acta seminarii neotestamentica upsaliensis
ATANT	Abhandlungen zur Theologie des Alten und Neuen Testaments
BA	*Biblical Archaeologist*
BAG	*A Greek-English Lexicon of the New Testament and Other Early Christian Literature,* ed. W. Bauer, rev. W. Arndt and F. Gingrich, 1967

BAGD	Same volume, ed. W. Bauer, rev. W. Arndt, F. Gingrich, and F. Danker, 1979
BARev	*Biblical Archaeology Review*
Barn.	*Epistle of Barnabas*
BBB	Bonner biblische Beiträge
b. Ber.	*Berakhot*, Babylonian Talmud
BDF	F. Blass, A. Debrunner, and R. Funk, *A Greek Grammar of the New Testament and Other Early Christian Literature*
Bel	Bel and the Dragon
b. Hag.	*Hagigah*, Babylonian Talmud
Ben.	The 18 Benedictions
Bib	*Biblica*
Bib. Ant.	*Biblical Antiquities* (Pseudo-Philo)
BibInt	*Biblical Interpretation*
BibKir	*Bibel und Kirche*
BibLeb	*Bibel und Leben*
BibToday	*The Bible Today*
BibZeit	*Biblische Zeitschrift*
BJRL	*Bulletin of the John Rylands Library*
BJS	Brown Judaic Studies
b. Mo'ed. Q.	*Mo'ed Qatan*, Babylonian Talmud
BN	*Biblische Notizen*
b. Nid.	*Niddah*, Babylonian Talmud
BNTC	Black's New Testament Commentary
b. Pes.	*Pesahim*, Babylonian Talmud
BR	*Biblical Research*
BRev	*Bible Review*
b. Qid.	*Qiddushin*, Babylonian Talmud
b. Sanh.	*Sanhedrin*, Babyonian Talmud
b. Shab.	*Shabbat*, Babylonian Talmud
b. Sot.	*Sotah*, Babylonian Talmud
b. Suk.	*Sukkah*, Babylonian Talmud
b. Ta'an.	*Ta'anit*, Babylonian Talmud
BTB	*Biblical Theology Bulletin*
BTZ	*Berliner Theologische Zeitschrift*
b. Yoma	*Yoma*, Babylonian Talmud
BZNW	Beihefte zur *Zeitschrift für die neutestamentliche Wissenschaft*
c.	about
Cant	Song of Solomon
CBQ	*Catholic Biblical Quarterly*

CD	*Damascus Document,* DSS
cent.	century
cf.	compare
chap(s).	chapter(s)
Col	Colossians
Comm.	*Commentary*
ConB	Coniectanea biblica
Contra Celsum	Origen, *Against Celsus*
CRINT	Compendia Rerum Iudaicarum ad Novum Testamentum
d.	died
Dan	Daniel
Deut	Deuteronomy
Dial. Sav.	*Dialogue of the Savior*
Dial. Trypho	Justin Martyr, *Dialogue with Trypho*
Did.	*Didache*
diss.	dissertation
DSS	Dead Sea Scrolls
Eccl	Ecclesiastes
ed.	edited
EDNT	*Exegetical Dictionary of the New Testament,* 3 vols., ed. H. Balz and G. Schneider
Eg. Pap.	*Egerton Papyrus*
EKKNT	Evangelish-katholischer Kommentar zum Neuen Testament
Ench.	*Enchiridion*
EncJud.	*Encyclopaedia Judaica,* 1971
Eng.	English
Ep. Ap.	*Epistula Apostolorum*
Eph	Ephesians
Epict. Disc.	Arrian, *Discourses of Epictetus*
Ep. Jer.	*Epistle of Jeremiah*
Ep. Pet. Phil.	*Epistle of Peter to Philip*
Ep. Pol. Phil.	*Epistle of Polycarp to the Philippians*
esp.	especially
EstBib	*Estudios Biblicos*
Esth	*Esther*
ETL	*Ephemerides theologicae Lovanienses*
ETR	*Études théologiques et religieuses*
EvT	*Evangelische Theologie*
Exod	Exodus
ExpTim	*Expository Times*

Ezek	Ezekiel
Ezra	Ezra
Gal	Galatians
GeistLeb	*Geist und Leben*
Gen	Genesis
gen.	general
Gk.	Greek
GNT	Grundrisse zum Neuen Testament
Gos. Bart.	*Gospel of Bartholomew*
Gos. Eb.	*Gospel of the Ebionites*
Gos. Eg.	*Gospel of the Egyptians*
Gos. Heb.	*Gospel of the Hebrews*
Gos. Mani	*Gospel of Mani*
Gos. Mary	*Gospel of Mary*
Gos. Naz.	*Gospel of the Nazarenes*
Gos. Nic.	*Gospel of Nicodemus*
Gos. Pet.	*Gospel of Peter*
Gos. Phil.	*Gospel of Philip*
Gos. Pseud.-Matt.	*Gospel of Pseudo-Matthew*
Gos. Thom.	*Gospel of Thomas*
Hab	Habakkuk
Hag	Haggai
HALOT	L. Koehler, W. Baumgartner, and J. J. Stamm, *The Hebrew and Aramaic Lexicon of the Old Testament*, trans. M. E. J. Richardson
HCNT	*A Hellenistic Commentary to the New Testament*, ed. M. Boring, K. Berger, and C. Colpe
Heb	Letter to the Hebrews
Heb.	Hebrew
Herm. Man.	*Shepherd of Hermas, Mandate*
Herm. Sim.	*Shepherd of Hermas, Similitude*
Herm. Vis.	*Shepherd of Hermas, Visions*
Hist.	Tacitus, *Histories*
Hist. Eccl.	Eusebius, *Church History*
HNT	Handbuch zum Neuen Testament
Hos	Hosea
HTKNT	Herders theologischer Kommentar zum Neuen Testament
HTR	*Harvard Theological Review*
Ibid.,	*ibidem,* in the same place
IBS	*Irish Biblical Studies*
ICC	International Critical Commentary

ABBREVIATIONS

IDB	*The Interpreter's Dictionary of the Bible,* 4 vols. plus Sup., ed. G. Buttrick
IEJ	*Israel Exploration Journal*
Ign. *Eph.*	Ignatius, *Letter to the Ephesians*
Ign. *Rom.*	Ignatius, *Letter to the Romans*
Ign. *Trall.*	Ignatius, *Letter to the Trallians*
Int	*Interpretation*
Isa	Isaiah
JAMA	*Journal of the American Medical Association*
Jas	James
j. Ber.	*Berakhot,* Jerusalem Talmud
JBL	*Journal of Biblical Literature*
JBTh	*Jahrbuch für Biblische Theologie*
Jdt	Judith
Jer	Jeremiah
JerusalemPersp	*Jerusalem Perspective*
JETS	*Journal of the Evangelical Theological Society*
JJS	*Journal of Jewish Studies*
j. Kil.	*Kil'ayim,* Jerusalem Talmud
Job	Job
Joel	Joel
John	John
Jonah	Jonah
Jos. Asen.	*Joseph and Aseneth*
Josh	Joshua
JR	*Journal of Religion*
JSNT	*Journal for the Study of the New Testament*
JSNTSup	*Journal for the Study of the New Testament, Supplement Series*
JSP	*Journal for the Study of the Pseudepigrapha*
JTS	*Journal of Theological Studies*
Jub.	*Jubilees*
Jude	Jude
Judg	Judges
KEK	Kritisch-exegetischer Kommentar über das Neue Testament (Meyer-Kommentar)
Lam	Lamentations
Lat.	Latin
LCL	Loeb Classical Library
LEC	Library of Early Christianity
Lev	Leviticus
Life	Josephus, *Life*

Life Apoll.	Philostratus, *Life of Apollonius*
lit.	literally
log.	Logion, reading
LSJ	*A Greek-English Lexicon*, ed. H. Liddell, R. Scott, J. Jones, and R. McKenzie
Luke	Luke
LXX	Septuagint, Gk. trans. of Heb. OT
m. Avot	*Avot*, Mishnah
Mal	Malachi
Mark	Mark
Mart. Isa.	*Martyrdom of Isaiah*
Mart. Pol.	*Martyrdom of Polycarp*
Matt	Matthew
m. B. Bat.	*Bava Batra*, Mishnah
m. Ber.	*Berakhot*, Mishnah
m. B. Qam.	*Bava Qamma*, Mishnah
Mek. Exod.	*Mekilta on Exodus*
Mem. Apost.	*Memoria Apostolorum*
m. Git.	*Gittin*, Mishnah
m. Hag.	*Hagiga*, Mishnah
m. Hul.	*Hullin*, Mishnah
m. Kel.	*Kelim*, Mishnah
m. Ker.	*Keritot*, Mishnah
m. Ket.	*Ketubbot*, Mishnah
m. Kil.	*Kilayim*, Mishnah
m. Mid.	*Middot*, Mishnah
m. Miqw.	*Mikwa'ot*, Mishnah
m. Ned.	*Nedarim*, Mishnah
m. Neg.	*Negaim*, Mishnah
m. Pes.	*Pesahim*, Mishnah
m. Ohal.	*Ohalot*, Mishnah
Mic	Micah
m. Rosh HaSh.	*Rosh HaShana*, Mishnah
m. Sanh.	*Sanhedrin*, Mishnah
m. Shab.	*Shabbat*, Mishnah
m. Sheq.	*Sheqalim*, Mishnah
m. Sot.	*Sotah*, Mishnah
m. Suk.	*Sukkah*, Mishnah
MT	Masoretic Text
m. Ta'an.	*Ta'anit*, Mishnah
m. Teh.	*Teharot*, Mishnah
m. Yad.	*Yadayim*, Mishnah

m. Yoma	*Yoma*, Mishnah
m. Zav.	*Zavim*, Mishnah
m. Zev.	*Zevahim*, Mishnah
n.	note
Nah	Nahum
n.d.	no date
Neh	Nehemiah
NHL	*Nag Hammadi Library*, ed. J. Robinson
Neot	*Neotestamentica*
NIBC	New International Biblical Commentary
NICNT	New International Commentary on the New Testament
NIDNTT	*New International Dictionary of New Testament Theology*, 3 vols., ed. C. Brown
NotesTrans	*Notes on Translation*
NovT	*Novum Testamentum*
nr.	number
NT	New Testament
NTApoc	*New Testament Apocrypha*, rev. ed., 2 vols., ed. W. Schneemelcher, trans. R. Mcl. Wilson
NTD	Das Neue Testament Deutsch
NTG	New Testament Guides
NTS	*New Testament Studies*
NTTS	New Testament Tools and Studies
Num	Numbers
Obad	Obadiah
Odes Sol.	*Odes of Solomon*
OT	Old Testament
OTP	*Old Testament Pseudepigrapha*, 2 vols., ed. J. Charlesworth
p.(p).	page(s)
Pan.	Epiphanius, *Refutation of All Heresies*
par.	parallel
Phd.	Plato, *Phaedo*
Phil	Philippians
Pol. *Phil.*	Polycarp, *Epistle to the Philippians*
Phlm	Philemon
pl.	plural
P.Oxy.	Oxyrhynchus Papyrus
Pr Azar	Prayer of Azariah
Pr Man	Prayer of Manasseh
Prot. Jas.	*Protoevangelium of James*

Prov	Proverbs
Ps (*pl.*: Pss)	Psalm(s)
Pss. Sol.	*Psalms of Solomon*
Quest. Bart.	*The Questions of Bartimaeus*
Rab. Exod.	*Rabbah on Exodus*
RB	*Revue Biblique*
Refut. Om. Haer.	Hippolytus, *Refutation of All Heresies*
repr.	reprinted
ResQ	*Restoration Quarterly*
Rev	Revelation
rev.	revised
RevBib	*Revue biblique*
RevistB	*Revista Biblica*
RevQ	*Revue de Qumran*
RIDA	*Revue internationale des droits de l'antiquité*
Rom	Romans
Ruth	Ruth
SBLDS	Society of Biblical Literature Dissertation Series
SBLSS	Society of Biblical Literature Semeia Studies
SBT	Studies in Biblical Theology
ScEs	*Science et Esprit*
Sib. Or.	*Sibylline Oracles*
Sir	Ecclesiasticus, or Wisdom of Jesus Ben Sira
SJLA	Studies in Judaism in Late Antiquity
SJT	*Scottish Journal of Theology*
SNTSMS	Society for New Testament Studies Monograph Series
SNT(SU)	Studien zum Neuen Testament (und seiner Umwelt)
Spec. Leg.	Philo, *Special Laws*
Str-B	*Kommentar zum Neuen Testament aus dem Talmud und Midrasch*, 6 vols., eds. H. Strack and P. Billerbeck
Sus	Susannah
T. Adam	*Testament of Adam*
TBei	*Theologische Beiträge*
T. Benj.	*Testament of Benjamin*
t. Ber.	*Berakhot*, Tosefta
TCGNT	B. Metzger, *A Textual Commentary on the Greek New Testament*
T. Dan	*Testament of Dan*
TDNT	*Theological Dictionary of the New Testament*, 9 vols., ed. G. Kittel and G. Friedrich, trans. G. Bromiley

ABBREVIATIONS

TDOT	*Theological Dictionary of the Old Testament*, 8 vols., ed. G. Botterweck and H. Ringgren
Testim. Truth	*The Testimony of Truth*
Tg. Ket. Qoh.	*Targum of the Writings, Qohelet*
TGl	*Theologie und Glaube*
Tg. Jon.	*Targum Jonathan*
THKNT	Theologische Handkommentar zum Neuen Testament
Thom. Cont.	*The Book of Thomas the Contender*
Tijd. Theol	*Tijdschrift voor Theologie*
T. Iss.	*Testament of Issachar*
Titus	Titus
T. Jud.	*Testament of Judah*
T. Levi	*Testament of Levi*
Tob	Tobit
trans.	translated
Treat. Res.	*Treatise on the Resurrection*
Treat. Seth	*The Second Treatise of the Great Seth*
T. Sol.	*Testament of Solomon*
TToday	*Theology Today*
TynBul	*The Tyndale Bulletin*
TZ	*Theologische Zeitschrift*
T. Zeb.	*Testament of Zebulun*
v(v).	verse(s)
Vita Apol.	Philostratus, *Life of Apollonius*
War	Josephus, *The Jewish War*
WBC	Word Biblical Commentary
WordWorld	*Word and World*
Wis	Wisdom of Solomon
WUNT	Wissenschaftliche Untersuchungen zum Neuen Testament
Zech	Zechariah
Zeph	Zephaniah
ZNW	*Zeitschrift für die neutestamentliche Wissenschaft*
ZTK	*Zeitschrift für Theologie und Kirche*

Frequently Cited Works

Achtemeier, Paul. *Mark*. Proclamation Commentaries. Philadelphia: Fortress Press, 1975.

Branscomb, B. H. *The Gospel of Mark*. London: Hodder and Stoughton, 1941.

Cranfield, C. E. B. *The Gospel According to Saint Mark*. Cambridge: University Press, 1974.

Drewermann, Eugen. *Das Markusevangelium. Erster Teil: Mk 1,1 bis 9,13*. Olten und Freiburg im Breisgau: Walter Verlag, 1989.

Grundmann, Walter. *Das Evangelium nach Markus*. 3. Auflage. THKNT. Berlin: Evangelische Verlagsanstalt, 1968.

Gnilka, Joachim. *Das Evangelium nach Markus*. 2 Teile. EKKNT II/1-2. Zürich, Einsiedeln, Köln: Benziger; Neukirchener Verlag, 1978.

Guelich, Robert A. *Mark 1–8:26*. WBC 34a. Dallas: Word Books, 1989.

Gundry, Robert. *Mark: A Commentary on His Apology for the Cross*. Grand Rapids: Eerdmans, 1993.

Haenchen, Ernst. *Der Weg Jesu. Eine Erklärung des Markus-Evangeliums und der kanonischen Parallelen*. 2. Durchgesehene und verbesserte Auflage. Berlin: Walter de Gruyter & Co., 1968.

Hengel, Martin. *Studies in the Gospel of Mark*. Trans. J. Bowden. Philadelphia: Fortress Press, 1985.

Hooker, Morna D. *A Commentary on the Gospel According to St Mark*. London: A & C Black, 1991.

Hurtado, Larry W. *Mark*. NIBC. Peabody: Hendrickson, 1989.

Klostermann, Erich. *Das Markusevangelium*. HNT. Tübingen: J. C. B. Mohr (Paul Siebeck), 1936.

Lagrange, M.-J. *Évangile selon Saint Marc*. Édition Corrigée et Augmentée. Paris: J. Gabalda, 1947.

Lane, William. *The Gospel According to Mark.* NICNT. Grand Rapids: Eerdmans, 1974.

Lohmeyer, Ernst. *Das Evangelium des Markus.* KEK. Göttingen: Vandenhoeck & Ruprecht, 1953.

Legasse, Simon. *L'Evangile de Marc.* Lectio Divina Commentaires 5. Paris: Les Editions du Cerf, 1997.

Lührmann, Dieter. *Das Markusevangelium.* HNT. Tübingen: J. C. B. Mohr (Paul Siebeck), 1987.

Nineham, D. E. *The Gospel of St Mark.* London: Adam & Charles Black, 1963.

Pesch, Rudolph. *Das Markusevangelium.* 2 Teile. HTKNT. Freibourg, Basel, Wien: Herder, 1976, 1977.

Pixner, Bargil, O.S.B. *Mit Jesus in Jerusalem.* Seine ersten und letzten Tage in Jerusalem. Rosh Pina: Corazin Publishing, 1996.

———. *With Jesus Through Galilee According to the Fifth Gospel.* Trans. C. Botha and D. Foster. Rosh Pina: Corazin Publishing, 1992.

Schlatter, Adolf. *Der Evangelist Matthäus. Seine Sprache, sein Ziel, seine Selbständigkeit.* Stuttgart: Calwer Verlag, 1959.

———. *Die Evangelien nach Markus und Lukas.* Erläuterungen zum Neuen Testament. Stuttgart: Calwer Verlag, 1954.

Schürer, Emil. *The History of the Jewish People in the Age of Jesus Christ (175 B.C.–A.D. 135).* Rev. and ed. G. Vermes and F. Millar. 3 vols. Edinburgh: T. & T. Clark, 1973-87.

Schweizer, Eduard. *The Good News According to Mark.* Trans. D. Madvig. London: SPCK, 1971.

Swete, Henry Barclay. *The Gospel According to St Mark.*[3] London: Macmillan, 1909.

Taylor, Vincent. *The Gospel According to St. Mark.*[2] New York: St. Martin's Press, 1966.

Zahn, Theodor. *Introduction to the New Testament.* Trans. M. Jacobus and C. Thayer. 3 vols. Edinburgh: T. & T. Clark, 1901.

Introduction

1. HISTORY OF THE INTERPRETATION OF MARK

Until modern times the Gospel of Mark has received considerably less attention than the other three Gospels. In comparison to John with its lofty theology, Matthew with its narrative structure, or Luke with its inimitable parables and stories, Mark has often been judged as a rather artless and pedestrian Gospel, even by scholars.[1] The eclipse of Mark goes all the way back to the dawn of the Gospel tradition, which, according to the general consensus of the church fathers, ascribed the earliest Gospel to Matthew.[2] Since Mark contains only three pericopes that are not found in either Matthew or Luke, or both (Mark 4:26-29; 7:31-37; 8:22-26), from the middle of the second century onward (e.g., Irenaeus, *Adv. Haer.* 3.1.1)

1. G. Dehn, *Der Gottessohn. Eine Einführung in das Evangelium des Markus* (Hamburg: Im Furche-Verlag, 1953), 18, declared that Mark was "neither a historian nor an author. He assembled his material in the simplest manner thinkable." R. Bultmann, *The History of the Synoptic Tradition,* trans. J. Marsh (New York: Harper & Row, 1963), 350, wrote that "Mark is not sufficiently master of his material to be able to venture on a systematic construction himself." E. Trocmé, *The Formation of the Gospel According to Mark,* trans. P. Gaughan (London: SPCK, 1975), 72, scoffed at Mark's literary achievement: "The point is settled: the author of Mark was a clumsy writer unworthy of mention in any history of literature."

2. Six fathers — Irenaeus, Clement of Alexandria, Origen, Eusebius of Caesarea, Epiphanius, and Jerome (and seven if one counts Papias) — state that the earliest record of Matthew was written in Hebrew (although no Hebrew Gospel text is extant today). The Islamic Hadith also preserves a tradition of an early Hebrew Gospel: "Kadija then accompanied [Muhammad] to her cousin Waraqa ibn Naufal ibn Asad ibn 'abdul 'Uzza, who, during the Pre-Islamic period became a Christian and used to write the writing with Hebrew letters. He would write from the Gospel in Hebrew as much as Allah wished him to write" (*Sahih al-Bukhari* 1:3).

1

Mark was placed second (and sometimes fourth) in the canon as a rather inferior abridgment of Matthew. Throughout the patristic period quotations from the Gospels were cited from Matthew and John, in that order; from Luke as a distant third; and from Mark last and only rarely. A dictum of Augustine with regard to the Gospel of Mark typifies not only the judgment of the fathers before him but also that of the succeeding centuries until the age of the Enlightenment: "Mark imitated Matthew like a lackey (Lat. *pedisequus*) and is regarded as his abbreviator."[3] As a consequence of this view, the Christian church has historically derived its picture of Jesus primarily from the Gospel of Matthew. Because Matthew appears first in the NT canon, and because it emphasizes Jesus' fulfillment of OT promises, for seventeen centuries the church regarded Matthew as the earliest and most reliable Gospel. Readings for Sundays and holy days were taken from Matthew, the other Gospels being utilized generally only when Matthew was thought to be deficient.

Opinion on the value of Mark underwent a radical shift in the first half of the nineteenth century when, on the basis of careful internal investigations of the first three Gospels, scholars[4] hypothesized that Mark was not a slavish follower of Matthew but rather the *earliest* of the Gospels, and a primary source for the Gospels of Matthew and Luke. This reevaluation has radically affected scholarly interest in Mark. For the past century and a half, Mark has received attention of celebrity proportions, and the resultant crest of scholarship on the Second Gospel is so prolific that no one scholar can claim to have read it all, let alone mastered it all. The theory of Markan priority, although not uncontested, continues to be held by a majority of scholars today, the present author included. The relationship of the four Gospels — and especially the first three — poses one of the most difficult problems in the history of ideas and cannot be rehearsed in this commentary.[5] The most that can be done in the present volume with respect to Markan priority is to draw attention to the significant number of passages where Mark reasonably can be supposed to precede, and to have influenced, the other Synoptic Gospels, and Matthew in particular. The spate of recent scholarship devoted to Mark has succeeded in laying to rest, I believe, the pejorative judgments of earlier

---

3. *De Consensu Evangeliorum* 1.2.4.

4. K. Lachmann, 1835; C. H. Weisse and C. G. Wilke, 1838; H. J. Holtzmann, 1863; B. Weiss, 1886; B. H. Streeter, 1924.

5. H.-H. Stoldt, *History and Criticism of the Marcan Hypothesis* (Macon, Ga.: Mercer University Press/Edinburgh: T. & T. Clark, 1980), 1: "The critical analysis of the sources of the Gospel is justifiably regarded as one of the most difficult research problems in the history of ideas. . . . One can truly say that no other enterprise in the history of ideas has been subjected to anywhere near the same degree of scholarly scrutiny."

scholars that Mark was a clumsy and artless writer. The position represented in this commentary is that Mark was a skilled literary artist and theologian. Although the style of Mark approximates everyday spoken Greek rather than affecting high literary quality, the Gospel nevertheless displays considerable sophistication in literary intention and design, as is evinced by Mark's sandwich technique, use of irony, and special motifs of insiders-outsiders, command to silence, and the journey. These and other literary conventions are employed by the author of the Second Gospel in order to portray a profoundly theological conception of Jesus as the authoritative yet suffering Son of God.

2. AUTHORSHIP AND PLACE OF COMPOSITION

Like the other canonical Gospels, the Gospel of Mark nowhere identifies its author, nor even, as is the case with Luke (1:1-4) and John (20:30-31), the occasion of writing. The titles of each of the four Gospels, which were assigned on the basis of church tradition, appear in the first half of the second century. The normal nomenclature is "Gospel According to Matthew" (Gk. *euangelion kata Maththaion*), "Gospel According to Mark" (Gk. *euangelion kata Markon*), and so on. With reference to the Gospel tradition, the early church used the word for "Gospel" (Gk. *euangelion*) regularly in the singular and rarely in the plural, indicating that it conceived of the Gospel tradition as a unity, that is, the *one* Gospel in four versions.[6]

The first reference to the author and circumstance of the Second Gospel comes from Papias, bishop of Hierapolis in Asia Minor, in a work entitled *Exegesis of the Lord's Oracles,* composed sometime prior to Papias's death in A.D. 130.[7] Although the *Exegesis* has since been lost, Papias's testimony has been preserved by Eusebius in the following version:

> Mark became Peter's interpreter and wrote accurately all that he remembered, not, indeed, in order, of the things said or done by the Lord. For Mark had not heard the Lord, nor had he followed him, but later on, as I said, followed Peter, who used to give teaching as necessity demanded but not making, as it were, an arrangement of the Lord's oracles, so that Mark did nothing wrong in thus writing down single

6. M. Hengel, *Studies in the Gospel of Mark,* trans. J. Bowden (Philadelphia: Fortress Press, 1985), 64-69; M. Hengel, *The Four Gospels and the One Gospel of Jesus Christ,* trans. J. Bowden (Harrisburg: Trinity Press International, 2000), 34-115.

7. W. R. Schoedel, "Papias," *ABD* 5.140, places Papias's literary activity in approximately 110.

points as he remembered them. For to one thing he gave attention, to leave out nothing of what he had heard and to make no false statements in them. (*Hist. Eccl.* 3.39.15)

Although this testimony was penned in the early fourth century, it comes from sources two centuries earlier and represents very reliable tradition. Eusebius derives the above tradition not only from Papias but also from the respected second-century church father Irenaeus. Eusebius includes a lengthy preface to the Papias testimony, noting that although the latter had not heard the apostles directly, he had made careful inquiry into the origins of the Gospel tradition and had received the above information through their immediate successors, a John the Elder and a certain Aristion, who were disciples of the apostle John. This dates the Papias tradition to between 90 and 100. The reliability of the Eusebius quotation is further enhanced by the fact that, in this instance, Eusebius is willing to trust the testimony of a man whom he did not automatically regard as a dependable source.[8]

The salient points of the Papias testimony are that the Second Gospel derives from Mark, who, although not an apostle, was a faithful interpreter of the apostle Peter's testimony. Papias further testifies that Mark wrote accurately and endeavored to make no false statements; that he wrote fully in setting down all he remembered; but that he did not write in entirely chronological order. The last statement shows that Papias was aware that, at least in some circles, Mark was being criticized for presenting a variant chronology of Jesus' life. That criticism probably derives from the fact that Mark's chronology departs in certain particulars from the Gospel of John, to whom the protégés of Papias adhered.

The reference to Peter "teaching as necessity demanded" is elaborated in a further testimony of Eusebius, the substance of which he attributes to the late-second-century church father, Clement of Alexandria:

When Peter had publicly preached the word at Rome, and by the Spirit had proclaimed the Gospel, that those present, who were many, exhorted Mark, as one who had followed [Peter] for a long time and remembered what had been spoken, to make a record of what was said; and that he did this, and distributed the Gospel among those that asked him. (*Hist. Eccl.* 6.14.6-7)

---

8. In one instance Eusebius dismisses Papias as "a man of very little intelligence, as is clear from his books" (*Hist. Eccl.* 3.39.13). Eusebius's willingness to trust the Papias tradition related to Mark indicates that he has reason to do so in spite of his estimate of Papias's reputation. For the whole discussion, see *Hist. Eccl.* 3.39.1-17.

To this account we may add the corroborating testimony of Irenaeus in the middle of the second century that after Peter and Paul had preached and laid the foundations of the church in Rome, "Mark, the disciple and interpreter of Peter, also himself handed on in writing the things that had been preached by Peter" (*Adv. Haer.* 3.1.1). The tradition that Peter was a key source for Mark's Gospel — indeed, that the Second Gospel was in many respects "Peter's memoirs" — found, as far as we know, unanimous agreement in the early church.[9] Thus, from a variety of traditions from the end of the first century onward we see a complementary testimony that the author of the Second Gospel is Mark, the interpreter of Peter, who composed the Gospel in Rome.

The Mark under consideration is evidently John Mark, son of a woman named Mary, in whose house the early church gathered in Jerusalem (Acts 12:12). The same dwelling was apparently the site of the Last Supper (Acts 1:13-14; Mark 14:14).[10] In the NT John Mark appears only in association with more prominent personalities and events. He accompanied Barnabas and Saul as an assistant on the first missionary journey (Acts 12:25; 13:4), evidently being responsible for travel arrangements, food, and lodging. At Perga he quit the journey for undisclosed reasons (Acts 13:13). The question whether Mark should participate in the second missionary journey in approximately A.D. 50 caused a rift between Paul and Barnabas: Paul, considering Mark's desertion of the first journey unjustifiable and being unwilling to take him on a second journey, took Silas and returned to Asia Minor; whereas Barnabas returned to Cyprus with Mark (Acts 15:37-41). John Mark is not heard from again until a decade later, when scattered references show him reconciled to Paul (Col 4:10; Phlm 24; 2 Tim 4:11). A final NT reference shows him laboring with Peter

9. The Anti-Marcionite Prologue; Justin Martyr, *Dial. Trypho* 106; Irenaeus, *Adv. Haer.* 3.1.1; Hippolytus, on 1 Pet 5:13; Clement of Alexandria (cited in Eusebius, *Hist. Eccl.* 6.14.6); Origen (cited in Eusebius, *Hist. Eccl.* 6.25.5); Jerome, *Comm. in Matt., Prooemium* 6). Further, see Eusebius, *Hist. Eccl.* 2.15; 5.8.2. See the material gathered in V. Taylor, *The Gospel According to St. Mark*, 1-8; W. Grundmann, *Das Evangelium nach Markus*, 22-23; and H. Koester, *Ancient Christian Gospels: Their History and Development* (Philadelphia: Trinity Press International, 1992), 289-90. To the above testimonies could also be added that of the Muratorian Canon, which contains a list of books recognized for their authority in Rome in the period 170-90. The initial part of the Muratorian Canon has been lost, the extant portion containing only a fragment of the final statement about Mark ("at which, however, he was present, and so he has set it down"). Despite its incompleteness, the above phrase is reasonably explained, as in the traditions preserved by Papias, Irenaeus, and Eusebius, as a reference to Mark's attendance on Peter's preaching, i.e., "at Peter's preaching, however, Mark was present and has set it down in writing."

10. Grundmann, *Das Evangelium nach Markus*, 21, suggests that the young man carrying the water jug in Mark 14:13 was Mark, the author of the Gospel. There is no further evidence either for or against this intriguing suggestion.

in Rome (1 Pet 5:13). According to patristic tradition, Mark evangelized in Egypt and there established churches characterized by asceticism and philosophic rigor, eventually becoming the first bishop of Alexandria (Eusebius, *Hist. Eccl.* 2.16).

Although we cannot prove that John Mark was the author of the Second Gospel, the weight of evidence rests firmly in his favor. The Gospel has numerous characteristics of an eyewitness account, and we shall have repeated occasion in the commentary to show where Mark's story plausibly relies on Peter's testimony. No early church tradition and no church father ascribes the Gospel to anyone other than Mark. Since books of the NT normally required authorship by an apostle to qualify for acceptance into the canon, it is unlikely that the early church would have assigned a gospel to a minor figure like John Mark, whose name appears in no apostolic list, unless he were its author. The unelaborated title "The Gospel According to Mark" suggests the only Mark known to us in the NT — John Mark.[11]

3. DATE

The date of the Gospel of Mark is as obscure as is its author. Nowhere does Mark, or any of the canonical Gospels, give specific information by which it can be dated. An approximate date of composition rests on a combination of what external sources report and what internal evidence within the Gospel suggests with respect to dating. In both cases the evidence is limited, and hence conclusions about the date of the Second Gospel must be tentative.

With respect to external evidence, Irenaeus reports that Mark did not reduce the Gospel to writing until after the "exodus" (Gk. *exodos*) of the apostles Peter and Paul in Rome (*Adv. Haer.* 3.1.1). The use of "exodus" in the passage connotes the death of Peter and Paul (so, too, the use of the word in 2 Pet 1:15; and Eusebius, *Hist. Eccl.* 5.8.2). This is confirmed by the testimony of the Anti-Marcionite Prologue — a source contempo-

---

11. Taylor, *The Gospel According to St. Mark,* 7, concludes a full review of ancient testimonies to the Gospel of Mark thus: "In sum, we may say that, from the beginning of the second century, the external evidence agrees in ascribing the authorship of the Gospel to Mark, 'the interpreter of Peter,' and . . . in assigning its place of composition to Rome." Likewise, J. Wenham, *Reading Matthew, Mark and Luke* (Downers Grove: InterVarsity Press, 1992), 142: "All these testimonies point to a solid core of tradition, which makes Mark the author of the gospel, which makes him a fellow-worker with Peter, and which makes his book a faithful record of what that apostle taught in Rome."

rary with Irenaeus, if not earlier — which explicitly mentions the death of Peter prior to Mark's composition of the Gospel (Lat. *post excessionem ipsius Petri*). This tradition is not unanimous, however, for two third-century fathers, Clement of Alexandria (Eusebius, *Hist. Eccl.* 6.14.6-7; 2.15.2) and Origen (Eusebius, *Hist. Eccl.* 6.25.5), while silent with respect to Paul, report that Mark composed the Gospel in Rome *during* Peter's lifetime. It is no longer possible to judge which of these two traditions is correct, but combined external evidence, at any rate, locates the composition of Mark toward the end of Peter's life or shortly thereafter. Early church tradition is unanimous that Peter died during the latter years of Nero's reign, who ruled from 54 to 68. External evidence thus suggests a date for Mark in the mid to late 60s of the first century.

Arguments from internal evidence for the dating of Mark rest on three and perhaps four possible relevant data. First, Mark's emphasis on Jesus as the *suffering* Son of God, and the concomitant emphasis on suffering *discipleship* (8:31–9:1; 13:3-13), suggest that the Second Gospel was written to Christians undergoing persecution. We know of two persecutions during the decades following Jesus' crucifixion, the first being Caligula's attempt to erect a statue of himself in the guise of Zeus in the temple of Jerusalem (Josephus, *Ant.* 18.261-309). Caligula's insane ambition was potentially catastrophic, but owing to his murder in A.D. 41 the whole affair was averted. The second persecution, both actual and barbaric, occurred under Nero in Rome. Seeking a scapegoat for the fire in Rome — a fire that the Roman historian Tacitus blamed on the orders of Nero himself — the emperor fastened the blamed on Christians and subjected them to the most gruesome horrors (Tacitus, *Annals* 15.44). The Roman conflagration occurred in the year 64, with Nero's persecution of Christians following soon thereafter. This coincides with both the place and approximate dating of Mark suggested by external evidence, and lends plausible support to the inference that the backdrop of persecution in Mark was the pogrom of Nero, under whom Christians experienced their first official persecution.

A second datum relevant to the dating of Mark is the statement in 13:14 about "'the abomination that causes desolation' standing where it does not belong." The Greek word for "standing" *(hestēkota)* is in the masculine gender, which has suggested to many commentators that the statement is an enigmatic reference to the destruction of the temple by Titus in A.D. 70. If this suggestion could be established, then the composition of Mark would obviously fall after that date. But it is very doubtful that the suggestion can be established. A comparison of the enigmatic reference in 13:14 with Josephus's detailed description of the capture and destruction of the temple in book 6 of *The Jewish War* finds no certain parallels and several actual disagreements. A climactic entry of the victorious Titus into the destroyed temple is nowhere narrated by Josephus in a way reminiscent of 13:14 (see *War* 6.409-13). On the other hand, Josephus repeatedly emphasizes the destruction of the temple by fire, which finds no mention in Mark 13. Above all, the reference to flee to the hills when "the abomination that causes desolation" is seen standing where it should not can scarcely refer to the Roman siege, for when Titus entered Jerusalem it had long been surrounded by the Roman siege wall, the *circumvallatio*, making flight from Jerusalem a virtual impossibility. The ambiguity of 13:14 is rather puzzling if Mark were composing his Gospel after the actual fall of Jerusalem. If Mark knew of the fall of Jerusalem, one would expect a more obvious correlation with the Roman siege, as is apparent in Luke 21:20, 24, for example. The evidence related to Mark 13:14 thus suggests a time prior to the fall of Jerusalem in 70.[12]

A third piece of evidence may perhaps be concealed in the opaque reference in the temptation scene to Jesus' being "with the wild animals" (1:13). This phrase is without any obvious parallel in the Bible and has not yet been satisfactorily explained. I am inclined to see in the phrase a veiled reference to the Neronian persecution, in particular to the state of affairs later described in Tacitus's statement that Christians were "covered with the skins of wild beasts and torn to pieces by dogs" (*Annals* 15.44). Given the above arguments for the Neronian persecution as the backdrop of Mark, it is not implausible that Mark includes a reference to wild beasts in the temptation account of Jesus in order to encourage Roman Christians undergoing Nero's atrocities that Jesus himself faced wild beasts — and in so doing was ministered to by angels.

A fourth possible piece of evidence relevant to the composition of Mark comes from the Roman rhetorician Quintilian, who lived in Rome from the brief reign of Galba (A.D. 68) through the reign of Domitian (81-96). In book 1 of his *Institutio Oratorio*, which is devoted to childhood education, Quintilian makes a passing reference to young students who are precocious but without maturity and depth. The reference is curiously reminiscent of the parable of the sower (Mark 4:3-9, par.) and the parable of the growing seed (Mark 4:26-29), the latter of which is unique to Mark.[13] At the time Quintilian was writing the *Institutio* he was tutor to

---

12. See further discussion of the issue at 13:14, plus Hengel, *Studies in the Gospel of Mark*, 18.

13. "Non multum praestant, sed cito; non subest uera uis nec penitus inmissis radicibus nititur, ut quae summo solo sparsa sund semina celerius se effundunt et imitatae spicas herbulae inanibus aristis ante messem flauescunt. Placent haec annis comparata; deinde stat profectus, admiratio decrescit" (*Institutio Oratorio* 1.3.5). H. E. Butler (LCL; 1963) translates the above as follows: "They have no real power, and what

two young princes, the sons of Domitilla, niece of Domitian, and her husband Clemens. "All we know about Quintilian goes to show that he would do his best to keep in close relation with the parents of his charges," writes F. H. Colson.[14] Quintilian's dutifulness in this instance is significant, for the mother of the boys (and perhaps the father as well) was a professed Christian. The affinities of Quintilian's metaphor with two stories about horticulture in the Gospels, one of which occurs only in Mark, may suggest that the rhetorician, perhaps through Domitilla and Clemens, had prior acquaintance with the Gospel of Mark.[15] Although this possibility does not allow us to further the degree of precision regarding the date of the Second Gospel, it may lend corroborative evidence that Mark was known in Rome sometime after 68.

In summary, although none of the foregoing arguments and evidence is conclusive in itself, a combination of external and internal data appears to point to a composition of the Gospel of Mark in Rome between the great fire in 64 and the siege and destruction of Jerusalem by Titus in 70, that is, about the year 65.[16]

---

they have is but of shallow growth: it is as when we cast seed on the surface of the soil: it springs up too rapidly, the blade apes the loaded ear, and yellows ere harvest time, but bears no grain. Such tricks please us when we contrast them with the performer's age, but progress soon stops and our admiration withers away." On the similarity of the above with Mark's version of the parable of the sower, H. J. Rose, "Quintilian, The Gospels and Comedy," *Classical Review* 39 (1925): 17, writes that "this passage gives us the closest parallel I know, not simply to the general trend of the Parable of the Sower, but to the working out of a detail thereof. . . . Here we have detailed parallelism extending even to wording, when we allow for the difference between the very plain style of St. Mark and the elaborate style of Quintilian."

14. F. H. Colson, "Quintilian, the Gospels and Christianity," *Classical Review* 39 (1925): 167.

15. *Ibid.,* 169: "I should have no hesitation in saying that the natural explanation was . . . that Quintilian had either through Domitilla or by direct reading borrowed from the Evangelist, and that we have here the first adaptation of the Gospels in a pagan writer and perhaps the first in any writer."

16. Wenham, *Reading Matthew, Mark and Luke,* 146-72, argues that Peter visited Rome early in the reign of Claudius (in 42-44), and that Mark was written shortly thereafter in c. 45. Despite the valiant arguments of Wenham and others (e.g., G. Edmundson; recently C. P. Thiede), neither external nor internal evidence for such a date is compelling. It is true that church tradition from the fourth century onward assumes Peter's early and long (twenty-five-year) tenure in Rome, but the NT is completely silent on the matter, and there is only sparse and ambiguous evidence about the matter until the fourth century (including Eusebius). At any rate, the issue to be resolved is not when Peter was in Rome but when the Gospel of Mark was written, and internal evidence in the Gospel appears to favor the Neronian persecution of the 60s rather than the relatively uneventful decade of the 40s.

4. HISTORICAL CONTEXT

Significant details in the Second Gospel corroborate the foregoing historical reconstruction that the intent of the Gospel of Mark was to portray the
person and mission of Jesus Christ for Roman Christians undergoing persecution under Nero. There can be little doubt that Mark wrote for Gentile readers, and Roman Gentiles in particular. Mark quotes relatively infrequently from the OT, and he explains Jewish customs unfamiliar to his
readers (7:3-4; 12:18; 14:12; 15:42). He translates Aramaic and Hebrew
phrases by their Greek equivalents (3:17; 5:41; 7:11, 34; 10:46; 14:36; 15:22,
34).[17] He also incorporates a number of Latinisms by transliterating familiar Latin expressions into Greek characters.[18] Finally, Mark presents
Romans in a neutral (12:17; 15:1-2, 21-22) and sometimes favorable (15:39)
light. These data indicate that Mark wrote for Greek readers whose primary frame of reference was the Roman Empire, whose native tongue
was evidently Latin, and for whom the land and Jewish ethos of Jesus
were unfamiliar. Again, Rome looks to be the place in which and for
which the Second Gospel was composed.

5. DISTINCTIVE LITERARY CHARACTERISTICS

5.1. Style

Mark is the shortest and most compact of the four Gospels. The brevity of
Mark owes to the fact that Mark includes fewer stories in his Gospel than
do the other Evangelists. The stories that Mark includes, however, are as
a rule narrated in fuller fashion than are the same stories in the other Gospels.[19] Mark composes his Gospel in a total of 1,270 different Greek
words, excluding proper names. This relatively modest vocabulary
range, which is nearly the same number of different Latin words used by

17. See Grundmann, *Das Evangelium nach Markus,* 23. Hengel, *Studies in the Gospel
of Mark,* 46, declares: "I do not know any other work in Greek which has as many Aramaic or Hebrew words and formulae in so narrow a space as does the second Gospel."

18. These words are Latin-based derivatives in Mark: *modius,* 4:21; *legio,* 5:9, 15;
speculator, 6:27; *denarius,* 6:37; *census* and *Caesar,* 12:14; *praetorium,* 15:16; and *centurio,*
15:39, 44. For a discussion of Greek phrases in Mark that derive from Latin originals, see
BDF, 4-6.

19. For example, Mark's story of Jesus' healing of Jairus's daughter and the
woman with a hemorrhage (Mark 5:21-43) contains 383 words in Greek. The parallels in
Matt 9:18-26 and Luke 8:40-56 contain 138 words (= 36% of Mark's length) and 285 words
(= 74% of Mark's length), respectively.

Caesar in the much longer *Gallic War,* indicates that Mark, like Caesar, utilizes ordinary spoken vocabulary in order to convey extraordinary events. Mark avoids the cultured and often affected style that characterizes the Attic masterpieces, and not a few Hellenistic Greek words as well. He writes in an unadorned though vivid style that communicates immediately with the reader. He maintains a vigorous tempo by ubiquitously beginning sentences with "and" (Gk. *kai*), as well as by linking coordinate clauses by *kai* rather than by the use of participles or subordinate clauses; by the equally ubiquitous use of the "historical present tense" of Greek verbs; and by frequent use of words like "immediately" (Gk. *euthys*), "again" (Gk. *palin*), and many words for astonishment or amazement. On occasion the haste of Mark's narrative is rivaled by its density of diction, as in 5:26-27, for example, where six participles in rapid succession precede the finite verb. Equally characteristic of Mark's style is a preference for diminutives, and, as noted earlier, a penchant for including Greek words and phrases that are indebted to Latin originals, whether transliterations of Latin words or echoes of Latin syntax and phraseology. Mark's allegro narrative leaves the impression of close proximity to the events described, and his pericopes are set side-by-side like building blocks with virtually no editorial mortar between them. Attendant narrative details — for example, where and when Jesus was at a given place, or who was with him — are pared to a minimum, the result of which approximates a modern play with a sparse setting and backdrop, so as to focus unwavering attention on Jesus.

5.2. Sandwich Technique

The Second Gospel frequently interrupts a story or pericope by inserting a second, seemingly unrelated, story into it. For example, in chap. 5 Jairus, a synagogue ruler, begs Jesus to heal his daughter (vv. 21-24). A woman with a hemorrhage interrupts Jesus en route to Jairus's house (vv. 25-34), and only after recording the woman's healing does Mark resume with the raising of Jairus's daughter, who had died in the meantime (vv. 35-43). This particular sandwich is about faith, but other sandwiches, which occur some nine times in the Gospel,[20] emphasize concomitant themes of discipleship, bearing witness, or the dangers of apostasy. Sandwiches are thus literary conventions with theological purposes. Each sandwich unit consists of an A^1-B-A^2 sequence, with the B-component functioning as the theological key to the flanking halves. There may have

---

20. 3:20-35; 4:1-20; 5:21-43; 6:7-30; 11:12-21; 14:1-11; 14:17-31; 14:53-72; 15:40–16:8.

been rudiments of the sandwich technique in the traditions that Mark received, but a comparison of Mark with the other Synoptics reveals that he employs the sandwich technique in a unique and pronounced manner to underscore the major themes of the Gospel.[21]

5.3. Irony

Mark is master of the unexpected. In addition to its allegro narrative style and sandwich technique, the Second Gospel is characterized by irony. The medium of irony is important for the Second Evangelist, who throughout the Gospel portrays Jesus as one who challenges, confounds, and sometimes breaks conventional stereotypes, whether religious, social, or political. Jesus' response to various persons and situations — and their response to him — is not at all what readers anticipate. The religious and moral leaders, as represented in the scribes and Sanhedrin, for example, are in running combat with Jesus throughout the Gospel, whereas a Syrophoenician Gentile woman of no reputation whatsoever is commended for her faith (7:29). Likewise, those closest to Jesus — his disciples (8:14-21, 33; 10:35-45) and even his own family (3:21, 31-35; 6:1-6) — perceive his mission and being only gradually and with difficulty, whereas outsiders like blind Bartimaeus (10:46-52) and a Gentile centurion (15:39) respond to Jesus more immediately and intuitively. In yet another example, Jesus restores alien outsiders such as a leper (1:40-45) and a hostile demoniac (5:1-20) to health and society — and becomes himself an outsider in so doing. Jesus enters into a great variety of settings in Mark, in each of which he remains his own person in sovereign freedom and authority, both challenging the way things are and extending hope for what they might become. Readers of Mark's Gospel find it necessary to drop their preconceptions of what God and God's Messiah are like in order to experience a "new teaching with authority" (1:27) and to learn that new wine requires new wineskins (2:22).

6. JESUS IN THE GOSPEL OF MARK

Every pericope in Mark is about Jesus except for two about John the Baptizer (1:2-8; 6:14-29), who is presented as the forerunner of Jesus. From

21. See J. R. Edwards, "Markan Sandwiches: The Significance of Interpolations in Markan Narratives," *NovT* 31 (1989): 193-216.

start to finish, Jesus is the uncontested subject of the Gospel of Mark, and he is portrayed as a man of action. The action of the Gospel is all-important to the meaning of the Gospel, for we learn who Jesus is not so much from what he says as from what he *does*. In this respect, Mark writes with a paintbrush. Unlike the Gospel of John, for instance, where major themes are made explicit, Mark has much more *implicit* major themes, requiring readers to enter into the drama of the Gospel in order to understand its meaning. Although Jesus is often referred to as a teacher, Mark seldom reports the content of his teaching. It is quickly apparent that the person of the teacher is more important than the content of his teaching. Mark is also the most ready of the four Evangelists to portray the humanness of Jesus, including his sorrow (14:34), disappointment (8:12), displeasure (10:14), anger (11:15-17), amazement (6:6), fatigue (4:38), and even ignorance (13:32). Gospel tradition subsequent to Mark reveals a subtle tendency to soften and mute Mark's stark portrayal of Jesus' humanity. Above all, Mark's portrayal of Jesus is characterized by three factors: his divine authority, his mission as the suffering Servant of God, and his divine Sonship.

6.1. The Authority of Jesus

The characteristic of Jesus that left the most lasting impression on his followers and caused the greatest offense to his opponents was his *exousia*, his sovereign freedom and magisterial authority. In his first public appearance in Mark, Jesus astounds the synagogue congregation by his supremacy over both the demonic world and the teaching of the Torah experts (1:21-28). Both effects — his teaching and his exorcisms — derive from his divine authority.

The *exousia* of Jesus comes to expression first of all in his presuming to reorder social and political priorities. His calling of twelve disciples, whose number corresponds to the twelve tribes of Israel (3:13-19), suggests a fulfillment of the destiny of Israel in the apostolic college of followers. Motherhood and sibling relationships are redefined according to doing the will of God rather than blood lineage (3:31-35; 6:1-6). In the political realm, Jesus presumes to declare what is — and what is not — owed to Caesar (12:13-17).

The *exousia* of Jesus also manifests itself in his presumption to redefine the Torah commandments. The responsibility of a son to provide for his parents is declared to supersede the legal option of Corban (7:8-13). Jesus unleashes a vehement critique of the rabbinic oral tradition (7:1-23), and in contrast to both the tradition of the elders and the Mosaic law he embraces a leper (1:40-45), tax collectors and sinners (2:13-17), and unclean Gentiles, including a Syrophoenician woman (7:24-30). Jesus contravenes the proscription of work on the Sabbath by plucking grain (2:23-26) and healing (3:1-6); and he redefines the very purpose of the Sabbath as a constitutive order of creation (2:27-28). Rabbinic discussions in first-century Palestine were oriented primarily around four compass points of law: Sabbath observance, ritual purity, foods, and marriage — each of which would later develop into either individual tractates or entire divisions of the Mishnah. Each of these four is also vigorously challenged by Jesus.

Finally and most importantly, the authority of Jesus exhibits itself in his laying claim to prerogatives that otherwise belong only to God. Jesus possesses the ability to cure the most varied and serious illnesses — an ability acknowledged even by his opponents (3:22; *b. Shab.* 104*b*; *b. Sanh.* 25*d*). His authority extends also to supremacy over nature. In his calming of the storm (4:35-41), his "rebuke" of the wind and "muzzling" of the waves are phrased in the language of exorcism, recalling the power of God over chaos at creation. Likewise Jesus' walking on the water (6:45-52) connotes that Jesus treads where only God can walk (Job 9:8, 11; Ps 77:19; Isa 43:16), and designates Jesus by the same expression (*egō eimi;* "I Am") used for God's self-disclosure to Moses (Exod 3:14, LXX). Further exhibitions of Jesus' divine authority include his binding of Satan, "the strong man" (3:27); his presumption to forgive sins (2:10); and his replacement of the temple in Jerusalem as the *locus Dei,* the place where God meets humanity (15:38-39). His speech to and about God is unique among Jewish rabbis: by his frequent prefacing of statements with *Amēn* ("Truly, I say to you . . .") he presumes to speak with the authority of God; and his reference to God as *"Abba"* (14:36) exhibits a filial closeness to God unparalleled in Judaism. When questioned about the source of his authority, Jesus points to his baptism by John, wherein the voice declaring him Son of God and the Spirit empowering him as the servant of God confer on him the *exousia* of God (11:27-33).[22]

6.2. Servant of the Lord

The authority of Jesus, which everywhere permeates his demeanor and bearing, is employed not for self, however, but in the service of others. Consequently, Mark depicts Jesus using the profile of a servant, espe-

---

22. J. R. Edwards, "The Authority of Jesus in the Gospel of Mark," *JETS* 37/2 (1994): 217-33.

cially as the fulfillment of Isaiah's suffering servant of God. The most important characteristic of Isaiah's Servant of the Lord is the effect of his vicarious and atoning suffering (Isa 53:5, 10), which is found nowhere else in the OT. It is precisely this aspect of the Servant that Jesus fulfills in his mission as Son of Man "'to give his life as a ransom for many'" (10:45). Echoes of the Servant of the Lord are interspersed at key junctures in Mark's portrayal of Jesus. Already in the baptism the voice from heaven (1:11) defines divine Sonship in servant categories (Isa 42:1; 49:3). Early in his ministry Jesus shows awareness that his life must be taken from him (2:20), and later Jesus understands his death as an essential part of his work, a "baptism" (10:38). A lavish chrism of an unnamed woman is received as an anointing for burial (14:8). Three passion predictions (8:31; 9:31; 10:33-34) serve as milestones in the journey to Jerusalem in the second half of the Gospel, to which may be added the revealing phrase in the parable of the vineyard that the beloved Son is surrendered into the murderous hands of wicked tenants (12:6-8). In the Last Supper Jesus again interprets his impending death in categories reminiscent of the Servant of the Lord as "the blood of the covenant which is poured out for many" (14:24).

6.3. Son of God

Mark refers to Jesus by various titles — teacher, rabbi, Son of David, Christ, Lord, Son of Man, and Son of God. Of these, the final title is unquestionably the most important. Son of God defines both the beginning and end of the Gospel: it occurs in the opening pronouncement of the Gospel, "The beginning of the gospel about Jesus Christ, the Son of God" (1:1), as well as in the concluding and climactic confession of the centurion at the cross, "'Surely this man was the Son of God!'" (15:39). The divine Sonship of Jesus is the theological keystone to the Gospel of Mark. At decisive points Mark gives clues to unlock the mystery of Jesus' person. At the baptism (1:11) and transfiguration (9:7) the Father in heaven calls Jesus "my Son, whom I love," indicating that Jesus shares a unique relationship of love and obedience with the Father. Demons also recognize Jesus as God's Son (1:24; 3:11; 5:7), testifying that he is endowed with divine authority.

Mark establishes not only *that* Jesus is the Son of God but also *what kind* of Son of God he is. Unlike the various heroes and divine men of the Hellenistic world who were elevated above the mundane, Jesus exhibits his divine Sonship in the midst of a troubled world. The surprise — and key — to understanding the Son of God is in his suffering. Jesus must be

15

obedient to the will of the Father, even to death on a cross (14:36). In the passion narratives Mark portrays Jesus chiefly according to the model of the suffering servant of Isaiah. Immediately before the passion Jesus tells a parable about the only son of a vineyard owner who suffers rejection and death at the hands of insolent tenants (12:1-12). The parable ultimately reflects Jesus' own fate, which transpires in the crucifixion account. Ironically, his death on the cross is the place where both his mission and his identity as Son of God converge, and as such the cross is the first place where humanity recognizes him as God's Son (15:39).[23]

7. DISTINCTIVE THEMES

7.1. Discipleship

There is a causal relationship in Mark between the ministry of Jesus and that of his disciples. As Jesus is with the Father, so his disciples are to be with him (3:13). Jesus empowers the disciples to undertake his own ministry of proclamation and power over the forces of evil (3:14; 6:7-13). As the Son of Man serves in humility without regard to self and even in suffering, so, too, must his disciples (10:42-45). "'If anyone would come after me, he must deny himself and take up his cross and follow me'" (8:34). Ironically, however, when one loses one's life for Christ, one finds it in Christ (8:35). Discipleship is repeatedly defined in Mark by simple proximity to Jesus: being with him (3:13), sitting around him (3:34; 4:10), hearing him (4:1-20), and following him "on the way" (1:16-20; 10:52). The simple but all-important act of hearing and following Jesus precedes and is more important than disciples' complete understanding of him. The disciples, and especially the Twelve, are not infrequently shown to lack understanding and even to be hard-hearted (8:14-26). Surprisingly, this does not compromise their discipleship. What Jesus has to teach can only be taught in an apprentice relationship, which necessitates the disciples' being with him more than their full understanding of him. Indeed, their understanding can come only from the vantage point of the cross, where the temple curtain is torn asunder and the meaning of Jesus' divine Sonship is finally and fully revealed (15:38-39).

---

23. Further, see the excursus on the Son of God at 15:39. J. R. Edwards, "The Son of God: Its Antecedents in Judaism and Hellenism, and Its Use in the Earliest Gospel," Ph.D. diss., Fuller Theological Seminary, 1978. For a digest, see *Studia Biblica et Theologica* 8/1 (1978): 76-79.

7.2. Faith

For Mark, faith and discipleship have no meaning apart from following the suffering Son of God. Faith is thus not a magical formula, but depends on repeated hearing of his word and participation in his mission. Mark shows two different faith responses to Jesus. On the one hand, a number of individuals display insights and acts of faith that are remarkable for their immediacy and lack of precedent. Ironically, these individuals as a rule come from outside Jesus' immediate circle of followers and are often women or Gentiles. Four unnamed companions of a paralytic are commended for their faith (2:5), as are a leper (1:40-42), an unclean, hemorrhaging woman (5:34), a Syrophoenician woman (7:24-30), the father of an epileptic son (9:24), a blind man (10:52), a penniless widow (12:41-44), a woman who anoints Jesus at Bethany (14:3-9), and, above all, the centurion at the cross (15:39). These individuals demonstrate great resolve and sacrifice in one form or another, and their faith in Jesus is not disappointed.

On the other hand, those who would seem to have a faith advantage — Jesus' family (3:31-35), his hometown (6:1-6), or the religious experts (11:27-33) — are, ironically, the least understanding and most resistant. Even the faith response of Jesus' inner circle, and particularly the Twelve, is halting and incomplete. For this group, faith comes slowly, even laboriously, by repeatedly hearing, receiving, and finally bearing fruit (4:10-20). The Twelve question who Jesus really is (4:41), and at times they exasperate him (9:19). Nevertheless, like the blind man at Bethsaida, they, too, can be made to see, but only by the sustained presence and repeated "touch" of Jesus (8:14-26).

7.3. Insiders and Outsiders

The themes of discipleship and faith are closely related to the theme of insiders and outsiders. Speaking to the inner circle, Jesus says, "'The secret of the kingdom of God has been given to you. But to those on the outside, everything is said in parables . . .'" (4:11). Among Jesus' followers are an inner group that is privy to the secret of the kingdom of God and an outer group that cannot be taken into its confidence. The surprise, however, is in who belongs to each group. We would expect Jesus' family, for instance, to be among the insiders. A disquieting episode early in the Gospel, however, reveals Jesus' mother and brothers standing outside, and a group of unnamed adherents on the inside, sitting around Jesus and doing God's will (3:31-35). Once again, "outsiders" — women, Gentiles, or

Jews considered "unclean" — frequently demonstrate understanding and faith in Jesus, whereas the religious leaders, his family, and even his disciples do not. Indeed, Mark frequently portrays Jesus as an "outsider" (1:45; 5:17; 8:23; 11:19; 12:8; 15:22). He fits none of the prevailing social categories, and throughout his ministry he faces misunderstanding, hardness, and rejection. The kingdom that Jesus proclaims and inaugurates is not identifiable with any existing social norms and institutions, but is uniquely centered in his own person.

7.4. Gentiles

Not only is Mark written for a Gentile audience (see **5. Historical Context**), but it also portrays Jesus ministering to Gentiles as well as to Jews. Mark's Jesus is a "northern" Jesus, oriented to regions beyond the orbit of Jerusalem-defined Judaism. Galilee, the center of Jesus' formative early ministry, lay at the northern extreme of the nation but still within the jurisdiction of Jerusalem, from which deputies were sent to spy on Jesus (3:8, 22; 7:1). Galilee, however, had a significant Gentile population (hence "Galilee of the Gentiles," Isa 9:1; Matt 4:15). According to Mark, Jesus frequently leaves Galilee for Gentile regions: in the Decapolis to the east of the Sea of Galilee he heals a demoniac (5:1-20) and feeds the four thousand (8:1-10), demonstrating the same power among Gentiles that he earlier demonstrated among Jews (6:31-44). He undertakes a long, circuitous journey northward to Tyre and Sidon in Phoenicia, where, among Israel's great pagan rivals, he encounters a woman of indefatigable faith (7:24-30) and later heals a deaf-mute (7:31-37). According to Mark, from Gentiles and in Gentile regions Jesus finds greater receptivity than he does from Jewish regions. Mark's two great christological confessions are related to Gentiles: in Caesarea Philippi Jesus is declared to be the Christ (8:27-30), and by the Gentile centurion at the cross Jesus is declared the Son of God (15:39).

7.5. Command to Silence

In the first half of Mark, Jesus frequently commands persons whom he has healed, onlookers, disciples, and even demons to be silent (1:25, 34; 1:44; 3:12; 5:43; 7:36; 8:26, 30; 9:9). It has long puzzled readers why Jesus, who came to make himself known, works at cross purposes with himself by remaining hidden. Three reasons may be given.

Jesus doubtlessly used the command to silence to protect himself from false messianic expectations. For most of Jesus' contemporaries, "messiah" conjured up images of a military hero like King David who would drive the Roman overlords from occupied Palestine. While Jesus embraced some aspects of Davidic messianism (2:25; 12:35-37), and was recognized for doing so (e.g., "Son of David," 10:47-48; 11:10), he eschewed militaristic methods of effecting his kingdom. Not the warrior's sword but the servant's towel, as foretold by the prophet Isaiah, was the model he embraced.

A further reason why Jesus concealed his miraculous power was that he knew that faith could not be coerced by a spectacle (e.g., Matt. 4:5-7). Not sight, but *insight* into Jesus' life and purpose could evoke true faith. Saving knowledge needed to come through experience of Jesus himself, not alone through proper formulas and titles, or reports of astounding deeds.

Finally, Mark employs the secrecy theme in order to teach that until the cross Jesus cannot be rightly known for who he is. The leper may be cleansed (1:44), but Jesus enjoins him to silence lest he proclaim Jesus merely as a wonder worker; the demons may call Jesus the "Son of God" (3:11-12), but Jesus silences them because those who oppose him cannot be his heralds; even the chief apostle is commanded to silence after confessing Jesus to be the Christ (8:30) — not because he was wrong but because he did not fully grasp the meaning of his confession. Nor could he. Only at the cross can Jesus be rightly known, not simply as a great moral teacher or as the most noble person who ever lived; nor only as a miracle worker or as an answer to this or that pressing question of the world. At the cross Jesus is revealed as the suffering Son of God, whose rejection, suffering, and death reveal the triumph of God. Only at Golgotha can Jesus be rightly known as God incognito who reveals himself to those who are willing to deny themselves and follow him in costly discipleship.[24]

7.6. Journey

A final theme in the Gospel is that of the journey. A quotation from Isaiah at the outset describes the gospel of Jesus Christ as "a way" (1:2-3). In the first half of the Gospel, the way is indeterminate and unfocused. Jesus frequently crisscrosses the Sea of Galilee and once makes a long, circuitous journey into Gentile regions to the north and east of Galilee. He is continually on the move, but there is no apparent destination to his movements. Only at the outer limits of Caesarea Philippi (8:27) do the

---

24. On the command to silence, see further at 1:34.

Galilee wanderings merge into a focused goal that determines the framework of the remainder of the Gospel. There Peter declares Jesus to be the Messiah, and thereafter Jesus sets his face and directs his steps toward Jerusalem. "On the way" becomes the thematic refrain of the second half of the Gospel (8:27; 9:33-34; 10:17, 32, 52; 11:8). "On the way" Jesus thrice declares the necessity of his going to Jerusalem to suffer rejection and execution, and finally to be raised from the dead (8:31; 9:31; 10:33-34). "On the way" is not only Jesus' destiny, however, but also the destiny of his disciples (10:32, 52). The "way" or journey thus describes the way Jesus must go and the way disciples must follow if both are to fulfill God's plan.

8. NARRATIVE STRUCTURE

The Gospel of Mark falls naturally into two halves, the first concerning Jesus' ministry in Galilee (1:1–8:26), and the second his journey to Jerusalem and his passion there (8:27–16:8). The first half begins with the declaration of the purpose of the Gospel (1:1), followed by the appearance of John the Baptist (1:2-8) and the baptism of Jesus (1:9-11). The temptation in the wilderness is mentioned but not elaborated (1:12-13), and the introduction concludes with a capsule of Jesus' message, "'The time has come. The kingdom of God is near. Repent and believe the good news!'" (1:14-15).

Then follows a series of thirteen carefully crafted vignettes depicting Jesus as a teacher, healer, and exorcist in and around Capernaum, often in conflict with Jewish authorities (1:16–3:25). Chapter 4 is a select assemblage of Jesus' parables, most of which are about growing seeds.

Mark resumes Jesus' ministry as an open-air preacher and healer in 4:35–8:26. Opposition to Jesus from Herod Antipas and from Jewish religious leaders forces him to quit Galilee and embark on a circuitous journey in the Gentile regions of Phoenicia and Decapolis. Gentile "outsiders" display remarkable openness and acceptance of Jesus and the gospel, whereas "insiders," especially the disciples, are as obdurate as the religious leaders, although not with evil intent.

The second half of the Gospel begins in 8:27 with Jesus no longer circumambulating the Sea of Galilee but "on the way" to Jerusalem. The way to Jerusalem begins with Peter's confession at Caesarea Philippi. Jesus asks his disciples, "'Who do people say I am?'" (8:27). Peter responds, "'You are the Christ'" (8:29). Jesus shocks the disciples by explaining that the Christ must suffer and die; moreover, that whoever desires to be his disciple must be prepared for discipleship (8:31–9:1). A glorious transfiguration of Jesus follows this dire pronouncement, which shows that the Father in heaven confirms Jesus' role as the suffering Son of Man (9:2-13).

Following Caesarea Philippi the narrative is directed resolutely to Jerusalem. "On the way" Jesus three times predicts his imminent suffering, death, and resurrection (8:31; 9:31; 10:33-34). The large crowds that attended him in Galilee fall away, and Jesus focuses on teaching the Twelve the meaning of discipleship. "'Whoever wants to be great among you must be your servant. . . . For even the Son of Man did not come to be served, but to serve, and to give his life as a ransom for many'" (10:43, 45). Although Jesus enters Jerusalem as a celebrated pilgrim (11:1-10), Mark signifies his breach with the Holy City by his nightly removal to Bethany outside Jerusalem (11:11) and by his judgment on the temple (11:12-21). Chaps. 11–13 contain a series of tests and traps in and around the temple, most of which evince the hostility of the Sanhedrin to Jesus and Jesus' corresponding rejection of the temple. In chap. 13 the destruction of the temple becomes a symbol for the woes that will beset the faithful before the Day of the Lord and the return of the Son of Man. Chaps. 14–15 comprise the heart of the passion account. A solemn Last Supper with the disciples is set in the midst of intrigue and treachery, not only by Jewish and Roman adversaries but even by his disciples. A clandestine arrest leads to two hearings, one by the Jewish Sanhedrin (14:53-72) and one by Pontius Pilate, the Roman governor (15:1-20). The accent on the crucifixion scene falls less on Jesus' physical suffering than on his abandonment (even by God, 15:34) and the mockery of his adversaries. At the moment of his death, a Gentile centurion confesses Jesus as God's Son (15:39). Defeat is thus transformed into victory as God's Son is revealed in suffering. The oldest form of the Gospel ends with an angelic announcement of the resurrection of Jesus (16:1-8); a later secondary ending includes various resurrection appearances of Jesus (16:9-20).

CHAPTER ONE

The Gospel Appears in Person

MARK 1:1-13

THE KEY TO MARK (1:1)

Ancient writings normally begin either with a formal dedication describing the purpose of the book or with an opening line treating the first subject discussed.[1] The formal introductions of the Gospel of Luke and the book of Acts follow the former pattern. The Gospel of Mark begins in the latter way, "The beginning of the gospel about Jesus Christ, the Son of God" (1:1). If Mark intended his work to have a title, this is it. Like Genesis, Hosea, and the Gospel of John, the first word of Mark is simply "beginning." Mark doubtlessly chooses it as a reminder of God's activity in history: in the beginning God created the world; so, too, the age of the gospel is manifest when the Son of God becomes a human being in Jesus Christ. The Greek word translated "beginning," *archē*, can incorporate two meanings: first in order of temporal sequence, or first in terms of origin or principle. It is the latter sense in which the term is here used, since Mark intends the whole Gospel, and not merely its opening part, to be incorporated by *archē*. "Beginning" thus identifies in the initial word of the Gospel the authority from whom the Gospel derives, God himself, the author and originator of all that is.[2] Lohmeyer is correct in saying that "beginning" signals the "fulfillment of God's everlasting word."[3] For Mark the introduction of Jesus is no less momentous than the creation of the world, for in Jesus a new creation is at hand.

---

1. H. Koester, *Ancient Christian Gospels* (Philadelphia: Trinity Press International; London: SCM Press, 1992), 14.
2. R. P. Martin, *New Testament Foundations* (Grand Rapids: Eerdmans, 1975), 1.27.
3. E. Lohmeyer, *Das Evangelium des Markus,* 10.

The **gospel** of which Mark speaks is not a book, as it is for Matthew (1:1, "A record [Gk. *biblos*] of the genealogy of Jesus Christ"). Rather, for Mark the gospel is the story of salvation in Jesus. The word for "gospel" (Gk. *euangelion*) literally means "good news." In both the OT and in Greek literature *euangelion* was commonly used of reports of victory from the battlefield. When the Philistines defeated the troops of Saul on Mt. Gilboa, "they sent messengers throughout the land of the Philistines to proclaim the news *(euangelizesthai)* . . . among the people" (1 Sam 31:9; see also 2 Sam 1:20; 18:19-20; 1 Chr 10:9). The messenger who brought the report was the deliverer of "good news" (2 Sam 4:10; 18:26). Among the Greeks the term was used likewise of victory in battle, as well as of other forms of good news. In 9 B.C., within a decade of Jesus' birth, the birthday of Caesar Augustus (63 B.C.–A.D. 14) was hailed as *euangelion* (pl.). Since he was hailed as a god, Augustus's "birthday signaled the beginning of Good News for the world."[4] In the Greco-Roman world the word always appears in the plural, meaning one good tiding among others; but in the NT *euangelion* appears only in the singular: *the* good news of God in Jesus Christ, beside which there is no other.[5] The concept of "good news" was not limited to military and political victories, however. In the prophet Isaiah "good news" is transferred to the inbreaking of God's final saving act when peace, good news, and release from oppression will be showered on God's people (Isa 52:7; 61:1-3). For Mark, the advent of Jesus is the beginning of the fulfillment of the "good news" heralded by Isaiah.

If, as seems probable, Mark is the first evangelist, then he also inaugurates a new literary genre in applying the term "gospel" to the life and

4. Taken from the calendar inscription of Priene; cited in A. Deissmann, *Light from the Ancient East,* trans. L. Strachan (London: Hodder and Stoughton, 1927), 366. The Greco-Roman world honored its heroes by elevating them to god-like status. The cult surrounding Caesar Augustus was particularly inclined in this regard. Augustus was believed, according to popular legend, to have been conceived by a serpent (which represented the *genius* of a god; see Suetonius, *Lives of the Caesars,* "The Deified Augustus," 94). His reign was celebrated as the fulfillment of the golden age, as the following encomium suggests: "The eternal and immortal nature of all things graciously granted the wonderfully good Caesar Augustus to perform good deeds in abundance to men in order that they might enjoy prosperity of life. He is the father of his divine homeland Rome, inherited from his father Zeus, and a savior of the common folk. His foresight not only fulfilled the entreaties of all people, but surpassed them, making peace for land and sea, while cities bloom with order, harmony, and good seasons; the productivity of all things is good and at its prime, there are fond hopes for the future and good will during the present which fills all men, so that they ought to bear pleasing sacrifices and hymns" (cited in H. Kleinknecht, ΠΑΝΘΕΙΟΝ: *Religiöse Texte des Griechentums* [Tübingen: Mohr, 1959], 40).

5. G. Stanton, Inaugural Lecture as Lady Margaret's Professor of New Testament, Cambridge, England, 27 April 2000.

ministry of Jesus Christ.[6] For Mark, the gospel refers to the fulfillment of God's reign and salvation in the fullness of time (Isa 52:7; 61:1). In the appearance of Jesus in Galilee, a new age has dawned that requires repentance and faith. Mark's written record of Jesus' life is itself called a Gospel, and thus this same Jesus who overcame the grave in the resurrection from the dead is now the living Lord who is at work in the church and world, calling people to faith in the gospel. In Mark's understanding, therefore, the gospel is more than a set of truths, or even a set of beliefs. It is a *person*, "the gospel of Jesus Christ."[7] The kingdom that God inaugurates is bodily present in Jesus of Nazareth.

Jesus, whose name in Hebrew is a variant of "Yehoshua" (Eng. "Joshua"), meaning "God is salvation," is defined in Mark's prologue as the "Christ" and "Son of God." (See the excursuses on **Christ** at 8:29 and on **Son of God** at 15:39.) Son of God is a more complete title for Jesus' person and mission than is Messiah, and is Mark's blue chip title for Jesus, the chief artery of the Gospel.[8] "The beginning of the gospel about Je-

---

6. "Gospel," *euangelion*, is a frequent and favorite expression of Mark, occurring seven times in Mark, only four in Matthew, and none in Luke or John or in the hypothetical sayings source "Q." Mark is thus not only the first to apply the understanding of "gospel" to Jesus, but he is also the first to invent the literary genre of "Gospel" to depict his life and death. See Martin, *New Testament Foundations*, 1.23-27.

7. W. Marxsen correctly notes that Jesus Christ can be substituted for "gospel," and, moreover, that "gospel," as employed by Mark, is a title or description for the entire narrative of Jesus from baptism through death and resurrection (see *Mark the Evangelist*, trans. J. Boyce, D. Juel, W. Poehlmann, and R. Harrisville [Nashville/New York: Abingdon Press, 1969], 130-31). Mark can scarcely have regarded a selection of sayings (e.g., the hypothetical sayings source "Q") or a depiction of Jesus as a mere teacher of wisdom (e.g., the *Gospel of Thomas* or the many gnostic documents of Nag Hammadi) as a "gospel" in the sense in which he introduced it into the Synoptic tradition. Nor could the early church, for whom the four Gospels were versions (e.g., "according to Matthew," "according to Mark) of the *one* gospel (see M. Hengel, *Studies in the Gospel of Mark*, trans. J. Bowden [London: SCM Press, 1985], 65). In a critique of the Jesus Seminar at this point, N. T. Wright correctly notes that "Calling [*Thomas* and Q] 'gospels' obscures the obvious difference of genre between them and the four ordinarily so called" ("Five Gospels but No Gospel: Jesus and the Seminar," in *Authenticating the Activities of Jesus*, ed. B. Chilton and C. Evans, NTTS 28/2 (Eiden, Boston, Koln: Brill, 1999), 92.

8. See O. Hofius, "Ist Jesus der Messias? Thesen," *JBTh* 8 (1993): 117, who rightly emphasizes that "Messiah" designates a human actor whereas "Son of God" is a fuller metaphysical term designating the deity of Jesus Christ: "The *metaphysical* title "Son of God," which appears as a title of exaltation for Jesus in the New Testament, presupposes the original and essential communion of Jesus with God, and with it his preexistent deity *(Gottsein)*" (italics in original). "Son of God" is omitted in two weighty uncial manuscripts, Sinaiticus (4th cent.) and Koridethi (9th cent.), although the sheer number, diversity, and weight of manuscripts support its inclusion in 1:1. Against its authenticity is the fact that scribes not infrequently succumbed to the temptation to expand titles and quasititles of books. Moreover, it is difficult to explain why a scribe would omit such an impor-

sus Christ the Son of God" (1:1) is the prologue, indeed the topic sentence, of Mark's Gospel. It may even be considered the title of the Gospel, as long as it is not divorced from what follows, as the connection with John the Baptist in v. 2 evinces. In v. 1 Mark declares the essential content of the *euangelion*, the "good news." The Gospel of Mark is thus not a mystery story in which readers must piece together clues here and there to discover its meaning; nor is it a pedestrian chronicle of dates and places without purpose or significance; nor is it reducible to a mere system of thought. Rather, from the outset Mark announces that the content of the gospel is the person of Jesus, who is the Christ and Son of God. It is a brief confession of faith, the meaning of which will unfold only as the reader follows Mark's presentation of Jesus in the Gospel.

JOHN THE BAPTIZER: FORERUNNER OF JESUS (1:2-8)

2-3 The Gospel of Mark was written for Roman Gentiles. Quite understandably, Mark makes sparing use of OT quotations, since proof texts from Hebrew prophecy would not carry the degree of authority with Gentile audiences that they would and did with Jewish audiences. It is all the more remarkable, therefore, that Mark begins his story with a reference to the OT. The quotation is introduced with an authoritative formula common in both the Greco-Roman and Jewish worlds, "It is written" (Gk. *kathōs gegraptai*). In the Hellenistic world the formula frequently appears in introductions to laws or declarations carrying legal force. In the OT it claims normative influence over hearers or readers by designating the authority of God, Torah, king, or prophet.[9]

The quotation of 1:2-3 is identified as coming from the prophet Isaiah, although it is actually a tapestry of three OT passages.[10] The refer-

---

tant title, were it original. In favor of its authenticity, on the other hand, is the possibility of scribal oversight in copying owing to the similarity of the genitive endings of the four preceding words. Furthermore, "Son of God" plays a key role in Mark's Christology and is present at critical junctures of the Gospel (baptism, 1:11; exorcisms, 3:11; 5:7; transfiguration, 9:7; trial of Jesus, 14:61; and especially the centurion's confession, 15:39). The overall manuscript evidence and purpose of Mark appear to argue in favor of the originality of "Son of God" in 1:1. See B. Metzger, *TCGNT*, 73. N. Perrin ("The Christology of Mark: A Study in Methodology," in *A Modern Pilgrimage of New Testament Christology* [Philadelphia: Fortress, 1974], 115) notes: "if [the title] was not part of the original superscription it should have been, and the scribe who first added it was Markan in purpose if not in name."

9. G. Schrenk, "*graphō*," *TDNT* 1.747-49.

10. A number of uncial manuscripts (A K P W Π) ascribe the quotation in vv. 2-3 to

ence to the sending of the messenger in v. 2 follows the first half of both Exod 23:20 and Mal 3:1, although there is no exact counterpart in the OT to the latter half of v. 2 ("who will prepare your way"). The greater part of the tapestry comes in v. 3, which reproduces Isa 40:3 nearly exactly. Isaiah 40:3 is quoted by all four Gospels with reference to John the Baptizer as the forerunner of Jesus (Matt 3:3; Mark 1:3; Luke 1:76; John 1:23). The Isaiah quotation in v. 3 was deemed the defining element of the tapestry of quotations.[11] Thus, the whole is attributed to Isaiah, who was considered the greatest of the prophets, and whose authority in the early church superseded that of both Exodus and Malachi.[12]

In both the MT and the LXX "in the desert" designates the place where God will prepare the way for his people; thus, "A voice of one calling, 'In the desert prepare the way for the LORD'" (Isa 40:3). Following this understanding, the DSS cite the verse in justification of founding a Torah community away from "the men of sin" (= Jerusalem) in the steppe or desert of Qumran (1QS 8:14). Mark, however, aligns "in the desert" with the herald ("a voice of one calling in the desert") rather than with the place of God's preparation, thus conforming to John the Baptizer's appearance in the Judean wilderness. The quotation introduces John the Baptizer as the "messenger sent ahead of you," the "voice of one calling in the desert" (1:2-3).

John's task is to "prepare the way" for the One to follow. In Exod 23:20, 23 the "messenger" who will lead the people is not a human guide or even Moses, but a divine messenger of Yahweh. Applying this text to the Baptizer indicates more than Mark's high estimation of John; it indicates his divinely ordained purpose. Likewise, the Malachi passage (also Mal 4:5-6) identifies the preparer of the way with Elijah, who, according to 2 Kgs 2:11, did not die but was taken to heaven in a chariot of fire. There was widespread expectation in Judaism that Elijah would return as a forerunner of God's eschatological kingdom in the final day.[13] It is often assumed that Elijah, whom Mark here identifies with John the Baptizer, would be the forerunner of the Messiah. But in pre-Christian Jewish texts

---

"the prophets" rather than specifically to Isaiah. This change can be explained by the desire of later copyists to make the introductory formula more comprehensive, since the quotation in vv. 2-3 is a composite. The ascription of the quotation to Isaiah is more strongly attested, however, and is to be preferred. See Metzger, *TCGNT*, 73; and E. Hoskyns and N. Davey, *The Riddle of the New Testament* (London: Faber and Faber, 1958), 44-46.

11. Str-B 2.1.
12. On the OT quotations in vv. 2-3, see J. Marcus, *The Way of the Lord* (Edinburgh: T. & T. Clark, 1992), 12-17, who argues that the composition stems from Mark.
13. Mal 3:1; Sir 48:10; Ps.-Philo, *Bib. Ant.* 48:1; 4 Ezra 6:26; *Sib. Or.* 2:187-89; *Apoc. Elijah* 5:32-33; 4Q558.

preserved in the OT and intertestamental literature Elijah prefigures not the Messiah but the appearance of God himself.[14] This fact considerably elevates the importance of the OT quotation in 1:2-3. In the quotation, several of the pronouns and "the way for the LORD" refer to God. Mark, however, applies these texts with reference to *Jesus*. This indicates that the Baptizer is not simply the herald of the Messiah but of God himself, appearing in Jesus of Nazareth

1:2-3 thus introduce John as the divinely ordained precursor of Jesus, and Jesus as the manifestation of God. The quotation has the further effect of linking the life and ministry of Jesus to the OT. Jesus is not an afterthought of God, as though an earlier plan of salvation had gone awry. Rather, Jesus stands in continuity with the work of God in Israel, the fulfiller of the law and the prophets (Matt 5:17). The introductory tapestry of OT quotations not only links the person and ministry of Jesus inseparably with the preceding revelation of God in the OT, but it makes the person and ministry of Jesus nonunderstandable apart from it. From a Christian theological perspective, this unites the NT uniquely and inseparably to the OT. The gospel is understandable only as the completion of something that God began in the history of Israel. This excludes the possibility of Christians either dismissing or diminishing the importance of the OT, or of attempting to "purge" the gospel of its Jewish origins and context.

A second effect of the tapestry of quotations offers a clue to understanding Jesus' person. Of paramount significance is that the quotations, which in their original Hebrew contexts refer either directly or indirectly to Yahweh, are here applied to Jesus. The opening quotation of Mark transfers the fulfillment of God's eschatological reign subtly but directly to Jesus. Already in 1:2-3 the groundwork is in place that will define and characterize Jesus' bearing throughout the Gospel, in which Jesus unpretentiously but authoritatively unites his way with God's way, his work with God's work, his person with God's person.[15]

Finally, the tapestry of quotations provides a clue to the nature of Jesus' ministry. Three times in 1:2-3 the word "way" or "path" occurs. The initial reference to "the gospel about Jesus Christ" (1:1) is thus a *way* (cf. Acts 9:2). From its outset the story of Jesus directs hearers not to metaphysics and mysticism, nor to ethical rules and systems, but to something practical and transforming, a *way* of salvation made possible by God.

---

14. M. Öhler, "The Expectation of Elijah and the Presence of the Kingdom of God," *JBL* 118 (1999): 641-76.

15. Marcus, *The Way of the Lord*, 31-41, correctly sees the christological import of the opening OT mosaic. "The way for the Lord" is not primarily a reference to ethical behavior, but to God's present inbreaking in Jesus. Mark thus signals that where God formerly acted, Jesus now acts.

Mark will resume and refine this theme in the second half of the Gospel, where "on the way" directs Jesus — and his disciples — to the fulfillment of his mission in Jerusalem. In Mark, the *way* of God is ultimately the way of Jesus to the cross.

4 Without so much as a conjunction following the quotation, John the Baptizer appears in 1:4.[16] The immediacy of John's introduction identifies him as the messenger of preparation for Jesus. The description of John in vv. 4-8 is more focused and defined than is the picture of John in the other Gospels. Omitted in Mark are the wondrous circumstances of John's birth (Luke 1), his thunderous challenge to the dominant Pharisaic and Sadducean schools of Judaism (Matt 3:7-10; Luke 3:7-9), and his call for social reform (Luke 3:10-14). Mark restricts his portrait of John to a single motif, depicting John as the fulfiller of Elijah's climactic role as the forerunner of "one more powerful" (1:7), whose sandals he is unworthy to untie.

Like Elijah (1 Kgs 17:2-3), John is identified with the wilderness — the vast and barren badlands of Judah, seared by wind and heat. The wilderness repeatedly represents in Israel's history a place of repentance, and hence a place of God's grace.[17] From the inception of Israel the wilderness is the place where God brings deliverance to his people, first in the wilderness of Sinai following the Exodus (Exod 15:22ff.) and thereafter in a symbolic wilderness of hope proclaimed by the prophets (Jer 2:2-3; Hos 2:14ff.). John's appearance in the wilderness fulfills both the Mosaic and the prophetic prototypes: it is a reenactment of the mighty inaugural event of Israel's history in the Exodus, and it also fulfills the promises of the prophets, since "all the country around the Jordan" (Luke 3:3) frequented by John is precisely the region associated with Elijah (2 Kgs 2:6-14). John summons people away from the routines and comforts of their urban domiciles, and especially from the statutory temple hegemony of Jerusalem, "to a baptism of repentance for the forgiveness of sins" in the wilderness.

As a symbol of moral and spiritual regeneration John calls people to **baptism**. The Greek word for "baptism," from the root *baptein,* means "to dip fully, to plunge or immerse." The precise origins of baptism are obscure, although rites of sacred baths and ritual washings are known throughout the ancient Near East.[18] Pre-Christian Judaism was agreed in

---

16. The manuscript tradition is divided in v. 4 whether *baptizōn* ("baptizing") should be arthrous or anarthrous, i.e., whether it is a title of John *the Baptizer* or a description of him *baptizing* in the wilderness. The latter is the preferred reading since (1) it claims stronger and more diverse manuscript support and (2) because "the Baptizer" can be explained as an assimilation to passages like 6:25 and 8:28. See Metzger, *TCGNT,* 73.
17. U. W. Mauser, *Christ in the Wilderness,* SBT (London: SCM Press, 1963), 46-52.
18. A. Oepke, "*baptō,*" *TDNT* 1.528-29.

the necessity of repentance before the eschaton when God would cleanse his people by the Holy Spirit (*Jub.* 1:22-25). Although *mikwa'ot* (ritual washings before worship) were a constitutive element of Judaism (see *m. Miqwa.*), and although there is some evidence for proselyte baptism in Judaism, the chief example of ritual washings in Judaism derived from the covenant community at Qumran near the Dead Sea, where daily lustrations symbolized the eschatological cleansing of God. "[God] will sprinkle over him the spirit of truth like lustral water (in order to cleanse him) from all the abhorrences of deceit and from the defilement of the unclean spirit" (1QS 4:21-22).

Whether, and to what extent, John's baptism reflects these various water-rite precursors is much debated. In several important respects John's baptism differs from what we know of proselyte baptism and Qumran washings. Unlike ritual *mikwa'ot* and Qumran baths, which were self-washings, John's baptism was administered to the penitent by John as a second party. Moreover, proselyte baptism and Qumran washings were rites of initiation into faith communities, whereas John's baptism signified moral and spiritual renewal. Assuming that John baptized in the general vicinity of the Qumran settlement, scholars often suppose that John had either been associated with or influenced by the Essenes.[19] From the meager evidence we possess, however, it appears that John baptized further north along the Jordan, near Galilee (see n. 23 below). There is, moreover, no evidence in the NT that John was associated with Qumran; and if he were, its customs left scant trace in his ministry. Given the differences between John's baptism and Jewish ritual washings in general, it is questionable whether John's baptism stems in any direct fashion from the Qumran Essenes. It seems more likely that John's baptism recalls and revives God's foundational covenant with Israel at Sinai in which the entire people were summoned to be a "kingdom of priests and a holy nation" (Exod 19:6; 23:22; also 1 Pet 2:9). This had been the unique and peculiar ideal (NIV, "treasured possession," Heb. *segullah*) of *all* Israel from its inception, and not just of the priesthood descended from Aaron. The Israelites signified acceptance of their covenant relationship with God by washing their clothes and purifying themselves before entering into the covenant at Sinai (Exod 19:10). Such washing symbolized the moral and spiritual transformation necessary to enter into cove-

---

19. The pros and cons of the influence of Qumran on John are discussed in O. Betz, "Was John the Baptist an Essene?" *BRev* 6/6 (1990): 18-25. Betz believes that John was raised at Qumran and strongly influenced by it, but that he later left the sect to preach to a wider community of Jews. John's association with Qumran remains conjectural, however, and the differences between John and the Essenes are more numerous and striking than their similarities.

nant relationship with God. John's "baptism of repentance" for all Jews (and not just the religious elite) corresponds favorably with the essential elements of preparation for the day of the Lord in the original Sinai covenant.

The key to understanding John's baptism is that it is *proclaimed*, which means that it is an action of God as opposed to a mere human action.[20] It is both a divine gift and a divine opportunity that is realized through repentance. "Repentance" (Gk. *metanoia*) is a compound word meaning "to change one's mind" or "to alter one's understanding," thus connoting rational decision and willful act as opposed to emotive feeling. But the Greek etymology of the word needs to be augmented by the concept of repentance and conversion in the OT, particularly in the prophets, if John's call to repentance is to be appreciated.[21] Repentance was the message of the Baptizer reduced to a word. It entailed, according to Mark's brief report in v. 4, a turning away from sin, and also, according to Matt 3:8 and Luke 3:8, a sign or "fruit," perhaps water baptism but more likely moral transformation. Above all, John's call to repentance is more urgent than that of the prophets; it is the only thing necessary to prepare people for the imminent judgment of God. Nor can John's call to repentance be compartmentalized. It lays claim to the totality of one's life, and not just for notorious sinners (Luke 3:12-13) or Gentiles (Luke 3:14) but even for righteous Jews (Matt 3:7-10).[22] In the only reference to John's baptism outside the NT, Josephus underscores the intention of reform inherent in John's call to repentance. "[John] exhorted the Jews to lead righteous lives, to practise justice towards their fellows and piety towards God, and so doing to join in baptism" (*Ant.* 18.116-18). Baptism in such a state of moral reform accomplished, in Mark's words, "the forgiveness of sins."

5 Exactly where along the Jordan River John baptized Mark does not say, although several factors suggest the stretches immediately to the south of the Sea of Galilee.[23] The "whole Judean countryside and all the

20. See Lohmeyer, *Das Evangelium des Markus*, 13-15; and Marcus, *The Way of the Lord*, 18-31, who argue that in the NT the object of the verb *kēryssein* ("proclaim") is an action of God.

21. *Metanoia* and *metanoeō* occur infrequently in the LXX, normally as translations of *naḥam*, "to regret" or "to be remorseful." The conditions of John's preaching of repentance, particularly as preserved by Matt 3:7-10 and Luke 3:7-9, reveal a pattern more reminiscent of Heb. *shub*, "to turn," which occurs in the MT more than a thousand times.

22. H. Merklein, "metanoia," *EDNT* 2.415-19; J. Behm, "*metanoeō*," *TDNT* 4.1,000-1,001.

23. The precise location of John's baptism is uncertain. Mark (1:5) and Matthew (3:6) say simply that John baptized in the Jordan River. Luke 3:3 reports that John "went into all the country around the Jordan," implying that John baptized at more than one

people of Jerusalem went out to meet [John]," according to Mark. The express mention of Jerusalem indicates that John's ministry drew attention (and perhaps converts) from the ruling elite of the temple in Jerusalem as well as from the countryside. John's notoriety, as Mark's description indicates, was widespread and impressive. Two or three decades later, about A.D. 55, the apostle Paul met disciples of John in distant Ephesus (Acts 19:1-7); and writing near the end of the first century Josephus devotes more attention to John than to Jesus (*Ant.* 18.116-19). John's attraction and influence, in other words, were history making. John's intention, however, was not to gain popularity but to initiate a movement of repentance and reform in Israel to prepare for "the one more powerful" to come (1:7; Luke 1:17).

6   The description of John's dress, nearly as unusual in John's day as it would be in ours, recollects the garb of a prophet (Zech 13:4), and particularly of the prophet Elijah, who wore "a garment of hair and a leather belt around his waist" (1 Kgs 1:8). The Hebrew of 1 Kgs 1:8 describes Elijah's clothing as a shaggy, goat-haired garment, which in Mark becomes a camel's hair robe on the Baptizer. Although offensive to some modern Western tastes, the eating of locusts fell within Jewish dietary regulations (Lev 11:22; *m. Hul.* 3:7) and provided a high source of protein and minerals. John's rustic dress and diet set him apart from the refined temple cult in Jerusalem and further identify him with "the desert region" (1:4). Not only does John's dress associate him with Elijah, but his fearless criticism of Herod Antipas (6:18) echoes Elijah's confrontations with King Ahab (1 Kgs 18:18).[24] Thus, in dress, setting, and proclamation Mark associates John with Elijah, the thundering prophet who renewed God's covenant with Israel on Mt. Carmel (1 Kgs 18:30-45). The stream of crowds that visit John are thus making a pilgrimage to a figure who is a harbinger of the fulfillment of Israel's destiny.

7   Unlike Matt 3:7-10 and Luke 3:7-9, which call attention to John's message of reform, Mark focuses on John's preaching of the "one more

---

place on the river and perhaps on the tributaries flowing into the Jordan. Taking Luke's description as a cue, B. Pixner suggests that John baptized at various places associated with Elijah (*With Jesus Through Galilee*, 19-20). The Gospel of John locates John baptizing at "Aenon near Salim, because there was plenty of water" (John 3:23). Both Aenon and Salim lie immediately to the west of the Jordan, some twenty-five miles south of the Sea of Galilee. This locates John's baptism in the Decapolis, close to Galilee. For a thorough discussion of the question, see R. Riesner, "Bethany Beyond the Jordan (John 1:28): Topography, Theology and History in the Fourth Gospel," *TynBul* 38 (1987): 29-63 (although Riesner's argument for Batanaea southeast of the Sea of Galilee is perhaps too speculative).

24. See M. Hengel, *The Charismatic Leader and His Followers*, trans. J. Greig (New York: Crossroad, 1981), 35-37.

powerful" to come. This description of Jesus anticipates the compact one-verse parable in 3:27, where Jesus refers to himself as the only one powerful enough to bind the strong one, Satan. According to a metaphor of the day, John thought himself unworthy to untie the sandals of the Coming One. The loosing of sandals and washing of feet were duties of slaves, indeed of only *Gentile* slaves, in first-century Judaism. The metaphor bespeaks John's humility and subordination in relation to the Messiah (see John 3:30).[25]

8 John's baptism was symbolic and provisional of a more permanent and powerful reality to come: "I baptize you with water, but he will baptize you with the Holy Spirit."[26] That is an extraordinary declaration, for in the OT the bestowal of the Spirit belongs exclusively to God. John's declaration, according to Mark, transfers the bestowal of the Spirit to *Jesus*, once again indicating that, as the Greater One, Jesus will come in the power and at the prerogative of God.[27] The spiritual power of the messianic baptism will thus supersede the symbol of water in human baptism. "*Holy* Spirit" identifies the spiritual power of Jesus with God, thus guarding the divine power from being misunderstood as something Satanic or evil (e.g., 3:22).

Although Mark's introduction of Jesus is considerably truncated in comparison to that of the other Gospels, its economy nevertheless testifies that the Christ-event is not a random and arbitrary occurrence. On the contrary, the dawn of the age of salvation in Jesus is the consummation of a purposeful history of revelation of God extending back to Israel's inception at the Exodus. From Sinai onward, and particularly in the prophets, God has been preparing for a new beginning in Jesus Christ.

---

25. See Str-B 2.557.

26. The manuscript tradition of v. 8 is divided whether John baptized "in water" or simply "by means of water." The first suggests immersion, whereas the second is more ambiguous. Although a slightly stronger field of manuscripts reads "in water," the simple *hydati* ("by means of water") is preferable (1) because of the support of the major Alexandrian manuscripts (‭א‬ B Δ) and (2) because scribes would tend to add *en* ("in") before *hydati* ("water") to agree with passages like Matt 3:11 and John 1:26. See Metzger, *TCGNT*, 74.

27. A few uncial manuscripts (B L) read *pneumati hagiǭ* ("with Holy Spirit"; followed by the NIV), and one (P) that Jesus will be baptized "in Holy Spirit and fire." The latter reading is an obvious assimilation to Matt 3:11 and Luke 3:16. The preferred reading, however, is represented by an overwhelming majority of manuscripts, "*in* Holy Spirit," which intensifies the union between Jesus and the Holy Spirit. See Metzger, *TCGNT*, 74.

THE BAPTISM OF JESUS (1:9-11)

Mark recounts Jesus' baptism in a mere fifty-three words in the original Greek. The significance of the event is vastly disproportionate to its size, however. As the inaugural event of Jesus' public ministry, the baptism tells us not what Jesus does but what God does to him. A reference in Acts 1:21-22 testifies that from the earliest days of the Christian movement the baptism was regarded as a defining and indispensable fact of Jesus' life. When the apostles found it necessary to choose a replacement for Judas, the main criterion was finding someone who had accompanied Jesus from his *baptism* onward. Although the Gospel of John commences with the preexistence of the Word of God and the Gospels of Matthew and Luke with the portentous circumstances surrounding Jesus' birth, Mark begins the story of Jesus with the inaugural event that the church from its very inception regarded as commencing the saving significance of Jesus' life and ministry, his baptism in the Jordan by John.

9 The introduction to the baptism in the first part of 1:9 has the ring of a Hebraism, suggesting an original Hebrew or Aramaic narrative. The mention that "Jesus came from Nazareth in Galilee" is the sole naming of Jesus' hometown in Mark, although Nazareth is alluded to again in 6:1. Mark links the baptism to the ministry of John the Baptizer by parallel wording in vv. 5 and 9.[28] Nevertheless, Jesus is not placed on the same plane as John. The strategic shift to the passive voice ("Jesus . . . was baptized by John in the Jordan") transfers John the Baptizer, who has been in the subject of vv. 4-8, to a mediatorial role, establishing Jesus prominently as the subject. Mark also shifts his verb tenses from the aorist (simple past tense) in v. 9 to the imperfect (continuous action in the past) in vv. 10-11, which has the effect of drawing the reader into the impending drama. When Jesus comes up from the water he experiences three things that in Jewish tradition signified the inauguration of God's eschatological kingdom: the heavens were opened above him, the Spirit descended into him, and the heavenly voice spoke to him. The concurrence of these momentous events at the baptism signals that Jesus is the "more powerful one" (1:7) promised in the OT and the inaugurator of God's eschatological kingdom.

---

28. 1:5: *exepereueto . . .*
   pasa hē Ioudaia chōra kai hoi Ierousolymitai pantes
   kai ebaptizonto hyp' autou en tǭ Iordanǭ potamǭ
   1:9: *ēlthen*
   Iēsous apo Nazaret tēs Galilaias
   kai ebaptisthē eis ton Iordanēn.
See Lohmeyer, *Das Evangelium des Markus,* 20

34

10 The prophet Isaiah (64:1) was the first to speak of the rending of the heavens and descent of the Messiah. Subsequent Jewish tradition elaborated Isaiah's imagery. The *Testament of Levi*, composed perhaps in 250 B.C., anticipates Mark's baptismal narrative by expressly mentioning all three eschatological signs noted above.

> The heavens will be opened,
> and from the temple of glory sanctification will come upon him,
> with a fatherly voice, as from Abraham to Isaac.
> And the glory of the Most High shall burst forth upon him.
> And the spirit of understanding and sanctification
> shall rest upon him [in the water].
> For he shall give the majesty of the Lord to those who are his sons in
> truth forever. (*T. Levi* 18:6-8; Charlesworth, *OTP,* 1.795)

A similar passage from the *Testament of Judah* speaks of the messianic king as the Star of Jacob, upon whom "the heavens will be opened . . . to pour out the spirit as a blessing of the Holy Father" (*T. Jud.* 24:1-3; Charlesworth, *OTP,* 1.801). The rending or opening of heaven is highly significant because Second Temple Judaism commonly believed that with the cessation of the great OT prophets the Holy Spirit had ceased speaking directly to God's people.[29] The absence of the Spirit quenched prophecy, and God was believed to speak to the faithful only in a distant echo, a *bat-qol* (Heb. "daughter of a voice"). The opening of the heavens at the baptism thus inaugurates the long-awaited return of God's Spirit. A period of grace begins in Jesus, in whom God reveals himself in the world in an unparalleled manner.

Especially significant is Mark's wording that the heavens will literally be "torn open" (Gk. *schizein*), a rendering softened by both Matt 3:16 and Luke 3:21 to "opened" *(anoigein)*. *Schizein* is the proper rendering of Heb. *qara* ("to tear") in Isa 64:1. *Schizein* also translates the Hebrew of the *Testament of Levi* and the *Testament of Judah* above. It appears in Jewish literature for cataclysmic demonstrations of God's power, such as the dividing

---

29. Ps 74:9; *T. Benj.* 9:2; *2 Apoc. Bar.* 85:3; 1 Macc 4:46; 9:27; 14:41; Josephus, *Ag. Ap.* 1.41. See J. Jeremias, *New Testament Theology,* trans. J. Bowden (New York: Scribner's, 1971), 80-81. See Str-B 1.125-34 for further evidence that at the death of the last prophets Haggai, Zechariah, and Malachi, the Holy Spirit (the Spirit of prophecy) disappeared from Israel and communicated henceforth only occasionally through an inferior Bath-Qol (further, Str-B 2.128-34). Qumran was an exception to this belief, however. For a counter view that the rabbis did not deny the presence of the Holy Spirit in Second Temple Judaism but that they were indifferent to it, partly owing to their desire to defend their authority from the challenge of nascent Christianity, see F. Greenspahn, "Why Prophecy Ceased," *JBL* 108 (1989): 17-35.

of the Red Sea (Exod 14:21), Moses' cleaving the rock (Isa 48:21), the splitting of the Mount of Olives on the Day of the Lord (Zech 14:4), or the descent of the heavenly man in *Joseph and Aseneth* (*Jos. Asen.* 14:3). Mark employs the word for similar effect at the baptism. *Schizein* occurs only once again in Mark, when the centurion confesses at the crucifixion that Jesus is God's Son, at which the temple curtain is "torn in two from top to bottom" (15:38). Both renderings — the first at his baptism and the last at his crucifixion — are supernatural occurrences revealing Jesus as the Son of God. Mark's strategic employment of this word indicates that the confession of Jesus as the Son of God does not arise from human resources but solely from divine revelation and empowerment (see 1 Cor 12:3).

The second sign attending the baptism is the descent of the Spirit. Scholars of a former generation rested too securely in Dalman's judgment that it was unheard of in Judaism to speak of "the Spirit" in an absolute sense, and that the presence of "the Spirit" in Mark 1:10 derived either from Hellenism or Christianity.[30] Dalman's dictum was an exaggeration even at the time, and it has been revealed so by further texts from the intertestamental period, and more recently from Qumran findings.[31] Above all, it was believed that in the eschatological age the Messiah would be endowed with God's Spirit.[32] This endowment is intensified in Mark's description of the descent of the Spirit. The NIV renders the phrase as "the Spirit descending on him," but the Greek intensifies the union of Jesus and the Spirit: "the Spirit was descending *into* him," indicating Jesus' complete filling and equipping for ministry by the Spirit. Likening the Spirit of God to a dove is unusual in Judaism (Str-B 1.124-25), but not wholly unknown. In Philo the dove symbolizes the wisdom and word of God; in the targum to Gen 1:2 the Spirit brooding over the water is seen as a dove (*b. Hag.* 15*a*); and in *Odes Sol.* 24:1 a dove flutters over the head of the Messiah (although this last passage is likely of Christian influence). Unlike Luke, who depicts the Spirit in "bodily form" (Luke 3:22), Mark sees the dove as a simile ("like a dove"), that is, as a visual image suggesting a dove. The imagery of a dove for the descent of the Spirit into Jesus is thus not a metaphor for spiritual enlightenment or even an inner mystical experience, but a supernatural occurrence that can be likened to empirical reality. Although Mark's account of the baptism focuses strictly on Jesus rather than on the bystanders, as do Matthew's and Luke's accounts, he does not describe a subjective inner experience

---

30. G. Dalman, *The Words of Jesus*, trans. D. M. Kay (Edinburgh: T. & T. Clark, 1909), 203.

31. *1 Enoch* 49:3; 62:2; 1QS 4:6; for a thorough discussion, see J. R. Edwards, "The Baptism of Jesus According to the Gospel of Mark," *JETS* 34 (1991): 46-47.

32. See the material gathered in E. Schweizer, *"pneuma," TDNT,* 6.384.

of Jesus. The emphasis on seeing and hearing attests to the empirical objectivity of the event.[33]

11 The final eschatological sign is the declaration from heaven, "'You are my Son, whom I love; with you I am well pleased.'" In Greek the voice is no longer the object of "saw" in v. 10, as are the first two signs. The voice is in the nominative case, making it the subject of what follows and signifying the climactic nature of the divine declaration. Only here and in the transfiguration (excepting John 12:28) do we see direct divine discourse with Jesus in the Gospels, and in each instance God addresses Jesus as "my Son."[34]

Beneath the divine declaration lies a wealth of OT imagery. One of its clearest antecedents is Isa 49:3, where the humble servant of the Lord, despite his feelings of utter futility, is declared to be the one in whom God displays his splendor: "You are my servant, Israel, in whom I will display my splendor." The parallelism between the declaration to the Servant of the Lord and the declaration to Jesus at the baptism is immediately apparent (also Isa 42:1). Like the Servant of the Lord, the Son also accomplishes God's will through hiddenness. Indeed, hiddenness is essential to the revelation of God, for only in divesting himself of his rightful prerogatives can the Son's life be transparent of God's will. Like the ministry of Isaiah's mysterious Servant, that of Jesus will be fraught with opposition and seeming defeat, but his vicarious service will have revelatory ("a light for the Gentiles") and salvific ("to bring my salvation to the ends of the earth," Isa 49:6) effect.

Beyond the concept of servanthood, the declaration at the baptism unmistakably identifies Jesus as God's Son by echoing the enthronement of the king of Israel in Ps 2:7. The filial intimacy and obedience that were imperfectly foreshadowed by the Israelite king are now fully completed in Jesus. Jesus is the perfect fulfillment of the original concept of sonship that was linked to Israel's call in Exod 4:22-23: Jesus is Israel reduced to one.

A third antecedent to the voice at the baptism is the concept of the *beloved* Son. Abraham's deep love for Isaac when he was called to sacri-

---

33. Note R. Bultmann's judgment: "There is not so much as a word about the inner experience of Jesus. . . . Matthew and Luke are quite right to take Mark's story as the description of an objective happening" (*The History of the Synoptic Tradition,* rev. ed., trans. J. Marsh [New York: Harper and Row, 1963], 247-48).

34. The Greek manuscript tradition is divided on how to describe the voice from heaven. The NIV follows the majority tradition that "a voice came from heaven" (א^c A B K L P W Δ Π), but the simpler reading of א* and D ("a voice from heaven") is impressive (1) because of the different traditions represented by the two manuscripts, and (2) because scribes would have tended to supply a verb. The reading of Θ, that a voice "was heard," is likely a later scribal improvement. See Metzger, *TCGNT,* 74.

fice him on Mt. Moriah is the clearest prototype for this aspect of the heavenly declaration (Gen 22:2, 12, 16). The divine proclamation expresses the steadfast love of the Father for the Son as well as their essential unity. Other NT writers (Rom 4:24; 8:32; Heb 11:17-19) and early church fathers (*Barn.* 7:3 onwards) also saw in the sacrifice of Isaac the prefigurement of the sacrifice of Jesus.

In the sublime declaration to Jesus at the baptism we encounter Fatherly love and filial obedience, kingship and suffering service. Each is a facet of what it means to be the Son of God. To no prophet had words been spoken such as the words to Jesus at the baptism. Abraham was a friend of God (Isa 41:8), Moses a servant of God (Deut 34:5), Aaron a chosen one of God (Ps 105:26), David a man after God's own heart (1 Sam 13:14), and Paul an apostle (Rom 1:1). Only Israel (Exod 4:23) — and the king as Israel's leader (Ps 2:7) — had been called God's Son before. But where Israel failed, Jesus takes its place.

The baptism is the keystone in the life and ministry of Jesus. The empowerment by the Spirit to be God's Servant, and the declaration from heaven, "'You are my Son,'" enable Jesus not only to speak and act *for* God but *as* God. This is demonstrated by his forgiveness of sins (2:5), acceptance of sinners (2:15), calling of tax collectors into discipleship (2:13), healing of the sick (1:40ff.) and casting out demons (1:24), recovery of the true intent of the Sabbath (2:28), and challenge to the Jewish religious establishment as represented in the oral tradition (7:1ff.), the temple (11:12ff.), and the Sanhedrin (14:61ff.). It is not coincidental that when Jesus is later confronted by the Sanhedrin asking, "'By what authority do you do these things?'" he drives his questioners back to his baptism (11:27-33). What Jesus does as God's servant ultimately has meaning only because of who he is as God's Son.

It is sometimes assumed that the baptism teaches adoptionism, that is, that Jesus first becomes God's Son at the Jordan. Although this view is possible, it is not very compelling. Assuming the originality of "Son of God" in 1:1, Mark has already announced Jesus' divine Sonship. The wording of the divine declaration, "'You are my Son, whom I love,'" does not establish a relationship so much as presuppose a relationship.[35] At

---

35. "Die Gottesstimme setzt nicht erst Jesu Sohnschaft, sondern setzt sie voraus." K. H. Rengstorf, *Das Evangelium nach Lukas*, NTD (Göttingen: Vandenhoeck & Ruprecht, 1965), 27. Further, "The New Testament authors desire to make clear: The one who is promised in the Scriptures as the Son of God is *in truth* according to his beginning and being, and therefore from his very inception, the *divine* Son who belongs at the side of God. Accordingly, *nowhere* in the New Testament is there talk of the man Jesus of Nazareth being adopted as Messiah" (Hofius, "Ist Jesus der Messias? Thesen," *JBTh* 8 [1993]: 125 — italics in original).

the baptism the heavenly voice declares and confirms first of all who Jesus is: God's Son, who as such is anointed and equipped with God's Spirit to express his filial status in terms of servanthood — indeed, suffering servanthood. The baptism signals the confirmation of Jesus' Sonship and the commencement of his servanthood.[36]

GOD'S SON MEETS GOD'S ADVERSARY (1:12-13)

Following the declaration of Jesus as God's Son and the inauguration of his public ministry, Jesus is not treated, as might be expected, to a reception or celebration. He is, rather, appointed by the Spirit to a much different task — to a meeting with Satan in the wilderness. Mark's description of the temptation, although less developed than the accounts of Matt 4:1-11 and Luke 4:1-13, makes clear that Jesus' status as God's Son and empowerment by the Spirit are given for the promotion of God's kingdom, foremost of which is the defeat of God's adversary, Satan.

12 Markan stylistic features are clearly evident in the temptation account. "At once" (Gk. *euthys*, occurring some forty times in Mark), the present tense of "send out" (NIV, "sent out"), and the skeletal brevity of the account are all vintage Mark. The haste and immediacy of the temptation on the heels of the baptism create a sense of imminence and fervency in the reader. There is no time to linger in the glory of the baptism. Without a moment to catch his breath, as it were, Jesus is thrust into the fray to pursue the ministry to which he is ordained and for which he is endowed. The apocryphal *Gospel of Philip* (74.29-31) has Jesus emerging from the baptism laughing in contempt at the world, as though his ministry were a melodrama. Not so in Mark, where dead earnestness pervades the temptation narrative. The same Spirit that descended on Jesus at the baptism has an appointment for him in the wilderness. The language is forceful and unambiguous. The Spirit "drives" Jesus or "thrusts him out" (Gk. *ekballein*) to confront Satan. The imagery is reminiscent of the scapegoat loaded down with the sins of Israel and expelled into the wilderness (Lev 16:21). Like the wording of 1:9 above, the passive voice ("being tempted by Satan") again establishes Jesus as the undisputed subject. The Spirit that empowers the Son for ministry now tests him to determine whether he will use his divine Sonship for his own advantage or submit himself in obedience to God.

The temptation of Jesus is not presented as an unfortunate circumstance or as a hardship resulting from a lapse or failure on Jesus' part.

---

36. Edwards, "The Baptism of Jesus in the Gospel of Mark," *JETS* 34 (1991): 43-57.

What happens to Jesus in the wilderness is as divinely orchestrated as what happened to him at the Jordan. The baptism, as we noted, is something that God did to Jesus; the temptation, likewise, is its necessary corollary, lest Jesus be imagined a divine clone or automaton who had no choice or desire of his own. The temptation establishes the free, sovereign agency of Jesus, who, like all human agents, must choose to make God's will his own. The significance of that choice can be realized only in the context of an alternative and opposite choice posed by God's adversary. Hence Jesus must be "tempted by Satan."

13 Like his description of John the Baptizer, Mark's story of the temptation is severely pruned, at least in comparison to the fuller temptation dramas of Matt 4:1-11 and Luke 4:1-13. Mark pares the narrative of the various tests in the latter Gospels in order to highlight the encounter with **Satan** in the wilderness. "Satan," from Heb. *śatan,* literally means "adversary"; but here as elsewhere in the NT it designates the personal and supernatural enemy of God. Mark does not employ the more functional term "devil" to refer to God's adversary, although the latter term occurs roughly the same number of times in the NT (thirty-four times) as does Satan (thirty-six times). Although explicit references to Satan are relatively infrequent in the Second Gospel,[37] Mark's use of "Satan" indicates his understanding of the personal agency of God's adversary, beneath whom are legions of subordinate "demons." As God's adversary, Satan endeavors to subvert God's reign as it is manifested through his beloved Son. In Mark, Jesus' first miracle (1:21-28) and parable (3:27) are offensives against Satan as "the strong one." The summary capsule of 1 John that "the reason the Son of God appeared was to destroy the devil's work" (3:8) is equally descriptive of Mark's Gospel.

The forty-day trial of God's Son continues the baptismal theme of Jesus as Israel-reduced-to-one. Israel was in the wilderness forty years (Deut 8:2), Moses was on Mt. Sinai forty days and nights (Exod 34:28), and Elijah was led for forty days and nights to Mt. Horeb (1 Kgs 19:8). In each instance the wilderness was a proving ground, a test of faithfulness, and a promise of deliverance. The same contrasts are present in Jesus' temptation, for in the wilderness Jesus is both tempted by Satan and attended by angels.

The wilderness as a place of testing and deliverance provides a clue to understanding the most curious element of Mark's temptation account, his reference to Jesus being "with the wild animals." There is no exact parallel to this statement in the Bible. One attempt to explain its meaning appeals to Adam's naming of the beasts in Eden (Gen 2:19), the

---

37. 1:13, 3:23, 26; 4:15; 8:33.

new covenant (Hos 2:18-19), and above all the transformation of hostile creation into a peaceable kingdom (Isa 11:6-9; Job 5:22-23). According to this interpretation, the wild beasts recall an image of redemption and new creation in which once hostile beasts are pacified and made subservient to Christ their Lord. Capitalizing on this theme, an apocryphal Gospel speaks of the wild beasts *worshiping* and protecting the baby Jesus in the wilderness (*Gos. Pseud.-Matt.* 19:1).

This is not an entirely satisfying interpretation, however. None of the OT passages cited above is close enough to the wording or thought of v. 13 to make it a convincing background or parallel.[38] Likewise, mention of the beasts follows immediately after the mention of Satan, the tempter and adversary, suggesting the beasts' alliance with Satan. Moreover, if the wild animals are meant to symbolize the new creation, then the following reference to the angels attending Jesus is a non sequitur, for Jesus scarcely needs ministering to (Gk. *diakonein*) in paradise.

All of these objections are relieved if we see the beasts as symbols of "the horror and danger" of the vast, haunting, and untamed Judean wilderness.[39] I am inclined to see in the reference to the wild beasts a very specific point of contact with Mark's Roman readers. Tacitus spoke of Nero's savagery toward Christians in the sixties of the first century in these words: "they were covered with the hides of wild beasts and torn to pieces by dogs" (*Ann.* 15.44).[40] Given the ravaging of Christians by ferocious animals during Nero's reign, it is not difficult to imagine Mark including the unusual phrase "with the wild beasts" in order to remind his Roman readers that Christ, too, was thrown to wild beasts, and as the angels ministered to him, so, too, will they minister to Roman readers facing martyrdom.[41] If this explanation is correct, then "with the wild

38. For an exposition of the wild animals as symbolizing the peaceable messianic kingdom inaugurated by Jesus, see R. Bauckham, "Jesus and the Wild Animals (Mark 1:13): A Christological Image for an Ecological Age," in *Jesus of Nazareth: Lord and Christ. Essays on the Historical Jesus and New Testament Christology,* eds. J. Green and M. Turner (Grand Rapids: Eerdmans/Carlisle: Paternoster, 1994), 3-21. Bauckham does not successfully show, however, that this is the meaning of the concept in Mark 1:13. Nor is his argument compelling that the preposition "with" (e.g., "*with* the wild animals") "cannot itself convey hostility," but only positive and friendly physical proximity (p. 5). In Mark 3:4, 6, e.g., *meta* ("with") is used of anger and of the death plot of the Herodians against Jesus.

39. Mauser, *Christ in the Wilderness,* 37, 100-101.

40. "ferarum tergis contecti laniatu canum interirent." The Latin "ferus" is the regular translation of the Gk. *thēr* ("beasts of prey"), a derivative of which, *thērion,* is used by Mark in v. 13. In the first decade of the second century, Ignatius (*Rom.* 5:2-3) uses the same Greek term *(thērion)* to refer to his impending martyrdom by beasts in Rome.

41. Ignatius (*Romans* 4–5) repeats the same word (*thēriōn;* "wild beasts") six times with reference to his impending martyrdom by wild beasts in Rome.

41

beasts" is an important piece of evidence for locating the provenance of Mark in Rome during the reign of Nero.

Although God leads Jesus into the test in the wilderness — as he leads Mark's Roman readers — God does not abandon either Jesus or them in it. The imperfect tense of the Greek verb for "attended" indicates that the angels ministered to Jesus not at the end of the test (so Matt 4:11), but throughout the forty days. This unassuming conclusion to the temptation is an example of the understated drama that characterizes Mark's Gospel. The way of the Son of God has the Father's blessing, and even in his trials by the archenemy Jesus is sustained by the Father's celestial attendants.

CHAPTER TWO

Beginnings of the Galilean Ministry

MARK 1:14-45

Mark only sparingly provides time and place designations in his Gospel. That he provides both at the commencement of Jesus' public ministry in 1:14 is therefore significant. Mark does not specifically mention a sojourn of Jesus in Judea as does the Gospel of John (3:22-36), but passing comments in his prologue that Jesus "came *from* Nazareth in Galilee" (1:9) and returned *"into* Galilee" (1:14) imply the possibility of a Judean sojourn. If Jesus' return to Galilee were a *consequence* of John's arrest in 1:14, then it might be possible to suppose, as John states (3:22), that Jesus collaborated in ministry in some form with John in Judea. But it is more likely that Mark intends 1:14 to be understood temporally, that is, *when* John was betrayed, *then* Jesus went public. At any rate, we should probably reckon with an interval of time between Mark 1:13 and 1:14, perhaps owing to an initial ministry in Judea.[1] Both Mark and John report that following an unspecified interval Jesus returned to Galilee (Mark 1:14; John 4:1-3). Mark seizes Jesus' return as a decisive moment and fashions it into a formal announcement in 1:14, a "press conference" of sorts, to signify the commencement of Jesus' public ministry.

---

1. See J. Murphy-O'Connor, "Why Jesus Went Back to Galilee," *BRev* 12/1 (1996): 20-29.

43

THE GOSPEL IN A NUTSHELL (1:14-15)

How remarkable that Jesus should choose Galilee in which to premier. "He did not prepare for a missionary campaign, first against Jerusalem and then into the rest of the world; no, he remained in insignificant Galilee."[2] Galilee, the Jewish settler region to the west of the Sea of Galilee, is where Jesus begins his ministry and, in terms of popular appeal, enjoys his greatest success (1:28; 3:7). Galilee is also where Jesus, following his death and resurrection, gathers his dispersed and defeated followers (14:28; 16:7) and recommissions them for ministry. Mark's depiction of Jerusalem, by contrast, characterized by unrelieved faithlessness and opposition of the temple and religious leaders, distinguishes Galilee, despite all its insignificance, as a place of promise and opportunity for the gospel.[3]

14 The baptism of Jesus by John and the arrest of John were milestones by which the early church demarcated the commencement of Jesus' public ministry (Acts 1:22; 10:37). Although the NIV speaks of John's being "put in prison," the Greek does not specifically mention imprisonment but rather John's "arrest" or "handing over." True, in Greek inscriptions and papyri the term is often found in police and legal jargon for "delivering up as a prisoner,"[4] but in Mark the term cannot be restricted to this sense alone. The word for "handing over" (*paradidomi*) plays a special role in Mark for the fate of the faithful. The same word will be used of Jesus' "handing over" as the Son of Man (9:31; 10:33; plus eight times in chaps. 14–15) and of Christian believers (13:9, 11, 12). "Handing over" combines not only the adversities to which the faithful are subjected but also the superintending will of God that is operative through them (14:21!).

The arrest of John and the beginning of Jesus' ministry are intentionally correlated to show that the gospel is proclaimed and known in adversity and suffering, not in ease and comfort. Jesus' announcement of "good news" (1:14) in the immediate context of the arrest and eventual

---

2. E. Schweizer, *The Good News According to Mark,* 47.

3. See R. Pesch, *Das Markusevangelium,* 1.104-5. S. Legasse, *L'Évangile de Marc,* 102-3, is correct in noting the sharp contrast between Galilee and Jerusalem in Mark, but he is wrong in supposing that Galilee represents the reception of the gospel by pagan Gentiles as opposed to its rejection by Jewish Jerusalem. Mark indeed emphasizes a Gentile impetus in Jesus' ministry (e.g., 7:24–8:10), but it is not represented by Galilee per se. The northwest shore of the Sea of Galilee, which was the focus of Jesus' early ministry, was the most *Jewish* region of Galilee, as evidenced by many synagogues (1:21ff., 39; 6:2), priests (1:44), and Jewish customs (2:16, 24; 3:4; 7:1-23).

4. C. E. B. Cranfield, *The Gospel According to Saint Mark,* 61-62.

execution of righteous John epitomizes Mark's presentation of the gospel. The Baptizer is the forerunner of Jesus not only in his message but also in his fate, which includes suffering and death. And the Baptizer is not a prototype for Jesus alone. As we shall see in the sandwich technique of 6:7-30, John's arrest and execution set a standard for disciples of Jesus as well. If, as seems probable, Mark's Gospel was composed in Rome in the mid-sixties, then the hortatory effect of linking the gospel with the arrest of the Baptizer would not be lost on Mark's readers who were suffering from persecutions under Nero.

The meaning of the term "gospel" *(euangelion)* has been discussed at 1:1.[5] As used in 1:14, the gospel refers to a narrative summary *of* Jesus' teaching, thus the content of his message. In early Christian tradition the term will increasingly include the proclamation *about* Jesus as the story of his life, death, and resurrection. Thus Jesus proclaimed the gospel, but he also *was* the gospel. The fact that early Christians referred to both the message of Jesus and the message about Jesus with this word — and bequeathed a third sense to the term by designating the written accounts of Jesus' life as "Gospels" — indicates how inseparably these various understandings are present in this one term.

This is the only reference in Mark's Gospel to "the good news *of* God," an expression that is reminiscent of Paul (Rom 1:1; 15:16; 2 Cor 11:7; 1 Thess 2:2, 8, 9; also 1 Pet 4:17). Since Mark has already introduced the gospel (Gk. *euangelion;* NIV, "good news") with reference to Jesus in 1:1, it is probable that by "the good news of God" he does not mean the good news *about* God, but rather the good news *from* God that is made known in Jesus Christ. "The good news of God" is thus the sum of Jesus' teaching and proclamation, and will be further elaborated by "the kingdom of God" in v. 15. The word for "proclaiming" (Gk. *kēryssein*) was used of John the Baptizer in 1:4, and its repetition here signifies the close association of Jesus' message with that of John. Although *kēryssein* is not used frequently in the OT prophets, it does occur in Isa 61:1 and Joel 2:1, two passages that announce the eschatological reign of God. The use of *kēryssein* in v. 15 suggests that in Jesus' proclamation of "the good news of God" the reign of God foreseen by the prophets has arrived.

15 1:14-15 are a synopsis of Jesus and his message, v. 14 providing the historical setting and v. 15 its interpretation. Mark is able to summarize the whole of Jesus' life and teaching in a single concept, **"the king-**

---

5. A respectable number of Greek manuscripts, including the majority Byzantine tradition, read "the good news *of the kingdom* of God" at v. 14. It is probable, however, that *of the kingdom* was inserted by copyists so as to conform to the common expression "the kingdom of God," as in v. 15. See B. Metzger, *TCGNT*, 74.

dom of God" (1:15). The kingdom of God takes its initial shape from Israel's concept of God as king (Exod 15:18; 1 Sam 12:12; Ps 5:2). As creator of the world, God is exalted above his creatures, rules in majestic splendor, mocks gods of wood and stone, and brings kingdoms to naught. The reign of God was initially manifested in Israel's history in the exodus from Egypt and the giving of the Torah at Mt. Sinai, but it would be supremely manifested in the advent of a future Messiah, whose reign would usher in the eternal and heavenly reign of God.

Jesus affirmed the above description of the kingdom of God. But he parted ways from other conceptions of the kingdom held by his contemporaries. Jewish literature of the period, not least the formulaic references to "the sons of light and the sons of darkness" in the DSS, shows a propensity to divide humanity into two classes, the righteous and the unrighteous. The righteous predictably took the yoke of obedience to the Torah on themselves, whereas the unrighteous did not; and because of their obedience the righteous could expect to be rewarded in the future after God annihilated the ungodly. According to the prevailing view, the kingdom ultimately depended on God, but its arrival was predicated on the prerequisites of human righteousness and obedience, which might be thought of as "matching funds" to the bargain.

In contrast to this understanding, Jesus' teaching is bold and innovative. He rarely — and never in Mark — speaks of God as king or of his sovereignty over Israel or the world. Rather, he speaks of *entering* the kingdom as entering a new state of being. The kingdom of God is not a result of human effort, nor does it evolve toward its completion, nor is it identical with a religious outlook or affiliation. As a mystery (4:11) that cannot be deciphered and calculated, it is best spoken of in analogies or parables (4:26, 30). At present the kingdom is hidden, although it awaits future manifestations of unprecedented proportions, including power and glory (9:1; 14:25, 61). Even in its hiddenness people must make a decision to receive it or reject it, and its future manifestation makes the present choice a matter of urgency. Even now in its embryonic form there are surprises. The rich and confident will scarcely find entrance (10:23-25), whereas the poor, insignificant, and outsiders — even children — find ready admittance (10:14-15). Even though the kingdom is not yet fully realized, the contrite and sincere already stand on its threshold (12:34). Thus, not only is the kingdom of God the substance of Jesus' teaching (1:15), it also corresponds to and is identified in the closest possible way with his own person and ministry. Mark's verb choice appears to reinforce the linkage of the kingdom with Jesus' person, for in declaring the kingdom "near" (v. 15) Mark employs a verb (Gk. *engizein*) that occurs frequently in the NT with reference to spatial rather than temporal nearness.[6] In Jesus of Nazareth the kingdom of God makes a personal appearance.[7]

"The time has come." The announcement of the kingdom at Jesus' debut in Galilee is presented by Mark as the definitive moment of history. The dawn of salvation, which Paul speaks of as "the fullness of time" (Gal 4:4; Eph 1:10), results from God's providence and timing, *kairos* in Greek, which means the "critical or opportune moment" (as opposed to progressive time). God has brought the time of prophecy as represented in the quotation of 1:2-3 to a close and has inaugurated the final phase of history. Jesus comes not hustling or selling the kingdom. Rather, he has submitted himself patiently to the divine timing and waited for the propitious moment, so long prepared for, of which he is the herald. The arrival of God's *kairos* demands a change in thinking. The new and unparalleled possibility presented to humanity in the gospel calls for a unique response. That response is contained in the word "repent" (1:15; see discussion of the term at 1:4), which demands a decisive change.

Coupled with the command to repent is the command to "believe." If repentance denotes that which one turns *from*, belief denotes that which one turns *to* — the gospel. Both verbs in Greek are present imperatives, that is, they enjoin living in a condition of repentance and belief as opposed to momentary acts. Repentance and belief cannot be applied to certain areas of life but not to others; rather, they lay claim to the total allegiance of believers. Repentance (Gk. *metanoein*) is used in the summary description of the proclamation of John (1:4), Jesus (1:15), and the disciples (6:12), and not again in Mark. The sequence of the terms "repent" and "believe" suggests that belief presupposes repentance and depends on it. Belief appears frequently in Mark, in both word and concept, and assumes the act of repentance.

Mark frames his introductory summary of Jesus' proclamation in

---

6. R. H. Fuller, *The Mission and Message of Jesus* (London, 1954), 20-25. The three occurrences of *engizein* in Mark (1:15; 11:1; 14:42) occur with respect to spatial nearness; thus, "in the appearance of Jesus the kingdom of God is *approaching*" (D. Dormeyer, "*engizō*," *EDNT* 1.371).

7. D. Flusser, *Jesus* (Jerusalem: Magnes Press, Hebrew University, 1997), 110-11, notes that "[Jesus] is the only Jew of ancient times known to us who preached not only that people were on the threshold of the end of time, but that the new age of salvation had already begun. . . . For Jesus, the kingdom of heaven is not only the eschatological rule of God that has dawned already, but a divinely willed movement that spreads among people throughout the earth. The kingdom of heaven is not simply a matter of God's kingship, but also the domain of his rule, an expanding realm embracing ever more and more people, a realm into which one may enter and find one's inheritance, a realm where there are both great and small. That is why Jesus called the twelve to be *fishers of men* and to heal and preach everywhere."

1:14-15 according to a characteristic OT schema that presents the revelation of God in terms of divine blessings and human obligations. The gracious activity of God evokes and demands an appropriate response from humanity (e.g., Exodus 19–20; Deut 29:2-8; 9-15). Likewise, the gospel, as it is proclaimed by and present in Jesus, can remarkably be summarized in a single indicative: the divine blessing is present in "the kingdom of God," and the human obligation is contained in two simple imperatives, "repent" and "believe."

CALLING THE FIRST DISCIPLES (1:16-20)

The first recorded act of Jesus' ministry in Mark is not something sensational — a spectacular miracle or a mighty sermon — but a simple summons of four common laborers into fellowship with himself. The setting is the **Sea of Galilee**, a picturesque lake some seven miles wide and thirteen miles long at the extremities. Lying nearly seven hundred feet below sea level, the Sea is confined by a rather precipitous bank of mountains on the east and by somewhat gentler slopes on the west. Seen from the heights, the lake has roughly the shape of a harp, from which it may have received its name in Hebrew, Kinnereth. Josephus extols the Sea of Galilee for its pure sweet water and many species of fish, its fertile soil and pleasing climate that supplies fruit and produce ten months of the year. The whole region, he says, is one in which "nature had taken pride" (*War* 3.516-21).

16-20 Mark does not specify where along the lake Jesus called the four.[8] The shoreline in the neighborhood of Capernaum, which presumably was the general location of the call, is a mass of broken black basalt, making for difficult walking and beaching of boats. Simon and Andrew were "casting a net into the lake" (1:16), according to Mark. The word for "casting a net" (Gk. *amphiballein*), meaning "to throw around," designates a circular net, an *amphiblēstron* according to Matt 4:18, measuring some twenty feet in diameter and with heavy bars of metal or rocks at-

---

8. Two scholars who have spent a lifetime investigating the Sea of Galilee, Mendel Nun and Bargil Pixner, place the call at Tabgha, some two miles south of Capernaum. The little Harbor of Peter, as it is known today, is commended as the site of the call of the four fishermen because of the small waterfall that plunges into the lake, where fishermen could wash their nets (Luke 5:2), and because warm springs entering the lake there attracted schools of musht in winter and spring, promising rewarding catches. See B. Pixner, *With Jesus Through Galilee,* 30-32; M. Nun, "Ports of Galilee," *BARev* 25/4 (1999): 27-28.

tached to the perimeter. With practice and dexterity the casting net could be handled by a single fisherman who, either standing in a boat or, as is the case here, wading out into the water, gathered the net on his arm and heaved it forcefully outward in a circular motion so that it would land like a parachute on the water, trapping fish as it sank to the bottom. Fish were retrieved by the fisherman diving to the bottom, gathering the weights of the net together, and dragging the net and its catch to shore.[9]

In the first century fishing was a thriving industry on the Sea of Galilee, which counted no fewer than sixteen bustling ports on the lake and several towns on the northwest shore, including Bethsaida ("house of the fisher"), Magdala ("fish tower"), and Taricheae ("salted fish"), named for the fishing trade. So numerous were fishing boats that Josephus was able to commandeer 230 of them during the war in Galilee in A.D. 68 (*War* 2.635). Nor was the catch consumed by local markets alone. It should be remembered that fish, and not meat, was the staple food of the Greco-Roman world. Fish from the Sea of Galilee were exported and prized in distant Alexandria in Egypt and Antioch in Syria. That fishermen in Galilee competed in the larger Mediterranean market testifies to their skill, prosperity, and ingenuity — and probably to their command of Greek, which was the international language of business and culture. The fishermen whom Jesus called were scarcely indigent day laborers. In order to survive in their market league, they needed to be — and doubtlessly were — shrewd and successful businessmen.[10]

Three aspects determine the call to discipleship. First and most importantly, Jesus is the unqualified subject of the call. As he passes along the shore and sees the two pairs of brothers, he issues a summons, "'Come, follow me.'" On this particular point Jesus was a very different leader from the rabbis and scribes of Judaism. There are no rabbinical stories analogous to the calling of the disciples, for rabbis did not consummate the teacher-student relationship by the summons, "Follow me." Unlike the decisive call that comes from Jesus, entry into a rabbinical school depended on the initiative of the aspiring student, not the call of a rabbi.[11] The personal prominence that Jesus assumes in the call of the four fishermen is highly unusual in Jewish tradition as a whole. The chief allegiance of rabbinic students was to the Torah rather than to a particular rabbi. In

9. See M. Nun, *The Sea of Galilee and Its Fishermen in the New Testament* (Kibbutz Ein Gev: Kinnereth Sailing Company, 1989), 23-27.

10. See J. Murphy-O'Connor, "Fishers of Fish, Fishers of Men: What We Know of the First Disciples from Their Profession," *BRev* 15/3 (1999): 22ff.; and Nun, "Ports of Galilee," *BARev* 25/4 (1999): 18-31.

11. K. H. Rengstorf, "*mathētēs*," TDNT 4.446-50; M. Hengel, *The Charismatic Leader and His Followers*, trans. J. Greig (Edinburgh: T. & T. Clark, 1981), 50-51.

the OT the idea of "following God" is rare, if not absent. Neither Moses nor the kings nor the various "men of God" nor the prophets call people, as a rule, to follow them. The summons, rather, is to walk in God's ways and according to his statutes (e.g., Deut 5:30). But Jesus calls the four to *himself*. The sole analogous OT precedent for a call to oneself is Elijah's call of Elisha in 1 Kgs 19:19-21, although even there the parallel is not complete, for Elijah allows Elisha to return home and say farewell to his mother and father, whereas the allegiance Jesus expects from disciples does not even permit a farewell to family (Luke 9:57-62).

The call to the four fishermen is rooted not in the Torah, nor even in the name of God, but in Jesus' messianic authority alone. No supporting evidence accompanies his call — no miracles or debate or moral persuasion. Unlike rabbinic aspirants, the fishermen are not required to do anything before they become disciples; they need not exhibit knowledge of the Torah or pass a qualifying examination in theology. What they need to learn and do can only be learned and done as they follow Jesus (10:52). For Mark, the act of following Jesus entails a risk of faith, and faith must be an act before it is a content of belief. Only as Jesus is followed can he be known.

The Gospel of John (1:35-42) notes that Peter and Andrew, and perhaps other disciples, had some prior acquaintance with Jesus before their call. Mark, however, omits reference to any such acquaintance and anchors the call of the disciples solely in the authoritative call of Jesus. They do not search for him, but he searches for them. It is in *their* world that discipleship begins. When Jesus as God's Son initiates human fellowship the encounter takes places not on his ground, or even on the holy ground of the synagogue or temple, but on their ground in the working world of boats and nets and labor from dawn to dusk. There is only one thing the fishermen can do, and that is to respond to the commanding word of Jesus, grounded solely in the authority of his person.

A second characteristic of the call to discipleship is that it is a call to service. "'Follow me,'" said Jesus, "'and I will make you fishers of men'" (1:17). The Greek wording is actually more nuanced, reading, "'I shall make you *become* fishers of men.'" The process of becoming disciples of Jesus is a slow and painful one for the Twelve; it is not easy to understand (8:14-21), to watch (14:37), to follow (14:50), to suffer persecution for the cause of Jesus (13:13). The life to which Jesus calls disciples requires a fundamental change of perspective, to have in mind the things of God rather than self (8:33). Only thus can disciples participate in and serve the kingdom. As the Servant whose goal is not to be served but to serve and give his life as a ransom for many (10:45), Jesus is the model of those who would follow him. This service is costly, requiring a separation from former allegiances in order to be free for the new allegiance to Jesus. Not only must the fishermen leave their nets behind, but they must also leave their own families.[12] There is nothing inherently wrong with nets, and less so with families. Nets are essential to fishing, and families to life. But even these must be abandoned if they become encumbrances that prevent one from heeding the call to the venture of discipleship with Jesus (see Matt 5:29-30).[13]

Finally, the call of the four fishermen indicates that the essential work of Jesus consists in forming a fellowship, and that only within fellowship is the call of Jesus heard and obeyed. The community that Jesus forms is not a nameless and faceless mass, but a community of individuals whose names are known — Simon, Andrew, James, and John, and others to come. Mark's emphasis on the call of the four fishermen, and his relatively modest account of the temptation scene (which pits Jesus in an individual battle with Satan), has the effect of making Jesus the initiator and center of a new, life-encompassing community.[14] It is not an exaggeration to say that the seeds of the Christian church originated in the first act of Jesus' public ministry in which he called four fishermen into community with himself.

THE AUTHORITY OF JESUS (1:21-28)

The introduction to Jesus' Galilean ministry in 1:16-45 exhibits Mark's economy of style by splicing several episodes together with only brief connectives ("and," "immediately," "then," etc.) and with little or no edi-

---

12. The transposition of *euthys* from the call of Jesus in Mark 1:20 ("Without delay [Jesus] called them") to the response of the Zebedee brothers in Matt 4:21-22 ("immediately they left the boat") is a syntactical refinement that argues for Matthew's use of Mark.

13. E. Schweizer, *Lordship and Discipleship*, SBT 28 (London: SCM Press, 1960), 12-13.

14. It is J. D. Crossan's thesis (*The Historical Jesus: The Life of a Mediterranean Jewish Peasant* [Edinburgh: T. & T. Clark 1991], 345-48) that Jesus was a representative of a "brokerless kingdom," a radical itinerant preacher of "unbrokered egalitarianism," who opposed any "brokering" of his message or ministry by Peter and the Twelve. Against this conception of Jesus, it should be noted that Mark's choice to begin his account of Jesus' public ministry with the calling of disciples clearly implies that Jesus has designs beyond those of healing, magic, and miracle working (as Crossan characterizes his ministry). Were the latter the sum of Jesus' agenda, then he, like Apollonius of Tyana or any number of the wandering preachers in the Greco-Roman world, could better accomplish them alone than in community. By all Gospel accounts, however, Jesus called and invested his disciples with his mission and authority (in Mark alone see, e.g., 6:7-13, 41; 8:6; 9:38-40!), as the catchword to become "fishers of men" (1:17) implies.

torial comment. Equally Markan, we learn through a variety of encounters (calls, exorcisms, healings, and travels) who Jesus is by what he *does*. In the synagogue in Capernaum, Mark demonstrates the authority of Jesus by showing what happens when a man with an unclean spirit meets the One anointed with God's Spirit. The story combines two episodes that make the same point. In the first, Mark shows that Jesus teaches with unique *authority*, unlike and indeed surpassing that of the scribes (vv. 21-22). The second part is an account of an exorcism (vv. 23-26). Both episodes are knit together by v. 27, in which Mark notes that all the people — and he emphasizes *all* — are astonished, for the authority by which Jesus expels a demon is the same authority by which he teaches. The combined stories demonstrate that *Jesus' word is deed.*

21 According to Matt 4:13; 9:1 (and ostensibly Mark 2:1; 9:33), **Capernaum** became Jesus' residence after leaving Nazareth. We are not told why he moved there, although it may have been because Capernaum was the home of his first converts. Capernaum was propitiously situated for a ministry in Galilee. It lay adjacent to the Via Maris, the main trade route between the Mediterranean coastal plain and Damascus in the north. It was also as distant as one could be in Galilee from the major Hellenistic cities of Sepphoris, Beth Shan, and especially Tiberias, where Herod Antipas made his capital, so that Jesus was able, at least initially, to avoid interference from political and religious leaders. Antipas's arrest of John the Baptizer (1:14; 6:14-29) made this second consideration not an insignificant one.

Capernaum, located on the north shore of the Sea of Galilee, took its name from Heb. *Kephar Nahum* ("village of Nahum"). Archaeological evidence indicates that in the first century a harbor extended along a 2,500-foot promenade that was supported by an eight-foot-wide seawall. Piers extended from the promenade a hundred feet into the lake. Capernaum was a border town between the tetrarchies of Philip and Herod, and hence the site of a customs office (2:14). Most (though not all) of its inhabitants were Jews, who labored as fishermen, farmers, artisans, merchants, and officials, including tax collectors. The already mixed population was augmented by a small Roman garrison that lived in better quarters than the locals and that enjoyed the amenities of a Roman bath, with caldarium, tepidarium, and frigidarium. Relations between Jews and Gentiles were evidently cordial since, according to Luke 7:1-10, a Roman centurion not only built a synagogue for the Jews in Capernaum, but on one occasion even found them pleading his case before Jesus. The commercial advantages of a location on a major trade route surrounded by fertile lands and plentiful fishing destined Capernaum to an enviable degree of economic prosperity.

Capernaum's prosperity continued for several centuries, for in the fourth century the city could afford to construct a synagogue — the most impressive to be excavated to date in the Holy Land — from imported white limestone rather than from the local black basalt, as was the case at neighboring Chorazin. The gleaming white limestone synagogue presents a striking contrast to the black basalt structures around it. This synagogue dates from the fourth century and is not the one visited by Jesus. A series of trenches cut beneath its floor in 1969 revealed a basalt stone pavement, however, which can be dated to the first century (it was strewn with first-century pottery and coins). This sub-pavement would appear to be the original floor of the synagogue visited by Jesus. The black basalt foundation of the synagogue Jesus knew is clearly visible at ground level beneath the fourth-century limestone synagogue.[15]

According to custom, Jesus enters the **synagogue** on the Sabbath and begins to teach. Unlike the temple in Jerusalem where animal sacrifice was practiced by priests, Jewish synagogues, according to rabbinic nomenclature, were "assembly halls" or auditoriums where the Torah was read and expounded. There was but one temple (in Jerusalem), whereas synagogues, the Greek derivation of which simply means "gathering places," could be found throughout the Mediterranean world wherever ten or more Jewish males, thirteen years of age or older, were present. The only official in charge of a synagogue was the "ruler of the synagogue," a position that included the responsibilities of librarian, worship committee, custodian, and perhaps schoolteacher. The ruler of the synagogue did not preach or expound the Torah, however, which meant that Sabbath teaching and exposition fell to the laity, and on this occasion to Jesus.[16]

22 The teaching the congregation hears from Jesus is unlike anything it has heard before. Reactions of those in attendance range from astonishment to incredulity — "The people were all so amazed that they asked each other, 'What is this? A new teaching — and with authority!'" (1:27). The only possible standard to which Jesus' teaching might be com-

---

15. On Capernaum, see S. Loffreda, *Recovering Capernaum* (Jerusalem: Terra Santa, 1985); R. Riesner, "Neues von den Synagogen Kafarnaums," *Biblische Umschau* 40 (1985): 133-35; V. C. Corbo, "Capernaum," *ABD* 1.866-59; M. Nun, "Ports of Galilee," *BARev* 25/4 (1999): 23-27. J. M. O'Connor's description of Capernaum as poor and undistinguished (*The Holy Land*[3] [New York: Oxford University Press, 1992], 223-25) is unjustifiably dismissive of the significance of the archaeological remains.

16. On synagogues, see S. J. D. Cohen, *From the Maccabees to the Mishnah*, LEC, gen. ed. W. Meeks (Philadelphia: Westminster Press, 1987), 111-15; G. F. M. Moore, *Judaism in the First Centuries of the Christian Era* (New York: Schocken, 1971), 1.29-36, 281-307; Str-B IV/1.115-88; E. Schürer, *History of the Jewish People*, 423-53.

pared is to that of the **scribes**. In the first century, before the advent of universal education and literacy, there was a great demand for scribes throughout the ancient world, and especially in Judaism where the written code of the Torah regulated Jewish life. The Hebrew word for scribes, *sopherim*, has to do with counting, reckoning, and keeping written documents, thus providing an initial understanding of the functions of a Jewish scribe. The term "scribe" occurs early in the Davidic monarchy for a royal official who was a general secretary and recorder (2 Sam 8:16-17; 20:24-25; 1 Kgs 4:3). In postexilic Judaism the word "scribe" came to designate an expert in the Torah, of whom Ezra was the first in an illustrious line (Ezra 7:6, 11). The importance and fame of scribes grew during the Hasmonean period when Hellenistic ideals began to rival Torah-learning among the Jews. Scribes were, first of all, experts in the Torah who were capable of issuing binding decisions on its interpretation. Scribal knowledge of the Torah, and the means by which it was attained, were often regarded as esoteric enlightenment, and hence the more authoritative. With the growth of the synagogue, scribes became, secondly, teachers of the Torah, whose reputation was honored by the title "rabbi," meaning "my great one." Finally, scribes were legal jurists in the broad sense of the term. "Scribe" thus combined the offices of Torah professor, teacher and moralist, and civil lawyer, in that order. Their erudition and prestige reached legendary proportions by the first century, surpassing on occasion that of the high priest (*b. Yoma* 71b). Only scribes (apart from the chief priests and members of the patrician families) could enter the Sanhedrin. Commoners deferred to scribes as they walked through the streets. The first seats in the synagogues were reserved for scribes, and people rose to their feet when they entered a room.[17]

Henceforth in Mark both synagogues and scribes will, for the most part, play oppositional roles to Jesus. The distance between Jesus and the synagogue is already hinted in v. 23 with the reference to *"their* synagogue."* Synagogues will appear another half-dozen times in Mark as places where demons are present (1:39), and where there is antagonism from religious leaders (3:1; 12:39), hardness of heart (6:2), and persecution (13:9). Likewise, there is but one positive reference to a scribe in Mark (see 12:28-34); the remaining eighteen references portray scribes as antagonists of Jesus and his mission. The general antagonism of synagogues and scribes thus foreshadows the coming rejection of Jesus from

---

17. On scribes, see G. F. M. Moore, *Judaism in the First Centuries of the Christian Era*, 37-47; E. P. Sanders, *Judaism: Practice and Belief, 63 BC–66 AD* (Philadelphia: Trinity Press International, 1992), 170-89; G. Baumbach, *"grammateus,"* EDNT 1.259-60; J. Jeremias, *Jerusalem in the Time of Jesus*, trans. F. H. and C. H. Cave (London: SCM Press, 1969), 233-45.

both temple and religious leaders in Jerusalem. The narrative effect of this is to reinforce the parable of 2:21-22, that the new wine of the gospel cannot be contained by the old wineskins of Judaism.

Mark's statement that "[Jesus] taught as one who had authority, not as the teachers of the law" (1:22) is less a disparagement of the scribes than an acclamation of Jesus. The word that Mark uses of Jesus' **authority**, *exousia*, is a preeminent term in his presentation of Jesus. In the latter portions of the LXX and in intertestamental literature, *exousia* is used more often than not of supernatural powers and authorities, especially of God and God's works, representatives, and emissaries, as expressed through kings, priests, and saints. The DSS follow suit, although at Qumran the Hebrew terms that lie behind *exousia* in the LXX[18] often refer to supernatural powers of a demonic nature. At any rate, *exousia* typically designates supernatural authority in literature immediately prior to the Christian tradition. In Mark *exousia* occurs nine times, six with reference to Jesus (1:22, 27; 2:10; 11:28, 29, 33) and three with reference to authority conferred by Jesus on the apostles (3:15; 6:7; 13:34). Every instance of *exousia* therefore reflects either directly or indirectly the authority of Jesus. Mark's use of this defining term at the outset of Jesus' public ministry establishes his authority over the highest authorities in both the temporal realm, as represented by the scribes, and the supernatural authorities, as represented by the demon in 1:23ff.[19]

The scribes derive their authority from the "tradition of the elders" (7:8-13) — the fathers of Judaism, we might say; whereas Jesus receives his authority directly from the Father in heaven (1:11). The authority of the scribes is contingent on the authority of the Torah and hence a mediated authority; whereas Jesus appeals to an immediate and superior authority resident in himself that he received at his baptism.[20] The amazement of the synagogue gathering at the teaching of Jesus is not solely owing to the fact that in Jesus they have seen a greater teacher than in the scribes. Rather, Jesus' teaching is qualitatively different, "not as the teachers of the law."[21] David Flusser, the Jewish scholar of Second Temple Ju-

---

18. *Mashal* and *shalat*.

19. On *exousia*, see further "The Authority of Jesus," Introduction 6.1; and J. R. Edwards, "The Authority of Jesus in the Gospel of Mark," *JETS* 37 (1994): 217-22.

20. "All [Jesus'] actions and words are connected with John and go back to the spirit of God's descent on him after he had accepted baptism at John's hand" (B. M. F. van Iersel, *Reading Mark* [Edinburgh: T. & T. Clark, 1989], 148).

21. D. Daube ("*exousia* in Mark 1 22 and 27," *JTS* 39 [1938]: 45-59) attempts to account for the opposition of the scribes to Jesus by arguing that two classes of scribes had developed in Jesus' day, an inferior class of elementary teachers called in Heb. *sopherim* (Gk. *grammateis*) and a smaller group of elite scribes who taught with *reshut* (*exousia*). Jesus belonged to the later group in Daube's judgment, and this accounts for the amaze-

daism, argues against the tendency in contemporary NT scholarship to relegate testimonies to Jesus' preeminent self-consciousness to later stages of the Gospel tradition. Flusser bases his arguments on evidence of the unusual self-prominence of Hillel and the Teacher of Righteousness from Qumran. Despite similarities between Jesus and Hillel, Flusser declares that "there is a great difference between the two. Hillel's self-understanding was not limited to his own person, but rather was a prototype for every person. Jesus' consciousness of his exalted worth was, like Hillel's, accompanied by personal humility and opposed to any hint of a 'personality cult,' but it was inextricably bound up with the knowledge that his own person was not interchangeable with any other person. He understood himself as 'the Son,' which meant that he had a central commission and task in the economy of God."[22]

Mark notes the amazement of the congregation at Jesus' teaching, but he does not recount the content of the teaching. The accent falls rather on Jesus the teacher. The word for "teaching" occurs in various forms thirty-five times in Mark,[23] and in all but one Jesus is the subject. In the synagogue of Capernaum, the "teaching" indeed amazes the congregation, but because of the authority of the teacher, which is so unlike that of the scribes. In the Gospel of Mark the person of Jesus is more important than the subject of his teaching. If we want to know what the gospel or teaching of Jesus consists of, we are directed to its embodiment in Jesus the teacher.

23-26 For Jesus' first public appearance in ministry Mark chooses an encounter in the synagogue of Capernaum in which the kingdom of God goes head-to-head with its unseen though ultimate opponent, the power structure of evil. The acid test of Jesus' authority comes in 1:23.

---

ment of the crowds in remote Galilee where only the lesser scribes were usually found. Against Daube's thesis, however, it must be said that the NT shows no awareness of a class of superscribes, nor that Jesus belonged to it. Since scribes are not mentioned in either Josephus or Philo, the NT witness becomes a weighty piece of counterevidence to Daube's thesis. Nor is Daube's attempt to equate *reshut* with *exousia* successful. *Reshut* occurs in only three fragmentary texts in the DSS (1QM 12:4; 4QM1 1+1:3; 4QM1 8+1:5), none of which carries the force of *mashal* or *shalat*.

22. D. Flusser, *Entdeckungen im Neuen Testament. Band 1: Jesusworte und ihre Überlieferung* (Neukirchen-Vluyn: Neukirchener Verlag, 1987), 210-15 [my translation]. Note further M. Hengel's judgment of Jesus' authority: "Jesus' claim to authority . . . goes far beyond anything that can be adduced as prophetic prototypes or parallels from the field of the Old Testament and from the New Testament period. . . . [H]e remains in the last resort incommensurable, and so basically confounds every attempt to fit him into the categories suggested by the phenomenology or sociology of religion" (*The Charismatic Leader and His Followers*, 68-69).

23. *Didaskein*, "to teach" (eighteen times), *didaskalos*, "teacher" (twelve times), *didachē*, "teaching" (five times).

Even more impressive than Jesus' authority as a teacher is his supremacy in the supernatural realm. Beginning with this story (see also 3:7-12; 5:1-20), the exorcisms in Mark depict the gripping conflict between the kingdom of God and the dominion of Satan, between the one anointed with God's Spirit and those held captive by unclean spirits. The inbreaking of God's kingdom in Jesus first begins, according to Mark, not in the human arena but in the cosmic arena, in order to bind the "strong man" (3:27) who exercises power over the natural order. Indeed, as supernatural powers themselves the demons recognize the mission and authority of Jesus before humanity does (1:24; 3:11; 5:7). The demons become the second party in Mark's presentation of Jesus, following the voice from heaven at the baptism (1:11), to announce Jesus' divine Sonship.

The demoniac cries out, "'What do you want with us, Jesus of Nazareth? Have you come to destroy us? I know who you are — the Holy One of God!'" (v. 24). "Unclean spirit" is a favorite expression of Mark (eleven times) for evil spirits, occurring roughly the same number of times as "demon" (thirteen times), both of which occur only in the first half of the Gospel. "Unclean" indicates that which is polluted or contaminated, which in a Jewish perspective is tantamount to ungodly. The plaintive appeal of the demoniac recalls the desperate words of the widow of Zarephath to Elijah (1 Kgs 17:18). "'What do you want with us?'" (lit. "What [is it] to us and you?") occurs not infrequently in the LXX and the NT.[24] With the exception of John 2:4, the phrase indicates that the two parties concerned have nothing to do with each other. The demon here, as elsewhere (5:9), refers to itself in the plural, perhaps because it reflects the subjective experience of the demon-possessed that a host of evil forces is at work within (so 5:9). Or perhaps the evil spirit knows that Jesus' mission is not simply to defeat one demon, but to lay waste the entire demonic power structure. The Greek word behind "said sternly" (v. 25, *epitiman*) is a technical term in Judaism "by which evil powers are brought into submission and the way is thereby prepared for the establishment of God's righteous rule in the world."[25] The first clash with Satan's minions following the temptation is a no-contest event. The strong Son of God prevails over evil and "binds the strong man" (3:27).

The demon refers to "Jesus of Nazareth" as "the Holy One of God." That may reflect the belief that speaking the name of a spiritual foe granted one mastery over it. The title "the Holy One of God" not only recalls the divine Sonship of Jesus' baptism (1:11), but apparently likens Je-

---

24. LXX: Judg 11:12; 2 Sam 16:10; 19:23; 1 Kgs 17:17; 2 Kgs 3:13; 9:18; 2 Chr 16:3; 35:21; NT: Mark 5:7 par.; Matt 27:19; Luke 4:34; John 2:4.
25. H. C. Kee, "The Terminology of Mark's Exorcism Stories," *NTS* 14 (1968): 235.

sus to Samson, the mighty vanquisher of the Philistines, who is the only other person in the Bible to be called "Holy One of God" (Judg 16:17). There may be an added correlation between Samson's "Nazarite" vow and the reference to Jesus from "Nazareth," both of which stem from the same Hebrew root.[26] Again anticipating the imagery of the "strong man" in 3:27, Jesus subdues the evil prince and his minions by the power of the kingdom of God.

27-28 The exorcism ends with the amazement of all present. "All" is emphatic in Greek (*hapantes*), meaning literally everyone. The word for "amaze" (Gk. *thambein*) derives from the root "to strike," meaning to astound or astonish.[27] The exhilaration of 1:27 has, interestingly, resulted in a Greek textual tradition confused by a welter of variant readings.[28] The impression of Jesus' authority goes deep, but it also "spread quickly over the whole region of Galilee" (v. 28). The initial report about Jesus from the synagogue in Capernaum is not simply of a victory of the Holy One of God over bent and evil forces, as though two chess players were manipulating pawns on the board for their own advantage. Jesus' defeat of the "strong man" (3:27) is not at the expense of Satan's victims but on their behalf. Not only are unclean spirits expelled, but broken people are restored to health and wholeness and to the possibility of restoration with their Creator, in whose image they are made. The *exousia* of Jesus is astonishing not as a display of Jesus' grandeur but as a power of redemption for captives.

A DAY IN THE LIFE OF JESUS (1:29-34)

Mark presents the events of 1:21-38 as comprising a single day whose activities are spliced together with five occurrences of *euthys* (vv. 21, 23, 28,

26. The correlation with Samson is made plausible by the designations "Nazarene" (NIV, "Nazareth") and "the Holy One of God," both of which are applied to Samson in Judg 16:17 (LXX), who in the A text is called *naziraios theou* and in the B text *hagios theou.* The Hebrew term behind *naziraios, nizir,* means "to be consecrated or devoted," hence the correlation with "the holy one of God." See E. Schweizer, "Er wird Nazoräer heissen," in *Neotestamentica. Deutsche und Englische Aufsätze 1951-1963* (Zürich/Stuttgart: Zwingli Verlag, 1963), 51-55. Lohmeyer's attempt (*Das Evangelium des Markus,* 37) to explain "the Holy One of God" with reference to the high priest Aaron is less plausible.

27. Mark regularly registers the public effect of Jesus' authority by superlatives: *ekplēssō* (6:2; 7:37; 10:26; 11:18); *thaumazō* (5:20; 15:5, 44); *ekthaumazō* (12:17); *thamboumai* (1:27; 10:24, 32); *ekthamboumai* (9:15; 16:5); *existēmi* (2:12; 5:42; 6:51); *phoboumai* (4:41; 5:15, 33, 36; 6:50; 9:32; 10:32; 11:18; 16:8). See Cranfield, *The Gospel According to Saint Mark,* 73.

28. See Metzger, TCGNT, 75.

29, 30; translated by the NIV variously as "just then," "as soon as," etc.). *Euthys*, which occurs eleven times in the first chapter (and more than forty times in the Gospel as a whole), seasons the account with a sense of urgency. The fast pace of the action and compressed time frame signal that the authority of Jesus as God's Son issues in decisive action. It is still the Sabbath (1:21, 32), and having left the synagogue Jesus enters the house of Simon and Andrew with James and John, the four fishermen called in 1:16-20. The healing of Peter's mother-in-law in vv. 30-31 is less exceptional than the majority of Jesus' miracles and might have been eclipsed by seemingly more significant works and wonders. The story, however, has the ring of a personal reminiscence and likely is included because of Peter's influence.[29] The inclusion of this humble miracle, and its subsequent multiplication among "the whole town" (1:33) and "throughout Galilee" (1:39), asserts Jesus' solidarity and engagement with common people and common needs.

29 Within a stone's throw of the Capernaum synagogue lies a structure that can reasonably be identified as the **house of Peter**. The house is part of a large "insula" complex, in which doors and windows open to an interior court rather than outward to the street. The court, accessed by a gateway from the street, was the center of the lives of the dwellings around it, containing hearths, millstones for grain, hand-presses, and stairways to the roofs of dwellings. The dwellings were constructed of heavy walls of black basalt over which a flat roof of wood and thatch was placed. Although the dwelling in question underwent various developments in succeeding centuries, archaeological investigations have discovered sacred and devotional graffiti in Greek, Latin, Syriac, and Aramaic scratched on the plaster walls, indicating that it was venerated as a gathering place for Christians, and perhaps as a church, from the end of the first century or the beginning of the second. There is a strong probability that the site preserves Peter's house.[30] No site, incidentally, has been identified in Scripture or tradition as Jesus' house, and it may be that Jesus lived with Peter in Capernaum.

---

29. T. Zahn (followed by many others) suggests that the account stems from a first-person report of Peter that ran thus: "We came direct from the synagogue to our house, and James and John accompanied us; and my mother-in-law lay sick of a fever, and we spoke with Him at once concerning her" (*Introduction to the New Testament*, 2.496-97). Zahn's suggestion may also shed light on the confused Greek textual tradition of v. 29. Although strong and numerous manuscripts support the singular pronoun ("he [Jesus] came into the house"), the plural reading ("we came into the house") better explains the variants and comports with the testimony of Peter suggested by Zahn. Further, see Metzger, *TCGNT*, 75.

30. Corbo, "Capernaum," *ABD* 1.867-68.

30 In the house Peter's mother-in-law lies ailing "with a fever." The word for "fever" (Gk. *pyressō*) is too infrequent in the NT and too general to identify the nature or cause of the ailment (see John 4:52; Acts 28:8). In the NT and rabbinic tradition fevers are often attributed to divine punishment or demon possession, and they still are among many bedouin in the Middle East. Our account gives no hint of either divine punishment or demon possession, but the parallel account in Luke identifies the miracle as an exorcism.[31]

31 Rather than discussing the nature of the fever, Mark emphasizes the all-sufficiency of Jesus as a healer. There are no spells and incantations typical of Hellenistic wonder-workers. Rather, hearing of the fever, Jesus "went to [Peter's mother-in-law], took her hand and helped her up." The Greek casts "helped her up" in the imperfect tense ("he was helping her up"), as though the healing were being relived, again suggesting a personal reminiscence of Peter. The healing depends solely on Jesus, whose personal touch and compassion restore the ailing woman to health.[32]

In response to the healing, Peter's mother-in-law "began to wait on them" (1:31). This verse has often been cited in support of relegating women to serving capacities. It cannot have connoted the idea of subservience or inferiority to Mark, for the word for "wait on" (Gk. *diakonein*) is the same word used for the angels' "attending" Jesus during the temptation (1:13). It is, moreover, the same word translated "to serve" in 10:45, where Jesus declares that the Son of Man comes "not to be served, but to serve, and to give his life as a ransom for many." Serving is the way of Jesus and those who attend him, and thus it describes an essential characteristic of the kingdom of God that Jesus introduces and exemplifies. For Mark, the proper response of one who has been touched by Jesus is to serve "them," that is, the Christian fellowship. (On serving, see further at 9:35.)

32-34 The compassion that Jesus demonstrated to Peter's mother-in-law is now extended to the crowds. The Sabbath extended from sunset

---

31. "[Jesus] . . . rebuked the fever, and it left her" (Luke 4:39). The Greek word for "rebuke," *epitiman*, is a common technical term for exorcisms. On "fever," see K. Weiss, "*pyressō*," *TDNT* 6.956-59.

32. It is interesting to note the factuality with which Jesus' miracles are described in contrast to those of familiar Hellenistic wonder-workers. In many Hellenistic accounts, the verb "seem" *(dokein)*, or a similar term, accompanies the description of a miracle. Thus the girl whom Apollonius was reputed to have raised from the dead only "seemed" dead, according to Philostratus (*Life Apoll.* 4.45). Asclepius "seemed" to have "brought back many to life who had died" (Diodorus, 4.71.1-2). People "assumed" *(hypolambanein)* that Heracles went to be with the gods after his cremation (Diodorus 4.38), and a thunderbolt "seemed" to fall at Apollonius's birth (Philostratus, *Life Apoll.* 1.4).

on Friday to sunset on Saturday, during which Jews were forbidden to work or travel. This explains why the crowds gather only after sunset on the Sabbath. The desperation of the sick and demon-possessed is expressed in simple Markan pathos: "The whole town gathered at the door." The door of Jesus' compassion and power is open to them, for he "healed many who had various diseases."[33] When Mark says Jesus "healed many," he does not mean to imply that Jesus healed only some but not others. He employs "many" in the Hebraic *(rabbim)* sense for "the whole community." Jeremias suggests a translation, "Great was the number of those healed."[34]

Demons (1:34) play an important role here and elsewhere in Mark's Gospel. Mark situates all demons and exorcisms in the first half of the Gospel, thereby helping the reader to understand Jesus' identity. The prophets foresaw that God would banish the names of idols on the Day of the Lord (Zech 13:2); for Mark the Day of the Lord is signified by Jesus' vanquishing and banishing the works and servants of Satan. At the baptism (1:11), the heavenly voice announces that Jesus is God's Son. This declaration is reinforced by a series of alternating questions and answers in succeeding chapters. The questions about Jesus' identity come from the human side (1:27; 2:7; 4:41; 6:2; 6:14-16), and the answers come, in part, from the demonic side (1:24; 1:34; 3:11; 5:7). The effect of the interplay between human questions and demonic answers reveals that the human participants do not yet understand Jesus' identity, whereas the demons do, for they, as he, belong to the spiritual world.[35]

Demons, in turn, are closely related to the **command to silence**, which occurs here for the second time (see 1:24-25). "[Jesus] would not let the demons speak because they knew who he was." The command to si-

33. A subtle change of wording in the parallel passage in Matthew argues in favor of Markan priority. Whereas Mark says that "all" were brought to Jesus, of whom "many" were healed (1:32, 34), Matt 8:16 says that "many" were brought, "all" of whom were healed. Mark's wording raises questions in readers' minds why Jesus did not heal all who were sick. It is more reasonable to suppose that Matthew changed Mark's text, thereby relieving it of a possible diminution of Jesus' power, than that Mark introduced such a diminution into Matthew's otherwise felicitous text.

34. In Talmudic literature, *harabbim* consistently designates "the whole community." Likewise, at Qumran the term designates the guild of fully qualified members. In Rom 5:15 Gk. *hoi polloi* ("the many") carries an equally universal and inclusive sense. The anarthrous adjective can carry the same connotation (e.g., *1 Enoch* 62:3, 5). See J. Jeremias, *The Eucharistic Words of Jesus,* trans. N. Perrin (London: SCM Press, 1964), 179-82.

35. A number of Greek manuscripts (B L W Θ C, plus corrections to ℵ) read that the demons recognized Jesus to be the Messiah *(Christos).* It seems unlikely, however, that Mark included *Christos,* which occurs very infrequently (seven times) in the Second Gospel. The inclusion of the title is most likely to be explained as an assimilation to Luke 4:41. Had the title been original with Mark, it is hard to imagine a scribe omitting it.

lence touches one of the most controversial nerves of the Gospel. Why does Jesus seemingly work at cross purposes with himself by forbidding the healed to make him known? The command to silence seems to frustrate the publication of the kingdom of God for which he has come (1:14-15).

An adequate explanation of the command to silence appears to require three components. First, on a practical and strategic level, it was necessary for Jesus to silence messianic utterances about himself since these carried connotations of military deliverance (see further on **Christ** at 8:29). Not only were such connotations inappropriate to his mission, but publication of the title "Messiah" (or an equivalent) would have invited swift intervention from the Roman occupation. Moreover, Jesus rejects any announcement of his person and mission by demons opposed to God's kingdom.

But the command to silence is rooted in more than strategic interests. Second and more importantly, it appears to derive from the profile of the Servant of the Lord to which Jesus consciously patterns his ministry. The Servant is defined by restraint and humbleness: "a bruised reed he will not break" (Isa 42:3). That restraint comes to fuller expression in Isa 49:1-6. Although the Servant feels that he "has labored to no purpose" and "spent his strength in vain," God assures him to the contrary that he will be "a light to the nations." The deftness of the Servant's message ("He made my mouth like a sharp sword") and the range of his influence ("he made me like a polished arrow") are concealed within hiddenness ("in the shadow of his hand he hid me . . . and concealed me in his quiver"). The Psalms know that the righteous one must be hidden (17:8; 27:5; 64:3), but the idea comes to fullest expression in the Servant hymns of Isaiah, where hiddenness becomes a defining element of the Servant's mission. The prototype of the Servant of the Lord appears to have exerted the strongest possible influence on Jesus' ministry (Matt 12:15-21). No other figure, whether Abraham, Moses, Samuel, or one of the kings or prophets, corresponds as closely to Jesus' ministry nor influenced it more profoundly than that of the Servant of the Lord.

The Servant motif is assuredly a key to the question why God's Son channels his authority and power in hiddenness. That which truly changes the human heart and ultimately compels one to recognize and follow Jesus can never come from coercion or a display of miraculous power. Jesus will have no allegiance exacted by amazement and astonishment. The faith of his disciples must be evoked through humility and ultimately through suffering. If one will not receive Jesus in this form, one will not receive Jesus in all his power and majesty.

The command to silence thus represents both strategic and typological interests in Jesus' historical ministry. But the silencing theme plays yet a third role in the Gospel of Mark.[36] In addition to its roles in Jesus' historical ministry, Mark employs the theme for his own christological purpose, namely, that until the consummation of Jesus' work on the cross all speculations about him are premature. Only on the cross can Jesus rightly be known for who he is. Until the confession of the centurion at the cross (15:39), all utterances about Jesus — and especially those coming from members of the rebellion — are either premature or false. Thus, strategic and typological motives in Jesus' life and christological motives in Mark's story cohere in Jesus' command to silence.

Excursus: The Secrecy Motif and Jesus' Messianic Self-Consciousness

The secrecy motif is an inherent part of the fabric of Mark's Gospel. On three occasions *demons* are enjoined to silence (1:25; 1:34; 3:11). Jesus commands silence after four *miracles* (cleansing of a leper, 1:44; raising of a dead girl, 5:43; healing of a deaf-mute, 7:36; healing of blind man, 8:26). Twice the *disciples* are commanded to silence (8:30; 9:9). Twice Jesus withdraws from *crowds* to escape detection (7:24; 9:30). Beyond these explicit admonitions to secrecy, Mark implies secrecy in other aspects of Jesus' public ministry. Only "inside" with the disciples does Jesus explain the mysteries of the kingdom, whereas in public the kingdom is cloaked in parables (4:10-12). He gives private instruction to his disciples on inner corruption (7:17-23), messianic suffering (8:31; 9:31; 10:33), and the second coming (13:24-27). Jesus chooses to reveal the mystery and glory of his divine Sonship only to intimate followers, and then in guarded settings (4:10-20; 8:27–9:13). But, ironically, the command to silence often results in the opposite: "the more he [commanded to silence], the more they kept talking about it" (7:36; 1:45; 5:20; 7:24).

In *The Messianic Secret*,[37] William Wrede attempted to argue that the admonitions to secrecy in Mark were only additions stemming from the pre-Markan tradition and from Mark himself. It was Wrede's belief that the early church was caught in a contradiction between what it *received* about Jesus and what it eventually *believed* about him. Wrede suggested

---

36. On the use of the Servant of Yahweh motif in portraying Jesus' ministry, see J. Marcus, *The Way of the Lord: Christological Exegesis of the Old Testament in the Gospel of Mark* (Edinburgh: T. & T. Clark, 1992), 186-94; and R. E. Watts, *Isaiah's New Exodus and Mark*, WUNT 88 (Tübingen: Mohr Siebeck, 1997), 119-21.

37. W. Wrede, *The Messianic Secret*, trans. J. Greig (Cambridge/London: Clarke, 1971).

that the most primitive traditions of Jesus' life were nonmessianic, although following Easter the church had come to believe that Jesus was indeed the Messiah. The presence of the secrecy material provided the key, in Wrede's estimation, to solve the contradiction. The church, and Mark the evangelist, inserted admonitions to secrecy at various points in the Gospel to explain why Jesus' earthly life appeared nonmessianic, as well as to explain how later generations after the resurrection (e.g., 9:9) came to regard him as messianic.

Wrede's theory, first proposed in 1901, has bewitched a century of scholarship on the Gospel of Mark. Its influence, however, has been disproportionate to its merit.[38] The theory is founded on the essential presumption that the historical Jesus neither believed himself to be nor was the Messiah. If Jesus' awareness of his divine Sonship can be reasonably established, Wrede's theory collapses. It is precisely this belief that the Gospel of Mark everywhere presupposes, for a nonmessianic stratum of the Gospel tradition has yet to be discovered. The messianic consciousness of Jesus is deeply imbedded in Jesus' speech, actions, and bearing, especially as expressed in his *exousia,* his divine authority that commenced at his baptism.[39] It must be remembered that the proclamation and writing of the gospel arose within Judaism. Given the foundational significance of the *Shema* (Deut 6:4) and monotheism in Judaism, it is scarcely conceivable that Jews who believed Jesus to be the Messiah would have fabricated his divine Sonship. The only reasonable answer for their incurring the odium of fellow Jews in proclaiming the gospel is that they believed Jesus to be God's Son and Messiah. Jesus could scarcely have been proclaimed as Messiah after the resurrection unless he had been recognized as such during his ministry. Moreover, it is a consid-

---

38. Already in 1926 Geerhardus Vos exposed and refuted the flaws in Wrede's thesis (*The Self-Disclosure of Jesus* [Grand Rapids: Eerdmans, repr. in 1954]). Further, see V. Taylor, *The Gospel According to St. Mark,* 122-24; O. Betz, "Die Frage nach dem messianischen Bewusstsein Jesu," *NovT* 6 (1963): 28-48; G. E. Ladd, *A Theology of the New Testament* (Grand Rapids: Eerdmans, 1974), 169-71; R. P. Martin, *Mark, Evangelist and Theologian* (Grand Rapids: Zondervan, 1972), 148-50; N. T. Wright, *The New Testament and the People of God* (London: SPCK, 1992), 391.

39. "In the last resort, the messianic secret goes back to the mysterious messianic authority of Jesus. So it is no invention of the gospel of the pre-Marcan community, but an expression of the mystery of Jesus himself which presses forward to the question of the Messiah. . . . The mystery of the messianic *exousia* of Jesus and the mystery of the kingdom in 4:11 are indissolubly connected in the historical person of Jesus himself. . . . With so unique a figure as Jesus, who bursts all historical frameworks, there could be no 'one-dimensional tradition,' without tensions and apparent contradictions. His person and activity cannot be forced into the confines of ready-made christological theories" (M. Hengel, *Studies in the Gospel of Mark,* trans. J. Bowden [London: SCM Press, 1985], 45).

erable leap of faith to believe that Jews would be willing to surrender their trump card of monotheism in exchange for acceptance of the gospel by "Gentile sinners" (Gal 2:15) and idolaters (Rom 1:23), as is often conjectured. Finally, the crucifixion is virtually unexplainable unless Jesus was suspected by Rome of being a messianic pretender.

Wrede's theory results in a thoroughly skeptical view of Mark's historical value and literary and theological coherence. In order to answer the question posed by Wrede it is unnecessary to resort to a theory fraught with questionable historical and literary assumptions. Evidence within the Gospels themselves is manifold and varied that the dominant genre of Jesus' messianic self-consciousness was transmitted to the early church and to Mark by Jesus himself. The secrecy motif arose from Jesus' conscious identification with the Servant of the Lord motif in Isaiah and from the need to guard his messianic identity from premature and false understandings. With regard to the command to silence, both historical and literary factors argue that Mark's presentation of Jesus stands in essential continuity with the Jesus of history.

JOURNEY INWARD, JOURNEY OUTWARD (1:35-39)

Mark now moves from the particular to the general. The healing of Peter's mother-in-law in 1:30-31 yields to a general summary of Jesus' mission in vv. 35-39, without details of location or duration. The effect of the summary is to show that Jesus' ministry extends beyond both the confines of Capernaum and the scope of the Gospel narrative so far. Despite its general nature, this brief historical summary advances Mark's theological purpose that in his ministry of teaching and healing Jesus remains essentially misunderstood, and not only by the religious leaders and crowds but also by his own disciples.

35 The awkward and redundant opening of 1:35 in Greek (*kai prōi ennycha lian;* NIV: "Very early in the morning, while it was still dark") sounds more colloquial than literary, perhaps reflecting a reminiscence of Peter. Jesus rises early and leaves Capernaum to pray in solitude. The Greek word for "solitary place" (*erēmos*) is the same word for the wilderness where John preached (1:4) and where Jesus was tempted (1:12). As we noted earlier, in Mark the word does not connote a desert waste but, reflecting Israel's sojourn in the wilderness following the Exodus, a place of repentance, restoration, and fellowship with God.[40] Mark records Jesus

---

40. "Israel's wanderings under the leadership of Moses were a march under the

praying only three times in the Gospel; here (1:35), following the feeding of the five thousand (6:46), and in Gethsemane (14:32-39). All three occur at night and in solitary places. All three also occur in contexts of either implied or expressed opposition to Jesus' ministry. Amid a whirlwind of activity, Jesus seeks a still point in prayer with the Father. There is a suggestive parallel in wording between Jesus going out to pray (v. 35) and his going out to preach and expel demons (v. 39). The work of the Son of God is both an inward and an outward work. Jesus cannot extend himself outward in compassion without first attending to the source of his mission and purpose with the Father; and, conversely, his oneness with the Father compels him outward in mission. The significance of Jesus' ministry consists not simply in what he does for humanity, but equally in who he is in relation to the Father. Jesus is, according to Mark's narrative, neither contemplative ascetic nor social activist. He does not promote an agenda but derives a ministry from a relationship with the Father. He is the Son, one in being with the Father; and the Servant, one in purpose with his will.

36 The NIV rendering ("Simon and his companions went to look for [Jesus]") is anemic compared to Mark's vigorous wording: Simon and company "pursued" (Gk. *katadiōkein*) him. The Greek verb can even connote "hunted." Luke 4:42 says that Jesus was pursued by "the people" rather than by Simon, perhaps to spare offense to Simon and the disciples. Mark, however, intentionally identifies the intruder as Simon Peter and the other disciples. This seemingly innocuous intrusion and Peter's more infamous opposition in 8:32-33, which forms a watershed in Mark, are curiously alike. In both passages Simon Peter is the only disciple named, and in both he tries to prevent Jesus from fulfilling his mission. In both instances the chief apostle is found to be the chief antagonist to God's Son. This episode foreshadows the more emphatic truth of 8:31-39, that discipleship consists not in attempting to control God's work but in following God's Son.[41]

37 When the disciples find Jesus they announce, "'Everyone is looking for you.'" Again, the language is deceptive. The Greek word be-

---

guidance of the Spirit of God (Isa 63:11), and the Spirit gave the people rest (Isa 63:14). As the first exodus had been a journey under the leadership of God's Spirit, it is not surprising that the prophet [Isaiah] expects a new outpouring in the time of the second exodus" (U. Mauser, *Christ in the Wilderness* [London: SCM Press, 1963], 52; see also 105-8).

41. J. Crossan (*The Historical Jesus,* 346-47) correctly recognizes the conflict between Peter and Jesus in 1:36, but there is no suggestion, either here or in the rejection of Jesus at Nazareth (6:1-6), that the conflict resulted, as Crossan argues, from the hope of Jesus' disciples and family to reap benefits from his fame and gifts. The problem is not "brokerage," to quote Crossan, but misunderstanding and disbelief.

hind "looking for" *(zētein)* occurs ten times in Mark, and in each instance it carries negative connotations. Its first two occurrences refer to interference of Jesus and obstruction of his ministry (1:32; 3:32); its next two refer to disbelief and faithlessness (8:11; 8:12); and the remaining occurrences refer to attempts to kill Jesus (11:18; 12:12; 14:1; 14:11; 14:55).[42] "Seeking" connotes an attempt to determine and control rather than to submit and follow. In this respect, seeking for Jesus is not a virtue in the Gospel of Mark. Nor are clamoring crowds a sign of success or aid to ministry. Here, as elsewhere in Mark, enthusiasm is not to be confused with faith; indeed, it can oppose faith.

38-39   The disciples evidently want Jesus to capitalize on his notoriety as a miracle worker. Already on the first day of public ministry, according to Mark, Jesus' mission is endangered, and by those closest to him. Jesus, however, remains undeflected from his purpose, responding simply and decisively, "This is why I have come." In this unassuming declaration Jesus reaffirms his baptismal commission of service that he fulfills by "proclaiming the good news of God" (1:14-15). In Mark the word for "proclaim" (Gk. *kēryssein*), occurring twice in vv. 38-39, is not reserved solely for the activity of Jesus or of John the Baptizer. A wide variety of heralds proclaim the gospel — Jesus, John the Baptizer, a cleansed leper, a healed demoniac, the disciples, even the crowds. The gospel is proclaimed by unexpected and unlikely sources, but the subject of its varied messengers is consistently the good news of Jesus.[43]

Mark locates Jesus' preaching and exorcisms in "their synagogues" (1:39).[44] The focus of Jesus' ministry to Jewish synagogues again (1:21) identifies him as a teacher of Israel. He is not, like the wandering philosophers in the Greco-Roman world, a maverick and unaligned individual-

42. The final occurrence of *zētein* in 16:6 is less pejorative, but here, too, it appears to question the women's search for Jesus. It is probably too speculative to suggest that Mark intends by this final more positive reference to imply that one can only seek Jesus after the resurrection.

43. There are two sets of textual variants in v. 39. The first concerns *ēlthen kēryssōn* ("he came preaching"), which is favored by ℵ B L Θ. The textual support for this reading is slightly inferior to the periphrastic imperfect *ēn kēryssōn* ("he was preaching"; A C D K W Δ Π), which is a typically Markan construction. A decision on the first set of variants cannot be rendered apart from the second set of variants, however. The second set concerns *eis tas synagōgas autōn* ("into their synagogues"), which is adopted by nearly all Markan manuscripts and is clearly superior to *en tais synagōgais autōn* ("in their synagogues"), which is attested only in late minuscule manuscripts. The well-attested *eis tas synagōgas autōn* requires a preceding transitive verb, and this argues for the originality of the transitive *ēlthen* over the intransitive *ēn* in the first set of variants.

44. The towns visited by Jesus were large enough to have synagogues, which required at least ten bar mitzvahed males. Mark's word for "villages" (v. 38), *kōmopoleis*, also suggests towns of at least moderate size rather than small villages. See Str-B 2.3-4.

ist. The gospel is not revealed in a vacuum, nor in ecstatic and voluntary movements, of which there were not a few in first-century Palestine. Jesus directs his ministry to practicing communities of faith in Judaism in fulfillment of an earlier history of revelation (1:2-3). His mission is defined and directed by the completion of God's purpose for Israel.

JESUS TRADES PLACES WITH A LEPER (1:40-45)

By appending this story to 1:35-39 Mark leads us to understand it as an example of Jesus' missionary outreach to "the nearby villages" (v. 38) of Capernaum. Like the previous narrative, and typical of Mark, it lacks geographical specificity. Just as an elaborate frame can detract from a great painting, Mark regularly omits contextual details so as not to detract from the essential focus of the narrative.

40 "A man with leprosy came to him" understates a highly provocative and offensive encounter. **Leprosy** was a widespread disease in Palestine. This is apparent not only from the several lepers whom Jesus encountered in his ministry but also from the plethora of instructions about the disease in the Mishnah. Leprosy was then as now a subject of superstition and fear. Leprosy is a skin disease, and like all skin diseases it is difficult to diagnose and heal. Its conditions are discussed in two lengthy chapters in Leviticus 13–14 that read like an ancient manual on dermatology. The Hebrew term *tsara'at* covers other skin diseases besides leprosy, including boils (Lev 13:18), burns (Lev 13:24), itches, ringworm, and scalp conditions. Scribes counted as many as seventy-two different afflictions that were defined as leprosy. In the OT leprosy was generally regarded as a divine punishment, the cure of which could only be effected by God (Num 12:10; 2 Kgs 5:1-2). The dread of its contagion is reflected in the following passage: "The person with such an infectious disease must wear torn clothes, let his hair be unkempt, cover the lower part of his face and cry out, 'Unclean! Unclean!' As long as he has the infection he remains unclean. He must live alone; he must live outside the camp" (Lev 13:45-46).

This is not simply the description of an illness. It is a *sentence,* the purpose of which was to protect the health of the community from a dreaded contagion. Elaborating Leviticus 13–14, Mishnah tractate *Negaim* ("Plagues") discusses the spread of leprosy not only among people but also among garments (*m. Neg.* 3:7; 11:1-12) and houses (*m. Neg.* 3.8; 12–13). Lepers were victims of far more than the disease itself. The disease robbed them of their health, and the sentence imposed on them as a consequence robbed them of their name, occupation, habits, family and fellowship, and worshiping community. To ensure against contact with society, lepers were required to make their appearance as repugnant as possible. Josephus speaks of the banishment of lepers as those "in no way differing from a corpse" (*Ant.* 3.264). The reference to Miriam's leprosy in Num 12:12 prompted various rabbis to speak of lepers as "the living dead," whose cure was as difficult as raising the dead.[45] The diagnosis of leprosy thus encompassed both medical and social dimensions. Leprosy contaminated Israel's status as a holy people (although it did not contaminate Gentiles since they were already considered unclean, *m. Neg.* 3:1; 11:1). Other illnesses had to be healed, but leprosy had to be *cleansed* (e.g., Matt 11:5). Mark's account of Jesus and the leper is a mirror image of these tragic realities, for there is no reference to "healing," but there are four references to "cleansing" in six verses.

The offense of the leper's action is immediately apparent. Lepers were required to "stand at a distance" (Luke 17:12) of fifty paces. If a leper's entrance into a house contaminated it (*m. Negaim* 12–13), or his standing under a tree polluted anyone who passed under it (*m. Neg.* 13:7), then this leper's approach compromises Jesus' ritual cleanliness. Nevertheless, the leper risks everything, breaking both law and custom, on the chance of being healed and restored by Jesus. No obstacle, not even the decrees of the Torah itself, prevents him from coming to Jesus. His obsequious approach and posture, "beg[ing] him on his knees, 'If you are willing, you can make me clean,'" betrays the long humiliation of his affliction.[46] But contained within the leper's plea are the beginnings of faith that Jesus can save him. His faith is revealed by the fact that he does not question Jesus' *ability* to save him, only his *willingness* to save him. The leper's longing is profoundly human, for it is not God's ability that we doubt, but only his willingness — *if* he will do what we ask.

41-42 Surprisingly, the response of Jesus is no less scandalous than the leper's audacity. In the face of such an intrusion, one would expect an observant Jew to recoil in protection and defense. But with Jesus compassion replaces contempt. Rather than turning from the leper, Jesus turns *to* him; indeed, he *touches* him, bringing himself into full contact with physical and ritual untouchability. The outstretched arm of Jesus is a long reach for his day . . . for any day. It removes the social, physical, and spiri-

---

45. Str-B 4/2.750-51; on leprosy in general, see 4/2.743-63.

46. The Greek textual tradition is confused whether "kneeled" is original or not. Manuscript tradition favors its exclusion, and it is a rare word, occurring only once again, in Mark 10:17. But if it were original, its omission could be explained by homoeoteleuton, i.e., a scribal error caused by the eye passing inadvertently from one word to another having the same sequence of letters. See Metzger, *TCGNT*, 76.

tual separations prescribed by the Torah and custom alike. The touch of Jesus speaks more loudly than his words; and the words of Jesus touch the leper more deeply than any act of human love. Jesus is not only able but desirous: "'I am willing,'" he says, "'be clean.'" Unlike an ordinary rabbi, Jesus is not polluted by the leper's disease; rather, the leper is cleansed and healed by Jesus' contagious holiness.

The NIV describes Jesus as "filled with compassion." What the NIV does not note is that a very old and important manuscript (D) reads "filled with anger." In this context and coming from Jesus, anger initially seems wrong. That may argue for its originality, however, since copyists tended to change difficult readings into more acceptable ones. Moreover, the fact that both Matt 8:3 and Luke 5:13 omit the word in their retelling of the story is more explainable if the original word were "anger" than if it were "compassion." Anger may not be as offensive as it first appears if one recalls that in Judg 10:16 "[God] became indignant over the misery of Israel" (RSV), much as Jesus does here. If "anger" was the original reading, it must clearly mean that Jesus was indignant at the misery of the leper (so John 11:33-38), for Jesus willingly healed him.[47] As though the leprosy were dispelled by holy wrath, Mark declares, "Immediately the leprosy left him and he was cured."

43-44 Abrupt and adamant, "Jesus sent him away at once with a strong warning: 'See that you don't tell this to anyone.'" The word for "strong warning" is literally "snorting" in Greek, deriving from the Hebrew word for anger (*'ap*), meaning "to flare the nostrils." The word for "send away" is likewise stronger in Greek than in the NIV. Often used of expelling demons, the expression (Gk. *ekballein*) means that Jesus sent him packing. The command to silence ("'*See* that that you don't tell this to anyone'") appears to be a literal translation of a spoken Hebrew injunction.[48] The no-nonsense charge to the healed leper reflects the same determination with which Jesus commanded the demons to silence at 1:25 and 1:34. Jesus is earnest and urgent about guarding the veil of his messianic identity to preserve it from misunderstanding and false responses (see **Command to Silence** at 1:34).

Jesus commands the man to follow the traditional rite of cleansing as specified in Leviticus 14, and later elaborated in *m. Negaim* 14 of the Mishnah. The leper must first show himself to the priest. Although priests were officially associated with the temple ninety miles south in Je-

---

47. The reading *splangnistheis* ("filled with compassion") remains, however, a very strong reading, as evidenced by Metzger's arguments in its favor (*TCGNT*, 76).

48. *Hora* = r'h (so Exod 28:40). See A. Schlatter, *Der Evangelist Matthäus* (Stuttgart: Calwer Verlag, 1959), 272.

rusalem, it was not unusual to find them in outlying regions like Galilee. The Aaronic **priesthood** was a hereditary office; priests, like Levites, in other words, were born, not made. Josephus reports that there were some 20,000 priests in Palestine in his day (*Ag. Ap.* 2.108). They were divided into twenty-four priestly families or "courses." Each course needed to be present in Jerusalem in order to serve pilgrims at the major festivals of Passover (spring), Pentecost (or the Feast of Weeks, late spring), and the Day of Atonement, followed by the Feast of Booths (or Tabernacles, fall). Thereafter each course of priests served in the temple for one week, twice annually. A priest's temple duties were thus fulfilled in a few weeks of every year. According to the *Epistle of Aristeas* (92–95), such duties included officiating at worship, burning incense, leading in liturgy, accepting sacrifices and offerings, hearing confessions, and, above all, butchery of animals for sacrifice. In normal rotations a priest's service would not have been overly taxing, but at festivals priestly service in the temple could be long and demanding. Once their temple duties were fulfilled, priests were free to return to their homes, even, as here, in distant Galilee. In off seasons they served as scribes, judges, and magistrates in their respective locales.[49]

One legal responsibility of priests entailed making pronouncements regarding diseases: "only a priest may pronounce [lepers] unclean or clean" (*m. Neg.* 3:1; also Lev 13:50; 14:2-4). Since it was a priestly duty to ensure the ritual cleanness of Israel, inspection of alleged leprosy cases played a natural role in their work. If a clean bill of health were rendered and certified in writing (*m. Neg.* 8:10), the healed person was instructed to present two birds, one of which was killed at the temple in Jerusalem. The other bird was then dipped in the blood of the slain bird and released. After a waiting period of eight days the healed person further brought to the priest three lambs, one a sin offering, one a guilt offering, and one a whole offering (Lev 14:10-11; *m. Neg.* 14:7). If a suppliant was too poor to afford three lambs, a reduction in offerings was allowed.

45 This was the protocol prescribed for a cleansed leper. The fact that Jesus commanded the man to follow it reveals that he honored the Mosaic law. Galilee, of course, was a long way from Jerusalem, and the prescribed sacrifice could be rendered the next time the man went to the temple, presumably at festival time. In the meantime news of his healing began to spread. Whether the man followed the prescribed rite of cleansing we are not told. What we are told is that he broke Jesus' command. "He went out and began to talk freely, spreading the news." After he has

---

49. On the priesthood, see E. P. Sanders, *The Historical Figure of Jesus* (London: Penguin Press, 1993), 41-43.

been healed by Jesus, the leper's earnestness and humility (1:40) turn to complacency, even disregard. An adverse irony results. Jesus has relieved the leper of his burden, but in broadcasting the news the leper imposes a burden on Jesus, for "he could no longer enter a town openly but stayed outside in lonely places."

Mark began this story with Jesus on the inside and the leper on the outside. At the end of the story, Jesus is "outside in lonely places." Jesus and the leper have traded places. Early in his ministry Jesus is already an outsider in human society. Mark casts him in the role of the Servant of the Lord who bears the iniquities of others (Isa 53:11) and whose bearing of them causes him to be "numbered with the transgressors" (Isa 53:12).

CHAPTER THREE

Trouble with the Authorities

MARK 2:1–3:12

Mark returns the action to Capernaum where, in a sequence of five compact narratives, he offers insight into the authority of Jesus. Each story reflects daily life in and around Capernaum, and, with the exception of the first story, each is approximately the same length. The first story begins as another healing, but it unexpectedly turns into a question of Jesus' identity (2:1-12). Then, in a most unprecedented move, Jesus calls a man of bad company, a tax collector, to join his band of followers (2:13-17). This is followed by pronouncements on fasting (2:18-22) and the Sabbath (2:23-28), two questions of considerable interest in Jesus' day. Mark completes the sequence back in the synagogue of Capernaum where a Sabbath healing brings a dire judgment against Jesus (3:1-6). In each story Jesus runs afoul of the religious authorities, primarily the Pharisees (2:16, 18, 24; 3:6) but also scribes (2:6) and Herodians (3:6). In each episode Jesus supersedes the Torah and the tradition of the elders, showing what happens when the Messiah goes public, exploding the customs and conventions of the day. The Gospel of John reports that "[The Word] came to his own, but his own did not receive him" (1:11). This collage of five stories is a good elaboration and commentary of that statement.[1] Mark concludes the series of stories with a summary of Jesus' authority over hostile powers, physical and spiritual, and a second confession from demons that he is the Son of God (3:7-12).

---

1. See D. E. Nineham's brief discussion of the five conflict stories in 2:1–3:6 in *The Gospel of St Mark*, 88-89.

THE AUTHORITY OF THE SON OF MAN (2:1-12)

The Greek verb tenses of this narrative may provide a clue to its composition. The healing of the paralytic looks like an older story introduced in the present tense (in Greek, 2:3-11) that Mark frames by an introduction and conclusion in the past tense (again in Greek, vv. 1-2/12). The present tense narrative in vv. 3-11 has an eyewitness quality to it that conceivably derives from Peter.

1 "A few days later" separates the present narrative from Jesus' preaching tour of 1:35-45. His notoriety is growing and word gets out that "he had come home." The Gk. *en oikō*, which might be rendered "at home," suggests a familiar location, presumably Peter's house of 1:29 (see description at 1:29). Roofs of Palestinian homes, which were accessible by outside stone staircases, were typically flat, supported by beams resting on the exterior walls of the house. The beams were cross-hatched by smaller poles and sticks, which were covered with thatch, which in turn was covered with a surface of mud (hence the reference to "digging through it," v. 4). The level roof, which needed resurfacing periodically by means of a roof roller, functioned much as a deck does today, offering relief from the dank quarters below, access to fresh air, and a place to dry laundry, eat, and even pray in solitude (see Acts 10:9).

2-4 A crowd of people jams the doorway of the house where Jesus is (1:33). **Crowds** play an important role in the Gospel of Mark.[2] Mark attests to Jesus' popularity in Galilee by referring to crowds nearly forty times before chap. 10. Crowds form audiences for his teaching and are the object of his compassion, but Mark never describes crowds turning to Jesus in repentance and belief, as the gospel requires (1:15). In respect to understanding and faith, crowds generally demonstrate passivity, and given their precipitous reduction following Jesus' teaching on suffering at Caesarea Philippi, they demonstrate even greater fickleness. The single most common attribute of crowds in Mark is that they obstruct access to Jesus. Thus, despite Jesus' popularity, crowds are not a measure of success in Mark. They constitute "outsiders" who stand either in ambivalence or opposition to Jesus. Hence Jesus masks his teaching to them in parables (e.g., 4:33-34; 7:17). Interestingly, the Greek words for "crowd" *(ochlos)* and "house" *(oikos)* produce an alliterative rhyme. Houses or private settings, by contrast, provide settings for special revelation and instruction to disciples and insiders

---

2. *Ochlos,* thirty-eight times; *polys,* in reference to crowds, fourteen times. On crowds in Mark, see J. D. Kingsbury, *The Christology of Mark's Gospel* (Philadelphia: Fortress Press, 1983), 78-80.

in Mark.[3] Only in private does Jesus explain things clearly to his disciples and allow glimpses, if at all, of his divine Sonship. The contrast between "crowd" and "house" helps illustrate a larger theme in Mark, that enthusiasm for Jesus and even proximity to him are not the same as faith — and may oppose it (e.g., 11:1-11).

What attracts such crowds to Jesus? Mark offers the simplest summary: "he preached the word to them." Mark occasionally describes Jesus' message simply as "the word" (2:2; 4:33; 8:32), by which he means the message of the "gospel of God" (1:14-15). More than any other expression in early Christianity, "the word" defines the essence of Jesus' ministry. Especially in Mark, who seldom records the content of Jesus' teaching, it may mistakenly be assumed that the amazement of the crowds is owing to spellbinding miracles and wonders. So essential, on the contrary, is the proclamation of the gospel to Jesus' purpose that Mark can subsume his entire ministry in the phrase, "he preached the word to them." The truth he proclaims is the same truth he embodies, before which his hearers cannot remain passive. The "word" exacts of his hearers a response of faithfulness that can only be rendered to Jesus himself.

The teaching of Jesus at home in Capernaum is the context for a more important story, however. Mark introduces the episode of the paralytic by the dynamic present tense (in Greek), which contemporizes the narrative and heightens its immediacy for the reader: "they bring a paralytic carried by four men" (2:3).[4] The throng in the courtyard is blocking a needy party from reaching Jesus. Being part of the crowd around Jesus is not the same as being a disciple of Jesus. The crowd stands and observes; disciples must commit themselves to action, as illustrated by the plucky squad of four. If an opening to Jesus cannot be found, one must be made. That is a description of faith: it will remove any obstacle — even a roof, if necessary — to get to Jesus.[5] The removal of the roof may have showered disrespect as well as dirt on the guests below. The Talmud (b. Mo'ed Q. 25a) tells a related story (although three centuries later) of the death of Rabbi Huna (A.D. 297), whose funeral bier was too big to go through the door of his house. It was suggested that the bier be taken up through the

---

3. *Oikos:* 2:1; 7:17; *oikia:* 7:24; 9:33; 10:10; *kata monas:* 4:10; *kat idian:* 4:34; 6:31, 32; 7:33; 9:2, 28; 13:3.

4. The awkwardness of this phrase in Greek, which both Matt 9:2 and Luke 5:18 improve, argues for Markan priority.

5. The textual tradition is divided among *prosenenkai* ("to offer"), *prosengisai* ("to draw near"), and *proselthein* ("to approach") in v. 4. Although the second reading claims the strongest manuscript support, it is likely, as Metzger suggests (*TCGNT*, 77), that the absence of a direct object (required by *prosenenkai*) prompted copyists to substitute the other two words that do not need direct objects.

roof, whereupon one of Huna's disciples remonstrated, "We learned from him that the honor of a teacher requires access through the door." In Rabbi Huna's case the door was enlarged.

5 Jesus is not offended by the roof removers, however, but encouraged. When he sees "their faith, he says to the paralytic, 'Son, your sins are forgiven'" (2:5). The address "son" (Gk. *teknon*; also 10:24; Luke 16:25; John 13:33; 1 John *passim*) likely reflects Heb. *beni*, "my son." It is more than a term of endearment or affection, although it is that. It is primarily a term of a superior who acts with authority and benevolence.[6]

The first mention of faith (2:5) in Mark significantly links it with acting rather than with knowing or feeling. We know nothing of the beliefs of the four friends of the paralytic except that they take action, including circumventing crowds and removing roofs to ensure that their charge is brought to Jesus. Faith is first and foremost not knowledge about Jesus but active trust that Jesus is sufficient for one's deepest and most heartfelt needs.

The question whether "their faith" includes the paralytic's faith is not addressed in the relevant Gospel texts (Matt 9:2//Mark 2:5//Luke 5:20). On the one hand, it is difficult to imagine the four porters bringing the paralytic to Jesus against his will; surely, as Lagrange notes, it would be a rare case that a person with paralysis would not hope to be healed of the malady.[7] Nevertheless, the plural pronoun ("*their* faith") includes the faith of the porters, and this should not wholly surprise us. The Gospels preserve several instances of Jesus fulfilling the petition of one party on behalf of another.[8] The power of Jesus is actually enhanced in intercessory healings, for the cure cannot be attributed to auto-suggestion or to the victim's inner preparedness.[9] Jesus thus reveals himself to the paralytic through faith; and the Gospels seem more concerned with the fact of faith than with the specific agents of faith.[10]

Of greater interest is the relationship between sin and illness implied in 2:5. It is not likely that Jesus raises the question of the paralytic's sins in order to provoke the scribes and provide an occasion to demon-

---

6. On *teknon* ("son"), see W. Grundmann, *Das Evangelium nach Markus*, 56-57.

7. M.-J. Lagrange, *Évangile selon Saint Marc*, 35.

8. For example, the father who petitions Jesus to heal his daughter (5:21-43); the Syrophoenician woman who begs Jesus to heal her demon-possessed daughter (7:24-30); the official who intercedes with Jesus for his son (John 4:46-53) or servant (Matt 8:5-13).

9. E. Schweizer, *The Good News According to Mark*, 61.

10. Note Schlatter's felicitous wording on this point: "Wird die Bitte zur Fürbitte, so wird sie dadurch nicht geschwächt; vielmehr gilt ihr gegenüber erst recht die Regel Jesu, dass er keinen Glauben zerstört" ("A petition is not weakened by becoming an intercession; an intercession even better illustrates the rule of Jesus, which is not to destroy faith"; *Der Evangelist Matthäus* [Stuttgart: Calwer Verlag, 1959], 297-98).

strate his authority. It is uncharacteristic of Jesus to use a person for an ulterior motive. Why, then, might Jesus expressly mention the man's sins? A majority of commentators typically denies that there was anything unusual or flagrant about the paralytic's sin, insisting rather that Jesus' response addresses the inevitable and organic connection between sin and illness characteristic of all humanity.[11] While affirming the general truth of this view, it is worth considering whether it fully explains why only here, of all Jesus' healings, he explicitly correlates sin and infirmity. Furthermore, "your sins" appears to speak to specific sins rather than to the general condition of sin. It appears possible that Jesus' address to the paralytic reflects knowledge of his particular sins, and their relationship to his paralysis. There is nothing more distinctive of a person than his or her sins. Jesus thus addresses the paralytic at the deepest level of his sins, which may be particularly appropriate lest the paralytic think the faith of his friends is an acceptable substitute for his own response to Jesus.

6-7 Mention of the forgiveness of sins creates a most unexpected twist in the story. The paralytic has not been brought because he believed his sins needed forgiving but because he wanted his paralysis healed. On hearing the forgiveness of sins, the story abruptly shifts from the paralytic to the scribes. Scribes did not claim to forgive sins, and they are scandalized when Jesus presumes to do so. Jesus and the scribes again run aground, although not over teaching as in 1:21-28, but over his presumption to forgive sins. What began as a heart-warming healing has suddenly become a perilous confrontation over religious authority.[12]

11. A problem with this line of thought is that it perpetuates (consciously or not) the idea that illness is the result of sin, which characterized the Judaism of Jesus' day (see the evidence gathered in Str-B 1.496). Some illnesses and misfortunes, of course, are the result of sin, but not all (e.g., Luke 13:1-5). According to John 9:2-3, Jesus denies a categorical equation of sin with illness. The fact that no other healing of Jesus expressly combines infirmity with sin seems to suggest that the paralytic's sin needs to be forgiven before his paralysis can be healed.

12. Klostermann attempts to downplay Jesus' forgiving sin by arguing that, like a priest, he simply mediates God's forgiveness to the paralytic: "The passive rendering of *aphientai* means 'God forgives you'! Thus, Jesus does not forgive from himself, but rather risks extending from himself divine forgiveness to one whose sickness marked him as a 'sinner against God'" (*Das Markusevangelium*, 23). This statement fails to do justice to the radical authority of Jesus in v. 5. Jesus does not say, e.g., as does Nathan in speaking to David, "'The LORD has put away your sins'" (2 Sam 12:13). Jesus claims to put away the sins himself, thus clearly presuming the place of God. Moreover, Jesus does not claim to forgive sins against himself (which would be within his human powers to do), but to forgive sins against *another* (vv. 5, 10). J. D. G. Dunn correctly notes: "it is impossible to soften the Christological force of 2:7, 10: Jesus is able and has authority to forgive sins, not merely to declare them forgiven" (*Jesus, Paul, and the Law: Studies in Mark and Galatians* [Louisville: Westminister/John Knox, 1990], 27).

Jews commonly believed that sin was the cause of illness (Job 4:7; John 9:2; Jas 5:15-16), but since forgiveness of sins was exclusively God's prerogative, Jewish healers seldom if ever pronounced forgiveness of sins in their healings.[13] Apart from the act of absolution on the Day of Atonement, not even the chief priest could forgive sins, or give promise of such, whether individually or corporately. "'Who can forgive sins but God alone?'" respond the scribes. They are right. Only God can forgive sins (Exod 34:6-7; Ps 103:3; Isa 43:25; Mic 7:18). Indeed, not even the Messiah would claim such power. The classic description of the Messiah in *Psalms of Solomon* 17–18 speaks of his overcoming demons, ushering in a perfect government, judging the godless, and of his righteousness and even sinlessness (17:36), but not of his ability to forgive sins. Strack and Billerbeck rightly conclude that "there is no place known to us in which the Messiah has the authority to pronounce forgiveness of sins from his own power ('Machtvollkommenheit'). Forgiveness of sins remains everywhere the exclusive right of God."[14] The reason is that in every sin, even in sins committed ostensibly only against one's neighbor, God is the party most offended. Thus in his adultery with Bathsheba and murder of Uriah, David, who in one affair breaks at least three and perhaps four of the Ten Commandments, confesses to God, "'against you, you only, have I sinned'" (Ps 51:4).

8-9 Without having been told, Jesus knows the crises in the minds of the scribes — and he apparently wills it! When Mark says, "Jesus knew in his spirit" (see 8:12; John 2:25), he implies more than human knowledge; Jesus not only knows the sins of the paralytic, but he also knows the hearts of the scribes. The scribes have nothing to say to the man's physical or spiritual condition. Jesus has something to say to both, but what he says causes the scribes the gravest possible offense. "'He's blaspheming'" (2:7), they cry.[15] Blasphemy was punishable by the death penalty (Lev 24:16).[16]

---

13. A recently published text from Qumran correlates the healing of an ulcer with the forgiveness of sins (4QPrNab). Although this is an exceptional text, the Jewish diviner forgives the sins for God, whereas Jesus pronounces forgiveness by his own authority. See R. Gundry, *Mark*, 116.

14. Str-B 1.495.

15. The apocryphal *Acts of Pilate* misses the authority of Jesus to forgive sins and recasts the healing of the paralytic as an example of Sabbath breaking: "Then one of the Jews came forward and asked the governor [Pilate] that he might speak a word. The governor said, 'If you wish to say something, say it.' And the Jew said, 'For thirty-eight years I lay on a bed in anguish and pain, and when Jesus came many demoniacs and those lying sick of various diseases were healed by him. And certain young men took pity on me and carried me with my bed and brought me to him. And when Jesus saw me he had compassion, and said to me, 'Take up your bed and walk.' And I took up my bed and

10-11 Jesus can heal a man of physical paralysis; the larger question is whether he can heal the scribes of spiritual paralysis. The scribes are no less dependent on Jesus than is the paralytic for the work of God, but their learning and status make them less aware of their need for it. Jesus wants them to *know* (v. 10), that is, to experience firsthand the authority by which he forgives sins (v. 9). In v. 7 the scribes ask who "can" (Gk. *dynatai*) forgive sins, that is, who has the ability. Jesus declares that the Son of Man not only has the ability but the *authority* to do so. The word for "authority" *(exousia)* is the same word used to describe Jesus' teaching and exorcism in the Capernaum synagogue (1:21-28). From a human perspective it is safe to pronounce the forgiveness of sins, since that statement cannot be falsified. Jesus, however, will provide evidence of the former by healing the paralytic, which can be verified by all. His authority to forgive, no less effective because of its invisibility, will be proved by healing the paralytic. The authority to heal and the authority to forgive are the same authority. "'But that you may know that the Son of Man has authority on earth to forgive sins. . . .' He said to the paralytic, 'I tell you, get up, take your mat and go home.'"

12 Mark reports that the paralytic "got up, took his mat and walked out in full view of them all." Thus, in answer to the question, "'Who can forgive sins but God alone?'" hearers and readers are invited to supply the name of Jesus. Jesus' victory over sickness and sin is complete, for Jesus does what only God can do. The singularity of the event is echoed in the exclamation of the crowd, "'We have never seen anything like this!'"

Excursus: Son of Man

"Son of Man," which occurs in v. 10 for the first time in Mark, is an ambiguous title, largely free of the political and military connotations associated with Messiah. In itself the title does not appear to have made any special claim in the ears of Jesus' contemporaries. Nowhere are people amazed that Jesus calls himself the "Son of Man," for example, nor do they take exception to his doing so. "Son of Man" thus offers the advan-

---

walked.' The Jews said to Pilate, 'Ask him what day it was on which he was healed.' The cured man said, 'On a Sabbath'" (*Acts Pil.* 6:1; quoted from J. K. Elliott, *The Apocryphal New Testament* [Oxford: Clarendon Press, 1993], 175).

16. The fear of blasphemy caused Jews to avoid pronouncing the divine name whenever possible. Following Num 15:30, the Mishnah decreed expulsion from the community as punishment for taking God's name in vain (*m. Ker.* 1:1-2; *m. Sanh.* 7:5). The same punishment was decreed at Qumran for uttering God's name frivolously (1QS 7).

tage of a title unencumbered by unwelcome associations, allowing Jesus the possibility of speaking of himself in public, indeed often in the face of opposition and hostility, in such a way that his hearers might discover his identity, if they would discover it at all.

"Son of Man" occurs fourteen times in Mark, and only from the mouth of Jesus. As in the other synoptic Gospels, "Son of Man" is divided into three categories in Mark. In three instances (8:38; 13:26; 14:62) it occurs in *apocalyptic* contexts, as in its usage in Daniel 7 and *1 Enoch* 37–69, where it refers to the Son of Man coming in judgment. Twice the title refers to Jesus' earthly *authority* to forgive sins (2:10) and supersede the Sabbath (2:28). Its most predominant usage, however, is with regard to Jesus' *suffering* (nine times: 8:31; 9:9, 12, 31; 10:33, 45; 14:21 [twice], 41). Each of the three categories refers to a divine attribute, or, as in the case with the third, fulfilling a divinely ordained purpose. It is thus apparent that "Son of Man" is not, as is often supposed today, merely a circumlocution for "the human one." In the present passage (2:10) "Son of Man" depicts Jesus' authority to forgive sins, thereby alluding to the "son of man" figure in Dan 7:13-14, who likewise is empowered with God's authority ("there before me was one like a son of man. . . . He was given authority [LXX, *exousia*], glory, and sovereign power").

The authority of the Son of Man is predominantly exhibited, however, in humiliation, suffering, and death.[17] Like Mark's more important title for Jesus, "Son of God," "Son of Man" includes suffering as its primary content. This is signified by the majority of its uses in the Gospel. In five of its nine uses related to suffering, Jesus is "betrayed" (Gk. *paradidonai*) into the hands of sinners. The betrayal of the Son of Man is not arbitrary, but it is the will of God and the means by which God's will is accomplished, for the Son of Man "must" (Gk. *dei*) suffer for the sake of his disciples and give his life a ransom for others (10:45).

It is noteworthy that Jesus chooses "Son of Man" to designate his offices as God's Son. He does not speak of his vocation in the first person, that is, "That is the way I do things," but in the third person, which

---

17. In an article remarkable for its brevity and sensibility, C. F. D. Moule, "'The Son of Man': Some of the Facts,'" *NTS* 41 (1995): 277-79, underscores the association of "Son of Man" with an individual (as opposed to a communal understanding of the term) who must suffer: "I still believe that the simplest explanation of the almost entire consistency with which the definite singular is confined to Christian sayings is to postulate that Jesus did refer to Dan 7, speaking of '*the* Son of man [whom you know from that vision]', and that he used Daniel's human figure as not primarily a title so much as a symbol for the vocation to victory through obedience and martyrdom to which he was called and to which he summoned his followers (so that they would together constitute 'the people of the saints of the Most High')."

thereby designates his humiliation, suffering, and exaltation as God's ordained way.

THE SCANDAL OF GRACE (2:13-17)

In content this story parallels the calling of the four fishermen in 1:16-20. Both stories describe Jesus passing along the Sea of Galilee, and in both Jesus calls people to follow him who stand either on the fringes of religious respectability or outside it. Like the fishermen, Levi follows Jesus without further information or discussion. In structure, however, the present story parallels the progression from particular to general in 1:29-34. There Jesus healed Peter's mother-in-law, followed by many others; here he calls Levi, followed by many others. Already in Jesus' ministry we see a pattern emerging. Jesus is not a footloose wandering philosopher without map and compass. Nor is fellowship with him something that happens by coincidence and caprice. Rather, there is a plan of itinerant teaching and healing already apparent in Jesus' ministry, from which he purposefully recruits a cadre of apprentices and followers.

13 "Jesus went out beside the lake." In the *Gospel of Thomas* and many gnostic Gospels discovered at Nag Hammadi, the sum of Jesus' life and work consists of sayings and pronouncements. In these documents there is virtually no reference to Jesus' ministry and itineration; he is, rather, a "talking head," a sedentary teacher, who occupies, quite literally, a chair of religion. Mark, on the contrary, devotes his Gospel almost entirely to Jesus' activity as an itinerant teacher. The gospel is not something merely spoken but lived, an *incarnation*. Hence Jesus is not sitting home taking calls but actively out making them.

Mark again summarizes Jesus' ministry in a word, "and he was teaching them" (*edidasken*; NIV, "and he began to teach them").[18] The term itself, and the way Mark repeatedly uses it to characterize Jesus' ministry, indicate the essential role that teaching played in Jesus' ministry (e.g., 10:1; 14:49). Jesus' teaching to large crowds, in this instance beside the lake, reveals him to be not an esoteric teacher of select initiates but a public teacher with a message for the masses (so 1:14-15).

14 Passing along the lake, Jesus sees Levi sitting at his tax table, and he calls him, "'Follow me.'" The word for "follow" (Gk. *akolouthein*) is used in the Gospels only of Jesus' disciples, never of those who oppose him. Occurring nineteen times in Mark, "following" is a load-bearing

---

18. *Didaskein* describes and summarizes Jesus' activity fifteen times in Mark.

term that describes the proper response of faith (10:52!), and is indeed practically synonymous with faith. "Following" is an act that involves risk and cost; it is something one does, not simply what one thinks or believes. Levi is probably to be identified with "Matthew" of Matt 9:9.[19] Not infrequently the same person is known by more than one name in the NT (e.g., Cephas/Simon/Peter). Mark records no dialogue in the call; like the four fishermen (1:16-20), Levi must respond solely to the authority of Jesus and his call.

It is not surprising that Jesus encounters **tax collectors** in Capernaum, a border town to neighboring Gaulanitis. The Mishnah describes tax collectors making daily rounds, "exacting payment of men with or without their consent," or, as here, sitting at tax stands with account books open and pen in hand (*m. Avot* 3:17). Travelers arriving in Capernaum from the territory of Herod Philip and the Decapolis to the east and north would be taxed by agents such as Levi, who were in the service of Herod Antipas, tetrarch of Galilee and Perea. The Roman tax system was complex and varied, even in a small country like Palestine. Land and poll taxes were collected directly by the Romans, but taxes on transported goods were contracted out to local collectors, most of whom were ethnic Jews but probably not observant Jews, since Torah-conscious Jews could not be expected to transact business with Gentiles.[20] Levi was one of these middlemen (or in the service of one) who made bids in advance to collect taxes in a given area. His own profit came from what he could mulct from his constituents, and a portion of his receipts stayed in his own pockets.[21] The Roman system of taxation depended on graft and greed, and it attracted enterprising individuals who were not adverse to such means.[22]

Tax collectors were obviously despised and hated. Anyone who is

---

19. Codices D and Θ read "James the son of Alphaeus" rather than "Levi the son of Alphaeus," but this reading is probably a subsequent harmonizing with 3:18 and not original.

20. Josephus (*War* 2.285-88) records a story in which the Jews of Caesarea called on a tax collector named John to intercede for them with Florus, prefect of Judea from A.D. 64 to 66. John was able to produce a bribe for Florus amounting to some eight talents of silver (= over $40,000), which illustrates the power and wealth some tax collectors possessed.

21. Note Philo's description of a tax collector in c. A.D. 40, only a decade after Jesus' death. "Capito is the tax collector for Judea and he holds the population in contempt. When he came there he was a poor man, but he has amassed much wealth in various forms by defrauding and embezzling (*nosphizetai kai pareklegei*) the people" (*Embassy* 199).

22. On the Roman tax system in Palestine, see E. Schürer, *History of the Jewish People*, 1.372-76.

familiar with "moles" and informants in Nazi and Communist regimes will have an appreciation for the loathing that first-century Jews felt for tax collectors. The Mishnah and Talmud (although written later) register scathing judgments of tax collectors, lumping them together with thieves and murderers. A Jew who collected taxes was disqualified as a judge or witness in court, expelled from the synagogue, and a cause of disgrace to his family (*b. Sanh.* 25*b*). The touch of a tax collector rendered a house unclean (*m. Teh.* 7:6; *m. Hag.* 3:6). Jews were forbidden to receive money and even alms from tax collectors since revenue from taxes was deemed robbery. Jewish contempt of tax collectors is epitomized in the ruling that Jews could lie to tax collectors with impunity (*m. Ned.* 3:4) — a ruling, incidentally, with which both the houses of Hillel and Shammai (who normally stood poles apart) agreed. Tax collectors were tangible reminders of Roman domination, detested alike for its injustice and Gentile uncleanness. Not a few Jewish extremists, including one among Jesus' own disciples (3:18), considered submission to the Roman yoke, as well as its system of taxation (see 12:13-17), an act of treason to God.

15-16 The Levi whom Jesus calls as a learner-apprentice belonged to this category of persons. Understandably, the call of Levi causes great consternation in the eyes of fellow Jews. It brings Jesus again into contact with unclean persons; not with unclean diseases as in the case of the leper (1:40), but with an individual who, because of his collaboration with the Gentile occupation, is both morally contemptuous and ritually unclean. It may be that contact with Levi was actually more offensive than contact with a leper since a leper's condition was not chosen whereas a tax collector's was.

Rather than stopping with Levi, however, the offense metastasizes. Jesus joins Levi for dinner at his house where there are "many tax collectors and 'sinners,'" signifying that the call of a sinner is not an exception to his mission but typical of it. In order to understand the term "sinners," we need to think of the "wicked" of the Psalms, which in the LXX appear as "sinners" (Gk. *hamartōloi*). The "wicked" are not occasional transgressors of the Torah but those who stand fundamentally outside it. They are categorically reprobate. The Mishnah describes "sinners" variously as gamblers, moneylenders, people who race doves for sport, people who trade on the Sabbath year, thieves, the violent, shepherds, and, of course, tax collectors (*m. Sanh.* 3:3). Some of the above are criminal elements, but many are simply laborers and commoners, who were too busy, too poor, or too ignorant to live up to the rules of the religious authorities. In our eyes, of course, listing common folks with thieves is like throwing jaywalkers into jail with hardened criminals, but it did not seem so to the Pharisees. Quoting Rabbi Meir, the Mishnah states that

> He that occupies himself in the study of the Law . . . is deserving of the whole world. He is called friend, beloved of God, lover of God, lover of mankind; and it clothes him with humility and reverence and fits him to become righteous, saintly, upright, and faithful; and it keeps him far from sin and brings him near to virtue, and from him men enjoy counsel and sound knowledge, understanding and might. (*m. Avot* 6:1)

This eulogy testifies that Torah is the standard of the "deserving" and "righteous." By inference, those who do not study Torah belong to an alien class, "sinners and tax collectors" (so Luke 15:1).

English translations leave the impression that Jesus was sitting at table in Levi's house, but the Greek of 2:15 indicates that he was reclining, the culinary posture customary especially at feasts and festivals, with head facing the table and feet extending outward from it. The word for "reclining" (Gk. *katakeimai*; NIV, "having dinner") occurs only four times in Mark, with reference either to reclining with sinners (2:15; 14:3) or with a malady (1:30; 2:4). Its four occurrences are subtle reminders of Jesus' solidarity with alienated and needy people. Jesus' acceptance of Levi sends a signal to others like him, for "many tax collectors and 'sinners'" joined him and the disciples. Jewish dietary laws were (and are) intended to exclude contact with Gentiles, especially in the intimacy of table fellowship. Jesus' disrespect for this essential Jewish boundary causes great offense to the scribes.

Jesus' behavior again exacerbates a latent tension into an open conflict with the scribes. In 2:1-12 the conflict resulted from his forgiveness of sins; here it results from his eating with sinners. In both instances Jesus could have accomplished the same or similar ends by avoiding the conflict. Both stories leave the impression, however, that the conflict is not the result of negligence but of provocation. The tax collectors and sinners invite him to dinner, whereas the scribes stand outside in judgment.[23] The cleft between Jesus and the scribes is accentuated by the word "followed": Levi follows Jesus (v. 14), as do the tax collectors and sinners (v. 15). But the "scribes of the Pharisees" do not follow Jesus.[24] The lesson is trenchant: fellowship with Jesus is based on a radically different stan-

---

23. A number of Greek manuscripts expand the question to, "'Why does he eat *and drink* with tax collectors and 'sinners'?'" (v. 16). The shorter reading is preferable, however. It claims stronger manuscript support, and the addition of "and drink" can be explained as a scribal accretion, perhaps in conformity with Luke 5:30 (see Metzger, *TCGNT*[2], 67).

24. On scribes, see at 1:22. Greek copyists apparently altered Mark's *hoi grammateis tōn Pharisaiōn* (so B ℵ L) to conform to the more traditional "scribes and the Pharisees" (Metzger, *TCGNT*[2], 67). For a discussion of Pharisees, see at 2:18.

dard from that of Torah. Whereas study of Torah, to quote Rabbi Meier again, makes one "deserving" and "righteous," Jesus calls and reclines with the blatantly undeserving and unrighteous. Fellowship with Jesus violates social and religious convention rather than promoting it. This story thus illustrates the truth of 2:1-12: there Jesus pronounced forgiveness of *sins*, here he forgives *sinners*, entering their houses in fellowship and reclining with them at table.

The reclining of sinners and tax collectors with Jesus suggests that he — rather than Levi — is the real host of the party. The basis of table fellowship is the forgiveness Jesus offers as Messiah, and it anticipates the messianic banquet at the end time.[25] Jesus' fellowship with tax collectors and sinners — and its condemnation by the scribes — illustrates the radical nature of grace. The "tradition of the elders" justifies a status quo of distinctions and erects barriers among people; the gospel seeks to transform and reconcile this condition by building a bridge between Jesus and human need. Jesus' call of Levi and dining with those like him are a graphic depiction of Rom 9:30-31: the righteousness of God escapes those who seek to establish their own righteousness; whereas those who are too far off to hope for the righteousness of God are graciously granted it.

It is a commonplace that the scribes and Pharisees opposed Jesus for eating with "sinners and tax collectors." But what exactly was it about Jesus' association with such people that offended them? Did Jesus eat with sinners on the condition that they change their lives? Was his association with tax collectors, prostitutes, and the reprobate predicated on their forsaking their wickedness and becoming godly persons? Jesus would certainly have been pleased if that were the result. But if that were his intention, we might expect the religious leaders to applaud him, not oppose him. We know, however, that they opposed him — always and everywhere. Their opposition is the more explainable on the ground that reform was the not the fundamental assumption of Jesus' ministry, as it had been for John the Baptizer, for instance. There is no word in the call to Levi and in the dinner with sinners about repentance. Repentance, in fact, is curiously absent from Jesus' proclamation in Mark.[26] The scandal of this story is that Jesus does not make moral repentance a precondition of his love and acceptance. Rather, Jesus loves and accepts tax collectors and sinners as they are. If they forsake their evil and amend their lives, they do so, as did Zacchaeus (Luke 19:1-10), not in order to gain Jesus' favor

---

25. See W. Lane, *The Gospel According to Mark* (Grand Rapids: Eerdmans, 1974), 106.

26. The verb "to repent" *(metanoein)* occurs but twice of Jesus in Mark (1:15; 6:12), and the noun never. Only in Luke, Acts, and Revelation does repentance play a prominent role in the gospel proclamation.

but because Jesus has loved them as sinners. Jesus' association with such people is not coincidental. He does not happen to be with them or wait for invitations. He initiates the fellowship, "'I must stay at your house today'" (Luke 19:5). We are not told how many sinners and tax collectors repented and reformed. We are only told that Jesus sowed love as profligately and uncalculatedly as the sower who threw seed in unpromising places (Mark 4:3-9). It is this that scandalized the religious leaders of his day, as it scandalizes those who define the gospel in terms of pure moral reformation and character formation of our day. Jesus communicates in word and deed that accepting and following him are more important than following Torah. When the unreformed and unregenerate do that, they will enter the kingdom of God before the scribes and Pharisees. In table fellowship with "sinners and tax collectors," Jesus scandalously asserts his *exousia*, his own person over Torah, and the profligate love of God over merit. That is the scandal of grace.[27]

17 The scene is summed up in a memorable saying, "It is not the healthy who need a doctor, but the sick. I have not come to call the righteous, but sinners." This verse was remembered and preserved in a number of early Christian sources, including Clement of Rome (*2 Clem.* 2:4), the *Didache* (4:10), the *Epistle of Barnabas* (5:9), and Justin Martyr (*Apol.* 1.15.8). The saying is a defense of Jesus' outreach to the disreputable, not a suggestion that there are some who are exempt from his call. The fact that Jesus can be found in the company of people such as Levi reminds us of the difference between his mission and that of the scribes. They come to enlighten; he comes to redeem. Given that mission, it is as senseless for Jesus to shun tax collectors and sinners as for a doctor to shun the sick. The grace of God extends to and overcomes the worst forms of human depravity. Ironically, in one sense great sinners stand closer to God than those who think themselves righteous, for sinners are more aware of their need of the transforming grace of God. "Where sin increased, grace increased all the more" (Rom 5:20).

FASTING AND FEASTING (2:18-22)

The five stories in 2:1–3:6 display a steady intensification of conflict between Jesus and the religious leaders, particularly the scribes and Pharisees. In the first story (2:1-12) the antagonism remained largely unspo-

---

27. See E. P. Sanders, *The Historical Figure of Jesus* (London: Penguin Press, 1993), 230-37.

ken. In the following three (2:13-17, 18-22, 23-28) the conflict results in verbal confrontations. In the final story (3:1-6) it erupts into a plot against Jesus' life. In each encounter the authority of Jesus explodes the formulas and categories into which people would press him. Like the vintage parable in v. 22, Jesus is like expansive new wine that needs its own wineskin.

18 Jesus' contemporaries saw possible analogies to his movement in two other movements of the day, namely, in that of the disciples of John and in that of the Pharisees. Mark makes only one other passing reference to John's disciples (6:29); further information about John's movement, which is limited, can be gleaned from scattered references in the NT and Josephus.[28] About the **Pharisees** much more is known. The exact origins of the Pharisees are not clear, but we know that they arose at the time of the Maccabean Revolt (168 B.C.), which means they had been in existence some two centuries by Jesus' day. Their name means either "separated one" or "holy ones," two interpretations that are not incompatible with each other. From their inception the Pharisees were staunchly opposed to Hellenism, that is, the tendency, outright or subtle, to accommodate Jewish life to prevailing Greco-Roman ideals. They stood decidedly on the rock of Torah, "the precious instrument by which the world was created," the perfect expression of God's wisdom and will, and the surpassing object of human existence (*Pirke Abot* 3:19). They were not a political party, and indeed they were rather indifferent to political rulers as long as they were permitted to pursue and establish their life according to Torah. Pharisaism was a lay movement numbering, according to an estimate of Josephus, about six thousand persons in the first century (*Ant.* 17.42), or approximately one percent of the population. Although small and but one party among several in Palestine, the Pharisees surpassed the Sadducees, Essenes, Herodians, and Zealots most probably in number and certainly in influence. Pharisaism was reputed for high ideals and was, in the words of Josephus, "extremely influential among the common people" (*Ant.* 18.14-15). The Pharisees were regarded as the authorized successors of Torah, who sat on "Moses' seat" (Matt 23:2). The strength and adaptability of the Pharisees were proven by the fact that of all the Jewish parties mentioned above, they alone survived the war with Rome in A.D. 66-70. All Judaism subsequent to that catastrophe owed its existence to Pharisaic origins. The foundational beliefs of the Pharisees, which were expounded by an illustrious rabbinic dynasty known as the

---

28. Matt 11:2; 14:12; Luke 7:18; 11:1; John 1:35, 37; 3:25. According to the Gospel of John, two of Jesus' disciples had originally belonged to the Baptizer's followers (John 1:35-42). John's fame and followers survived his death, perhaps even competing in some sectors and in some degree with the movement of Jesus (John 1:19-23; Acts 19:1-7; Josephus, *Ant.* 18.116-19).

"tradition of the elders" (7:5), included belief in the sovereignty of God coupled with human accountability for virtue and vice; the resurrection of the dead; angels and demons; and scrupulous adherence both to the written Torah and to the oral traditions based on it, coupled with expressed disdain for those who were ignorant, negligent, or violators of Torah.[29]

Jesus himself stood closer to the foundational beliefs of the Pharisees than to those of any other party of Judaism. The Gospels record only sporadic and coincidental exchanges between Jesus and the Sadducees, Herodians, and Zealots, and none between Jesus and the Essenes; but throughout his ministry Jesus is in a standing debate with Pharisaism, primarily over the issue of *tradition*. The essential difference is especially evident in Mark 7:1-23, in which Jesus accuses the Pharisees of overvaluing oral tradition and undervaluing the *intent* of the law itself. By Jesus' day the original fervor and vitality of Pharisaism had calcified into a formalism at myriad points of practice and observance, in which conformity to legal prescriptions replaced the disposition of the heart, thus distorting the true intent of the law. Believing that Torah was prescriptive for all of life, the Pharisees wove an increasingly intricate web of regulations around it, whose purpose may have been to honor Torah, but whose effect was a confining and even crushing burden on human existence.[30]

In 2:18 the Jesus movement is compared to the movements of the Baptizer and Pharisees on the question of **fasting**. The three main pillars of Judaism were prayer, almsgiving, and fasting. Judaism required but one fast on the Day of Atonement (*Yom Kippur*, Lev 16:29-30; *m. Yoma* 8:1-2). But the Mishnah tractate *Ta'anit*, which is devoted to proper observances of fasting, specifies at least three other types of fasts. One type

---

29. On the Pharisees, see Str-B 4/1.334-52; Schürer, *History of the Jewish People*, 2.381-403; S. J. D. Cohen, *From the Maccabees to the Mishnah*, LEC (Philadelphia: Westminster Press, 1987), 143-64; G. F. M. Moore, *Judaism in the First Centuries of the Christian Era* (Cambridge, Mass.: Harvard University Press, 1927), 1.56-71.

30. Two modern Jewish interpreters have produced significant studies of Pharisaism, both of whom conclude that the NT portrait of the Pharisees is not a misrepresentation of the movement or rooted in anti-Jewish biases, but essentially faithful to other witnesses to Pharisaism of the time period. Jacob Neusner, *The Idea of Purity in Ancient Judaism*, SJLA (Leiden: Brill, 1973), 65, writes: "The legal matters attributed by later rabbis to the pre-70 Pharisees are thematically congruent to the stories and sayings about Pharisees in the New Testament Gospels, and I take them to be accurate in substance, if not in detail, as representations of the main issues of Pharisaic law." Likewise, E. Rivkin, *A Hidden Revolution* (Nashville: Abingdon Press, 1978), 123-24, 147-79, argues that the picture of the Pharisees in the Gospels and Paul conforms in essential respects with that of the Mishnah and Talmud; and, moreover, that various rabbis, Johanan ben Zakkai among them, criticized some rabbis, and particularly Sadducees, no less severely than did Jesus.

was fasts that lamented national tragedies, such as the destruction of the temple by Nebuchadnezzar (Zech 7:3-4; 8:19); another was fasts in times of crises, such as war, plague, drought, and famine; and a third type was self-imposed fasts for any number of personal reasons (2 Sam 12:16; Ps 35:13). The Pharisees normally fasted on Mondays and Thursdays (*Did.* 8:1; *b. Ta'an.* 12*a*), although this was not required. The required fast on the Day of Atonement lasted a full twenty-four hours, whereas voluntary fasts as a rule extended only from dawn to dusk. Although not a legal requirement except in one instance, fasting had become in Jesus' day a prerequisite of religious commitment, a sign of atonement of sin and humiliation and penitence before God, and a general aid to prayer. The rabbis often referred to fasting as "an affliction of the soul," thereby designating it as a characteristic and sacrificial act of piety.[31]

Those who challenge Jesus on the issue of fasting are identified by Mark in the most general terms ("Some people"). They evidently were commoners rather than Pharisees, which reinforces the impression that fasting was regarded as part and parcel of true piety in the Jewish world of Jesus' day. Their question, "'How is it that John's disciples and the disciples of the Pharisees are fasting, but yours are not?'" insinuates that if Jesus and his followers intend to be taken seriously they had better pay greater attention to fasting protocol.

19 Against the somber backdrop of fasting Jesus volunteers a festive picture of a **wedding** feast. A wedding celebration in a Jewish village normally lasted seven days for a virgin bride or three days for a remarried widow. Friends and guests had no responsibility but to enjoy the festivities. There was an abundance of food and wine, as well as song, dance, and fun both in the house and on the street. Even rabbis were expected to desist from Torah instruction and join the celebration with their students. "The guests of the bridegroom" (Gk. *hoi huioi tou nymphōnos,* "sons of the bridegroom," a literal Semitism) pictures the gathering of the wedding party, waiting impatiently to eat. Any thought of fasting at such a moment is out of the question!

The use of wedding imagery with regard to a question about fasting radically alters the challenge to his authority. Jesus has no complaint with fasting per se as it is practiced by the disciples of John and the Pharisees. He grants that when the bridegroom is taken away, "on that day [his disciples too] will fast." The difference between Jesus and the disciples of John and the Pharisees pertains to an attitude toward Jesus' ministry. Jesus describes his mission as a wedding — himself the bridegroom and his disciples "guests of the bridegroom." A wedding is not a time to abstain

31. On fasting, see J. Behm, *"nēstis,"* TDNT 4.924-35; Str-B 2.241-44; 4/1.77-114;

but to live it up. Jesus again thrusts his person and mission prominently, inescapably, to center stage. If the disciples of John and the Pharisees grasp the significance of his person they will understand why they should celebrate rather than fast.[32] Their noncompliance with the party, however, attests to their nonacceptance of his person.

The wedding imagery is unusually provocative, although its full significance is often missed. The fact that the Messiah is nowhere in the OT presented as a bridegroom, and only rarely outside the OT,[33] has led a number of scholars to doubt the christological significance of Jesus' use of the bridegroom imagery in 2:19.[34] Although a firm link between Messiah and bridegroom cannot be established, that does not exclude or diminish the christological significance of the bridegroom imagery. In this instance, in fact, it appears to heighten it, for in the OT Israel's husband and lover is not the Messiah but God (Isa 5:1; 54:5-6; 62:4-5; Ezek 16:6-8; Hos 2:19). This same nuptial imagery increases in later Judaism.[35] The divine associations inherent in the bridegroom imagery are consonant with Mark's Christology, whose chief christological category is not Messiah but Son of God. The latter conveys not simply messianic service of God but shared nature and essential union with God. At the baptism Jesus is declared to be God's Son and is endowed with God's Spirit. His divine status and empowerment combine in his *exousia,* his divine authority, to defeat demonic powers (1:25) and even to forgive sins (2:10). The imagery of the bridegroom recalls not a messianic function but the person of God himself. In this suggestive metaphor Jesus continues, naturally and without arrogance, to presume the prerogatives of God to himself. The upshot of the wedding imagery is thus not unlike the forgiveness of sins in 2:7, which invited hearers to supply their own answer to Jesus' identity. Both episodes are provocations to see that the role and mission of God are now present in Jesus.[36]

20   Although it is still early in his ministry, Jesus is under no illu-

32. In the *Gospel of Thomas* 104 Jesus instructs his hearers to fast and pray when they see him coming from the wedding chamber. This saying conflates two competing sets of imagery and appears to subordinate Jesus to fasting, whereas according to Mark Jesus subordinates fasting to himself.

33. A Jewish midrash on Exod 12:2 says, "In the days of the Messiah the wedding will take place" (*Exodus Rabbah* 15 [79b]). The NT, of course, employs the bridegroom image messianically (Rev 19:7-9).

34. For example, Nineham, *The Gospel of St Mark,* 103.

35. W. Eichrodt, *Theology of the Old Testament,* trans. J. Baker (London: SCM Press, 1961), 250-58; J. Jeremias, "*nymphē,*" *TDNT* 4.1,101-3.

36. In the gnostic *Tripartite Tractate* from Nag Hammadi the bridegroom imagery is shorn of its relationship with God and Jesus' earthly ministry and spiritualized as the union of the soul with Christ in the bridal chamber of election (122:14-30).

sions about potential opposition. Mention of "the bridegroom [being] taken from them" is an abrupt and dismaying image. In a normal wedding it is the guests who finally leave the groom and bride to begin life together. But Jesus interjects the alien thought of the groom being forcibly removed from the wedding celebration. Mark's linkage of the debut of Jesus' ministry with the arrest of John the Baptizer in 1:14 has already projected storm clouds over Jesus' ministry. Those storm clouds increased in the consternation of the scribes over Jesus' presumption to forgive sins in 2:10. The reference to the bridegroom being "taken from them" reveals that Jesus himself is aware of the future consequences of the malice of the authorities (so 3:6). In the first of many reminiscences and allusions to Isaiah's Servant of the Lord, Mark intimates that Jesus, too, will be "cut off from the land of the living" (Isa 53:8).

The kingdom of God makes a personal appearance in Jesus, but the final victory is far from realized. In order to overcome sin and death the bridegroom must become their victim. Christ's followers, moreover, must experience in some way the fate of Jesus their Lord, especially the experience of the hiddenness and silence of God. The reference to the bridegroom being taken from the disciples, and their subsequent fasting, was surely a reminder of perseverance and faithfulness to Mark's congregation in Rome, itself the victim of Nero's depraved persecution. There will be days when Jesus is far from them, as was the Father from Jesus in his passion (14:36; 15:34). "Conflicts on the outside, fears within," is how Paul described the long haul and lonely watches of Christian discipleship (2 Cor 7:5). It was with reference to sustaining the life of faith and growth into Christ-likeness that fasting continued to be practiced in early Christianity.[37] The discipline of physical privation in fasting was an aid to watchfulness, contrition, and strength and sensitivity in Christian life.

21-22 The messianic wedding imagery is followed by two crisp parables of Jesus, the first in the Gospel of Mark. Their placement following v. 20 appears to link them closely with Jesus' ministry rather than specifically with fasting or as general illustrations of the kingdom of God, which is not mentioned (see 4:26, 30). Like all Jesus' parables, both incorporate common images of the day. The first pictures a new patch of cloth sewn on an old garment. When washed, the new patch will shrink, causing a tear in both the garment and the patch (see Job 13:28).[38] The second

---

37. Acts 13:2-3; 14:23; 1 Cor 7:5; 9:25-27; 2 Cor 6:5; 11:27; *Did.* 8:1.

38. Greek manuscripts show unusual diversity in wording in v. 22 (see R. W. Swanson, ed., *New Testament Greek Manuscripts: Variant Readings Arranged in Horizontal Lines Against Codex Vaticanus: Mark* [Sheffield: Academic Press, 1995], 32-33). The reconstruction offered by Metzger appears to be the best resolution of the numerous possible readings (*TCGNT*[2], 67-68).

depicts used wineskins filled with new wine that ferments and expands, bursting the old and brittle skins (see Job 32:19). Both wine and wineskins come to ruin.

The chief impression of both parables is their finality. The unshrunken patch "will pull away" from the old garment, "making the tear worse." The Greek word for "pull away," *airein,* is the root of the word in v. 20 describing the bridegroom being "taken from them" (Gk. *apairein*). Likewise, the wineskins will be "burst" and "ruined" (Gk. *apollymi,* "destroyed"). In both instances something once serviceable is destroyed and of no further worth.[39] The new patch and new wine are incompatible with the old cloth and wineskins; and if the attempt is made to combine them, the new substances will destroy the old.

"Both parables are about the relation of Jesus, of Christianity indeed, to traditional Judaism."[40] The parables illustrate the radical posture and presumption of Jesus. Jesus is the new patch and the new wine. He is not an attachment, addition, or appendage to the status quo. He cannot be integrated into or contained by preexisting structures, even Judaism, Torah, and the synagogue. He is, of course, neither ascetic nor anarchist, and thus he participates as a human being in human structures. He goes to the synagogue, but not as everyone else goes to the synagogue. Jesus goes with a new teaching (1:27). He is like the scribes in that he teaches, but his authority surpasses theirs (1:22). He honors Torah by sending the healed paralytic to make the offering required by Moses, but he is not bound by Torah; he breaks it when it impedes his ministry (2:24; 3:1-6), and he subordinates it to himself (Matt 5:17; Rom 10:4). His contemporaries exclaim, "'We have never seen anything like this!'" (2:12). He relinquishes himself completely, though never surrendering his divine authority. He gives himself in service, though rendering allegiance to none but God. He gives his life to the world, but he is not a captive of the world. The question posed by the image of the wedding feast and the two atom-like parables is not whether disciples will, like sewing a new patch on an old garment or refilling an old container, make room for Jesus in their already full agendas and lives. The question is whether they will forsake business as usual and join the wedding celebration; whether they will become entirely new receptacles for the expanding fermentation of Jesus and the gospel in their lives.

39. The *Gospel of Thomas* 47 includes the two parables in Mark 2:21-22 in a cluster of short parables about the impossibility of riding two horses or stringing two bows or serving two masters. The *Gospel of Thomas* employs the parables as a warning against divided allegiances, thereby missing their violent and final effect in Mark.
40. J. Drury, *The Parables in the Gospels: History and Allegory* (London: SPCK, 1985), 45.

LORD OF THE SABBATH (2:23-28)

Most of the world's religions venerate sacred places: Islam honors Mecca, Hinduism the Ganges River, and Shintoism the island of Japan. Judaism also venerated Jerusalem and especially the temple as sacred space, but it venerated something beyond it, and perhaps above it: *time*, the Sabbath.

The present pericope, although different in content from the previous story about fasting, is generally similar in construction. In both narratives Jesus is put to the test by the Pharisees because of the behavior of his disciples, and both conclude with two sayings of Jesus (although not parables in the present narrative). Formal similarities like this are clues of conscious shaping in narration and transmission. The fact that each of the four stories in 2:13–3:6 contains roughly the same number of words may posit their length and form to the stage of oral transmission.

23-24 Western indifference toward Sabbath observance puts modern readers at a disadvantage in understanding the importance of Sabbath in Judaism. Two observances above all defined Jews and set them apart from the nations: circumcision and the **Sabbath**, which extended from sunset Friday until sunset Saturday. The Fourth Commandment, the longest of the Ten Commandments (Exodus 20; Deuteronomy 5), enjoins Jews to abstain from every kind of labor since God himself had rested on the seventh day of creation (Exod 20:8-11). Included in Sabbath rest were not only observant Jews but also slaves and animals, and even vegetation, which could not be cut, plucked, or uprooted (Philo, *Life of Moses* 2.22). Alone of the Ten Commandments, the Sabbath is rooted in the order of creation and attests to the divine order of the universe (*Mek. Exod.* 20:17). According to Jewish tradition, God chose Israel from all the peoples of the earth and instituted the Sabbath as an eternal sign and blessing of Israel's unique status (Ezek 20:12; *Jub.* 2:18-33). Tractates *(Shabbat)* of both the Mishnah and the Talmud offer prolific guidance on what was deemed permissible on the Sabbath. The Talmud describes the Sabbath as a holy ordinance of God and ordains that whoever observes the Sabbath becomes a partner with God in the creation of the world and brings salvation to the world (*b. Shab.* 118-99b). The DSS preserve the most rigorous Sabbath regulations in Judaism, forbidding even the carrying of children, giving of help to birthing animals, or the retrieval of an animal fallen into a pit on the Sabbath (CD 10–11). The Pharisaic and rabbinic traditions were only slightly less rigorous in their interpretation. Amplifying Exod 35:1-3, the Mishnah lists thirty-nine classes of work that profane the Sabbath, including those we might expect, such as plowing, hunting, and butchering, and those we would not, such as tying or loosening knots, sewing more than one stitch, or writing more than one letter (*m. Shab.* 7:2). The general rule of observance was not to begin a work that might extend over to the Sabbath, and not to do any work on the Sabbath that was not absolutely necessary — by "necessary" meaning life endangering (*m. Yoma* 8:6). Such scrupulousness inevitably resulted in novel rulings. For example, it was forbidden to set a dislocated foot or hand on the Sabbath (*m. Shab.* 22:6), or to repair a fallen roof (though it might temporarily be propped up; *m. Shab.* 23:5). The rabbis endeavored to offer a rule, or at least a precedent, for every conceivable Sabbath question. The comprehensiveness of the tradition is revealed in the following ruling: if a building fell down on the Sabbath, enough rubble could be removed to discover if any victims were dead or alive. If alive, they could be rescued, but if dead, the corpses must be left until sunset (*m. Yoma* 8:7).[41]

The controversy in the present passage reflects the Pharisaic determination to uphold and honor the Sabbath. It appears that Jesus and his disciples actually violate two categories of work, the first of which is *traveling*. Walking more than 1,999 paces (= 800 meters) was considered a journey and hence a breach of the Sabbath (CD 11:5-6). Curiously, the Pharisees leave this infraction unmentioned. Their grievance is that in plucking ears of grain the disciples are "reaping" (Exod 31:13-17; 34:21). According to Deut 23:25, snitching grain from a neighbor's field was permissible — but not on the Sabbath, according to later rabbinic ruling (*m. Shab.* 7:2). Hence the reproach of Jesus, "Why are [your disciples] doing what is unlawful on the Sabbath?"

25-26 The Pharisees' complaint had been about Jesus' disciples, but Jesus answers on their behalf, much as the Holy Spirit will answer for the church in the hour of persecution (13:11). Jesus normally appeals to his own *exousia* or authority when making pronouncements or judgments. But on occasion he follows the rabbinic precedent of appealing to scripture in settling a controversy, as he does here (also 12:35-37). "'Have you never read what David did when he and his companions were hungry and in need?'" asks Jesus. "'In the days of Abiathar the high priest, he entered the house of God and ate the consecrated bread, which is lawful only for priests to eat.'" The precedent to which Jesus appeals comes from the desert-fox years of David's life when he and his men were outlaws from King Saul (1 Sam 21:1-6). In hunger and desperation, David entered "the house of God" (i.e., the tabernacle) in search of food. The bread in question refers to the twelve loaves that were placed on the altar Sabbath by Sabbath as food for the priests (Exod 40:23; Lev 24:5-9). Mention of Abiathar is problematic in the account because the priest at Nob from whom David procured the loaves was Ahimelech (1 Sam 21:1), not

41. On Sabbath, see Schürer, *History of the Jewish People*, 2.467-75; Str-B 1.610-22.

94

Abiathar his son (1 Sam 22:20), who succeeded to the high priesthood during David's reign. The NIV rendering "in the days of Abiathar the high priest," although not technically as accurate as the NRSV's "when Abiathar was high priest," nevertheless seems better to capture Mark's intention, for the event under consideration appears to have been associated in popular memory with the high priesthood of Abiathar.[42]

The weight of Jesus' argument rests not on the priest of Nob, however, but on David. The messianic echo hidden in the bridegroom imagery in 2:19 is again present here in much bolder relief. David was Israel's greatest king and the precursor of the Messiah (2 Sam 7:11-14; Ps 110:1). "'The days are coming,' declares the LORD, 'when I will raise up to David a righteous Branch, a King who will reign wisely and do what is right in the land. In his days Judah will be saved and Israel will live in safety'" (Jer 23:5; see also *Pss. Sol.* 17:21). The Davidic messianic hope was enshrined in the Eighteen Benedictions recited in the synagogue, "Cause the Branch of David thy servant speedily to sprout, and let his horn be exalted by thy salvation" (Ben. 15 [14]). In scripture, tradition, and liturgy David was enshrined as the inaugurator of a future messianic reign that would be even more glorious than his historical reign.

Jesus' allusion to the episode at Nob is only approximate, for his re-

---

42. The problem with Abiathar in 2:26 does not seem to be resolved by simply attributing an error to Jesus or Mark. On the one hand, the fact that David appeared before Ahimelech in 1 Sam 21:1-6, and the added fact that both Matt 12:4 and Luke 6:4 omit the reference to Abiathar in their parallels, seem to argue in favor of an error. Such an error could easily be explained as a slip of memory, especially given the fact that complete manuscripts of the OT were rare and unwieldy (so Schweizer, *The Good News According to Mark*, 72). But the problem is more complex than this. The most helpful discussions of the issue are those of Lagrange (*Évangile selon Saint Marc*, 53-54) and E. Lohmeyer (*Das Evangelium des Markus*, 64). Already in the OT Abiathar and Ahimelech appear to be confused. In 1 Sam 22:20 Ahimelech is said to be the son of Achitub and the father of Abiathar, but in 2 Sam 8:17 and 1 Chr 18:16 Zadok is said to be the son of Achitub and Ahimelech the son of Abiathar! 1 Chr 24:6 also calls Ahimelech the son of Abiathar. The family genealogy is ostensibly: Achitub, father of Ahimelech, father of Abiathar, father of Ahimelech (1 Chr 24:3, 6, 31). There appear to be two Ahimelechs, grandfather and grandson, with Abiathar between; but, as noted above, the second and third members of the line are sometimes reversed. Abiathar is by all accounts the dominant member of the genealogy since he survived the massacre of his father by Doeg and fled to David. There he became high priest for the duration of David's reign (so Josephus, *Ant.* 6.269-70), which may account for the association of David with him in Mark 2:26. Mark's wording, *epi Abiathar archiereōs*, employs *epi* technically to mean "in the time of" (so 1 Macc 13:42; Luke 3:2; Acts 11:28; *Martyrdom of Polycarp* 21). The NIV rendering, "in the days when Abiathar was high priest," thus appears to render Mark's intended sense. Although David in fact ate the bread of presentation under Ahimelech, the event seems to have been remembered and transmitted in association with the dominant high priesthood of Abiathar.

telling differs in detail from the original. Nevertheless, the reference to David's visit to Ahimelech is significant. David had eaten the consecrated bread as an exception when he and his men were starving. Jesus, however, does not raise the incident in order to plead for a Sabbath exception for his hungry disciples. He cites David's violation of the Torah not as an excuse for his action but as a *precedent*. In making the allusion to David, Jesus is inviting a comparison between his person and Israel's royal messianic prototype. This is the first of several references or allusions to David in Mark's Gospel that help define what kind of Son of God Jesus is. Blind Bartimaeus will call Jesus the "Son of David" (10:47), and later in the temple — at the heart of Israel — Jesus will broach the issue by questioning the religious leaders how it is possible for the Messiah to be both David's "son" and "lord"? (12:35-37). The implication is that the Messiah is the "son" of David because he is descended from David but the "lord" of David because he is of higher authority. The appeal to David in our passage begins to define Jesus' authority as the royal Son of God anticipated since the reign of David (see the excursus on **Divine Man** at 3:12).

27-28 Mark concludes the grainfield controversy with two sayings of Jesus. 2:27 clarifies the relationship between human life and the Sabbath: people are not made for Sabbath rules, but the Sabbath was instituted in order to bless humanity and enhance its well-being. This ruling expresses a principle remarkably similar to that of the wine and wineskins in 2:22: as wineskins must conform to wine, so must the law confirm human life. Jesus corrects a mistaken interpretation that makes of Torah a burdensome yoke on human existence and recovers its true intent as an aid and guardian of life. Jesus' ruling on the Sabbath was not without analogy in Judaism. A late second-century rabbi essentially agreed, "The Sabbath has been given to you; you have not been given to the Sabbath" (*Mek. Exod.* 31:13).

By what authority, however, does Jesus contravene Sabbath convention and presume to redefine it? The answer is given in the Promethean pronouncement of v. 28. True lordship over the Sabbath is invested in the Son of Man. Some scholars argue that Son of Man in v. 28 is essentially a circumlocution for "man" in v. 27; thus, if the Sabbath has been made for humanity, humanity is consequently lord over it.[43] This argument may be attractive on humanistic grounds, but it faces formidable objections. If, as

---

43. For example, R. Funk, R. Hoover, and The Jesus Seminar, *The Five Gospels: What Did Jesus Really Say?* (San Francisco: HarperSanFrancisco, 1997), 49, translates Mark 2:27-28 thus: "'The sabbath was created for Adam and Eve, not Adam and Eve for the sabbath day. So, the son of Adam lords it ever over the sabbath day." By "Adam and Eve" and "son of Adam," the Jesus Seminar means any member of the human race. See the discussion and critique of this reading in R. Guelich, *Mark 1–8:26*, 125-27.

we have noted, the Sabbath was grounded in creation and was the most distinctive characteristic of Judaism, it is inconceivable that Jesus or any other rabbi would declare human supremacy over it.[44] Second, this solution fails to answer the question of the Pharisees in v. 24, "'Why are they doing what is unlawful on the Sabbath?'" If "Son of Man" means simply "man," then v. 28 is not an answer to the Pharisees but a mere tautology. Finally, there are no instances of the use of "Son of Man" in the Gospels with reference to humanity in general. Here, as always when "*Son of Man*" appears on the lips of Jesus, it carries the definite article, "*the* Son of Man*," referring to Jesus' unique vocation as the Son of Man with divine authority and power from Dan 7:14.[45] Even when "Son of Man" refers to Jesus' human suffering, as it frequently does, it nearly always refers to that suffering as a fulfillment of *divine* appointment (see the excursus on **Son of Man** at 2:12). The title can signify various offices of Jesus, but it does not in the Gospels (as, e.g., in the Psalms and Ezekiel) mean simply "man."

The only plausible understanding of "Son of Man" in v. 28 is with reference to Jesus. The Greek syntax of v. 28 is bold. The word for "Lord" (Gk. *kyrios*) is shifted prominently to the beginning of the sentence, which in Greek makes it emphatic, accentuating *who* the true Lord of the Sabbath is. We might render it, "And who is Lord of the Sabbath? The Son of Man is!" In the Gospels, "Son of Man" is used only by Jesus of himself, either of his present status, both of humiliation and authority, or of his future glory. Here, too, it is a reference to the authority of Jesus and not a circumlocution for humanity in general. God, as we noted earlier, had instituted the Sabbath (Gen 2:3), and Jesus now presumes preeminence over it! Once again Jesus puts himself squarely in the place of God. Thus v. 27 offers the principle, and v. 28 the effective authority behind it; that is, the principle of v. 27 is true because the Son of Man of v. 28 is Lord! The authority of Jesus as the Son of Man extends over the Sabbath itself.

2:27-28 preserve an important clue concerning the relationship of Jesus and the Torah, gospel and law, which have long been a point of controversy in Christianity. The extremes of both legalism and antinomianism are avoided. The law is not here regarded as an autonomous revelation, which in legalism tends to replace the person of God. Nor is Jesus a free agent who abrogates the Sabbath or the moral order or the revealed will of God, as in antinomianism. Rather, the sayings of vv. 27-28 teach that the righteous purpose of God as manifested in the Torah can be recovered and fulfilled only in relation to Jesus, who is its Lord.

44. F. W. Beare, "The Sabbath Was Made for Man," *JBL* 79 (1960): 130-36; Nineham, *The Gospel of St Mark*, 108.
45. Moule, "'The Son of Man': Some of the Facts," *NTS* 41 (1995): 277-79.

A QUESTION OF LIFE AND DEATH (3:1-6)

In style this account repeats a pattern of previous episodes. Mark sets the stage for the narrative in the Greek aorist (past tense, v. 1) and then draws the reader dramatically into the ongoing action by using Greek imperfects and presents (vv. 2-5). The immediacy of the narrative again suggests personal reminiscence, perhaps from Peter.[46] With this episode Mark concludes the conflict stories begun in 2:1. In each story Jesus charts a sovereign course, free alike from societal norms and the expectations of scribes, Pharisees, and rabbinic interpretation of the Torah. His allegiance is exclusively to the good news of God (so 1:14-15), which in these five stories is directed to needy and alienated people. His mission has not gone unopposed, however. The proclamation and practice of the good news occur amid resistance and even hostility, as Mark signified by linking the commencement of Jesus' ministry with the arrest of John the Baptizer (1:14). Already Jesus has a reputation as a blasphemer (2:7), a colleague of sinners (2:16), an apostate from religious custom (2:18), and a Sabbath breaker (2:24). These sentiments will become manifest in a contract on his life in this the final conflict story, for "the Pharisees went out and began to plot with the Herodians how they might kill Jesus" (3:6). With his entire road still before him, Jesus must conduct his journey in the shadow of the cross.

1-2 It is the Sabbath, and Jesus is again in the synagogue, presumably at Capernaum. A man is present with "a shriveled hand." The word translated "shriveled" (Gk. *xērainein*) occurs several times in Mark, with meanings ranging among "dried up" (5:29), "withered" (4:6; 11:20-21), and "stiff" (9:18). A stiff and deformed hand seems to fit the present context. "They watched him closely" is in the imperfect tense (Gk. *paretēroun*), meaning "hanging in suspense." Aware that Jesus has already healed there on the Sabbath (1:21-28), all eyes are riveted "to see if he would heal [the man with the shriveled hand] on the Sabbath." Among the congregation some are not simply neutral and impartial observers. They are, rather, motivated "to accuse Jesus." Markan irony is again present: the authorities deny Jesus the right to do good on the Sabbath while they conspire to do evil on the Sabbath.

As we have noted, Sabbath regulations could be overridden only in cases of endangerment to life (*m. Yoma* 8:6). Otherwise, the various schools of Judaism were agreed that the Sabbath must be fully upheld.[47]

---

46. So V. Taylor, *The Gospel According to St. Mark*, 220; C. E. B. Cranfield, *The Gospel According to Saint Mark*, 119.

47. See the discussion of Sabbath observance at 2:23.

First aid was deemed permissible to prevent an injury from worsening, but efforts toward a cure were regarded as work and must wait the passing of the Sabbath. A withered hand was obviously not life-threatening and did not qualify as an exception to the Sabbath rules. Indeed, "they may not straighten a deformed body or set a broken limb [on the Sabbath]" (*m. Shab.* 22:6).

3-4 Jesus, however, orders the "dexterously challenged" man to "'Stand up in front of everyone.'" One can almost feel the man's horror. Had he dreamed his handicap would be made a public spectacle he surely would never have braved attending synagogue. Rather than escaping notice, the dread of most persons who bear handicaps or deformities is having people stare them in the face: the man is summoned by Jesus to the center of the synagogue. Jesus asks, "'Which is lawful on the Sabbath: to do good or to do evil, to save a life or to kill?'"

The first part of the question about doing good or evil obviously refers to healing the handicapped man. For Jesus human need poses a moral imperative. Where good needs to be done, there can be no neutrality, and failure to do the good is to contribute to the evil. It is thus not simply permissible to heal on the Sabbath but *right* to heal on the Sabbath, whether or not it is "lawful." A litmus test of true versus false religion is its response to injustice. In the face of the man's need the religious authorities are "silent," but Jesus is "angered and deeply distressed" (v. 5). The silence of the authorities is evidence that for them religion is about fulfilling stipulations, like driving the speed limit (to use a modern analogy), even though they would very much like to drive faster. This kind of religion can easily be separated from human need. For the conniving observers proper religion is not about the intent of the heart but about things that can be empirically tested and measured, about questions of theological correctness, matters of purity, and fulfilling legal requirements. The observers are willing to tolerate the lamentable condition of another human being and in this instance to use it as possible leverage against Jesus. But Jesus does not use people, whether powerful or powerless, for ulterior purposes. For Jesus the gospel of God (1:14) is different from proper religion in that it is about the disposition of the heart, which cannot remain unmoved in the face of suffering. Only in Gethsemane (14:34) is Jesus' grief and anguish expressed more forcefully in Mark than in the face of the callousness of the synagogue gathering to the suffering of this man. Questions of theological orthodoxy and moral behavior cannot be answered in the abstract, but only by responding to the concrete call of God in one's life and to specific human needs at hand. The test of all theology and morality is either passed or failed by one's response to the weakest and most defenseless members of society. For Jesus the call of God presents itself urgently in the need of this particular man.

At this point in the story the focus abruptly changes, as it did in the healing of the paralytic (2:5-6). The second part of the question comes as a surprise. What is meant by "to save life or to kill?" The issue in the synagogue is about whether or not Jesus will heal on the Sabbath, not about living and dying.[48] Or so it seems. But Jesus again knows the intentions of those who have followed this event (2:8; John 2:28), perhaps even planned it. The second part of the question no longer refers to the disabled man but to Jesus himself. The man with a bad hand is a pawn. If Jesus makes a habit of violating the Sabbath,[49] the authorities will have reason to dispatch him. Subtly but powerfully, the framing of the question in v. 4 links Jesus' fate inextricably with the man with the bad hand. "To do good or to do evil" refers to Jesus' response to the unfortunate man; "to save life or to kill" refers to the observers' response to Jesus. His response to the man with the bad hand will determine their response to him. "But they remained silent." For once an argument from silence is conclusive.

5 Jesus "looked around," according to Mark. The Greek *periblepesthai*, a favorite of Markan vocabulary, describes a summary and commanding survey, which is usually followed by an authoritative pronouncement (3:5, 34; 5:32; 10:23; 11:11). Mark's description of Jesus' anger at the callousness of the observers is graphic and passionate. He uses three strong Greek words that appear nowhere else in the Gospel. Having surveyed the crowd, Jesus is "angry" (Gk. *met' orgēs*); and he is "deeply distressed" *(syllypoumenos)* at their "stubborn" *(pōrōsei)* hearts. The word translated "stubborn" does not mean malicious (although in this instance it appears to include that) as much as unwilling to understand.[50] Nor is such stubbornness isolated to Jesus' opponents; it will equally describe

---

48. Matthew's version of the story (Matt 12:9-14) omits the reference to "to save life or to kill," thus maintaining the focus of the story on the healing. The same is true of the version of the story preserved in Jerome (*Comm. on Matt* 12:13), with inclusion of the man's vocation: "In the Gospel which the Nazarenes and the Ebionites use, which we have recently translated out of Hebrew into Greek, and which is called by most people the authentic [Gospel of] Matthew, the man who had the withered hand is described as a mason who pleaded for help in the following words: I was a mason and earned my livelihood with my hands; I beseech thee, Jesus, to restore to me my health that I may not with ignominy have to beg for my bread" (*NTApoc* 1.160).

49. In Mark, the Sabbath is a day of contention for Jesus. His healings (1:21; 3:2, 4), "working" (2:23, 24, 27), and redefining Sabbath (2:28) draw opposition, as does his visit to Nazareth (6:2). Only in the grave does Jesus rest on the Sabbath (16:1, 2, 9)!

50. See K. L. and M. A. Schmidt, *"pōroō,"* TDNT 5.1,025-28. The Greek word for "stubborn" occurs in both verbal and noun forms in 3:5; 6:52; 8:17; John 12:40; Rom 11:17, 25; 2 Cor 3:14; and Eph 4:18 of Jews, Gentiles, and disciples.

his own disciples (6:52; 8:17). Jesus' anger is a description of righteous indignation. The greatest enemy of divine love and justice is not opposition, not even malice, but hardness of heart and indifference to divine grace, to which not even disciples of Jesus are immune.

Jesus does not equivocate. He does not decide whether or not to act depending on his standing in the polls or on personal consequences to himself. "'Stretch out your hand,'" he commands. The thing the man with the bad hand most fears is before him. A choice must be made. He may refuse and spare himself humiliation. But in so doing he will only be like the religious leaders who refuse to open themselves to the word of Jesus. Or he may take the risk of faith and act on the command of Jesus. "He stretched it out," says Mark, "and his hand was completely restored." In exposing himself to Jesus he is healed. Once again Mark describes faith without using the word. Faith is not a private wager but a public risk that Jesus is worthy of trust when no other hope can be trusted.

6 The compassion of Jesus is free but costly. The hand is restored, but the Pharisees and Herodians "began to plot . . . how they might kill Jesus." The reasons for their resolve are not stated, but the evidence against Jesus has been compounding: Sabbath violations (1:21-25; 2:23-28), fraternizing with sinners (1:40; 2:13-17), disregarding rabbinic custom (2:18-22), and presumption to forgive sins (2:10-11).

Mark lodges the plot against Jesus with the Pharisees and Herodians. In contrast to that of the Pharisees (see on 2:18), the identity of the Herodians is extremely elusive.[51] Matthew 12:14 and Luke 6:11 both omit the Herodians from their versions of the story. Apart from three passing references in the NT (3:6; 12:13 [8:15?]; Matt 22:16), the term "Herodians" is absent in ancient literature. The reference in Josephus to "partisans of Herod (the Great)" (*Ant.* 14.447) may refer to this group without identifying them further.[52] In a separate reference, Josephus notes that Herod (the

51. Standard reference works are generally negligent of the Herodians, largely because of the dearth of information about them. Good discussions can be found in H. H. Rowley, "The Herodians in the Gospels," *JTS* 41 (1940): 14-27; S. Sandmel, "Herodians," *IDB* 2.594-95; and Guelich, *Mark 1–8:26*, 138-39.

52. Rowley notes that the Syriac Peshitta understands Herodians likewise, rendering 3:6 as "those of the house of Herod" ("The Herodians in the Gospels," *JTS* 41 (1940): 23. C. Daniel, "Les 'Herodiens' du Nouveau Testament sont-ils des Esseniens?" *RevQ* 6 (1967): 31-53, makes the highly unsustainable proposal that the Herodians were Essenes who gained the nickname "Herodians" from Herod's enemies who resented the latter's patronage of the Essenes. The virtual absence of objective data on the Herodians puts Daniel's thesis and his conjectural supports of it in serious doubt. See the rebuttal by W. Braun, "Were the New Testament Herodians Essenes? A Critique of an Hypothesis," *RevQ* 14 (1989): 75-88.

Great) "showed special favor to those of the city's populace who had been on his side while he was still a commoner" (*Ant.* 15.2). These allusions suggest that the Herodians were not a distinct sect or political party as were the Pharisees or Sadducees or Essenes, for example, but rather sympathizers and supporters of Herod's cause and the Herodian dynasty. In the NT Herodians always appear in alliance with the Pharisees. This is a curious and unexpected alliance, for the Pharisees staunchly opposed Hellenism and had precious little in common with those who freely compromised with Hellenistic influences and Roman politics.[53] The alliance of these two otherwise antagonistic parties must argue for the magnitude of their opposition to Jesus. The inclusion of Herodians in v. 6 is a forewarning that the opposition ranged against Jesus is not only religious but perhaps political as well (6:14-29; 12:13; 15:1-2).

Common to each of the five stories in 2:1–3:6 is the showcasing of Jesus' authority: to forgive sins (2:1-12), to eat with sinners and tax collectors (2:13-17), to dispense with fasting (2:18-22), to supersede the Sabbath (2:23-28), and to heal on the Sabbath (3:1-6). Parallel to the authority of Jesus is the opposition of the authorities, which begins with silent accusation (2:6-7), intensifies to questioning (2:16; 2:24), and concludes with a plot against his life (3:2, 6). The greater the opposition, however, the greater is Jesus' authority. His authority is both the near and helpful presence of God and a stumbling block. This same authority — and the conflicts resulting from it — will be replayed with the Jerusalem religious leaders in the temple (11:27–12:37). The reference to the "bridegroom being taken from them" (2:20) and the plot against Jesus' life (3:6) already lay the cornerstone for the passion and death of God's Son.

---

53. Sanders, *The Historical Figure of Jesus*, 130-32, views the mention of Herodians as anachronistic in 3:6. He regards the conflicts in 2:1–3:6 as "fairly minor," and doubts Herodian opposition so early in Jesus' ministry. He explains their mention here by supposing that 2:1–3:6 originally was a preface to the passion account that Mark has transposed to the beginning of his Gospel! This is an extreme and unwarranted hypothesis. The conflicts in 2:1–3:6 are scarcely "minor"; blasphemy (2:7) already lays the foundation for a capital case against Jesus. The supposition that 2:1–3:6 once functioned as a preface to a passion narrative is entirely conjectural. Finally, Sanders' dogmatic suggestions about the Herodians are surprising given the latter's obscurity. We know that Herod the Great initially ruled Galilee before he displaced his brother Phasael in Jerusalem. It is entirely reasonable to suppose that his supporters continued to constitute a significant political presence in Galilee, and that the Pharisees, perceiving Jesus' threat to their religious hegemony, should ally themselves with the politically savvy Herodians in plotting Jesus' death.

THE OPEN-AIR PREACHER (3:7-12)

This editorial summary of Jesus' ministry beyond Capernaum is without exact parallel in the Gospels, although it is similar to Mark's earlier summary description of Jesus' ministry in 1:35-39. The Gospel of Mark is unusually particular and concrete, narrating what Jesus did and said in specific situations. But Mark cannot provide an "unabridged life" of Jesus, and general summary reports such as this one inform and remind readers that Jesus' ministry surpassed the stories included in Mark's Gospel. Jesus' ministry and reputation enjoyed extensive geographical influence and dominion over demonic as well as mundane opposition.

7-8 "Jesus withdrew with his disciples to the lake." Although this is the only instance of "withdraw" (Gk. *anachōrein*) in Mark, its many occurrences in Matthew suggest withdrawal for retreat and solitude. Given the battery of tests Jesus has faced in 2:1–3:6, it may be that he desires to escape further harassment from the religious authorities. Mark's description of withdrawing "to the lake" is puzzling because Capernaum, the ostensible site of 3:1-6, is on the lake. The phraseology perhaps implies that Jesus quit Capernaum for the more deserted stretches of the shore to the north where the Jordan River enters the lake.

"A large crowd" gathers from extensive geographical regions, not only from Galilee but from Judea (including Jerusalem), from Idumea 120 miles due south, from points east of the Jordan, and from Tyre and Sidon fifty miles to the north. Equally remarkable is the ethnic diversity of the crowd. Galilee, Judea, and Jerusalem were principally Jewish territories; Idumea and Transjordan were mixed Jewish-Gentile regions; and Tyre and Sidon were largely if not entirely Gentile regions (see Luke 6:17; Matt 11:21-22).[54] The fame of Jesus is far reaching and all encompassing, which is all the more remarkable given the social cleavages of the day. The range of Jesus' influence exceeds that of John the Baptizer, who had attracted crowds only from Jerusalem and Judea (1:5). In this reputation and magnetism Jesus is again "more powerful" (1:7) than John. Like Isaiah's portrayal of the Servant of the Lord, Mark's description of Jesus' geographical influence designates him as a "light for the Gentiles" (Isa 49:6).

9-10 The sizable crowd attracted by Jesus' fame is again an ambivalent force, providing both an opportunity and impediment to Jesus' teaching and ministry (see the discussion of **crowd** at 2:2). The press of the crowd necessitates the readiness of "a small boat . . . to keep the people from crowding him." Pastoral and folksy stereotypes of Jesus sur-

---

54. The Greek text of vv. 7-8 is unusually disparate in details and word order, perhaps owing to Mark's prolix summary of locations. See Metzger, *TCGNT*[2], 68.

rounded by lambs and children are skewed caricatures of Mark's description of Jesus' early ministry in Galilee. The arrival of a popular leader jostled by crowds and hassled by reporters is more appropriate. The crowd is actually described rather menacingly. The word for "crowding" (Gk. *thlibein*) would better read "pressing" or "crushing"; and "pushing forward" suggests in Greek "mobbing" or "falling upon" Jesus. The crowd is a paradox. Its needs command Jesus' attention, and Jesus is fully attentive to the misery present in its numbers, but its clamor is not a response of faith.

11-12 The crowds may fall upon Jesus, but the evil spirits "fall before" him. The word for "fall before" (Gk. *prospiptein*) occurs eight times in the NT, and in each instance save one it conveys the image of an inferior prostrating himself in homage before a superior. The word for "evil spirits" is in Greek "unclean spirits," which is a Jewish formulation.[55] The Greek word used to describe their sight of Jesus is *theōrein*, a word that is used frequently in John's Gospel to connote inner comprehension, indeed almost faith. Its meaning falls short of this sense in Mark, however. In the seven uses of the term in Mark, it connotes a rather detached observation or spectating, without any sense of conviction in what is beheld. As spiritual forces themselves, the evil spirits recognize the one filled with God's Spirit, but they do not participate in the object of their sight (see further on *theōrein* at 15:40-41). They declare Jesus' full divine identity, "'You are the Son of God'" (see **Son of God** at 1:1; 15:39). In addition to the Father (1:11), the demons are the only other party so far in Mark to confess Jesus' divine Sonship (1:24; 3:11; 5:7). Their doing so in the presence of the disciples in this instance accentuates the incompleteness of the disciples' knowledge of Jesus. Some scholars suggest that the demons expose Jesus' identity in order to escape his authority over them, even to rob him of his strength and prevail over him.[56] But this passage, as in 5:7, suggests a no-contest event, reminiscent of Jas 2:19, "Even the demons believe [that God exists] and *shudder*." The emphasis falls not on exorcism per se but on Jesus subduing the demon world to his authority (see the **Command to Silence** at 1:34). Characteristic of Jesus' divine authority over evil is Gk. *epitiman* ("he gave them strict orders"). Used in the OT of the word of God that prevails over both natural (Ps 106:9) and demonic

---

55. A. Y. Collins, "Mark and His Readers: The Son of God Among Jews," *HTR* 92/4 (1999): 398-99, suggests that "unclean spirits" recalls fallen angels from Gen 6:1-4; *1 Enoch* 15:3-4, *Jub.* 7:21; 10:1; and *Testament of Solomon*. The demons in *Testament of Solomon*, however, are merely devious pests, and those of Genesis, *1 Enoch*, and *Jubilees* are unclean owing to sexual transgressions. Neither category seems to do justice to the more sinister and oppressive power of the demonic in Mark.

56. Grundmann, *Das Evangelium nach Markus*, 75-76.

(Zech 3:2) forces, *epitiman* represents the sovereign command of God to rebuke and subdue evil (1:25; 4:39; 9:25). Jesus' authority over the demonic realm is total. Demonic forces are left with no other choice than to confess his sovereignty by their subjection.

Although portions of the present account are present in Matt 4:24-25; 12:15-16; and Luke 6:17-19, neither of the latter includes the confession of Jesus as God's Son. For Mark the confession is a necessary completion of Jesus' healings and exorcisms. There is no compatibility or coexistence between Jesus and the demonic. When the More Powerful One meets unclean spirits it is in the capacity of complete supremacy over them. Their house is plundered, to anticipate the imagery of 3:27. So final is Jesus' supremacy that it is acknowledged by *their* confession of him as "the Son of God."

Excursus: Divine Man

A key issue in the study of the Gospel of Mark relates to titles and nomenclature for Jesus. It has become practically axiomatic in modern NT scholarship to regard as secondary statements in the Gospels that attribute messianic titles or status to Jesus. The Christology of the Gospels, whether explicit (e.g., in titles) or implicit (e.g., as in *exousia*), is generally considered either to have arisen as a result of the early church's encounter with the categories of Greek thought in the Gentile mission (such as "divine man" and "Son of God"), or to have been projected onto the Gospel accounts by the early church as a result of its desire to attribute to the historical Jesus an honor commensurate to the church's postresurrection experience of his Lordship. Although recent NT scholarship has concentrated more on investigating the Jewish background of the NT, the supposition of Hellenistic and Greco-Roman influences on NT Christology continues to be strong.[57] The "divine man" theory has especially

57. The history of this interpretation is extensive. In the early part of the twentieth century (1913) it was given classic expression by W. Bousset, *Kyrios Christos: A History of the Belief in Christ from the Beginnings of Christianity to Irenaeus*, trans. J. Steely (Nashville: Abingdon Press, 1970). It subsequently became a commonplace in NT Christology. Bultmann says, "In Mark he [Jesus] is *theios anthrōpos*" (*The History of the Synoptic Tradition*, trans. J. Marsh [New York and Evanston: Harper and Row, 1963], 241). Later T. J. Weeden writes, "In the past decade an increasing number of Markan scholars have recognized that a large amount of Markan material is steeped in a christology drawn in the tradition of the Hellenistic *theios anēr* (divine man)." Further, "There is absolutely no hint in the first half of the Gospel [of Mark] that authentic messiahship should contain any other christological dimension [than *theios anēr*]" (*Mark — Traditions in Conflict* [Philadelphia: Fortress Press, 1971], 55-56). A recent reference work casts Jesus entirely in the mold

been used to explain the exorcisms of Jesus and his subjugation of demonic forces.[58] According to this theory, Mark depicts Jesus according to miracle-worker models of Hellenism.

Despite the readiness with which some scholars associate Mark's Jesus with a Hellenistic "divine man," the theory is beset with obstacles and has not succeeded in gaining a consensus of opinion among scholars.[59] The first problem is with nomenclature itself. "Son of God" was not a common title in Hellenism. More frequent and important titles were *neos* ("new," accompanied by a name), *epiphanēs* ("epiphany"), *euergetēs* ("benefactor"), and *sōtēr* ("savior"). This terminology is strikingly absent in the NT. "Divine man" does not occur in the NT, and the adjective *theios* ("divine") appears only three times (Acts 17:29; 2 Pet 1:3, 4), and then only of God, not of human beings. "New" occurs twenty-four times in the NT, but never with reference to Jesus as a "New" something. "Epiphany" appears only once in a textual variant (Acts 2:20) in a quotation of Joel 3:4. "Benefactor," which was commonly used of emperors and outstanding figures of antiquity, also occurs but once in the NT, where it is expressly rejected (Luke 22:25-26). Finally, *sōtēr* occurs twenty-four times in the NT, but only three times in the Gospels (Luke 1:47; 2:11; John 4:42); otherwise, it appears mainly in Paul. It is used only of Jesus, or in the Pastoral Epistles of God.[60] Thus, the load-bearing vocabulary of "divine men" in Hellenism is conspicuously absent in the NT, and in one instance dismissed contemptuously.

More problematic than nomenclature, however, is the concept of "divine man" itself. "Divine man" is a term that occurs only rarely in ancient literature. It is not a fixed concept but a collective abstract of modern derivation for a series of semi-related phenomena, including gifted or

---

of *theios anēr* ("divine man"): "Jesus' action in the Gospel story (in Mark 3:1-6) therefore corresponds completely to the contemporary picture of the public benefactor. Like a philosopher king, he lays claim to the right to determine the criteria for right and wrong conduct himself" (*HCNT*, 86).

58. L. Keck argues that the miracle stories in 3:7-12; 4:35–5:43; 6:31-52; and 6:53-56 stem from Hellenistic sources since they are devoid of references to conflicts with Judaism, debates over the Sabbath, or Jesus' authority, and since they have no connection with the kingdom of God or forgiveness of sins. He concludes, "the supernatural power is resident within Jesus in a way to make him different from other men. . . . They are direct manifestations of the Son of God, and in a particular way — the *theios anēr*" ("Mark 3:7-12 and Mark's Christology," *JBL* 84 [1965]: 341-58).

59. See P. Achtemeier, "Gospel Miracle Tradition and the Divine Man," *Int* 26 (1972): 174.

60. On "savior" and "benefactor," see A. D. Nock, "Soter and Euergetes," in *Essays on Religion and the Ancient World*, ed. Z. Stewart (Cambridge, Mass.: Harvard University Press, 1972), 1.720-35.

unusual rulers, warriors, philosophers, poets, heroes of various sorts, and miracle workers. The Hellenistic world designated any number of unusual persons with one or more of the above titles, which modern scholars rather indiscriminately refer to as "divine men." Given the ambiguity of the concept, it is insufficient to assume or argue, without further identification and precision, that this collective genre lies at the root of Mark's portrait of Jesus.[61] Jesus shared little in common with the poet inspired by the Muses or with the flamboyant and decadent Caesar cult. The heroic feats of Heracles are scarcely prototypes for the carpenter of Nazareth. Even the prototype of the Hellenistic miracle worker, which is the closest analogy to Jesus, is of questionable usefulness. It must be remembered that the model of the "divine man" that is supposed to have influenced Mark's story of Jesus is a post-Christian model. Stories of wonder workers do not begin to appear until the latter half of the second century A.D., and then, at least in the cases of Philostratus, Porphyry, Iamblichus, and Diogenes Laertius, with anti-Christian polemic intent.[62] But even assuming such accounts preserve earlier traditions, such traditions are far from parallel to the Jesus tradition in the Gospels. Although healings or resuscitations are frequently found in Hellenistic literature, exorcisms were uncommon among Hellenistic "divine men."[63]

By contrast, Mark pictures demons as Jesus' arch opponents and the *first* party to recognize and confess him as Son of God. With regard to healing miracles, miracle workers of antiquity normally practiced their craft with ostentation, for "everywhere in the ancient world signs were demanded to substantiate the claim to being a 'son of God.'"[64] Typical of such ostentation is the story of Apollonius of Tyana, who, having "passed away from among men," appeared in a dream to a young atheist to convince him of the immortality of the soul (Philostratus, *Life Apoll.* 8.31).[65]

---

61. See D. L. Tiede, *The Charismatic Figure as Miracle Worker,* SBLDS (Missoula: Scholars Press, 1070), 289; W. von Martitz, *"huios," TDNT* 8.339.

62. E. Schweizer, *Jesus Christus im vielfältigen Zeugnis des Neuen Testaments* (München/Hamburg: Siebenstern Taschenbuch Verlag, 1968), 127.

63. See the material gathered in H. D. Betz, *Lukian von Samosata und das Neue Testament* (Berlin: Akademie-Verlag, 1961). Betz, who otherwise is sympathetic to the "divine man" motif, admits that Lucian's reports of exorcisms and those reported of Jesus in the NT are fundamentally different.

64. G. P. Wetter, *Der Gottes Sohn* (Göttingen: Vandenhoeck & Ruprecht, 1916), 64-65.

65. Apollonius of Tyana, the most publicized of ancient miracle workers, is a distant analogy to Jesus. Philostratus produced his account of Apollonius a full 150 years after Jesus, with the apologetic aim of rehabilitating Apollonius from the charge of charlatanism. The *Life of Apollonius* lacks the proximity to its subject that characterizes the Gospel accounts of Jesus, and is thoroughly legendarized. Apollonius knows all lan-

Mark, however, portrays Jesus as the humble servant whose authority is not employed for self-display or aggrandizement.[66] In contrast to Jesus, no Hellenistic wonder worker presumes to forgive sins. Philostratus recounts the story of Apollonius to demonstrate his difference from normal humanity. With Philostratus as with other writers of antiquity, it was important to demonstrate the hero's *moira* ("merit") as a basis for the hero's eventual apotheosis to godhood. But the Gospels emphasize Jesus' identification and solidarity with humanity (Mark 10:42-45). The revelation of Jesus' unique filial relationship with God within the context of human relationships defined by trust and discipleship is essentially different from the formulaic role of "divine man" in the official cult, as exemplified by references to departed pharaohs as "divine father" or to Roman emperors as "savior and benefactor of the inhabited world."

The one place where the Hellenistic "divine man" concept influenced early Christianity was in the apocryphal Gospels, not in the canonical Gospels. In the apocryphal Gospels we observe elaborations of Jesus reminiscent of "divine man" motifs, and most especially in those accounts that find no parallels in the canonical Gospels.[67] This indicates that the canonical Gospels exerted a restraining influence on depicting Jesus as a "divine man." With regard to the canonical Gospels themselves, the foregoing evidence indicates that Mark and the NT evangelists resisted the vocabulary and concepts associated with "divine man" in their presentations of Jesus. The formative model of Jesus' divine Son-

---

guages (even of birds and animals) without having learned them, knows events past and future, and even remembers former incarnations. The twenty-one miracles reported of him are intended to evince his preternatural status. In Egypt he was gazed on as a god, and people everywhere marveled at his goodness. Apollonius, however, did not claim the title of god for himself, nor does Philostratus call him a son of god. Philostratus equivocates in recording a number of his miracles, recounting that Apollonius "seemed" to effect cures, etc. Philostratus is also nebulous about the death of Apollonius, vaguely referring to it as "passing." Apollonius is, in short, the classic Hellenistic sage or prophet who is accordingly apotheosized.

66. Athanasius (fourth century), who knew Hellenistic wonder workers firsthand, differentiated Jesus thus: "Now, if they ask, Why, then, did [God] not appear by means of other and nobler parts of creation, and use some nobler instrument, as the sun, or moon, or stars, or fire, or air, instead of man merely? Let them know that the Lord came not to make a display, but to heal and teach those who were suffering. For the way for one aiming at display would be, just to appear, and to dazzle the beholders; but for one seeking to heal and teach the way is, not simply to sojourn here, but to give himself to the aid of those in want, and to appear as they who need him can bear it; that he may not, by exceeding the requirements of the sufferers, trouble the very persons that need him, rendering God's appearance useless to them" (*On the Incarnation* 43).

67. Achtemeier, "Gospel Miracle Tradition and the Divine Man," *Int* 26 (1972): 174-97.

ship is not that of the Greco-Roman "divine man," in whatever expression. Jesus' divine Sonship is defined by OT concepts of filial love and obedience, and expressed according to the Servant of the Lord motif in Isaiah.[68]

68. On "divine man," see J. R. Edwards, "The Son of God: Its Antecedents in Judaism and Hellenism and Its Use in the Earliest Gospel" (Ph.D. diss., Fuller Theological Seminary, 1978), 48-81, 125-35. Among those who rightly resist the Siren song of the "divine man" concept are O. Betz, "The Concept of the So-called 'Divine Man' in Mark's Christology," in *Studies in New Testament and Early Christian Literature: Essays in Honor of Allen P. Wikgren* (Leiden: Brill, 1972); C. H. Holladay, *Theios Anēr in Hellenistic Judaism: A Critique of the Use of This Category in New Testament Christology,* trans. J. Bowden (Philadelphia: Fortress Press, 1976); W. Liefeld, "The Hellenistic 'Divine Man' and the Figure of Jesus in the Gospels," *JETS* 16 (1973): 195-205; E. Schweizer, "Neuere Markus-Forschung in USA," *EvT* 33 (1973), 533-37; J. D. Kingsbury, "The 'Divine Man' as the Key to Mark's Christology — The End of an Era?" *Int* 35 (1981): 243-57.

CHAPTER FOUR

Insiders and Outsiders

MARK 3:13–4:34

The rapid-fire sequence of stories in 2:1–3:12 depicted Jesus' authority in a variety of public settings. Mark now focuses on Jesus' authority with respect to his followers, first in the formal constituting of the Twelve (3:13-19), but also with respect to groups related to Jesus in other ways, including associates (3:21; 4:10) and family (3:31-35). In the present section Mark develops with special attention the theme of insiders and outsiders, which is important throughout his Gospel. This is not a separate theme from the authority of Jesus, however, but a subtheme, for the status of insider or outsider is determined by one's proximity and receptivity to Jesus.

THE NEW ISRAEL (3:13-19)

Next to the themes of the divine Sonship and authority of Jesus, the theme of following Jesus is the most important one in the Gospel of Mark. From the beginning of his Galilean ministry Jesus calls people to fellowship with himself in order to implant his message and mission among them. The word for "disciple," in both its Greek and Hebrew roots, means "student" or "learner," specifically one who learns in active fellowship, hence an apprentice. Jesus has already gathered some disciples prior to this episode. From beside the lake he called four fishermen (1:16-20) and a tax collector (2:13-14). These and other followers are mentioned in passing throughout the early chapters of Mark. Jesus' retinue, however, exceeds the disciples named so far, as his choosing the Twelve from a larger group of unnamed followers indicates. Some of the names in this larger retinue are still preserved, including those of Joseph Barsabbas and

Matthias, who had been with Jesus from his baptism onward (Acts 1:21-23). Others were women, "Mary Magdalene, Mary the mother of James the younger and of Joses, and Salome" (15:40). The early church also counted the names of Paul, Barnabas, and James, the brother of Jesus, as later disciples who had not been among the Twelve.

Early in his ministry Jesus elected twelve men from his wider following to join him as formal apprentices.[1] This inner circle is distinguished as "apostles," that is, commissioned followers to Jesus. In 3:13-19 Mark describes more exactly what discipleship to Jesus entails. Vv. 13-15 explain the function of the Twelve, and vv. 16-19 their identity.

13 "Jesus went up into the hills and called to him those he wanted, and they came to him." The language of this sentence is more solemn and symbolic in Greek than it appears in English. The first clue is Jesus' going up "into the hills." Although the setting of the call of the Twelve was probably the western hills overlooking the Sea of Galilee, "the hills" is an inadequate translation of Gk. *oros* ("mountain") in v. 13. Mountains are often in Mark sites of revelation or significant junctures in Jesus' ministry (3:13; 6:46; 9:2; 11:1; 13:3; 14:26), as they are sites of revelation in the OT.[2] Jesus' ascent of a mountain to call the Twelve has the significance of Moses' ascent of Mt. Sinai to receive and transmit the Ten Commandments (Exod 19:1-25; 20:18-20).

Jesus "called to him those he wanted." The Greek is more emphatic; the sense is that he *summoned* those whom he *willed*. Jesus determines the call. Disciples do not decide to follow Jesus and do him a favor in so doing; rather, his call supersedes their wills, summoning one who does not intend to follow (10:21) and debarring one who would (5:19). The society into which he calls them is determined not by their preferences but by his summons. Its members have nothing in common except his sovereign

1. The calling and commissioning of Twelve by Jesus is a virtual historical certainty. Apart from a reference to twelve council elders at Qumran (1QS 8:1), twelve is not a common number for Jewish fellowships (see Acts 6:3, e.g., where the apostles choose *seven* deacons). Nor is it likely that the Twelve were retrojected into the life of Jesus by the Christian community, for it would scarcely be conceivable that the early church would have included the betrayer of Jesus in such a circle of followers. Finally, Paul's awareness and recognition of the Twelve (1 Cor 15:5; Gal 2:9) attests to its foundation in Jesus' ministry. See E. Schweizer, *The Good News According to Mark*, 127-28.

2. The OT frequently associates mountains with God's presence and revelation: From Mt. Ebal and Mt. Gerizim come blessings and curses (Deut 11:29; 27:12-13; Josh 8:33); Isaac is offered on a mountain (Gen 22:2); Moses prays on a mountain (Exod 17:9-10), as does Elijah (1 Kgs 18:42); the ark is set on a hill (1 Sam 7:1; 2 Sam 6:3); and Yahweh dwells on mountains (1 Chr 16:39). Above all, God gives the commandments on Mt. Sinai (Exodus 19–20), Mt. Zion is God's dwelling place (Pss 15:1; 24:3); and God will judge the earth from the Mount of Olives (Zech 14:4). See W. Foerster, *"oros," TDNT* 5.475-87.

call, apart from which the community cannot exist. As we noted at 1:16-20, the embryo of the church is already signified in the call of apprentice-followers to form a new community around Jesus.

Finally, the apostles come "to him." Rabbis, as we noted at 1:16-20, did not call disciples, but were chosen by their disciples, much as students today choose a college. Nor would a rabbi dare leave the impression that his person superseded the Torah. Rabbinic disciples would ideally see in their tutor a means of mastering the Torah and a model of what they themselves might become. But as described by Mark, Jesus' program is of a different order. Jesus is the sole and exclusive subject of the call. Nothing — not even the Torah or God — is presented as more important than Jesus. Unlike a rabbi, Jesus is not a means to an ulterior good but is himself the final good. As for equaling or surpassing Jesus, that possibility does not exist. The question is what Jesus can make of his disciples, not what they can be on their own.[3]

14-15 In every respect the new community is Jesus' doing. The NIV says, "He appointed Twelve," but the Greek says, "he *made* Twelve." To appoint is to select from an existing lot and raise to a new status, but to *make* means to bring into existence. Mark's verb *(epoiēsen)* is the same as that of Gen 1:1 (LXX). Although this is a common verb, it is very conceivable that Mark intends to recall the opening line of Genesis, "In the beginning God *made* heaven and earth," signifying that the Twelve are a new creation.[4] Discipleship does not consist in what disciples can do for Christ, but in what Christ can *make* of disciples.[5]

---

3. On the radical nature of Jesus' call, see K. H. Rengstorf, *"mathētēs," TDNT* 5.444-47, who declares that "[The initiative of Jesus] dominates all the Gospel accounts of the way in which [disciples] began to follow Jesus." The distinctiveness of Jesus' call is captured by Schweizer, *The Good News According to Mark,* 49: "This concept of discipleship is Jesus' own creation. The Greeks and the later rabbis spoke of 'disciples of God'; however they meant by this 'becoming like him' in an ethical sense, or the obedience to his commandments. The relationship of the rabbis to their students seems to be a closer parallel to this discipleship. The primary difference is that the rabbi does not call his disciples — he is sought by them. Above all, the rabbis never could have conceived of a call so radical as to make clear that being with Jesus is more important than all of God's commandments. A disciple of a rabbi might dream of some day becoming even better, if possible, than his master; but a disciple of Jesus could never expect that some day he himself might be the 'Son of Man.' Jesus never debates with his disciples as a rabbi would have done. Thus the word 'follow' received a new sound when Jesus said it, a sound which it has nowhere else in those passages of the Old Testament which declare that one must follow either Baal or Yahweh."

4. See E. Lohmeyer, *Das Evangelium des Markus,* 74-75.

5. The gnostic *Letter of Peter to Philip* (133-34) at Nag Hammadi is oblivious to the authority of Jesus to call and determine the disciples. Contrary to Mark, The *Letter of Peter to Philip* makes the disciples the subject of the relationship, and they gather not to the

The new status of the disciples is signified by their being *named* (NIV, "designates") "apostles." This again may recall the creation theme, where Adam names the animals (Gen 2:19). In the biblical world the right to name belonged to a superior — maker, master, parent — who determined the essence and purpose of the thing named.

The setting of the call of the Twelve in vv. 13-14 underscores in every conceivable way the authority of Jesus to determine and constitute his followers. In vv. 14b-15 the call is further defined by two purpose clauses. The Twelve are constituted *to be with him*, and *to be sent*; the latter purpose likewise divides into two further responsibilities: to preach and to have authority over demons. Apostleship is thus a matter of *being* and *being sent*, of who one is in relationship to Jesus and of what one does as a result of that relationship.

The simple prepositional phrase "to be with him" has atomic significance in the Gospel of Mark. Discipleship is a relationship before it is a task, a "who" before a "what." If, as Gen 3:4-5 indicates, the essence of sin is substituting a false god for the true God, being with Jesus becomes the way of forsaking human idols and honoring the true God, thus recovering the image of God (Gen 1:26-27). To be with Jesus is the most profound mystery of discipleship. From now on his person and his work determine the existence of the Twelve.

The second purpose of the call is to be "sent." In Greek the verbal form of the word for "apostle" *(apostolos)* is *apostellein*, meaning "to commission" or "send with a specific purpose." The emphasis in Mark is not on designating a special category of super-followers who are distinct from other followers, that is, apostles versus disciples. This is made evident by the fact that the word "apostle" occurs only once for certain in Mark 6:30,[6] whereas the word "disciple/s" occurs forty-five times, with still other expressions for Jesus' followers (3:34; 4:10; 10:32; 11:9).[7] The call and commission of the Twelve is representative of that of all Jesus' followers.

The Twelve are sent by Jesus specifically "to preach" and "to have authority to drive out demons." The Greek word rendered "preach" *(kēryssein)* is the same word used of Jesus' proclamation of the gospel of God in 1:14. It carries the meaning of public discourse, hence proclama-

---

person of Jesus but only to a "great light" and "voice" for enlightenment from the Pleroma.

6. It is not certain that the explanatory phrase "designating them apostles" *(hous kai apostolous ōnomasen)* was penned by Mark. Although it is present in several old manuscripts (B ℵ C θ), it is omitted in many important manuscripts. Its presence here may be owing to an interpolation from Luke 6:13.

7. See W. R. Telford, *Mark*, NTG (Sheffield: Sheffield Academic Press, 1995), 141.

tion. The gospel is not an ineffable mystery beyond words, but a story — the story of Jesus — that can be articulated and understood in common language. The proclamation is not the verbalizing of the subjective experience of the believer but the making known of the saving activity of God in Jesus. Not what disciples think and feel but what they have seen and heard is the subject of proclamation; "thus we proclaim, and so you believe" (1 Cor 15:11). Hence one does not proclaim the gospel either in one's own words or by one's own powers; rather, one must be sent by Jesus (5:19; 6:7).

In addition to verbalizing the message, apostles are empowered to act with authority to expel demons. This constitutes the second reason for their sending. Until now the power of proclamation and exorcism has been the sole possession of Jesus, who has "traveled throughout Galilee, preaching in their synagogues and driving out demons" (1:39). In an intentional act of empowerment, Jesus confers on the Twelve *his* authority to proclaim the good news and prevail over demonic powers (Acts 5:12-16; 16:16-18). This constitutes them as peers, not as servile followers or doting fans, and lays the foundation for their later mission in his name (6:7). The symbolic force of this empowerment is as important as its actual effect. Popular Judaism believed that the subduing of demons would characterize the messianic age.[8] This is another example of Mark's "implicit Christology," namely, that Jesus' authority and bearing point to the divine source behind his words and deeds.

The apostolic commission encompasses the three constitutive elements of human experience — the relational, verbal, and behavioral. Discipleship is a matter of being *with* Jesus, of *speaking* his message, and of *acting* in his name by casting out demons and opposing evil. With regard to the third characteristic, the behavioral, disciples are not simply defined by what they stand for but also by what they stand against. They are commissioned to confront demonic and evil powers — however they manifest themselves — and to confront them not only in thought and word but in action.

16-19 Immediately following the job description, the names of the disciples are given.[9] The order of deed-doers is important: tasks are not fashioned to fit disciples, but disciples are defined and formed by the commission of the gospel (so Rom 6:17). Significant is the number

---

8. "And Beliar shall be bound by [the high priest of the messianic age] and he (the high priest) shall give power to his children to tread upon the evil spirits" (*T. Levi* 18:12).

9. The best textual reconstruction of v. 16 is again difficult to decide. The manuscript evidence for *kai epoiēsen tous dōdeka* is no better than it was for the variant reading in v. 14 (see n. 5 above). Contrary to B. Metzger (*TCGNT²*, 69), the omission of the phrase does not impair the sense of the text.

Twelve. The NT provides four lists of the twelve apostles (3:16-19; Matt 10:2-4; Luke 6:14-16; Acts 1:13).[10] The significance of each list is less in the specific names (there are minor differences in names and order) than in their *number,* which always is Twelve. In v. 14 the Greek reads literally, "he made Twelve," a curious wording since Twelve is something one counts or numbers rather than "makes." The phrase indicates a fixed, complete unit or college.[11] The number Twelve, of course, recalls the twelve tribes of Jacob (Gen 35:22-26; 49:1-28). Jesus' summons of the Twelve in fellowship and service to himself signifies a reconstituting of Israel. According to Matt 19:28 and Luke 22:30, the Twelve are not only an extension of Jesus' earthly ministry, but their function extends beyond time when they will sit in judgment over Israel. The call of the Twelve was surely significant to Mark's first Roman readers, both Gentiles and Jews. For Gentiles, it is a reminder that "salvation is from the Jews" (John 4:22), that is, that the only savior proclaimed to the world is the one pre-pared for in Abraham and now present in Jesus. For Jews, likewise, the Twelve is a reminder that Israel fulfills its destiny only in the fellowship and service of Jesus.

Concerning the names of the Twelve, Peter's name heads every NT apostolic list, followed by the Zebedee brothers (usually James followed by John). Peter, James, and John form an inner circle among the Twelve that accompany Jesus on special occasions (5:37; 9:2; 14:33). Simon is nicknamed "the rock" (Aram. *Cephas;* Gk. *Petros*), although it will be some time before he lives up to it. It is often supposed that Simon's nick-name reflects his rocklike character. Firmness and stability do not charac-terize Peter's portrayal in Mark, however, and not even always after Pen-tecost (see Gal 2:11-14). The nickname is better explained as a clue to Peter's fundamental role among the apostles. The distinction of being a cornerstone of the community is communicated solely by Jesus' call, not by Peter's merit.[12] Only in Mark are James and John called "Boanerges,"

10. Epiphanius (*Pan.* 30.13.2-3) gives a separate list of disciples that he claims de-rives from the *Gospel of the Ebionites:* "And when [Jesus] entered into Capernaum into the house of Simon who was called Peter, he opened his mouth and said: While I was pass-ing along the lake of Tiberias I chose John and James, sons of Zebedee, and Simon and Andrew and Thaddeus and Simon the Zealot and Judas Iscariot; and you, Matthew, I called while you were sitting at your tax table and you followed me. It is you whom I wish to make Twelve apostles for a witness to Israel" (my translation). Epiphanius's list of the disciples differs from the NT lists in several respects: it is the only list narrated in the first person, only eight names are mentioned, it highlights Matthew, and Simon's name does not head the list.

11. In the NT Pseudepigrapha "Twelve" is occasionally used when only eleven apostles are meant; see, e.g., *Gospel of Peter* 59; *Asc. Isa.* 3:17; 4:3.

12. See E. Klostermann, *Das Markusevangelium,* 34-35.

which in Hebrew suggests "the loud ones," or perhaps "hot-tempered pair," which Mark renders "Sons of Thunder."[13] The appropriateness of the nickname is evidenced by the descriptions of the brothers in 9:38 and Luke 9:54! The position of James in the Synoptic lists suggests a status second in command to Peter.[14] Matthew is apparently the Levi of 2:13 (so Matt 9:9). Of Andrew, Philip, Thomas, and Judas Iscariot we hear only occasionally again; and of Bartholomew, Matthew, James the son of Alphaeus, Thaddeus, and Simon the Zealot nothing further. The meaning of "Iscariot," the surname of Judas, is obscure. "The man of Kerioth" (Heb. *ish Keriot*) is perhaps the most likely meaning, identifying Judas with the town of Kerioth, some twenty miles due east of the Dead Sea (Jer 48:24; Amos 2:2). Another suggestion, less likely but not impossible, derives from *sicarius* ("dagger [man]"), which would identify Judas with a radical fringe of Zealot assassins.[15]

Beyond the names themselves, the list of the Twelve is significant in at least three respects. First, apart from various pious but unreliable legends, our knowledge of several of the names of the apostles is meager or non-existent.[16] What their specific contributions were to the advancement of the gospel we do not know. Their names, however, like the even longer list of names in Rom 16:1-16, stand as silent witnesses to the truth that the existence of the church is indebted to the labors of those who for the most part remain unknown and unnamed.

Second, as far as we know, none of the apostles comes from the Jewish religious establishment and leadership. They all derive from the broad and diverse common folk known as the *am-ha'aretz*, "people of the land." Within that nondescript category, names like Peter, Andrew, James, and John represent the respectable (or acceptable) middle;[17] with

---

13. See C. E. B. Cranfield, *The Gospel According to Saint Mark,* 130-31.

14. Andrew's name intervenes in Matt 10:2 and Luke 6:14 only because he is Peter's brother.

15. On the reading *Iskariōth* (or *Iskariōtēs*), see Metzger, *TCGNT*[2], 21-22. The various options of explaining the name are explored in R. Guelich, *Mark 1–8:26,* 163. B. Pixner makes the intriguing but speculative suggestion that the connection of Judas's name with "Simon the Zealot" (also Luke 6:15-16) can be explained by supposing that both came from Gamala, the Zealot eagle's nest northeast of the Sea of Galilee (*Wege des Messias und Stätten der Urkirche,* Herausgegeben von R. Riesner [Basel: Brunnen Verlag, 1991], 76). M. Hengel, however, cautions against assuming that Judas was a Zealot (*The Zealots,* trans. D. Smith [Edinburgh: T. & T. Clark, 1989], 338).

16. See W. Bauer and M. Hornschuh, "The Picture of the Apostle in Early Christian Tradition," in *New Testament Apocrypha,* ed. E. Hennecke and W. Schneemelcher, 2.35-74; and W. Bienert, "The Picture of the Apostle in Early Christian Tradition," in *NTApoc,* 2.5-27.

17. *Barn.* 5:9, on the contrary, says that the disciples were "iniquitous above all sin," in order to demonstrate that Jesus called the unrighteous.

the opposite extremes present in Matthew, the collaborating tax collector, and Simon the Zealot, who is (or had been) a member of a movement committed to holy war against Rome. The differences of the latter two especially exceed anything that might conceivably unite them, except for the authoritative call of Jesus.

Finally, the name of "Judas Iscariot, who betrayed [Jesus]" is especially significant. "Betrayed" recalls John's betrayal in 1:14, and is yet another hint (2:7, 16, 18, 23, 3:6) of Jesus' foreboding destiny (14:10). Writing some thirty years after Judas's defection and death, Mark must have been tempted to strike from the list of the Twelve a name that had caused such scandal. That he does not do so is a testimony both to his historical veracity and to his understanding of the church. Even the Christian fellowship recruited and trained by Jesus is not an untarnished and utopian society. Judas stands as a reminder that the followers of Jesus are not perfect, nor do they have to be to accomplish the purposes for which he calls them. Rather, Jesus accomplishes his purposes in spite of their failure, perhaps even through it. It will, in fact, be on the night in which Jesus is *betrayed* (14:18) that Jesus will inaugurate the new covenant.

THE BINDER OF THE STRONG MAN (3:20-35)

One of Mark's signature literary techniques is the sandwiching of one story in the middle of another story. In so doing, Mark not only signifies a relationship between the two stories, but by their combination succeeds in making an entirely new point. The present unit is an example of this A^1-B-A^2 "sandwich" technique. The setting of both A-parts is a "house" in which Jesus is surrounded by a "crowd" (vv. 20, 32). In both A-parts the companions of Jesus try to control Jesus, perhaps even to suppress him — in v. 21 by "taking charge of him" (Gk. *kratein*); and in vv. 31-32 when Jesus' mother and brothers stand outside "calling" (Gk. *kalein*) and "looking for" (Gk. *zētein*) him. In the flanking A-parts, the followers of Jesus attempt to bind him, whereas in the central B-part Jesus binds the strong man, Satan, and frees his captives to become followers of the strong Son of God. The central B-part of Markan sandwiches holds the key to their meaning. In the present sandwich Mark signifies that the authority of Jesus binds even the prince of demons, but Jesus' followers must not and cannot bind him. He is the binder of the strong man who is himself unbounded.[18]

18. On Mark's sandwich technique, see the Introduction, 5.2; and J. R. Edwards,

Jesus allows neither "his own people" (v. 21) nor "mother and brothers" (v. 31) to take priority over the new society he has formed in the Twelve. The Greek of v. 21 *(hoi par autou)* is vaguer than the NIV's "his own people." It simply means "the ones around Jesus" and appears to be a calculated ambiguity. Mark contrasts the associates of Jesus who believe they have a claim to him in v. 21 with the true followers of Jesus ("those seated in a circle around him," *hoi peri auton kyklō kathēmenoi*, v. 34; similarly 4:10), who allow Jesus to have a claim on them! The latter are sitting in his presence and doing the will of God, thus fulfilling the ideal of 3:14-15. These are the true "brother and sister and mother" of Jesus (3:34-35).

20-21 Mark concluded the preceding story on the note of Judas's betrayal (v. 19). He now describes, if not a betrayal, a grievous misunderstanding within Jesus' inner circle. With typical economy of language Mark returns the scene to "a house."[19] The only house identified in the Gospel thus far has been Peter's house in Capernaum (1:29), the ostensible site of the healing of the paralytic (2:1-12). The same house may be intended here. Jesus' magnetism attracts people in great throngs. As in the story of the healing of the paralytic, the house is so crowded that Jesus and the disciples are "not even able to eat." The crowd is again an obstacle rather than an asset to Jesus' mission.

"When his family heard about this, they went to take charge of him, for they said, 'He is out of his mind.'" This startling statement is omitted by the parallels in Matt 12:22 and Luke 11:14. The Greek wording is even more explicit: "they went to seize him, believing that Jesus had gone berserk" (John 10:20). The word for "seize" (Gk. *kratein*) is regularly used by Mark in the sense of attempting to bind Jesus and deprive him of freedom, which is its sense here.[20] There is obviously more to this incident than Mark relates. Exactly who is threatening Jesus is not entirely clear. English translations normally read "family," but the Greek is a simple and ambiguous prepositional phrase, "those of him" *(hoi par autou)*, which could mean associates, kin, or followers as well as friends or family.[21] According

---

"Markan Sandwiches: The Significance of Interpolations in Markan Narratives," *NovT* 31/3 (1989): 209-10.

19. Several important manuscripts read *erchontai* ("they arrive") rather than the singular *erchetai* ("he [Jesus] arrives"). The singular verb is to be preferred because it has support from a diversity of text types, plus the plural verb can be explained as an accommodation to the plural subjects of vv. 16-19.

20. *Kratein* occurs fifteen times in Mark. In three instances it refers to Jesus' grabbing the hand of a healed person (1:31; 5:41; 9:27), but in eight instances it occurs in contexts openly hostile to Jesus (3:21; 6:17; 12:12; 14:1, 44, 46, 49, 51). The remaining instances of "holding to the tradition of the elders" (7:3, 4, 8) or "kept the matter to themselves" (9:10), though not hostile, are adversarial to Jesus.

21. On the role and vocabulary of disciples in Mark, see Telford, *Mark,* 141.

to John 2:12, Jesus' mother and brothers visited Jesus and his disciples in Capernaum early in his ministry. Perhaps there was a connection between that visit and the attempted intervention here. Or perhaps they intervened from Nazareth itself. At any rate, those closest to Jesus believe his conflicts with the authorities to be mistaken and they come to retrieve him, perhaps even to "deprogram" him (Zech 13:3!).[22] The disconcerting reference that Jesus "is out of his mind" reminds Mark's readers that the religious authorities are not alone in their mistaken apprehensions of Jesus. Their opposition is the more explainable, for as outsiders they may be victims of ignorance, false reports, jealousy, or misguided zeal. The opposition of insiders is more troubling, for Jesus' associates ought to be advocates, not adversaries. The very ambiguity of Mark's wording, "the ones of him," is a calculated reminder that those closest to Jesus may indeed oppose him, and that proximity to Jesus — even blood relationship or being called by Jesus — is no substitute for allegiance to Jesus in faith and following.

22   The scribes are default opponents of Jesus in Mark (see the discussion of the scribes at 1:22). Their coming from Jerusalem in this instance (also 7:1), the seat of temple authority, plus their frequent mention with the chief priests (8:31; 10:33; 11:18; 11:27; 14:1, 43, 53; 15:1, 31), signifies *official* opposition arrayed against Jesus. Their opposition is bolder and more confrontational in the present narrative. No longer do they pose insinuating questions ("Why does this fellow talk like that?" 2:7). They have formed a virulent judgment: Jesus "is possessed by Beelzeboul," and "by the prince of demons he is driving out demons." The precise nature of their opposition is important to note. They do not deny Jesus' power to perform miracles, nor do they accuse him of being an imposter. They indeed recognize his power to perform miracles, but they impugn the *source* of his power, ascribing it to Beelzeboul rather than God.

The malicious judgment of the scribes is evidence that faith and unbelief are not the result of proofs. There is a mistaken view abroad that if only we saw the undisputed miracles of Jesus we would believe — or believe more. The scribes, however, have seen precisely such evidence — but they do not believe. Faith, in other words, is not an automatic, inevitable, or necessary consequence of witnessing the acts of God. The words and deeds of Jesus are indeed evidence of God's presence, but the evidence demands a decision from the beholder as to its source and significance. Faith judges that the person and work of Jesus stand in continuity

22. See B. Pixner, *With Jesus Through Galilee*, 49-51. A few Greek manuscripts (D W) make "the scribes and the others" the culprits, but the weight and majority of manuscripts rightly identify the culprits as Jesus' own associates.

with the character of God and hence have saving significance; disbelief judges that the person and work of Jesus derive not from God but, as the scribes suggest in this instance, from the devil.

The exact meaning of "**Beelzeboul**" is difficult if not impossible to recover, partly owing to its various spellings. The term "Beelzebub" appears only rarely in Jewish literature, and the term "Beelzeboul" (which is the reading in v. 22) nowhere outside the Gospels. Beelzebub, a Syrian god of Ekron (2 Kgs 1:2), originally meant something like "Lord of the Dwelling (= Temple)," but already in the LXX it is made into a term of contempt, *Baal muian*, "Lord of carrion or flies," that is, something rotten and repulsive. This has led many interpreters to suggest that "Beelzebub," the rendering of the NIV in v. 22, perpetuates the OT slur, meaning "Lord of the dung heap."[23] Although this is a frequent explanation of the term, it appears to have the argument of etymology against it, for the Greek of v. 22 reads *Beelzeboul*, not Beelzebub. The Heb. *zeboul* occurs five times in the OT (1 Kgs 8:13; Isa 63:15; Hab 3:11; Ps 49:14; 2 Chr 6:2). In each instance it refers to an exalted prince or ruler, or to his dwelling place. The targums corroborate this meaning, as do the two occurrences of *zeboul* in the DSS (1QM 12:1-2; 1QS 10:3). The best suggested meaning of Beelzeboul thus appears to be "Baal the prince" or, correspondingly, "Baal's abode or dynasty." Not only during the OT monarchy but also in the succeeding Hellenistic period, the chief rival of Yahweh faith was the cult of the heavenly Baal. Biblical writers commonly explained foreign gods as demons (Ps 96:5; 1 Cor 10:20), and in this instance Beelzeboul is seen as the arch ruler of a dynasty of demons and evil spirits (v. 30).[24] Although Satan is nowhere called Beelzeboul in Jewish literature, vv. 22-23 clearly equate Beelzeboul with Satan, who is "the prince of demons" (so too Matt 9:34; 10:25; 12:24; Luke 11:15).[25] This understanding of Beelzeboul as Baal, ruler of a demonic dynasty, is reinforced by the ensuing

23. So BAGD, 139; Str-B 1.631-35; followed by V. Taylor, *The Gospel According to St. Mark,* 238. See the overall discussion of the problem in T. Lewis, "Beelzebul," *ABD* 1.638-40.

24. See L. Gaston, "Beelzebul," *TZ* 18 (1962): 247-55; E. C. B. MacLaurin, "Beelzeboul," *NovT* 20 (1978): 156-60. Gaston's article has made an important contribution to the understanding of the term "Beelzeboul." His concluding argument that the Beelzeboul controversy stems from Jesus' claims over the temple is, however, overly speculative. On "Baal the prince," see W. Herrmann, *Dictionary of Deities and Demons in the Bible*[2], eds. K. van der Torn, B. Becking, and P. W. van der Horst (Leiden: Brill/Grand Rapids: Eerdmans, 1999), 154-56.

25. *T. Sol.* 3:5-6; 6:1-11 also call Beelzeboul the "Prince of Demons," the highest-ranking angel in heaven. The Beelzeboul in the *Testament of Solomon* is more comical than ferocious, however, for King Solomon subdues him with a magic ring, and when the fiend complains Solomon forces him to cut marble for the construction of the temple!

interchange between Jesus and the scribes in vv. 23-27, where Jesus speaks of Satan's realm as a "house" and "kingdom," which his stated purpose is to ransack and vanquish.

23-27 In response to the accusation of being in cahoots with Satan, Jesus begins with a series of examples grounded in simple logic. "Jesus called them together." Mark's verb (Gk. *proskaleomai*) occurs in eight instances when Jesus makes solemn and important pronouncements. The force of Jesus' logic is here delivered "in parables." If the work of Jesus is diametrically opposed to Satan, then how can Jesus be empowered by Satan? If what the scribes say is true, then Satan is clearly working at cross purposes with himself, which will only hasten his fall. "If a kingdom is divided against itself, that kingdom cannot stand." There is no caricature of the devil here, as is common in the modern world. "Kingdom" and "house" denote powerful and despotic realms ruled by Satan.

The imagery of the "strong man's house" in v. 27 is likely a word-play on "Beelzeboul" in v. 22, that is, "the house or dynasty of Baal, the evil god."[26] "No one can enter a strong man's house and carry off his possessions unless he first ties up the strong man. Then he can rob his house." In this brief but nuclear parable Jesus recalls the mission of the messianic high priest to bind Satan: "And Beliar shall be bound by [the messianic high priest], and he shall grant to his children the authority to trample on wicked spirits" (*T. Levi* 18:12). As we noted at 1:10, this passage plays an important role in illuminating Jesus' baptism by John. In the discussion of the command to silence at 1:34, we further noted the importance of Isaiah's Servant of the Lord for Jesus' conception of ministry. Even more important than the *Testament of Levi* is the call to the Servant of the Lord to rescue captives from cruel warlords:

> "Can plunder be taken from warriors,
>   or captives rescued from the fierce?
> But this is what the LORD says:
> 'Yes, captives will be taken from warriors,
>   and plunder retrieved from the fierce;
> I will contend with those who contend with you,
>   and your children I will save. . . .
> Then all mankind will know that I, the LORD, am your Savior,
>   your Redeemer, the Mighty One of Jacob.'" (Isa 49:24-26)

---

26. Taylor's (*The Gospel According to St. Mark*, 240-41) view that v. 27 is a new argument and was originally a separate saying is, in our understanding of Beelzeboul, unnecessary and incorrect. Rather than introducing a new argument, the parable of plundering the strong man's house in v. 27 is patterned according to the image introduced in v. 22 of Beelzeboul as the master of a house of demons.

According to *Pss. Sol.* 5:3, "No one takes plunder away from a strong man." But that is precisely what Jesus as the strong Son of God does. He alludes to himself as the "Mighty One," as prophesied by John the Baptizer (1:7), who fulfills Yahweh's mission of plundering the house of the oppressor and liberating his captives (Tob 3:17). The parable of v. 27, which is also carefully preserved in the *Gospel of Thomas* 35, offers an unusually clear insight into Jesus' self-understanding. As the Son of God, Jesus does something *for* humanity before doing something *to* it. He must liberate humanity from the power of evil (1 John 3:8) before restoring it to the image of God. Not coincidentally, Mark's first miracle story was an exorcism (1:21-28). The healing of the paralytic in 2:1-12 illustrates a similar principle: Jesus first forgives, then heals. The mission of Jesus is not fulfilled in compromise or coexistence, but in invading and conquering Beelzeboul, "the head of the house" (Matt 10:25), "binding" (Gk. *deomai;* NIV, "ties up") Satan and "plundering" (Gk. *diarpazein;* NIV, "carry off") his "possession." Following the image of Beelzeboul as the master of the house, the "possessions" of the strong man must refer to demonic spirits, who, like their master, have met a superior master in Jesus.

28-30 A solemn pronouncement of Jesus follows the graphic and picturesque language of vv. 23-27. The pronouncement is introduced by the solemn formula, "I tell you the truth" (Gk. *Amēn legō hymin*), used more than a dozen times in Mark to preface an earnest admonition. Here it signifies the seriousness of the charge that Jesus is in league with Satan. Vv. 28-29 display a number of Hebraic elements and can be readily translated back into Hebrew, which suggests careful transmission of Jesus' sayings on the part of the early church. The sin against the Holy Spirit is one of the most disturbing statements of Jesus in the Gospels. It may have been disturbing for Mark's community as well. In a rare editorial insertion, Mark provides the key to its understanding when he says that Jesus was being accused of having an evil spirit (v. 30). The word for "sins" in vv. 28-29 is not the normal Greek word for "sin" *(harmatia)*, but a derivative *(hamartēma)*. The latter carries a slightly different nuance of sins as sinful *acts* and wrongful deeds as opposed to the nature and motives of sin.[27] Such sin is called "an eternal sin" (v. 29), that is, a sin with an eternal consequence.[28] "Blasphemy," meaning to slander or defame, is used predominantly in the NT of infractions against the true God.

The sin against the Holy Spirit must be understood in light of the

---

27. G. Stählin, *"hamartanō,"* *TDNT* 1.293-94.

28. The phrase "an eternal sin" is an unusual expression. The scribes tended to alleviate this strange reading by substituting eternal "judgment" or "torment." The manuscript evidence strongly favors "an eternal sin," however.

opening testimony of John the Baptizer. John heralded the messianic era by foretelling the coming of a More Powerful One who would baptize with the Holy Spirit (1:7-8). Jesus here depicts himself as that More Powerful One who by the power of God's Spirit binds Satan and routs his minions (v. 27). The gravity of the offense of the scribes, as Mark declares in v. 30, is that they accuse Jesus of having an evil or unclean spirit. The sin against the Holy Spirit is thus not an indefinable offense against God,[29] but a specific misjudgment that Jesus is motivated by evil rather than by good, that he is empowered by the devil rather than by God.

From his baptism onward Jesus as God's Son has been authorized by God's Spirit. Whoever, like the scribes, can look at him and say, "This is the devil"; or, conversely, whoever can look at the devil and call him God's Son, as does Milton's Satan, who "felt how awful goodness is" and said, "Evil, be thou my Good,"[30] that person is hopelessly lost. This is "an eternal sin" (v. 29) since anyone who, willingly or not, cannot distinguish evil from good and good from evil, darkness from light and light from darkness, is beyond the pale of repentance. "Woe to those who call evil good and good evil, who put darkness for light and light for darkness" (Isa 5:20).

In addressing the warning of 3:28-30 to the scribes (see v. 22), Mark signifies the unique pitfall that this sin can pose for *religious* people. Sinners and tax collectors are less likely to commit this sin than are the learned, religious, and moral. In this respect, wickedness poses a lesser problem to the grace of God than do pride and self-righteousness. The early church, of course, recognized the role that the Jewish religious leaders played in Jesus' death.[31] Mark's sandwiching of this warning between two episodes related to Jesus' followers and associates, however, is a sober reminder that the danger before the scribes, which was obvious, is in fact a paradigm of a similar danger before Jesus' disciples, which was not so obvious.[32] Nor is Mark alone in this sober admonition. There is evi-

29. For example, *Gos. Bart.* 5:3-4, "And Bartholomew said: 'What is the sin against the Holy Spirit?' Jesus answered, 'Everyone who decrees against any man who serves my Father has blasphemed against the Holy Spirit. For every man who serves God with reverence is worthy of the Holy Spirit, and he who speaks any evil against him shall not be forgiven.'"

30. *Paradise Lost* 4.846 and 4.108, respectively.

31. Not surprisingly, the early church was struck by the Jewish leaders' condemnation of the very one whom they awaited as Messiah. Note the warning Luke ascribes to Paul in Acts 13:27, "The people of Jerusalem and their rulers did not recognize Jesus, yet in condemning him they fulfilled the words of the prophets that are read every Sabbath."

32. Cranfield's words on v. 29 remain continually valid: "Those who most particularly should heed the warning of this verse (29) are the theological teachers and the official leaders of the church" (*The Gospel According to Saint Mark*, 143).

dence from other sectors of the early church that *Christians* received essentially the same warnings that had been delivered to the Jews (Heb 6:4-6; 10:26; 1 John 5:16; *Gospel of Thomas* 44). How wrong the church has been to single out Jewish rejection of Jesus as something distinctive! It is a human problem, and Jesus' closest confidants are as liable to misjudging and rejecting Jesus as are the scribes. Finally, it is imperative to note that Mark places this saying as a warning, not as a condemnation or cause for anxiety. The same saying that warns against ascribing evil to Jesus also assures of God's willingness to forgive "all the sins and blasphemies of men." Anyone who is worried about having committed the sin against the Holy Spirit has not yet committed it, for anxiety of having done so is evidence of the potential for repentance. There is no record in Scripture of anyone asking forgiveness of God and being denied it!

31-32   Mark concludes the sandwich unit by returning to Jesus' followers in 3:31-35, who are no longer simply "those around him" (v. 21) but his "mother and brothers." The setting remains the crowded house of v. 20. At some point in the colloquium a message is passed to Jesus, "'Your mother and brothers are outside looking for you.'" The scene is devoid of details except for a few clues. Twice we are told that Jesus' mother and brothers are outside (vv. 31 and 32) and that the crowd is on the inside with Jesus. That is ironic since households normally have family members on the inside and crowds on the outside. But here the order is reversed: Jesus' family is outside "calling" (Gk. *kalein,* v. 31) him. Elsewhere in Mark Jesus is the subject of the verb "to call" (1:20; 2:17), but here his family is attempting to assert a claim on him. They are also "looking for" him. The Gk. *zētein* occurs ten times in Mark, and in each instance it describes an attempt to determine Jesus and gain control over him (see the discussion of the term at 1:39). Like his followers in vv. 20-21, his family assumes it has rights that Jesus is obliged to honor.

33-35   Jesus, however, does not share their assumption. "'Who are my mother and my brothers?'" he asks.[33] This sobering rejoinder is not exactly an insult to his family, but it is not an unequivocal affirmation either. Jesus' hearers must ponder its implications for them: those who assume that they are close to Jesus should think again; those who assume that they are far from him should take hope. The question disquiets the comfortable and encourages the dejected. Again, in an authoritative survey (Gk. *periblepomai,* 3:5), Jesus "looked around at those seated in a circle." "'Here

---

33. According to the *Gospel of the Ebionites* (log. 5), Jesus' question, "'Who are my mother and my brothers?'" (v. 33) was evidence to some early Christians that Jesus was not fully human. That is scarcely the purpose of vv. 31-35, however. The question is set in a context of discipleship, not of Jesus' self-disclosure.

are my mother and my brothers!'" he declares. In so doing, Jesus redefines family. Without spite, Jesus alerts his natural family that blood relationship cannot claim privilege. At the same time the statement indicates that those who sit around him and do God's will are his family. There are only two kinds of people: those who sit on the inside at Jesus' feet and those who stand on the outside with false assumptions. Discipleship depends on being in Jesus' presence and doing God's will, which are the essential characteristics of apostleship outlined in 3:14-15 (also Luke 11:27-28!).

The addition of "sister" in the final declaration emphasizes the rightful place of women in the Christian fellowship.[34] The fact that Jesus does not add "father" probably indicates that Joseph has died. But the absence of "father" may further indicate that the role of father cannot be transferred symbolically to others. No one except God can be called Father by Jesus. The divine Sonship of Jesus is unshared, and his unique relationship with God as Father is nontransferable. Jesus' provocative question, "'Who are my mother and my brothers?'" was especially poignant by the time Mark wrote his Gospel some forty years after the death of Jesus, when James, Jesus' brother, had assumed leadership of the Jerusalem church, and his mother Mary had attained honorific stature. If Mark is willing to put such people to the test, surely no one can presume to be "in" with Jesus apart from faith and commitment. There is, so to speak, no proxy membership in God's kingdom. If "those around Jesus" (v. 21), even the holy family, are placed under question, then Mark places under question all who grow up amid the trappings of Christianity, whether through baptism, Christian homes, confirmation, church attendance, or charitable giving. Anyone can be an insider who sits at Jesus' feet and does the will of his Father, and no one can be an insider who does not.

This returns us in conclusion to the composite sandwich in 3:20-35. The sandwich makes a trenchant though unspoken statement about true versus false discipleship. True disciples are with Jesus (so 3:13) and do the will of God. They are Jesus' true family.[35] False disciples attempt to restrain Jesus from his mission or redirect him to another. This is danger-

34. Two significant manuscripts (A D) add "sisters" in v. 32, i.e., "'Your mother and brothers and sisters are outside looking for you.'" The weight and majority of manuscripts omit "sisters," however, which was likely added by a later scribe at v. 32 in accommodation to the pronouncement of Jesus in v. 35. Moreover, Metzger is probably correct to suggest that "it is extremely unlikely that Jesus' sisters would have joined in publicly seeking to check him in his ministry" (Metzger, *TCGNT*, 82). If "sisters" did not originally belong in v. 32, the addition of "sisters" by Jesus in v. 35 is a dominical witness for the role of women in Christian fellowship, and without distinction from "brothers."

35. Note the saying preserved in *Gos. Eg.* 9:11: "For the Lord also says: 'My brethren are those who do the will of my Father.'"

ously mistaken and potentially as blasphemous as confusing Jesus with Satan. To seek to avert Jesus from his mission is satanic, as Jesus' stinging rebuke of Peter later indicates, "'Out of my sight, Satan! You do not have in mind the things of God, but the things of men'" (8:33).

THE PARABLE OF THE SOWER AND THE MYSTERY OF THE KINGDOM (4:1-20)

Only two chapters in the Gospel of Mark depart from narrative format to include sizeable blocks of Jesus' teaching; one is the collection of parables in chap. 4, and the other is a discourse on the end time in chap. 13. 4:1-20 is another Markan sandwich in which the parable of the sower (vv. 3-9) and its explanation (vv. 14-20) are divided by private instruction by Jesus on the mystery of the kingdom of God. The sandwich construction signifies that Mark intends the whole to be understood as a unit. The center of the sandwich in vv. 10-13 is the key to understanding the whole, that only in fellowship with Jesus do parables disclose the meaning of the kingdom of God.

1 The setting beside the Sea of Galilee is by now familiar territory for Mark's readers (1:16; 2:13; 3:7). The large crowd attracted by Jesus' magnetism is again both an obstacle and an opportunity. It is an obstacle in that it forces Jesus to use a boat as a floating pulpit (see 3:9). But the crowd also provides Jesus an opportunity for teaching. Exactly where Jesus taught cannot be said for sure, but a possible location is a natural amphitheater situated halfway between Capernaum and Tabgha to the south where the land slopes gently down to a lovely bay. Israeli scientists have verified that the "Bay of Parables" can transmit a human voice effortlessly to several thousand people on shore.[36] Mark's description of the scene is awkward in Greek, "[Jesus] got in a boat and sat on the sea." Matthew (13:2) improves the wording and Luke omits it, both of which argue for the earlier provenance of Mark's Gospel. Mark's awkward wording may nevertheless intend a theological point, for according to Ps 29:10, "The LORD sits enthroned over the flood." If Mark intends this allusion, then Jesus is again put in the place of God.

2 For the first time in the Gospel Mark reports more than a saying or two of Jesus' teaching, the content of which is given in **parables**. The

---

36. See B. C. Crisler, "The Acoustics and Crowd Capacity of Natural Theaters in Palestine," *BA* 39 (1976): 137. On the location of the Bay of Parables, see Pixner, *Wege des Messias und Stätten der Urkirche*, 88-89; the same author, *With Jesus Through Galilee*, 41-42.

reference to parables in the plural, plus the large number of parables in Matthew and Luke, is a reminder that parables were Jesus' preferred form of public teaching. Jesus did not invent the parable genre, for there are occasional examples of such in the OT (2 Sam 12:1-14; Ezek 17:1-10) and among Jewish rabbis from the second century onward. There were, of course, also many stories and fables in Greco-Roman antiquity, some of which resemble parables.[37] But in quantity and excellence Jesus' parables are without parallel in the ancient world. The Gospels record some sixty different parables of Jesus, most of which are found in Matthew and Luke, fewer in Mark, and none in John. The word "parable" means something that is placed alongside something else for the purpose of clarification. The most common subject of Jesus' parables is the kingdom of God, which he illustrated by episodes from everyday life — fishing and farming, housekeeping and family life, royalty and banquets. Jesus' parables required of his hearers no special knowledge or vocabulary to understand. Parables may reflect daily life, but they are not simple and easily understood. Many of Jesus' parables are confounding, knocking hearers off balance so that that they must see things in a new light. Although some of Jesus' parables can and do have allegorical qualities, the allegory is not a simple equation between an element in the parable and a deeper reality that, once decoded, causes the story to lose further significance. An allegory can be understood from the "outside," but parables can be understood only from within, by allowing oneself to be taken into the story and hearing who God is and what humans may become. Parables are like stained glass windows in a cathedral, dull and lifeless from the outside but brilliant and radiant from within. Or to borrow an analogy from Jesus (1:17), they are like fishing. There is a hook hidden in the bait. The hook is the word of God, which is personified in Jesus. Parables cannot be understood apart from the one who tells them. Parables are not simply good advice, they are good news; for the life of Jesus is itself a parable, indeed the greatest parable.

3-9 The parable of the sower begins and ends with the summons to "hear" (NIV, "listen!"; vv. 3, 9), which occurs fully ten times in Mark 4. "Listen!" (v. 3) is in the imperative mood, which underscores its urgency and importance. Similar to Israel's foundational confession, "Hear, O Is-

---

37. Parables are found only among Palestinian rabbis, not among Babylonian rabbis. The subject of such parables is invariably the Torah, not the kingdom of God. According to Str-B 1.654, the single rabbinic parable known to antedate Jesus is from Hillel (c. 20 B.C.). For examples of Hellenistic stories that resemble parables, see HCNT, 89-92. The differences in the latter are noteworthy, however. Hellenistic "parables" are not about the kingdom of God, they nearly always have a moral appended, and they do not need to be "entered" to be understood.

rael: The LORD our God, the LORD is one" (Deut 6:4), <u>hearing is the only possible way of understanding Jesus' parables</u> (so Rom 10:17). Hearing, or better *heeding*, requires engagement and receptivity to what is said.

The parable speaks of a sower who scatters seed on the ground. Some seed falls on pathways, some on rocky ground, some among thorns, and some on good soil.[38] This typifies the austere farming conditions prevalent in the rocky terrain and scrub vegetation of Galilee. Farming in Palestine was a hardscrabble affair (Jer 4:3; Jas 1:11), and the farmer sows unsparingly. Farming instructions in the Mishnah decreed that farming should be orderly, methodical, and with special care given not to mix seeds (*m. Kil.* 2:3ff.). But the sowing in Jesus' parable is far from orderly and methodical; it is profligate, almost wasteful. The indiscriminate sowing of seed has often been explained as a result of plowing *after* sowing in first-century Palestine. This is an attractive hypothesis, for it would help explain why seed is sown in unpromising places. Taken as a whole, however, the evidence suggests that ancient farmers, as today, plowed prior to sowing — although there is at least some evidence that they not infrequently plowed afterward as well to provide a protective layer of soil for the seed.[39] So intent is the farmer on a harvest that he sows in every corner of the field "in hopes that good soil might somewhere be found," said Justin Martyr in his retelling of the parable over a century later (*Dial. Trypho* 125.1-2).[40] Even so, rocks, thorns, and adverse elements render three-quarters of the labor lost.[41]

38. This same order of sowing in preserved in the *Gospel of Thomas* 9.

39. J. Jeremias, *The Parables of Jesus*, rev. ed., trans. S. H. Hooke (London: SCM Press, 1963), p. 11, asserts that "in Palestine sowing precedes ploughing." K. D. White makes a forceful rebuttal of this assertion in "The Parable of the Sower," *JTS* 15 (1964): 300-307. The issue has been reexamined by P. B. Payne, "The Order of Sowing and Ploughing in the Parable of the Sower," *NTS* 25 (1978): 123-29. Payne is able to sustain his conclusion that "ploughing regularly follows sowing in order to bury the seed" (127) only by admitting that spring plowing preceded fall sowing in Palestine. As Isa 28:24, Hos 10:12, Jer 4:3, and other OT texts indicate, plowing normally preceded sowing, and sometimes following in order to cover the seed. See J. Drury, *The Parables in the Gospels* (London: SPCK, 1985), 57-58.

40. The power and the purpose of the sower are lost in the apocryphal *Memoria Apostolorum*, in which the disciples accuse Jesus of being a bad farmer for having sown seed where it cannot grow (see *NTApoc* 1.376).

41. The enemies of the harvest are legion. See G. E. M. Suess, "Enemies of the Harvest," *JerusalemPersp* 53 (1997): 18-23, who lists some 125 species of thistles in Palestine that choke the harvest. Similarly, M. P. Knowles, "Abram and the Birds in *Jubilees* 11: A Subtext for the Parable of the Sower?" *NTS* 41 (1995): 145-51, draws attention to similarities between the ravishing crows in *Jub.* 11:10 and the role of birds in the parable of the sower. In *Jubilees* the crows are sent by Mastema/Satan, prince of demons. This might provide a possible link of the parable of the sower with the preceding Beelzeboul controversy.

Those are discouraging odds. But the parable, ironically, does not end on a discouraging note. "Growing, increasing, and bringing forth," the good soil yields a breathtaking harvest. The Greek verbs of v. 8 mount in a crescendo of momentum. A harvest of one-hundred fold was extraordinary in Palestine, a sure sign of divine blessing (Gen 26:12). Mark hints at the marvelous harvest by a subtle change in the number of "other." In vv. 4, 5, and 7, the "other" seed that is lost is singular, but in v. 8 the "other" seed that yields "thirty, sixty, or even a hundred times" is plural.[42] For "produced a crop" the Greek reads "giving fruit" (*edidou karpon*), a Semitism that may reflect Jesus' speech. Clearly, this is no ordinary harvest! Not infrequently in Jewish literature, "the harvest" is a metaphor for the inbreaking of the kingdom of God (Isa 9:3; Ps 126:6). The parable of the sower, like the parables of sowing to follow (4:26-29, 30-32), reports astounding results in spite of inauspicious beginnings.

The parable of the sower is usually interpreted as a parable of soils, seeing the hardened ground, rocks, thorns, and good soil as examples of wrong or right discipleship. But the parable is more than a metaphor of human psychology or attitudinal states, as interesting as those are to us.[43] The parable represents the historical inbreaking of God's kingdom in Jesus, the sower of the gospel. The astounding harvest in v. 8 is an important clue that the growth is not owing to human activity but to God's providential power.[44] God is at work — hidden and unobserved — in Je-

---

42. "Fold" means the increase of number of grains harvested over the number sown. *Gospel of Thomas* 9 increases the harvest in the parable of the sower to "sixty-fold and even one hundred and twenty-fold." The size of an average harvest in first-century Palestine is still debated. Jeremias, *The Parables of Jesus*, rev. ed., 150, following G. Dalman, *Arbeit und Sitte in Palästina* (Hildesheim: G. Olms, 1964), 153-65, maintained that a seven-and-one-half yield was average in first-century Palestine, and thirty-fold or more was unheard of. W. D. Davies and D. Allison dispute this judgment in *A Critical and Exegetical Commentary on the Gospel according to Saint Matthew*, ICC (Edinburgh: T. & T. Clark, 1991), 2.385, saying that the figures given in the parable of the sower "do not seem obviously out of the ordinary." Both positions are probably overstated. There is evidence from Varro, Theophrastus, Strabo, and Pliny, as well as from Gen. 26:12, that huge crops were possible in some place in some years. But the average harvest seems to have been far less, perhaps even as low as three- and four-fold (see R. K. McIver, "One Hundred-fold Yield — Miraculous or Mundane? Matthew 13:8, 23; Mark 4:8, 20; Luke 8:8," *NTS* 40 [1994]: 606-8, who surveys the literature and maintains that "a yield of thirty-fold . . . was not only exceptional, it was miraculous in first-century Palestine"). There is no evidence in ancient literature that the figures in the parable of the sower were normal. Thirty-, sixty-, and one-hundred-fold signal a remarkable, if not miraculous, harvest.

43. See Drury, *The Parables in the Gospels*, 51.

44. The reference to the parable of the sower in *Ap. Jas.* 8:15 at Nag Hammadi reflects the tendency to separate the parable from the ministry of Jesus and focus on instead on seeds and soils.

sus and the gospel to produce a yield wholly disproportionate to human prospects and merit. The sower's earnest and profligate sowing, which at first looked mistaken and futile, is vindicated by a bumper crop. Throughout the Gospel Jesus teaches, preaches, and proclaims (2:2; 4:33; 8:32; 9:10; 10:22, 24; 11:29; 13:31; 14:39) as tirelessly as the sower sows. The farmer's "going out" to sow seed (4:2) is the same word in Greek (exēlthen) with which Jesus declares his purpose in 1:38.[45] Despite resistance and rejection, there is an irrepressible empowerment behind the work of Jesus, as momentous as the generative agency of the seed that "grows, produces, and multiplies." Let not hearers suppose the opposition of scribes, Pharisees, crowds, and even his own associates, as adversarial as the hardpan, rocks, and thorns of Galilee, will be the last word. Despite discouraging odds, the harvest in Jesus' ministry will be beyond compare. The framing of the parable of the sower in vv. 3 and 9 by the Greek word akouō indicates that only one thing remains for disciples to do: to hear! Discipleship is not what we can make of ourselves, but allowing both the Sower and the seed to produce a harvest of which we alone are incapable. Near the end of the first century, Clement of Rome rightly detected the providence of God in the ministry of Jesus, noting that as the Master raises up decayed seeds from parched and barren soil, so, too, would he raise up Jesus from death and the grave (1 Clem. 24:5).

10 Between the parable of the sower and its interpretation in 4:13-20, Mark inserts Jesus' rationale for speaking in parables in vv. 10-12. This insertion is both the key to understanding the sandwich in 4:1-20 and one of the most important sections in the Gospel. It is also one of the most difficult passages in the Gospel to interpret. As noted in the Introduction, 3-4, Papias reported that Mark took certain liberties in arranging his stories. An example of that rearrangement is apparent in vv. 10-34, which are not part of the lakeside sermon (note the presence of the boat in 4:1, 36) but are given in private to the disciples at another time ("When he was alone," v. 10). Vv. 10-20 are thus a Markan insertion in order to comment on the purpose of the parables.

Mark commences the insertion by declaring that Jesus was alone with "the Twelve and the others around him." Jesus' inner circle is defined as the chosen Twelve (3:14-19) and "the others around him." This latter group repeats the wording of 3:34 (hoi peri auton) and intends those who are in fellowship with Jesus and do the will of God. These two groups — "the Twelve and the others around him" — hear the parable as Jesus commanded and inquire privately as to its meaning. Private set-

---

45. See J. Marcus, "Blanks and Gaps in the Markan Parable," BibInt 5 (1997): 255.

tings, as we have noted, are often opportunities for revelation in Mark, and in such a setting Mark offers the interpretive key to the parable of the sower in vv. 10-20.

11 In 1:27 Mark announced that Jesus brought a "new teaching." Jesus delivers this new teaching in vv. 10-12 to two separate audiences, "to you" and "to those." Mark's placement of these two groups at the head of their respective clauses in Greek makes them emphatic, thus accentuating the difference between the two audiences. Each audience receives a different form of teaching. "The Twelve and the others around him" are insiders, "members only," to whom "the secret of the kingdom of God has been given." This last phrase is a "divine passive," meaning that the knowledge of the mystery is a gift from God and not a human achievement. The secret, or "mystery" (Gk. *mystērion*), means a knowledge of God that cannot be attained by natural means (Dan 2:27-28; Wis 2:22).[46] Hence the mystery is "given," not attained. Here again is a great irony, for although Jesus is the fulfillment of the mystery, people do not see it; indeed, according to the Gospel of John, it is precisely *because* Jesus tells the truth about himself that they do not believe (John 8:45!). "It is the secret that the kingdom of God has come in the person and words and works of Jesus. That is a secret because God has chosen to reveal himself indirectly and in a veiled way. The incarnate Word is not obvious. Only faith could recognize the Son of God in the lowly figure of Jesus of Nazareth. The secret of the kingdom of God is the secret of the person of Jesus."[47]

As its author, God of course knows the mystery (1:11; 9:7). Demons

---

46. In the present passage, and in the NT as a whole, *mystērion* ("mystery") does not refer, as it does in Iamblicus, *Life of Pythagoras* 23.104-5, e.g., to esoteric knowledge reserved for select initiates; nor, as in modern detective stories, to unknown information that must be pried out by stealth and wit. Rather, "mystery" means the truth of God that is available only as a revelation of God. No amount of research can unlock the mystery of God, for in the NT, as in Judaism itself, the mystery must be revealed from heaven in order to be known, and hence it is received by faith as a result of *hearing*. Its purpose is not simply to reduce ignorance but to produce *awe*. Especially in Mark 4:11, both the mystery and the kingdom of God are inescapably present and fulfilled in the words and works of Jesus. On "mystery," see H. Krämer, *"mystērion,"* EDNT 2.446-49; J. Marcus, "Mark 4:10-12 and Marcan Epistemology," JBL 103 (1984): 558-61; M. Bockmuehl, *Revelation and Mystery in Ancient Judaism and Pauline Christianity,* WUNT 2/36 (Tübingen: Mohr-Siebeck, 1990). K. Barth (*Church Dogmatics,* I/1, trans. G. T. Thomson [Edinburgh: T. & T. Clark, 1960], 188) says, "*Mysterium* signifies not simply the hiddenness of God, but rather His becoming manifest in a hidden, i.e., in a non-apparent way, which gives information not directly but indirectly. *Mysterium* is the veiling of God in which He meets us by actually unveiling Himself to us: because He will not and cannot unveil Himself to us in any other way than by veiling Himself."

47. Cranfield, *The Gospel According to St Mark,* 153.

also know it because they belong to the spiritual realm (1:24, 34; 3:11; 5:7; 9:20). The inner circle of v. 10 is made privy to the mystery only by a dispensation of Jesus, not by virtue of human intelligence or merit. The mystery in v. 11 is the point of the parable of the sower — that the providence of God is effective in Jesus to produce a fruitful harvest in the world. It is revealed to them precisely because they are *hearers*. Matt 13:11 and Luke 8:10 speak of the disciples "knowing" the mystery, but Mark is more guarded: the disciples have been given the mystery, but they do not fully understand it (6:52; 8:18!).

"To those on the outside," by contrast, "everything is said in parables." There are a dozen references to parables in Mark, and each is set in a context of opposition (e.g., 3:23). Parables are thus a way for Jesus to speak to "outsiders" who have ears to hear but do not hear. Outsiders include the public gamut, from declared opposition in the scribes and Pharisees to those who may even sympathize with Jesus but who hear only casually or carelessly and "do not bear fruit" (v. 8). The parable of the sower thus recapitulates the insider-outsider motif of 3:20-35. The categories of insiders and outsiders were familiar enough to Jesus' hearers, who thought it self-evident that observant Jews (scribes, Pharisees, Zealots, and perhaps Sadducees and Essenes) were insiders, and that lapsed Jews, "am-ha'aretz" (common people), and Gentiles were outsiders. But this division is of no help in understanding insiders and outsiders in relation to Jesus; in fact, it is often reversed.[48] In both his person (3:20-35) and parables (4:1-20), Jesus precipitates a crisis among his hearers, dividing them along quite different lines. Insiders are those for whom the fellowship and will of Jesus take precedence over everything else (so 3:14-15, 34-35). They "hear, believe, and bear fruit" (4:20), which is Mark's definition of faith. They can hear only by being with Jesus, and to them the mystery is revealed.

Insiders and outsiders, in other words, correspond to the seed sown on good and bad soil. Those who hear in faith (even if they do not fully comprehend) are given the mystery of the kingdom. The word of God causes fruit to grow and increase in them, thirty, sixty, or even a hundred times (v. 8). Those who fail to hear remain befuddled outsiders. "'Whoever has will be given more; whoever does not have, even what he has will be taken from him'" (4:25).[49] The difference between the lost seed and fruitful seed depends on *hearing in faith*.

48. J. Donahue, S.J., *The Gospel in Parable* (Minneapolis: Fortress Press, 1990), 42-44, rightly notes that insiders-outsiders does not refer to disciples versus crowds or disciples versus hostile Jews, but that it crosses all categories and depends solely on hearing.
49. Matt 13:12 transposes this verse into his explanation of the purpose of parables, thus underscoring the necessity of faith in understanding parables.

Mark does not regard insiders and outsiders as immutable distinctions, however. Their status is determined solely by their hearing and believing that, as the Sower, Jesus brings the fruitful gospel of God (1:14). Some outsiders will become insiders — the Gerasene demoniac (5:1-20), the woman with a flow of blood (5:25-34), the Syrophoenician woman (7:24-30), a Gentile centurion (15:38-39), perhaps even a scribe (12:28-34). Likewise, some insiders, such as Judas, will become outsiders (14:1-2, 10-11, 21, 43-46). Like the seeds in the parable, faith is dynamic, not static: it matures by hearing, receiving, and bearing fruit (4:20) — or it withers and decays.

12 This brings us to the quotation from Isa 6:9-10 in v. 12, in which parables are presented not as windows through which outsiders perceive the kingdom of God but as doors debarring them from it. This perplexing verse presents a Jesus rather at variance from the rationalizing and moralizing Jesus of the Enlightenment. Mark's quotation, as is often noted, follows the Targum[50] rather than the Hebrew version of Isaiah, or its Greek translation in the LXX.[51] It has often been suggested that Mark accentuated or even mistranslated a milder Aramaic original from the mouth of Jesus. Consequently, various commentators offer conjectural emendations of the quotation[52] that bring vv. 11-12 into general agreement with the corresponding versions of Matt 13:10-17 and Luke 8:9-10, where the hardness of heart of the hearers is the cause of their failure to understand the parables, not the result of God's preventing their hearing, as implied by Mark.[53]

50. Aramaic paraphrases of OT texts used in synagogue readings.

51. This is made apparent by Mark's use of the third person plural instead of the second person plural in Isa 6:9; his use of "forgive" rather than "heal" in Isa 6:10; and the passive "it should be forgiven." On these points Mark and the Targum agree against the Hebrew and Greek forms of Isaiah.

52. Many scholars accept T. W. Manson's proposal that Jesus' Aramaic saying reflected the Targum and read, "To you is given the secret of the Kingdom of God; but all things come in parables to those outside who

See indeed but do not know,
And hear indeed but do not understand,
Lest they should repent and receive forgiveness."

See T. W. Manson, *The Teaching of Jesus: Studies in Its Form and Content* (Cambridge: Cambridge University Press, 1963), 75-81; also J. Jeremias, *Die Gleichnisse Jesu*[7] (Göttingen: Vandenhoeck & Ruprecht, 1965), 9-14.

53. Matthew, in particular, attributes the failure to receive the mystery to the people's hardness of heart, as is evinced by the longer Isaiah quotation in Matt 13:14-15 that speaks of the hard hearts of the people. Moreover, immediately prior to the quotation, Matthew speaks of "this wicked and adulterous generation" (12:39, 45) that stands under greater judgment than does Nineveh (12:41).

Appealing as this proposed solution may be, it is rendered improbable on several counts. First and most importantly, there is no textual evidence of a mistranslation in 4:12. Had Mark misunderstood or mistranslated a saying of Jesus at this point, we would expect variants and emendations in the textual tradition. But there are none; in fact, the manuscript evidence in vv. 10-12 is remarkably agreed.[54] Further, even Matthew's and Luke's more nuanced versions are not entirely free of the mysterious correspondence of the hardened heart with God's will. Finally, the Isa 6:9-10 quotation occurs six times in the NT, always in contexts of unbelief and hardness of heart. Despite its difficulties, the received text of v. 12 is the one deserving our attention. The sense of 4:11-12 is that Jesus' parables confirm the states of people's hearts: insiders who are with Jesus will be given the understanding of the mystery, and outsiders who are not with Jesus will be confirmed in their disbelief.[55]

Mark is unwilling to relax the tension between divine sovereignty and human free will in the accomplishment of God's will.[56] Rather, he holds them in juxtaposition. The tension was already present in Isaiah 6, where God sent his prophet to a people who would not respond. It was evident in Pharaoh's hardness, which is attributed alternatively to his

54. See the critique of Manson's argument in M. Black, *An Aramaic Approach to the Gospels and Acts*[3] (Oxford: Clarendon Press, 1967), 211-16, who concludes that "nothing is more certain than that Mark wrote and intended" the text as it stands.

55. Note, by contrast, *Gospel of Thomas* 62 where Jesus discloses his mysteries to the *worthy*, shifting the focus from God's sovereignty to human merit. See E. Kellenberger, "Heil und Verstockung. Zu Jes 6,9f. bei Jesaja und im Neuen Testament," *TZ* 48 (1992): 268-75, who argues that Mark properly understands Isa 6:9-10 to show the inseparable tension between salvation and judgment, both of which are proclaimed in Isa 6:9-10 without reference to human merits. Kellenberger argues that even the disciples in Mark are hardened (6:52; 8:17), but that Christ will make them see (8:22-26), just as Paul believed God will make it possible for unbelieving Jews to see (Rom 11:26, 32). Both Kellenberger and Cranfield (*The Gospel According to Saint Mark,* 157-58) argue, however, that God's hardening is penultimate, not final, and that his ultimate purpose is salvation.

56. This tension is frequently abandoned by commentators. B. H. Branscomb, *The Gospel of Mark,* 78, argues entirely for human free will, maintaining that a division between insiders and outsiders determined by God's will "totally misrepresents" Jesus' attitude toward common people and the purpose of parables, which was to reveal. This is a popular view, represented already by Chrysostom and Victor in the patristic period, but it fails to take the text seriously. On the other hand, Marcus, "Mark 4:10-12 and Marcan Epistemology," *JBL* 103 (1984): 566, argues entirely for predestination: "Some people are good soil but others are wayside, rocky, or thorny soil; the former group can receive the word, but the latter cannot. There is no suggestion that one can alter the sort of soil one is." Such determinism fails to take seriously Jesus' call to *hear* (4:3, 9) and to do the will of God (3:35). The Markan sandwich of 4:1-20 avoids both these extremes. The mystery of divine providence, which is manifest in the ministry of Jesus, is given to those who are with Jesus (3:14, 34) and who hear (4:3, 9) his word.

own choice (Exod 7:14, 22; 8:15, 19, 32; 9:7, 35; 13:15) and to God's will (Exod 4:21; 7:3; 9:12; 10:1, 20; 11:10). It is evident in the parable of the sower where a farmer sows seed on ground that cannot produce a yield. The tension is preserved in Mark's reflection on the defection of Judas, one of Jesus' chosen, who betrayed him: "'On the one hand, the Son of Man must be betrayed as it is written, but woe to that man through whom he is betrayed'" (14:21). The disbelief and rejection experienced by Jesus were later experienced by the early church as well, and again Isa 6:9-10 (along with Jer 5:21) spoke to the problem of the hardened heart (Acts 28:26-27; John 12:40).

In the inscrutable interplay between the expressed purposes of God and the contrary facts of history, Mark and the early church saw more than a tug-of-war between equal and opposite forces. Rather, the sovereign God was exercising a teleological purpose. The God who "gives" the mystery (v. 11) also blinds the eyes of the unwilling. Like Jesus' own ministry, parables are hidden and mysterious, and only as such can they reveal to those who really hear.[57] Jesus presented the kingdom of God in such a way that it created a crisis and division, a "sword" according to Matt 10:34, for these are the necessary prerequisites of decision and repentance. Jesus' person and ministry create a dividing line between insiders and outsiders, and this corresponds to the will of God. The Gospel of John well expresses Mark's understanding of this crisis, "'For judgment I have come into this world, so that the blind will see and those who see will become blind'" (9:39).

13 "'Don't you understand this parable? How then will you understand any parable?'" With this question Mark returns to the second half of the sandwich in the interpretation of the parable of the sower. The presence of this verse, which Matt 13:18 and Luke 8:11 omit, indicates the importance of the parable of the sower for Mark. Failure to hear *this* parable means failure to understand parables in general. What is it about the parable of the sower that makes it the paradigm for all parables? The answer, which becomes apparent in the interpretation of vv. 14-20, is that the parable of the sower combines the two elements that form the core of Mark's story and that are necessary for understanding the gospel,

---

57. Note M. Hengel's insight: "What we have [in the parables] is what I would want to call a 'revelatory concealment.' Revelation can conceal and concealment can reveal. . . . There are circumstances which can only be expressed adequately in the form of a revelation which conceals, and I believe that the 'mysteries' of Jesus are such situations. Not because the one who talks about such circumstances wants to be mysterious, . . . but because the nature of these circumstances does not allow any other kind of language as an adequate expression" (*Studies in the Gospel of Mark,* trans. J. Bowden [London: SCM Press, 1985], 95-96).

namely, Christology and discipleship. The first telling of the parable in 4:3-9 explains the meaning of Jesus, and the second telling in 4:14-20 explains the meaning of discipleship.

14-19 The shift to the theme of discipleship in the explanation of the parable is unmistakable. A careful reading of 4:14-20 reveals that the seed, which in v. 14 is identified as the word (= gospel), becomes in vv. 15ff. the hearers. Many scholars regard this shift as evidence of a later interpretation of the church projected onto Jesus. This is a possible conclusion, but it is not as necessary as many scholars suppose. There are several instances in Jewish tradition where the faithful are planted, exactly as they are here (Hos 2:23; Jer 31:27; 1 Enoch 62:8; 2 Esdr 8:41).[58] The apostle Paul also speaks of the sowing of people (1 Cor 15:42-48), as does the Shepherd of Hermas (*Herm. Sim.* 9:20:1; *Herm. Vis.* 3:7:3).

Another characteristic of the explanation of the parable is the presence of words and expressions that are unique. These words, which do not occur elsewhere in Mark but do occur particularly in Paul, suggest to many scholars that the explanation of the parable stems from the early church rather than from Jesus. The vocabulary statistics, however, are not as compelling as their proponents suggest. There are only five terms that occur only here in Mark and nowhere else in the Synoptics outside the explanation of the parable of the sower.[59] That is a notable figure, but it is not proof of a later provenance of the text.

Finally, the various obstacles to hearing are supposed to reflect a later time period. "Trouble and persecution" (v. 17), "falling away" (v. 17), "worries of this life, the deceitfulness of wealth and the desires for other things" (v. 19) are thought to fit the circumstances of the early church better than Jesus' itinerant ministry. Once again, although they could possibly be true, the same data also fit with Mark's narrative of Jesus' ministry. For example, the reference to Satan taking away the word that is sowed (v. 15) transpires in the experience of Peter in 8:32; the falling away because of trouble and persecution (v. 17) is realized in 14:43-50

---

58. L. Ramaroson, "Jesus semeur de parole et de peuple en Mc 4:3-9 et par.," *ScEs* 47 (1995): 287-94, examines nine passages where God sows the people of his kingdom and argues that the explication of the parable of the sower in 4:14-20 is faithful to Jesus' thought.

59. C. H. Dodd, *The Parables of the Kingdom* (London: Collins, 1965), 14-15, and Jeremias, *The Parables of Jesus*, rev. ed., 78, present a combined list of fourteen words that are unique to the explanation of the parable of the sower. That is a very loose count. In actuality, there are only five terms that occur only here in Mark and nowhere else in the Synoptics outside the explanation of the parable: *akarpos* ("unfruitful"), *apatē* ("deceitfulness"), *paradechomai* ("accept"), *ploutos* ("wealth"), and *proskairos* ("short time"). Mark 4:14-20 consists of a hundred words in Greek; five unique words among them are insufficient to prove the later provenance of the passage.

when Judas and his posse cause the disciples to flee; and the cares of the world and deceitfulness of wealth are brought to pass in the story of the rich man in 10:17.[60]

Is, then, the interpretation posited in vv. 14-20 an authentic explanation of Jesus or an addition of the early church? The artificial placement of the explanation of parables in vv. 10-20 into Jesus' lakeside sermon, new vocabulary, the shift from seeds to people, and the life-setting reflecting the early church can, of course, be read as evidence for a provenance in the early church. But they need not be read that way.[61] The foregoing discussion offers both data and reasons that can equally plausibly locate the explanation of the parable in the life of Jesus. In any case, the explanation of the parable, which at first appears troubling, forces us to reconsider what a parable is and does. Parables are a plastic rather than a static medium. They are not bricks, dried hard and fast in the sun, but wet clay that invites new impressions. Whether the new impressions are made by the hands of the potter or by later apprentices is very difficult to say, and for Mark's purposes unimportant. What is important to assert is that the new impressions are not errors or aberrations. It is mistaken to suppose that a parable has a single meaning, fixed and static, and that any change from the assured *ipsissima vox Jesu*, the word of Jesus himself, is of secondary provenance and importance. A parable presents a certain quantum before hearers that has the potential to address them in various ways and at different levels. The dialectic between the spoken word of Jesus and the understanding hearing of believers is the revelatory intent of the parable. The telling and interpretation of the parable of the sower combines within one story Mark's two central themes, the meaning of Jesus and the meaning of discipleship.[62]

The paramount purpose in the interpretation of vv. 14-20 is the stress on *hearing*. Discipleship hangs on this term, for everything depends on receptivity. Disciples — insiders — are those who have received the mystery of the kingdom (v. 11) and who hear what Jesus says. Mark's vocabulary is unambiguous. The "word" (Gk. *logos*) appears eight times in vv. 14-20, and the command to "hear" (Gk. *akouein*) half that number. The first three types of hearing — those from whom Satan steals the word

60. Drury, *The Parables in the Gospels*, 51.

61. Cranfield's sensible discussion of vv. 14-20 in *The Gospel According to Saint Mark*, 158-61, is evidence that the case against the authenticity of 4:14-20 is far from established.

62. M. Fishbane's *Biblical Interpretation in Ancient Israel* (Oxford: Clarendon Press, 1985) offers a helpful perspective on the way authoritative tradition *(traditum)* was transmitted *(traditio)* in ancient Israel. Drury's *The Parables of the Gospels* offers an equally helpful perspective on the way parables function in the Gospels.

(v. 15), those with no root who fall away in difficulty (v. 17), and those whose wealth and worldly desires choke the word (v. 18-19) — are described by Mark in the aorist tense in Greek. The Greek aorist connotes punctiliar action, something done simply and finally. The first three types of hearing thus imply a quick, superficial hearing, in one ear and out the other, without effort or heeding. Satan, persecution, and the cares of the world spell havoc for those who give the gospel only a casual hearing. Their failure to hear confirms them as outsiders, and the word of God becomes fruitless to them (v. 19). But in v. 20 a different kind of hearing is implied. The aorist tense is suddenly replaced by the present tense of the verb, signifying a continual, ongoing hearing as opposed to a careless or inattentive hearing. People who are engaged in the fourth kind of hearing are insiders who "hear . . . receive . . . and bear fruit." Hearing, receiving, and bearing fruit are the marks of a disciple of Jesus. A responsive hearing produces a miraculous harvest — "thirty, sixty, or even a hundred times what was sown"!

What is the overall meaning of the Markan sandwich in 4:1-20? The key to its interpretation is the central B-part in vv. 10-12. The clue to receiving the mystery of the kingdom of God is found in Jesus. Those are with Jesus and do the will of God (3:34-35) are insiders to whom the mystery of the kingdom of God is revealed. Those who are not with Jesus are outsiders, for whom the parables seal their unbelief. The parable of the sower is like the cloud that separated the fleeing Israelites from the pursuing Egyptians, bringing "darkness to the one side and light to the other" (Exod 14:20). That which was blindness to Egypt was revelation to Israel. The same event was either a vehicle of light or of darkness, depending on one's stance with God. The parable of the sower holds Christology and discipleship in symbiotic union, just as Mark will again hold them in union in the teaching at Caesarea Philippi (8:27-38). Right confession of Jesus leads to right discipleship. The parable of the sower informs and warns disciples that although the ministry of Jesus is beset by obstacles, it will produce a harvest beyond compare. Disciples, too, will be sent to sow the word, and they, too, will know the tremendous frustration of sowing where chances of a harvest seem next to impossible. But as they have experienced in their own lives, the seed will unexpectedly find good soil in the lives of others. Those who *hear* will understand the mystery of the kingdom of God and will, by the grace of its generative power, produce a harvest beyond belief.

HIDDENNESS THAT REVEALS (4:21-25)

The sayings in this unit can be found scattered elsewhere in Matthew and Luke as well as in early church tradition.[63] This indicates that Mark assembled the material in this section from a pool of Jesus' sayings that had been gathered prior to his writing and that probably circulated in oral form afterward for a considerable time. The sayings are employed in different contexts and for different purposes by the above writers. Mark weaves them into the present context of chap. 4 to comment on the meaning of parables. Although it is not specifically stated, the resumption of parabolic speech in v. 21 leads us to assume that Jesus is again teaching publicly beside the Sea of Galilee.

21 The awkwardness of this verse in the original Greek is a clue to its meaning. The NIV puts the lamp in the objective case in order to make the verse more felicitous ("'Do you bring in a lamp to put it under a bowl or on a bed?'"). Matt 5:15, Luke 8:16, and the *Gospel of Thomas* 33 all preserve the saying and place the lamp in the objective case as well. Mark makes the lamp the subject of the sentence, however, doubtlessly for theological reasons: "'Does the lamp come in order that it might be placed under the bowl or under the bed?'" In the OT, a lamp is not infrequently a metaphor for God (2 Sam 22:29) or the Davidic Messiah (2 Kgs 8:19; Ps 132:17) or the Torah (Ps 119:105). Not only does Mark distinguish the lamp by making it the acting subject, but he refers to it with the definite article, *the* lamp. Finally, reference to the lamp *coming* (Gk. *erchetai*) is more suitable of a person than an object, and has indeed been used of Jesus earlier (1:7; 3:20). These particulars signal that this is no ordinary lamp. The image points to Jesus as the implied agent, for whom the lamp is a metaphor. Jesus is the lamp of God who has come to bring light and revelation (John 1:5; 8:12).

Oil lamps, one of the most common artifacts discovered by archaeologists, give optimum light when elevated in the open rather than when placed under something like "a bowl[64] or a bed." The saying may have been prompted by the placement of the lampstand in the tabernacle for all to see (Exod 25:37). 4:21 repeats the thought of 2:21-22, although in different imagery. As Jesus cannot be conformed to old garments and wineskins, neither can he be placed under "a bowl or a bed." Perhaps bowls and beds (Gk. *klinē*) recall the pitchers and kettles and beds (Gk. *klinē*) of 7:2. If so, the parable again declares Jesus' independence from

63. Verse 21: Matt 5:15; Luke 8:16; *Gospel of Thomas* 33; v. 22: Matt 10:26; *Gospel of Thomas* 5–6; *P.Oxy.* 654, no. 4; v. 23: Matt 11:15; *Acts of Thomas* 82; v. 24: Matt 7:2; *1 Clem.* 13:2; Pol. *Phil.* 2:3; v. 25: Matt 13:12; *Gospel of Thomas* 41; 4 Ezra 7:25?

64. The Greek word for "bowl" *(modios)* was a container common to Palestinian houses, with a volume of about two gallons.

and sovereignty over Jewish purification rites. At any rate, the lamp on the lampstand asserts that Jesus is not subordinated to anything but supreme over all things, and the light by which people are enabled to see. The lamp, coupled with the theme of disclosure in vv. 21-25, testifies that God's purpose in Jesus is to enlighten and reveal.[65]

22 For the present, however, the kingdom of God, and Jesus' role in it, remain largely hidden (4:22). Yet even the concealment of the present hour (reflecting back on vv. 11-12) contains the seeds of what will be revealed. If the beginnings of the kingdom look inauspicious and unpromising, that serves God's purpose. The very humanness of Jesus governs the glory of God from overwhelming and blinding the world, and invites people to discover the kingdom by experience.[66] The rather baffling activity of God in Jesus is like hide-and-seek: only that which is first hidden can be found.

23-24 Jesus is hidden *in order* to be manifested. Concealment intends disclosure. The kingdom of God — and the parables that witness to it — are like a piece of embroidery: one side is a mass of knots and tangles, while the other is a finished pattern. So, too, is the figure of Jesus. To outsiders he is a homespun rabbi without the credentials of a rabbinic school, a Galilean upstart. How might one detect in the ordinary threads of such a life the emerging pattern of the kingdom of God? Only by *hearing*. The point is repeated to redundancy in vv. 23-24, where the command to hear occurs in Greek three times in two verses. The explanation of the parable of the sower warned against allowing life to become leached by the demands and attractions of the world, leaving no soil in which to nourish the seeds of life. "'Consider carefully what you hear,'" says Jesus, for you are like a prisoner whose one chance of escape depends on hearing and solving a riddle. As in the parable of the sower, the entryway into the kingdom of God is through hearing.

To the theme of concealment and revelation, Mark appends a saying of Jesus in 4:24 about being measured by the standard one sets for others. This is an old Jewish proverb that occurs in a variety of forms, one of which ran, "In the pot in which you cook for others, you'll be cooked."[67]

---

65. Klostermann, *Das Markusevangelium*, 42-43, sees a contradiction between the idea of revelation in v. 21 and concealment in v. 11. But R. Gundry, *Mark*, 212, is correct in noting that "the saying about hiddenness and manifestation naturally means that nothing is hidden in a parable spoken to the huge crowd that will not be made manifest to Jesus' disciples in a private explanation."

66. *P.Oxy.* 654, no. 4, expands the saying in v. 22 to include ". . . and nothing buried that will not be raised." This addition connotes that the veil and concealment of Jesus' earthly ministry will be lifted at his resurrection from the dead.

67. Str-B 1.445 [my translation].

Vv. 23-24 betray unmistakable signs of having been framed and transmitted in a Jewish milieu. They are Hebrew wording in Greek dress and can be easily translated back into Hebrew.[68] A literal translation of the Greek would be: "In whatever measure you measure it will be measured to you and will be added to you."[69] The passive voices of the two verbs are "divine passives," meaning, "God will measure it out and add it to you." The frequent use of the passive voice in such sayings preserves the Jewish convention of avoiding the name of God for fear of profaning it.

25 Mark applies this Jewish wisdom saying to the understanding of parables. It seems illogical that more can be given to one who has than to one who has not, but two later sayings from the Talmud essentially agree.[70] The degree to which one hears the parables, the extent to which one allows the kingdom to break upon oneself, will determine the measure of one's understanding. Those who hear, those who knock until the door is opened, will find the kingdom disclosed to them. But those of hurried search, whose knock at the door of life is tentative or brief, will find a once joyous invitation to enter the kingdom to have faded into a mirage of disbelief. In particular, the saying invites application to Jesus, for the same verb ("given"; Gk. *didomi*) links the giving of the kingdom in v. 11 with v. 25. Those to whom the mystery of the kingdom of God is given in Jesus will receive even greater capacity to enter it. On the other hand, those who fail to receive the mystery in Jesus will discover that "even what he has will be taken from him" (see Prov 1:5-6; 9:9). Understanding the kingdom of God is not a human ability but a capacity created by Jesus Christ within the heart of the believer.

68. The source and context that best explain the meaning of vv. 21-25, according to J. Jeremias, *Abba: Studien zur neutestamentlichen Theologie und Zeitgeschichte* (Göttingen: Vandenhoeck & Ruprecht, 1966), 99-102, is Jesus himself.

69. The concluding phrase, "and will be added to you," is missing in the Western text (D), perhaps owing to homoeoteleuton (when the eye of a copyist inadvertently omitted a word owing to its similarity to another word). That is a potential for error in vv. 24-25, where four words end in *ēsetai* in Greek. See Metzger, *TCGNT*, 83-84. On the other hand, a copyist may have omitted the added words because they destroyed the parallelism of the preceding words and seemed redundant.

70. God "puts more into a full vessel, but not into an empty one; for it says 'If hearkening you will go on hearkening (Exod. 15.26), implying, If you hearken you will go on hearkening, and if not you will not hearken'" *(b. Ber. 40a)*; "According to the standards of mortal man, an empty vessel is able to contain [what is put into it], and a full vessel cannot contain it, but according to the standards of the Holy One, blessed be He, a full vessel is able to contain it while an empty one cannot" *(b. Suk. 46a-b)*. Cited from M. Hooker, *The Gospel According to St Mark*, 134.

FROM THE INSIGNIFICANT TO THE INCOMPREHENSIBLE (4:26-34)

Mark concludes Jesus' teaching in parables with two parables about the kingdom of God (4:26-29, 30-32) and a summary of the purpose of parables (4:33-34). The first parable (4:26-29) is unique to Mark and found nowhere else in the Gospels. The two parables illustrate the plasticity inherent in parabolic teaching that we noted in the explanation of the parable of the sower. Both parables repeat the image of a person sowing seed (cf. 4:3ff.), but to wholly different effects. In the first parable the emphasis falls on the process of growth, whereas similar imagery in the second accentuates the contrast between small beginnings and great results. Both parables are stories of surprise. One could never imagine the conclusion from the beginning. Such is the kingdom of God.

26 "'This is what the kingdom of God is like. A man scatters seed on the ground.'" A more banal comparison could not be imagined. The kingdom of God should be likened to something grand and glorious: to shimmering mountain peaks, crimson sunsets, the opulence of potentates, the lusty glory of a gladiator. But Jesus likens it to *seeds*. The paradox of the gospel — indeed, the scandal of the Incarnation — is disguised in such commonplaces. The God whom Jesus introduces will not be kept at celestial arm's length. Jesus does not tell us how high and lofty God is but how very near and present he is, and how the routines of planting and harvesting are mundane clues to the nature and plan of God.

27-28 Jesus likens the kingdom of God to a process of growth. A seed is not spectacular, nor does its laborious growth attract attention. Night and day a farmer waits for seeds;[71] "he sleeps and gets up," and life goes on as it always has. But simultaneously and independent of the farmer another process is at work. Slowly, imperceptibly, "the seed sprouts and grows." The seed is wholly unlike the worldly quest for power where, as in Jotham's parable of the thornbush (Judg 9:7-15), raw ambition secures a place for itself by violence and revolution. Jesus will later warn against that pursuit and temptation (10:42-45). Rather, the seed is so harmless and negligible that the farmer at first may be unaware of its growth. "He does not [even] know how" it happens. Despite the farmer's absence and ignorance, however, the soil brings forth "all by itself" (Gk. *automatē*), from which we derive the word "automatic."[72] The

---

71. The order of events in v. 27, "Night and day, whether he sleeps or gets up," reflects the Jewish custom of reckoning the new day at sundown.

72. See G. Theissen, "Der Bauer und die von selbst Frucht bringende Erde," *ZNW* 85 (1994): 167-82, who locates the crux of the parable in *automatos* ("by itself").

seed contains within itself a power of generation and an orderly process of growth — "first the stalk, then the ear, then the full kernel in the ear" — that transpires quite apart from the farmer.[73]

An earlier theology tended to emphasize the role of human activity in ushering in the kingdom of God.

> Rise up, O men of God! His kingdom tarries long;
> Bring in the day of brotherhood, And end the night of wrong.[74]

This hymn could not have been written by Jesus or Mark. Apart from sowing, the only human activity in this parable is waiting in faith, confident of a harvest to come (see Jas 5:7). The coming of the kingdom of God is likened to a process of growth but a process strangely independent of human activity. Despite inauspicious beginnings and the absence of human involvement, the seed contains within itself fruit-bearing potential. The seed, like the gospel, prospers of itself, and once sown sets in motion a process that leads to harvest.[75]

29 Putting forth the sickle for the harvest often symbolizes the arrival of God's kingdom, especially in judgment (Joel 4:13; Rev 14:15; *Gospel of Thomas* 21). This parable admonishes that alongside and within "business as usual" the kingdom of God is present and growing, even if unobserved. The world may bemoan, "Where is this 'coming' he promised?" (2 Pet 3:4). Such skepticism is the result of awaiting the arrival of God's kingdom as if it were a bolt of lightning, commanding and overwhelming. God does not hurl the kingdom as Poseidon does his thunderbolt. God plants it as a seed, present even now in the ministry of Jesus, hidden and imperceptible, but portending both a harvest and judgment.

73. A similar order of growth appears in *1 Clem.* 23:4-5, and *2 Clem.* 11:3. The *Apocryphon of James* 12:20-30, a third-century gnostic text, shifts the point of the parable from the kingdom as God's work to humanity's responsibility to reap and appropriate: "For the kingdom of heaven is like an ear of grain after it has sprouted in a field. And when it had ripened, it scattered its fruit and again filled the field with ears for another year. You also: hasten to reap an ear of life for yourselves that you may be filled with the kingdom."

74. More recently, J. D. M. Derrett writes, "The parable of the Seed Growing Secretly indicated that good deeds and good intentions are meritorious, even though the 'sower' (the man) isn't aware of his eventual sharing in the profits" ("Ambivalence: Sowing and Reaping at Mark 4:26-29," *EstBib* 48 [1990]: 489-510). How this humanistic interpretation is derived from 4:26-29 is puzzling. V. 27, in particular, relegates humanity to an entirely passive role in the realization of the harvest. The parable has three subjects (sower, seed, earth), and the responsibility of the only human subject is simply to wait in faith.

75. On the possible relevance of 4:26-29 for the dating of Mark, see Introduction, 8.

The Zealots[76] tried to force the kingdom on stage by revolution; apocalypticism hoped by careful observations and reckonings to portend the future; the Pharisees believed that the emergence of the kingdom could be midwifed by scrupulous legal observance. The parable of the growing seed warns against wedding the coming of the kingdom to forecasts, projections, timetables, and strategies. Throughout the Gospel of Mark, Jesus sunders all attempts to capture him in categories, formulas, and agendas. So it is with the kingdom of God. To anchor it to human dreams is to lose it, for God has ordained what "no ear has perceived, no eye has seen" (Isa 64:4). Like the patient farmer, Jesus is supremely confident in the coming kingdom. Though beset by opposition from religious leaders and misunderstanding from followers, Jesus is not disheartened, distraught, or desperate. Nor should there be anxiety among his disciples. The faith that Jesus requires of disciples is to sleep and rise in humble confidence that God has invaded this troubled world not with a crusade but with a seed, an imperceptible "fifth column" that will grow into a fruitful harvest.[77]

30-32 The parable of the mustard seed appears similarly in Matt 13:31-32, Luke 13:18-19, and *Gospel of Thomas* 20. In wording reminiscent of Isa 40:18, Jesus again likens the kingdom of God to the sowing of seeds. The parable of the mustard seed is similar in meaning to the parable of the growing seed, although the point of the mustard seed lies in *contrast* rather than in growth. The mustard seed, which is an annual and proliferates anew each spring, is not actually the tiniest of seeds, but it stood for something proverbially small in Palestine (Matt 17:20). Microscopic though it is, the mustard seed produces a large shrub in which birds may nest.

76. The Zealots were a Jewish faction that combined the theology of the Pharisees (see at 2:18) with the military aspirations of the Maccabean freedom fighters who liberated Palestine from the Seleucid yoke in the second century B.C. According to Josephus, the movement began with Judas the Galilean in 6 B.C. (*Ant.* 18.22-25). The Zealot revolt against Roman control of Palestine in A.D. 66 resulted in the catastrophic defeat of the nation four years later and the extermination of the Zealot movement.

77. "One day, perhaps, when we look back from God's throne on the last day we shall say with amazement and surprise, 'If I had ever dreamed when I stood at the graves of my loved ones and everything seemed to be ended; if I had ever dreamed when I saw the specter of atomic war creeping upon us; if I had ever dreamed when I faced the meaningless fate of an endless imprisonment or a malignant disease; if I had ever dreamed that God was only carrying out his design and plan through all these woes, that in the midst of my cares and troubles and despair *his* harvest was ripening, and that every thing was pressing on toward his last kingly day — if I had know this I would have been more calm and confident; yes, then I would have been more cheerful and far more tranquil and composed" (H. Thielicke, *The Waiting Father*, trans. J. Doberstein [San Francisco: Harper & Row, 1959], 88).

With the hyperbole of a good storyteller, Jesus fashions the prover-bial mustard seed into an illustration of the kingdom. As with the preced-ing parable, the advent of the kingdom is not something humanity brings about but something God gives. The greater point, however, is that the kingdom of God arises from obscurity and insignificance. That which no one would imagine — or if one did would seem utterly impossible — will in time loom inescapably before us. God's reign will not only be more real than the world can imagine, but it will also be larger and more encom-passing.[78] But as in the previous parable, the emphasis lies on its small, obscure beginnings. It is now hidden and easily overlooked. Had Jesus desired to emphasize the power and glory of the kingdom of God he could have told a parable about a cedar, which was a symbol of might (Ps 80:10; 9:10; Zech 11:2) and splendor (Cant 1:17; Jer 22:23). But the mystery of the kingdom is not present in the cedar; it is present in a tiny mustard seed. "What appears to be the smallest is nevertheless the greatest. In that which is hidden, the foundation of a work is laid that will encompass the whole world."[79]

The OT prophets occasionally use the image of birds nesting in branches to allude to the inclusion of the Gentiles in God's chosen people (Ps 104:12; Ezek 17:23; 31:6; Dan 4:9-21).[80] This offers a clue to v. 32, "the birds of the air can perch in its shade." In addition to the surprising growth of the kingdom, the parable of the mustard seed contains a hint of God's grace to *all* peoples. This may explain its anchor position in chap. 4, for it would have signaled to Mark's Roman Gentile readers that their in-clusion in the kingdom was foreordained by the Lord. "Out of the most insignificant beginnings, invisible to human eyes, God creates his mighty Kingdom, which embraces all the peoples of the world."[81]

33-34   Mark concludes his medley of parables with an explanation of their purpose that recalls 4:10-12. The parables included in chap. 4 are but a sampling of "many similar parables Jesus spoke." For the tenth time in chap. 4 Mark emphasizes the importance of *hearing:* "[Jesus] was speak-

---

78. Seneca, a contemporary of Jesus, likened human words and reason to seeds that when scattered grow from insignificance to "greatest growth" (*Epistles,* "Letter to Lucilius," 4.38.2; cited in *HCNT,* 94). Seneca's analogy celebrates the power inherent in human reason and language, whereas similar imagery of Jesus affirms the miraculous irony of God to produce his kingdom in the world from insignificant beginnings.

79. A. Schlatter, *Die Evangelien nach Markus und Lukas,* 48.

80. A similar idea is preserved in *Joseph and Aseneth,* a Jewish novella dating from perhaps the time of Mark: "And your name shall no longer be called Aseneth, but your name shall be City of Refuge, because in you many nations will take refuge with the Lord God, the Most High, and under your wings many peoples trusting the Lord will be shel-tered" (*Jos. Asen.* 15:7).

81. Jeremias, *The Parables of Jesus,* rev. ed., 149.

ing to them the word, as they were able to hear." The last part of the description is important, "as they were able to hear" (see also 1 Cor 3:1). Parables enlighten or obscure depending on the ability to hear. Those who hear find them revelatory — and even more will be given to them (vv. 24-25). Those who are unable to hear find parables opaque. Hearing determines whether one is an insider or an outsider. It is the all-important first step that leads to fellowship with Jesus, where fuller understanding becomes possible, for "when he was alone with his own disciples, he explained everything." "Only in association with Jesus can one learn to understand the language about God."[82]

Parables were the public persona of Jesus the teacher. By means of graphic images from everyday life, Jesus teased, tantalized, and tested his audiences, inviting them to an insider experience of the kingdom and of fellowship with himself.

82. Schweizer, *The Good News According to Mark,* 106.

CHAPTER FIVE

"'Who Then Is This?'"

MARK 4:35–6:6a

The material in 3:13–4:34 consists of conversations, controversies, and parables. Readers are suddenly transferred in 4:35 to the resumption of Jesus' public ministry around the lake. The four stories in this section, longer and more detailed than many of Mark's pericopes, all highlight Jesus as a miracle worker. His mighty acts evoke a judgment from those who witness them. The disciples in the foundering boat must choose between faith and fear (4:35-41); the witnesses of the healed Gerasene demoniac must choose between acceptance and rejection of Jesus (5:1-20); both Jairus and the hemorrhaging woman must choose between faith and despair (5:21-43); and even Jesus' hometown in Nazareth must choose between belief and disbelief. The initial step of faith may not seem like one at all, for the presence of Jesus is first of all an unsettling presence. His disciples ask, "'Who then is this?'" (4:41), and his family and acquaintances in Nazareth ask, "'How can this man do these things?'" (6:2). The right judgment of Jesus cannot be made by following convention, for Jesus supersedes the powers of nature, demons, illness, death, and family influence. Confining Jesus within such categories and stereotypes is to misunderstand him; acknowledging his supremacy to such categories is the first act of discipleship.

JESUS — STILLER OF STORMS (4:35-41)

The calming of the storm is full of vivid details, many of which are flattened or omitted in the versions of the story in Matt 8:23-27 and Luke 8:22-25. Mark's version is replete with eyewitness characteristics: the hour of day (v. 35), the reference that the disciples took Jesus from the

147

boat in which he was sitting (v. 36), the presence of other boats (v. 36), the boat's drawing water (v. 37), Jesus' sleeping on the cushion (v. 38), the disciples' sarcasm (v. 38) and Jesus' rebuke (v. 40).[1] Moreover, the description of the disciples' fear in v. 41 is redundant in Greek (smoothed out in the NIV, "they were terrified"), reflecting an underlying infinitive absolute in Hebrew. Particulars such as these are evidence of firsthand narration, and Peter is again a likely source. These historical details are not related randomly and inchoately, as one might find in a diary entry, for example. The story exhibits sophisticated theological thought and reflects in particular the influence of Jonah 1 and Ps 107:23-32.[2] The calming of the storm illustrates Mark's larger purpose of interpreting historical events theologically so as to show Jesus as God incarnate and his significance for discipleship.

35-36 Mention of "other boats with him" may allude to the larger circle of disciples beyond the Twelve who were with Jesus in 3:34 and 4:10. The curious detail that "they took [Jesus] along, just as he was, in the boat" probably reflects the memory of the disciples that Jesus was taken directly from the boat in which he was teaching the crowd (4:1), without his having returned to the shore.

In 1986 the hull of a fishing **boat** was recovered from the mud on the northwest shore of the Sea of Galilee, about five miles south of Capernaum. The boat — 26½ feet long, 7½ feet wide, and 4½ feet high — corresponds in design to a first-century mosaic of a Galilean boat preserved in Migdal only a mile from the discovery site, and to a sixth-century mosaic of a similar boat from Madeba. Carbon 14 technology dates the boat between 120 B.C. and A.D. 40. Both fore and aft sections of the boat appear to have been covered with a deck, providing space on which to sit or lie. The boat was propelled by four rowers (two per side) and has a total capacity of about fifteen persons. The Galilee boat corresponds to the particulars of the boat described in this story and to depictions in various ancient artistic renderings. A similar boat accommodated Jesus and his disciples on their crossings of the Sea of Galilee.[3]

37 The disciples and Jesus launch out eastward across the lake. Mark does not state their purpose, but Jesus' desire to preach elsewhere (so 1:38) may apply here. The Sea of Galilee (see at 1:16) lies nearly seven hundred feet below sea level in a basin surrounded by hills and mountains that are especially precipitous on the east side. Thirty miles to the

---

1. V. Taylor, *The Gospel According to St. Mark,* 272-73; C. E. B. Cranfield, *The Gospel According to Saint Mark,* 172.

2. R. Pesch, *Das Markusevangelium,* 1.267-75.

3. See S. Wachsmann, "The Galilee Boat," *BARev* 14/5 (1988): 18-33.

northeast Mt. Hermon rises to 9,200 feet above sea level. The interchange between cold upper air from Mt. Hermon and warm air rising from the Sea of Galilee produces tempestuous weather conditions for which the lake is famed. The "furious squall" of v. 37, which in Greek can mean "hurricane," fits the stories of Galilean fishermen even today, to whom the early evening easterly is known as "Sharkia" (Arabic for "shark").[4] Although the Greek word for the "furious squall" *(lailaps)* is not used in Jonah, in other respects the description of the storm in v. 37 echoes the violent storm that befell the ship in which Jonah was fleeing (Jonah 1:4).

38 As Jonah retired to the bowels of the ship and fell into a deep sleep (Jonah 1:5), Jesus is also described by Mark sleeping on a sailor's cushion in the stern of the boat. Ironically, the only place in the Gospels that we hear of Jesus sleeping is during a storm. The scene depicts his complete trust in God in the midst of adversity, like the farmer in the preceding parables (4:3-9, 27) who trusts God's providential working over all obstacles and adversities.[5] As in the Jonah story, the disciples, some of them veteran seamen, are terrified by the ferocity of the storm. The captain of Jonah's ship upbraids Jonah for sleeping while the crew is perishing (LXX, *apollymi*); likewise the disciples reproach Jesus, "'Teacher, don't you care if we drown (Gk. *apollymi*)?'" Matt 8:25 softens the reproach to a prayer, and Luke 8:24 to a plea for help. The rudeness of Mark's wording reflects the way frustrated and desperate people speak (cf. Luke 10:40) and is probably a verbatim reminiscence of the disciples' response in the crisis. A later editor is not likely to have made Jesus the object of such a reproof. The divine humility of Jesus is made evident by his tolerance of the reproaches of his disciples.[6] That same humility will be evinced later when verbal reproach turns to outright abandonment (14:50).

39 The disciples are not abandoned to watery peril, however. Jesus "got up, rebuked the wind and said to the waves, 'Quiet! Be still!' Then the wind died down and it was completely calm." When Jonah is thrown overboard, the sea becomes calm (Jonah 1:15); so also in the tempest on the Sea of Galilee, nature is made to conform to the repose of its Master. The grateful change is effected not by prayer or incantation, but by the authoritative *word* of Jesus, just as God produced order from chaos in the beginning (Gen 1:2).

Mark's description of the stilling of the storm exceeds the Hebrew penchant for personalizing nature (e.g., Ps 104:3-6). In particular, the lan-

---

4. On weather conditions on the Sea of Galilee, see M. Nun, *The Sea of Galilee and Its Fishermen in the New Testament* (Kibbutz Ein Gev: Kinnereth Sailing Company, 1989), 52-57.

5. So Lev 26:6; Pss 3:5; 4:8; Job 11:18-19; Prov 3:21-26.

6. So Cranfield, *The Gospel According to St. Mark*, 174.

guage of v. 39 is, strictly speaking, proper to that of exorcism. The wind is "rebuked" (or "censured"). The Gk. *epitiman* has been used twice earlier in Mark of the rebuking of evil spirits (1:25; 3:12). The word is not used in Hellenistic exorcisms; it is rather a technical term in Jewish exorcisms for "the commanding word, uttered by God or by his spokesman, by which evil powers are brought into submission and the way is thereby prepared for the establishment of God's righteous rule in the world."[7] To the waves Jesus orders, "'Quiet! Be still!'" and they "obey him" (v. 41). The Greek word for "'Be still!'" *pephimōso*, carries the sense of "muzzled." It occurs in the second person singular, as though Jesus were addressing a personal being. Its unusual perfect passive imperative form indicates that the condition shall persist, that is, "Be still, and stay still."

Such language is more appropriate of demonic forces than of inanimate nature (1:25; 3:12; 9:25; cf. 8:33!). Not uncommonly in the OT wind and waters symbolize hostile forces over which God prevails.[8] The stilling of the storm is often regarded simply as a "nature miracle" told with hyperbole and metaphor so as to emphasize Jesus' extraordinary power. The language of v. 39, however, depicts Jesus as the Strong Man (3:27; 1:7) who vanquishes Satan and plunders his evil minions (3:27; cf. 1:7). Jesus' power over the forces of nature, and the language in which it is described, foreshadows his power over the forces that disrupt human nature in the story of the Gerasene demoniac (5:1-20). In both stories Jesus vanquishes hostile forces that attempt to prevent him from extending his ministry into Gentile regions.

The description of the stilling of the storm in the language of exorcism is intended not simply to demonstrate that Jesus possesses power over nature as well as over illness and demon possession. Its ultimate purpose is to show that Jesus does what only God can do.[9] Mark's narra-

---

7. H. C. Kee, "The Terminology of Mark's Exorcism Stories," *NTS* 14 (1968): 323-46.

8. Exod 14:21ff.; Job 12:15; 28:25; Pss 33:7; 65:7; 77:16; 107:23-30; 147:18; Prov 30:4; Amos 4:13; Nah 1:3ff.

9. In an insightful investigation of the language of 4:35-41, Gisela Kittel, "'Wer ist der?' Markus 4,35-41 und der mehrfache Sinn der Schrift," in *Jesus Christus als die Mitte der Schrift. Studien zur Hermeneutik des Evangeliums,* Herausgegeben von Ch. Landmesser, H.-J. Eckstein, und H. Lichtenberger, BZNW (Berlin: Walter de Gruyter, 1997), 517-42, draws attention to the mythic proportions of Mark's language in this story. In the OT, God alone can save people from the storms of chaos (Pss 33:7; 65:8; 89:11; 104:7; Job 26:12; 38:8). Hence this is not simply a miracle story of salvation; rather, it is a story of Jesus as the Epiphany of God who does what only God can do. Kittel asks the provocative question posed by the story, "Who is this who in the middle of the storm stands at one and the same time with his own and also at the side of God? Who is this, in whom God's creative and redeeming power invades the world of chaos and snatches people from its destructive force? This question must now accompany the disciples."

tion invites comparison with Ps 107:23-32 as well as with Jonah 1. Psalm 107 speaks of God's stirring up a tempest at sea that causes sailors to melt in fear. They cry to the Lord in their distress, and "He stilled the storm to a whisper; and the waves of the sea were hushed" (107:29). The language and pattern of this psalm are unmistakably reflected in Mark's story. In the OT God alone possesses power to quell natural storms such as this (Pss 65:7; 89:9; 104:7; also *T. Adam* 3:1). In this story, Mark informs us that the same power and authority belong to Jesus. In a final allusion to the Jonah story in v. 41, Mark says that the disciples were terrified at the calming of the storm. Their exceeding fear repeats verbatim the fear of the sailors in the Jonah story (*ephobēthēsan phobon megan*, Jonah 1:10, 16). The pagan sailors in the Jonah story recognized God in the presence of the miracle and offered sacrifice to him. In the calming of the storm on the lake Jesus does again what only God can do (so 2:7-10), and Mark invites disciples, then and now, to recognize in Jesus the same presence of God.[10]

40-41 Typically in Mark, whenever the person and work of Jesus are highlighted, so, too, are discipleship. For Mark, the revelation of Jesus as God's Son is not an isolated datum that transpires in a vacuum. Jesus' self-disclosure occurs in the presence of insiders so that they may be enabled to hear, comprehend, and increase in faith. Who Jesus is lays a claim on what his disciples may become. These two elements of Christology and discipleship are evident in the present story.

Throughout the stilling of the storm Mark gives clues that the purpose of the miracle is for the disciples. The story is told from their perspective: it is they who take Jesus with them (v. 36) and raise him from sleep (v. 38); they are afraid (v. 41), and their probing question concludes the story (v. 41). This is an unusual perspective for Mark, who normally is an anonymous narrator. In addition, the narrative focus of the story is on faith. In the eye of the storm the disciples panic and accuse Jesus of forsaking them (v. 38). In their response Mark may intend a parallel between the situation of the disciples in the boat and those of his church in Rome

10. The christological purpose of the stilling of the storm, i.e., that in the person and word of Jesus the purpose of God is effective, sets this miracle apart from other stories of calming waters in antiquity. The legend of a Jewish boy in *j. Ber.* 9:1 (4th cent. A.D.) who saved a boatload of Gentiles from peril at sea is essentially about the superiority of Judaism over paganism. Plutarch's story of the Dioscuri (*Moralia*, "Obsolescence of Oracles," 30) simply recognizes the sons of Zeus as protectors and patrons of mariners. The same theme is present in Lucian's "The Ship" or "The Wishes" 9. Both Philostratus (*Life Apoll.* 4:13) and Porphyry (*Life of Pythagoras* 29) relate stories about calming of waves so imperiled travelers could arrive safely, but the purpose of both is the exoneration of Apollonius and Pythagoras as miracle workers. See *HCNT*, 66-68. In addition to their different emphases, all the stories noted above (with the exception of Porphyry) postdate Mark and cannot have been prototypes of Mark 4:35-41.

who lived under the dominion of pagan powers and gods, and who suffered hot persecution in the later years of Nero's reign (A.D. 64-68). Like the disciples, Mark's first readers may have thought God indifferent to their hardship and suffering. This story assured them, as it assures us, that even seismic revolt against God's Son cannot swamp the boat in which he is gathered with his disciples. In the midst of their consternation the authoritative word of Jesus that has muzzled rebel powers asks the disciples, "'Why are you so afraid? Do you still have no faith?'"[11] This will not be the last time Jesus questions the disciples' lack of faith.[12] The disciples may indeed be insiders (4:10-11), but they do not yet fully understand Jesus — nor can they until the cross and resurrection. Jesus does not reproach the disciples for their lack of knowledge, however, but for their fear, the Greek word for which means "losing heart" or "cowardice" (see 6:50-51). The real threat to faith comes not from lack of knowledge but from doubt and fear.

Mark concludes the stilling of the storm with a question that is a doorway to faith. The disciples, we are told, "were terrified." This will not be the last time that the mighty acts of God will produce fear in them. The women at the tomb will be equally terrified (16:8). Ironically, the terror of the disciples at what Jesus has done exceeds their initial fear of the storm. The presence of the supernatural is more frightening to humanity than the most destructive of natural disasters. Jesus is still a stranger to his own followers, for they are better able to handle the possibility of their own death than the possibility of the presence of God among them. In this instance, God's nearness in Jesus is not something reassuring but something profoundly unsettling, even terrifying. Yet such consternation produces the one question that makes faith possible. It is a question that was first asked by the crowd in 1:27. Now it is present on the lips of the disciples, "'Who then is this?'" Following the Exodus, the Israelites had also feared God. "And when the Israelites saw the great power of the LORD displayed against the Egyptians, the people feared the LORD and put their trust in him" (Exod 14:31). The question before the disciples and Mark's readers is this: Will their fear lead them also to "put their trust in him"?

---

11. Among the textual variants of v. 40, the shorter version of the question *deiloi este? oupō* ("'Why are you afraid? Do you still have no faith?'") has the strongest textual support and is preferable to the NIV, "Why are you *so* afraid?" (Metzger, *TCGNT*, 84).

12. 7:18; 8:17, 21, 33; 9:19; [16:14].

CREATION FROM CHAOS (5:1-20)

Jesus has just calmed a violent storm at sea (4:35-41); he now meets a man with an equally violent storm inside him. In both cases the power of Jesus prevails over chaos and destruction. The purpose of the healing of the Gerasene demoniac, as with the stilling of the storm on the lake, is not simply to leave readers awestruck at Jesus' power, however, but to prompt them to consider "'how much the *Lord* has done for you, and how he has had mercy on you'" (5:19). Once again Jesus is connoted with God, for the *Lord* who has healed the demoniac is none other than *Jesus* (v. 20).

1 Mark locates the exorcism and healing of the demoniac in "the region of the Gerasenes." The place name is puzzling because the city of Gerasa (modern Jerash) lay not on the eastern shore of the Sea of Galilee but thirty-seven miles inland to the southeast. A two-day commute by foot between Gerasa and the Sea where our episode takes place is obviously out of the question. Skeptics have made sport of the pigs running the great distance from Gerasa (or even from Gadara, according to Matt 8:28, five miles to the southeast) across steep ravines and wadis before plunging into the lake.

If "the region of the Gerasenes" is the original reading in v. 1, then Mark may mean the *region* associated with Gerasa, which may have extended to the Sea of Galilee, rather than the city itself. But "Gerasenes" is not a certain reading. The name of the location in v. 1 appears in different manuscripts as "Gerasa," "Gadara," or "Gergesa."[13] None of the three locations is clearly superior to the other two in terms of textual support.[14] As we have noted, both Gerasa and Gadara lay too far inland to be suitable sites for the story. We cannot say for certain, but a town named Gergesa apparently existed on the northeast shore of the lake. Both Origen (*Comm. on John* 6:41, chap. 24) and Eusebius (*Onomasticon* 64.1) identified the swine miracle with a town named Gergesa on the eastern side of the lake. Moreover, a midrash to Song of Songs (*Zuta* 1:4) mentions a form of the name in the following reference, "the graves of Gog and Magog will be open from south of the Kidron Valley to Gergeshta on the eastern side of Lake Tiberias." Although the *Zuta* midrash is late, this particular saying is ascribed to Rabbi Nehemiah, an acclaimed disciple of Akiba in the second century A.D. This quotation preserves an independent tradition a century

---

13. *Gerasēnōn, Gadarēnōn, Gergesēnōn.* See the brief discussion of the terms in Metzger, *TCGNT,* 84.

14. "Gergesa," however, possesses the most *diverse* attestation, including uncial and minuscule manuscripts, ancient versions, and patristic citations. "Gergesa" is also the corrected reading in Sinaiticus (ℵ).

earlier than Origen and two centuries before Eusebius that a town named Gergesa (or Gergeshta) existed along the northeast shore of the lake. In 1970 a bulldozer cutting a road along the eastern shore of the lake unearthed the remains of an ancient town immediately south of Wadi Samak in the Valley of Kursi ("Gersa" or "Gursa," as known in local dialect). The location of the town and the similarity in the place names suggest an identification of Kursi with Gergesa. By the early third century both archaeology and church tradition locate the swine miracle at this site. The date is important, for pre-Byzantine site identifications are generally more trustworthy than those that stem from the Byzantine period. Although the foregoing evidence is not conclusive, it is both respectable and reasonable. The "Gerasa" of Mark 5:1 was probably Kursi/Gergesa, which lay within the administrative district of Hippos, one of the major cities of the Decapolis situated on the commanding promontory to the south.overlooking the Sea of Galilee.[15]

2-5 The healing of the Gerasene demoniac is Mark's third and most graphic exorcism so far (1:25; 3:11). Matt 8:28-34 and Luke 8:26-39 also recount the story, but drastically reduce it. Matthew, in particular, crops Mark's story from twenty verses to six verses, leaving only the core of an exorcism. Mark's wealth of personal interest material makes the demoniac a rounded character and his salvation a complete story. The description of the demoniac in vv. 2-5 is one of the most lamentable stories of human wretchedness in the Bible. He is a terror to himself and others, and his violence is hammered home in three resounding negatives in the Greek: "*not even* by chains could *anyone any longer* restrain him" (v. 3). Even in life he is consigned to the land of the dead. There, wailing among the tombs, he wreaks havoc on himself day and night. Mark's vocabulary is raw and brutal; even "bindings," "chains," and "irons" are unsuccessful "to subdue" the demoniac. Mark's description is more fitting of a fero-

---

15. On the identification of Kursi with Gergesa, see V. Tzaferis, "A Pilgrimage to the Site of the Swine Miracle," *BARev* 15/2 (1989): 45-51; B. Pixner, *Wege des Messias und Stätten der Urkirche*, Herausgegeben von R. Riesner (Giessen/Basel: Brunnen Verlag, 1991), 142-48. In a long discussion, M.-J. Lagrange, *Évangile selon Saint Marc*, 132-38, argues forcibly that Origen was mistaken in placing Gergesa along the eastern shore of the lake. The quotation from midrash *Zuta*, however, and the subsequent discovery of the village of Kursi, appear to mitigate Lagrange's critique and rehabilitate the credibility of Origen and Eusebius on this question. The Zuta reference comes from Z. Safrai, "Gergesa, Gerasa, or Gadara?" *JerusalemPersp* 51 (1996): 16-19. Safrai's explanation for the variant readings of Gerasa and Gadara in 5:1 is not implausible. He posits that Origen's mention of Gergesa as "an ancient city" indicates that already by his day it was in decline. When Gergesa became unknown, it was altered to the well-known "Gerasenes." The great distance of Gerasa from the lake, however, invited the alteration to "Gadarenes" (modern Umm Qeis), closer to the lake.

cious animal than of a human being; indeed, the Greek word for "subdue," *damazō*, is used of taming a wild beast in James 3:7. The evil forces that torment the man among the tombs equal and parallel the violent tempest that beset the boat on the lake (4:37).

From a Jewish perspective, the story is replete with elements of uncleanness. The setting is the eastern shore of the lake, the Gentile Decapolis. The Decapolis (lit. "Ten Cities") was a loose geographical term for a number of cities east of the Jordan River (with the exception of Beth Shan, which lay west of the Jordan). These cities were severed from Hasmonean rule by Pompey when he invaded Palestine in 63 B.C. and were reestablished as showcase cities of pagan Hellenistic culture and ideals (Josephus, *War* 1.155; *Ant.* 14.74-75). The existence of an important Roman settlement and harbor in Kursi/Gergesa also established the latter as a Gentile city, a suburb of the citadel of Hippos immediately to the south. In this region there lived a man who, according to Mark, had been commandeered by "an unclean spirit" (v. 2). His banishment to the tombs rendered him unclean according to OT law, where contact with the dead defiled one for seven days. According to Num 19:11-14, anyone who failed to purify himself from the pollution of tombs "must be cut off from Israel." Expanding on this Torah teaching, rabbinic interpretation extended uncleanness from contact with the dead to include contact with anything associated with them, including their bier, mattress, pillow, or tombs.[16] In the region there were also swine herders. Following the OT proscription against swine (Lev 11:7; Deut 14:8), the Mishnah states categorically: "None may rear swine anywhere" (*m. B. Qam.* 7:7). Although the staple food of the Roman army was grain and corn, meat was a prized supplement, when available. If the swineherds where supplying the Roman legions with pork, then the raising of unclean food for the detested Roman occupation was doubly offensive. Thus Jesus meets a man with an unclean spirit living among unclean tombs surrounded by people employed in unclean occupations, all in unclean Gentile territory.

6-7 Mark's narrative framework implies that demonic powers are intent on prohibiting Jesus from entering the region. First, the demonic nature of the storm on the lake nearly capsizes the boat; now a demon-possessed man powerful enough to break irons hurls himself at Jesus and the disciples. This is a place where no one would want to go for any reason. Contrary to all reason and expectation, however, Jesus goes there.

16. For Mishnaic regulations regarding tombs, see *m. Kel.* 23:4 and *m. Ohalot* 17–18. The city of Tiberias had been constructed over graveyards, and this, declares Josephus, "was contrary to the law and tradition of the Jews because [it] was built on the site of tombs, . . . and our law declares that such settlers are unclean for seven days" (*Ant.* 18.38).

He penetrates both the ritual wall of uncleanness and the formidable reputation of the demoniac. For once, however, the explosive terror of the demoniac does not prevail, for rather than falling on Jesus he "fell on his knees . . . [and] shouted at the top of his voice, . . . 'Swear to God that you won't torture me!'" The Greek verb for "fell on his knees," *proskynein*, denotes prostrating oneself before a person to whom reverence or worship is due, even kissing his feet or the hem of his garment. When demoniac meets divine, it is a no-contest event.[17]

The demoniac's address to Jesus, "'Swear to God that you won't torture me,'" is a curious mixture of imploring and pleading. On the one hand, "'Swear to God'" (Gk. "I adjure you as God") sounds like an exorcism formula (see 1 Kgs 2:42; 2 Chr 36:13).[18] But the plea not to be "tortured" or tormented by Jesus is an admission of subservience. (On the phrase, "'What do you want to do with me?'" [lit. "What [is it] to me and you?"], see at 1:24.) Most important is the reference to Jesus as "Son of the Most High God." In Judaism, "Most High God" is an epithet emphasizing the transcendence and exaltation of Israel's God over pagan gods and goddesses and rival powers.[19] In Gentile territory on the east side of the lake, the strength of this God is demonstrated in the vanquishing of a legion of demons powerful enough to destroy a herd of swine. The reference to "Son of the Most High God" rather than "Son of God" is typical of Gentile polytheism, designating Jesus as the Son of the one true God transcendent over all others. "Son of the Most High God" establishes the *uniqueness of Jesus' position* in relation to God Almighty and the *universality of his power.*

8-10 The unclean spirit is expelled from the demon-possessed man solely by the authoritative word of Jesus. The discovery of Greek magical papyri in Egypt informs us of the long and convoluted formulas, spells, conjurations, and catchwords that ancient exorcists employed as they sparred with demonic opponents to gain advantage over them.

---

17. The *Testament of Solomon*, a Jewish-Christian demonological text dating from the first to third centuries A.D., presents a panoply of demons in the form of a folktale. The exorcism of the Gerasene demoniac fascinated its author and provided grist for several episodes contained therein (see *T. Sol.* 1:13; 11:1-7; 17:2-3).

18. See similar formulas gathered in BAGD, 581, and A. Deissmann, *Bible Studies*, trans. A. Grieve (Edinburgh: T. & T. Clark, 1901), 281-83: *horkizō se, daimonion pneuma, ton theon tou Abraam* ("I adjure you, demonic spirit, by the God of Abraham").

19. Gen 14:18; Num 24:16; Isa 14:14; Dan 3:26; Luke 1:32, 35, 75; 6:35; Acts 7:48; 16:17; Heb 7:1; *Acts of Thomas* 45. The Heb. *'el 'elyon* ("Most High God") is found fifteen times in the DSS and seldom in rabbinic literature. It occurs thirty-one times in the OT, and increases in frequency after the Maccabees in order to show the supremacy of Israel's God over pagan gods and goddesses. G. Bertram, *"hypsos," TDNT* 8.602-20; E. Lohmeyer, *Das Evangelium des Markus*, 95.

Likewise, Philostratus describes a long and involved conversation of Apollonius with a demon, including empirical signs that the exorcism had actually been effective.[20] But with Jesus there is no elaborate protocol, nor is the effectiveness of the exorcism dependent on the words he utters. The power to prevail over the demonic resides within Jesus himself. He speaks and the demons are expelled; his word is deed.

Asked who he is, the demoniac identifies himself as "Legion, for we are many."[21] The grip of demons resembled the grip of the Roman legion on Palestine, which had been subjugated by Pompey less than a century earlier. The Greek term "Legion" is a military term borrowed from Latin. A *legio* designated the largest troop-unit in the Roman army, some 5,600 soldiers.[22] The demoniac is not a split personality but a multiple or shattered personality equal to the number and force of a Roman legion occupying him. "Legion" adds another militant facet to the demoniac's violent history and is a chilling reminder of the number, power, and intention of the demons. The plea of the demons not to be sent from the area is perhaps rooted in the illusion that there they are safe from the authority of Jesus. At any rate, it is a further clue that the Decapolis is dominated by demonic forces of darkness hostile to the arrival of Jesus. Nevertheless, the demons offer no challenge to Jesus, but plead for his mercy as the only alternative to experiencing his wrath.[23]

20. See *HCNT*, 69-72, 331-32.

21. The healing of the Gerasene demoniac has spawned a plethora of psychological interpretations. E. Drewermann attempts to explain "legion" from the perspective of depth psychology as the loss of an individual personality in a group personality. "This type of demonic never shudders so much as when a person begins to say 'I' and becomes an individual. The realm of such demonic control is always the crowd, the many, the collective, in which one loses oneself, escapes one's individuality, forsakes one's own decisions. This demonic is the spirit of the masses, the pressure to deny oneself — which is present from infancy to the grave" (*Das Markusevangelium*, 1.318). As recounted by the Gospels, however, the demoniac's struggle is not with social pressures and masses, as Drewermann supposes, but with superhuman forces capable of great destruction to himself and others. P. Horsfield, "The Gerasene Demoniac and the Sexually Violated," *St. Mark's Review* 152 (1993): 2-7, sees the demoniac's "possession" as a metaphor of those who have been sexually abused as children or who have been victims of sexual violence. Again, E. Frick, "Der Besessene von Gerasa. Ein Bibliodrama zu Mk 5,1-20," *GeistLeb* 64 (1991): 385-93, sees the story as a psychodrama of psychotic individuals as well as more global evil forces. Not all these interpretations do justice to the text, but they indicate, as do a growing number of interpreters interested in manifestations of spirits and demons among primal people groups, that a text that is problematic for historical-critical interpreters may be fertile soil for other theological approaches and fields of inquiry.

22. F. Annen, *"legiōn,"* EDNT 2.345.

23. R. Bultmann, *The History of the Synoptic Tradition*, rev. ed., trans. J. Marsh (Oxford: Basil Blackwell, 1972), 210, regards the demoniac's self-identification in v. 9 as a boast, hoping to outwit Jesus by its strength and numbers ("Legion" and "we are

11-13 On their own initiative, "the evil spirits came out and went into the pigs. The herd, about two thousand in number, rushed down the steep bank into the lake and were drowned." The destruction of the pigs plagues or embarrasses many modern interpreters. Some, arguing that the element of the pigs was not part of the earliest tradition, dismiss it as a later addition to the narrative.[24] There is, however, no objective evidence of such developments within the story. In fact, apart from the place name in 5:1, the twenty verses of the story are more textually certain than perhaps any similar section in Mark. Moreover, the destruction of the swine poses a moral problem (see below) that its omission would avoid. If the drowning of the pigs were a later addition we might expect greater harmonizing: for example, the number of pigs might be correlated to the number of men in a Roman legion. Finally, if the stampede and destruction of pigs is omitted from the story, there is no reason for the people to drive Jesus from their region (v. 17).[25] The story coheres as written and should be read and interpreted as a complete unit.

About two miles south of Kursi/Gergesa a ridge extends from the eastern slopes of the Decapolis practically to the lake. The ridge terminates in a steep embankment and fits the description of 5:13: "The herd, about two thousand in number, rushed down the steep bank into the lake and were drowned." The greatest dilemma posed by the stampede of swine, in my judgment, is the moral question. Two thousand pigs repre-

---

many"). Neither the dialogue nor the context appears to support Bultmann's conclusion, however, for in every way the demon acquiesces to Jesus. The self-identification of v. 9 is not a challenge but a surrender. So, too, the recounting of the same story in *Epistula Apostolorum* 5 (cited in *NTApoc* 1.253).

24. For example, J. Craghan, "The Gerasene Demoniac," *CBQ* 30 (1968): 522-36. Craghan charts an evolutionary development of an original story of Jesus expelling a demon that was then augmented by "the community's contribution" of the tombs and pigs (vv. 3-5, 9, 12-13) as a "haggadic midrash" on Isaiah 65, and finally to Mark's redaction in vv. 18-20. Craghan elaborates the position of E. Schweizer, *The Good News According to Mark*, 111-13, who suggests that the drowning of the pigs is a later addition to delight Jewish readers. Schweizer argues for "an ancient story about Jesus casting out a demon [that] has been enlarged by the addition of various legendary features, but primarily through the addition of the folksy description of the pigs which rushed into the water." Such reconstructions are, of course, hypothetical. There is no evidence of the stages of development as suggested above. Nor is the supposed "unevenness" of the canonical story compelling. Indeed, Bultmann, who is not adverse to dismembering texts, declares that "it is hardly possible to establish what is editorial work. Clearly the story is essentially intact in its present form" (*The History of the Synoptic Tradition*, 210). Such polarities of opinion caution us against fanciful reconstructions of this text.

25. See J. L. P. Wolmarans, "Who Asked Jesus to Leave the Territory of Gerasa (Mark 5:17)?" *Neot* 28 (1994): 87-92, who argues that the people who asked Jesus to leave were probably the swineherds so as to defend themselves from culpability in the loss of the swine.

sented an enormous livelihood, and their loss an economic catastrophe. The good done to the demoniac results in great misfortune for the swineherds. Ironically, both Jesus and Mark pass over the obvious plight of the swineherds without comment.[26] As it stands, the story directs undivided attention to the rescue of one man from a tragic and torturous fate. Here perhaps is the essential moral of the miracle, surpassing even the dilemma of the loss of pigs. In the eyes of Jesus, the rescue and restoration of one person is more important than vast capital assets. Compared to the redemption of a human being, the loss of the swineherds, considerable though it is, does not rate mentioning.

14-17 The remainder of the story centers on the reaction of the locals to the exorcism. The swineherds "reported this in the town and countryside" (5:14). The nearest town was Kursi/Gergesa, but also in the region was Hippos, a citadel city of the Decapolis situated on a commanding summit on the east side of the lake. The report summons people from the surrounding area to see what has happened. And they see something quite astounding: the infamous demoniac is in a wholly altered state, "sitting there, dressed and in his right mind." That is a picture of discipleship and salvation: a restored individual sitting at the feet of Jesus.

The corollaries of the healing of the demoniac with the stilling of the storm in 4:35-41 are now wholly apparent. Both stories end in *fear.* At the crossing of the lake, the disciples were more terrified at Jesus' power to still the storm than at the storm itself (4:41); here the inhabitants are more frightened by Jesus' power to expel the demons than they are by a terrifying demoniac himself. Further, like the disciples, the townspeople witness a stupendous miracle, but it does not lead to faith — at least not yet. In the latter story, the residents of the Decapolis resent the intrusion of Jesus into their region and ask him to leave. Such is the response of the human heart to Jesus. Most people, if they were asked, would probably say that they would like to see a manifestation of God. But this story is a cold shower for such religious pipe dreams: when God manifests himself in Jesus most people ask him to leave (see John 1:11). Finally, there is a clear parallel in the outcomes of both stories. The composure of the healed demoniac ("dressed and in his right mind") is a counterpart to the great calm on the lake after the storm. Both outer and inner storms have been quelled by the authority of Jesus. Like the Spirit wresting order from depths and darkness (Gen 1:2-3), Jesus brings creation out of chaos.

26. As with the story of God's commandment to Abraham to sacrifice Isaac on Mt. Moriah (Genesis 22), Søren Kierkegaard may have counted this incident as an example of the "teleological suspension of the ethical," i.e., an instance where an ultimate good or command of God overrides all other goods.

18-20 The story concludes with the former demoniac asking to *be with him*. The request is worded in the vocabulary of discipleship of 3:14, indicating his wish to join Jesus. Jesus forbids him, however, probably because a Gentile would have been a stumbling block in his mission to Israel (Matt 10:5-6). The mission and call of Jesus are owing to his will alone. Curiously, however, Jesus does not swear the man to silence as he has heretofore. It may be supposed that the command to silence is unnecessary in Gentile territory where there is no fear of false messianic expectations. This is not the case, however, for in 7:31-37 Jesus swears a man to silence after a healing in the Decapolis. The reason Jesus sends the man to announce what happened to him may be related to the fact that Jesus has been banished from the region. Mark would not leave us with a false stereotype, however, that Gentiles are receptive to the gospel whereas Jews are not. The response to Jesus in the Decapolis is essentially no different from the Jewish response in Galilee. But human response alone, even hardness of heart, is not the final word. "'Go home to your family and tell them how much the Lord has done for you, and how he has had mercy on you,'" Jesus commands. Their banishment of Jesus does not rid them of Jesus, for Jesus is present in the message of the gospel proclaimed by his followers. In the concluding verses of the story Mark leaves us with another clue to Jesus' divine status. "'Tell them how much the *Lord* has done for you,'" commands Jesus. The man then went out and told "how much *Jesus* had done for him." For this man, the Lord and Jesus are one and the same. In the Gospel of Mark, the healed demoniac becomes the first missionary-preacher sent out by Jesus. Remarkably, he is a Gentile sent to Gentiles.

FAITH THAT DEFIES DEFEAT (5:21-43)

This dramatic story is another example of a Markan sandwich in which the healing of Jairus's daughter (5:21-24, 35-43) is interrupted by a woman with the hemorrhage (vv. 25-34). The middle story of the hemorrhaging woman provides the key to understanding the combined stories. Mark delimits the middle insertion by casting it in the aorist (past) tense in Greek, whereas the flanking halves tend to be in imperfect and present tenses. In addition to using the A^1-B-A^2 sandwich structure, Mark signifies the relationship between the two stories by several common elements. Both stories are of females healed by the touch of Jesus; both are called "daughter" by Jesus; and the woman's illness and the girl's age are both given as twelve years. In both stories Jesus is met by rebukes (vv. 17, 40), and both stories bring Jesus into contact with uncleanness (the menstrual hemorrhage of the woman and the corpse of the child). The aspect of uncleanness connects the present sandwich narrative with the previous story (5:1-20). All three characters in Mark 5 transfer their uncleanness to Jesus, and to each Jesus bestows the cleansing wholeness of God. Mark 5 might be called the "St. Jude chapter" (the saint of hopeless causes), for the Gerasene demoniac, the menstruating woman, and Jairus each find hope in Jesus when all human hopes are exhausted.

21 After being expelled from Kursi/Gergesa, Jesus crosses back to Jewish territory on the western shore of the lake.[27] Compared to the voyage eastward, the westward crossing is uneventful. Mark does not locate the point of disembarkation other than to say it was "by the lake." The lakeside is by now a familiar theme in Mark, for in the first six chapters there are some fifteen references to Jesus' public ministry on the western shore of the lake. The "large crowd gathered around him" is more receptive than the gathering in the Decapolis.

22-24 Immediately a ruler of the synagogue cuts through the crowd. A **ruler of the synagogue** was the president or "head" of the local Jewish worshiping community, *rosh ha-keneset* in Hebrew (*m. Yoma* 7:1; *m. Sot.* 7:7-8). The title is found throughout the Mediterranean world in the first century, although it does not occur in Josephus or Philo. In a synagogue the conducting of public worship, reading of Scriptures, preaching, and public prayer were performed not by a professional class of officials but by lay synagogue members. The ruler of the synagogue, accordingly, was not a worship leader or a professionally trained scribe or rabbi but a lay member of a synagogue who was entrusted by the elders of the community with general oversight of the synagogue and orthodoxy of teaching. His responsibilities included building maintenance and security, procuring of scrolls for Scripture reading, and arranging of Sabbath worship by designating Scripture readers, prayers, and preachers. Ordinarily, a synagogue had only one ruler, but not always. Acts 13:15 speaks of at least two rulers in the same synagogue. In v. 22, however, "one of the synagogue rulers" should probably be taken to mean "one from the class of synagogue presidents." Inscriptional evidence from the first century A.D. ascribes the title to a surprisingly diverse lot of individuals, including individuals who bore Greek names and who wrote in Greek. Moreover, nearly two dozen Greek and Latin inscriptions dating from the first century B.C. onward from both Palestine and the Diaspora bestow the title on women, and even occasionally on children.[28]

---

27. For a discussion of the minor textual variants of v. 21, see Metzger, *TCGNT*, 84-85.

28. See E. Schürer, *History of the Jewish People*, 2.433-37; and J. T. Burtchaell, *From*

Mark preserves the name of the ruler of the synagogue as "Jairus."[29] In general, Mark does not burden his Gospel with proper names. Why he has chosen to include the name of Jairus is not entirely clear, but it is not impossible that Jairus was known to Peter in Capernaum and that his name owes its presence to a reminiscence of Peter.[30] On this occasion the ruler's posture and speech are not officious but desperate and pleading (7:25; John 11:32). Jairus "fell at his feet and pleaded . . . , 'My little daughter is dying. Please come." The daughter's condition is critical: the Gk. *eschatos echei* (NIV, "is dying") is a colloquialism for "at death's door" or "sinking fast."[31] Despite the fawning crowd Jesus shows himself to be interruptible, and he enters the desperation of this lonely parent (see 1 Kgs 17:17-24; 2 Kgs 4:17-37). "So Jesus went with him." In that simple statement, which recalls the equally simple description of Jesus' purpose in 1:38 ("This is why I have come"), Mark testifies to Jesus' commitment to minister to human need and to the inestimable worth of the human individual for Jesus.

Synagogue to Church: Public Services and Offices in the Earliest Christian Communities (Cambridge: Cambridge University Press, 1992), 240-46. On first-century Greek inscriptions, see *HCNT*, 316. The significance of the title "ruler of the synagogue" applied to women (and children) is difficult to assess. B. Brooten, *Women Leaders in the Ancient Synagogue: Inscriptional Evidence and Background Issues*, BJS 36 (Chico: Scholars Press, 1982), has amassed nearly two dozen inscriptions that refer to women as "head of the synagogue," "leader," "elder," "mother of the synagogue," "priestess," and "presiding officer." Exactly how these titles are to be understood is not yet clear. Brooten has been followed by many when she argues that such nomenclature is not simply honorific but functional, i.e., that women were *bona fide* rulers of synagogues. Burtchaell argues to the contrary that the titles were honorific, indicating only that women bearing such titles were married to men who were rulers of synagogues; and likewise that children bearing such titles were children of rulers of synagogues, but scarcely rulers themselves. Burtchaell reasons that Philo would not have been surprised that the Therapeutae admitted women into their Sabbath assemblies if there were Jewish women rulers of synagogues. Further, that "there was absolutely no participation by females in the Jewish priesthood, yet there are epitaphs of Jewish priests in the feminine." Finally, "how is it likely in a culture where women were legally forbidden to be counted as members of the worship fellowship, to study Torah, to join in the communal recitation of grace (and by many rabbis to read Torah in public), that women could have been officers of the community's public affairs?" Beyond the inscriptional evidence there is no indication that women acted as officers in synagogues. Given these facts and observations, there is reason to be cautious, and perhaps skeptical, that women (and children) were actual rulers of synagogues in ancient Judaism.

29. Two uncial manuscripts (fifth-century W and ninth-century Θ) and two minuscule manuscripts omit the name of Jairus from v. 22. Metzger discusses the omission in detail and rightly argues for the inclusion of the name (*TCGNT*, 85-86).

30. For the Palestinian-Aramaic roots of 5:21-42 and its historical reliability, see S. Sabugal, "La resurreccion de la Hija de Jairo (Mc 5,21-24a. 35-43 par.). Analisis historico-tradicional," *Estudio Agustiniano* 26 (1991): 79-101.

31. In the parallel account in Matt 9:18 the girl has just died.

25-26 With not a moment to spare, Jesus is forced to spare it, for there is another suppliant in the crowd. A woman with a menstrual hemorrhage, whose desperation is quieter but scarcely less urgent, moves unobtrusively toward Jesus in the jostling crowd (3:9; 4:1). In v. 29 Mark describes her condition as a *mastix*, a graphic expression meaning "whip, lash, scourge, or torment" (see Acts 22:24; Heb 11:36). The term combines physical suffering and shame, hence something akin to punishment. In a dramatic volley of Greek participles, v. 26 graphs the woman's condition precipitously: *having* a blood flow, *having suffered* from many doctors, *having exhausted* all her wealth, *having not improved* but *having gotten* worse. The same verse is equally emphatic and categorical: she suffered *much* from *many* physicians, exhausted *all* her resources, and gained *nothing*. Clearly, the woman's prospects are no better than the dying girl's.[32]

According to the Torah, a woman was unclean for seven days after her monthly period, but if she had a protracted gynecological problem, as does this woman, she remained unclean throughout its duration. Anyone who came into contact with her during menstruation would be banished until evening (Lev. 15:19-27). Josephus's testimony that "the temple was closed to women during their menstruation" (*War* 5.227) indicates that this particular Torah ruling was carefully observed in Jesus' day. Accordingly, a menstruating woman — and whoever touched her — was banished from the community until purification.[33]

27-29 Mark does not explain what was in the woman's mind as she attempted to touch Jesus. Particularly rulers in the ancient world were believed to possess power to bless those who touched them. Alexander the Great was often mobbed by crowds who "ran to him from all sides, some touching his hands, some his knees, some his garment" in hopes of being baptized with his aura and power.[34] Sometimes the approach was made with a more specific intent, for healing or fulfillment of a request.[35] The woman may have approached Jesus with a similar intent, perhaps mixed with superstition. Perhaps, however, she saw in Jesus something more than the aura of a ruler. She may have seen in Jesus a

---

32. In *The Golden Bough,* J. Frazer argues for the evolution of magic to religion, and religion to science. In this instance, however, Mark gives an alternative flow chart from science to religion!

33. 1QSa 2:2-4; *Bib. Ant.* 7; *Spec. Leg.* 3.32-33. Menstrual blood, along with other "fluxes" (semen, spittle, urine, and pus), rendered one unclean, a *zab* according to rabbinic tradition (*m. Zavim* 1–5).

34. Arrian, *Anabasis of Alexander* 6.13.3. So, too, Plutarch, *Life of Sulla* 35 (474 C). Both passages are cited from *HCNT,* 78.

35. Tacitus, *Hist.* 4.81.1, also cited from *HCNT,* 78.

representative of God who, like the altar of the tabernacle, would render holy those who touched him (Exod 29:37). That she reaches for his clothes may indicate that she associates him with the God of Israel, for the reference to clothing probably refers to the tassels on the corners of his outer garment worn by all observant Jews (Num 15:38-39; Deut 22:12).[36] Mark makes no judgment on her orthodoxy or lack thereof, however. Rather, he relates that she does the one and only important thing for a disciple to do: she "heard," she "came," she "touched" (v. 27).[37] To act on what one hears about Jesus is always in Mark the sign of a disciple, and this the woman does. In striking contrast to her deplorable straits in v. 26, Mark narrates the result of her action concretely and graphically in v. 29, which can be literally translated: "And immediately the flow of her blood was dried up and she knew in her body that she had been healed from her curse." As in the story of the man with the shriveled hand (3:1-6), in bringing her infirmity to Jesus she is healed.[38] Twelve years of shame and frustration are resolved in a momentary touch of Jesus.

30 At the same moment Jesus also knows "within himself," to translate the Greek literally, that healing has gone out from him.[39] An act of faith has occurred before the woman fully understands its meaning. Considering the woman's social stigma, Jesus' response to her is remarkable. Her being in public and touching him, both of which were viola-

36. The parallel passage in Matt 9:20 expressly mentions "tassels" (Gk. *ta kraspeda;* Heb. *ṣîṣit*). Tassels normally consisted of four woolen threads, three white and one blue, worn on outer garments by all observant Jews — priests, Levites, women, and even slaves, as reminders of the commandments of the Lord and Israel's election. See Str-B 4/1.277-92.

37. A majority of Greek manuscripts read that the woman "heard about Jesus," whereas a small but weighty number of manuscripts (א, B, C, Δ) read that the woman "heard what Jesus had done." Metzger (*TCGNT,* 86) opts for the former reading, suggesting that the latter reading is an "Alexandrian refinement." Context, however, may argue for the latter reading, for the woman appears attracted to Jesus' miracle-working ability, after which she hopes to escape unnoticed.

38. H. Kinukawa, "The Story of the Hemorrhaging Woman (Mark 5:25-34) Read from a Japanese Feminist Context," *BibInt* 2 (1994): 283-93, argues that the woman challenged Jesus' power, and that the true miracle would have been for Jesus to accept the woman as she was, even if bleeding. This interpretation seems incongruous with the narrative. The woman is not seeking recognition but help; she is desperate and frightened rather than seeking empowerment; and, finally, vv. 33-34 do not imply that Jesus' acceptance of the woman depends on her first being healed. Rather, he desires to meet a person, not simply to dispense a cure.

39. The second-century *Epistula Apostolorum* 5 paraphrases the story of the healing of the woman with a hemorrhage from the perspective of the disciples. V. 30 is rendered as "And [Jesus] answered and said to us, 'I notice that a power went out from me.'" The casting of the quotation in first person and the reference to "power" are reminiscent of gnostic tendencies in Christian traditions (*NTApoc* 1.253).

tions of the Torah, are not the subject of reprimands from Jesus.[40] Rather, she is the central figure of the story who tells "the whole truth" (v. 33), and thus she becomes the model of faith for Jairus![41]

31-34 Mark carefully singles out the woman from the multitude, perhaps to indicate that a true encounter with Jesus distinguishes one as a unique individual from the crowd. Jesus insists in knowing who touched him. The Greek verb of v. 32 implies that he *"kept* looking to see who had done this." The chance of finding the suppliant in such a large crowd exasperates the disciples, but ironically they are more out of touch with Jesus than is the woman. The persistence of Jesus in discovering who touched him rivals the woman's persistence in reaching Jesus. She wants a cure, however, a some*thing,* whereas Jesus desires a personal encounter with some*one*.[42] He is not content to dispatch a miracle; he wants to encounter a person. In the kingdom of God, miracle leads to meeting. Discipleship is not simply getting our needs met; it is being in the presence of Jesus, being known by him, and following him. Unable to evade Jesus' searching gaze, the woman "fell at his feet, trembling with fear." Her obsequious behavior reflects her humiliation from her long illness. Perhaps the public meeting with Jesus is as necessary to overcome her social ostracism as is his power to cure her physical disease. Her fear and trembling are not met with reproach or censure but with tender compassion (also 1:41), "'Daughter, your faith has healed you'" (cf. 2:5). The Greek word for "healed," *sōzein,* can mean either "heal" or "save" depending on context. The spoken Hebrew and Aramaic term behind it, *yashaw,* is actually a variant of the Hebrew name of Jesus, *Yeshua.* In a way the woman cannot yet know, the desire for healing and wholeness is the desire for Jesus. Jesus' final word to the woman is a veritable benediction, "'Go in peace.'"[43] In the statement

---

40. For the woman's violations of Torah purity prescriptions, see M. J. Selvidge, "Mark 5:25-34 and Leviticus 15:19-20: A Reaction to Restrictive Purity Regulations," *JBL* 103 (1984): 619-23.

41. According to later tradition, the woman's name was either Bernice or Veronica (*Acts of Pilate* 7; Eusebius, *Hist. Eccl.* 7.18). Eusebius claims to have seen a bronze statue of her in Caesarea Philippi, where she was reputed to have lived. Both sources above are late (fourth century A.D.), however, and exhibit legendary characteristics. If, by chance, they represent trustworthy tradition, the role of the woman in the Markan sandwich would be further enhanced, for a bronze statue of such an event would only be conceivable in a Gentile milieu. This would mean that the woman was a Gentile, in which case a Gentile woman's faith would be used by Mark as a paradigm of faith for a Jewish ruler of a synagogue!

42. The different intents of the woman and Jesus are good illustrations of M. Buber's distinction between "I-It" encounters and "I-Thou" relationships.

43. "Go in peace" was a Hebrew blessing (*leki leshalom,* 1 Sam 1:17; 20:42; 2 Sam 15:9; 2 Kgs 5:19; Luke 7:50; Acts 16:36; Jas 2:16; *Ep. Ap.* 51).

"'be freed from your suffering,'" the woman hears from Jesus' mouth what she has already experienced from his person. His word interprets her experience; again, Jesus' deed and word are one.

35-36 The drama now intensifies. While Jesus speaks with the woman, attendants of the ruler of the synagogue arrive to announce that his daughter has died. The interruption, so profitable to the woman, has cost the life of Jairus's daughter. Hope is now lost, and the inevitable conclusion follows, "'Why bother the teacher any more?'" The remainder of the story swings like the pendulum of a clock between the extremes of human despair and divine possibility. Jesus overhears the report of the attendants, but curiously he does not speak to the circumstances of the little girl's death. Mark's word choice for Jesus' hearing the report in v. 36 is masterful. The Gk. *parakouein* (translated in the NIV as "ignoring) has three distinct meanings: (1) to overhear something not intended for one's ears, (2) to pay no attention to or ignore, and (3) to refuse to listen or to discount the truth of something. All three meanings apply to Jesus in v. 36.[44] He does not rehearse what has happened, why, or what might have been. Instead, he speaks directly to Jairus. There is still one thing Jairus can do, but he must shift his focus from the circumstances of his daughter's death to Jesus himself. "'Don't be afraid; only believe.'" This is the challenge before Jairus, and before everyone who meets Jesus: to believe only in what circumstances allow, or to believe in the God who makes all things possible? One thing only is necessary — to believe. The present tense of the Greek imperative means to *keep* believing, to hold onto faith rather than give in to despair. With respect to his daughter's circumstances, Jairus's future is closed; but with respect to Jesus it is still open. Faith is not something *Jairus* has but something that has *Jairus*, carrying him from despair to hope. Jesus' authoritative word to Jairus is not to fear but to believe.[45]

37-40 Mark now returns to his insider-outsider theme. Only Peter, James, and John, Jesus' trusted inner circle of disciples, and the father and mother of the child, are allowed to accompany Jesus to the dead girl's side.[46] No one else is allowed to follow Jesus. Through dirge and dance

44. The ambiguity of *parakousas* led to its replacement by the more obvious *akousas* in a number of manuscripts. See Metzger, *TCGNT,* 87.

45. The second- (or third-)century *Acts of Thomas,* a gnostic Hellenistic romance, tells an apocryphal story of the apostle Thomas's visit to India, where he is thrown into prison for building a palace of good works rather than of stone for King Gundaphorus. As Thomas is delivered to prison, he quotes v. 36, "Fear nothing, but only believe."

46. The inner circle of Peter, James, and John among the Twelve bears a curious (though probably coincidental) similarity to the leadership of Qumran, where "in the Community council (there shall be) twelve men and three priests" (1QS 8:2).

the mourners have begun their doleful commentary on death in the house of Jairus. Mourners formed a professional guild in first-century Judaism and were required at funerals; "Even the poorest person in Israel should hire at least two flute players and one wailing woman," said Rabbi Judah a century later. The mourners, usually women, accompanied the bier from the house to the grave, clapping their hands together and wailing haunting laments.[47] When Jesus says the girl is but sleeping, lamentation turns to derision. "They laughed at him." The professional mourners represent the hard-core realists of every age who decide when empirical realities have foreclosed on divine possibilities.

Several commentators argue that the statement about the child's sleeping should be taken literally, that is, that this story is really about a resuscitation rather than a resurrection from the dead. Especially in the nineteenth century the miracle was rationalized as a "deliverance from premature burial" rather than a raising from the dead.[48] The statement is surely meant to be understood figuratively, however, for professional mourners were not in the habit of being deceived by comatose patients. The reference to sleeping may indicate to Jairus the way Jesus wants him to see the girl, and hence the way God would have us regard those who die in faith.

41-42   As with the hemorrhaging woman, hand and mouth, physical contact and spoken word, raise the child. *"Talitha koum"* is Aramaic; *talitha* is a feminine form of the word for "lamb" or "youth," and *koum* an imperative meaning "arise!"[49] The Greek translation indicates that

47. Str-B 1.521-23.
48. H. E. G. Paulus, *Das Leben Jesus als Grundlage einer reinen Geschichte des Urchistentums* (Heidelberg: C. F. Winter, 1828). Paulus, a thoroughgoing rationalist, believed in the impossibility of miracles and regarded the laws of nature as coextensive with God. See the discussion of his work in A. Schweitzer, *The Quest of the Historical Jesus*, trans. W. Montgomery (London: Adam and Charles Black, 1911), 48-57. For Paulus, the achievement of Jesus in the present story was the presentiment to know the girl was comatose rather than dead. In this Paulus essentially follows an ancient hermeneutic extending from Celsus (*On Medicine* 2.6) back to Apuleius of Madaura (*Florida* 19.2-6) and finally back to Pliny (*Natural History* 7.37), who applauded the Greek physician Asclepiades for recognizing by careful observation that a man carried in a funeral procession was actually alive. The Asclepiades tradition is only a distant parallel to the present story, however. Its purpose is to commend a wise physician rather than to appeal for faith in him; indeed, there is no role or necessity of faith in the Asclepiades tradition. The raising of Jairus's daughter, on the contrary, is about a dead child brought back to life. The tradition of Apollonius's raising of a young girl from "her seeming death" probably belongs in a similar category of heroic resuscitations (Philostratus, *Life Apoll.* 4.45; cited in *HCNT*, 203-4). The Apollinius traditions, which were produced by Philostratus in the third century A.D., were influenced at least in some degree by the Gospels.
49. F. Horton, "Nochmals *ephphatha* in Mk 7:34," *ZNW* 77 (1986): 101-8, is mistaken

167

Mark's first readers in Rome were not native Hebrew or Aramaic speakers, who otherwise would not need a translation. The Greek translation, "little girl," is endearing. The word *korasion,* a diminutive of *korē* (a stately young woman or maiden), indicates prime childhood, perhaps "little lady." Such nomenclature reveals the vast difference in Jesus' perspective of the girl from the mourners' perspective. References to the child's walking and eating attest to her total restoration. The effect of the cure on those who witnessed it is, as in earlier instances (1:28; 2:12), ecstatic. The Greek rendering of "completely astonished," *exestēsan ekstasei,* probably translates an infinitive absolute in Hebrew, thus reflecting an underlying Hebrew or Aramaic source. (For the **command to silence**, see at 1:34.)

What does Mark accomplish by sandwiching the woman's story into the story of Jairus? Jairus and the woman have only one thing in common: both are victims of desperate circumstances who have no hope apart from Jesus. Otherwise their stories diverge sharply. Jairus has a name and a position. As ruler of the synagogue, he has enough clout to summon Jesus to his house. The woman has none of these. Her name is not given (or remembered), and she has no position. Her only identification is her shame, a menstrual hemorrhage. She must approach Jesus from behind, whereas Jairus approaches Jesus face to face. Jairus, in other words, is a person of status and privilege. But in typical Markan irony, he does not hold an advantage regarding the one thing that matters. It is the woman who exemplifies faith, and in this respect their roles are reversed. Despite her embarrassing circumstances, she pushes through both crowd and disciples to reach Jesus. Her gender, namelessness, uncleanness, and shame — none of these will stop her from reaching Jesus. To this undaunted woman comes the healing and liberating word, "'Daughter, your faith has healed you; go in peace.'" When Jesus says, "'Don't be afraid; just believe,'" how should Jairus understand the command to believe? What kind of faith should he have? The answer is that he must have the kind of faith the woman has (v. 34)! The woman exemplifies and defines faith for Jairus, which means to trust Jesus despite everything to the contrary. That faith knows no limits — not even the raising of a dead child![50]

---

in arguing that *ephphatha* in 7:37 and *talitha koum* in v. 41 are magical commands. Neither expression is otherwise typical of exorcism commands. Both are plain Aramaic, relevant to their contexts, not secret magical spells. Moreover, the miracles of Jesus are not determined by the words he speaks but by the authority of his filial relation to God.

50. See J. R. Edwards, "Markan Sandwiches: The Significance of Interpolations in Markan Narratives," *NovT* 31 (1989): 203-5.

PROPHET WITHOUT HONOR (6:1-6A)

Jesus now leaves the Sea of Galilee to visit his hometown of Nazareth (1:9), some twenty-five miles to the southwest of Capernaum. Nearly four miles to the southwest of Capernaum, at Gennesaret, Jesus would have joined the major trade route that continued some seven miles further south to Magadan, and then west through the break in the precipitous cliffs of Arbel and up to the Horns of Hattin, where it bent southward to Nazareth.[51] The Via Maris (Way of the Sea), as the road was known, was the main route between the Mediterranean Sea and Damascus to the north. With the change in location comes a change in the tenor of the narrative. In the preceding stories Jesus has displayed lordship over nature, demons, and death. But among his own people in Nazareth he encounters misunderstanding and rejection. Heretofore the crowds are amazed at Jesus' authority (1:22; 5:20; 6:2), but in Nazareth it is Jesus who is amazed at their disbelief. The disbelief and opposition at Nazareth prepare for the Baptist's fate before Herod Antipas (6:14-29) and for Jesus' later fate before the Sanhedrin and Pilate (14:43ff.).

1 Mark's report that Jesus "went to his home town, accompanied by his disciples" is a classic description of an itinerant Jewish rabbi with his retinue of apprentice-disciples. About his hometown there is less to say. The apostle Paul could boast that his hometown of Tarsus was "no insignificant city" (Acts 21:39), but no such boast could be made for **Nazareth**. Nazareth is not mentioned in the OT, in Josephus, or in the rabbinic literature of the Mishnah and the Talmud. Outside the dozen references to it in the NT, it is first mentioned by an obscure writer, Julius Africanus, some two centuries after Jesus' birth. No church was built in Nazareth until the time of Constantine (A.D. 325). Archaeological excavations beneath the imposing Churches of the Annunciation and St. Joseph in Nazareth have uncovered a series of grottoes that date to the time of Jesus. The resultant picture is of an obscure hamlet of earthen dwellings chopped into sixty acres of rocky hillside, with a total population of five hundred — at the most.[52]

During Jesus' youth, Herod Antipas, tetrarch of Galilee, recruited artisans from surrounding villages for the construction of his capital at Sepphoris, about four miles north of Nazareth. Whether Antipas utilized the services of Joseph and Jesus we cannot say, although it seems doubt-

---

51. D. A. Dorsey, *The Roads and Highways of Ancient Israel* (Baltimore: Johns Hopkins University Press, 1991), 104.

52. On Nazareth, see J. Strange, "Nazareth," *ABD* 4.1050-51; J. Murphy-O'Connor, *The Holy Land: An Archaeological Guide from Earliest Times to 1700*[4] (Oxford/New York: Oxford University Press, 1992), 374-77.

ful.[53] That Jesus would have had at least some contact with Gentiles, in Nazareth or beyond, seems highly likely, however. For centuries after the Assyrian conquest of the Northern Kingdom in 721 B.C., Galilee had been converted to a predominantly Gentile populace, with a modicum of Jewish settlers entering the area only after the Maccabean revolt in the second century B.C. The Gospel of Matthew still referred to the region as "Galilee of the Gentiles" (4:15).

2-3 According to his custom, Jesus addresses his teaching "in the synagogue," that is, to the heart of the Jewish community. Jesus' wisdom and mighty works again captivate the townspeople. The reports of his extraordinary charisma and influence as a teacher are more significant than they might first appear. No people could boast of more prophets, learned scribes and rabbis, and savants than the Jews. The field in which Jesus distinguished himself as a teacher was, in other words, crowded and competitive. His prestige caused a dilemma for those acquainted with him, however, for he had not been apprenticed to a famous rabbi, nor could his wisdom be accounted for at home (John 7:15).[54] We read earlier of the amazement of the synagogue in Capernaum at Jesus' teaching (1:22). Nazareth is also amazed, but negatively. We have already noted an obstruction to Jesus' ministry in 3:21 that may have come from Nazareth. The present text follows in a similar vein. Rather than celebrating Jesus' success, the townspeople are skeptical and attempt to discredit his ministry. They do not refer to Jesus by name but with distance and suspicion, as "this man."[55] Moreover, "they took offense at him," they fail to honor him as a prophet (v. 4), and they exhibit an amazing "lack of faith" (v. 6).

The skepticism of Nazareth is most evident in v. 3: "'Isn't this the carpenter? Isn't this Mary's son?'" The earliest versions of this verse alter

---

53. The recent excavation of Sepphoris has prompted some scholars to emphasize its influence on surrounding villages like Nazareth, but the actual influence was probably minimal, at least on Jesus and his family. The NT never records Jesus going to Sepphoris or Tiberias, the other major Herodian center of Galilee. Village life was dominated by hard work six days a week, and Sepphoris lay beyond the one-thousand-yard limit for a Sabbath journey. E. P. Sanders, *The Historical Figure of Jesus* (London: Allen Lane/Penguin Press, 1993), 104, is probably correct in saying that "It is not likely that many residents of Nazareth spent much time in Sepphoris."

54. Not having studied with a rabbi then was like not having an academic degree today. "Even though a man has read Scripture and learned the Mishnah, but not served *talmidai hakamim* ('apprentice of a master'), he is an *am-ha'aretz* ('commoner')" (*b. Ber.* 47b). Further, see K. H. Rengstorf, *"mathētēs," TDNT* 4.434.

55. R. Gundry, *Mark,* 290, capitalizes on the contemptuous tone of the pronouns in vv. 2-3: "From where does this guy have these things? And what is the wisdom given to this guy and the miracles such as are taking place through his hands? This guy is the carpenter, isn't he, the son of Mary. . . ."

the wording, making Jesus neither a carpenter nor Mary's son, for example, "'Isn't this the carpenter's son?'" (Matt 13:55).[56] The Greek word for "carpenter," *tektōn*, literally means one who makes or produces things — usually of wood, but sometimes also of stone, hence a stonemason (2 Sam 5:11, LXX). Given the scarcity of wood and prevalence of stone in Palestine, it would not be surprising if Jesus' trade included stonework as well as woodwork.[57] In Jewish society there was absolutely nothing demeaning about manual labor. Hence, it was not an insult to call Jesus a carpenter. Among the duties a father owed his son, according to the Talmud, were circumcision, instruction in the Torah, teaching a manual trade, and procural of a wife.[58] But in the Gentile world — and this included the world of Mark's readers — designating Jesus a "carpenter" was not particularly complimentary and could have been regarded as an attempt to discredit him.[59]

Even more questionable is the expression "the son of Mary." Judaism was a patronymic culture. The name of a father attached to the name of a male child was as usual and necessary as is a surname today (e.g., Luke 4:22; John 6:42), and the father's name was retained, as is a family name today, even when the father was no longer living. The absence of Joseph's name in v. 3 may indicate that Joseph had died, although this is not as certain as many commentators suppose, for John 6:42 assumes that he is still alive. In Jesus' day men were occasionally called by the names of their mothers, particularly when the woman was the better-known

---

56. Luke 4:22 reads, "'Isn't this Joseph's son?'" (see also John 6:42). There were sporadic attempts to assimilate the text of Mark 6:3 to the wording of Matt 13:55, but the weight of textual evidence, including "all uncials, many minuscules, and important early versions," supports the reading of 6:3 as printed (see Metzger, *TCGNT,* 88-89). The tendency to refine Mark's wording argues in favor of the priority of Mark, for we can explain why, if Matthew and Luke follow Mark, they would endeavor to relieve possible offense to readers by altering Mark's wording, whereas we cannot explain why, if Mark follows Matthew and Luke, he would alter an acceptable reading to make it more offensive.

57. Justin Martyr, *Dial. Trypho* 88.8, however, says Jesus made "ploughs and yokes," thus understanding *tektōn* in the sense of carpenter.

58. Str-B 2.10-11.

59. The outspoken detractor of Christianity in the second century, Celsus, scoffed that the founder of the new religion was nothing but "a carpenter by trade" (Origen, *Contra Celsum* 6.34, 36). R. MacMullen, *Roman Social Relations: 50 B.C. to A.D. 384* (New Haven/London: Yale University Press, 1974), 107-8, 138-41, shows that occupations such as weavers and carpenters betrayed plebeian origins and were grist for "the range of prejudice felt by the literate upper classes for the lower." This judgment should not be unduly pressed, however. The snobbery of the elite patrician minority cannot be assumed of the broader populace as a whole, most of whom, like Mark's readers presumably, were also working-class people.

parent, and evidently without the opprobrium of illegitimacy attached to it.[60] In the OT, for instance, Joab, Abishai, and Asael are repeatedly (twenty-six times) referred to as "the three sons of Zeruiah" (2 Sam 2:18), who was David's sister (1 Chr 2:16). One suspects, however, that the name of Zeruiah owes its presence in this instance to her famous brother. Even the obvious narrative link with David is not sufficient to remove suspicions about the reference in the minds of most modern scholars.[61] In actual practice, calling a person the son of a woman, as the Nazarenes do here, was not normal in Judaism, and was almost certainly insulting. The claim of some scholars that calling Jesus "son of Mary" was tantamount to calling him a bastard is probably overstated,[62] but "son of Mary," along with the rebuff that Jesus otherwise receives at Nazareth (see vv. 5-6), is clearly questionable, probably disrespectful, and may even insinuate illegitimacy. Subsequent Jewish polemic will indeed accuse him of illegitimacy when, in answer to the Christian teaching of the virgin birth, it charges that Jesus was born out of wedlock, his mother having been seduced by a Gentile named Pandera.[63]

It is sometimes supposed that Mark's reference to Jesus as the "son of Mary" is an oblique reference to the virgin birth. This seems doubtful, however. Otherwise in Mark there is no reference to the virgin birth, nor does the present text attempt to explain Joseph's role in the family, as in Luke 3:23, for instance.[64] Moreover, the dismissive context in which "son of Mary" occurs scarcely comports with the honor of the virgin birth.

Along with Mary, mention is made of **Jesus' brothers and sisters**. The sisters are unnamed, which, according to Jewish custom, normally meant they were married. Of James, Joseph, Judas, and Simon, only James, who later headed the church in Jerusalem, and Jude are men-

---

60. See Tal Ilan, "'Man Born of Woman . . .' (Job 14:1): The Phenomenon of Men Bearing Metronymes at the Time of Jesus," *NovT* 34 (1992): 23-45. Also, P. Head, *Christology and the Synoptic Problem: An Argument for Markan Priority*, SNTSMS 94 (Cambridge: Cambridge University Press, 1997), 66-83.

61. "More might be involved than a narrative link with David." So P. L. McCarter, *Second Samuel*, AB (Garden City, N.Y.: Doubleday, 1984), 96.

62. E. Klostermann, *Das Matthäusevangelium*[2], HNT 4 (Tübingen: J. C. B. Mohr, 1927), 126; E. Stauffer, "Jeschu ben Mirjam: Kontroversgeschichtliche Anmerkungen zu Mk 6,3," in *Neotestamentica et Semitica: Studies in Honour of Matthew Black*, eds. E. Ellis and M. Wilcox (Edinburgh: T. & T. Clark, 1969), 19-28; F. W. Beare, *The Gospel According to Matthew: A Commentary* (Oxford: Basil Blackwell, 1981), 319.

63. *EncJud* (1971), 10.14-17. See also R. T. Herford, *Christianity in Talmud and Midrash* (London: Williams and Norgate, 1903), 112-15.

64. "[Jesus] was the son, so it was thought (*nomizein*), of Joseph" (Luke 3:23). Likewise, Justin Martyr, *Dial. Trypho* 88.8: "When Jesus came to the Jordan, being thought (*nomizein*) to be the son of Joseph the carpenter. . . ."

tioned again.[65] By the second century A.D. a reverence for the holy family, and especially for the sanctity of Mary, resulted in the brothers and sisters of Jesus being regarded as children of Joseph by a former marriage.[66] Both the Roman Catholic and Orthodox traditions, in dependence on creeds from the fourth century and later, call Mary "ever virgin" and follow the view that Jesus' siblings were half-brothers and half-sisters. Arguments that Jesus was an only child are based on later dogma, however. The plain sense of v. 3, and of the NT in general, is that Jesus was the oldest of five brothers and at least two sisters, all of whom were the natural children of Joseph and Mary.[67]

"And they took offense at him," says Mark. The word for "offense" comes from Gk. *skandalon*, meaning a "stumbling block." The verb (Gk. *skandalizein*) means to "cause to stumble," and in the present context to be "put off" or even "repelled" by Jesus. *Skandalizein* occurs eight times in the Gospel of Mark; in each instance it designates obstructions that prevent one from coming to faith and following Jesus.[68] A stumbling block to faith, a signature motif in Mark, is a grave problem. The "offense" of v. 3 verifies that the amazement of the people in Nazareth is not one of faith but of incredulity and opposition.

---

65. James: Matt 13:55; Luke 5:16; Acts 12:17; 15:13; 21:18; 1 Cor 15:7; Gal 1:19; 2:9, 12; Jas 1:1; Jude 1; Josephus, *Ant.* 20.200. Jude: Jude 1(?).

66. *Prot. Jas.* 9:2; and the *Gospel of Peter*, as quoted in Origen, *Comm. on Matt.* 10.17. R. Bauckham, "The Brothers and Sisters of Jesus: An Epiphanian Response to John P. Meier," *CBQ* 56 (1994): 686-700, suggests that "son of Mary" may have been intended to distinguish Jesus from the children of Joseph by a former marriage. This otherwise interesting suggestion is opposed by the context of vv. 2-3, however, which discredits Jesus. The meaning Bauckham suggests would scarcely have been a reason to "take offense at him."

67. In addition to the above references to James, the NT mentions Jesus' siblings in 3:32; Matt 13:55-56; John 2:12; 7:5. The argument that *adelphos* means "cousin" in v. 3 is unsustainable. The Greek has a distinct word for "cousin" (*anepsios*; e.g., in Col 4:10). Although neither Hebrew nor Aramaic had a word for "cousin," both customarily spoke of a cousin as "a son of an uncle" (Heb. *ben dod*; Aram. *bar dad*). Moreover, the LXX never translates either expression as "brother" or "sister." It is true that *adelphos* sometimes means more than a blood brother, e.g., Gen 29:12; Rom 9:3 (kinsman); Matt 5:22-23 (neighbor); Mark 6:17-18 (step-brother). In such instances the context must determine the meaning, but in 6:3 there are no indications that *adelphos* should be translated other than in its natural sense as "blood brother." Various arguments have been advanced to suggest that the James and Joses mentioned in 15:40 are not the same brothers mentioned in 6:3, nor the Mary mentioned there the mother of Jesus. See M. Barnouin, "'Marie, mere de Jacques et de Jose' [Marc 15.40]," *NTS* 42 [1996]: 472-74; R. Brown, *Responses to 101 Questions on the Bible* (New York: Paulist Press, 1990), 92-97; and J. Fitzmyer, *BRev* 7/5 (1991): 43. This latter question cannot be answered for certain, but in my judgment the context favors the view that the Mary, James, and Joses of 15:40, 47; 16:1 are the same individuals mentioned in 6:3. See further discussion of this issue at 15:40.

68. 4:17; 6:3; 9:42, 43, 45, 47; 14:27, 29.

4 In the face of disbelief and rejection, Jesus quotes a proverb that a prophet is honorable everywhere but at home. The idea and even wording of the saying were not uncommon in antiquity, including both Jewish and Greco-Roman contexts.[69] Jesus thus takes over a piece of wisdom current in his day and applies it to three concentric social circles in Nazareth: to his hometown, relatives, and his own house. Each of the circles becomes more restricted and more personal, extending to his own home. According to John 7:5, Jesus' own brothers did not believe in him during his ministry, and we hear of only James (and perhaps Jude) coming to faith after his death and resurrection. We saw in 3:19 that opposition to Jesus would infiltrate his chosen circle of apostles; here, too, it infiltrates his own home. Once again (3:31-35) Jesus' family are outsiders and he is a stranger in his own home. Thus, exposure to Jesus and the gospel is no guarantee of faith; indeed, apart from faith, exposure to the gospel inoculates as often as it enlivens.

5-6a Mark says openly that Jesus "could not do any miracles there."[70] Mark is more willing to ascribe unapologetic humanness to Jesus than any other Gospel writer. Unlike the later gnostic Gospels that kept Jesus untarnished by humanity,[71] Mark's Jesus walks the same road that peasants and tax-collectors walk, facing weariness (4:38), disappointment (vv. 5-6), ignorance (13:32), fear (14:34) — and even the inability to influence his own family.

The concluding accent falls on the townspeople's unwillingness to believe. We are again confronted with the mystery of the kingdom of God: some of those who have every opportunity to believe do not, and some who, like the Gerasene demoniac, would never be expected to believe do. No one can predict who will be insiders and outsiders, perhaps not even Jesus, "who was amazed at their lack of faith."

"Amazed at their lack of faith." What amazes God about humanity is not its sinfulness and propensity for evil but its hardness of heart and unwillingness to believe in him. That is the greatest problem in the world, and herein lies the divine judgment on humanity.[72] Humanity

69. In the NT: Matt 13:57; Luke 4:24; 13:33; John 4:44. Elsewhere: *Gos. Thom.* 31; *P.Oxy.* 31:1; Philostratus, *Life Apoll.* 1.354.12 (Letter 44); Plutarch, *Moralia,* "Exile," 7.13; Dio Chrysostom, *Discourses* 47.6.

70. Matt 13:58 shifts the failure from Jesus' inability to the townspeople's "lack of faith." This again argues for the priority of Mark, for we can easily explain why Matthew would alter Mark, but not the reverse.

71. Compare the fanciful accounts in the third-century *Acts of John* (93), where Jesus, whose "substance was immaterial and incorporeal, as if it did not exist at all," left no footprints in the sand.

72. In January 1982 I asked Helmut Thielicke if he could identify the worst evil he experienced in the Third Reich in Germany. His answer: "The unredeemed human heart!"

wants a spectacular sign of God, or, like the devil, a great display of divine power (Matt 4:1-11; Luke 4:1-13). But it does not want God to become a human being like one of us (John 1:11). The people of Nazareth see *only* a carpenter, *only* a son of Mary, *only* another one of the village children who has grown up and returned for a visit. If only God were less ordinary and more unique, then they would believe. The servant image of the Son is too prosaic to garner credulity. God has identified too closely with the world for the world to behold him, too closely with the town of Nazareth for it to recognize in Jesus the Son of God. Humanity wants something other than what God gives. The greatest obstacle to faith is not the failure of God to act but the unwillingness of the human heart to accept the God who condescends to us in only a carpenter, the son of Mary.

CHAPTER SIX

Witness to Jews

MARK 6:6b–7:23

Having been rebuffed at Nazareth (also Luke 4:29), Jesus begins his third preaching tour in Galilee, according to Mark (1:14, 39). In this tour he begins to shift responsibility to his disciples. Jesus had no intention of being a solo artist in the work to which God had called him. Rather, from the outset he called (1:16-20), designated (3:13-19), and taught (4:10-12) a select group of followers. In 6:7-13 he continues their training in a trial mission in which they go as his representatives or deputies, commissioned, empowered, and instructed by him.

All the stories in this section are set in the vicinity of the northwest shore of the Sea of Galilee. In addition to the mission of the Twelve, they include the feeding of the five thousand (6:31-44), the appearance of Jesus to the Twelve in the midst of a storm on the lake (6:45-52), a healing of the crowds (6:53-56), and a concluding conflict between Jesus and the Pharisees over "the tradition of the elders" or oral tradition (7:1-23). These stories form the final witness of Jesus in Jewish Galilee, for after the controversy with the Pharisees over the tradition of the elders in 7:1-23 Jesus quits the region, returning only intermittently and secretly before the final journey to Jerusalem.

THE COST OF DISCIPLESHIP (6:6b-30)

The mission of the Twelve is the defining theme of 6:6b-30. This is signified by another Markan sandwich, in which the martyrdom of John the Baptizer (6:14-29) is placed between the sending (6:6b-13) and return (6:30) of the Twelve. John the Baptizer was last mentioned at 1:14, when

176

Mark announced the commencement of Jesus' public ministry in conjunction with John's arrest. Mark has yet to report on John's fate at the hands of Herod Antipas. The fact that Mark inserts the execution of the Baptizer in the context of the sending and return of the Twelve on their first mission journey forces readers to consider what John's death means for discipleship and mission with Jesus.

6b-7 Jesus again embarks on a mission circuit, "teaching from village to village" (1:14, 39; also Matt 9:35). As earlier, the defining element of his ministry is teaching. Jesus is popularly conceived of as undertaking a ministry of "presence" or of compassion and healing. These were indeed important elements of his ministry, but they do not identify the dominant purpose of his ministry, which, according to Mark, was *teaching*. The doing of a deed, even the performing of a miracle, does not necessarily exact any commitment from those who behold them. They may, if they choose, remain simply impressed, without considering the possible significance of the event for their lives. Even if they consider the event further, they may be mistaken in its significance (e.g., 3:22). But teaching involves "the word" (2:2), which affords a clearer and more precise window into Jesus' person and mission, and with it the possibility of greater understanding and commitment.

With filial authority, Jesus summons and sends the disciples. Both summoning (Gk. *proskalein*; NIV, "calling") and sending (Gk. *apostellein*) defined the apostolic commission in 3:13-14 (see the discussion of terms there), and they are actualized in the present mission. Beyond what was said of "sending" at 3:13-14, we should add that there is little evidence that Jewish rabbis sent out disciples, as Jesus does here, in the name but without the person of their master. There were at least some efforts at proselytizing among Jews (Matt 23:15), but these appear to have been private initiatives rather than authorized by a commissioning body.[1] Thus, not only is Jesus unique in calling the disciples to himself as opposed to the Torah, but he is unique in *sending* them in his name and in his authority.

The sending of the Twelve appears premature and may catch us by surprise, for the record of the disciples to date has not been reassuring. Heretofore they have impeded Jesus' mission (1:36-39), become exasperated with him (4:38; 5:31), and even opposed him (3:21). Their perception

---

1. See K. H. Rengstorf, *"apostolos," TDNT* 1.418: "It must be emphasized most strongly that Jewish missionaries, of whom there were quite a number in the time of Jesus, are never called *sheluḥim* ["apostles"], and that in relation to them the words *shelaḥ* ["to send"] and *apostellein* ["to send"] play no part. Their work took place without authorization by the community in the narrower sense, and it thus had a private character. . . . Thus we cannot really speak of Jewish 'apostles' at the time of Jesus."

of Jesus has been — and will continue to be — marked by misunderstanding (8:14-21). The willingness of Jesus to abide the intractable nature and behavior of his followers is further testimony to his divine humility. The sending of these particular individuals — and at this stage of their understanding of Jesus — testifies to the beleaguered believers in Mark's church, indeed to believers of every age, that the fulfillment of the word of God depends not on the perfection or merit of the missionaries but on the authoritative call and equipping of Jesus.[2]

Sending the disciples in pairs conformed to Jewish custom (e.g., Eccl 4:9-10) and was continued in the early church.[3] Traveling in pairs was advantageous in several respects: it provided company and common counsel, and it augmented each partner with complementary gifts. It also benefited their hearers, for in the Jewish world "a matter must be established by the testimony of two or three witnesses" (Deut 19:15).[4]

Although the Twelve are sent to proclaim the gospel (v. 12), the accent in Jesus' instructions, according to Mark, falls on subduing evil spirits. The conferral on the Twelve of "authority over evil spirits" (3:15) clearly signals the inbreaking of the messianic reign. The authority with which Jesus has acted (1:27) and which was promised to the Twelve (3:13) is now made available to them according to the prophecy of *T. Levi* 18:12, in which the messianic high priest would "grant to his children the authority to trample on wicked spirits." The authority given the Twelve is an authority to *act*. Here as elsewhere in early Christianity there is no proclamation of the gospel without powerful deeds, and no powerful

---

2. The apostle Paul later reflects on this same paradox: "Brothers, think of what you were when you were called. Not many of you were wise by human standards; not many were influential, not many were of noble birth. But God chose the foolish things of the world to shame the wise; God chose the weak things of the world to shame the strong. He chose the lowly things of the world and the despised things — and the things that are not — to nullify the things that are. . . . It is because of him that you are in Christ Jesus" (1 Cor 1:26-30).

3. Acts 3:1ff.; 8:14ff.; 11:30; 12:25; 13:2; 15:39-40; 1 Cor 9:6. J. Crossan, *The Historical Jesus: The Life of a Mediterranean Jewish Peasant* (Edinburgh: T. & T. Clark, 1991) 335, suggests that "two by two" means an unmarried man and woman traveling together in Christian mission. Crossan virtually negates this suggestion by confessing, "I am utterly aware of how tentative that suggestion must remain." Not only tentative, indeed, but scarcely conceivable. There is no evidence whatever for his suggestion (1 Cor 9:5 means *wives*, not female consorts); unmarried women traveling with male partners would not only have besmirched the character of the woman, in particular, but hopelessly compromised the gospel. For a solid and readable refutation of the profile of Jesus advanced by Crossan and the Jesus Seminar, see G. A. Boyd, *Cynic Sage or Son of God?* (Chicago: Victor Books, 1995).

4. This same principle is presumably the reason why *two* witnesses, Moses and Elijah, appear to Jesus on the Mount of Transfiguration (9:4).

deeds without proclamation of the gospel.[5] The Twelve are not sent to do a new work but to continue and extend the work begun by Jesus (1:34; 3:11-12; 5:8). That even includes the places in which they minister, for they are not sent to urban centers like Tiberias or Sepphoris but to the "villages" (Gk. *kōmē*) where Jesus has been. The accent falls not on innovation but on the full representation of the one who commissioned them. Jesus bestows authority on believers so that they may participate in and further *his* ministry.

8-9 The mission instructions fall into two parts, with a report of the outcome appended in 6:12-13. The first set of instructions in vv. 8-9 concerns what to take. The Twelve are allowed a staff as a walking stick and protection against wild animals, a tunic and belt, and sandals for the stony road, but nothing more. Bread, knapsack, money, and even a second tunic must all be left behind. The prohibition against taking "an extra tunic" is in Greek direct discourse (second person plural) in an otherwise third person narrative and likely reflects Jesus' original command.

It is fashionable in some circles today to portray the early Jesus movement according to the model of radical Cynic philosophers and preachers who wandered the ancient world.[6] The mission instructions to the Twelve have often been viewed as evidence that Jesus emulated the ideal voiced by a younger contemporary, Musonius Rufus (A.D. 30-100), who advocated a life of asceticism and deprivation: "Wearing one tunic is preferable to needing two, and wearing none but only a cloak is preferable to wearing one. Also going barefoot is better than wearing sandals, if one can do it, for wearing sandals is next to being bound, but going barefoot gives the feet great freedom and grace when they are used to it."[7] The resultant picture of Jesus is that of a countercultural peripatetic who flaunts societal norms and encourages others to do so as well.

The correspondence of Jesus and his followers to wandering radical philosophers is a modern fantasy, however. There is, for instance, no evidence for the presence of Cynics in Galilee in Jesus' day. This fact alone goes a long way toward refuting the Cynic hypothesis. But there is further conclusive evidence against it. More than one scholar has unmasked the ideological agendum in those who ply the Jewish-Cynic argument.[8] A

---

5. E. Lohmeyer, *Das Evangelium des Markus*, 113.
6. See J. Crossan, *The Historical Jesus*, esp. chap. 4, and Part III, who sees Jesus and his followers as "hippies in a world of Augustan yuppies" (421).
7. *HCNT*, 81.
8. So H. D. Betz, "Jesus and the Cynics: Survey and Analysis of a Hypothesis," *JR* 74 (1994): 460: "Is not the aim of this entire venture to make sure that there was 'nothing unique' about [Jesus], that he was 'not a beginning' of anything, and that his identity simply was 'internal to the culture'? Removed from both Judaism and Christianity,

closer examination of Cynic dress, practices, and ideals reveals the correspondence between Cynicism and Jesus to be superficial, at best. The standard apparel of Cynic philosophers was a cloak, knapsack or travel bag (NIV, "bag"), and staff, but no shoes. The instructions to the Twelve, on the contrary, require staff, belt, sandals, and one tunic, but no travel bag. The differences in items are important, and not only because the recognizable Cynic travel bag is omitted. The four items required of the Twelve are, in fact, identical to the belongings that God instructs the Israelites to take on their flight from Egypt: cloak, belt, sandals, and staff in hand (Exod 12:11). The parallel in dress, in other words, is identical with the Exodus apparel but only loosely similar to Cynic dress. These four items of clothing recall the haste and expectation of the Exodus. They suggest that the mission of the Twelve announces something as foundational and revelatory as the Exodus from Egypt, and that the disciples must be as free from encumbrances as were the Israelites, to serve their God in a new venture.

The purposes of wandering Cynic preachers were foreign to Jesus not only in dress but also in teaching and instructions. Cynicism was essentially an attack on civilization. The Cynic preacher made himself uncouth and unkempt to protest the privilege and refinements of the patrician class, in particular. Above all, Cynicism sought emancipation from all forms of authority, and submission to nothing but the "royalty" of one's own conscience. For Cynics, itinerancy and lack of attachments were ends in themselves. This is quite different from the program of Jesus and his disciples. The mission of the Twelve is not a crusade against civilization, nor is it free from authority. The mission of the Twelve is not carefree nonattachment but fraught with danger, as we shall see in the subsequent story (vv. 14-29). It is participation in a new authority conferred by Jesus. Its minimal baggage is not itself a virtue but a means for greater service and dependence on God, and its purpose is not protest but rather proclamation of God's coming rule.[9]

The most startling particular in the mission of the Twelve is the instruction on what *not* to take. The journey on which Jesus sends them is

---

stripped of the traditions, and fitted into the 'social role' of a Cynic, the historical Jesus as a phenomenon to be interpreted has simply vanished."

9. See J. A. Draper, "Wandering Radicalism or Purposeful Activity? Jesus and the Sending of the Messengers in Mark 6:6-56," *Neot* 29 (1995): 183-202, in which Draper ably argues that the purposefulness of the mission of the Twelve distinguishes it from wandering radicalism. Moreover, he protests the stereotype and idealization of the term "peasant" in Crossan and others: "If New Testament scholars are to use this designation 'peasant,' then they will have to pay a lot more attention to what social anthropologists say about peasant societies and peasant behaviour."

unlike any other, for it must be made without an elaborate support apparatus and with only the barest provisions. The Twelve are not angels, so they need cloak, sandals, belt, and staff. The barest of essentials, however, ensures that they place their trust not in their supplies and training but rather than in the one who sends them. It would be like laying out on your bed everything you planned to take on a trip and then leaving everything but your coat and toothbrush behind. True service of Jesus is characterized by dependence on Jesus, and dependence on Jesus is signified by going where Jesus sends despite material shortfalls and unanswered questions. Like the Israelites fleeing Egypt (Exod 12:11), the Twelve must travel light lest worldly cares blunt the urgency of the message. Like Gideon's troops with their reduced numbers before the battle with Midian (Judges 6–7), they must go in dependency on God. Like birds of the air and lilies of the field (Matt 6:25-34), they must trust him alone who sends them. Jesus' severe instructions ensure that the Twelve seek not their own advancement but that of the gospel. If they go with an elaborate support system and provisions for every eventuality, then they need not go in faith, and apart from faith their proclamation is not believable.

10-11 A second set of directives concerns how to act. The Twelve are to be grateful guests by staying put where they are received. Trust in the Jesus who sends them into mission includes trust in those whom he has designated to meet their needs. Moving from house to house dishonors their hosts and creates invidiousness among them. If the disciples are rebuffed they are instructed to "'shake the dust off your feet when you leave, as a testimony against them.'" This is a searing indictment since Jews traveling outside Palestine were required to shake themselves free of dust when returning home lest they pollute the holy land.[10] This commandment is tantamount to declaring a *Jewish* village *heathen*. Jesus' reference to Israel by a Gentile figure of speech has the effect of desacralizing Eretz Israel, thus eliminating the presumption of salvation on the basis of ethnicity, nation, or race. Even in the Promised Land there will be those who reject the Promised One. "Not all who are descended from Israel are Israel" (Rom 9:6). Nevertheless, as v. 12 indicates, the purpose of the warning is not to damn but to induce repentance.

It is sometimes suggested that Mark's mission instructions do not originate with Jesus but reflect Christian mission practices of a later period. A comparison of the mission of the Twelve with the *Didache*, a manual of church instruction from the latter first century, does not sustain the

---

10. See Neh 5:13; Acts 18:6. For further references from the Mishnah and the Talmud, see Str-B 1.571.

suggestion, however.[11] The *Didache* is occupied with the question of true versus false prophecy, a widespread problem in early Christianity, particularly as Gnosticism made inroads into the church (so 1 John 4:1-3). This suggests that the *Didache* is fairly representative of early Christian mission concerns. Mark's description, by contrast, emphasizes the mission of the Twelve as representatives of Jesus. The Twelve are dependent on Jesus' authority, which corresponds with the ministry of Jesus in Galilee. T. W. Manson was doubtlessly correct when he declared that "the mission of the disciples is one of the best attested facts of the life of Jesus."[12]

12-13 The summary of the mission in v. 12 is a catalogue of favorite Markan terms: proclamation, repentance, casting out of demons, and healing. Preaching and repentance (see the discussion of both terms at 1:4 and 1:14-15), which were not included in the opening instructions in vv. 7-9, remind us that the apostolic mission was one of word and deed. Both realities also characterize the story of Jesus. New, however, is the anointing with oil, found in the NT only here and in Jas 5:14. Olive oil (Gk. *elaion*) was a staple of life in antiquity, serving as food, anointing, sacrifice, lamp fuel, and medicine. Rabbinic sources frequently cite the medicinal value of olive oil for curing illnesses as well as for exorcising demons.[13] In our passage anointing with oil is more than a means of healing but equally a sign of the inbreaking of the good news, an anointing with "the oil of gladness" (Ps 45:7).

The sending of reluctant and timorous disciples into mission is, on

---

11. The *Didache* preserves the following instructions regarding visiting missionaries:

(1) Those who teach false doctrine should not be received (11:2).
(2) A missionary who stays three or more days is a false prophet (11:4).
(3) An apostle who asks for money or more than bread to eat is a false prophet (11:6).
(4) Speaking "in a spirit" is not a sign of a true apostle unless the behavior of the apostle is genuine and godly; and no apostle who asks for food or money in a spirit is a true apostle (11:7-12).
(5) A traveling missionary who has no trade by which to earn a living should be avoided (12:3-4).
(6) A true prophet is worthy of the first fruits of field and flock (13:1-3).

The differences in particulars between the *Didache* and Mark 6:6a-13 are immediately apparent, as well as of frame of reference. In the *Didache* the instructions are to the community, whereas in Mark they are to the disciples.

12. T. W. Manson, *The Sayings of Jesus* (London: SCM Press, 1950), 73. On the historicity of the mission, see C. E. B. Cranfield, *The Gospel According to Saint Mark*, 201-3; and E. Schillebeeckx, *Jesus: An Experiment in Christology*, trans. H. Hoskins (London: Collins, 1979), 219-23.

13. Olive oil was prescribed for hip pains, skin diseases, headaches, and wounds. See Str-B 2.11-12; and H. Schlier, "*aleiphō*," *TDNT* 1.229-32.

the face of it, completely mistaken. Uncomprehending and ill-prepared disciples nevertheless typify believers in every age and place who are sent out by the Lord of the harvest. No matter how much exegesis, theology, and counseling one has studied, one is never "prepared for ministry." A genuine call to ministry always calls us to that for which we are not adequately prepared. It is only in awareness of such that the Christian experiences the presence and promise of Jesus Christ, and learns to depend not on human capabilities but on the one who calls and in the power of the proclamation to authenticate itself. "This brief description," writes Eduard Schweizer, "shows how important the genuineness of the proclamation is. Everything, even the poverty and simplicity of the messenger, indeed even the courage to be rejected, must conform to the Word that affirms that God is infinitely more important than all else."[14]

We now proceed to the center of the Markan sandwich in the martyrdom of John the Baptizer. There are only two passages in the Gospel of Mark that are not about Jesus. Both are about John, and both foreshadow Jesus (see 9:11-13). In the first (1:2-8) John is the forerunner of Jesus' message and ministry. The second (6:14-29), the passage before us, might be thought of as Mark's first passion narrative, for here John is the forerunner of Jesus' death. The parallels between the deaths of John and Jesus are especially clear.[15] Both John and Jesus are executed by political tyrants who fear them but vacillate and finally succumb to social pressure. In John's case Antipas acquiesces to Herodias, and in Jesus' case Pilate acquiesces to the mob. Both John and Jesus die silently as victims of political intrigue and corruption, "as sheep silent before their shearers" (Isa 53:7). And, most obviously, both die as righteous and innocent victims.[16]

John's martyrdom prefigures more than Jesus' crucifixion, however. It also exemplifies the consequences of following Jesus in a world of greed, decadence, power, and wealth. Mark sandwiches the brutal and moving account of the martyrdom of the Baptist between the sending of the Twelve (6:7-13) and their return (6:30) in order to impress upon his readers the cost of discipleship.

14-17 The account begins with "king" Herod's paranoia that John, whom he had imprisoned (1:14) and killed (v. 16), has returned in Jesus to haunt him. The story of John's death contains the names of several mem-

---

14. E. Schweizer, *Das Evangelium nach Markus*, 73.

15. Compare 6:17 and 14:46, 15:1; 6:19 and 14:1; 6:29 and 15:45ff.

16. The death of the Baptist is narrated in the simple aorist tense instead of Mark's preferred historical present, and there are several *hapax legomena* (words occurring only once in Mark) in the narrative, which is more cultivated than is characteristic of Mark. These observations may indicate a preformed narrative incorporated into Mark's Gospel. See Lohmeyer, *Das Evangelium des Markus*, 117-21.

bers of the Herodian family, and it will be helpful to identify them. The Herodian family tree was as twisted as the trunk of an olive tree. No fewer than four rulers bear the name "Herod" in the NT. The Herod of our story, Herod Antipas, was the second of the four, who ruled from the death of his father Herod (the Great) in 4 B.C. until A.D. 39. His official title was *tetrarch* of Galilee and Perea (Matt 14:1; Luke 9:7; Josephus, *Ant.* 18.109), although he popularly enjoyed the title "king" (Justin Martyr, *Dial. Trypho* 49.4-5; *Gospel of Peter* 1; *Acts of Pilate,* Prologue). "Tetrarch" (lit. "ruler of a fourth part" [of Palestine]) was the title given to Herod's sons who ruled over the four divisions of his kingdom after his death. Herod the Great (Matthew 2) had ten wives, Antipas being son of the fourth wife, Malthace. Herodias was the daughter of Aristobulus, Antipas's half-brother who was murdered by his father Herod. Herodias was thus a granddaughter of Herod the Great through his second wife, Mariamne I, and hence a niece of Herod Antipas.

Antipas is less infamous than Herod the Great largely because he was less able rather than less ruthless. It was not without reason that the early church mentioned Antipas's name *before* Pilate's when recalling the crucifixion of Jesus (Acts 4:27). Like his father, Antipas was shrewd, pitiless, and a lover of luxury, particularly of magnificent architecture. He built two cities in Galilee, Tiberias and Sepphoris. Jesus' reference to Antipas as "that fox" (Luke 13:32) bears eloquent testimony to the latter's cunning and malice. Antipas revealed his avarice when he persuaded Herodias, wife of his half-brother Herod Philip, son of Herod the Great's third wife Mariamne II (not the tetrarch Philip of Luke 3:1), to divorce her husband and marry him.[17] In order to marry Herodias, however, Antipas had to jilt his own wife, the daughter of Aretas, king of Nabatea east of the Dead Sea. In reprisal, Aretas inflicted a crushing defeat on Antipas in A.D. 36. Three years later Antipas and Herodias were banished to Gaul by the emperor Caligula.[18]

According to Mark, the growing reputation of Jesus was an uneasy reminder to Antipas that he had not silenced John's message by severing his head. "King Herod heard about this, for Jesus' name had become well known." Herod's hearing of Jesus follows immediately on the mission of the Twelve and may have been the result of it. Herod thinks of Jesus as John the Baptizer returned to life; or as Elijah, the forerunner of the Day of the Lord who in popular Judaism was a helper of the needy (further on Elijah, see at 1:6); or as one of the great prophets long silent. These were the three prevailing opinions of the day about Jesus (also 8:28). Although

17. Herodian family relations are explained in Josephus, *Ant.* 18.136-37.
18. For greater elaboration of these events, see Josephus, *Ant.* 18.109-19.

Jesus is not reckoned as the Messiah in the popular mind, he clearly ranks among the greatest figures of Israel. He is above all a prophet — and would suffer a prophet's fate (12:10-12). The glowing estimate of Jesus in v. 15 reminds us that holding a high opinion of Jesus is not the same thing as faith.[19] Considering Jesus to be Elijah or one of the prophets, or, as we hear today, to be the greatest person ever to have lived or the finest moral example of humanity, does not necessarily bring one a step closer to faith. Indeed, it may be a graver danger to faith, for it is easier to be content with a noble opinion that is wrong than with a base opinion that is wrong. Mark has already shown that familiarity with Jesus, even familial relationship with him, is of no ultimate advantage — and may, in fact, hinder faith (6:1-6a). It is nevertheless ironic that Herod, master of *Realpolitik*, apparently holds a higher opinion of Jesus than do his own relatives in Nazareth.

17-20 Mark now supplies the conclusion to the story of John's arrest that he mentioned in 1:14, and with which he identified the beginning of Jesus' ministry. Herod's association of Jesus and John shows that even in the common mind there was a correlation between the Baptizer and the Galilean Preacher. As "the stronger one to follow" (1:7), Jesus triggers Mark's flashback on John's execution. The treacherous marriage of Antipas and Herodias forms the backdrop for the death of the Baptist. According to Mark, Antipas imprisoned John for criticizing his marriage, which was forbidden by Jewish law (Lev 18:16; 20:21). Josephus also provides an account of John's death at the hand of Antipas, though a somewhat more political version, reporting that Antipas, fearing John's influence on the people, "decided to strike first and be rid of him before his work led to an uprising" (*Ant.* 18.116-19). The two accounts of Mark and Josephus look like two sides of the same coin, both attesting to John's righteousness and piety and Herod's paranoia and ruthlessness.[20] Mark chooses to emphasize the

---

19. Whether this was Antipas's personal opinion or opinion at large is difficult to say. Variants in the Greek manuscript tradition give both readings. It may be that Mark intends to reflect opinion at large (thus the pl. *elegon;* "they were saying"), for it can be explained why that reading would be altered to the third person singular *elegen* ("he was saying") to agree with the preceding third person singular *ēkousen* ("he was hearing"). See F. Neirynck, "ΚΑΙ ΕΛΕΓΟΝ en Mc 6,14," *ETL* 65 (1989): 110-18.

20. Compare Mark 6:17, 20 with Josephus, "For Herod had put [John] to death, though he was a good man and had exhorted the Jews to lead righteous lives, to practice justice towards their fellows and piety towards God" (*Ant.* 18.117). John's proclamation of the coming day of judgment (Matt 3:7-10; Luke 3:7-9) was doubtlessly a further irritant to Antipas. "If we combine Antipas' fear of insurrection (Josephus) and John's prediction of a dramatic future event that would transform the present order (the gospels), we find a perfectly good reason for [John's] execution" (E. P. Sanders, *This Historical Figure of Jesus* [London: Allen Lane/Penguin Press, 1993], 93).

moral charges that John brought against Antipas, whereas Josephus stresses the political fears that John aroused in him.

The Baptizer himself is merely a pawn in the events leading to his death. The story is entirely dominated by the personalities of Antipas, Herodias, her daughter Salome,[21] and the guests. Antipas, Herodias, and Salome are also fascinating studies in deviant psychology. Antipas is a house divided against himself. He cannot risk allowing John to remain free, but he cannot bring himself to eliminate him either. He even finds a certain fascination with his nemesis, listening with puzzlement and yet interest to an individual and message that he detests.[22] Antipas hopes to achieve an expedient end by doing a limited injustice. But like anyone who lives by such a philosophy, he can choose to do a limited act of injustice, but he cannot determine the greater injustice to which it will lead.

In this (as in other events in his life), Antipas's weakness of character and vacillating actions are exploded and exploited by Herodias. She is the prime mover in the story. In contrast to Antipas, who is shortsighted and impetuous, Herodias nurses her antipathy against John with shrewd and calculating patience, entirely willing to sacrifice even the honor of her daughter to achieve her design. T. W. Manson put it well, "Herodias felt that the only place where her marriage-certificate could safely be written was on the back of the death-warrant of John the Baptist."[23] Salome is merely an extension of her will, a compliant pawn in a game of intrigue and power. Salome, young and talented, is willing to sell her services to the highest bidder, without regard for their consequences.[24]

21. The daughter is unnamed in Mark, but Josephus identifies her as Salome, daughter of Herodias and Herod Philip, whom Herodias divorced to marry Antipas (*Ant.* 18.136).

22. Greek manuscripts are divided over the wording of the end of v. 20, some saying Antipas was "puzzled" by John, others that he heard "the many things he was doing." Diversity of external evidence favors the latter reading, but I am in some doubt whether it was Mark's original wording (so, too, B. Metzger, *TCGNT,* 89). The unusual contrast between puzzlement *(ēporei)* and gladness *(hēdeōs),* which would have prompted a scribe to alter the former for the banal *epoiei,* corresponds surprisingly well with Herod's cognitive dissonance in the account as a whole.

23. *The Servant-Messiah* (Grand Rapids: Baker Book House, 1977), 40.

24. Herodias's ambition and ruthlessness are further corroborated by Josephus. Of her liaison with Antipas and divorce of Herod Philip, Josephus says she took "it into her head to flout the way of our fathers" (*Ant.* 18.136). Following his defeat by Aratus of Nabatea, Antipas was goaded by Herodias to sail to Rome and receive from the emperor, Gaius Caligula, fortunes equal to those received by her brother, Agrippa I. "She never flagged till she carried the day and made [Antipas] her unwilling partisan, for there was no way of escape once she had cast her vote on this matter," says Josephus. The event backfired, however, and Caligula banished Antipas to Lyons in Gaul. To her credit, however, Herodias chose exile with Antipas rather than clemency from Caligula (*Ant.* 18.240-54).

21-23 Events come to a climax at a party thrown by Antipas. The exact translation of the Greek term *genesia* (NIV, "birthday") is disputed, meaning either the celebration of a birthday or the accession of a throne. Either translation is possible, but the custom of celebrating birthdays of princes is much better attested, especially in the Roman world where the emperor's birthday and the anniversary of his accession of the throne were public holidays.[25] We should not be surprised to see Antipas aping imperial custom, and "birthday" is the probable meaning of the term. The guest list includes the top brass and upper class of Galilee, "the high officials and military commanders and leading men." They — the wealthy, powerful, and prestigious — say not a word in the story, indeed do not need to, for their influence is greatest when unspoken. They are critical to the outcome of the story, however. For Salome they are a fawning audience; for Herodias, the leverage to force Herod's trembling hand; for Herod himself, a power bloc before whom every allegiance must be sacrificed.

This party ends not in gaiety, however, but in tragedy, in "great distress" (v. 26), and in death.[26] We can only imagine what kind of dance prompted Antipas to promise "up to half my kingdom" to Salome.[27] If Antipas meant the promise to be understood literally, it was a sham, for Rome would not allow him to part with an acre of land.[28] The promise,

25. E. Schürer, *History of the Jewish People*, 1.346-48 has a three-page-long footnote (#26) discussing the meaning of *genesia*.

26. As a symbol of sexual attraction and death, Salome has enflamed the (male?) imagination in both art and literature. See A. Bach, "Calling the Shots: Directing Salome's Dance of Death," *Semeia* 74 (1996): 103-26.

27. Mark refers to Salome only as "the girl" (*to korasion*). It is the same word Jesus used of the little girl in 5:41, meaning a young woman of statuesque beauty. The bewildering relationships within the Herodian family surface in the Greek wording of v. 22. Although it is not apparent in the NIV, several weighty Greek uncial manuscripts (א B D L Δ) identify the girl as *thygatros autou Hērōdiados* ("his [Herod's] daughter Herodias"). Although this is the more difficult reading, and therefore theoretically preferable, it is confusing to the point of meaninglessness. In v. 24 the girl is called the daughter of Herodias, not Antipas; and if she were the daughter of Herodias, it is difficult even in the Herodian family to imagine mother and daughter sharing the same name. The confusion in the reading is probably to be explained by the grammatical difficulty making the name Herodias possessive, which is already in the genitive case owing to the genitive absolute at the beginning of v. 22. Contra Metzger, *TCGNT*, 89-90, it seems advisable to opt for the reading *thygatros autēs Hērōdiados* ("the daughter of Herodias herself"), which is supported by several important uncials (A C K W) and many minuscule manuscripts, plus the Vulgate and Syriac versions.

28. The textual evidence for the inclusion in v. 23 of *polla* ("many things") is so evenly divided that it is nearly impossible to imagine whether it was original or not (see Metzger, *TCGNT*, 90). It *perhaps* should be accepted, since there is no reason for a scribe to have added it, and its omission might be explained by a scribe's desire to tighten the meaning of v. 23.

which is absent in Matthew's and Luke's version of the story, recalls a similar promise of King Xerxes to Esther that resulted in the unmasking of Haman's evil plot (Esth 5:3, 6; 7:2). Here the promise unmasks an equally evil plot, hatched not by Haman but by Herodias. "Up to half my kingdom" appears to be a figure of speech (see 1 Kgs 13:8), however, and cannot have been meant literally.

24-29 The whole scene reeks of treachery. Herodias's power over Antipas in plotting the death of John reads like Jezebel's power over King Ahab in persecuting Elijah and plotting the death of Naboth (1 Kings 19, 21). Family affairs in the Herodian line could supply the grist for a long soap opera series. Given the widespread decadence of the Herodian lifestyle, one is somewhat amazed that John bothered to challenge it in the first place. Should he not have played his hand in a more important game? John, however, was a prophet without price whose thundering call exposed unrighteousness in any quarter. Like the courageous prophets before him, John understood that the proclamation of God's word included moral responsibility. There were no sacred cows in his herds; he did not read the polls before speaking and acting; he protected no special interests; nor did he predicate what he said and did on chances of success. John's was a costly courage. In so doing, he risked a swift end, which eventually came from a cold sword wielded by petty functionaries.

Mark does not say where John was executed.[29] Josephus identifies the place as Machaerus on the austere heights east of the Dead Sea. Situated on the frontier between Arabia and Nabatea, Machaerus was one of Herod the Great's palace-fortresses that combined military defense with the opulence of "magnificently spacious and beautiful apartments," in Josephus's words (*War* 7.170-77; *Ant.* 18.119).[30] If John were beheaded at Machaerus — and there seems no reason to doubt it — the place name was sadly appropriate for the gruesome deed, for "Machaerus" derives from the Gk. *machaira*, "sword."

Mark focuses solely and dramatically on John's beheading. A suspensefully constructed v. 26 (not reproduced in the NIV) has Salome making her deadly request of Antipas by withholding the object of her desire until the very end of the sentence: "'I desire that you give me immediately on a platter the head of John the Baptizer!'" Stunned alike by the malevolence of the request and his own entrapment, the king never-

---

29. Nor does Justin Martyr, *Dial. Trypho* 49.4-5, who also summarizes John's martyrdom.

30. Herod the Great built and/or expanded a series of fortresses around the north shore of the Dead Sea for refuge in case the populace revolted against him. They included (from north to south) Alexandrium, Cyprus, Hyrcania, Herodium, Machaerus, and Masada. Machaerus was the only fortress east of the Jordan valley.

theless "beheaded John in prison" and brought "his head on a platter to the girl."[31] It is a bitter commentary on the inability of tyrants to tolerate righteous individuals — a fact no less true today than in John's day. The one whom Jesus called the greatest man born of woman (Matt 11:11) is sacrificed to a cocktail wager! The only act of decency in the account of John's martyrdom is the arrival of his disciples to give his body a proper burial. Like the "valiant men" of Jabesh Gilead who buried Saul and Jonathan (1 Sam 31:11-13), and especially like Joseph of Arimathea who will bury Jesus' body (15:42-47), John's disciples risk the wrath and recrimination of Antipas in honoring their slain leader.

30 Mark follows the martyrdom of the Baptizer with a one-sentence summary of the mission of the Twelve: "The apostles gathered around Jesus and reported to him all they had done and taught." Mark normally refers to Jesus' followers as "disciples" rather than as "apostles," which he does only here and at 3:14. "Apostles" may be accounted for in the present context as a specific link to the Twelve (apostles, so 3:14) who have returned from the mission of 6:6a-13. The report of their return, which one would expect after v. 13, has been placed following the death of John, producing an A^1-B-A^2 sandwich construction. What does Mark intend by bracketing the martyrdom of the Baptizer by the mission of the Twelve? The sandwich structure draws mission and martyrdom, discipleship and death, into an inseparable relationship. This is precisely what Jesus will teach in 8:34, "'If anyone would come after me, he must deny himself and take up his cross and follow me.'" There, as here, both words are addressed to disciples. Whoever would follow Jesus must first reckon with the fate of John. John's martyrdom not only prefigures Jesus' death, but it also prefigures the death of anyone who would follow him.

FEEDING THE FIVE THOUSAND (6:31-44)

Mark follows the account of Herod's banquet with a banquet of a very different sort. At this banquet Jesus presides. It is held not in a fortress or palace but in the open air and rolling hills of Galilee, and the invitation is not restricted to important people. Unlike Herod's banquet, the primary purpose of which was to bolster his position with the crowds, Jesus' banquet is not provided to boost his standing with the crowds but rather to minister to their needs, both perceived and otherwise. Jesus' compassion

31. In a wordplay on "head," the gnostic *Ap. Jas.* 6:30 (c. third cent. A.D.) says, "the head of prophecy was cut off with John."

on the multitudes and the manner in which he satisfies their needs are a dramatic contrast to Herod's self-serving and deadly party. Jesus' banquet became even more renowned in the memory of the early church than Herod's banquet. It is the only miracle recorded in all four Gospels, and its significance is signaled by a sequel in 8:1-10, two subsequent reflections in 6:52 and 8:17-21, and a final banquet in the Last Supper, of which the feeding of the five thousand is a foreshadowing (cf. 6:41 with 14:22).

31-32 The first prerequisite of discipleship is being with Jesus (3:14). The life of the disciple is not only mission for Jesus but also mission with Jesus. The enlisting of the disciples' services cannot usurp or eclipse their fellowship with Jesus. This latter truth is signified by Jesus' call to "'Come away with me by yourselves.'" The priority of Jesus' relationship with the Twelve is signified by the repetition in vv. 31-32 of two Greek phrases, *kat' idian* (NIV, "by yourselves/by themselves"), and *eis erēmon topon* (NIV, "a quiet place"/"a solitary place"). The latter phrase means a deserted or lonely place away from towns and villages. The gathering of the disciples to Jesus means that in the midst of business and busyness they are accountable to him alone. And the greater the demands on them, the greater their need to be alone with Jesus.

The reason they need to recuperate with Jesus is "because so many people were coming and going that they did not even have a chance to eat." This is a curious remark, for which there has been no preparation in the narrative. Mark has regularly noted the crowds around Jesus (e.g., 2:2), but the wording here is unusual and slightly more specific. Mark does not use his customary word for large crowd (Gk. *ochlos*), but rather another word meaning "many people" (Gk. *polloi*), perhaps even many *men*.[32] We shall revisit this phrase when we consider v. 44. Because of the commotion, Jesus and the Twelve withdraw from an undisclosed location on the western shore of the lake and go by boat to a deserted area.[33] Where the feeding of the five thousand occurred we do not know, but the hill country north of Capernaum and west of Bethsaida (see Luke 9:10) is a reasonable suggestion.[34]

33 The solitude Jesus and the disciples want they cannot have.

---

32. The masculine plural ending can denote either people in general or men specifically.

33. Boats were used not only to cross the lake but also and perhaps even more frequently to sail along the coast. See John 6:24-25 where a voyage from Tiberias to Capernaum is referred to as "the other side of the lake."

34. M. Nun, "The 'Desert' of Bethsaida," *JerusalemPersp* 53 (1997): 16-17, 37, offers insufficient evidence for proposing that "desert" means the green fields of Bethsaida rather than "wilderness."

Earlier the disciples had interrupted Jesus' need for privacy (1:35-39); now the crowd interrupts theirs. The crowd, seeing Jesus and the Twelve set off by boat, hurries overland to intercept them. The exact wording of v. 33 is uncertain in Greek, some manuscripts reading that the crowd gathered to the disciples once they landed, others that the crowd got there *before* them, and still others a combination of the two.[35] The manuscript evidence slightly favors the second reading, "before." If this is the correct reading, then we must reckon with a remarkable intentionality on the part of the crowd, anticipating Jesus' movements and awaiting his arrival. Either they suspect where Jesus will land, or Jesus veers the boat toward land when he sees the throngs along the shore.[36]

34 Despite the fact that the crowd interrupts Jesus' much-needed repose with the Twelve, Jesus looks upon it with "compassion." The Greek word for "compassion," *splangnizesthai,* is used in the NT only of Jesus, and here his compassion is expressed in "teaching them many things." They were to Jesus, reports Mark, "like sheep without a shepherd." Although this image elicits pictures of Jesus helping weak and helpless sheep (Matt 9:36), a pastoral connotation is not its primary connotation in Jewish tradition. As a metaphor, the shepherd of sheep was a common figure of speech in Israel for a leader of Israel like Moses (Isa 63:11), or more often of a Joshua-like military hero who would muster Israel's forces for war (Num 27:17; 1 Kgs 22:17//2 Chr 18:16; Jer 10:21; Ezek 34:5; 37:24; Nah 3:18; Zech 13:7; Jdt 11:19). It is, in other words, a metaphor of hegemony, including military leadership and victory. In his compassion, Jesus sees a whole people without direction, without purpose, without a leader. Jesus utilizes the opportunity to teach the people, but as is usual in Mark, it is not the content of the teaching but the one who teaches who is the focus of interest.

35-36 As distance grows with darkness, the disciples become uneasy. For the third time in the account of the feeding of the five thousand Mark notes the distance and desertion of the surroundings (Gk. *erēmos,* vv. 31, 32, 35). The theology of Jesus and the practical instincts of the disciples come to loggerheads (Luke 10:38-41). The disciples make what ap-

35. The difference in meaning depends on a single letter in Greek, i.e., *prosēlthon* ("they came to") and *proēlthon* ("they preceded"). Which reading is original cannot be said for sure, but probability favors the NIV reading "got there ahead of them" (see Metzger, *TCGNT,* 90-91).
36. The description of people gathering "from all the towns" (v. 33) again suggests a place along the northwest shore of the Sea of Galilee where several towns were located. A crossing to the eastern shore is unlikely. Not only was the distance too great to follow by foot (15-20 miles), but the Jordan is too high and swift in springtime to make a crossing feasible, especially by such a large crowd.

pears to be an imminently reasonable suggestion: dismiss the crowd and allow them to disperse among the surrounding villages to buy food and provisions. Given the lateness of the hour and number of people, even this suggestion had its limits, but it seems to them preferable to doing nothing and allowing a need to escalate into a crisis.

37 Rather than relieving the crisis, Jesus intensifies it: "'You give them something to eat,'" he orders. To their minds that is an unreasonable, if not impossible, command. As in the case of all the Lord's commands, however, they will in the end do exactly what he says, although they cannot now imagine how. The disciples consider buying food for the crowd, but whether they had the money to pay a two-hundred-denarii grocery bill is a question worth considering.[37] The disciples are swept away by the magnitude of the problem, just as Moses had been when confronted with the need to feed the Israelites in the wilderness (Num 11:13, 22).

38-40 Everything now depends on Jesus. "'How many loaves do you have?'" he asks. The disciples complain about what they lack; Jesus focuses on what they possess. The problem will not be resolved by something beyond them but by something from among them. Jesus sees possibilities where his disciples see only impossibilities, for God can multiply even the smallest gifts if they are made available to him.[38] Despite the pitiful resources, Jesus orders the crowd to sit in groups "of hundreds and fifties." Groups of such size made the crowd manageable enough to serve, but they may have had more than a utilitarian function. Moses had arranged the Israelites in groups of 1,000, 500, 100, and 10 under their respective leaders (Exod 18:25; Num 31:14), and similar formations were practiced at the Qumran community (1QS 2:21-22; CD 13:1). The arrangement certainly recalls God's miraculous provision for Israel in the wilderness, and it may hint at the eschatological gathering of God's people on the last day. Jesus presides over the multitude like a Jewish father over the family meal.

41 We are not told the content of his prayer, but we can imagine Jesus beginning with the words of the table prayer common to Judaism: "Praise be to you, O Lord our God, king of the world, who makes bread to come forth from the earth, and who provides for all that you have created."[39] Not surprisingly, the early church saw a parallel between the feeding of the five thousand and the Last Supper, both accounts of which

---

37. According to Matt 20:2 a denarius was a day's wage; two hundred denarii is thus nearly a year's wages.

38. A point emphasized in the apocryphal *Acts of John* 93: "every man was satisfied by that little (piece)."

39. Str-B 1.685.

contain the sequence of "taking bread . . . blessing . . . breaking . . . giving to the disciples" (cf. 14:22). The inability of the disciples to understand (6:52) does not prevent their *acting* on the command of Jesus, which is signified here in their mediating between Jesus and the crowd. The miracle that Jesus performs requires both human resources, inadequate though they are, and the disciples.

42-44 In typical Markan brevity and understatement, we are told, "They all ate and were satisfied." The word "all" is significant. Nowhere did the Torah and the oral tradition regulate Jewish life more than at table. The effect of kosher was to ensure that only proper foods that were properly prepared were eaten by the properly clean; unclean foods and unclean persons were necessarily excluded. At the wilderness banquet, however, the ritual hierarchy of kosher is abandoned in favor of an open invitation and inclusiveness of all people. "They *all* ate and were satisfied." The meal provided by Jesus does not tide them over until something more substantial can be had.[40] The bread of Jesus *satisfies* because it is an expression of his compassion, and it is given in such measure that there is a basket of leftovers for each of the disciples.[41] In conclusion, Mark notes that those who ate were "five thousand men." "Men" in this instance is gender specific. The Gk. *andres,* unlike the more usual *anthrōpoi,* is not inclusive of women and children; it means five thousand males. Matthew's wording underscores this fact by reading "five thousand men, besides women and children" (Matt 14:21).

The feeding of the five thousand is sometimes explained not as a true miracle of Jesus but as a triumph of sharing on the part of the crowd: Jesus' selfless spirit inspires an outpouring of generosity from the crowd that suffices for the needs of all. This interpretation makes the feeding of the five thousand into a moralistic story: when each shares what he or she has, there is enough for all. The moral is a good one, and is taught elsewhere in Scripture (e.g., Acts 2:44-45; 4:34-35), but it is neither the purpose of this story nor sufficient to explain the feeding of the five thousand. The facts of the story are clear. There are thousands of hungry people, and there are insufficient means of feeding them. Were there sufficient provisions among the crowd, the disciples, in their anxiety about the situation, surely would have known of them; or the provisions would have been broken out by now. Help is either nonexistent or distant, and

---

40. The second-century *Epistula Apostolorum* 5, in attempting to answer the claims of Gnosticism, spiritualizes the bread, making it a metaphor for the doctrines of the creed — Father, Jesus Christ, Holy Ghost, the church, and forgiveness.

41. BAG, 448, describes the basket *(kophinos)* as a "large, heavy basket for carrying things." Josephus (*War* 3.95) uses the word for the kind of basket in which Roman soldiers carried daily rations.

the hour is growing late. A problem of enormous proportions is rapidly developing into a crisis. It is Jesus, not the disciples or the crowd, who meets the need. Like the superabundant harvest in the parable of the sower (4:9, 20), the feeding of the five thousand supersedes any human harvest.

The feeding of the five thousand is one of the most familiar stories of the Bible, immortalized in children's Bibles and storybooks as a pastoral miracle of Jesus surrounded by children and happy families. This picture is a misleading stereotype of what appears to have happened in the Galilean hill country, however. Several clues in the account suggest something much less bucolic and idyllic, namely, the makings of a revolutionary uprising.

Rural Galilee was a stronghold of the Zealot movement (Acts 5:37). The Zealot movement was founded in A.D. 6 by Judas *the Galilean,* who hailed from Gamala in the hills to the east of Bethsaida (Josephus, *War* 2.118). Two of his grandsons, Menahem and Eleazar, perished in the battle for Masada in the early 70s of the first century (*War* 2.433; 7.253). Even before Judas, the independent sentiments of Galilee had resulted in stiff resistance against Herod the Great prior to his accession of the throne in 37 B.C., and when he died in 4 B.C. Sepphoris in Galilee revolted against the transferal of his throne to his sons. Josephus, who commanded the forces in Galilee in A.D. 66-67 against Vespasian, speaks of the valiant resistance of Galilee against the Roman invasion. Galilee — and particularly this part of Galilee which lay within eyeshot of Gamala — was, in other words, the spearhead of freedom movements against Rome, and particularly of the Zealot movement.[42]

Further clues in the account suggest populist and revolutionary sentiments within the crowd. The reference to "sheep without a shepherd" (6:34), is, as we saw, a predominantly military image. Mention of the "many people [who] were coming and going" (v. 31) is unusual, even suspicious, and suggests a clandestine movement afoot, especially if the "many" (Gk. *polloi*) is to be understood as predominantly or exclusively masculine, as are the five thousand "men" of v. 44. Also, if the verb of v. 33 reads "got there ahead of them," as we suppose, the context suggests a populist anticipation of Jesus. An unusual number of signs thus suggest that the wilderness commotion was aflame with messianic fervor, and that the crowd hoped to sweep Jesus up as a guerrilla leader.

---

42. On the origins and ideals of the Zealots, see M. Hengel, *The Zealots: Investigations into the Jewish Freedom Movement in the Period of Herod I until 70 A.D.,* trans. D. Smith (Edinburgh: T. & T. Clark, 1989), 56-59; and S. G. F. Brandon, *Jesus and the Zealots: A Study of the Political Factor in Primitive Christianity* (Manchester: Manchester University Press, 1967), 26-64.

These clues are confirmed in John's account of the feeding of the five thousand, where we are told that the people "intended to come and make him king by force" (John 6:15).[43]

It is nevertheless clear from the account that Jesus will not march to a populist and militarist drumbeat.[44] He will not be a militant-messianic shepherd of the sheep (so Isa 40:11; Mic 5:4; *Psalms of Solomon* 17). His model as host of the wilderness banquet is not that of Barabbas, a Zealot chieftain, but that of Moses. The repeated references to the wilderness (6:31, 32, 35) recall Israel's sojourn in the wilderness following the Exodus from Egypt; the multiplication of loaves (v. 41) recalls the gift of manna (Exod 16:14-15); and Jesus' leading the people as a shepherd (v. 34) recalls Moses' leading a fledgling nation. Like Moses (Exod 18:21, 25), Jesus divides the crowd into groups (vv. 39-40). The shepherd that this wayward flock needs is not a guerrilla Messiah but a Moses to teach them (Num 27:17) and a David to lead them (Ezek 34:1-31). It is their work that Jesus has come to fulfill.

In literature a "comedy" is a story that begins on a bad note and ends on a good one. The feeding of the five thousand is a true comedy, for all the problems at the beginning of the story are resolved in the end.[45] Even though there were five thousand men apart from women and children, "they all ate and were satisfied" — and there was a great quantity of leftovers. Moreover, Jesus ministers to the need *through* the disciples: it is from them that he receives the initial offering of bread and fish; they are instructed to settle the crowd into groups,[46] and they distribute the

43. See Manson, *The Servant-Messiah*, 70-71; more recently, J. B. Fuliga, "The Man Who Refused to be King (Matthew 14:13-21)," *AsiaJournTheol* 11 (1997): 140-53.

44. The feeding of the five thousand is a crucial text for those who believe that Jesus intended to be a political-militaristic Messiah. For example, Brandon, *Jesus and the Zealots*, esp. chaps. 5–7, argues largely on the basis of circumstantial evidence that Jesus was a Zealot sympathizer and that he was crucified as such by Rome. Evidence for Brandon's thesis is conspicuously absent, however. Had Jesus entertained political and military aspirations, the feeding of the five thousand was a golden opportunity to express them, for the crowd appears poised and prepared to conscript him as a messianic military leader. That Jesus refuses their overtures is strong evidence for his disavowal of the Zealot model of liberation. Not surprisingly, Brandon never refers to this passage!

45. The blanket dismissal of the historicity of the feeding of the five thousand by R. Pesch, *Das Markusevangelium*, 1.355 ("Der Erzähler greift nirgendwo erkennbar auf konkrete Überlieferung aus dem Leben Jesu zurück" [The narrator nowhere makes a recognizable reference to concrete tradition from the life of Jesus]), is wholly unwarranted. Particular references to the green grass, specific numbers in the story, the type of basket used, plus the populist Zealot undercurrent, all testify to a historical provenance of the story. It is hard to conceive of all four Gospels recording a story that was simply spun from OT motifs, as Pesch imagines.

46. A textual variant at v. 39 has Jesus himself seating the crowd into groups. *Ana-*

195

multiplied bread and fish to the crowd. The disciples are the hands of Jesus in the feeding of the five thousand. The miracle brings the divine will to perfect expression, for God wills to fill his creatures with himself, to meet their needs with his surplus, to expand their smallness by his greatness, and to transform mundane life into abundant life (John 10:10). The turning point in the story is traceable to the moment when Jesus looks on the crowd with *compassion,* desiring to fill it with the abundance of grace within himself. "From the fullness of his grace we have all received one blessing after another" (John 1:16).

THE "I AM" IN THE MIDST OF A STORM (6:45-52)

Mark 6:45-52 was the object of intense interest in post-Enlightenment lives of Jesus. Starting from the premise that the "laws of nature" are inviolable and that all things in the universe must be capable of rationalistic explanation, the most improbable and far-fetched theories were advanced to explain Jesus' walking on the Sea of Galilee. Albert Schweitzer's *The Quest of the Historical Jesus* (1906) documents the opinions of scores of scholars who judged this story an optical illusion caused by Jesus walking along the shore, or a deception caused by his walking on a sandbar. For solely rationalist interpreters, the story was a code to be cracked, a conundrum to be resolved. If Jesus walked on water, it was like Xerxes crossing the Hellespont or Alexander's siege of the island fortress of Tyre: solid underfooting had to be found somewhere. The effect of this preoccupation was to limit the possibilities of the story and virtually eclipse its meaning.

45-46 6:45-46 must be read in tandem with the conclusion of the feeding of the five thousand. "Immediately Jesus made his disciples get into the boat and go on ahead of him to Bethsaida, while he dismissed the crowd." There is an unmistakable urgency to this verse. The Gk. *euthys ēnankasen* is unusually forceful, meaning that the disciples were "compelled posthaste" to depart the scene. They arrived at the place of the feeding of the five thousand with Jesus, but now, when darkness is close at hand or already upon them, he hustles them away alone. Jesus wants to be rid of the disciples so he can dismiss the crowd by himself. Why?

---

klithēnai in the passive voice means "he commanded them that they all should recline by companies." A stronger field of manuscripts, however, attests to the active voice, *anaklinai,* which implies that Jesus instructed the disciples to cause the crowd to be settled. See Metzger, *TCGNT,* 91.

The answer follows from the clues in the feeding of the five thousand. The disciples are not unsusceptible to the messianic contagion of the crowd. The Gk. verb *ēnankasen* suggests that the disciples are reluctant to leave. The apparent sense is that Jesus must expeditiously remove them from the scene in order to persuade the crowd to disperse peaceably and thus avert a revolutionary groundswell (John 6:14-15).[47]

Having dismissed the crowd, Jesus retreats to the hills to pray. The mention of prayer in this context is a further clue of a messianic groundswell, for Mark notes Jesus praying at only three points in his ministry (1:35; 6:45; 14:35-39). Each prayer is at night and in a lonely place, each finds the disciples removed from him and failing to understand his mission, and in each Jesus faces a formative decision or crisis. Following the feeding of the five thousand, Jesus reaffirms by prayer his calling to express his divine Sonship as a servant rather than as a freedom fighter against Rome.

The feeding of the five thousand must have taken place in the hill country northwest of the Sea of Galilee, and if Luke 9:10 is an indication, somewhere west of Bethsaida. From the site of the open-air banquet, Jesus sends the disciples by boat across the northern part of the lake to Bethsaida (a similar crossing is noted in John 6:25).[48] Bethsaida, meaning "house of the fisher," was named for its chief industry and lay east of the mouth of the Jordan at the north of the lake in the tetrarchy of Philip.

47-50 The focus of the story now shifts from Jesus to the disciples. The "boat was in the middle of the lake, and [Jesus] was alone on land." Whenever the disciples are separated from Jesus in the Gospel of Mark, they fall into distress. Even in poor conditions the Sea of Galilee could normally be crossed in six to eight hours, but the disciples are helpless in the face of a hard wind blowing against them from the northeast. The description of the gale fits that of the well-known easterly known as the "Sharkia" (Arabic, "shark"), which usually starts in early evening and is good cause for apprehension among fishermen.[49] According to the NIV the disciples "were straining at the oars." The

47. See C. H. Dodd, *The Founder of Christianity* (London: Collins, 1971), 131-35.

48. The parallel accounts in Matt 14:22 and John 6:17 omit "Bethsaida," perhaps because of the rather trivial voyage from the site of the feeding of the five thousand to Bethsaida. The omission of difficult readings such as this argues for the priority of Mark. The voyage may be defended on two grounds, however: the disciples cannot leave their boat behind, and it is probably easier to sail past the mouth of the Jordan than crossing it by foot in spring when the water was high.

49. M. Nun, *The Sea of Galilee and Its Fishermen in the New Testament* (Kibbutz Ein Gev: Kinnereth Sailing Company, 1989), 52-54.

Greek word for "straining," *basanizein*, means "to torment." The word often means the torment of demon possession (Matt 8:6; Mark 5:7), but it can also refer to dire straits in other forms (contractions of childbirth, Rev 12:2; suffering in hell, Rev 14:10; or the torment of a righteous soul forced to live among the unrighteous, 2 Pet 2:8). In the present context, however, *basanizein* does not appear to carry connotations of demon possession but to depict vividly the force of the wind and waves against the disciples (4:37).

In their distress Jesus comes to them at "the fourth watch of the night," that is, between 3 A.M. and 6 A.M. In dividing the night into four watches Mark follows the Roman custom rather than the threefold Jewish division, ostensibly for the benefit of his Roman readers.[50] Jesus now looks on the disciples with the same compassion with which he earlier looked on the hungry crowds (6:34). Like Yahweh in the OT, Jesus comes to deliver his people in need, and the deliverance becomes a self-revelation. The centerpiece of the story is the description of his "walking on the lake . . . about to pass by them." There is no possibility of translating "walking on the lake" in any other way. The Greek preposition *epi (tēs thalassēs)* means "on," "upon," or "on top of" the water (just as the Gk. *epi tēs gēs* in v. 47 means "on land"). The phrase cannot be retranslated to avoid the problem of open water sustaining a human body. If such an attempt is made, the point of the story is forfeited, for in the OT only God can walk on water.[51] In walking on the water toward the disciples, Jesus walks where only God can walk. As in the forgiveness of sins (2:10) and in his power over nature (4:39), walking on the lake identifies Jesus unmistakably with God. This identification is reinforced when Jesus says, "'Take courage! It is I.'" In Greek, "'It is I'" *(egō eimi)* is identical with God's self-disclosure to Moses.[52] Thus Jesus not only walks in God's stead, but he also takes his name.

The latter part of v. 48 is not immediately clear, however. "He was about to pass by them" is baffling, suggesting that Jesus intended to walk past the disciples. In the OT, however, this nondescript phrase is charged with special force, signaling a rare self-revelation of God. At Mt. Sinai the transcendent Lord "passed by" Moses (Exod 33:22; also 33:19 and 34:6) in order to reveal his name and compassion. Again, at Mt. Horeb the Lord revealed his presence to Elijah in "passing by" (1 Kgs 19:11). The most important antecedent of the idea, however, comes in Job 9:8, 11:

---

50. Str-B 1.688-89. Mark names the four watches evening, midnight, cock crow, and dawn (13:35).

51. Job 9:8; 38:16; Ps 77:19; Isa 43:16; Sir 24:5-6, *Odes Sol.* 39:10.

52. Especially Exod 3:14, but also Exod 6:6; Isa 41:4; 43:10-11; 48:12.

> [God] alone stretches out the heavens
>   and treads on the waves of the sea.
> When he passes me, I cannot see him;
>   when he goes by, I cannot perceive him.

This quotation bears linguistic as well as thematic similarities with v. 48, for "treads the waves of the sea" contains the same wording as Mark (Gk. *peripatōn epi* [*tēs*] *thalassēs*), and the same crucial word for "pass by" (Gk. *parerchesthai* in the aorist; also in Exod 33:19; 34:6).

The Job quotation summarizes a passage that begins in 9:1ff. by recounting the awesome separation between God and humanity. God can do what humanity cannot do and can never conceive of doing. His wisdom is beyond compare, he moves mountains, shakes the earth, obscures the sun, arrays the heavens in splendor, and "treads on the waves of the sea." This God cannot be conceived of in human categories, and any "natural" explanation of his acts is foolish and pointless. The God described by Job is wholly God, wholly Other, and can never be confused with human beings.

When read from this perspective, the futility of trying to explain Jesus' walking on water by a "natural" phenomenon becomes apparent. The glory of the transcendent God who reveals himself in Jesus literally "passed by" the overconfident rationalistic theologians of a former generation — and those of our day who follow their lead. God "performs wonders that cannot be fathomed, miracles that cannot be numbered" (Job 9:10). But when Jesus "passes by" the disciples on the lake he does something differently from the revelation of God in the OT: he intends to make the mysterious and enigmatic God of Job visible and palpable as it had not been and could not have been to former generations. The God of Israel, majestic and awesome but unknowable face to face, is now "passing by" believers in Jesus of Nazareth. Jesus' walking on the water to his disciples is a revelation of the glory that he shares with the Father and the compassion that he extends to his followers. It is a divine epiphany in answer to their earlier bafflement when he calmed the storm, "'Who is this?'" (4:41). In this respect Mark's Christology is no less sublime than is John's, although John has Jesus *declaring* that he is the Son of God (John 10:36), whereas Mark has him *showing* that he is the Son of God. In Mark one must, like the disciples, be in the boat with Jesus and enter into the drama in order to behold who Jesus is. The one who calmed the storm is the one who now appears in the storm, the "I Am" of God.[53]

53. P. J. Madden, *Walking on the Sea: An Investigation of the Origin of the Narrative Account,* BZNW 81 (Berlin/New York: de Gruyter, 1997), argues that the story of Jesus walking on the water is a postresurrection story that has been retrojected into the minis-

The reaction of the disciples in the boat parallels their earlier consternation when Jesus quelled the storm on the lake (4:41). Once again they misperceive and misunderstand, shrieking in terror and mistaking him for a ghost. The word for "ghost" (Gk. *phantasma*) occurs in the NT only here and in the parallel in Matt 14:26. In classical Greek it means the appearance of a spirit or apparition, hence a "ghost."[54] Its rarity in the NT is a sanguine reminder that the supernatural world was neither a commonplace nor a comfort to the first disciples.[55] This speaks against the presumption that the vision is the result of superstition on their part. It should be remembered that the lake was where the disciples earned their livelihood; it was, in other words, not unknown and unusual for them but as familiar and ordinary as our own places of business are to us. The only other occurrence of the word as a verb is in Heb 12:21, where it refers to the awesome portents — fire, smoke, darkness, thunder — that accompanied the revelation of God to Moses on Mt. Sinai. In the rare occasions where apparitions are attested in Jewish literature they often occur in relation to the sea, which Jews regarded as a vestige of chaos, untamed and overwhelming.[56] *Phantasma* is thus a clue to the awesome appearance of Jesus walking on the water. It testifies that the empirical boundaries of the disciples have been broken.

51-52 Only when Jesus joins the disciples in the boat does the storm abate. Being *with* Jesus (3:14) is not simply a theoretical truth; it has practical and existential consequences, one of which is the safety and peace of disciples. If separation from Jesus brings the disciples into distress, Jesus' presence with them overcomes storms in their lives. The response of the disciples to their rescue by Jesus is one of perplexity and bewilderment, however. They are not only "completely amazed,"[57] but they

---

try of Jesus. The thesis of postresurrection retrojections into the life of Jesus is easier to assert (or assume) than to evince, and I do not follow Madden in this particular of his thesis. He is correct in noting, however, that what happens on the lake is incapable of being explained by naturalistic categories, and that various sea-walking narratives from pagan, Hellenistic, and Jewish sources pale in comparison to this account.

54. R. Bultmann/D. Lührmann, *"phantasma," TDNT* 9.6.

55. Contra J. J. Pilch, "Walking on the Sea," *BibToday* 36 (1998): 117-23, who asserts that experience of alternate reality was common to Mediterranean cultures. This generalization is not supported by the biblical material as a whole, where ghosts and apparitions are rare and unusual, and even the appearance of angels is not particularly common.

56. See the examples gathered in Str-B 1.691.

57. The Greek text behind "completely amazed" is uncertain. Although *existanto* ("amazed") is the shorter reading and thus theoretically preferable, and although the longer *existanto kai ethaumazon* ("amazed and marveled") may have been copied from Acts 2:7 (so Metzger, *TCGNT*, 92-93), the longer reading claims a stronger and more diverse array of manuscript support and is possibly original.

are bereft of understanding and "their hearts were hardened." Hardened hearts last appeared at the synagogue in Capernaum when Jesus healed the man with a deformed hand (3:5). There it occurred with reference to ostensible "outsiders" — members of the synagogue, Pharisees, and Herodians; here it occurs of "insiders," of Jesus' own disciples. Mark again (3:20-21) reminds us that faith is not an inevitable result of knowing about Jesus, or even of being with Jesus. Faith is not something that happens automatically or evolves inevitably; it is a personal decision or choice. In the Gospel of Mark it is more often than not a decision that must be made in the face of struggle and trepidation. Discipleship is more endangered by lack of faith and hardness of heart than by external dangers (3:5; 4:41; 5:17).

Some commentators suggest that Mark has formed the account of Jesus walking on the lake by combining two independent stories, a rescue story and an epiphany story. This conclusion runs contrary to the essential purpose of the story, however, which attests that it is in the midst of storms, hardships, and adversities that Jesus reveals himself to disciples. These two facets of trial and revelation combine to form a unified purpose, just as they did in the Exodus, where God disclosed himself as "I AM" (Gk. *egō eimi*, LXX) in the midst of Israel's oppression in Egypt. Jesus likewise declares himself "I Am" (Gk. *egō eimi*) in the storm on the lake. Mark will reassert this point supremely in chap. 15, where in the catastrophe of the cross the centurion recognizes Jesus as God's Son (15:39). In storms, adversities, and defeat, human self-sufficiency is revealed for what it is — human *in*sufficiency. When the defenses of human pride are breached, people sometimes see God's presence among them — even if it at first appears in troubling and perhaps terrifying ways.

THE MAN FOR OTHERS (6:53-56)

Mark concludes the events surrounding the feeding of the five thousand with Jesus' healing among the villages on the west side of the lake. This is a summary report, as evidenced by the fact that, apart from Gennesaret in v. 53, there are no proper nouns in the report. The "people" are not further identified, nor is "the whole region," nor "the villages, towns, or countryside." Mark reports that there is great commotion around Jesus, but he does not further specify who or what causes it. There are only two parties: Jesus and throngs of needy people. This is Mark's third summary report (1:35-39; 3:7-12), which again reminds readers that Jesus' ministry surpassed the particular stories included in this or other Gospels.

201

Throughout his Galilean ministry Jesus showed engagement and solidarity with crowds of suffering humanity.[58]

53 "When they had crossed over, they landed at Gennesaret and anchored there." This sentence is not a little problematic, and more so in Greek than in the above translation. The most natural translation of the verse would be: "And when they had crossed over on the land, they came into Gennesaret and anchored there."[59] The problem, of course, is that Mark has Jesus and the disciples "crossing on the land to Gennesaret" rather than crossing the sea to the land. This is another example of Mark's occasional awkward wording (see on 4:1), which must mean: "When they had crossed over, they beached the boats and came overland to Gennesaret."

A second problem with 6:53 is apparent to anyone who knows the geography of the lake. In v. 45 Jesus sent the disciples across the lake in the direction of Bethsaida. We do not know the exact location of the feeding of the five thousand, but the general vicinity appears to have been in the hill country north of Capernaum and west of Bethsaida. A boat crossing from there to Bethsaida leads due east (or perhaps slightly northeast) along the north coast of the lake. Gennesaret, however, lay some eight miles southwest of Bethsaida and some four miles south of Capernaum on the west side of the lake. Mark does not account for this triangular voyage. One way to make sense of it is to assume that the battering wind from the northeast (v. 48) blew the boat southeast in the direction of Gennesaret, where Jesus and the disciples then put ashore.[60]

---

58. C. P. Thiede, *The Earliest Gospel Manuscript? The Qumran Fragment 7Q5 and Its Significance for New Testament Studies* (Guernsey: Paternoster Press, 1992), 25-41, argues that the above-named Qumran fragment preserves a reading of Mark 6:52-53 in Greek. If true, this would necessitate dating Mark prior to the Jerusalem war (A.D. 66-70), at which time the Qumran community was wiped out by the Roman Tenth Legion. Unfortunately, the fragment has only twenty Greek letters on four or five lines, and of the letters only ten can be read with certainty. Given the illegibility of several letters, Thiede's reconstruction of the text is overly optimistic. Significant doubt remains whether the proposed text is, in fact, Mark 6:52-53. See rebuttals from G. Stanton, "A Gospel Among the Scrolls?" *BRev* 11/6 (1995): 36-42; and M.-E. Boismard, "A propos de 7Q5 et Mc 6,52-53," *RevBib* 102 (1995): 585-88.

59. Matthew 14:34 alleviates the problem of Mark's wording by rendering the sentence thus: "And when they had crossed over, they came on land to Gennesaret" (my translation). This improvement in wording again argues that Matthew knows Mark and occasionally improves his working.

60. S. H. Smith, "Bethsaida via Gennesaret: The Enigma of the Sea-Crossing in Mark 6,45-53," *Bib* 77 (1996): 349-74, following E. S. Malbon, *Narrative Space and Mythic Meaning in Mark* (Sheffield: Sheffield University Press, 1986), 27-29, argues that the problem of locations is a literary technique of Mark. Following Aristotle's *Poetics*, Smith suggests that failure to reach Bethsaida is a "plot suspension," signifying that until the disci-

54-56 Gennesaret (Heb. *Gennesar*) was a fertile plain three miles long by a mile wide on the west shore of the lake between Capernaum and Tiberius. It was the name of a town as well as a region, which was densely populated. Wherever Jesus puts his foot "in villages, towns, or countryside," the sick and needy clamor for his attention. The Gk. *krabbatos* (NIV, "on mats") refers to the mattresses or pallets owned by poor people and indicates that Jesus' influence is extended to the *am-ha'aretz*, the common and poor.

Unlike other healing stories in Mark, this one contains no teaching of Jesus, no dialogue with the ill, indeed no word from him at all. The accent falls on the throngs of people flocking to Jesus (see also 3:7-12; 3:20; 4:1; 5:21-31; 6:34). Their sole point of contact with him is begging "to let them touch even the edge of his cloak." "The edge of the cloak" again designates Jesus as an observant Jew (also 1:44; 5:28), for it refers to the tassels that Jews were commanded to sew on the four corners of their outer garments as reminders of the commandments of God (see at 5:28).

"And all who touched him were healed." This is a fitting conclusion to Jesus' ministry among the crowds from 6:31-56, for the last word, "healed" (Gk. *sōzō*), can mean either "healed" or "saved." The compassion of Jesus has fed, satisfied, and healed the crowds, but the blessings of his compassion raise the ultimate question whether those who experience them will enter further into Jesus' saving purpose. The physical blessings of Jesus are not an end in themselves, but a fork in the road, one branch of which leads to Jesus' final saving purpose, the other to a false understanding of Jesus as simply a wonder worker. Schlatter rightly notes, "In the zeal with which the people brought their sick to Jesus we recognize not only how deeply the untiring goodness of Jesus touched Israel, but also how distant Israel remained from Jesus, because it sought from him nothing but the healing of its sick."[61]

---

ples can accept the Gentile mission of Jesus they cannot reach the "other side." The fact that the disciples have already been to "the other side" in 5:1-20 should cast at least some doubt on this proposed interpretation, plus the fact that purely structuralist theories such as this reduce geographical place names to mere metaphors and allegories of deeper realities. Smith rejects the reasonable solution that the boat was blown off course by confidently stating that once the wind abated, "reaching Bethsaida would no longer have been a problem." I doubt that the situation seemed so simple to the disciples in the boat. After straining at the oars for the better part of the night, I suspect, they were happy to put in at Gennesaret rather than row another eight miles to Bethsaida.

61. A. Schlatter, *Die Evangelien nach Markus und Lukas*, 71.

RECOVERING THE TRUE INTENT OF THE LAW (7:1-23)

Jesus' confrontation with the Pharisees in 7:1-23 over the question of the oral tradition has no obvious connection to the preceding episodes. Placing stories together like bricks in a row with little if any editorial cement is not unusual in Mark. This particular unit shows signs of Mark's editorial hand throughout. The need to define "unclean hands" in v. 2, along with the parenthetical explanation of the Jewish custom of washing in vv. 3-4, would be quite unnecessary if Mark were writing to Jews. Passages such as these are unmistakable evidence that Mark is writing for non-Jews, and likely for Roman Gentiles. Mark's editorial shaping is further evinced by the reference to leaving the crowd and entering the house in v. 17, which typically allows Mark opportunity to clarify Jesus' teaching for the benefit of disciples and readers (2:1; 3:20; 4:10; 9:28; 10:10). An editorial hand may also be evident in the direct admonitions of vv. 14 and 18 ("'Listen to me, everyone, and understand this'"; "'Are you so dull?'"), which again underscore the dullness of the crowds and disciples (also 6:52; 7:17-21). Finally, the editorial addendum to v. 19 that "Jesus declared all foods clean" makes clear for Mark's Roman readers that the matters of ceremonial cleansing and kosher foods, so important to observant Jews, are not binding for followers of Jesus.

The editorial crafting of 7:1-23 has at least two purposes. One is to show the diametrical opposition between Jesus and the Pharisees on the question of the oral tradition. The oral tradition, which was the defining element of Pharisaic and rabbinic Judaism, is in the present pericope categorically nullified. The second effect is to underscore for Mark's readers the radical difference between Christians and Jews on questions of foods, cleansing, and the essential meaning of morality and what is pleasing to God. The difference between inner motives (v. 21) and ceremonial observances (v. 18) is honed to a fine edge in the present passage. This distinction will exert a defining influence in the early church, as is evinced in the story of Peter and Cornelius in Acts 10, or in Paul's teaching "that no food is unclean in itself. But if anyone regards something as unclean, then for him it is unclean" (Rom 14:14). In the framework of Mark's Gospel, the sharp cleavage between Jesus and the Pharisees on the oral tradition signals a cleavage between Jesus and Jewish Galilee as well, for henceforth Jesus quits the northwest quadrant of the Sea of Galilee and, apart from two subsequent appearances (8:11; 9:33), directs his focus to predominantly Gentile regions, and later to Judea and Jerusalem.

1 The account begins with the opposition of the Pharisees (last seen in 3:6) and scribes (last seen in 3:22). (On the Pharisees, see further at 2:18; on the scribes, at 1:22.) They again come from Jerusalem (3:22), which heretofore has been the primary source of opposition to Jesus, and which lay some ninety miles south of Capernaum. We cannot say for certain, but if Jesus quits Galilee *because of* this episode, then the dispute with the Pharisees is probably not an isolated dispute but a measure of wider opposition against him.

2-5 The conflict between Jesus and the Pharisees can best be understood by examining two points on which they differed. One is the idea of "**uncleanness**" (vv. 2, 5, 15, 18, 20, 23). Rituals concerning cleanness and uncleanness reflect rabbinic developments more than actual Torah prescriptions. According to the OT, only priests were required to wash before entering the tabernacle (Exod 30:19; 40:13; Lev 22:1-6); otherwise the washing of hands — the point of contention in v. 2 — was prescribed only if one had touched a bodily discharge (Lev 15:11). As Judaism's encounter with Gentile culture increased in the postexilic period, however, the question of ritual cleanliness took on new significance as a way of maintaining Jewish purity over against Gentile culture. This reached its extreme extent at the Qumran community described in the DSS. The physical separation and daily washings of the Qumran community cleansed its members not only from the defilements of Gentiles, Samaritans, and common folk *(am-ha'aretz)*, but also from other Jewish sects that for various reasons and in varying degrees were regarded as unclean, including Sadducees and even Pharisees and the Jerusalem temple. Next to the Qumran community, the Pharisees were the most scrupulous sect of Judaism with regard to matters of cleanness. Unclean for Pharisaic rabbis were any form of human excretion (spittle, semen, menstruation, etc.), women after childbirth, corpses, carrion, creeping things, idols, and certain classes of people, such as lepers, Samaritans, and Gentiles. This list implicates both Jesus and the disciples of several earlier violations of ritual uncleanness, since they have been with lepers (1:40), tax collectors (2:13), Gentiles (5:1), menstruating women (5:25), and corpses (5:35). Ritual washings were a means of cleansing and protecting observant Jews from the above defilements. (Further on the Pharisees, see at 2:18.)

It is important to understand that "cleanness" was not limited to or even primarily concerned with matters of hygiene, nor are distinctions between clean and unclean entirely understandable on the basis of rational explanation alone.[62] The Mishnah, for instance, declared that the Aramaic sections of Daniel and Ezra rendered the hands of anyone who

---

62. Note the judgment of Maimonides that the Talmudic laws of cleanness "are included among the arbitrary decrees." See *Mishnah Torah: The Book of Cleanness*, VIII. *Immersion Pools 11:12*, trans. H. Danby, *The Code of Maimonides, Book Ten: The Book of Cleanness* (New Haven: Yale University Press, 1954), 535.

touched them unclean, as did the Holy Scriptures themselves if they were translated into Assyrian. On the other hand, translating the Aramaic sections of Scripture into Hebrew made them clean (*m. Yad.* 4:5). This text is one of many instances indicating that "cleanness" was a ritual or cultic distinction as opposed to a practical or hygienic distinction.[63] To be sure, many Torah prescriptions regarding cleanness and defilement did promote hygiene, but the practical effects of avoiding germs or contagion was not their only, or even primary, concern. For moderns reared in a world of empirical realities, this may be difficult to grasp. One way to convey the power of the Jewish distinction between clean and unclean, perhaps, is to draw a parallel with authoritarian societies and organizations, where people avoid all contact with a person who is under suspicion or who has been fired, for example, so as not to endanger their own position.

Ideas such as these determine 7:2-5. For the sake of his Gentile readers, Mark spells out several types of cleansings.[64] The Pharisees recoil from Jesus' disciples, who eat without first washing their hands. The washing of hands before eating was expected of Jews, and during lengthy meals several hand washings might be required. The NIV translation of v. 3 avoids the special difficulty of *pygmē*, "fist," in the original Greek. This is the only instance in extant Jewish and Christian literature of washing the fist, and its meaning is particularly elusive.[65] Various suggestions have been advanced to explain it, including washing with a

63. Commenting on the distinction between cleanness and dirtiness, J. Neusner, *The Idea of Purity in Ancient Judaism,* SJLA 1 (Leiden: Brill, 1973), 1, writes: "If you touch a reptile, you may not be dirty, but you are unclean. If you undergo a ritual immersion, you may not be free of dirt, but you are clean. A corpse can make you unclean, though it may not make you dirty. A rite of purification involving the sprinkling of water mixed with the ashes of a red heifer probably will not remove a great deal of dirt, but it will remove the impurity."

64. On clean and unclean in the first century A.D., see Neusner, *The Idea of Purity in Ancient Judaism,* 32-71.

65. The oddity of "fist" is reflected in the manuscript tradition. Two uncial manuscripts (ℵ W) and several ancient versions read *pykna* ("often") rather than *pygmē* ("fist"). This makes better sense, but the vastly superior textual support for "fist," in early and diverse manuscripts alike, argues for its originality. T. C. Skeat, "A Note on *pygmē* in Mark 7:3," *JTS* 41 (1990): 525-27, argues that the term is a scribal error resulting from a corruption of the preceding *ean mē.* That would be a remarkable scribal blunder. Str-B 2.13-14 rejects the reading of "fist" on the grounds that washing hands in the form of a fist is unknown in Jewish literature. While this is true, it is an argument from silence, for Jewish literature does not prescribe whether the hand should be open or closed in washing. See the full discussion in R. Guelich, *Mark 1–8:26,* 364-65, who favors the meaning "with cupped hands." Ritual hand washings in modern Judaism and Islam, incidentally, tend to be done with a closed rather than open hand.

handful of water, washing hands while clenched as fists, or rubbing the fist of one hand into the hollow of the other. Which (if any) of these is correct can only be guessed. The first hypothesis may be slightly preferable on the ground that unclean hands are a "first-grade uncleanness" (e.g., *m. Yad.* 3:1), that is, one that can be cleansed by a minimal amount of water — perhaps the amount held in "cupped hands" (*m. Yad.* 2:1).

Graver "second-grade impurities" could only be cleansed by thorough immersion in water. Returning from the "marketplace" would ostensibly incur a second-grade uncleanness, where contact with various unclean things and people would render one unclean. This may be the meaning of the unusual word for "washing" in v. 4 (Gk. *baptizesthai/ baptismos*), which literally means "baptizing."[66] Second-grade uncleanness required more thorough cleansing, hence immersion, perhaps scrubbing. The concept of transference of uncleanness from an object to a person in contact with the object rules the thought of v. 4, "the washing of cups, pitchers, and kettles." Several factors contributed to whether an object was clean or unclean. A curved or cupped surface that could contain something within it — such as the objects above — could become defiled and needed washing, whereas a flat surface could not.[67] Also, surfaces and substances that were porous (e.g., pottery) were susceptible to uncleanness, whereas hard surfaces (metals, uncut stone, glass) were usually clean. A number of Greek manuscripts add "beds" in v. 4 to the list of objects needing washing.[68] Although beds may appear surprising in the list of objects, a bed was a soft surface that accepted impurities (discharges from men; menstrual flow from women, Lev 15:4, 20). Unless washed and cleansed, the bed defiled anyone who sat on it or came into contact with it.

To modern readers the cleansing of objects listed in 7:2-5 may appear exaggerated. Some may even suspect Mark of anti-Jewish polemic. Neither appears to be the case, however. A variety of evidence from the first century essentially corroborates the Pharisaic obsession with purity as described by Mark. Jacob Neusner notes that the dominant trait of Pharisaism before A.D. 70, as depicted in both rabbinic traditions and the Gospels, concerns conditions regarding ritual purity.[69] It is worth remem-

---

66. The two major uncial manuscripts (**א** B) read *rhantisōntai* ("sprinkling") rather than *baptisōntai* ("dipping/immersing"), but the number and diversity of manuscripts favoring the latter reading virtually assure its originality.

67. Schürer, *History of the Jewish People*, 475-78.

68. Omitted in the NIV because several very important manuscripts (p^{45} **א** B L Δ) lack the word. The evidence of the manuscripts that omit the reading is considerable. On the other hand, the unusualness of the word in the list of objects argues in favor of its inclusion, as do a respectable field of uncials, minuscules, and especially church fathers.

69. Neusner, *The Idea of Purity in Ancient Judaism,* 65.

bering that fully twenty-five percent of the Mishnah is devoted to questions of purity.[70] Archaeological excavations continue to discover Jewish *mikwa'ot* or cleansing pools that were a standard feature of Jewish homes and settlements in the first century (see Mishnah, tractate *Mikwa'ot*). *Mikwa'ot* have even been uncovered on the summit of Masada, one of the most arid places on earth.

The contention between Jesus and the Pharisees over clean and unclean was, however, only symptomatic of a deeper cleavage, the crux of which concerned the **"tradition of the elders"** (vv. 3, 5, 8, 9, 13). In distinction from the Sadducees for whom the written law of the Torah alone was authoritative, Pharisees accepted the evolving *oral* law as equally authoritative (Josephus, *Ant.* 13.297). Along with the above cleansing rituals, the oral tradition also became more pronounced after the close of the OT. Indeed, the accusation of the Pharisees and scribes in v. 5 that Jesus' disciples ate with unclean hands could not have been made or sustained on the basis of the Torah, but only on the basis of oral tradition. By Jesus' day, adherence to the unwritten oral tradition was as important for the Pharisees as was adherence to the Torah itself. Although the claim cannot be sustained from the OT itself, rabbis promoted the idea that Moses had received *two* laws on Mt. Sinai, the written Torah and the oral Mishnah. The Mishnah was believed to preserve an unbroken chain of authorized tradition extending from Moses to the "Great Synagogue" of Jesus' day (*m. Avot* 1:1-13). The Mishnah called the oral interpretation "a fence around the Torah" (*m. Avot* 3:14) — "fence" being understood as preservation of the integrity of the written law by elaborating every conceivable implication of it. In general, the Torah was understood as *policy.* Its commandments declared *what* God decreed, but not always *how* they were to be fulfilled. The Torah alone, according to advocates of the oral tradition, was believed to be too ambiguous to establish and govern the Jewish community. The oral tradition as preserved in the Mishnah, on the other hand, prescribed in infinite detail how the intent of the Torah ought to be fulfilled in actual circumstances.[71]

The rigor of the oral tradition was an indication of the seriousness with which Pharisees intended to uphold the Torah. The oral tradition, at least in theory, intended to express the intent of the law and extend it to matters of everyday life. In practice, however, "the tradition of the elders" tended to shift the center of gravity from the intent of the Torah to an increasing array of peripheral matters that either obscured or per-

---

70. *Ibid.*, 8.
71. On the role and significance of the Mishnah in relation to the Torah, see the material gathered in *HCNT*, 100-104.

verted that intent. It is this latter effect that falls under Jesus' withering critique in vv. 6ff.

6-9 The sarcasm of v. 6 (and v. 9) in the NIV is also present in the original Greek: "You have a fine way of setting aside the commands of God in order to observe your own traditions." When Jesus refers to the Pharisees as "hypocrites," he takes a term from the theater meaning to play a part on stage. Especially in Greek theater, actors wore various masks according to the roles they impersonated. The word "hypocrite," accordingly, comes to mean someone who acts a role without sincerity, hence a pretender. The quotation from Isa 29:13 (LXX) rightly defines "hypocrite" as one who voices lofty and even noble sentiments that are divorced from the intentions of the heart. People who do this "'worship me in vain,'" according to the quotation. The result of the pretense is that "'their teachings are but rules taught by men,'" thus idolatry, that is, the replacement of the divine by the merely human. With regard to the oral tradition, the Pharisees substitute interpretations of the law for the law it-self, indeed interpretations at variance with the intent of the law.

It would be a mistake to assume that in calling the Pharisees "hypo-crites" Jesus accuses them of lack of dedication. In the judgment of both Jesus and Mark they were gravely mistaken in the course they pursued, but they were not, as far as we can tell, either superficial or uncommitted. On the contrary, it was their commitment to the oral tradition — and Je-sus' equal commitment to recovering the intent of the written law — that made their differences so earnest. They may, to return to the metaphor of "hypocrite," confuse drama with reality, but they do so with vigor and rigor — and hence are the more dangerous because of it.

In 7:8-9 Jesus sets the oral interpretation in acid contrast to God's will. The "tradition of the elders" (vv. 3, 5, 8) is declared "*your own* tradi-tion" (vv. 8, 13) in contrast to the revealed "commandments of God" (vv. 8-9) or "the word of God" (v. 13). The verbs in v. 9 are more concrete and forceful than in the NIV translation. The Pharisees do not simply "set aside" God's commandments, that is, favor something in their place; they "reject" (Gk. *athetein*) them by making a conscious choice *against* them. Again, the NIV says that the Pharisees do this in order "to observe your own commandments." If the Gk. *stēsēte* is the proper reading in v. 9, then it is more definite and stronger: the Pharisees do this to erect (*stēsēte*) or cause something to stand in the place of the Torah.[72] Moreover, the pres-

---

72. The NIV's "observe" follows the reading *tērēsēte*, which is contained in an im-pressive group of manuscripts (ℵ A B [*tērēte*] K L X Δ Π), whereas the reading *stēsēte* is at-tested by fewer uncials (D W Θ), no minuscules, and various fathers and versions. On the whole, it would appear that *tērēsēte* is the preferable reading (contra Metzger, *TCGNT*, 94).

ent tense of the Greek verbs in vv. 8-9 implies that the Pharisees *continue* to uphold human traditions and *continue* to reject the commandments of God. The oral tradition is thus exposed and censured as a willful substitution of human contrivance for the word and will of God.

10-13 Not only is it a human contrivance, but it is also a distortion of the law. The example of "Corban" brings Jesus' critique of the oral tradition to concrete expression. The commandment to honor parents illustrates Jesus' radical divergence from the rabbis. The fifth commandment in the Decalogue is "Honor your father and mother" (v. 10; Exod 20:12; 21:17; Lev 20:9; Deut 5:16). But *you,* says Jesus, sidestep it by the contrivance of Corban. Jesus appeals to the original ruling of Moses in order to correct the oral tradition gone awry, that is, he is making the Decalogue a "fence against the rabbinic tradition," as it were. Not unlike the reference to *"your* tradition" in v. 9, the "you" of v. 11 is emphatic in Greek, implying that the interpretation of the Pharisees is not a faithful development of the law of Moses but a perversion of it, something other than the commandment itself. Corban, from the Hebrew word for "offering," was a rabbinic custom derived from the practice of devoting particular goods to the Lord as specified in Lev 27:28 and Num 18:14. Mishnah tractate *Nedarim* ("Vows") develops the general policy of devoting specific goods to the Lord into an elaborate panoply of rulings and regulations. Corban was similar to the concept of deferred giving. Today a person may will property to a charity or institution at his or her death, though retaining possession over the property and the proceeds or interest accruing from it until then. In the case of Corban, a person could dedicate goods to God and withdraw them from ordinary use, although retaining control over them himself. In the example of v. 11, a son declares his property Corban, which at his death would pass into the possession of the temple. In the meantime, however, the son retains control over the property — and his control deprives his parents of the support that otherwise would have been derived from the property in their old age. T. W. Manson's description of the practice is particularly trenchant: "A man goes through the formality of vowing something to God, not that he may give it to God, but in order to prevent some other person from having it."[73] This was not the end of the matter, however. Once property had been offered to God, priests discouraged anyone from withdrawing it from Corban in order to return it to human use. According to Josephus, priests required fifty shekels from a man, and thirty from a woman, to cancel Corban (*Ant.* 4.73). The practice of Corban resulted in egregious casuistry by annulling

---

73. *The Teaching of Jesus: Studies of Its Form and Content* (Cambridge: Cambridge University Press, 1951), 317.

a moral commandment of the Torah (honor of parents) by a ritual practice of the oral tradition (Corban). A concrete and unambiguous moral good, "'Honor your father and mother,'" is not simply thereby nullified but actually reversed by *forbidding* a child to do "'anything for his father or mother.'"[74]

The spate of second person plural pronouns of 7:12-13 reveals that in promoting Corban the rabbis are knowingly perpetrating a moral casuistry. "'Then *you* no longer let him do anything for his father or mother. Thus *you* nullify the word of God by *your* tradition that *you* have handed down.'" Corban is not simply a bad apple in the barrel, whose removal would salvage the whole lot. Rather, it typifies a comprehensive perversion promoted by the attitudes and methods of the Pharisees and scribes. "'And *you* do many things like that,'" says Jesus (v. 13). The verb "do" (Gk. *poieite*) is present tense, signifying that Corban is not an anomaly but standard procedure among Pharisees.

14-16 The wholesale perversion of the Torah by the oral tradition is met with a sharp and urgent appeal by Jesus. "'Listen to me, everyone, and understand.'" The verb for "listen" (Gk. *proskaleomai*) occurs nine times in Mark in the context of solemn pronouncements.[75] Mark again emphasizes that faith and understanding result from *hearing*. The Jews were fully agreed that eating forbidden or defiled food contaminated one and necessitated a cleansing bath (Lev 17:15). But Jesus reverses the direction of flow: it is actually *inner* impurities that defile things outside. Addressing the original accusation that the disciples were eating with unwashed hands (v. 2), Jesus pronounces that "Nothing outside a man can make him 'unclean' by going into him. Rather, it is what comes out of a man that makes him 'unclean'" (see Matt 23:25).[76] This simple pronouncement actually assumes the rabbinic theory that interior spaces

---

74. The Mishnah records a ruling similar to vv. 10-12 (though reversing the roles of father and son): "If a man said to his son, '*Konam* be any benefit thou hast of mine!' and he died, the son may inherit from him; [but if, moreover, he said] 'both during my life and at my death!' when he dies the son may not inherit from him and he must restore [what he had received from his father at any time] to the father's sons or brothers; and if he has nothing [with which to pay] he must borrow, and the creditors come and exact payment'" (*m. B. Qam.* 9:10). On the question of Corban, see Str-B 1.711-17. The Mishnah tractate *Nedarim* is replete with examples similar to vv. 10-12, in which persons and property are exempted from their usual functions simply by the utterance of "Konam" (a reverential substitute for "Corban").

75. 3:13, 23; 6:7; 7:14; 8:1, 34; 10:42; 12:43; 15:44. All but the last are pronouncements of Jesus.

76. This pronouncement is preserved in the *Gospel of Thomas* 14: "For what will go into your mouth will not defile you, but what comes out of your mouth, that is what will defile you."

were the most susceptible of defilement and thus most in need of cleansing.[77] In a brilliant reapplication and extension of his opponents' guiding principle, Jesus applies the theory of vessel defilement to *persons*, as if to say, "If the inside of vessels contaminates them, how much more so the inside of persons?" Uncleanness and defilement are matters of intention and the heart, not the violation of cultic rituals and formalities.[78]

17-19 The importance of this ruling is underscored by a private audience with the disciples in v. 17. Mark commonly places moments of divine revelation in a house, removed from the interference and mixed motives of the crowds. This convention is accentuated by an alliterative contrast in Greek: Jesus "left the crowd (Gk. *ochlos*) and entered a house (Gk. *oikos*)" (v. 17). The disciples are again impervious to the truth, however. Jesus appeals to them in exasperation, "'Are you so dull? Don't you see . . . ?'" Their failure to understand is not the result of stupidity, nor are they in need of enlightenment by means of esoteric instruction, as in Gnosticism. Their lack of perception is related to a false understanding of "this parable" (v. 17), similar to that of the outsiders in 4:12.[79] A parable cannot be understood from the outside but only by entering into it and seeing the reality that depicts from within. The disciples are like a dog looking at the pointed finger of its master rather than the object to which the finger points. They are like people looking at the stained-glass windows of a cathedral from the outside. Their sight and understanding are correspondingly dull and lifeless.

The understanding of the law that Jesus desires is not related to physical sight or to mental awareness but to the "heart" (v. 19). The heart is the center of human personality, the *will*, whose separation from God was bemoaned in the Isaiah quotation of v. 6: "their heart is far from me." For the benefit of those who cannot see but need to know, Jesus explains the imagery. Food may enter the mouth, but it all ends up in the same place. Mark understands Jesus thereby to declare all food clean. This is a revealing editorial insertion, for Mark seldom steps on stage as an actor in his drama. On the rare occasions (e.g., 3:30) when he does so his inter-

---

77. With regard to vessels, *m. Kel.* 2:1-7 expounds the general theory that a flat surface is normally clean, whereas a hollowed surface or receptacle is susceptible of uncleanness. See Schürer, *History of the Jewish People,* 2.476-77.

78. A majority of Greek manuscripts includes v. 16 after v. 15: "'If anyone has ears to hear, let him hear,'" although the verse is omitted by manuscripts of the Alexandrian tradition (א B L Δ). Manuscript evidence thus argues in favor of including the verse. Nevertheless, the decision to omit v. 16 is probably justified on the assumption that the verse was a scribal gloss from vv. 9 and 23. See Metzger, *TCGNT,* 94-95.

79. On similarities between 7:14-23 and Mark 4, see E. S. Malbon, "Echoes and Foreshadowings in Mark 4–8: Reading and Rereading," *JBL* 112 (1993): 218.

pretations should be accorded special significance. When Mark wrote his Gospel, questions related to kosher foods and dietary regulations were prominent in the minds of converts to Christianity, particularly from paganism (e.g., 1 Corinthians 8). Less than a decade earlier, in all likelihood, Paul had also addressed the question of clean and unclean foods at Rome (Romans 14–15), the probable location of Mark's Gospel. Mark's parenthetical declaration that "all foods [are] 'clean'" (v. 19) thus reveals his understanding of Jesus' position on the matter of clean versus unclean foods. This declaration takes precedence over the dietary regulations of both the oral and written laws (e.g., Leviticus 11; Deuteronomy 14).[80] Again in Mark, the teaching of Jesus is supremely authoritative, superseding the Torah itself. Similar to the earlier pronouncement on the Sabbath (2:27-28), in presuming to render a definitive judgment on a matter of divine revelation, Jesus assumes the role of God.

Rabbis frequently catalogued infractions of legal observances, but Jesus catalogues the deeper evils of the heart. The list in 7:21-22 shows a definite pattern in Greek. The first six terms occur in the plural, denoting evil *acts*. The first is "sexual immorality" (Gk. *porneia*), which can be found in Greek literature with reference to a variety of illicit sexual practices, including adultery, fornication, prostitution, and homosexuality. In the OT it occurs for any sexual practice outside marriage between a man and woman that is prohibited by the Torah. This sense is retained and intensified in the NT, which "is characterized by an unconditional repudiation of all extramarital and unnatural intercourse."[81] Subsequent terms in the list are generally self-explanatory: "theft, murder, adultery, greed, malice." The final term (Gk. *ponēria*) is less specific than the preceding terms, meaning simply "evil" or "wickedness."

The last six terms occur in the singular, denoting evil *attitudes*: "deceit, lewdness, envy, slander, arrogance, and folly."[82] All twelve terms are lodged in the evil thoughts of the heart, thus illustrating the point of the

80. B. Pixner, *With Jesus Through Galilee*, 77, suggests that the editorial interpretation of v. 19 was added "because Jesus was planning to leave Galilee, in order to spend a longer period of time with his disciples among the Gentiles." This understanding is commendable for its attempt to locate the saying in Jesus' historical ministry, but it appears to relegate the interpretation to a simple strategy on Jesus' part, and perhaps to reduce it to only temporary validity. On the contrary, the wording and placement of v. 19 give the pronouncement of Jesus definitive and final authority over food laws.

81. Hauck/Schulz, "*pornē*," *TDNT* 6.579-95.

82. Cranfield, *The Gospel According to Saint Mark*, 241, notes that the word for "greed" (*pleonexia*), which follows "adultery," often in the NT denotes sexual sins such as lust (Eph 4:19; 5:3; Col 3:5; 2 Pet 2:3). "Envy" translates "evil eye," a common rabbinic expression for envy and covetousness. The contrasting virtue of goodwill was known as the "benevolent eye."

parable in v. 15, that real defilement is what emits from the heart (see Matt 6:23). "All these evils," Mark concludes, "come from inside and make a man 'unclean.'" That restates the conclusion of the parable of v. 15, which in turn identifies the "commandment of God" (v. 8) and "word of God" (v. 13) with the essential matters of the heart. It is precisely the heart that the tradition of the elders fails to address, and because of this it fails to represent either the commandment or the will of God.

7:1-23 are the longest conflict speech in the Gospel of Mark. The length of the section is a clue to its importance. Mark labors to clarify that the essential purpose of the Torah, and hence the foundation of morality, is a matter of inward purity, motive, and intent rather than of external compliance to ritual and custom. The controversy thus cannot be interpreted as a case for Christian antinomianism but rather for the recovery of the true intent of the Torah. "Uncleanness" can no longer be considered a property of objects but rather a description of inner attitudes, a condition of the heart. The goodness of a deed depends not solely on its doing, but primarily on its *intent*. The judgment of Jesus stood in sharp contrast to that of the Essenes, for whom purity was determined by allegiance to the community; and also in contrast to that of the Pharisees, for whom purity consisted of a directory of observances and proscriptions. The approaches of the Essenes and Pharisees leached the law of its intended purpose and resulted in attempts to establish human substitutes for divine judgment and grace (Rom 10:3). Jesus, on the contrary, and not the "traditions of men," is able to declare what is pleasing to God. Mark profiles Jesus as the one who, in contrast to the oral tradition, is the true revealer of God, for Jesus can produce the inner transformation that the law requires but cannot effect.

CHAPTER SEVEN

Witness to Gentiles

MARK 7:24–8:9

Following the controversy with the Pharisees over purity matters and the oral tradition in 7:1-23, Jesus embarks on a long and circuitous journey through Tyre (7:24), Sidon (7:31), and the Decapolis (7:31). It is not immediately clear in either Mark or Matthew, both of whom record the venture, why Jesus embarks on this itineration among the Gentiles in what today is modern Lebanon and Syria. We can consider several clues, however, and draw at least a tentative conclusion from them. One clue comes from Jesus' desire for secrecy in all three stories in this unit (7:24, 33, 36; 8:9-10). A second clue is the placement of the Gentile itineration immediately following the controversy with the Pharisees in 7:1-23. A third clue, perhaps, is the reference in 6:16 that Herod Antipas considered Jesus to be John the Baptizer returned to life. Combined, these clues suggest that Jesus and the disciples quit Galilee to escape the harassment of the Pharisees and perhaps also of Herod, who ruled Galilee and Perea and who had killed John.[1]

This is only a hypothesis, but it appears justified from the above evidence. The hypothesis is further supported by the fact that Jesus does not teach in the Gentile itineration. Given the fifteen references thus far in Mark to Jesus' teaching in Galilee, the omission of his teaching among the Gentiles invites explanation. It is clear that the circuitous itinerary in Tyre, Sidon, and the Decapolis is governed by a more restricted purpose than Jesus exercised among Jewish towns and villages. Among the Gentiles he does mighty works of exorcism (5:1-20; 7:24-30), healing (7:31-37), and

---

1. So, too, B. Pixner, *Wege des Messias und Stätten der Urkirche. Jesus und das Judenchristentum im Licht neuer archäologischer Erkenntnisse*, Herausgegeben von R. Riesner (Giessen/Basel: Brunnen Verlag, 1991), 68-71.

feeding the hungry (8:1-10), but he does not teach and evangelize. According to 7:27, the witness to the Jews must take priority over the witness to the Gentiles. Jesus' itineration and ministry among the Gentiles signify that the kingdom of God is also addressed to the latter, but, as other NT witnesses attest,[2] the mission to the Gentiles does not take place before or apart from the prior witness to Israel. As the OT quotation at the outset of the Gospel in 1:2-3 signified, the proclamation of the gospel to the Gentiles is the fulfillment of the history of salvation begun in Israel. The Gentile itineration of 7:24–8:9 reinforces and furthers the truth of 7:1-23: there are no unclean foods (7:19), and there are no unclean people.

Nevertheless, a paradox results, for the response of the Gentiles is more favorable than is the response of the Jews in Galilee. If the previous story of the controversy with the Pharisees in 7:1-23 typified the resistance of official Judaism to Jesus, the three stories in the present section reveal a surprising openness to Jesus among the Gentiles. The Gentile response anticipates the confession at the cross where the first human to acknowledge Jesus as God's Son is a Gentile (15:39). It also assured Mark's Roman readers that their inclusion in salvation was not an accident but part of God's providence, deriving from the ministry of Jesus himself (Rom 11:29-32).

A GENTILE WHO WAS A "TRUE ISRAELITE" (7:24-30)

The encounter between Jesus and the Syrophoenician woman stands in stark contrast to the controversy with the Pharisees in the preceding story. The previous story revolved around Jewish men concerned with the law. The present story concerns a non-Jewish woman without the law. The tradition of the elders presupposed that there could be no salvation apart from law. In the present story, Mark shows that a Gentile pagan can find in Jesus what the tradition of the elders mistakenly thought could only be found in the Torah.

24 "Jesus left that place and went to the vicinity of Tyre."[3] Mark leaves Jesus' point of departure vague. The last place name mentioned was Gennesaret (6:53), which assumes a tour beginning in Galilee. The verb for "went" (Gk. *apēlthen*) is somewhat stronger than the normal Greek verb *erchesthai* and in Mark tends to signal a decisive departure. Its

---

2. Matt 10:5-6; 15:24; John 12:20-26; Acts 3:26; Rom 1:16-17.
3. A strong field of manuscripts reads "Tyre *and Sidon.*" Although manuscript support for this reading surpasses the shorter reading, B. Metzger, *TCGNT*, 95, is probably correct in judging Sidon a later assimilation to Matt 15:21 and Mark 7:31.

use may be another clue that Jesus is departing Galilee due to opposition from Pharisees and Antipas.

Tyre (modern Lebanon), which lay directly west and north of Galilee, was a Gentile region with a long history of antagonism to Israel. The region of Tyre (formerly Phoenicia) had been the home of Jezebel, who in Elijah's day had nearly subverted the Northern Kingdom with her pagan prophets and practices (1 Kgs 16:31-32). During the Maccabean Revolt in the second century B.C., Tyre, along with Ptolemais and Sidon, fought on the side of the Seleucids against the Jews (1 Macc 5:15ff.). The prophets decried the wealth and terror of Tyre (Ezek 26:17; Zech 9:3). Josephus concluded opprobriously that the inhabitants of Tyre were "notoriously our bitterest enemies" (*Ag. Ap.* 1.13).

The paganism of Tyre was not wholly unknown in Israel, however. Even in the first century paganism flourished in parts of Israel, especially at Beth Shan (Scythopolis), Mt. Carmel, and Jaffa, where the cult of Andromeda existed. The Jews in Palestine lived among pagans, sometimes next door to them, and Jesus could assume familiarity with the prayers of pagans among his Jewish audiences (Matt 6:7).[4] Nevertheless, Tyre probably represented the most extreme expression of paganism, both actually and symbolically, that a Jew could expect to encounter. According to *Pss. Sol.* 17:23-30, the Messiah would be ordained to expel and subdue the Gentiles, not to visit and embrace them. In journeying to "the vicinity of Tyre," and particularly in receiving a Syrophoenician woman, Jesus expands the scope of his ministry beyond anything conceivable of the Messiah. From a socioreligious perspective, Jesus' visit to Tyre universalizes the concept of Messiah in terms of geography, ethnicity, gender, and religion in a way entirely unprecedented in Judaism.

The initial report of Jesus' activity in the vicinity of Tyre is enigmatic. Why Jesus "entered a house and did not want anyone to know it" is unclear. It is sometimes supposed that Galilee's disappointing response to Jesus caused him to entertain a substitute mission to the Gentiles instead. This suggestion is not entirely persuasive, however, for in the dialogue with the Syrophoenician woman Jesus affirms the priority of his mission to Israel (v. 27). It seems more probable that Jesus hopes for a respite from the vice grip of opposition exerted by the Pharisees and Antipas (see the introduction to this chapter). Once again in Mark, Jesus does "not want anyone to know where they were" (9:30) so that he might

---

4. On Jewish exposure to paganism, see D. Flusser, "Paganism in Palestine," in *The Jewish People in the First Century: Historical Geography, Political History, Social, Cultural and Religious Life and Institution,* ed. S. Safrai and M. Stern, CRINT (Amsterdam: Van Forcum, Assen, 1976), 1,065-1,100.

teach the disciples (9:31-32). Given the disciples' general failure to understand his mission (6:52; 7:18; 8:17-21), we can understand Jesus' desire for enforced solitude far from harassment in order to instruct the disciples.

25-26 But even in foreign Tyre the magnetism of Jesus makes his retirement short-lived, for "he could not keep his presence secret" (7:24). As soon as she hears of him, an importunate woman shatters his privacy, as the disciples had done earlier (1:35). The woman "fell at his feet," begging for Jesus to heal her demon-possessed daughter. The last person in Mark to fall at Jesus' feet in supplication was Jairus (5:23; earlier 3:11; 5:6). The contrast between the Syrophoenician woman and Jairus, the president of a Jewish synagogue, could scarcely be more extreme. Despite Jairus's enviable qualifications, however, he does not hold an advantage with Jesus, for the woman's deficit with regard to qualifications will be compensated for by her depth of faith. For all their differences, *both* suppliants — Jew and Gentile — find fulfillment in Jesus, for Jesus sees not human status but human need.[5]

An encounter between this woman and a scribe or Pharisee would be hard to imagine in the "tradition of the elders."[6] Of all the people who approach Jesus in the Gospel of Mark, this individual has the most against her from a Jewish perspective. V. 26 reads like a crescendo of demerit: she is a woman, a Greek Gentile, from infamous pagans of Syrian Phoenicia. Even Levi the tax collector must have raised his eyebrows at this woman who has the pluck to beg "Jesus to drive the demon out of her daughter." Despite her notorious credentials, she does not apologize or cower in obsequiousness. This woman can claim none of the credits that a good Jew might bring to the Prophet of Nazareth. Her only cover letter is her desperate need.[7] Her prospects are as bleak as those of another Syrophoenician centuries earlier whose life ran out with the next meal — until she met a man of God.[8] Despite such obstacles, the woman's "heart" (to refer back to 7:19) is true, even if her credentials are wrong. She illustrates in the

---

5. See R. Guelich, *Mark 1–8:26*, 385.

6. In comparison to Mark, the version of the account in Matt 15:21-28 shows greater deference to Jewish sensibilities: the woman stands outside rather under the same roof; she calls Jesus "Son of David"; the disciples mediate by asking Jesus to send her away; and Jesus defends his reserve by declaring that he is sent only "to the lost sheep of the house of Israel."

7. J. Gundry-Volf, "Spirit, Mercy, and the Other," *TToday* 51 (1995): 508-23, notes that God's mercy responds to human need in such a way that it breaks societal patterns of exclusion.

8. The story of Elijah's meeting with the widow of Zarephath (1 Kgs 17:7-24) shares several similarities with our story: both Jesus and Elijah encounter women (widows?) in great need, both heal their children, and both stories take place in Syrophoenicia.

most unmistakable way the truth of the previous encounter with the Pharisees that if foods are not unclean, then neither are people! It is reasonable to suspect Peter as the source of this story, whose later experience with Cornelius reinforced the truth of this encounter: "'I now realize how true it is that God does not show favoritism but accepts men from every nation who fear him and do what is right'" (Acts 10:34-35).

27-28 The heart of the story is the "duel of wits"[9] in 7:27-28. Jesus responds with a brief parable to the woman's plea for healing her daughter: "First let the children eat all they want, for it is not right to take the children's bread and toss it to their dogs." The reference to the woman as a **dog** ranks among the most offensive sayings of Jesus. How is it to be understood? It would be an overstatement to say that "dog" was a thoroughly pejorative expression in the ancient world. There are instances of dogs being associated with the positive virtues of humility or service or watchfulness.[10] Nevertheless, "almost all OT passages . . . illustrate the loathing that devout Israelites felt toward dogs."[11] Dogs were associated with uncleanness because they ate garbage, carrion, and corpses (Exod 22:31; 1 Kgs 21:23; 22:38; 2 Kgs 9:36). Likewise, the expression was a term of opprobrium for people judged worthless and dispensable (1 Sam 24:15; 2 Sam 16:9; Isa 56:10). In the NT its contemptuous force is scarcely mitigated. Jesus warns against entrusting what is sacred to dogs (Matt 7:6), he describes human wretchedness in terms of a street mongrel licking the sores of a beggar (Luke 16:21), and Paul refers to his opponents as dogs (Phil 3:2). In the rabbinic tradition "dog" remained a term of reproach, referring to "the most despicable, insolent, and miserable of creatures."[12] It was in this opprobrious sense that "dog" was applied to Gentiles. The metaphor was common and varied in rabbinic speech, a fit description in the minds of Jews for Gentiles who were regarded as ignorant, godless, and pagan idolaters. "The peoples of the world are like dogs," declared the rabbis.[13]

9. R. Gundry, *Mark*, 374.

10. In the Lachish and Amarna letters "dog" is a stereotype of humility; in Mesopotamia a symbol of service; in Egypt dogs were valued as pets and for their ability to hunt; and in Assyria and Babylonia they were valued for watchfulness at the gate or even regarded as symbols of healing. See J. Botterweck, *"keleb,"* TDOT 7.147-52. There are also isolated instances among Jews where dogs are viewed favorably (Tob 6:1; 11:4; perhaps Eccl 9:4). F. Dufton, "The Syrophoenician Woman and Her Dogs," *ExpTim* 100 (1989): 417, overstates the case in saying that "no Jew would have allowed dogs to be [inside his house]."

11. *Ibid.*, 154.

12. Str-B 1.722.

13. *Ibid.*, 1.725. The particular image of dogs eating scraps under the table is found in *Jos. Asen.* 10:13; 13:8 and in Philostratus, *Life Apoll.* 19, both of which are pejorative.

In Jesus' place and time "dog" was thus scarcely a compliment. The question is whether Jesus thought of the woman with the above associations, and if he did not, why he referred to her with a term that carried them? Three points may be offered. First, if Mark's purpose in juxtaposing this story to the previous controversy with the Pharisees is to show that there are neither defiled objects nor *persons*, then it would clearly defeat his purpose if Jesus regarded this woman as an unclean dog. It would be hard to imagine Jesus so strenuously opposing the rabbinic view of defiled *things* in 7:1-23 while maintaining a perception of defiled *people* here. Second, the Greek word for "dog" is not the usual word for an unkempt street dog (Gk. *kyōn*), but a diminutive (Gk. *kynarion*), meaning a small dog that could be kept in the house as a pet.[14] In casting the word in the diminutive form Mark essentially empties it of opprobrium, for one feels entirely differently of a house pet than of an unclean street mongrel. The fact that the woman refers to her daughter and herself with the same term in her reply to Jesus shows that she does not take *kynarion* in a hostile or contemptuous sense. Third, "dog" signifies a traditional distinction between the Jews and the Gentiles that is important to the story. In the thought-world of the day, the Jews considered themselves "children" of God (Exod 4:22; Deut 14:1; Isa 1:2). They differed from other nations because of their inclusion in the covenant of Abraham (Genesis 17) and because they possessed the Torah (Exodus 19). The issue at stake between Jesus and the woman is whether Jesus is sent to "the children" or "to the dogs." The woman maintains the same distinction between "children" and "dogs" in her reply to Jesus, though with one slight change. Whereas Jesus refers to Israel as *teknōn* ("biological children"), the woman refers to Israel as *paidiōn*, which is more inclusive, implying both children and servants in a household. The change in terminology suggests that the woman understands the mercies of God to extend beyond ethnic Israel.

The basic issue in the repartee between Jesus and the woman is not whether Gentiles have a claim on God's mercies, but the relation of that claim to the Jewish claim. Jesus does not deny the woman's request. "*First* let the children eat all they want" simply establishes a priority of mission; it does not exclude other hungry mouths. In the present context it implies the messianic priority of Jesus' ministry to Israel to his ministry to the Gentiles, particularly, as we suggested earlier, with regard to teaching about the kingdom of God. But the priority of Israel in Jesus' mission does not imply the exclusion of the Gentiles. The Servant of the Lord must first "restore the tribes of Jacob," and then be "a light to the nations"

14. O. Michel, "*kyōn*," *TDNT* 3.1,104.

(Isa 49:6; also 42:1; 61:1-11). The choice of *kynarion* implies the dogs are *house* pets; that is, they belong to the household and will be fed along with the children. Indeed, the analogy of the children and dogs suggests a relationship to Jesus himself, for who might be the "father" who feeds the children — and their dogs — if not Jesus?

The woman's reply to Jesus in v. 28 shows her understanding and acceptance of Israel's privilege.[15] Indeed, she appears to understand the purpose of Israel's Messiah better than Israel does. Her pluck and persistence are a testimony to her trust in the sufficiency and surplus of Jesus: his provision for the disciples and Israel will be abundant enough to provide for one such as herself. Mark provides a clue to this understanding in the Gk. *chortazō* (NIV, "eat all they want"). This word occurs only twice elsewhere in Mark, in the feedings of the five thousand (6:42) and four thousand (8:4, 8). In its present location, the word bridges Jesus' feeding of the Jews (6:31-44) and his subsequent feeding of the Gentiles (8:1-10). When dogs eat crumbs from the table they do not rob children of their food; they simply eat what is theirs from the surplus of the children.[16] *God's provision overflows to Gentiles.*

29-30 This believing woman submits her cause entirely to Jesus, and she is not disappointed. "'For such a reply, you may go,'" says Jesus, "'the demon has left your daughter.'" What an irony! Jesus seeks desperately to teach his chosen disciples — yet they are dull and uncomprehending; Jesus is reluctant even to speak to a walk-on pagan woman — and after one sentence she understands his mission and receives his unambiguous commendation (loftier yet in Matt 15:28: "'Woman, you have great faith!'"). How is this possible? The answer is that the woman is the first person in Mark to hear and understand a parable of Jesus. The brief parable of the children and dogs at the table has disclosed to her the mystery of the kingdom of God. She is not distant and aloof, attempting to maintain her position and control. She does what Jesus commands of those who would receive the kingdom and experience the word of God: she enters the parable and allows herself to be claimed by it. That she an-

---

15. According to the NIV, the woman affirms Jesus' parable by saying "'Yes, Lord,'" and then adds her interpretation of it. In the Greek manuscripts, "'Yes'" is disputed. Although it is included by a superior number and diversity of manuscripts, it may not have been original, since *nai* ("yes") nowhere else occurs in Mark's Gospel. Metzger, *TCGNT*, 95, is probably correct in suspecting that *nai* was added by a later scribe who desired to make Mark conform to Matt 15:27 at this point.

16. The idea (and wording) of crumbs falling from the table to feed the poor and needy finds a close parallel in the story of poor Lazarus, who "longed to eat what fell from the rich man's table" (Luke 16:21). But what Lazarus cannot expect from the rich man the poor woman can expect from Jesus.

swers Jesus from "within" the parable, that is, in the terms by which Jesus addressed her, indicates that she is the first person in the Gospel to *hear* the word of Jesus to her.[17]

Within the parable she has met a living Lord with whom she has struggled and contended. She has sparred with Jesus as Jacob sparred with God at Peniel, "'Your name will no longer be Jacob, but Israel, because you have struggled with God and with men and have overcome'" (Gen 32:28). She is a female Jacob. She, too, has overcome. Jesus sends her home, assuring her that the healing of her daughter has already transpired.[18] This woman's contending with Jesus is a fulfillment of Israel's vocation; she, a Gentile, is a true Israelite. Martin Luther, who himself contended much with God, found in the story of the Syrophoenician woman a great wonder and comfort. She, said Luther, asked for no more than her due. "She took Christ at his own words. He then treated her not as a dog but as a child of Israel."[19]

The story of Jesus and the Syrophoenician woman is of great theological significance for Mark. This Gentile woman is not offered a separate revelation of God or a righteousness apart from Israel. She fully accepts the authenticity and uniqueness of God's revelation to Israel. So fully does she appreciate that revelation that she trusts its superabundance to spill over and include her people and others like her.[20] This reminded Mark's readers, as it does us today, that salvation is offered to the world, both to Jews and to estranged Gentiles like this woman, through Jesus who fulfills God's revelation to Israel.

17. See M. Hengel, *Studies in the Gospel of Mark,* trans. J. Bowden (London: SCM Press, 1985), 97-98.

18. The Gk. *exelēlythen* ("has [already] gone out") in v. 29 implies that the demon left her daughter prior to the moment of speaking. The intrepid story of the Syrophoenician woman appears to have shaped the later story of "The Life of St. Pelagia the Harlot." See *The Desert Fathers,* trans. and ed. H. Waddell (New York: Vintage Books, 1998), 181-96.

19. R. Bainton, *Here I Stand: A Life of Martin Luther* (Nashville: Abingdon, 1950), 362.

20. Certain feminist interpretations of Mark 7:24-30 see Jesus as a villain and the Syrophoenician woman as a heroine, often implying that the word of salvation comes from outside Christ or in contrast to him (e.g., J. Perkinson, "A Canaanitic Word in the Logos of Christ; or The Difference the Syro-Phoenician Woman Makes to Jesus," *Semeia* 75 [1996]: 61-85). While it is true that the woman wrests a blessing from Jesus that he might not otherwise have given, it is not true that the blessing derives from a source other than Jesus. The blessing comes from within the parable spoken by Jesus, and the exorcism results from his authoritative word. That the woman responds to Jesus from "within" the parable he speaks indicates that she fully affirms the conditions implied in the parable, i.e., that Jesus has brought salvation to Israel, from whose abundance Gentiles may also partake.

"THEY WILL SEE THE GLORY OF THE LORD" (7:31-37)

Episode two in Jesus' Gentile itineration is the healing of a hearing- and speech-impaired man in the Decapolis. This is one of only three stories in Mark that finds no counterpart in the other three Gospels, although Matt 15:29-31 provides what appears to be a brief summary of Mark 7:31-37. Matthew speaks of Jesus healing "great crowds" of the blind, crippled, dumb, and "many others," which would indicate that Mark's story is only one instance of a much larger healing ministry in the Decapolis. The clamor of the crowds on Jesus' second visit to the Decapolis contrasts noticeably with the ingratitude he suffered on his first visit there (5:17). That may simply be due to his works of mercy, but it is not impossible that Jesus' fame in the Decapolis is due to the report of the Gerasene demoniac (5:20). If so, the first Gentile missionary was not unsuccessful.

31 From the region of Tyre Jesus travels over twenty miles north to Sidon, then southeast across the River Leontes, and from there further south through Caesarea Philippi to the Decapolis on the east side of the Sea of Galilee. The horseshoe-shaped itinerary is not a step shy of 120 miles in length. It is a puzzling itinerary, rather like going from Washington, D.C., to Richmond, Virginia, by way of Philadelphia! Not surprisingly, all the other Gospels omit it.[21] The circuitous journey has elicited various attempts to explain it. Some commentators suggest that the disappointing response of Galilee caused Jesus to experiment with a further and perhaps substitute mission to the Gentiles.[22] Given the expressed purpose of his mission to Israel in 7:27, this suggestion seems unlikely. Other commentators suggest that Mark was either ignorant of Palestinian geography[23] or that the journey is a fiction to underscore that the gospel is also available to Gentiles.[24] Both of these suggestions are very improbable. It is difficult to imagine Peter, who is arguably a key source of Mark's Gospel (see Introduction, 3-6), and who elsewhere is the probable source of information that is problematic (e.g., 9:1) or disquieting (14:66-71), allowing such a fabrication. Moreover, it would be highly unusual for Mark to fabricate a journey that makes him look ignorant of geography, and perhaps

---

21. The textual tradition reflects similar uncertainty about the roundabout journey of v. 31. Three older manuscripts (p[45] A W) and various minuscules read that Jesus "went from the regions of Tyre and Sidon and came to the Sea of Galilee" (rather than going *through* Sidon; so the NIV). A journey through Sidon is to be preferred, however, because it claims the stronger manuscript support (ℵ B D L Δ Θ) and because it is the more difficult reading, i.e., it would have been less likely to have been added by a scribe. See B. Metzger, *TCGNT*, 95-96.

22. Pixner, *With Jesus Through Galilee*, 79.

23. D. Lührmann, *Das Markusevangelium*, 132.

24. E. Schweizer, *The Good News According to Mark*, 154.

even foolish. Contrary to the judgments of some scholars, I find Mark's geographical designations to be both defensible and accurate in every instance where they can be checked. That includes the present description. The journey of v. 31 may be odd, but it is not without precedent in Scripture. 2 Kings 2 records not one but two equally remarkable hairpin journeys, neither of which is entirely explainable.[25] Jesus' ministry in Galilee has been distinguished by constant movement around and across the lake, and the present journey continues the same strategy in Gentile regions. This journey, in fact, can be plausibly explained by a desire on Jesus' part to escape the growing opposition of the Pharisees and Antipas. Jesus is not simply evading opposition or buying time, however. The journey deep into Gentile territory — indeed notorious Gentile territory — indicates his willful inclusion of the non-Jewish world in his ministry.

32 In the Decapolis to the east of the Sea of Galilee "some people brought a man to [Jesus] who was deaf and could hardly talk" (similarly, 8:22). In the original Greek this description is cast in the present tense, suggesting an eyewitness reminiscence. The description of the man with the speech impediment (NIV, "could hardly talk") uses a Greek word, *mogilalos,* that occurs only once elsewhere in the Bible. In the description of the revelation of the glory of the Lord to the nations in Isaiah 35 we read: "Then will the eyes of the blind be opened and the ears of the deaf unstopped . . . and the tongue of the dumb *(mogilalos)* shout for joy" (Isa 35:5-6). The presence of *mogilalos* in v. 32 links our story unmistakably to the Isaiah quotation. Since Mark is writing for Roman Gentiles, he only infrequently appeals to OT proof texts. On the few occasions when he fortifies his literary architecture with OT reinforcements, however, they are load-bearing beams. The reference to Isaiah 35 is no exception. Isaiah 35 is essentially the final chapter of the first part of Isaiah. It follows a series of chapters declaring God's judgment of Edom, Egypt, Tyre, Israel, and Jerusalem. In chap. 35, however, the theme shifts from judgment to eschatology, and to the joy not only of the redeemed but of all creation at the revelation of the Lord. The allusion to Isaiah 35 is of supreme significance for Mark's presentation of Jesus, not only because the restoration of speech to a *mogilalos* signals the eschatological arrival of the Day of the Lord but also because the desert wastelands of *Lebanon* (Isa 35:2) will receive the joy of God. The regions of Tyre and Sidon are, of course, precisely the Lebanon of Isaiah 35. Jesus' healing of this particular *mogilalos* in the Decapolis becomes the firstfruit of the fulfillment of Isa 35:10, that Gentile Lebanon will

---

25. In 2 Kgs 2:1-6 Elijah and Elisha walk from Gilgal due west up to Bethel and then due east back to Jericho and the Jordan; again, in 2 Kgs 2:23-25 Elisha walks from Bethel northwest to Mt. Carmel and then backtracks to Samaria.

join "the ransomed of the Lord [and] enter Zion with singing"! Salvation thus comes to the Gentile world in Jesus, who is God's eschatological redeemer from Zion. As we have noted before, the only categories adequate for Mark to describe the person and work of Jesus are ultimately the categories of God. Once again, as in the story of the Syrophoenician woman (7:24-30), "salvation is from the Jews" (John 4:22).

33-34 In narrating the healing of the deaf-mute, Mark accentuates the empathy of Jesus for the man with hearing and speech impairments. By himself the needy man is simply another face in a crowd of Gentiles. But in removing him from the crowd, Jesus signifies that he is not simply a problem but a unique individual. Then Jesus "put his fingers into the man's ears. Then he spit and touched the man's tongue." In touching the man Jesus repeats his radical identification with needy, and sometimes ritually unclean people (1:31; 1:41; 3:5; 5:33, 41; 6:56). Schlatter is right to suggest that physical contact is an expression of Jesus' compassion. Love seeks intimacy, and the touch of Jesus is a tangible prelude of the fellowship that believers experience with him through faith.[26]

But why the particular contact of touching the man's tongue with spittle? As a bodily excretion, spittle normally fell under the category of polluting fluxes, along with menstrual blood, semen, urine, and pus (*m. Zavim* 1–5). The spittle of certain persons, however, was considered by the Jews to have healing power, especially when it was accompanied by conversation, applied to the area of sickness or injury, and accompanied by a formula or prayer.[27] These signs occur in our healing, thus implying their healing effect. Jesus does not minister from a safe distance but looks to heaven, heaves "a deep sigh" of engagement (see 5:30), and orders "'Ephphatha,'" for which Mark gives a Greek translation "'Be open.'"[28] The Semitic expression *ephphatha*, which would not derive from a Gentile region, apparently derives from Peter's witness of the healing.[29] Hellenistic healers were noted for attempting cures by the application of various balms, some of which were rather unpleasant.[30] It is not impossible that Jesus adopts such protocol in the Gentile Decapolis in order to

26. A. Schlatter, *Die Evangelien nach Markus und Lukas,* 78.

27. Str-B 2.16-17.

28. The need to translate an Aramaic saying into Greek again indicates that Mark is writing for non-Jews.

29. Whether the word is Hebrew or Aramaic is discussed by J. Jeremias, *New Testament Theology, Part One: The Proclamation of Jesus,* trans. J. Bowden (Chatham, Eng.: W & J Mackay, 1971), 7. Whatever the original language of the word, it is best explained as Jesus' actual expression.

30. A second-century inscription in Rome orders a three-day application of a balm made from the blood of a white rooster mixed with honey and eye salve for the recovery of sight. See *HCNT,* 284.

convey to the man what he might expect from him. Although Jesus may have used common means, he uses them to uncommon effect, however.[31] The anointing of Jesus' spittle might be considered an elementary and provisional foretaste of his own blood that will also be placed on the tongues of sinful men and women (14:24). The spittle thus seems to carry quasi-sacramental significance. The cure, however, is not effected by the material sign or any magical powers attached to it, but by Jesus' intimate compassion for this needy man and by the authority of his word.[32]

35-37 Like God's breaking the chains of darkness and gloom (Ps 107:14), at the word of Jesus "the man's ears were opened and his tongue was loosened and he began to speak plainly." The original Greek is more vivid and concrete, saying that "the chain of his tongue was broken." In the NT, the word for "chain" (Gk. *desmos*; NIV, "loosened") most frequently means a chain or fetter that binds a prisoner (Luke 8:29; Acts 16:26; 20:23; 26:29; Phil 1:7; Col 4:18). The breaking of the fetter by Jesus is a figure of liberation (Luke 13:16).[33] Likewise, the man was speaking "correctly" (Gk. *orthōs*; NIV, "plainly"), meaning that the difficulties and impediments of v. 32 are removed.

Jesus commands the crowd to silence. "But the more he did so, the more the people kept talking about it." (See the **Command to Silence** at 1:34.) This is the only instance in Mark of Jesus commanding Gentiles to silence. The reception of Jesus in his Gentile mission has been favorable, and in the case of the Syrophoenician woman even faithful. Nevertheless, the repetition of the command to silence among Gentiles indicates that the problems inherent in understanding and faith are essentially no different for Gentiles than for Jews. Neither group has an automatic "in"; nor is either automatically "out." The command to silence to both Jew and Gentile is a reminder that knowledge of Jesus by his wonders alone is inadequate knowledge. Adequate knowledge of Jesus — and hence proclamation about him — must await the revelation of the ultimate mystery that can come only through suffering and the cross (15:39). The commandment to silence in v. 36 is clear and blunt; it is not a suggestion and it is not ambiguous. Nevertheless, like the Jews, the Gentiles also break it. For all their differences, in this respect the Jewish and Gentile response to Jesus is remarkably similar. The great differences between Jews and Gentiles on points of

---

31. S. Cunningham, "The Healing of the Deaf and Dumb Man (Mark 7:31-37), with Application to the African Context," *Africa Journal of Evangelical Theology* 9 (1990): 13-26.

32. See Str-B 2.17.

33. A. Deissmann (*Light from the Ancient East*, trans L. Strachan [Grand Rapids: Baker Book House, 1978], 305-7) draws attention to the "bond of his tongue" as a technical expression. "The writer will not merely say that the dumb man was made to speak — he will add further that the daemonic fetters were broken, a work of Satan undone."

law, purity, and ethnicity fade before the truly *human* question and most significant issue of all, which is the question of faith in Jesus.

Mark concludes with the amazement of the crowd (also 1:22) and their confession that "'He has done everything well.'" This summary confession recalls God's surveying his works at creation and declaring them good (Gen 1:31). It is a further instance of Jesus fulfilling the role of God. The Son's work in redemption is like the Father's work in creation: it is done well and leaves nothing to be desired.

In 7:14 Jesus implored, "'Hear me, everyone, and understand.'" Mark now relates the story of a Gentile who, because of the touch of Jesus, can *hear* Jesus. Like the Syrophoenician woman (7:24-30), another Gentile outsider has been included in the company of Jesus. Mark is here resuming his insiders-outsiders theme. The hearing and understanding commanded by Jesus are made possible only by Jesus. Faith in Jesus is a difficult matter; indeed, it is the most difficult matter in all the world. Some, like the disciples, are in close and constant contact with Jesus but still cannot see. Others like the Syrophoenician woman and this speech- and hearing-impaired man are in dark and distant lands. Still others like Mark's readers in Rome may struggle with bearing witness to their faith with their lives. What does it mean for all these to hear and understand (7:14)? It means that whether Jew or Gentile, near or far, knowledgeable or neophyte, only the touch of Jesus can enable true hearing, seeing, understanding, and witness.

THE FEEDING OF THE FOUR THOUSAND (8:1-9)

The feeding of the four thousand and the feeding of the five thousand share more in common than any two stories in the Gospel of Mark. Both stories occur in deserted settings. Both emphasize Jesus' compassion on the crowds. Both repeat the question, "'How many loaves do you have?'" The command to recline is similar in both, as is the prayer and participation of the disciples. In both the words and serving of the loaves follow the same sequence, and in both "the people ate and were satisfied." Leftovers were gathered after both meals, and both conclude with Jesus dismissing the crowd and taking a boat trip. These similarities, combined with the unlikelihood that the disciples would have forgotten the previous feeding miracle, lead a majority of modern scholars to assume that the feeding of the four thousand is a doublet of the feeding of the five thousand rather than a separate historical event.[34]

34. For example, S. Legasse, *L'Évangile de Marc,* 463, opens his discussion of 8:1-10 with pronouncements rather than evidence: "The second account of the multiplication of

227

Although this is a feasible conclusion, it should not be simply assumed, for there are an equally telling number of differences. The first feeding began with five loaves and two fish, the second with seven loaves and "a few small fish" (v. 7). The word for fish is different in each account; in the feeding of the four thousand it is a diminutive in Greek, *ichthydia*, perhaps best rendered "sardines," which, along with bread, made up the staple diet of the local population.[35] The numbers of people fed also differ. In the first account, "five thousand *men*" (6:44) were present, which would amount to a larger number when women and children were included; in the second story, "four thousand" (v. 9) is a total estimate. In the first feeding the crowd was with Jesus one day (6:35); in the second, three days (v. 2). The first feeding was in springtime (the word for "green grass" [Gk. *chlōros,* 6:39] means the light green of spring), whereas there is no mention of the season in the second. In the second feeding, the people are not broken into groups as they are in the first feeding, but are simply seated "on the ground" (v. 6). The numbers of baskets of leftovers also differ, as do the Greek words for "basket."[36] Finally, the backdrop of a revolutionary uprising, apparent in the feeding of the five thousand, is missing in the second story.

Another important difference is the role of Jesus in the two accounts. In the feeding of the four thousand the person of Jesus is more prominent. He directs rather than responds to events, and with less help from the disciples. Also in the second feeding Jesus' dialogue is recorded in the first person, which corresponds with his speech at the Last Supper (14:22-26).[37] In the feeding of the five thousand the disciples play a more prominent role and the words of Jesus are narrated in the third person, thus being a narrative *about* him rather than *from* him. The first person dialogue in the second narrative has the effect of declaring Jesus' compassion directly to the Gentile crowd — and, by extension, to Mark's Roman readers.

---

the loaves is a doublet of the first and the two versions of the one account saw the light of day before Mark."

35. M. Nun, *The Sea of Galilee and Its Fishermen in the New Testament* (Kibbutz Ein Gev: Kinnereth Sailing Company, 1989), 51. Also, A. Schlatter, *Der Evangelist Matthäus,* 494-95.

36. An exact distinction between the two words for "basket" is unclear. The *kophinos* of the first feeding in 6:43 may have been smaller, perhaps of stiff wicker, whereas the *spyris* in 8:8 is larger and of more flexible mat. The latter was big enough to lower Paul through an opening in the city wall of Damascus (Acts 9:25). See Gundry, *Mark,* 398.

37. The sequence of "thanking, breaking, and distributing to the disciples" (8:6) also corresponds more closely to the "breaking, thanking, and distributing" in the Last Supper (14:22-23).

Is the feeding of the four thousand then a doublet or separate historical event? The agreements between the two feedings are indeed considerable, and a sound reason can be supplied for creating a doublet, namely, to show that Jesus "satisfies" the Gentiles as well as the Jews. This *may* indicate a doublet, but it is less assured than often supposed. Agreement between two accounts — even substantial agreement — is not proof of dependency. With regard to the two feedings, the specific differences in numbers and details argue in favor of separate events, as does the subsequent reflection on the two events in 8:18-20. Nor is the forgetfulness of the disciples in the second feeding a necessarily compelling argument for the doublet theory.[38] In the narrative flow of Mark, the feeding of the four thousand is not intrusive, nor is it demanded by the context. Considered as a whole, the evidence seems to lean toward a second miracle of multiplication of loaves.

1-3 "During those days" links the feeding of the four thousand generally to Jesus' sojourn in the Decapolis (7:31). Mark does not explicitly locate the second miraculous feeding in Gentile territory (nor did he explicitly relate the feeding of the five thousand to the Jews), but the context places the event in Gentile territory on the east side of the Sea of Galilee. The "large crowd" gathered around Jesus (7:33; Matt 15:29-31) has accompanied him for three days and begins to run short of food. In describing the crowd Mark uses a rare and intensified form of the word for "remain," *prosmenein,* connoting a special adherence and commitment to Jesus. The crowd has not been coincidentally present but intentionally *with* him.[39] This is an unusually positive description of a crowd in Mark. Jesus again finds a reception among Gentiles that he has not found among Jews.

In the feeding of the five thousand the disciples brought Jesus' attention to the impending crisis among the crowd (6:35-36), but here it is Jesus who perceives the problem. He "summons" (Gk. *proskaleomai*) the

---

38. The argument that the disciples' perplexity in 8:4 would be impossible after witnessing the feeding of the five thousand is noteworthy but not conclusive. C. E. B. Cranfield, *The Gospel According to Saint Mark,* 205, notes with justification that even mature Christians (which the disciples are not yet) often doubt the power of God after having experienced it; and, moreover, that enough time may have elapsed to have dulled their memory. As to why the disciples do not simply ask Jesus to repeat the miracle here that he did with the five thousand, M.-J. Lagrange, *Évangile selon Saint Marc,* 202, makes the insightful comment that the question of v. 4 rests less on the impossibility of Jesus doing such a miracle than on the disciples' embarrassment in asking for one. The most rigorous argument for two separate historical events comes from Gundry, *Mark,* 398-401, whose evidence and arguments must be countered before the doublet theory is further assumed.

39. F. Hauck, *"menō,"* TDNT 4.579.

229

disciples, a favorite Markan clue to the significance of Jesus' impending intervention. Jesus not only recognizes the objectivity of the need but personally identifies with it. He declares in the first person singular, "'I have compassion for these people.'" The Greek word for "compassion," *splangnizomai*, comes from *splangnon*, meaning entrails or vital organs. In ancient animal sacrifice, the *splangnon* — heart, lungs, liver, and kidneys — were eaten by priests and sacrificers before a sacrificial animal was offered on the altar.[40] As a consequence of this practice, *splangnizomai* takes on a metaphorical meaning of being moved deeply within, in the seat of emotions (Matt 9:36). "'I have compassion for these people'" expresses Jesus' gut-wrenching emotion on behalf of the crowd. Equally importantly, in Mark this word is not used of people for whom one would naturally feel compassion (such as friends or compatriots), but for those far removed and even offensive: lepers (1:41), revolutionaries (6:34), Gentiles (8:2), and demon-possessed (9:22).

The detail that "'some of them have come a long distance'" fits entirely with the austere and rugged geography of the Decapolis, which has fewer towns and settlements than does the west side of the lake. It is no place to be without provisions. In their condition, "'they will collapse on the way.'"

4 The perplexity of the disciples ("'But where in this remote place can anyone get enough bread to feed them?'") is a primary reason why many scholars suppose this story to be a doublet rather than a separate event. Surely, it is claimed, having earlier witnessed the feeding of a similar crowd, the disciples could not be so forgetful or dense to ask such a question. Again, had they experienced one such miracle, should they not have expected another in this instance? The more one reflects on this criticism the less convincing it becomes, however, especially in light of Mark's presentation of the obduracy of the disciples. Although Mark records proportionally more miracles than the other evangelists, he certainly does not portray Jesus as a vendor of miracles. With but few exceptions in Mark, Jesus' miraculous activity comes to people — and especially to the disciples — as wholly wondrous and unanticipated activity. Hankering for miracles is a sign of Jesus' opponents, not of his followers, as the request for a sign by the Pharisees in the story immediately following evinces (8:11-13). Although the disciples fail in essential ways to understand Jesus, they know his servant posture sufficiently well not to prod him for miraculous intervention. The assumption that the disciples should have lobbied for a miracle in the Decapolis is as great a misunderstanding of them as is their misunderstanding of Jesus.

40. LSJ, 1628.

5-7 Unlike the feeding of the five thousand where Jesus has the disciples seat the crowds (6:39), Jesus personally seats the crowd in the Decapolis. Likewise, in the feeding of the five thousand the description of Jesus' prayer follows Jewish custom ("looking up to heaven, he gave thanks [Gk. *eulogein*]," 6:41), whereas the description in the feeding of the four thousand employs the Gentile-Christian form of blessing, *eucharistein* ("given thanks," 8:6), from which Christians derived the name *Eucharist* for the Lord's Supper. When asked how many loaves of bread exist among the crowds, the disciples report, "'Seven.'" Whether this number can be seen to symbolize the totality of the Gentile nations (e.g., Deut 7:1) is difficult to say.[41] Unlike the Gospel of John or the Revelation, for example, Mark does not major in symbolic meanings (as he does, e.g., in irony), and in general it is unwise to load his details, and particularly his numbers, with symbolic value.[42] In addition to the bread, "a few small fish" are included in the meal.[43] The separate mention and blessing of the fish differ from the account of the feeding of the five thousand, where both bread and fish are mentioned together (6:41). Once again (6:41), however, the disciples are called upon to assist and extend Jesus' ministry by distributing the provisions to the crowd.

8-9 The NIV says "about four thousand men were present" for the feeding. "Men" here is not gender specific, for unlike the five thousand "men" of 6:44, the masculine plural ending of "four thousand" (Gk. *tetrakischilioi*) implies "people," including men, women, and children. The size of this crowd was thus considerably smaller than the mathematical difference between four thousand and five thousand suggests.

Mark concludes the account with a brief but telling statement: "The people ate and were satisfied." The use of "satisfied" (Gk. *chortazein*) re-

41. The number includes the Hittites, Girgashites, Amorites, Canaanites, Perizzites, Hivites, and Jebusites who dwelled in the land of Canaan. So Pixner, *With Jesus Through Galilee*, 83. However, whereas the Israelites were commanded to destroy the nations, Jesus feeds them!

42. Likewise, v. 3 ("some of them have come a long distance") is sometimes taken to symbolize the spiritual distance from paganism to Christianity. The numerology of A. Seethaler, "Die Brotvermehrung — ein Kirchenspiegel?" *BibZeit* 34 (1990): 108-12 (seven = totality; four [thousand] = people from the four corners of the earth; three days = perfect journey), is overly speculative.

43. The parenthetical nature of v. 7 is apparent in several textual variants, i.e., *tauta eulogēsas* ("[Jesus] blessed these [small fish]"; so A K Π), or *eulogēsas* ("blessed"; so X), or *eucharistēsas* ("gave thanks"; so D). The strongest reading, however, which is followed by the NIV, is *eulogēsas auta* ("having blessed [the small fish]"), which claims strong manuscript support (א B C L Δ Θ). The unusualness of Jesus blessing fish rather than God's name further commends the reading since it is not a reading one would invent. See Metzger, *TCGNT*, 96-97.

peats the same word used in the disciples' question of v. 4, "'Where in this remote place can anyone get enough bread to feed (Gk. *chortazein*) them?'" The Greek of v. 4 might better be translated, "'For *who* is able in this remote region to satisfy these [people] with bread?'" In the miracle of the multiplication of the loaves, the answer to the question is supplied: only Jesus can satisfy the people!

From the church fathers onward the church has rightly perceived that in the feeding of the four thousand Jesus brings saving bread to the Gentiles, as he brought it earlier to the Jews in the feeding of the five thousand. The journey to the Gentiles in 7:24–8:9 has evinced that they are neither beyond the reach of salvation nor inured to it. Like the book of Jonah, the three vignettes in Mark 7:24–8:9 reveal that supposed Gentile outsiders are in fact surprisingly receptive to the word of God in Jesus. The journey of Jesus to Tyre, Sidon, and the Decapolis proves that although the Gentiles are ostracized by the Jews, they are not ostracized by God. Jewish invective against the Gentiles does not reflect a divine invective. There is a lesson here for the people of God in every age, that its enemies are neither forsaken by God nor beyond the compassion of Jesus. On the contrary, the Gentiles, like others "a long distance" away, are the objects of Jesus' compassion. The difference between the Jews' response to the Gentiles and Jesus' response can be seen in Mark's concluding phrase, "And [Jesus] sent them away." The Greek word for "send away," *apolyein*, can mean either "to dismiss" or "get rid of"; or "to release" or "liberate." The first is the Jewish response; the second is Jesus' response, who satisfies the hungry outcasts and liberates them.

CHAPTER EIGHT

Removing the Veil

MARK 8:10–9:29

Mark's story of Jesus reaches a climax in chap. 8, at the center of which stands Peter's declaration of Jesus as the Messiah (8:29). Peter's declaration at Caesarea Philippi stands at roughly the midpoint of the Gospel and, like a continental divide, separates the Gospel into two major watersheds. In the first half of the Gospel Jesus crisscrosses the Sea of Galilee without apparent purpose, but after Peter's confession he is staunchly "on the way" to Jerusalem. Prior to Caesarea Philippi Jesus directs his teaching to the masses of Galilee, but after Peter's confession he leaves Galilee and deliberately instructs his disciples on the journey to Jerusalem. His didactic resolution is signified by the fact that only once in the first half of the Gospel does Jesus preface a teaching with the solemn formula, "'I tell you the truth'" (Gk. *Amēn legō hymin*, 3:28), whereas in the second half of the Gospel the formula occurs a dozen times. In the first half of the Gospel Jesus forbids people from announcing his identity and he is frequently in combat with demon-possession, but after 9:29 there are no further commands to silence and no further mention of demons or exorcisms. In the first half of the Gospel the disciples fail completely in their understanding of Jesus, whereas after Caesarea Philippi their fledgling understanding is expressed in their confession of his Messiahship, although they will struggle with the fact of a *suffering* Messiah rather than a royal Messiah. The first half of the Gospel takes Jesus outside Israel to Tyre, Sidon, Caesarea Philippi, and the Decapolis; the second half brings him to Jerusalem, the heart of Israel. The first half of Mark is a journey outward in which Jesus casts broadly; the second half is a journey inward to the source, to Jerusalem and the temple. Both halves of the Gospel conclude with christological confessions, and both confessions are associated with Roman Gentiles: the first is Peter's tentative confession at the Roman stronghold of Caesarea Philippi that Jesus is the Christ (8:29); the second is the full confession of the Roman centurion at the cross that Jesus is the Son of God (15:39). Both confessions teach that Jesus' true identity is revealed only through suffering — and that those who are called to follow Jesus must be prepared to participate in his suffering.

A SIGN OF DISBELIEF (8:10-13)

In a final conflict with the Pharisees in Galilee, Mark uses their request of a heavenly sign from Jesus as a negative object lesson on faith.

10 After feeding the four thousand, Jesus and the disciples cross the Sea of Galilee "to the region of Dalmanutha." This is the only mention of Dalmanutha in the NT and the only extant occurrence of the name in ancient literature.[1] Its location has never been identified for certain, but it probably was near or identical with "Magadan" (or a variant "Magdala"), which occurs in the parallel in Matt 15:39. Magadan was a fishing center, hence its Greek name, Tarichea, meaning "salted or pickled fish." A combination of the names in the Talmud (*b. Pes.* 46*b*), Migdal Tarichea, means "tower of [salted] fish." Schürer argues for a location of Tarichea south of Tiberias,[2] but this seems doubtful, since in none of the Gospels does Jesus visit the southwest quadrant of the lakeshore in which Tiberias lay. Magadan, however, which lay five kilometers north of Tiberius, is adjacent to Gennesaret, where Jesus and the disciples put in after the feeding of the five thousand (6:53). An anchorage discovered slightly north of Magdala in 1971 could possibly be the site of Dalmanutha.[3] The Hebrew radicals of Dalmanutha, *dylm`*, are found in the Talmud (*j. Kil.* 32*d*) with the meaning "wall." That could be a further clue to identifying Dalmanutha with Magadan since the latter lay directly below the massive wall or cliff of Arbel overlooking the western shore of the lake. This last suggestion is corroborated by Josephus, who places Tarichea near Gennesar at

---

1. For the variant readings in v. 10, see B. Metzger, *TCGNT,* 97.

2. E. Schürer, *History of the Jewish People,* 1.494-95, argues on the basis of Josephus, *War* 3.462 and 4.11, that Ammathus and Tarichea are the same place. In *War* 4.11 Josephus does not say Ammathus is south of Tiberias, however, but "in front of Tiberias." In the more complete description in *War* 3.462-67 Tarichea appears north of Tiberias, for Josephus identifies it with Gennesar and locates it "at the foot of a mountain" *(hypōreios),* which must refer to the imposing rampart of Arbel directly above Magadan/Tarichea. In locating Ammathus "in front of Tiberias," Josephus must be speaking from a perspective *north* of Tiberias, rather than south, as Schürer supposes.

3. J. Strange, "Dalmanutha," *ABD* 2.4.

the foot of a mountain (*War* 3.462-67). Dalmanutha is thus reasonably identified with Magadan, located on the westernmost part of the Sea of Galilee at the strategic juncture of the Via Maris beneath the cliffs of Arbel.

11 At Dalmanutha Jesus is accosted by the Pharisees, asking "him for a sign from heaven." Several Greek words in v. 11 are more antagonistic than the NIV indicates, leaving no doubt of the Pharisees' opposition. For "came," Mark reads "came out" (Gk. *exēlthon*), as if in military rank. They not only "question" him, but they "dispute" or "oppose" him, according to the Gk. *syzētein*, a staple in the Markan narrative (1:27; 8:11; 9:10, 14, 16; 12:28). The word for "asked" (Gk. *zētein*), another regular of Markan vocabulary, means to attempt to gain control of (see the discussion of term at 1:37). Likewise, the word for "test" (Gk. *peirazein*) does not mean an objective test to discover the merit of something, but an obstacle or stumbling block to discredit. It occurs only four times in Mark, once of Satan's temptation of Jesus in the wilderness (1:13) and three times of the opposition of the Pharisees (8:11; 10:2; 12:15). It is thus apparent in v. 11 that the Pharisees represent a challenge and confrontation of Jesus.

The Pharisaic expectation of "a sign from heaven" is echoed by Paul's statement that "Jews demand miraculous signs" (1 Cor 1:22). Even in the OT, however, signs were not regarded as proof positive of God's will. A prophet who commanded something contrary to the Torah but performed a miraculous sign was still a false prophet, for example (Deut 13:1-5). On the other hand, true prophecy was corroborated by the fulfillment of what a prophet predicted (Deut 18:22). A Jewish commentary on Deuteronomy 18 runs: "If a prophet begins to prophesy, listen to him if he does a sign and miracle; but it he does not do them, do not hear him."[4] The sign requested by the Pharisees is not simply for a miracle, however, for in the Synoptic Gospels a "sign" is not a miracle, nor is a miracle called a sign. Moreover, Jesus has done miracles all along, with which the Pharisees cannot have been unfamiliar. The word Mark normally uses for "miracle" (Gk. *dynamis*) is in fact absent here. Rather, the Pharisees request "a sign (Gk. *sēmeion*) from heaven," that is, a confirmation of Jesus' ministry from God himself, an "outward compelling proof of divine authority."[5] They reason that if Jesus is working in God's name, then God should divinely authorize his work.[6]

12 "[Jesus] sighed deeply and said, 'Why does this generation ask for a miraculous sign? I tell you the truth, no sign will be given to it.'" Although it is not entirely apparent in the NIV, this verse records a nadir of

4. Sifre Deut 18:19 § 177 (108a); see Str-B 1.727.
5. C. E. B. Cranfield, *The Gospel According to St Mark*, 257.
6. K. H. Rengstorf, *"sēmeion,"* TDNT 7.234-36.

dismay in the Gospel of Mark. The original Greek reads that Jesus "groaned in his spirit." The word for "groaned" (Gk. *anastenazein*) is a rare word, occurring only here in the NT, and fewer than thirty times in all of Greek literature. A survey of its uses reveals that it is not an expression of anger or indignation so much as of dismay or despair. *Anastenazein* is used to describe persons who find themselves in situations where they are pushed to the limit of faithfulness.[7] The antagonism of the Pharisees parallels the antagonism of the Israelites to Moses in the wilderness — and Jesus' groaning in dismay seems to reflect God's disgust with the bent and recalcitrant Israelites (Exod 33:5!). The reference to "this generation" signals the Pharisees' alienation from Jesus and recalls the disbelieving generation of Noah's day (Gen 7:1) and the stubbornness of the Exodus generation in the wilderness (Ps 95:10-11). The latter was a generation that turned its back on God, "in whom is no faithfulness" (Deut 32:20). Ironically, the Gentiles in the previous story who were "far off" (8:3; Eph 2:13-14) are closer to Jesus than those of his own faith and people like the Pharisees. The solemn declaration, "'I tell you the truth,'" has been used only once before in Mark with reference to the scribes' accusing Jesus of complicity with the devil. The repeat of the declaration here suggests that the Pharisees' antagonism is in league with the opposition of 3:22. The last part of v. 12 is an unusual grammatical construction in Greek. It is a Semitic construction — which roots it in Jesus or the early church — implying categorical denial. It means: "If a sign shall be given to this generation, may I die!"[8] Israel's disobedience in Moses' day (Deut 32:5-20) has been bequeathed to Jesus' day.

13 "Then he left them, got back into the boat and crossed to the other side."[9] That is a physical description of Jesus departing from one place to another, but it also appears to symbolize Jesus' parting ways with the Pharisees. Why does Jesus refuse to grant a sign? Is it because of the messianic secret (see at 1:34)? Probably not, for the issue in Dalmanutha is not Jesus' need for concealment but the Pharisees' disbelief. In the Synoptic Gospels the demand for "signs" is itself a sign of attempting

7. J. B. Gibson, "Another Look at Why Jesus 'Sighs Deeply': *anastenazō* in Mark 8:12a," *JTS* 47 (1996): 131-40.

8. For the expression, see Gen 14:23; Num 32:11; Deut 1:35; 1 Kgs 3:14; 6:31; Ps 94:11. The *ei dothēsetai* ("it will not be given") is a Semitism for *'m yinaten*. Matt 16:4 replaces the *ei* with a standard *ou*. This explanatory change, as well as the substitution of Magadan (Matt 15:39) for Mark's difficult Dalmanutha, argues in favor of Matthew's use of Mark rather than the reverse.

9. Manuscript evidence is rather evenly divided whether to include or omit "into the boat." Nor are arguments from probability conclusive, for a scribe may have omitted the phrase as redundant after "embarked" *(embas)*; or, conversely, "embarked" may have suggested the addition of "into the boat" to a scribe. See Metzger, *TCGNT,* 97.

to gain by empirical means what can only be gained by faith and trust. It is the false prophet who seeks to deceive by signs and wonders (13:22). Jesus forsakes signs, for "to force the evidence upon one would make a faith response by its very nature impossible."[10] Faith that depends on proof is not faith, but only veiled doubt. If a man hires a private eye to spy on his wife while he is away in order to "prove" her faithfulness, the detective's "proofs" will scarcely guarantee the husband's faith. Faith, like love itself, cannot be proven; it can only be demonstrated by trust and active commitment. The Pharisees turn and walk away; the disciples follow Jesus into the boat. Eduard Schweizer draws an insightful conclusion from this closing description: "faith comes when one steps into the boat with Jesus and does not prefer to remain in safety on the shore."[11]

THE ENEMY WITHIN (8:14-21)

The Pharisees' intractable opposition and Jesus' utter dismay in the previous story (8:11-12) marked a nadir in the Galilean ministry. Mark follows this brief and sadly unredemptive encounter with a conversation between Jesus and the disciples in the boat. The disciples' wholesale misunderstanding of Jesus' reference to "yeast" indicates that Jesus has not left the opposition behind with the Pharisees on the lakeshore. It is with him in the boat, if not in outright opposition at least in the bewildering misunderstanding of his own disciples. Jesus is moved to exasperation. Like the prophet Ezekiel, he is an exile among his own people. "'Son of man, you are living among a rebellious people. They have eyes to see but do not see and ears to hear but do not hear'" (Ezek 12:2).

14-15 In the boat the disciples discover that they have no bread with them except one loaf.[12] The topic of bread dominates this pericope, although Jesus and the disciples speak of two different kinds of bread. The disciples lament the shortage of bread (vv. 14, 16), whereas Jesus warns about "the yeast of the Pharisees and that of Herod." Matthew identifies the metaphor of the yeast of the Pharisees and Herod as the *teaching* of the Pharisees and Sadducees (Matt 16:12), and Luke identifies

10. R. A. Guelich, *Mark 1–8:26*, 415.

11. *The Good News According to Mark*, 160.

12. It is sometimes suggested that the one loaf refers to Jesus, who is able to offer himself as nourishment for all. Most recently, see E. LaVerdiere, "'Who Do You Say That I Am?'" *Emmanuel* 96 (1990): 454-63. Such an interpretation is unusually symbolic for the Gospel of Mark. Moreover, it is disjunctive with the subsequent "yeast" of the Pharisees and Herod, which is the thrust of the story.

it as the *hypocrisy* of the Pharisees (Luke 12:2). Mark leaves the metaphor unexplained, and its exact meaning is a matter of debate since the Pharisees and Herod Antipas apparently had little in common. The seriousness of the danger is clear. The word for "warned" (Gk. *diastellein*) means to "order" or "command," and twice Jesus says, "'Be careful'" and "'Watch out for'" the "yeast."

Yeast is a leaven that ferments, causing dough to rise. The image of yeast arises from the feast of unleavened bread at the Exodus (Exod 12:18). One would expect a metaphor deriving from Israel's foundational salvation experience to carry positive connotations, but it does not. In rabbinic literature "yeast" as a metaphor frequently refers to the tendency or intention of the human heart, sometimes in a good sense, but most often in a bad sense.[13] Similarly, in only one instance in the NT does "yeast" carry a positive metaphorical sense (Matt 13:33//Luke 13:21). In its dozen remaining uses "yeast" connotes corruption, unholiness, and danger.[14] The present use of "the yeast of the Pharisees and that of Herod" is clearly a negative warning.

But what is its meaning? The Pharisees and Antipas, after all, shared little in common.[15] Some see the metaphor as a warning against a political Davidic messianism that would attempt an overthrow of Rome in order to unite the Jewish people.[16] But this is unlikely on two counts. First, Antipas owed his position to Rome, and he had nothing to gain and everything to lose by rebelling against Rome. And second, in comparison with the Zealots, Sadducees, and Herodians, the Pharisees were relatively unambitious politically, and were not discontent with Roman rule as long as it did not interfere with the study and application of the Torah. Both the Pharisees and Antipas, in other words, had reasons to support rather than thwart Roman rule. Other scholars regard the metaphor as a warning against the demand for signs.[17] This interpretation fits with the Pharisees' demand for a sign in the previous story, although it is less clear in Mark that Antipas seeks a sign of Jesus.[18] The metaphor probably

13. See Str-B 4/1.466-83.

14. Matt 16:6, 11, 12; Luke 12:1; 1 Cor 5:6 (2x), 7, 8; Gal 5:9 (2x).

15. Some manuscripts (p[45] W Δ Θ) substitute "Herodians" for "Herod," thus bringing the saying into conformity with the Pharisees and Herodians in 3:6 and 12:13. The difficulty of "Herod," however, combined with the considerably superior manuscript evidence for it, argues strongly for the NIV reading.

16. For example, E. Lohmeyer, *Das Evangelium des Markus*, 157; R. Pesch, *Das Markusevangelium*, 1.413.

17. For example, W. Grundmann, *Das Evangelium nach Markus*, 163.

18. According to Luke 23:8, Antipas "hoped to see a sign from Jesus," but this request is not found in Mark. It is true that Antipas saw Jesus' miracles as a sign of John the Baptizer returned to life (6:14), but this was a superstition rather than a test of Jesus.

points in a slightly different direction. The one point at which the Pharisees and Antipas are united is in their opposition to Jesus. We have noted that the circuitous journey to Tyre, Sidon, and the Decapolis in 7:24–8:9 may have been motivated at least in part by harassment of both Antipas (6:14-29) and the Pharisees (7:1-23). Their opposition is the result of disbelief in Jesus, and disbelief is also fermenting among the disciples in the boat.[19] The "yeast of the Pharisees and that of Herod" appears to be the misunderstanding or even disbelief of the disciples that would be in effect as adversarial as that of Antipas and the Pharisees.

16 The disciples are unaware of their actual condition. They quibble about the meaning of "bread" without realizing that they are being infected by a deadly cancer. Their failure to comprehend can produce a hardness of heart that is tantamount to the declared opposition of the Pharisees and Herod. The danger is the more deceptive in their case since they are in daily contact with Jesus; and, as in the case of Jesus' mother and brothers (3:31-35), the fact that they are in physical proximity "with" Jesus (3:14) may lead them to presume they are also with him in purpose and mission. Their proximity to Jesus must grow into understanding, and understanding into faith, or else, like Judas, it will in the end inoculate them to the meaning of his person and work.

17-21 "Aware of their discussion," Jesus musters a counteroffensive. The word translated "discussion" (Gk. *dialogizesthai*), which can also mean to "reason" or "consider," occurs seven times in Mark,[20] but never positively. In each instance it describes various parties — scribes, disciples, Sanhedrin — attempting to resolve the meaning of Jesus on their own. Apart from the illuminating word of Jesus himself, however, human ruminations are futile and do not lead to understanding. Jesus presses the disciples in a fusillade of seven questions combining pleading with censure: Do you still not see?, do you still not understand?, are your hearts hardened? (8:17), can you not see?, can you not hear?, don't you remember? (v. 18), do you still not understand? (v. 21). And if this is not enough, Mark concludes with a painful reminder of the results of the feedings of the five and four thousands (vv. 19-20). The question about the leftovers in the two mass feedings shifts the subject back to actual bread, which departs somewhat from Jesus' initial point about the metaphorical meaning of the "yeast" of the Pharisees and Herod. But the point of the question is lost on the obdurate disciples, for they who have wit-

---

19. E. Haenchen, *Der Weg Jesu*, 288, is correct in noting the common bond between the Pharisees and Antipas in their "hostility" to Jesus, but Guelich, *Mark 1–8:26*, 422-24, is even closer to the mark in seeing "unbelief" as the danger looming with the disciples.
20. 2:6, 8 (2x), 8:16, 17; 9:33; 11:31.

nessed baskets full of bread doubt Jesus' sufficiency in the boat. The prophetic lamentation against the unbelief of Israel is echoed in Jesus' lamentation against the disciples' failure to comprehend: "'Do you have eyes but fail to see, and ears but fail to hear?'" (Jer 5:21; Ezek 12:2; also quoted in *Acts of Thomas* 82). The gist of this quotation was applied to *outsiders* in 4:12, but now it is applied to the disciples!

Failure to understand leads to hardness of heart (8:18). The plea for understanding is a reminder that faith is not separate from understanding, but possible only through understanding. This passage is a good apology for a proper understanding of Christian education. If intellectual and spiritual blindness lead to hardness of heart, *blind faith* without content must inevitably lead there as well. The faith for which Jesus appeals is a faith born of understanding and insight. The disciples are not chastised for not believing but for not *seeing* and *understanding*.

The hardened heart is a particular problem for religious and moral people (e.g., Rom 2:5). An ignorant heart cannot harden itself. Only a knowing heart can harden itself, and that is why those closest to Jesus — the Pharisees (3:5-6) and the disciples (6:52; 8:17) — stand in the gravest danger. The disciples mirror humanity-at-large, which is so stuck in its own world and cares that it is blind and deaf to God. The disciples are anxious about lack of bread, but Jesus is anxious about their lack of faith.

Despite the sorry showing of the disciples in the boat, Mark does not end the story here, nor end it in despair. Jesus has called the disciples (1:16-20; 2:13-14; 3:13-19), and his self-revelation comes only as they follow him. If their itineration with Jesus has revealed the gravity of their misunderstanding, even seemingly effected a regression in their faith, that has at least the negative benefit of ridding them of misconceptions and false expectations of Jesus.[21] Indeed, their failure necessitates and

21. J. B. Tyson, "The Blindness of the Disciples in Mark," *JBL* 80 (1961): 261-68 (repr. in *The Messianic Secret*, Issues in Religion and Theology 1, ed. C. Tuckett [Philadelphia: Fortress Press, 1983], 35-43), proposes that Mark emphasizes the stupidity and recalcitrance of the disciples in order to challenge and unmask a powerful apostolic hierarchy in Jerusalem, which consisted largely of Jesus' family at the time Mark wrote his Gospel. According to Tyson, Mark opposes the Jerusalem elite because it is closed to outside leadership (e.g., Paul and Mark himself) and to the Gentile mission. Tyson's thesis would be more persuasive in a modified form, e.g., that the leaders of the church in Jerusalem did not merit their position by their performance as disciples. But as proposed, Tyson's thesis is open to criticism. For one, it does not account for the rehabilitation of Peter in 14:28 and 16:7. For another, the Jerusalem leadership included a number of influential leaders beyond Jesus' immediate family, including Peter, James, John, and Stephen. Finally, Tyson's thesis fails to deal with the historical probability that Peter is one of the chief sources for the Gospel of Mark. If so, Mark's picture of the disciples is anchored to a historically reliable source rather than in literary apologetic.

makes possible an entirely new understanding of Jesus. Jesus has seemingly reduced them to naught so as to make of them something truly worthy (Rom 11:32!). They will not resolve the mystery of faith on their own. Rather, the one who called them will, by his repeated touch, enable them to see.

THE TOUCH THAT GIVES SIGHT (8:22-26)

After arriving by boat in Bethsaida, Jesus and the disciples are met by people requesting the healing of a blind man. This miracle and the miracle of healing of the deaf-mute in 7:31-37 are similar to one another and are the only two miracles in Mark that are omitted by Matthew and Luke.[22] We are immediately struck by Mark's emphasis on sight in the present miracle as opposed to the emphasis on blindness and lack of comprehension in the previous story (8:14-21). The juxtaposition of the two stories is a clue that the lingering blindness of the disciples may also be relieved, as is the blindness of the man at Bethsaida, by the continued touch of Jesus.

22 The boat journey mentioned in 8:13-14 brings Jesus and the disciples to Bethsaida. Located on the north shore of the Sea of Galilee, Bethsaida lay immediately to the east of the outflow of the Jordan into the

---

22. Similarities between the two accounts include the following: in both accounts Jesus cures the individual away from the crowd, both make use of spittle and the laying on of hands, and in both Jesus has an interest in secrecy. R. Bultmann, *The History of the Synoptic Tradition*, rev. ed., trans. J. Marsh (Oxford: Blackwell, 1972), 213, regards 8:22-26 as a variant of 7:31-37. Bultmann's dismissal of 8:22-26 ("We must take Jesus' journey north as a phantasy, and eliminate it from history," p. 65) is unduly cavalier. Despite the external similarities of the accounts, there are significant differences, including the influence of Isaiah 35 (present in 7:31-37 but absent in 8:22-26), the different maladies and locations of each account, and the second touch in the latter account, which is unique among Jesus' healings. An argument for a doublet requires more proof than noting general similarities between two accounts. In a slightly different vein, J.-F. Baudoz, "Mc 7,31-37 et Mc 8,22-26. Geographie et Theologie," *RB* 102 (1995): 560-69, argues that Mark received from tradition two healing accounts associated with Bethsaida and placed them at 7:31-37 and 8:22-26, respectively, to emphasize a universalist theology and a preparation for Peter's confession. Arguments from "tradition" are necessarily speculative in Mark's case since (if one holds to Markan priority) we do not have a pre-Markan tradition (or the means of definitely reconstructing one) with which to compare canonical Mark. Baudoz's redactional observations are not implausible, but neither do they evince his thesis. For discussions of the differences between the two accounts, see V. Taylor, *The Gospel According to St. Mark*, 369-70; D. E. Nineham, *The Gospel of St Mark*, 217; and C. E. B. Cranfield, *The Gospel According to Saint Mark*, 263-64.

lake. Like several towns surrounding the lake, Bethsaida, meaning "house of the fisher," derived its name from its chief industry. It lay in Gaulanitis in the tetrarchy of Philip, just east of the Galilee border. Along with Caesarea Philippi, Bethsaida-Julias had been built by Philip and named after Caesar Augustus's daughter, Julia.[23]

23-25 Jesus personally takes the hand of the blind man and conducts him outside the village.[24] We are not told explicitly that Jesus desires to be alone with him (as in 7:33), although he does desire to separate him from the village, perhaps because of its unbelief (see 6:45). In several instances in Mark the essential work that Jesus does with individuals necessitates his separating them from crowds. As in 7:33, Jesus heals the man by applying spittle to his eyes. Such gestures, as we noted at 7:33, were not unknown to Hellenistic healers. Tacitus records a story of Vespasian (Roman emperor, A.D. 69-79), who was importuned by a person whose sight was failing to "moisten his cheeks and eyes with his spittle."[25] Unlike the account of Vespasian, however, with Jesus there is no calculation, no hesitation, and no use of the infirm individual for ulterior ends.

Especially distinctive of this story are the references to **touching** and **laying on of hands**. What is the significance of Jesus' tactile contact with people? In the OT, laying on of hands occurs for three purposes: the dedication of sacrifices to God (its most frequent use; Exod 29:10, 15; Lev 1:4; 3:2ff.); installing of Levites to the office of priest (Num 8:10); and a means of blessing (Gen 48:17ff.; Num 27:18, 23; Deut 34:9). There is only one instance in the OT where the laying on of hands is linked with heal-

---

23. Josephus, *Ant.* 18.28. Josephus says that Philip "raised the village of Bethsaida . . . to the status of a city (Gk. *polis*) by adding residents and strengthening its fortifications"; Mark, however, refers to it simply as a village *(kōmē)*. Bethsaida was the home of at least three of Jesus' apostles: Philip, Andrew, and Peter (John 1:44; 12:21). It furnished a quarter of the apostolic college, but there is no indication that Jesus' ministry was unusually successful there ("'Woe to you, Korazin! Woe to you, Bethsaida!'" [Matt 11:21//Luke 10:13]). See M. Avi-Yonah, "Bethsaida," *IDB* 1.397.

24. The manuscript tradition is divided on how Jesus escorted the man outside the village. Three important uncials (A D W) read *exēgagen* ("led out"), but a stronger cohort of manuscripts (א B C L) reads *exēnenken* ("brought out"). The latter is the preferable reading, accentuating the role of Jesus in conducting the man outside the village.

25. Tacitus, *Hist.* 4.81. The story is repeated in a shorter form by Suetonius, "The Deified Vespasian" (7), *The Lives of the Caesars*. Both Tacitus and Suetonius agree that Vespasian initially ridiculed the request out of disbelief in such cures. Only after his advisors reasoned that a failed attempt would make the blind man look foolish whereas a success would crown him with glory did Vespasian consent to the healing. The restoration of the man's sight (which was diminished but not completely gone) was regarded by both Tacitus and Suetonius as something less than a true miracle, perhaps owing to autosuggestion.

ing, and that was the vain hope of Naaman, the Syrian general, for a cure from leprosy at the hands of Elisha (2 Kgs 5:11). Whether Jesus takes over the laying on of hands from the OT is unclear, for he lays on hands for different purposes than for those prescribed in the OT. If he is indebted to the OT for the practice (which would not be surprising), it receives an entirely new emphasis in his ministry. Particularly in Mark, where there are more references to laying on of hands than in any other Gospel, all but one instance occur in the context of healings. The terminology, however, varies. In some instances the infirm and troubled seek to touch Jesus (3:10; 5:27-31; 6:56), and in others Jesus extends a healing touch to them (1:41; 7:33; 8:22). Sometimes healing is accompanied by the actual laying on of Jesus' (5:23; 7:32; 8:23, 25) or the disciples' hands (6:5; 16:18). The only instance of laying on of hands as a blessing is the blessing of the children in 10:13.[26] The two primary purposes of laying on of hands in the Old Covenant were to transfer either animals or persons from the profane to the sacred by consecrating them to God. When Jesus lays hands on people the effect is rather the opposite, however, for the profane is no longer elevated to the sacred, as in the OT, but rather by bestowing God's holy and healing presence on ordinary, common, and even sinful people, Jesus brings the sacred to the profane.

In Mark's account of the healing of the blind man at Bethsaida not only the climax of the story but the entire narrative is constructed on the motif of "seeing." In English translations several of the words used for sight are the same, but in the original Greek there are eight different words used for nine instances of seeing in 8:23-25![27] The redundancy of references to sight and seeing provides a counterbalance to the redundancy of accusations of blindness and misunderstanding in the previous story. Yet another link between this miracle and the previous story occurs in the speech of Jesus to the blind man. At a miracle Jesus normally speaks an authoritative word or makes a pronouncement. Here, however, he asks a question, "'Do you see anything?'" (v. 23). That unusual question looks like an echo of Jesus' pleading questions of the disciples in the previous story, the first of which was "'Do you still not see?'" (8:17). The blind man's response that he can see people who "look like trees walking around" (v. 24) is a clue that the disciples themselves will be enabled by Jesus to begin the process of moving from blindness to sight.[28]

26. See C. Maurer, "tithēmi," TDNT 8.159-61; R. Grob, "haptō," NIDNTT 3.859-61.

27. Among the words for "sight," it should be pointed out that anablepsas ("he looked up," v. 24) means to "regain sight," not simply to "look up." See the evidence from the NT, LXX, classical Greek literature, and the church fathers gathered in E. S. Johnson Jr., "Mark VIII.22-26: The Blind Man from Bethsaida," NTS 25 (1979): 376-77.

28. R. S. Sugirtharajah, "Men, Trees and Walking: A Conjectural Solution to Mk

The healing of the blind man of Bethsaida is the only miracle in the Gospels that proceeds in stages rather than being instantly effected. Matthew and Luke omit this miracle, likely because it suggested that Jesus was unsuccessful on the first attempt.[29] The necessity of repeated touches cannot imply for Mark insufficiency on Jesus' part, however, since elsewhere Jesus performs more difficult miracles (from a human perspective) without fail, such as healing the Gerasene demoniac (5:1-20) or raising a dead girl (5:35-43). The two-stage cure in the present miracle thus suggests a *process* of revelation — as much for the disciples, we suspect, as for the blind man at Bethsaida.

26 The account concludes with Jesus sending the healed man home rather than back to the village. The textual tradition is splintered as to whether Jesus commanded him to silence,[30] but it is clear that Jesus does not want the man to broadcast the miracle (see the **Command to Silence** at 1:34).

This story brings us to the continental divide of Mark's narrative. By the gradual healing of the blind man, Jesus shows how the disciples, in particular, may come to faith. Like the blind man, the disciples, who "have eyes but fail to see, and ears but fail to hear" (8:18), can also be made to see and hear. But it will not happen on their own. The ability to

---

8:24," *ExpTim* 103 (1992): 172-74, sees the reference to walking trees in v. 24 as a critique of a Davidic political Messiah, based on Jotham's fable of the trees in Judg 9:7-15. The concept of a Davidic political Messiah, suggests Sugirtharajah, is like the unworthy bramble or thornbush in Jotham's parable that must be uprooted if the disciples are rightly to understand Jesus. Sugirtharajah's conjecture is consonant with Mark's emphasis on a suffering Messiah (e.g., 8:29-31; chap. 15, where the title "king of the Jews/Israel" occurs six times of the suffering Jesus), but whether the opaque reference of v. 24 intends it is debatable, since Jotham's fable speaks of the trees talking rather than walking.

29. Johnson, "Mark VIII.22-26: The Blind Man from Bethsaida," *NTS* 25 (1979): 370-83, argues that Matthew and Luke omit the story because they do not wish to emphasize the blindness of the disciples. This is possible, but it is not as compelling as the argument of omission because of the successive touches of Jesus. That Mark includes a story about healing a blind man immediately following a story about the disciples' blindness (8:14-21) suggests a relationship between the two stories. In itself, however, the story of the healing of the blind man at Bethsaida need not be connoted, as Johnson suggests, with the disciples' blindness. Thus Matthew and Luke could have used the story for other purposes. Since they did not have to reject it because of its connotation of the disciples' blindness, it is more probable that they omitted it because of its *denotation* of Jesus' insufficiency to heal.

30. It appears that the earliest form of the saying, which is well attested (א B L), was the reading adopted by the NIV, "'Don't go into the village.'" An Old Latin manuscript, however, reads "'Don't speak to anyone in the village,'" and this reading appears to have been conflated with the former to produce a longer reading that was often followed in the manuscript tradition, "'Don't go into the village and don't speak to anyone in the village.'" See Metzger, *TCGNT*, 98-99.

see, both physically and spiritually, is a gift of God, not of human ability. We hear nothing of the man's faith or behavior in the present story. There is no hint that as his faith grew his healing progressed. His healing from failed sight to partial sight to complete sight comes solely from the repeated touch of Jesus. His healing exemplifies the situation of the disciples, who move through the same three stages in Mark, from non-understanding (8:17-21) to misunderstanding (8:29-33) to complete understanding (15:39).[31] The first "healing touch" for them will come on the road to Caesarea Philippi (8:27ff.) when Peter declares that Jesus is Messiah. The disciples will be no longer blind, but their vision will remain imperfect and blurred, for they do not understand the meaning of Messiahship. Only at the cross and resurrection will they, like the man at Bethsaida, see "everything clearly" (v. 25).

PETER'S DECLARATION OF JESUS' MESSIAHSHIP (8:27-30)

With Peter's declaration at Caesarea Philippi Mark's story of Jesus reaches a denouement. Heretofore the disciples, like the crowds and especially the religious leaders of the Pharisees and scribes, have been ranged against Jesus on a scale from misunderstanding to opposition. They have been slow of understanding and hard of heart. Responses of faithfulness to Jesus have been few and sporadic, and when faithfulness has been found, it has surprisingly come from "outsiders" — from an unclean woman (5:25-34), a Syrophoenician woman (7:24-30), and a Gentile deaf-mute (7:31-37). Declarations of Jesus' true identity as God's Son have been given by Mark as narrator (1:1), by God (1:9-11), and by demons (1:25; 3:11; 5:7), but not yet by humans. Caesarea Philippi is the first breakthrough in the human plot of the Gospel. Peter's declaration is the first attempt on the part of the disciples to identify and define the *exousia*, the divine authority, with which Jesus has taught and acted.

27 The freeing of the logjam of the disciples' misunderstanding begins with Jesus and the disciples en route to **Caesarea Philippi**. Caesarea Philippi lay twenty-five miles due north of Bethsaida, a full day's walk from the latter site. Not to be confused with the better-known Caesarea on the Mediterranean coast, "Philip's Caesarea" lay in the north of the tetrarchy of Philip at the foot of Mt. Hermon, bordering on Syria.

31. So A. Kuby, "Zur Konzeption des Markus-Evangeliums," *ZNW* 49 (1958): 52-64.

The city had been refurbished by Philip and named in honor of Caesar Augustus, who ruled the Roman Empire for fifty-seven years (Josephus, *Ant.* 18.28; *War* 2.168). Caesarea Philippi was an unlikely place for the first proclamation of Jesus as Messiah, for its population was chiefly non-Jewish. It was also the site of two painful memories to Jews. It was in Caesarea Philippi that Antiochus IV gained a decisive victory over Egypt in 200 B.C., causing Palestine to fall to the Seleucids and plunging the whole region into twenty years of war following the Maccabean Revolt in 168 B.C. The city was also famous for its sanctuary to Pan (from which the city gained the name Caesarea Panias). Half man and half goat, Pan was revered as the guardian of flocks and nature and worshiped in a grotto at the foot of Mt. Hermon next to the cave from which one of the three major tributaries of the Jordan River gushes forth. It is here in the outer regions of paganism and even hostility to Judaism that Jesus is first proclaimed Messiah!

Mark's initial verb, to "set out" (Gk. *exēlthen*), implies a deliberate beginning. Peter's confession is identified with "the villages around Caesarea Philippi" (Matt 16:13, "the region around Caesarea Philippi"), and not necessarily with the city itself. "On the way" Jesus asks for a judgment from the disciples. Beginning with this verse, "on the way" occurs nine times in chaps. 8–12 as a designation that the "way of the Lord" proclaimed by John the Baptist at the outset of the Gospel (1:2-3) is fulfilled in Jesus' going to Jerusalem. Significantly, Jesus raises the question of faith, according to Mark, "on the way" of humiliation, rejection, suffering, and death. Faith and discipleship cannot be rendered from the sidelines, removed from risk. Jesus asks for a judgment about him in the midst of the journey, not at the end of it when all questions are answered and proof is finally in hand. Faith is a judgment about Jesus, and a willingness to act on the judgment in the face of other possible judgments. Indeed, for the disciples at this point in the Gospel faith will necessitate a choice *contrary* to the prevailing consensus of crowds and religious leaders. Faith means actively following Jesus *on the way,* not demanding signs (8:11-13) or turning to go one's own way (10:22).

Ordinarily in Judaism, it was disciples who posed questions to their rabbis rather than the reverse. But Jesus is no ordinary rabbi, and so far as we know the question he puts to the disciples has been asked by no rabbi before. "'Who do people say I am?'" Normally, people ask what others *do*, not who they *are*. The latter question is more unusual and more profound, and in this instance it reflects the question the disciples have harbored at least since the stilling of the storm, "'Who is this? Even the wind and waves obey him?'" (4:41).

"'Who do people say I am?'" Jesus puts the question to the disciples in two stages: what others say and what the disciples themselves say (v. 29). There is a psychological astuteness in intensifying the question thus, for it is usually less daunting to venture the opinions of others than to risk declaring our own thoughts. But there is more than psychology in Jesus' question. The judgments of others about Jesus have ranged from sympathy to hostility and have thus not been univocal. The two stages of the question require the disciples to form and express their own judgment about Jesus rather than merely seconding the views of others. They must separate themselves from the majority opinion and risk a personal confession. Faith expresses itself in a public confession of Jesus, and neither faith nor confession is a proxy vote. There is a difference between judgment and confession: we may be instructed by the judgments of others, but the declaration that Jesus is the Christ depends on a believer's personal confession.

28 The disciples' initial answer echoes popular opinion about Jesus, that he is John the Baptist returned to life, or Elijah, or one of the prophets. This is the same judgment voiced earlier by Herod Antipas (6:14-15). No OT personality held such fascination for first-century Judaism as **Elijah**. The reason lay not in his deeds, for the accomplishments of other OT figures — Abraham, Moses, David, even Joshua — exceeded Elijah's. The reason lay in the report that Elijah had been taken bodily to heaven (2 Kgs 2:11) where he was believed to oversee the deeds of mortals, to comfort the faithful and help the needy, and, above all, to return as forerunner of the great and terrible Day of the Lord (Mal 3:1; 4:5-6).[32]

As for John the Baptist, Antipas had drawn a direct correlation between Jesus and John, suspecting that John, whom he had beheaded, was reincarnated in Jesus (6:14-15). And as for the prophets, common currency was not simply that Jesus was a prophet in general, but "one of *the* prophets" hallowed in the Old Covenant. Ever since Moses had foretold that God would "raise up for you a prophet like me from among your brothers" (Deut 18:15, 18), Israel had awaited a final prophet who would stand in the category of the OT prophets and declare God's word conclusively to the people.

To liken Jesus to John, Elijah, or a prophet was to rank him among the stellar figures in Israel's long and illustrious history. That is an indication of Jesus' preeminent standing in the popular mind. Yet even these comparisons are inadequate. Even if Jesus were a new Moses or Elijah, it would simply designate him as the reemergence and fulfillment of an earlier prototype. To say that Jesus is like Elijah, John the Baptist, or a

32. See Str-B 4/2.764-98.

great prophet — or, as we so often hear today, that he is the greatest teacher or moral example who ever lived — may seem like an honor and compliment, but it is ultimately to deny his uniqueness and to press him into the service of old categories. It is "to pour new wine into old wineskins" (2:22). The authority that Jesus has demonstrated throughout Mark's narrative does not allow him to be defined by something other than himself and his relationship with the Father.

29-30 Jesus is not content to know what others think and say of him. His mission is not decided by his standing in the polls but by the judgment of each follower whom he has called. "'But what about you? Who do you say I am?'" The intensification of the question from what others think to what the disciples think repeats Mark's "outsider-insider" theme. If the disciples are to fulfill the role of insiders and understand "the secret of the kingdom of God" (4:11), they can do so only by penetrating Jesus' true identity and understanding the purpose for which he has come. The categories of John the Baptizer or Elijah or one of the prophets are no closer to the real Jesus than are the various "Jesus" figures of historical criticism or Enlightenment rationalism or feminism or Aryan and racist theories or the Jesus Seminar or the various sociological models in our day.[33] Jesus' comrades are asked to render a judgment about his remarkable *exousia*, his divine authority, which they have witnessed and experienced. This judgment cannot be rendered by collecting more evidence and data, or by further deliberations, observations, discussions, and explanations. The disciples must move from the status of passive recipients to active participants. At some point the colleagues of Jesus — and everyone who has heard his name — must look deep within Jesus and deep within themselves and risk a decision that will entail either a commitment to or a severance from the identity and mission of this Jesus.

Jesus has not rushed this moment. How long the disciples have been with him we cannot say, but it has been several months, perhaps a year or longer. Jesus wills that their choice be based not on hearsay or feelings but on experience. They have seen him teach, heal, and interact with the authorities. If they are to continue "on the way" with him, they cannot remain spectators and bystanders but must themselves become

---

33. The question "'Who do you say I am?'" is of central significance with regard to the upsurge of interest in the "historical Jesus." According to the NT, who Jesus is cannot be discovered or recovered by new historical data or theories or better sociological models but only from the apostolic testimony itself, of which Peter's declaration is the beginning. "One cannot learn who Jesus from Nazareth is by 'the quest of the historical Jesus,' but only by recourse to the apostolic witness to Christ in the New Testament." O. Hofius, "Ist Jesus der Messias? Thesen," *JBTh* 8 (*Der Messias*, 1993): 104.

participators. The way to Jerusalem involves the way of suffering, and for the disciples to participate in that way requires a fellowship based on faith. "'Who do you say I am?'" This is the central question of Mark's Gospel — and of every presentation of the gospel. The essential meaning of faith is contained in the answer given.

Peter answers that Jesus is the Christ, the Messiah of God.[34] Only God and demons have recognized Jesus as Messiah in Mark so far. No human actor has yet declared Jesus to be Messiah.[35] Mark is correct to credit Peter with the insight, but Peter's confession represents the confession of the Twelve as well, as shown by Jesus' public rebuke of Peter in v. 33, whose false understanding of Messiah is shared by the Twelve and threatens to corrupt them.

Excursus: Christ

The Greek word "Christ" translates the Heb. "Messiah," meaning "to anoint." In the OT, three classes of people received anointing: prophets, priests, and kings. The third class, kings, influenced the development of the concept of the Messiah in Judaism (e.g., 2 Samuel 7; Psalm 2). Especially as the monarchy failed and eventually fell to Nebuchadnezzar in 586 B.C., an expectation grew in Israel that God would raise up a new and even greater king like David. "'The days are coming,' declares the LORD, 'when I will raise up to David a righteous Branch, a King who will reign wisely and do what is just and right in the land'" (Jer 23:5).[36] The OT does not use "the Messiah" in an absolute sense, nor does it develop or present a formal doctrine of the Messiah. This also remains generally true for the subsequent intertestamental period, when the concept of Messiah is less frequent and developed than is often supposed. The earliest known instance of the absolute use of the term "the Messiah" comes from Qumran

34. The historicity of Peter's declaration is supported by Jesus' reserve with regard to the title (v. 30) and by his sharp rebuke of Peter's falsification of the title (v. 33). See E. Schweizer, *Theologische Einleitung in das Neue Testament*, GNT 2 (Göttingen: Vandenhoeck & Ruprecht, 1989), 19.

35. According to the *Gospel of Thomas* 13, Jesus is not only a "messenger" (so Peter) or a "wise philosopher" (so Matthew), but someone ineffable who cannot be captured in human thought and words (so Thomas). The Gnosticism of the *Gospel of Thomas* is especially apparent in log. 13, which holds that Jesus escapes and defies human conception. This is in direct contrast to the Gospel of Mark and the NT portrait of Jesus as a whole. In becoming truly human, Jesus enters human categories rather than eschewing them, and requires human judgments about him.

36. OT messianic texts include Isa 9:1-6; 11:1-10; Jer 30:8-11; 33:14-18; Ezek 17:22-24; 34:23-31; 37:15-28; Mic 5:1-5; Zech 9:9-13.

(1QSa 2:12).[37] The most common conception of the Messiah in pre-Christian texts is as an eschatological king. Otherwise, the messianic hope remained fairly general. Through the Messiah God would establish and protect an everlasting kingdom over all the earth. The Messiah would be the perfect king chosen by God from eternity, through whom God would first deliver Israel from its enemies and then cause Israel to live in peace and tranquillity thereafter (*Sib. Or.* 3:286-94). It may also be noted that neither the Servant of Yahweh nor Son of Man concept in the OT is associated with messianic connotations.

Disappointment with the Hasmonean princes who ruled over Israel in the second century B.C. after the Maccabean revolt, and disillusionment following Pompey's seizure of Jerusalem in 63 B.C., caused messianic expectations to increase in both specificity and compass. Though entirely human,[38] the Messiah would nevertheless be far greater than God's earlier messengers to Israel, "powerful in word and deed before God and all the people" (Luke 24:19). He would be endowed with miraculous powers, and be mighty and wise in the Holy Spirit. The Messiah would be holy and free from sin, the final Anointed One and true king of Israel who would destroy God's enemies by the word of his mouth. He would deliver Jerusalem from the Gentiles, gather the faithful from dispersion, and rule in justice and glory. This hope comes to full flower in the *Psalms of Solomon*:

> O Lord, raise up their king, the son of David,
>> that he may reign over Israel thy servant.
> Gird him with strength that he might shatter unrighteous rulers,
>> that he may purge Jerusalem from nations
>> that trample her to destruction.
> Wisely, righteously he shall thrust out sinners from the inheritance;
>> he shall destroy the pride of the sinner as a potter's vessel.
> With a rod of iron he shall break in pieces all their substance,
>> he shall destroy the godless nation with the word of his mouth;
>> at his rebuke nations shall fall before him,
>> and he shall reprove sinners for the thoughts of their heart.
> He shall gather together a holy people, whom he shall lead
>> in righteousness,
>> and he shall judge the tribes of the people that have
>> been sanctified by the Lord his God.

---

37. See F. G. Martínez, "Messianische Erwartungen in den Qumranschriften," *JBTh* 8 (1993, *Der Messias*): 171-208.

38. The Jew Trypho declares that the Messiah will be *anthrōpos ex anthrōpōn genomenos* ("a human born of humans") (Justin Martyr, *Dial. Trypho* 67.2 [cf. 48.1; 49.1]).

And he shall not allow unrighteousness to lodge any more in their
  midst,
nor shall there dwell with them any man who knows wickedness,
for he shall know them, that they are all sons of their God.
(Pss. Sol. 17:23-30)[39]

This was the popular concept of the Messiah in Jesus' day. It may
not be purely coincidental that Peter comes to this conclusion at this time
and place, and that "Jesus warned them not to tell anyone about him."
(On the **Command to Silence**, see at 1:34.) En route to Caesarea Philippi
the disciples had passed to the west of the pinnacle of Gamala, the home
of Judas the Galilean, whose sons, attempting to fulfill the prophecy of
Psalms of Solomon 17, took up arms against Rome in A.D. 66 and plunged
the nation into a catastrophic defeat by the armies of Vespasian and Titus.
Josephus referred to Judas as the founder of "the fourth philosophy" of
the Jews (in addition to the Pharisees, Sadducees, and Essenes), the
Sicarii, "whose passion for liberty is almost unconquerable, since they
think that God alone is their leader and master" (*Ant.* 18.23). Judas had
founded the movement in opposition to the census of Quirinius in A.D. 6,
and in the following years the *Sicarii* (= dagger men, assassins) had joined
forces with the Zealots in order to liberate the Holy City from Roman occupation. Their goal was to secure the temple for purity of worship and
to affirm God alone as the ruler of Israel.[40]

Gamala may have been one of "the villages around Caesarea
Philippi" (v. 27) that Jesus visited. Or perhaps its proximity and associations prompt the disciples to see Jesus in a new light. We cannot know exactly what prompted Peter to declare Jesus the Messiah, but Jesus will cut a
different profile from the popular stereotype. Jesus will of course identify
with some of the ideas associated with Messiah, such as liberation and

---

39. For discussions of the messianic expectation, see Str-B 4/2.799-1,015; G. F. M.
Moore, *Judaism in the First Centuries of the Christian Era* (New York: Schocken Books,
1971), 2.323-76; Schürer, *History of the Jewish People*, 2.488-54; Hofius, "Ist Jesus der
Messias? Thesen," *JBTh* 8 (*Der Messias*, 1993): 103-29. Qumran expected two Messiah figures: a son of David as military deliverer and a son of Aaron as high priest (1QS 9:11).
The expectation of a messianic high priest seems to have been limited to Qumran, however, and to have exerted little if any influence on subsequent Judaism. The texts and allusions to the Messiah in Mark all appear to reflect a military conqueror. These include
the apparent aspirations of the crowd at the feeding of the five thousand (6:31-44), the
reference to Jesus as the "son of David," the enthusiasm of the crowd at the triumphal entry (11:8-10; in the parallel passage in Luke 19:38 Jesus is called "king"), and Rome's execution of Jesus as "king of the Jews" (15:26).

40. Simon and Jacob, the sons of Judas, were later crucified by Rome as insurrectionists, and Judas's nephew Menahem — and Menahem's nephew Eleazar ben Jair
— both died in the last stand at Masada. See Schürer, *History of the Jewish People*, 598-606.

peace, but he will eschew others, especially those associated with military power and rule. In declaring Jesus as the Christ, Peter has supplied the proper title, but he has the wrong understanding.[41] His "vision," to use the imagery in 8:22-26, is improved but still blurry. Jesus will don the servant's towel rather than the warrior's sword; he will practice sacrifice above vengeance. He will not inflict suffering, but suffer himself as a "ransom for many" (10:45). As God's servant, Jesus must remain hidden if he is to complete God's appointment (Isa 49:1-6). This Peter does not know, and consequently Jesus swears him to silence (v. 30), lest a false report arouse revolutionary fervor. Jesus must now begin to teach the *true* meaning of Peter's confession. For this, Peter and the disciples are quite unprepared.

MESSIAHSHIP AND DISCIPLESHIP (8:31–9:1)

At the beginning of the Gospel, Mark announced Jesus to be the Christ (1:1), but until now he has kept the theme under wraps. For the first time we are now told that Jesus "spoke plainly about" his purpose and mission (v. 32). The word for "plainly" (Gk. *parrēsią*), which in John's Gospel often refers to Jesus' bold disclosure of his purpose (7:26; 11:14; 16:25, 29; 18:20), appears only here in the Synoptic Gospels and, ironically, only in connection with impending suffering. Peter has called Jesus "Messiah" (8:29), and Jesus now begins to explain what it means. The explanation results in bewilderment and dismay, not only because of its implications for Messiahship but equally because of its implications for discipleship.

31 "He then began to teach them that the Son of Man must suffer many things and be rejected by the elders, chief priests and teachers of the law, and that he must be killed and after three days rise again." (On Son of Man, see at 2:10.) The phrase "he began to teach" reads like a Greek translation of an underlying Semitism. It also suggests the arduous task that lay before Jesus in teaching the disciples the true meaning of Messiahship. 8:31 is the first of three passion predictions in Mark (8:31; 9:31; 10:33-34; on the **passion predictions**, see at 10:34). It is a stupefying pronouncement. When Jesus finally speaks of his messianic status it is not to claim the common understanding but to redefine it practically beyond recognition. Jesus is not the expected messianic teacher who would expound and reinstitute the Torah in Jewish life; rather, he teaches in puzzling and probing parables about the surprising inbreaking of God's

41. R. P. Martin, *Mark: Evangelist and Theologian* (Exeter: Paternoster Press, 1972), 129.

kingdom and the nearness of his love and forgiveness of sinners. Nor does Jesus exhibit stereotypical messianic authority, such as royal dominion, reestablishing and purifying the temple cult and above all expelling Gentiles from Jewish life; rather, his *exousia* is rooted in *who* he is. As God's Son he reconstitutes Israel in the call of the Twelve (3:13-19), reinterprets God's commandments (2:27-28), presumes to forgive sins (2:10), has power over nature (4:39; 6:48), and speaks for and as God.[42]

Not only does Jesus not fit the messianic stereotype, but he defines his mission in scandalous contrast to it. The meaning of his life and mission is not about victory and success, but about rejection, suffering, and death. When Jesus finally speaks to the issue of his identity and mission it is summed up in "The Son of Man must *suffer* many things." Never in Israel was it heard that the Messiah should suffer. There is of course the image of the suffering servant in Isaiah, but as noted in the excursus on Christ there is no evidence that the Servant of the Lord texts were ever associated with the Messiah.[43] Nor is there any allusion to the expiatory suffering of the Messiah. The suffering foreseen by Jesus is not regarded as is suffering in the Psalms, for instance, as a lamentable misfortune contrary to God's will. Rather, the way to Jerusalem and the bitter end that awaits Jesus there are affirmed as God's ordained way for him: he *must* suffer. Eduard Schweizer perceives the revelatory significance of Jesus' suffering:

> God is therein precisely God in that he can do what humanity cannot do: God can allow himself to be rejected, to be made low and small, without thereby being driven into an inferiority complex. . . . Whoever understands the suffering of the Son of Man understands God. It is there, and not in heavenly splendor, that one sees the heart of God.[44]

42. On Jesus' authority, see J. R. Edwards, "The Authority of Jesus in the Gospel of Mark," *JETS* 37 (1994): 223-25; and Hofius, "Ist Jesus der Messias? Thesen," *JBTh* 8 (*Der Messias*, 1993): 119-21.

43. Isa 42:1-4; 49:1-6; 50:4-11a; 52:13–53:12. The *Targum of Jonathan* does associate the Servant of Yahweh with the Messiah in Isaiah 53, but it interprets the verses that refer to suffering as *not* referring to the Messiah! (See Schürer, *History of the Jewish People*, 2.547-49.) This tradition of interpretation generally continues in Jewish interpretations until today. As one example, A. Heschel's otherwise excellent discussion of prophecy passes over the Suffering Servant passages in silence and never raises the issue of the Messiah (*The Prophets*, 2 vols. [New York: Harper Torchbooks, 1962], 1.145-58).

44. *Das Evangelium nach Markus*, 98 (my translation). Compare a similar thought of the divine humility in Dante:

> Limited man, by subsequent obedience,
> could never make amends; he could not go
> as low in his humility as once,
> rebellious, he had sought to rise in pride. (*Paradiso*, Canto 7, lines 97-99)

The prediction of Jesus' passion conceals a great irony, for the suffering and death of the Son of Man will not come, as we would expect, at the hands of godless and wicked people. The suffering of the Son of Man comes rather at the hands of "the elders, chief priests and teachers of the law." It is not humanity at its worst that will crucify the Son of God but humanity at its absolute best. The death of Jesus will not be the result of a momentary lapse or aberration of human nature, but rather the result of careful deliberations from respected religious leaders who will justify their actions by the highest standards of law and morality, even believing them to render service to God (John 16:2). Jesus will not be lynched by an enraged mob or beaten to death in a criminal act. He will be arrested with official warrants, and tried and executed by the world's envy of jurisprudence — the Jewish Sanhedrin and the *principia iuris Romanorum.*

The Jewish **Sanhedrin** consisted of elders, chief priests, and scribes. The elders comprised seventy lay members of the ruling council, both Sadducees and Pharisees. The chief priests included the current high priest of the Sanhedrin and his predecessors, as well as their family members. The chief priests all belonged to the sect of the Sadducees, and in Jesus' day they included Caiaphas, who ruled from A.D. 18 to 36; his father-in-law Annas, who ruled from A.D. 6 to 15; and Caiaphas's successor Jonathan and his brother Theophilus (see Acts 4:6; Josephus, *Ant.* 18.26, 95, 124). The scribes were legal experts and advisors to the Sanhedrin (further, see **scribes** at 1:22). These three groups — elders, chief priests, and scribes — comprised the Sanhedrin, which represented the official seat of religious power among the Jews.

32 The suffering, rejection, death, and resurrection of the Son of Man, though shocking and offensive, are the essential content of Jesus' messianic identity. "He spoke plainly about this" carries more theological freight in the original Greek than in the NIV translation. The word for "plainly," *parrēsia,* occurring only here in the Synoptic Gospels, means "boldly" or "confidently." The perspicacity with which the blind man finally saw in 8:22-26 is the perspicacity with which Jesus now identifies his mission (John 10:24!). In so doing Jesus boldly declares "the word" (Gk. *ton logon*).[45] This is one of the few instances in Mark where "word" is

---

45. G. Aichele, "Jesus' Frankness," *Semeia* 69-70 (1995): 261-80, understands v. 32 to refer to the title of the Son of Man, which she finds absurd since in her opinion one cannot speak plainly about such an ambiguous concept. Mark, however, does not say that Jesus was frank about the Son of Man but about "the word," which here refers to his *suffering.* E. Cuvillier, "'Il proclamait ouvertement la Parole.' Notule sur la traduction de Marc 8/32a," *ETR* 63 (1988): 427-28, is closer to the truth in noting that "word" refers to the content of proclamation, not specifically to the Son of Man. He would be absolutely correct, however, to recognize the association of the "word" here with Jesus' passion!

used in an absolute sense (1:45; 2:2; 4:33; 8:32; 9:10). Heretofore it has more or less signified "the secret (or mystery) of the kingdom" (4:11), but now for the first time the word is specifically identified with the necessity of Jesus' *passion and suffering*. The "word" is thus not a religious abstraction but the proclamation of the cross (1 Cor 1:18–2:5).

True to his heritage, Peter recoils at the thought of a suffering Messiah. Given the popular stereotype of a triumphant Messiah, it is natural and understandable that Peter should feel obliged to correct Jesus. For once Peter takes his obligation as seriously as Jesus takes his to train the disciples in the meaning of Messiahship. That Peter "began to rebuke" clearly parallels the words of Jesus, "began to teach," in v. 31. The word for "rebuke" (Gk. *epitiman;* see further at 4:39) is customarily used for rebuking demons, that is, the worst and most ultimate form of evil. The use of this word with reference to Peter's rebuke of Jesus indicates the degree of Jesus' error about suffering messiahship in Peter's mind.

33 If Peter was a key source for Mark's Gospel, and if the story of the rebuke of Peter by Jesus derives from Peter himself, then we surely have before us an eyewitness account in v. 33. In trying to avert Jesus from suffering, Peter, in a way he cannot know, opposes a deep mystery of God, for suffering is the only way to destroy the stronghold of Satan, which is Jesus' declared purpose from early in the Gospel (1:24; 3:27). Jesus sees in Peter's rebuke an opposition to the essential design of the Incarnation. To think in human terms — when human terms conflict with the things of God — is no longer to be disciple of Jesus but a disciple of Satan. Satan derives from the Hebrew word of the same pronunciation, meaning literally "an adversary" (1 Kgs 11:14; on Satan, see further at 1:13).[46] Jesus seizes Peter's rebuke and turns it on him; "he rebuked (Gk. *epitiman*) Peter, 'Out of my sight, Satan!' he said." Jesus' concept of Messiah is not satanic, as Peter suspects; but Peter's attempt to avert him from it is. According to Matt 4:10, Jesus rebuked Satan in the wilderness in the same words with which he rebukes Peter here. The sharp reprimand of Peter recalls and intensifies the earlier reprimand of the disciples in 8:14-21. The greater severity of the second reprimand suggests that a near-truth is more dangerous than an obvious error, since a partial truth is more believable. When disciples play God rather than follow Jesus, they inevitably become satanic. Jesus and Peter, God and humanity, as Ralph Martin says, "are at 'cross' purposes, since at the heart of the discussion is the cross. For Peter, the indication that the Son of man will die is unthinkable. For Jesus, it is inevitable."[47]

46. 1 Kgs 11:14 says that Hadad the Edomite was an adversary (*śaṭan*) to Solomon.
47. *Where the Action Is* (Glendale: Regal Books, 1977), 72.

34 A wrong view of Messiahship leads to a wrong view of discipleship. This is the point of v. 34, where the subject turns from Jesus to his followers. Mark abruptly reintroduces "the crowd," by which he implies that what Jesus now says he says to all disciples, and not only to the Twelve.[48] The gravity of the teaching is signaled by reporting that Jesus *summoned* (Gk. *proskaleomai;* NIV, "called") the crowd. "'If anyone would come after me, he must deny himself and take up his cross and follow me.'" An apocryphal Gospel preserves this saying as "whoever will not take up his cross as I do, will not be worthy of me" (*Gospel of Thomas* 55). The idea of worthiness is absent in Mark: following Christ in self-denial and even in suffering is a necessary means of salvation, not of being worthy or of becoming worthy by so doing.[49] One cannot follow Jesus except "on the way" of self-denial and the cross.

Modern culture is exposed to the symbol of the cross primarily in jewelry or figures of speech (e.g., "bearing a cross" as putting up with an inconvenience or hardship). How vastly different was the symbol of the cross in the first century![50] An image of extreme repugnance, the **cross** was an instrument of cruelty, pain, dehumanization, and shame. The cross symbolized hated Roman oppression and was reserved for the lowest social classes. It was the most visible and omnipresent aspect of Rome's terror apparatus, designed especially to punish criminals and quash slave rebellions. In 71 B.C. the Roman general Crassus defeated the slave-rebel Spartacus and crucified him and six thousand of his followers on the Appian Way between Rome and Capua. A century later in Mark's day, Nero would crucify and burn Christians who were falsely accused of setting fire to Rome.

The image of the cross signifies a total claim on the disciple's allegiance and the total relinquishment of his resources to Jesus (10:17-31). In Mark's day that was not merely a theoretical truth, for the Gospel of Mark was probably written in Rome near the time of Nero's crucifixion of Christians. Jesus' call to self-denial and suffering by the use of this image would remind Mark's community that their adversity under Nero was not a sign of God's abandonment but rather of their identification with and faithfulness to the way of Jesus himself.[51]

---

48. So Grundmann, *Das Evangelium nach Markus,* 225.

49. *Ap. Jas.* 5:30–6:10 also preserves a saying of the saving effects of the cross. The *Epistle of Peter to Philip* 138, on the contrary, states that Jesus does not suffer (although the text is corrupt at this point), whereas disciples must suffer because of their "smallness."

50. See M. Hengel, *Crucifixion in the Ancient World and the Folly of the Message of the Cross,* trans. J. Bowden (Philadelphia: Fortress Press, 1977).

51. For a discussion of the possible effects of the call to self-denial in a collectivist first-century Mediterranean culture versus effects of the same call in modern individual-

35 Mark includes four statements on the meaning of discipleship in vv. 35-38. Each is prefaced in Greek with a conjunction of purpose, "for," indicating that each statement is adduced in support of v. 34. There are four reasons, in other words, for taking up the cross and following Jesus. The first statement in v. 35 is a perfect chiasmus (A-B-B'-A'):

A "For whoever wants to **save** his life"
B   "will **lose** it,"
B'   "but whoever **loses** his life for me and the gospel"
A' "will **save** it."[52]

The word for "life" (Gk. *psychē*) can simply mean physical existence (e.g., Acts 27:37), but its more common and important sense is that of "personhood," "being," or "soul," that is, the core of one's existence that is not limited to boundaries of time and space. *Psychē* carries this latter sense in vv. 35-37, for the call to take up the cross in v. 34 obviously implies the possible loss of physical life, but it cannot connote the loss of one's "soul." Indeed, as vv. 36-37 assume, the attempt to preserve physical life will jeopardize the more essential being or soul of the disciple; whereas the willingness to lose even one's physical life for the sake of the gospel will guarantee one's eternal being. To lose one's life is to lose physical existence, but to lose one's soul has eternal consequences. The irony of v. 35 is that this one thing cannot be saved by preserving it but only by forsaking it in favor of following Jesus on the way of the cross.[53] The one for whom the way of Jesus is more important than his own existence will secure his eternal being; but the one whose existence is more important than Jesus will lose both Jesus and his existence.[54]

---

ist Western culture, see B. J. Malina, "'Let Him Deny Himself' (Mark 8:34 & Par): A Social Psychological Model of Self-Denial," *BTB* 24 (1994): 106-19.

52. The *Gospel of Thomas* 110 preserves this saying thus: "Jesus said: He who has found the world and become rich, let him deny the world."

53. W. Rebell, "'Sein Leben verlieren' (Mark 8.35 parr.) als Strukturmoment vor- und nachösterlichen Glaubens," *NTS* 35 (1989): 202-18, correctly applies the criteria of dissimilarity and multiple attestation to trace v. 35 back to Jesus. Rebell seems to be in error, however, in asserting that losing one's soul in the present context refers to the kingdom of God, and only after Easter to Jesus himself. 8:27–9:1 is not about the kingdom of God per se, but about Jesus as the suffering Messiah and the Son of Man, thus closely correlating discipleship with Jesus' impending fate. See C. Breytenbach, "Christologie, Nachfolge/Apostolat," *BTZ* 8 (1991): 183-98, for a discussion of the relationship between discipleship/apostleship and Christology.

54. A point immortally captured in a motto of Jim Elliott, who died a martyr's death at the hand of the Auca Indians in South America, "He is no fool who gives up what he cannot keep in order to gain what he cannot lose."

Equally important is the statement about losing one's life for the sake of the gospel (on gospel, see at 1:1).[55] Discipleship is not a mystical, unmediated union with Jesus, a spirituality severed from historical knowledge of Jesus' life, death, and resurrection. For believers after the Incarnation, Jesus Christ is known through the proclaimed word of the gospel. When confronted by the call to discipleship, disciples do not have a "both . . . and" choice — both Christ and their own lives. They stand before an "either . . . or" choice. The claim of Jesus is a total and exclusive one. It does not allow a convenient compartmentalization of natural life and religious life, of secular and sacred. The whole person stands under Christ's claim.

36-37 The second and third statements in vv. 36-37 belong together. They place the question of discipleship in the context of the ultimate realities of life: the soul and the world. Suppose one were to gain "the whole world" — everything one could possibly hope for — at the cost of one's soul (also *2 Clem.* 6:2; Justin, *Apol.* 1.15.12)? It would be a poor bargain, according to Jesus. "The world" one can live without, but when one loses one's personhood or being, what can one give in exchange for it (see Ps 49:6-8; Sir 26:14)? There is a further paradox in this verse, for those who strive desperately to preserve their souls do not in fact know the value of the soul. Apart from God, the soul is the one thing without compare. It takes the word of Jesus to teach the infinite worth of the human soul, and he alone is sufficient to preserve it.[56]

38 The fourth and final statement concerns those who are ashamed of the Son of Man (Matt 10:33; 12:39).[57] In calling his contempo-

---

55. Two important manuscripts (p[45] D) omit the reference to Jesus in v. 35, reading "whoever loses his life for the gospel will save it." A vastly superior field of witnesses includes Jesus in the verse, however, as followed by the NIV translation. The NIV reading is to be favored (see Metzger, *TCGNT*, 99), especially since a copyist would have tended to omit the reference in order to produce parallelism in the verse.

56. An illuminating illustration of vv. 34-37 appears in the Stasi files — the voluminous secret police records of former East Germany. "A contact [who was approached to become an informant] writes, 'After a thorough and intensive examination of my religious convictions as a Christian I must tell you that I cannot compromise the fundamentals of what I believe by what you are asking me to do. I cannot justify such behavior with what the New Testament requires of me: Matthew 16:26, 'What good will it be for a man if he gains the whole world, yet forfeits his soul?'" (J. Gauck, *Die Stasi-Akten. Das unheimliche Erbe der DDR* [Hamburg: Rowolt, 1991], 59).

57. Two important manuscripts (p[45] W) omit "words" from v. 38, leaving the reading: "'whoever is ashamed of me and my [followers].'" Not only does this result in an unusual reading, but the vast majority of manuscripts include "words," thus uniting (as in v. 35 above) Jesus and the gospel. The same two manuscripts (p[45] W) alter the end of v. 38 to read, "'when [the Son of Man] comes in his Father's glory *and* the holy angels' [glory]." The thought of Jesus coming in the glory of the angels rather than *with* them

raries "a sinful and adulterous generation," Jesus repeats the language of the prophets, who accused Israel of infidelity, hardness of heart, and spiritual adultery (Isa 57:3-13; Ezek 16:32-41; Hos 2:2-6). Jesus' words also echo his earlier accusation that "'These people honor me with their lips, but their hearts are far from me'" (7:6). However his contemporaries assessed their spiritual well-being, Jesus finds them wanting. Their status remained one of infidelity to the covenant and alienation from God. Such a people cannot know the glory of God. If they are to know God, God must reduce himself to their level, yet when he does they scoff at the glory that appears in the only way in which it might be known — incognito in Jesus Christ. Their situation is desperate in yet another way, for unless Jesus is received "in this generation," the Son of Man will not receive them in his future glory. The future begins now.

9:1 Mark closes the testament of Messiahship and discipleship with a puzzling statement that "'some who are standing here will not taste death before they see the kingdom of God come with power.'" The very difficulty of the saying argues strongly for its authenticity, for the early church would scarcely have attributed what appeared to be an unfulfilled prophecy to Jesus. The saying asserts that the arrival of the kingdom of God in power will transpire within the lifetime of the persons addressed. This saying is often combined with sayings of similar effect in the NT,[58] all of which are commonly understood as evidence of the expectation of the Parousia or return of Christ during the lifetime of Jesus' contemporaries.[59] Obviously that did not happen, and many scholars consequently believe Jesus to have been in error with regard to the expectation of the imminence of the Parousia. We cannot here examine all that Jesus believed and taught about eschatology as reflected in his various statements on the subject, but in what follows we shall argue that it is doubtful that the statement in 9:1 is necessarily a reference to the Parousia.

One of Mark's chief hermeneutical signals is the placement and framing of passages in his narrative. The placement of the saying in 9:1 is

---

may reflect Luke 9:26. At any rate, the textual tradition favors the NIV reading, "with the holy angels." See Metzger, *TCGNT*, 99-100.

58. 13:26; 14:61; 1 Thess 4:15–5:3; 1 Cor 15:51; 16:22; Phil 4:5.

59. See the discussion in T. W. Manson, *The Teaching of Jesus: Studies in Its Form and Content* (Cambridge: Cambridge University Press, 1963), 277-84. Manson reviews various interpretations of 9:1, e.g., that it refers to the transfiguration, or to the fall of Jerusalem, or to the coming of the Holy Spirit at Pentecost. He rejects these possibilities, however, concluding that "Jesus expected the consummation of the Kingdom to take place at some time in the immediate future, and that this expectation was not realized" (p. 282). Manson believes Jesus to have been in error on this matter, as Manson also believed him to be in error with regard to belief in demons, to the Davidic authorship of the Psalter, and to the historicity of the book of Jonah.

crucial to its understanding. The introductory phrase, "And he said to them" (Gk. *kai elegen autois*) looks as though it introduces a saying from elsewhere in the tradition that Mark received. Moreover, v. 1 is only loosely related to the previous verses. These two observations suggest that Mark has taken a free logion from tradition and spliced it into its present location. The insertion appears to be governed by two reasons: (1) that it is compatible with the theme of glory and angels in v. 38; and, more importantly, (2) that the saying introduces the subsequent transfiguration narrative. All three Synoptic Gospels, in fact, preface the account of the transfiguration with the saying (Matt 16:28; Mark 9:1; Luke 9:27).

The significance of v. 1 is signaled by a solemn preface characteristic of Jesus, "'I tell you the truth.'" The OT prophets customarily prefaced their sayings with "'Thus says the LORD'" as a guarantee of Yahweh's authority, but Jesus assumes that authority himself, earnestly pronouncing, "'I tell you the truth.'" Jesus' use of *Amēn* as an introductory formula rather than as a concluding prayer response (as was customary in Judaism) is, in the words of Joachim Jeremias, "without any parallel in the whole of Jewish literature and the rest of the New Testament."[60]

The context of 9:1, as 8:31 establishes, is not the Parousia as is often supposed, but the death and resurrection of Jesus, which did transpire in the lifetime of the hearers. The interpretation of 9:1 with reference to the resurrection claims a long history of support that goes back to many fathers in the early church. "'The kingdom of God come with power'" thus appears to point to the resurrection of Jesus from the dead, of which the subsequent story of the transfiguration is a prolepsis.[61]

---

60. J. Jeremias, *New Testament Theology*, trans. J. Bowden (New York: Scribner's, 1971), 35-36; so, too, H.-W. Kuhn, *"amēn," EDNT* 1.69-70; H. Schlier, *"amēn," TDNT* 1.335-38. *Amēn*, from the Heb. *'āmēn* ("it is true or faithful"), occurs thirteen times in Mark (3:28; 8:12; 9:1, 41; 10:15, 29; 11:23; 12:43; 13:30; 14:9, 18, 25, 30), all but two of which appear in the latter half of the Gospel, and all but one of which (8:12) is found in the formula *Amēn legō hymin* ("I tell you the truth").

61. So, too, the Nag Hammadi tractate *Treat. Res.* 48:9-10, which correlates the transfiguration with the resurrection. The interpretation that "the kingdom of God come with power" refers to the transfiguration has been ably argued by G. H. Boobyer, *St Mark and the Transfiguration Story* (Edinburgh: T & T Clark, 1942), and has since been followed, among others, by Taylor, *The Gospel According to St. Mark*, 385-86; Cranfield, *The Gospel According to Saint Mark*, 287-88; Pesch, *Das Markusevangelium*, 2.67; J. Gnilka, *Das Evangelium nach Markus*, 2.2; and D. Wenham and A. D. A. Moses, "'There Are Some Standing Here . . .': Did They Become the 'Reputed Pillars' of the Jerusalem Church? Some Reflections on Mark 9:1, Galatians 2:9 and the Transfiguration," *NovT* 36 (1994): 148-51. With regard to Wenham's and Moses' larger thesis that *tines hōde tōn hestēkotōn* ("some who are standing here") refers to the three disciples who were *styloi* ("pillars") in Gal 2:9, I am more skeptical, for the phrase that they contend refers to Peter, John, and James in 9:1 occurs in essentially the same form in 11:5 with reference to non-disciples, in

Mark 8:27–9:1 is a continental divide between the first and second halves of the Gospel. It unites Christology and discipleship in a unique and symbiotic relationship. It teaches that a proper confession of Jesus involves a new understanding of discipleship. When believers confess who Jesus is, they also and inevitably confess what they must become. Jesus is not an objective datum that, like a rock under a microscope, can be observed and examined in supposed neutrality. The statement "'You are the Christ'" (v. 29) imposes a claim on the one who says it. The Son of Man calls those who would know him to *follow* him.

REMOVING THE VEIL: THE TRANSFIGURATION OF JESUS (9:2-8)

Mark's presentation of Jesus reached a decisive stage at Caesarea Philippi. Until Caesarea Philippi, Mark portrayed Jesus teaching, healing, and interacting in Galilee and the Decapolis. Until this point in his ministry the disciples have not yet been challenged to commit themselves to his person. The question of Jesus on the way to Caesarea Philippi, "'Who do you say I am?'" (8:29) will, in effect, set the direction for the second half of the Gospel. Peter's confession that Jesus is the Christ is, as we have seen, correct in name but not in content. Jesus radically reinterprets messianic triumphalism by means of the humiliation of the Son of Man, indeed, by his suffering and death. This climactic disclosure is immediately followed by the account of the transfiguration and linked inseparably to it. Peter's confession in 8:29 might be seen as Mark's way of portraying believers' *initial* response to the "scandal" of the cross (1 Cor 1:23). The transfiguration, likewise, is his way of indicating what their understanding must become if they are to see Jesus from God's perspective. In Peter's confession Mark teaches how disciples should *think* about Jesus (8:33), and in the subsequent transfiguration narrative he allows them to *behold* his true nature.[62]

The transfiguration of Jesus falls near the midpoint of Mark's Gospel. After repeated ignorance and misunderstanding, the disciples receive a visible manifestation of the true nature of Jesus that has until now

---

13:14 with reference to the great tribulation at the end of time, and perhaps also in 15:35 (so A B) with reference to bystanders at the crucifixion.

62. In *Acts of John* 90, the transfiguration is presented as a theophany; Jesus is no longer man but God, of whom John can see only "his hinder parts" (so Exod 33:23). Likewise, in *Acts of Peter* 20, Peter is blinded, as was Paul on the road to Damascus, and cannot see the glory of Jesus.

eluded them. The vision is not of their doing, but is a divine revelation to them, modeled after the greatest revelation of God in the OT on Mt. Sinai. True insight into the mysterious Son of Man is afforded not by human wisdom but by divine revelation. The first passion prediction (8:31) has thrown the disciples into a tailspin of bewilderment. What transpires on the Mount of Transfiguration is both a divine assurance in the midst of their consternation and a divine ratification of Jesus' way to the cross.

2-3 "After six days Jesus took Peter, James, and John with him and led them up a high mountain, where they were all alone." Peter, James, and John appear elsewhere in the Gospel (5:37; 13:3; 14:33) as Jesus' inner circle. As we shall see, Mark's transfiguration narrative, in distinction from Matthew's and Luke's, accentuates their participation with Jesus in the meaning of the event. The specific reference to a six-day interval between Caesarea Philippi and the transfiguration is somewhat curious, for nowhere outside the passion narrative (14:1, 12) does Mark delimit time so specifically. The "six days" expressly link the transfiguration to Peter's confession. The tradition that Mark received was familiar with the time span of about a week between the two events, as Luke's "about eight days" (Luke 9:28) indicates. Mark's "six days" is most probably a chronological parallel with Moses' six-day sojourn on Mt. Sinai (Exod 24:16), thus establishing the first of many points of contact with that seminal event in Israel's history.[63]

A second allusion to Mt. Sinai is the "high mountain." In the Gospels mountains figure prominently in Jesus' ministry: on mountains he prays (6:46; Luke 6:12; John 6:15), preaches (3:13; Matt 5:1), performs miracles (Matt 15:29; John 6:3), is tempted (Matt 4:8), calls his disciples (3:13; Luke 6:12), sends them into mission (Matt 28:16), and accomplishes his passion (11:1; 14:32; 15:22). Like mountains elsewhere in Scripture, the Mount of Transfiguration is a place where God and humanity encounter each other, indeed, where God reveals himself to humanity.[64] In distinction from the aforesaid mountains, however, the Mount of Transfiguration is a mountain of *glory* (e.g., Rev 14:1), whose prominence in Jesus' experience is signified by the description, "high mountain." Mark does not specify the location of the Mount of Transfiguration, but the most natural

63. J. Schreiber, "Die Christologie des Markusevangeliums," *ZTK* 58 (1961): 161-63, regards the six-day reference as a symbolic link to the passion, since Jesus was crucified on the seventh day of the week. The six-day interval is more likely a reference to Moses' six-day sojourn on Mt. Sinai (Exod 24:16), however, since Sinai figures so prominently in the transfiguration narrative.

64. Gen 22:2; Exod 24:15; Deut 34:1; 1 Kgs 18:20; 19:11; Ezek 40:2; Matt 5:1; 14:23; 28:16; Mark 6:46; John 4:20; 6:3, 15; Acts 1:12; Rev 14:1; 21:10. See H. Riesenfeld, *Jesus Transfigured,* ASNU 19 (Copenhagen, 1947): 243-45.

supposition is Mt. Hermon, which dominates the region of Caesarea Philippi where Peter's confession occurred.[65] Although Mt. Tabor, a dome-shaped mountain rising from the Esdraelon plain that separated Galilee from Samaria, is the traditional site of the transfiguration, it is in fact a less probable site for the transfiguration than Mt. Hermon. For one, Mt. Tabor is a great distance to the south from the region of Peter's confession in Caesarea Philippi. Moreover, Mt. Tabor is not a particularly "high mountain," nor did it promise solitude ("they were all alone," v. 2), since in Jesus' day the summit of Mt. Tabor was inhabited (Josephus, *Ant.* 13.396) and surrounded by a wall. Josephus himself erected a fortress on the site to withstand the siege of Vespasian in the war of A.D. 66-70. Like all the cities in the region, however, Tabor fell to the Roman onslaught (Josephus, *War* 4.54-61).

The centerpiece of the transfiguration narrative is presented with typical Markan brevity and understatement, "There he was transfigured before them." The "them" must refer to the disciples, since Elijah and Moses have not yet been introduced. Luke 9:29 mentions only that Jesus' appearance was changed, but Mark, who is followed by Matt 17:2, records that Jesus not only was transfigured before his disciples but also on account of them. "To transfigure," from the Gk. *metamorphoun,* carries the root meaning "to change." The verb occurs only four times in the Greek Bible (9:2; Matt 17:2; Rom 12:2; 2 Cor 3:18), and in each instance it denotes a radical transformation. Referring to the transfiguration in 2 Cor 3:18, Paul says that as a consequence of beholding the glory of the Lord we were transformed (Gk. *metamorphoun*) from glory into glory. Similarly, *Asc. Isa.* 7:25 reads that the glory of Isaiah's "countenance was being transformed" as he ascended from heaven to heaven.[66] In Mark's transfiguration narrative, *metamorphoun* does not signify a change in Jesus' nature but rather an outward visible transformation of his appearance to accord with his nature. As a result of his transformation, Jesus' clothing becomes "dazzling white, whiter than anyone in the world could bleach it." Despite its faltering description, v. 3 succeeds in conveying that the transfiguration is so complete that Jesus' clothing as well as his person is transformed. Matt 17:2 and Luke 9:29 add that Jesus' face shone as well

65. The Hebrew radicals of *Hermon, ḥrm,* meaning "sacred" or "holy," may find an echo in the reference to the Mount of Transfiguration as "the sacred mountain" in 2 Pet 1:18. For arguments favoring Mt. Hermon as the site of the transfiguration, see A. M. Ramsay, *The Glory of the God and the Transfiguration of Christ* (London, New York, Toronto: Longmans, Green and Company, 1949), 113.

66. This reference occurs in close proximity to *Asc. Isa.* 8:25, where, as in the transfiguration, Jesus is referred to as the beloved Son. For a similar description of glorification, see *2 Apoc. Bar.* 51:3-12.

(see 2 Cor 4:6), which heightens the comparison with Moses, whose face shone because it reflected the presence of God (Exod 34:35). The diaphanous garments and brilliant face of Jesus signify total transformation and suffusion with the divine presence.[67]

4 "Elijah and Moses" are first mentioned in 9:4, but their presence is implied throughout the narrative.[68] Both are firmly rooted to the account,[69] but the reason for their presence in the transfiguration narrative is not so obvious. A review of their roles in pre-Christian Judaism is not particularly illuminating; never before do we find two precursors of the Messiah, nor do Moses and Elijah ever appear together as precursors of the end time.[70] Only once elsewhere in the NT (Rev 11:3-11) do the two appear together, but in a quite different context (in Revelation 11 they are slain by enemies, raised after three days, and taken to heaven in a cloud). The Revelation passage postdates the transfiguration narrative, however, and cannot have influenced it. Other figures emerge from apocalyptic literature as precursors of the Messianic Age: Ezra (4 Ezra 14:9), Baruch (*2 Apoc. Bar.* 76:2), Jeremiah (2 Macc 2:1), Enoch, Noah, Shem, Abraham, Isaac, and Jacob (*T. Benj.* 10:5-6), and Enoch (2 Esdr 6:25). As we noted at 1:2-3, Elijah does not appear in the OT as a forerunner of the Messiah but of the final Day of the Lord. Moses likewise plays only a peripheral role eschatologically in later Judaism.[71] This presumably stems from the fact that, unlike Elijah and Enoch who were believed not to have died, Moses was known to have died and been buried.[72]

Pre-Christian Jewish tradition thus does not provide an obvious key as to why Moses and Elijah appear on the Mount of Transfiguration with

---

67. In Scripture brilliant garments are often signs of heavenly beings: Dan 10:5; Matt 28:3; Mark 16:5; John 20:12; Acts 1:10; Rev 3:4; 4:4; 6:11; 7:9, 13; 14:14; 19:14.

68. See M. Thrall, "Elijah and Moses in Mark's Account of the Transfiguration," *NTS* (1969/1970): 305, who equates the high mountain (v. 2) with Mt. Sinai; the white garments of v. 3 with Moses' appearance after being in God's presence; the three tents in v. 7 with tabernacles in the wilderness; and the cloud, voice, and "hear him" in v. 7 with Moses as well.

69. Despite R. Bultmann's objection that the transfiguration account is unrelated to Exodus 24 in *The History of the Synoptic Tradition,* trans. J. Marsh (New York and Evanston: Harper and Row, 1963), 260.

70. See Str-B. 1.756; J. Jeremias, *"Ēl(e)ias,"* TDNT 2.938-39.

71. J. Jeremias, *"Mōyses,"* TDNT 4.856-57.

72. Although a Sifre on Deut 34:5 reads that "Moses did not die, rather he dwells and serves above," the majority tradition in Judaism believed that Moses died like other mortals. He was esteemed as the lawgiver and deliverer of Israel, but seldom as an eschatological precursor. Josephus, *Ant.* 4.323-26, also believed that Moses died, but he includes an intriguing legend with some similarities to the transfiguration story: "As Moses dismissed Eleazar and Joshua, and yet while he conversed with them, suddenly a cloud came to stand over him and he disappeared into a certain valley."

Jesus. On the one hand, both Moses and Elijah were great deliverers of Israel. In the transfiguration narrative of Luke (9:31), Jesus' passion is described as an "exodus," in obvious allusion to the exodus from Egypt under Moses. For Luke, Moses' deliverance of the Israelites from Egypt and formation of them into a nation are prototypes of Jesus' passion, through which he would deliver people from the power of sin and form a new people in the church. Elijah also was a deliverer of Israel, although from false gods of Baal worship rather than from foreign oppressors (1 Kings 17–18). Despite the common thread of deliverance, it is doubtful if this accounts for the presence of Moses and Elijah in the transfiguration, however, for the OT knew other and more important deliverers in the figures of Joshua, David, and Josiah.

It is more probable that Moses and Elijah appear in the transfiguration narrative as representatives of the prophetic tradition that, according to the belief of the early church, would anticipate Jesus. "All the prophets testify to [Jesus]" (Acts 10:43). It is probably too specific to maintain that Moses stands for the law and Elijah for the prophets, because each figure was associated with both the law and prophets. According to Deut 18:15, 18, a passage that is recalled in v. 7, Moses is considered the prototype of the eschatological Prophet, and Moses is frequently regarded as the representative figure of the prophetic tradition in Judaism.[73] Likewise, Elijah was associated with Mt. Sinai (1 Kgs 19:1-9), where he also received the word of God, though in a different fashion from Moses. Although the NIV introduces "Elijah and Moses" equally in v. 4, the Greek has Elijah appearing *with* Moses, which seems to imply a certain subordination of Elijah to Moses.[74] In only one passage do Elijah and Moses appear together before the Day of Yahweh. In Mal 4:4-6, Israel is commanded to remember the "instruction" (Heb. *torah*) of God's servant Moses. Immediately following, Elijah is introduced as the prophet who turns the hearts of people to repentance on the Day of Yahweh. The appearance of Moses and Elijah in the transfiguration narrative likely recalls this passage and their prophetic roles as joint preparers of the final Prophet to come (so Deut 18:15, 18 [see also 4Q175, lines 5-8]; Mal 4:5-6). Their joint preparation for Jesus is further signified by Mark's description of them "talking with Jesus"; that is, they hold an audience with Jesus as a superior.

The presence of Moses and Elijah thus signifies that Jesus is not a "walk on" in the divine economy, nor is his revelation as the Son of God

73. J. A. Ziesler, "The Transfiguration Story and the Markan Soteriology," *ExpTim* 81 (1969-70): 266.

74. On the centrality of Moses in the transfiguration, see J. Marcus, *The Way of the Lord* (Edinburgh: T. & T. Clark, 192), 80-93.

(v. 7) an anomaly or arbitrary expression of the divine will. Rather, the presence of Moses and Elijah as forerunners attests to the culmination of a purposeful revelation of God's Son with the history of Israel. Moreover, although Moses and Elijah speak with Jesus, they do not remain with him, for when the cloud is removed in v. 8 both figures vanish. Thus, the witness of Moses and Elijah points to Jesus and culminates in him, but their witness does not rival his. Their word and work are consummately fulfilled in Jesus (Rom 10:4; 2 Cor 1:20). They are servants of God and prophets of God, indeed, nothing less than divine witnesses to Jesus as the Son of God. If it be queried how the three disciples, especially in their lethargic state, recognized the attendants as Elijah and Moses, it might be suggested that in the realm of God, which is momentarily breaking into the life of the disciples on the summit of the mountain, all things are known for what they are (1 Cor 13:12). In God's Son the Day of Yahweh is at hand, and all that has gone before bears witness to him.

5-6 As a hollow mortal in the searing light of the eternal, Peter suggests building shelters. Peter's proposal, especially in light of Mark's editorial comment that "he did not know what to say," is often thought foolish.[75] The suggestion was not foolish in one sense, however, for Judaism held onto the hope that God would once again tabernacle with his people as in the Exodus. "Make a right confession to the Lord and bless the King of the ages, so that once again his dwelling [Gk. *skēnē*] may be erected with you in joy" (Tob 13:11). Josephus also records the hope of a new and literal tabernacle in the wilderness (*Ant.* 20.167; *War* 2.259). In Zech 14:16-19 the Feast of Booths assumes eschatological proportions. In this respect, Peter's proposal of tabernacles on the Mount of Transfiguration was fitting for a pious and knowledgeable Jew. What Peter must come to understand, however, is that God is providing his own tabernacle in which to dwell. Origen remarked that the cloud replaced the tents that Peter proposed.[76] That is close but not correct. Before Peter's very eyes God's dwelling with humanity is present, for Jesus is the new tabernacle of God dwelling with humanity.[77] Peter cannot establish Jesus; rather, it is Jesus who establishes Peter by his call to discipleship (1:17) and fellowship to be *with him* (3:14). The revelation of Jesus' divine nature before the disciples attests that "the dwelling place of God is with men, and he will live with them" (Rev 21:3). The transfiguration draws Mark's Christology remarkably close to John's

75. According to the *Apocalypse of Peter* 16, Jesus rebukes Peter for desiring to build tabernacles: "And [Jesus] said to me in wrath, 'Satan maketh war against thee, and has veiled thine understanding, and the good things of this world conquer thee.'"

76. Cited in M.-J. Lagrange, *Évangile selon Saint Marc*, 230, and followed by him.

77. So Ziesler, "The Transfiguration Story and the Markan Soteriology," *ExpTim* 81 (1969-70): 266; G. B. Caird, "The Transfiguration," *ExpTim* 67 (1955-56): 293.

understanding of the Incarnation, "The Word became flesh and lived [Gk. *skēnoun*, lit. "tabernacled"] for a while among us" (1:14).

7 A further key to understanding the transfiguration is the cloud, which throughout Scripture is the symbol of God's presence and glory. The Moses–Mt. Sinai typology again provides an illuminating parallel: "When Moses went up on the mountain, the cloud covered it, and the glory of the LORD settled on Mount Sinai. For six days the cloud covered the mountain" (Exod 24:15-16).[78] According to Mark, the cloud "enveloped" or overshadowed (Gk. *episkiazein*) them. This verb occurs only rarely in the Greek Bible, but it is used in Exod 40:35 to describe the cloud that filled the tabernacle with the glory of God and in 1 Kgs 8:10-11 to describe the cloud filling Solomon's temple. A passage that throws especial light on its use in the transfiguration is the overshadowing (Gk. *episkiazein*) of Mary by power of the Most High at the annunciation (Luke 1:35).[79] The cloud symbolizes the divine presence that speaks to Jesus and the disciples. The cloud is the impregnating presence of God, symbolizing that in Jesus, even more than in the tabernacle of old, God dwells bodily with humanity.[80]

The transfiguration reaches its climax in the heavenly voice, "'This is my Son, whom I love. Listen to him!'" This pronouncement recalls the declaration of Jesus as the Son of God at the baptism and carries the full content of meaning that we noted there (see at 1:11). At the baptism, however, the declaration was directed to Jesus ("'You are my beloved Son'") as a confirmation of his divine Sonship; here it reveals his Sonship *to the disciples*. "'*This is* my beloved Son,'" as well as the command to "'*hear him*,'" is thus a divine revelation to the disciples. The declaration from heaven sets Jesus apart from Moses and Elijah and designates him

78. For other references to the cloud as the symbol of God's presence, see Exod 13:21; 16:10; 19:9, 16; 40:35; Lev 16:2; Num 11:25; Ezek 1:4.

79. The cloud is sometimes seen to refer not to the divine presence in Jesus but to the Parousia, as in 13:26; 14:62; Luke 21:27; Acts 1:9; 1 Thess 4:17; Rev 1:7; 4:11; 5:12; 7:12; 11:12; 15:18; 19:1. So G. H. Boobyer, *Saint Mark and the Transfiguration Story* (Edinburgh: T. & T. Clark, 1942), 79ff.; L. Legrand, "L'arriere-plan neotestamentaire de Lc 1,35," *RB* 70 (1963): 172; and Riesenfeld, *Jesus Transfigured*, 248-49. The Parousia is not the most plausible interpretation of the cloud at the transfiguration, however. The usual use of clouds at the Parousia is coming *on* them, not being overshadowed *by* them and enveloped *in* them, as here. Even 2 Macc 2:8, a classic proof-text for the Parousia interpretation, refers to the cloud overshadowing Moses on Sinai and filling Solomon's temple, thus signifying divine presence rather than the Parousia. Exod 40:35 remains the more natural background of the cloud in v. 7, especially in light of the other Exodus motifs present in the transfiguration.

80. This point is made supremely in the Gospel of John, "The Word became flesh, and dwelled among us" (1:14). The word for "dwelled," *eskēnōsen*, is the verbal form of "tabernacle or tent," *skēnē*. In Jesus, God "pitched his tent among us."

uniquely as God's Son.[81] Only the Father can impart the mystery of Jesus' divine Sonship to believers. The disciples have not come to the recognition of Jesus as God's Son on their own (so Matt 16:17; 2 Pet 1:17-18). Understanding the nature of God and God's work in the world is not a human accomplishment. Faith is always and only our assent to the truth that has been *revealed* to us, apart from which it cannot be known.

Equally important is the conclusion to 9:7, "'Listen to him!'" This, too, recalls a word of Moses, "The LORD your God will raise up for you a prophet like me. . . . You must listen to him" (Gk. *autou akouesthe*)" (Deut 18:15). "'Listen to him (Gk. *akouete autou*)'" in v. 7 is identical in wording to the Deuteronomy quotation (though differing in forms and syntax). What exactly are the disciples to hear? Throughout the Gospel, Mark portrays Jesus pleading with people to hear and understand.[82] The voice from heaven now makes the same plea of the disciples. The divine injunction is necessary for the disciples to grasp the one point they cannot accept — that the Son must suffer![83] This injunction links the transfiguration inseparably with Peter's confession: the Messiah must suffer (8:31), and so, too, must the disciples (8:34-38). This the disciples must understand if they are to understand the person and mission of Jesus. Christology leads to discipleship; discipleship flows from Christology. "'Listen to him'" designates Jesus not only as the prophet who would follow Moses but also as the Son who must suffer, and who calls disciples to share his suffering.[84] It is God's ratification of the way to the cross — for Jesus and the disciples. The road to glory leads through the valley of suffering.

8 The story does not end on this ominous note, however. The uniqueness of Mark's transfiguration account is seen in its conclusion: "When [the disciples] looked round, they no longer saw anyone with them except Jesus." Elijah and Moses, the greatest figures of the OT, have vanished; in relation to Jesus they have no permanent standing. Jesus alone remains. Rather than escaping with his heavenly visitants to glory, Jesus remains to complete his journey to Jerusalem.[85]

81. Thrall, "Elijah and Moses in Mark's Account of the Transfiguration," *NTS* 16 (1969-1970): 308-9, notes that one purpose of the voice is to distinguish Jesus uniquely from Moses and Elijah because Peter's proposal to build tabernacles to all three implied equality among them.

82. 4:9; 6:52; 7:16(?), 18; 8:17-21, 32.

83. By contrast, the Nag Hammadi tractate *Ep. Pet. Phil.* 134:15-19 applies the injunction "'Listen to him'" to Jesus' eternal existence, not to the necessity of the cross.

84. The necessity of the disciples' suffering is forsaken in the *Gospel of Philip* 58, where the disciples themselves are elevated along with Jesus.

85. In the *Apocalypse of Peter* 15–17 the transfiguration is depicted as a return to Eden, at the end of which — in stark contrast to the canonical accounts — Jesus ascends with Moses and Elijah into the second heaven!

9:8 reinforces the unique role that the disciples play in Mark's transfiguration narrative. In Luke, the transfiguration happens primarily for Jesus' sake, for only Jesus ascends the mountain (9:28), only he prays (9:29), and, following the voice, only Jesus is left (9:36). Matthew's account includes the disciples to a greater degree, but at the end of Matthew's account Jesus remains "alone" (17:8). Mark, by contrast, puts the disciples fully into the event. This is all the more remarkable given that Mark's depiction of the disciples is grimmer than either Matthew's or Luke's. Jesus takes the three "up a high mountain, where they were all alone" (v. 2); he is transfigured "before them" (v. 2); Elijah and Moses appear "before them" (v. 4); the divine voice speaks to them (v. 7); and at the end, despite the ominous ring of suffering and death, Jesus stands alone with them! In the depths of their bewilderment, Jesus is with the disciples. The disciples — then as now — are not expected to go it alone in this hard and joyous thing of discipleship. Precisely where they hear the gospel, where they see both its glory and their own inadequacy, there Jesus is with them. The one who calls disciples to follow him does not abandon them for glory, but turns from glory to accompany them "on the way" to Jerusalem and the cross.

Excursus: How Should the Transfiguration Be Understood?

The transfiguration of Jesus is a singular event in ancient literature. It has no analogy in the Bible, or in the extrabiblical literature from the Apocrypha, Pseudepigrapha, rabbinic literature, Qumran, Nag Hammadi, or in Hellenistic literature as a whole. In light of this uniqueness, how should it be understood?

The literature on the origins and nature of the transfiguration is, not surprisingly, long and extensive. The most we can do in this brief excursus is to offer general directives that support our foregoing conclusions and expose the errors of interpretations foreign to them.

One position that is untenable is the supposition that the transfiguration narrative was fashioned according to "divine man" motifs in the Greco-Roman world (see the excursus on **Divine Man** at 3:12). This interpretation is occasionally adopted on the ground that the transfiguration, in contrast to the more functional Christology of the early Jewish-Christian church, portrays a metaphysical apotheosis of Jesus similar to the apotheoses of divine men in Hellenism.[86] The artificial distinction be-

---

86. See F. Hahn, *Christologische Hoheitstitel, Ihre Geschichte im frühen Christentum* (Göttingen: Vandenhoeck & Ruprecht, 1963), 309-11.

tween metaphysical Hellenistic and functional Jewish Christologies makes this hypothesis questionable from the outset, however. The Jesus of the transfiguration is certainly not metaphysically removed, for rather than being translated into heaven (so *Apocalypse of Peter* 17!), he remains with the disciples to continue "on the way" to Jerusalem and the cross. There is no precedent for divine men or Hellenistic sons of God willingly embracing the fate of suffering as Jesus does in 9:12-13. Moreover, the demand for silence (9:9) is typical of no divine man, and the presence of Moses, Elijah, and the Mt. Sinai typology represents Jewish rather than Hellenistic motifs. The Son of God in the transfiguration calls to mind no Greco-Roman divine man known to us.

A second position has been to interpret the transfiguration as a vision similar to Peter's vision in Acts 10[87] or as an epiphany or angelophany similar to the appearance of Yahweh in Genesis 18.[88] The supposed parallels between the transfiguration and these texts are no closer than those regarding divine man, however. The various visions and epiphanies recorded in Scripture are typically individual rather than communal, as they are at the transfiguration. Moreover, a vision or epiphany is a momentary inbreaking of the divine into the human "from above," whereas the transfiguration is a momentary revelation "from below" of the divine in the human Jesus. The parallels between the transfiguration and either visions or epiphanies elsewhere in Scripture are not close enough to constitute a meaningful analogy.

The most frequently posited explanation of the transfiguration is that it is a resurrection story retrojected into the life of Jesus.[89] The primary strength of this suggestion rests in the glorified body common to Jesus in both the transfiguration and Easter modes. Careful examination of the two modes of appearance substantially diminishes the initial attraction of the hypothesis, however. If the transfiguration were a retrojected resurrection appearance, we would expect to find evidence of dislocation and disruption of the body of Mark's Gospel. But the transfiguration does not appear extrinsic to Mark's narrative; it is organically linked to the preceding episode at Caesarea Philippi, and it connects the beginnings of the Gospel in the baptism with the end of the Gospel in the passion.[90] Jesus' appearance in the transfiguration also differs from

87. For example, A. Harnack, cited in Grundmann, *Das Evangelium nach Markus,* 180.

88. J. A. T. Robinson, "The Most Primitive Christology of All," *JTS* 7 (1956): 180.

89. So J. Wellhausen, cited in Grundmann, *Das Evangelium nach Markus,* 178; Bultmann, *The History of the Synoptic Tradition,* 39, 260.

90. For example, Caird, "The Transfiguration," *ExpTim* 67 (1955-56): 292: "A satisfactory explanation of the Transfiguration must do justice to its connexion with the Bap-

the resurrection appearances recorded in the Gospels. In the Easter narratives Jesus appears alone, whereas in the transfiguration he is accompanied by heavenly companions; in the Easter narratives Jesus speaks, but here he is silent; in no resurrection appearance is there a divine voice as there is in the transfiguration; in no resurrection appearance is there a description of Jesus' visual glory as here; in the resurrection appearances there are signs from Jesus to his disciples, but here there is no sign; in only one Easter narrative does Jesus appear on a mountain (Matt 28:16) as at the transfiguration; and the cloud that receives Jesus into glory (Acts 1:9) leaves him to be with the disciples at the transfiguration.[91] In light of such numerous and substantial differences, it is difficult to maintain that the transfiguration is an Easter story retrojected into earlier Gospel narratives.

The uniqueness of the transfiguration of Jesus deprives it of any adequate external standard or frame of reference by which to judge it. Given this fact, the judgment that readers make about the nature of the transfiguration will ultimately derive from their estimate of Jesus himself. Mark has endeavored throughout his Gospel to portray the divine authority, the *exousia*, with which Jesus teaches and acts. Anyone who has found Mark's presentation of Jesus credible will not find the transfiguration narrative incredible, for the transfiguration is a momentary empirical revelation of the divine authority that Jesus has manifested throughout his ministry. Given the crisis in the minds of the disciples, it is hard to imagine anything keeping them in fellowship with Jesus short of the Father's visual witness to his Son and ratification of his mission. That is the essence of the transfiguration. "If the view of [Jesus] person which was held by the evangelists and the apostolic Church in general is true, then a frankly supernatural occurrence in the course of His earthly ministry will be credible."[92] The location of the transfiguration within Mark's narrative scheme and the meaning inherent in it make its most plausible interpretation an *anticipation* of the resurrection within the ministry of Jesus for the purpose of encouraging the disciples to believe and follow Jesus on the way to the cross.[93]

---

tism, Caesarea Philippi, Gethsemane, the Crucifixion, the Resurrection, the Ascension, and the Parousia; and with the persecution of the disciples and their share, present and future, in the glory of the risen and ascended Christ."

91. See Schweizer, *The Good News According to Mark*, 180; J. Murphy-O'Connor, "What Really Happened at the Transfiguration?" *BRev* 3 (1987): 9.

92. Ramsay, *The Glory of God and the Transfiguration of Christ*, 106.

93. See Thrall, "Elijah and Moses in Mark's Account of the Transfiguration," *NTS* 16 (1969-70): 310-11.

PROFILES IN SUFFERING (9:9-13)

The Greeks honored a pantheon of heroes who, because of their great achievements, were promoted to heaven without dying. The term used to describe this was *apotheosis,* the making of mortals into gods. The apocryphal *Apocalypse of Peter* 15–17, as we have seen, conceived of Jesus as some kind of divine man who was whisked into heavenly glory from the summit of the Mount of Transfiguration. Mark's Jesus, to the contrary, refuses the upward mobility of the divine man. True, the transfiguration anticipates the glorious existence the Son of Man will enter after he is raised from the dead (9:9). And, yes, the transfiguration is a prolepsis of the resurrection, a present momentary representation of a glorious future event. But the resurrection and the glorious restoration of all things heralded by Elijah must not be either the first or the only thing in the disciples' thinking. Mark uses the dialogue in 9:9-13 between Jesus and the disciples to steer readers away from the concept of messianic triumphalism implied in Peter's declaration of 8:29. In vv. 11-13 three separate figures are introduced or alluded to — Elijah, the Son of Man, and the Suffering Servant of Isaiah, each of whom attests to the same truth: that suffering must precede glory.

Mark structures the present passage generally parallel to the dialogue between Jesus and the disciples following Peter's confession in 8:29. After both Peter's confession and the transfiguration Jesus swears the disciples to silence (8:30; 9:9). The disciples are likewise resistant to both events. After the passion prediction of 8:31 Peter tried to dissuade Jesus (8:32); and after the resurrection prediction of 9:9 the disciples "kept the matter to themselves, discussing what 'rising from the dead' meant" (v. 10). Finally, the disciples are in consternation following both events (8:31; 9:9), and Jesus uses their consternation to teach them the way that he as the Son of Man must go — and that they must follow.

9-10 On the descent from the mountain "Jesus gave [the disciples] orders not to tell anyone what they had seen until the Son of Man had risen from the dead" (see **Command to Silence** at 1:34). This is the final command to silence in the Gospel of Mark (although see 9:30), and the only one of the nine commands that is provisional. The commands heretofore have been absolute, but now for the first time the disciples are informed that the veil of silence must remain in effect only until the resurrection, after which they may speak. Ironically, at the empty tomb the women will finally be commanded to proclaim the resurrection — but they will flee in fear and bewilderment and say nothing to anyone (16:7-8).

The obtuseness of the disciples reemerges in 9:10. Their failure to grasp the meaning of the resurrection from the dead is not a little puzzling. True, the OT has only a vague and undeveloped concept of resurrection from the dead — at the most. Nevertheless, for at least two centuries prior to Jesus the doctrine of the resurrection had been an article of faith in Jewish theology, particularly among the Pharisees. Twice elsewhere in Mark resurrection is mentioned without question (6:14; 12:18-27). The puzzlement of the disciples at the resurrection must therefore be regarded as a further sign of their blindness. This is signaled more clearly in Greek than in English, where Mark says that they "seized" (Gk. *kratein*) Jesus' word and "sought among themselves" (Gk. *syzētein*) its meaning. These two words are typically used by Mark with pejorative connotations. Mark's vocabulary suggests that the disciples not simply kept the secret to themselves, as Jesus demanded, but quashed it. They appear to misunderstand and perhaps even to resist Jesus' command. And we can imagine why. If the Son of Man is to be raised, he must first *die*. The disciples are unprepared for any thought that the Messiah must suffer and die before his entrance into glory.[94]

The effect of the command to silence in vv. 9-10 is twofold. First, it reinforces that the cross and resurrection are the only vantage point from which Jesus' life and ministry can be understood according to their divine purpose, and that until the cross and resurrection all other knowledge of Jesus is inadequate and peripheral. The command to silence is especially pertinent in the afterglow of the transfiguration, lest the disciples succumb to the glory and emotional adrenaline of the mountain rather than the necessity of the way to Jerusalem and the cross. The transfiguration is indeed a preview of the resurrection, but the disciples inherit the *gloria resurrectionis* only through the *via dolorosa crucis.*

The second effect of the command to silence is to underscore the continued blindness and inertia of the disciples. Once again Mark reminds readers that disciples are not in fellowship with Jesus because of their knowledge, virtue, or abilities. They are in fellowship solely because of Jesus' sovereign call, and they remain in fellowship only because of his faithfulness to them. They are indeed misunderstanding and even stubborn. Their discipleship does not depend on their knowl-

94. Murphy-O'Connor, "What Really Happened at the Transfiguration?" *BRev* 3 (1987): 9, dismisses the historicity of the transfiguration by asking how Peter could have denied Jesus in the courtyard of the chief priest if he had earlier witnessed Jesus' glory on the Mount of Transfiguration. For Murphy-O'Connor, Peter's denial of Jesus at the trial of Caiaphas effectively refutes the historicity of the transfiguration. A very plausible refutation of Murphy-O'Connor's supposition emerges from the conversation in vv. 9-11, however, in which the euphoria of the transfiguration is effectively subordinated to the necessity of suffering. Thus, foremost in the disciples' minds as they journey to Jerusalem is the impending suffering of Jesus, not his resurrection.

edge and understanding, however, but simply on continuing to follow where Jesus leads.

11-13 The disciples' question in 9:11 about Elijah's return (see at 8:28) appears to be offered in order to counteract or even rebut the implication of suffering in v. 10. The gist of the question in v. 11 is more subtle than Peter's blatant attempt to rebut Jesus following the first passion prediction (8:31-32). Nevertheless, the question "'Why do the teachers of the law say that Elijah must come first?'" is a leading question, the intention of which is to suggest that Elijah's return to restore all things should obviate the need of the Son of Man to go to the cross. The reference is to the final verses of Malachi, where Elijah is sent by God before the "great and terrible day of the LORD" to restore righteousness and harmony in human relationships (Mal 4:5-6; also Sir 48:10).

Jesus indeed affirms Elijah's role of restoration. "'To be sure, Elijah does come first, and restores all things.'"[95] The hope of the disciples, in other words, is ultimately correct. But something equally essential must happen *before* the final restoration on the Day of Yahweh. There is another testimony in Scripture, less welcome but no less important. It is raised in a counterquestion of Jesus in 9:12b. If the restoration of righteousness and peace for which all people long is immediate and impending, then why do the Scriptures testify that a righteous suffering figure must necessarily precede the final restoration of the Day of the Lord?

Jesus refers to this righteous sufferer in three images. The first is as the Son of Man, about whom "it is written." The formula "it is written" attests to the divine will ordained and prescribed for the Son of Man (see the discussion of the term at 1:2). The suffering of the Son of Man is not a misunderstanding on Jesus' part or an aberration of the divine will, but an inherent part of his identity. The statement that the Son of Man "must suffer much and be rejected" appears to recall the suffering Servant of the Lord of Isaiah. We cannot be absolutely certain of this because the fate of the Servant of the Lord is not described in exactly these words. Nevertheless, it looks as though the description of v. 12 recalls the Servant of the Lord, despised and rejected, "a man of sorrows, and familiar with suffering" (Isa 53:3). If this is the case, Jesus claims the vocation of Isaiah's suf-

---

95. J. Marcus (following J. Wellhausen) suggests that v. 12a should be read as a question, i.e., "'When Elijah comes, will he restore all things?'" (*The Way of the Lord,* 99). The implication would be: No, Elijah will not come to restore all things but to suffer. Since early Greek manuscripts did not contain punctuation, it is possible to read the sentence as a question. In my judgment, however, the context of the passage argues against punctuating v. 12a with a question mark. It is not the final restoration of all things that Jesus challenges, but the idea that the restoration can be achieved apart from the suffering of the Son of Man. Hence the question in v. 12b.

fering servant as his own role as Son of Man. (On Servant of the Lord, see Introduction, 6.2.)

Finally, Elijah, too, must suffer. "'Elijah has come, and they have done to him everything they wished.'" This statement surely sent a shock wave to Jesus' hearers, for they were as unprepared for the suffering of Elijah as for the suffering of the Son of Man. Apart from only vague references (1 Kgs 19:2, 10), there was no hint that Elijah would suffer before the Day of the Lord. The reference to the suffering of Elijah is, of course, a reference to the death of John the Baptist, as Matt 17:13 makes explicit (followed by Justin Martyr, *Dial. Trypho* 49.17). If Herod had dealt severely with the forerunner of the Messiah (6:14-29), should there be any surprise about the fate of the Messiah?[96]

"'They have done to [Elijah] everything they wished.'" That phrase must have resonated with Mark's first audience, which itself was subjected to the savageries of Nero's persecution. It resonates today with the persecuted church in various parts of the world. Whenever Christians follow Jesus on the way of the cross, they find themselves exposed to the world and vulnerable to its machinations. The inevitable suffering that results in discipleship to Jesus is not a sign of abandonment by God, however, but of *fellowship* (Phil 3:10) with the Son of Man, who "must suffer much and be rejected."

Is it not instructive that the only reference to Jesus' earthly work in the Apostles' Creed is "he suffered"? That single, all-important truth is engrained in the disciples' consciousness in 9:12-13 by allusions to the Son of Man, the Suffering Servant of Isaiah, and Elijah. Elijah was remembered for various virtues and roles, but Jesus here designates his primary role as one of suffering, as represented in John the Baptist. The Elijah who goes before the Son of Man, and the disciples who come after him, must do so on the road to the cross. "'Did not the Christ have to suffer these things and then enter his glory?'" asks the resurrected Jesus in Luke 24:26? So, too, in Mark, the longed-for redemption of the Day of the Lord can be purchased only through the suffering of the Son of Man.

---

96. The intricate web of argumentation in vv. 11-13 is often attributed to Mark's redactional synthesis rather than to Jesus himself. In this view, "it is written" (v. 12) is the result of Mark's exegetical conclusions rather than the authority of Jesus. See, e.g., Marcus, *The Way of the Lord*, 97-107; J. Taylor, "The Coming of Elijah, Mt 17,10-13 and Mk 9,11-13: The Development of the Texts," *RB* 98 (1991): 117. I should not like to sever the essence of the conclusion from Jesus, however, even though the wording of vv. 11-13 may derive from Mark. In my judgment, the radical reinterpretation of Elijah's role advanced in v. 13 (like the reinterpretation of the Sabbath in 2:27-28) is more naturally explained by Jesus' *exousia* ("authority") than by innovation on the part of the early church.

FRAIL FAITH IN A STRONG SAVIOR (9:14-29)

The interplay between the journey inward to God and the journey outward to the world is common to Scripture (see the comment on 1:35-39). Moses descends from his hallowed sojourn on Mt. Sinai to confront rebellion and idolatry (Exodus 32); Elijah leaves the quiet strength of Horeb to face the paganism of Jezebel and Ahab (1 Kings 19); Jesus himself is driven from the unction of baptism to temptation in the wilderness (1:9-13). Similarly, on the descent from the Mount of Transfiguration with Peter, James, and John, Jesus is immediately confronted by a dispute between the scribes and his disciples, and by a lonely father struggling desperately for both the life of his son and the existence of his faith. Mark 9:14-29 is more than twice as long as the parallel accounts in Matt 17:14-20 and Luke 9:37-43. The flurry of activity and wealth of human interest detail in Mark's account leave the impression of a firsthand account, again perhaps from Peter.

14-15 In the absence of Jesus, Peter, James, and John, the remaining disciples, have not been idle. The circumstances of their sojourn at the base of the mountain are obscured until the moment they are rejoined by Jesus and the three disciples — a circumstance that is explainable if Peter, who was absent from them, is Mark's source for the story. Jesus and the three disciples discover their colleagues beset with crowds, scribes, and the demon-possessed — the same three groups that have attended Jesus' ministry all alone. Thus the remaining disciples are continuing Jesus' ministry — but without Jesus present (a condition that more than one minister of the gospel has experienced!). As we noted at 1:45-52, whenever the disciples are separated from Jesus they fall into crises.

The absence of Jesus is sorely felt, for when "all the people saw Jesus, they were overwhelmed with wonder and ran to greet him." In Mark, the astonishment of the crowds normally comes at the conclusion of Jesus' teaching or healing activity, whereas here it comes at the beginning. The reason the crowd is "overwhelmed with wonder" is not immediately apparent. This expression translates a single Greek word *(ekthambeomai)* that occurs only in Mark (9:15; 14:33; 16:5, 6), meaning trembling astonishment that verges on alarm. It is sometimes suggested that the amazement is owing to the glory of Jesus' countenance, like the radiance of Moses' face after returning from Mt. Sinai (Exod 34:29). Mark's syntax could be taken to support this interpretation, that is, the people were astonished because of what they saw in Jesus. On the other hand, if Jesus' countenance still radiates the glory of the transfiguration, the command "not to tell anyone" (v. 9) seems rather pointless. Moreover, if Jesus' countenance is substantially affected, we might expect the crowd to retreat in fear (Exod 34:30) rather than advance in avid pursuit. Again, the suggestion that *ekthambeomai* is Mark's way of portraying "the coming of Jesus as an epiphany of the Lord for believers"[97] seems overstated, for there seems to be no explanation why Jesus should appear epiphanous here and not elsewhere? On balance, the astonishment of the crowd appears to owe to Jesus' unexpected appearance and the hopes it raised. The crowd's wholesale shift of attention from the scribes to Jesus once again accentuates his authority over the scribes, who are cross-examining the disciples. The crowd's dissatisfaction with the disciples is offset by its hopes and satisfaction at seeing Jesus.[98] This unusual introduction to the pericope may remind Mark's readers that Jesus is competent to satisfy whatever longings remain unsatisfied by the church.

16-18 9:14-15 describe a scene without focus: crowd, scribes, and disciples intermingle inchoately and without purpose. But as soon as Jesus arrives he immediately commands attention by asking the scribes, "'What are you arguing with [the disciples] about?'" The word for "argue" (Gk. *syzētein*) carries combative connotations and is often used by Mark of altercations with religious authorities (8:11; 9:14, 16; 12:28). He commands the scribes to direct their questions to him rather than to the disciples.

A confrontation between Jesus and the scribes is preempted, however, by a desperate father who brings to Jesus his son "possessed by a spirit that has robbed him of speech" (similarly, 7:37). The father's description of the malady carries all the pathos of a parent's fear and dismay for his child's safety. His son is not simply ill but assaulted. The attacks on the defenseless boy are recounted four times in the ensuing account (vv. 18, 20, 22, and 26). Convulsions, foaming at the mouth, outcries, lockjaw, and bodily rigidity followed by loss of consciousness are the symptoms of tonic-clonic (grand mal) seizures, rightly identified as epilepsy in Matt 17:15.[99] Mark's terminology is not as medically objective

97. G. Bertram, *"thambos," TDNT* 3.6.

98. The references to the disciples' inability to heal the possessed boy (vv. 18, 28) are a strong argument for the historicity of the account, for the later church is unlikely to have invented a story that cast the apostles in a negative light. For two studies that defend the essential historicity of 9:14-29, see P. J. Achtemeier, "Miracles and the Historical Jesus," *CBQ* 37 (1975): 471-91; and especially the comprehensive analysis of G. Sterling, "Jesus as Exorcist: An Analysis of Matthew 17:14-20; Mark 9:14-29; Luke 9:37-43a," *CBQ* 55 (1993): 467-93.

99. Matthew 17:15 identifies the boy's affliction as epilepsy, but 17:18-19 also calls it a *daimonion* ("demon"). Again, Matthew's account can be explained assuming his use of Mark, for the reference to epilepsy improves Mark, whereas the retention of demon preserves Mark's original reading. For further evidence of Matthew's use of Mark's version of the narrative, see Sterling, "Jesus as Exorcist," *CBQ* 55 (1993): 477.

as Matthew's, but his description of both the boy's plight and the father's distress is more graphic and empathetic.[100] Even the disciples are powerless in the face of the child's condition. Again in Mark, when all human hopes are exhausted, hope can be expected from Jesus.

19-20 At the father's report, Jesus exclaims in exasperation, "'O unbelieving generation, how long shall I stay with you? How long shall I put up with you?'" The confusion and unbelief of the crowd parallels that of the disciples earlier (8:14-21). But, despite Jesus' prior rebuke of the disciples, the present judgment of Jesus does not appear to include them. The "unbelieving generation" is ostensibly a reference to the crowd apart from the disciples, for "generation" (Gk. *genea*) occurs five times in Mark (8:12 [2x], 38; 9:19; 13:30), but never with reference to the disciples. Even though the disciples are insufficient for the task of healing the demon-possessed boy (vv. 18, 28), Jesus does not chastise them. Inability is simply a limitation, not a fault, as are hardness of heart (3:5; 6:52) and misunderstanding (8:14-21). The crowd is included in the latter, however. How reminiscent is Jesus' lament of the prophetic grievances against unbelieving Israel (Deut 32:5, 20; Num 14:11; Isa 65:2).

The doubts and disbelief of the crowd do not determine Jesus' willingness or ability to act, however. On the contrary, the authority of Jesus' mission and person exerts sovereign influence in human affairs; "Let God be true, and every man a liar" (Rom 3:4). Jesus calls for the child. When the boy is brought, the condition described by the father becomes reality before Jesus' eyes: he is seized with convulsions and thrown to the ground, writhing and foaming at the mouth. The seizure is not coincidental, for Mark reports that "when the spirit saw Jesus, it immediately threw the boy into a convulsion." The boy may indeed be epileptic, but the epilepsy is portrayed as a front or vehicle of a malevolent engineering force. The language approximates earlier episodes in the Gospel where the demonic erupts in fits in the presence of Jesus (1:26; 5:6-10), or when natural phenomena are conceived as hosts of demonic opposition (4:39; 6:48). The present episode again testifies to the mission of Jesus to confront and to defeat the powers of evil, whether manifested in penultimate

---

100. A long account of a demon-possessed boy in Philostratus's *Life Apoll.* 3.38 provides an instructive contrast to Mark 9:14-29. In the Philostratus account, the demon is of primary concern and the possessed child is incidental. Thus Philostratus provides a complete history of the demon and the circumstances contributing to its habitation of the child. But the child is of interest only as a host of the demon. Indeed, the child is not even present, but is exorcised by a letter from Apollonius! Mark's story, by contrast, is not essentially concerned with the demon but with human need, i.e., the wretched straits of the boy and the anxiety of the father. Philostratus did not publish his work until the early part of the third century A.D., so the Gospel accounts cannot have been influenced by it.

conditions or ultimate causes. Since the temptation by Satan in the wilderness (1:12-13), Jesus appears as the More Powerful One (1:7) whose chief mission is to bind the strong man and liberate the captives (3:27; 1 John 3:8). The initial result of the effective presence of Jesus is not peace, however, but conflict; not resurrection, but suffering. Eduard Schweizer's insight is correct: "This indicates how the presence of God can produce storm and stress before anything constructive is accomplished."[101]

21-24 The important conversation between Jesus and the father in 9:21-24 is omitted by Matthew's and Luke's versions of the narrative. For the latter two Gospels the significance of the narrative is the miraculous, whereas for Mark the miraculous is penultimate to faith, and faith to discipleship. For Mark the significance of Jesus cannot be fully conveyed by *what* he does, but only by *who* he is. One can be amazed by a miracle, but one can only trust and believe a person.

The father's tremulous pilgrimage to faith begins in a simple dialogue that is triggered by Jesus' question, "'How long has he been like this?'" The question allows the father to tell his story that the boy has been afflicted since childhood, with near fatal effect. But it also allows the father to declare his heart. The question of Jesus invites the father to come to him as a total person, with hard facts and with human hopes. The father stakes his existence on the latter: "'If you can do anything, take pity on us and help us.'" The original Greek reads, "'Help us and have compassion on us.'" Help is the object of the father's request, but the source of his hope is rooted in the compassion of Jesus. The Greek word for "compassion" (*splangnizesthai*) points to the deepest reserves of Jesus (see further on the term at 1:41).

Jesus can expel demonic forces at a word, but the evoking of faith is a much harder matter. Disbelief of Jesus, whether from scribes, crowds, disciples, or desperate fathers, is both a greater opposition and more serious obstacle than all the hosts of pandemonium. The father has only the mustard-seed beginnings of faith. "'If you can'?" replies Jesus in surprise![102] The problem is not divine unwillingness (1:40) or divine inability but human unbelief! What is impossible to humans is possible to God (10:27). "'Everything is possible to him who believes.'" What Jesus commands of

---

101. *The Good News According to Mark*, 188.
102. The Greek manuscript tradition is very disparate in v. 23. The compressed response of Jesus troubled copyists, who added "to believe," i.e., "'If you are able to believe.'" This addition entirely alters the meaning of the response. Whereas in the best tradition (followed by NIV) Jesus repeats the father's words in order to remind him that with God all things are possible, the various alterations make for a burdensome moralism, requiring of the father what he confesses he lacks — greater belief. See Metzger, *TCGNT*, 100.

the father is what he earlier commanded of the hemorrhaging woman (5:34) and the synagogue ruler (5:36). The sole bridge between frail humanity and the all-sufficiency of God is *faith*. The means by which the *exousia* of Jesus, his divine authority and legitimacy, becomes effective in human life is faith. The statement that "'everything is possible to him who believes'" must appear to the father as an elusive hope, however, for the faith he needs to heal his son is a faith he does not have — or so he thinks.

True faith is always aware how small and inadequate it is. The father becomes a believer not when he amasses a sufficient quantum of faith but when he risks everything on what little faith he has, when he yields his insufficiency to the true sufficiency of Jesus, "'I do believe; help me overcome my unbelief!'" The risk of faith is more costly to the father than bringing his son to Jesus, for he can talk about his son but he must "cry out" (Gk. *krazein*) for faith.[103] True faith takes no confidence in itself, nor does it judge Jesus by the weakness of his followers. It looks to the More Powerful One (1:7) who stands in the place of God, whose authoritative word restores life from chaos. True faith is unconditional openness to God, a decision in the face of all to the contrary that *Jesus is able.*

25-27 Seeing the crowd gather and not wishing to make a display of his power, Jesus "rebuked" (Gk. *epitiman*) and "commanded" (Gk. *epitassein*) the evil spirit to leave the lad and never return. These two verbs express Jesus' authority, particularly over demonic forces.[104] In contrast to earlier exorcisms in 1:25-26 and 5:6-10, the demonic asserts itself violently, though no more successfully, against Jesus. The evil spirit abandons the boy in a deathlike condition, and onlookers take him for dead. The intervention of Jesus, in other words, has made things worse rather than better. Is the result of the father's fledgling faith the death of his son? Salvation is a process in which things must sometimes become worse before they become better (e.g., Exod 5:21–6:1). The first test of the father's faith is to trust the word and promise of Jesus alone, not the immediate empirical consequences of it. Jesus then (lit. in Greek) "raised him, and he was resurrected" (see at 5:41). The disciples have just asked what it means to be raised from the dead (v. 10). In the raising and restoring of the catatonic boy Jesus provides the first object lesson on the meaning of his own death and resurrection.

103. The NIV's "exclaimed" is insufficiently emphatic. *Krazein* appears eleven times in Mark, and in no instance can it be translated with less emphasis than "shout" or "cry out." According to several later manuscripts, the father "cried out *with tears*," thus heightening his emotional outburst. The addition is probably not original, however, for there is no adequate reason to explain why a copyist would delete it. See Metzger, *TCGNT*, 100.

104. On *epitiman* ("rebuke"), see at 4:39; on *epitassein* ("command"), at 1:27; 9:25.

28-29 The story closes with Jesus gathered privately in a house with the disciples. In Mark's Gospel, private gatherings in houses are typically settings of further instruction and revelation for the benefit of disciples.[105] In the present instance the disciples ask why they could not expel the demon. "'This kind can come out only by prayer,'" says Jesus.[106] This is the first injunction to **prayer** in the Gospel of Mark. There are three references to Jesus praying in Mark (1:35; 6:46; 14:32-39); in each he is alone and facing critical junctures in his ministry (see further at 6:46). Otherwise in Mark there are only passing references to prayer as a constituent element of faith. Prayer is twice commended to disciples for spiritual strength against temptation (13:33; 14:38). Other references include prayer against adverse circumstances (13:18), warnings against ostentation and pride in prayer (12:40), and Jesus' pronouncement that the purpose of the temple is for prayer (11:17). The most important passage devoted to prayer in Mark is the snippet in 11:24-25 where Jesus teaches that prayer must be accompanied by faith (v. 24) and by forgiveness (v. 25). The present passage also introduces prayer in the context of faith, connecting it with spiritual power. Grundmann correctly notes that "prayer is faith turned to God."[107] Prayer is the focusing and directing of faith in specific requests to God. Both faith and prayer testify that spiritual power is not in oneself but in God alone, and both wait in trust upon his promise to save.

A recurrent theme in this passage is the inadequacy of the disciples in ministry with Jesus. Service in fellowship with Christ is characterized by constant awareness of the inadequacy of the servant. As this story illustrates, Jesus calls disciples to tasks beyond their abilities, and the fact that the tasks surpass their abilities is evidence that the ministry is Christ's, not theirs. The inadequacy of disciples is not their fault, nor should it have the effect of impairing either their faith or fellowship with Christ. Rather, inadequacy drives the disciples to prayer, which is God's gift to them and another form of fellowship with Jesus as their Lord.

---

105. There are four occurrences in Mark where public teaching becomes private instruction of the disciples: 4:1-2, 10; 7:14, 17; 9:14, 28; 10:1, 10. For further discussion of the theme of private instruction in Mark, see D. B. Peabody, *Mark as Composer*, New Gospel Studies 1 (Macon: Mercer University Press, 1987).

106. A large number of manuscripts add "prayer *and fasting* (p45 ℵ A C D K L W X Δ Θ Π Ψ). Noting a similar textual tendency in 1 Cor 7:5, Metzger (*TCGNT*, 101) attributes the addition to the stress on fasting in the early church. Given Jesus' negative teaching on fasting earlier (2:19), it would be surprising if fasting were included in his teaching here. Despite the heavy manuscript tradition in its favor, internal factors argue against the originality of *and fasting*.

107. Grundmann, *Das Evangelium nach Markus*, 256.

CHAPTER NINE

Mere Discipleship

MARK 9:30-50

At first glance the material in this unit seems to be a sundry patchwork of unrelated sayings lacking a unifying theme. Closer inspection, however, reveals an underlying theme of humility and suffering that is demonstrated by Jesus, in word and deed, as he is with the disciples on the way to Jerusalem. Jesus establishes the theme by a second reminder of his own impending rejection and death (9:30-32). He follows this with lessons intended to inculcate an attitude of humility in the Twelve: warnings against pride and an exhortation to receive the small and powerless (vv. 33-37), appeals for clemency and mercy for outsiders (vv. 38-41), warnings against causing "little ones to stumble" (v. 42), and the necessity of suffering in fulfillment of God's kingdom (vv. 43-50). This collage of instructions and object lessons forms an extended commentary on Jesus' call to self-denial and cross-bearing (8:34), which was ratified by the divine ultimatum at the transfiguration for the disciples to "'hear him'" (9:8).

THE SECOND PASSION PREDICTION (9:30-32)

The second passion prediction introduces a unit of material extending from 9:30 to 9:50. The unit is composed of various vignettes in which Jesus focuses his teaching decidedly on the disciples. The passion prediction announces not only Jesus' impending fate; it is also an exemplar of the life of service to which he calls the disciples.

    30 "They left that place and passed through Galilee. Jesus did not want anyone to know where they were" (cf. Luke 17:11; John 7:1). We as readers do not know exactly where they were either.[1] 9:30 appears to pre-suppose a journey beginning outside Galilee that proceeds through Gali-lee. This fits with the location of 8:27–9:30 in the region of Caesarea Philippi (8:27) and strengthens the deduction that Mt. Hermon was the Mount of Transfiguration.[2]

9:30 is the last reference to Galilee in Mark until after the passion and resurrection (14:28; 16:7). Galilee has been Jesus' center of operations, the place where he has called disciples and taught great crowds. There is a certain melancholy in the note that Jesus is now only passing through a place he once lived, for Galilee is no longer in his sights. Reasons for the guarded and anonymous journey are not mentioned, but they are not dif-ficult to surmise. The opposition of Antipas and the Jewish authorities has not abated. Jesus' longing for privacy also appears to be dictated by his desire to teach the one essential truth of his ministry, that "'the Son of Man is going to be betrayed into the hands of men.'" Finally, Jesus is "on the way" to Jerusalem (see further on the expression at 8:27). Each of the three passion predictions occurs in the context of this expression (8:27; 9:33-34; 10:32), signaling that Jesus has turned his focus away from Gali-lee and set his face (so Luke 9:51) toward Jerusalem.

31 Mark's three passion predictions (8:31; 9:31; 10:33-34) share in common a three-part skeletal structure: (1) The Son of Man must suffer, (2) be killed, and (3) after three days be resurrected. The second predic-tion is the simplest and least specific of the three. It begins with a play on words, which would have been clearer in spoken Aramaic than it is in Greek: "'The Son of Man is going to be betrayed into the hands of men.'" "Man" is used in two striking senses: he who lives as a man among men, a human among humans, will be rejected by them; in fact, the one who gives himself for others will die at their hands. In the first prediction the responsibility for Jesus' suffering is attributed to Jewish leaders, "the el-ders, chief priests and teachers of the law" (8:31). But in the second pre-diction the enemies of the Son of Man are not Jewish leaders but all hu-manity. Human beings will do "everything they wish" to the Son of Man as they did to Elijah (= John the Baptizer, 9:13). "Man's inhumanity to

1. E. Lohmeyer, *Das Evangelium des Markus*, 191-92, suggests that the secrecy of lo-cation in v. 30 corresponds with Jesus' private instruction of the disciples. The suggestion would be more persuasive were it not for the fact that Mark frequently gives only vague geographical descriptions.

2. The major alternative to Mt. Hermon as the site of the transfiguration is Mt. Ta-bor. V. 30 seems to argue against Mt. Tabor, however, since the latter is in Galilee. Tabor, moreover, lies in southern Galilee, which would require Jesus and the disciples to back-track some twenty miles northward to Capernaum in v. 33. See A. Schlatter, *Der Evange-list Matthäus*, 537; M.-J. Lagrange, *Évangile selon Saint Marc*, 243.

man" became inescapably apparent in the twentieth century, but it was certainly no less inhuman in Jesus' day. One recalls David's fear of falling into the unmitigated hands of humanity: "'I am in deep distress. Let us fall into the hands of God, for his mercy is great; but do not let me fall into the hands of men'" (2 Sam 24:14).

In the second prediction, God is involved in a way not apparent in the first prediction. The Greek word for "betrayed" can also mean "handed over." The passive voice of the verb conceals its subject. It looks like a "divine passive," i.e., a reference to God without using God's name (for fear of defiling it). If it is a divine passive it conveys that God is handing over his Son to humanity. The verse reflects the language of the Servant of Yahweh in Isa 53:6, 12 (LXX) and hints that Jesus will die for the sins of others. "It is just this meaning that Christian proclamation finds in Christ's death: His incomprehensible fate is for the benefit of the very ones at whose hands he died, and that benefit is in accordance with God's salvific will for humankind."[3] But here, as elsewhere in Scripture, God's will does not absolve humanity of its responsibility. "'The Son of Man will go just as it is written about him. But woe to that man who betrays the Son of Man!'" (14:21).

32 Although Mark often refers to Jesus as a teacher, he seldom reports what Jesus taught. This pericope is an exception, however. In the passion predictions Jesus directs his teaching to an unswerving course and design: it is God's will for the Son of Man to suffer, die, and be raised. This Jesus must teach the disciples. But once again they cannot grasp it: "They did not understand what he meant and were afraid to ask him about it." The Gk. *agnoein* might be translated, "They were ignorant," or "the meaning escaped them." This is the sole use of *agnoein* in Mark, and it is used of those with the greatest access and opportunity to know — the disciples! They are also "afraid," a word that will occur at the third passion prediction as well (10:32). Mark's irony is rich and heavy: when the word of God is finally spoken, the human response — even from hand-picked followers — is one of ignorance and fear. How difficult for disciples to understand, to believe, and to follow. If we have difficulty imagining the obduracy of the Twelve, let us ask how many of us truly understand, believe, and follow Jesus? The degree of the disciples' misunderstanding becomes further apparent in the following story.

---

3. P. J. Achtemeier, "Mark 9:30-37," *Int* 30 (1976): 180.

. . . AND THE SECOND MISUNDERSTANDING (9:33-37)

The location of this pericope is a clue to its meaning. In the second passion prediction above (9:30-32), Jesus spoke of the humiliation and suffering of the Son of Man. Here Mark records a debate among the disciples about who is the greatest! The juxtaposition of the two pericopes reveals a jarring contrast between Jesus' humility and the disciples' desire for distinction and recognition. A similar contrast is, in fact, present in all three passion predictions. Peter's rebuke of Jesus following the first passion prediction (8:31) was prompted by the assumption that Messiahship entails privilege, not suffering. Likewise, the third passion prediction (10:33-34) is followed by the request of James and John to sit with Christ in glory (10:35-45). In all three passion predictions, Jesus speaks of the necessity of his rejection, suffering, and death; and following all three the disciples voice their ambitions for status and prestige. Jesus speaks of surrendering his life; the disciples speak of fulfilling theirs. He counts the cost of discipleship; they count its assets. The disciples have yet to learn that the rewards of discipleship come only as a consequence of following Christ on the costly way to Jerusalem.

33-34 For the last time in the Gospel of Mark Jesus returns to Capernaum (1:21; 2:1). The house he enters carries the definite article in Greek, which indicates a particular house, perhaps Peter's (1:29).[4] Houses are often settings of private instruction and revelation in Mark.[5] The house setting thus plays a role in Mark's larger "insider-outsider" theme, in which Jesus chooses private settings to teach the inner circle what the crowds cannot know and understand.

Once in the house Jesus asks the disciples, "'What were you arguing about on the road?'" The direct discourse in second person plural appears to preserve the original wording of Jesus' question to them. 9:34 is Mark's editorial explanation of Jesus' question and could rightly be placed within parentheses. "But they kept quiet." Mark's description of the silence of the disciples is exactly the same as his account of the silence of the Pharisees at the healing of the man with the deformed hand in 3:4 (Gk. *hoi de esiōpōn*). Both Pharisees and disciples are silenced before Jesus because of guilt and shame, just as both are guilty of hardness of heart

---

4. This point should not be unduly pressed, however, for in Mark *oikos* (house) is usually anarthrous (2:1; 3:20; 7:17; 9:38), whereas *oikia* (house) tends to be arthrous (1:29; 2:15; 9:33; 10:10; though 7:24 is anarthrous). One might argue that 1:29, 2:15, and 9:33 all refer to Peter's house, but 10:10 is also arthrous, and it cannot refer to the same house.
5. 2:1-2; 2:15-16; 3:20; 4:10(?); 7:17, 24; 9:28, 33; 10:10; 11:17(?), 14:3. For further discussion of houses, see at 2:2.

(3:5; 6:52). How little difference there is even at this point in Jesus' ministry between his disciples and his opponents.

The silence of the disciples is a wordless confession, "because on the way they had argued about who was the greatest."[6] Their preoccupation with rank and standing is in character with what we know of Judaism in general. Rabbinic writings frequently comment on the seating order in Paradise, for example, and argue that the just would sit nearer to the throne of God than even the angels.[7] Earthly orders of seating at worship and meals, or authority within the community, or dealings with inferiors and superiors were seen as preparation for the eternal order to come (also Ps 68:24-25). The *Rule of the Community* at Qumran, likewise, prescribed the proper order of procession in entering the Rule. First priests, then Levites, and "in the third place all the people shall enter the Rule, one after another, in thousands, hundreds, fifties and tens, so that all the children of Israel may know their standing in God's community in conformity with the eternal plan. And no one shall move down from his rank nor move up from the place of his lot" (1QS 2:19-23).

"So that all the children of Israel may know their standing." In Rom 10:3 Paul will accuse unbelieving Jews of attempting "to stand" in their own righteousness. That is uppermost in the minds of the disciples as well. They have imbibed the wine of rank, placement, and self-importance, and they import it into their fellowship with Jesus. True, their reticence when asked about it reveals at least a budding awareness of the incompatibility of their ambitions with the way of Jesus. Nevertheless, and not surprisingly, the journey to Jerusalem has been fanning the flames of messianic and eschatological hopes in their minds. Surely the kingdom would break forth in Jerusalem, with Jesus — and they with him — at its head!

35 The ambitions of the Twelve imperil their fellowship and following of Jesus. In an unusual expression, Mark says that Jesus sat down and called the Twelve to himself. To sit and instruct is to assume the posture of an authoritative teacher (12:41; Matt 5:1; 23:2; John 8:2). Jesus responds to the fantasy of the Twelve by a pronouncement in v. 35, which

6. Several Greek manuscripts (A D Δ) omit "on the way" in v. 34, evidently because it seemed superfluous in light of its occurrence in v. 33. The overall textual tradition argues for its inclusion, however.

7. Str-B 4/2.1,130-1,165. In answer to the question, Who is greatest in God's kingdom? some scribes accorded the honor to the just and righteous (so Ps 11:7). Others ranked knowledge of Torah or performance of good deeds in first place, and still others accorded first place to teachers who led the faithful to righteousness by their teaching. It was generally agreed, however, that martyrs were the greatest in the kingdom of God (Str-B 1.773).

he reinforces by example in vv. 36-37. "'If anyone wants to be first, he must be the very last, and the servant of all.'" The idea of subservience to others is so central to the thought of Jesus that it was remembered and recorded in nearly every stratum of early Christianity.[8] The model of service and humiliation that Jesus teaches the disciples can be heard only on the road of humiliation to Jerusalem — if it can be heard at all. At no point does the way of Jesus diverge more sharply from the way of the world than on the question of greatness. Jesus does not exactly repudiate prominence and greatness, but he redefines them. The challenge is to be great in things that matter to God. Nothing is greater in God's eyes than giving, and no vocation affords the opportunity to give more than that of a servant (10:43).

The word for **servant** is *diakonos*, the ordinary Greek word for waiting tables (Luke 17:8; John 12:2; Acts 6:2). It refers to personal devotion in service as opposed to service as a slave or for hire or as a priest, for example. The Greek world generally considered service demeaning and undignified; "How can a man be happy when he has to serve someone?" (Plato, *Gorgias* 491e) expressed the basic Greek attitude toward service and servants. In Jesus' teaching, to the contrary, the concept of service grows out of his concept of love for one's neighbor. Jesus' selfless service of others fills the concept of servant with entirely new content; the posture of the servant is a visible manifestation of the reality of God's love. Greatness in God's economy is not reserved for the gifted and privileged; rather, it presents itself to every believer in the common and simple tasks of serving others. Indeed, the more common and humble the task, the greater the deed, for humility is the essence of him who said, "'For I am among you as one who serves'" (Luke 22:27). Service to others is *the* primary way in which believers imitate and fulfill the mission of Jesus (10:43-45).[9]

36-37 The simple profundity of this truth is better *enacted* than spoken. Jesus "took a little child and had him stand among them. Taking him in his arms, he said to them, 'Whoever welcomes one of these little children in my name welcomes me.'" We are mistaken if we imagine that

---

8. Mark 10:43-44; Matt 20:26-27; 23:11; Luke 22:26; Phil 2:1-11; *Ep. Pol. Phil.* 5:2; *Herm. Man.* 2:1; *Herm. Sim.* 9:29:3; *Gospel of Thomas* 22; *Acts of Peter* 38. On the entire concept of humility, see E. Schweizer, *Erniedrigung und Erhöhung bei Jesus und seinen Nachfolgern*, ATANT 28 (Zürich: Zwingli Verlag, 1962). To say that the idea of humility is central to Jesus is not to say that it was unique to him. Twenty years before the ministry of Jesus, Rabbi Hillel said, "By lowering myself I exalt myself, and by exalting myself I lower myself" (Str-B 1.774). Variants of the same idea were present in Hellenism as well. "In public life one must escape . . . [from] the desire to be first and greatest" (Plutarch, *Moralia* 8).

9. On the concept of servant and service, see H. Beyer, *"diakoneō," TDNT* 2.81-87.

Greek and Jewish society extolled the virtues of childhood as do modern societies in general. Societies with high infant mortality rates and great demand for human labor cannot afford to be sentimental about infants and youth. In Judaism, children and women were largely auxiliary members of society whose connection to the social mainstream depended on men (either as fathers or husbands). Children, in particular, were thought of as "not having arrived."[10] They were good illustrations of "the very last" (v. 35).

The conclusion Jesus draws from the child in his arms is subtle and surprising. The child is not used, as is often supposed, as an example of humility, but as an example of the "little" and insignificant ones whom followers of Jesus are to receive. "'Whoever *welcomes* one of these little children in my name welcomes me; and whoever welcomes me does not welcome me but the one who sent me.'" Disciples are thus not to be like children, but to be like Jesus who embraces them. It is Jesus, not the child, who here demonstrates what it means to be "the servant of all." It is in the small and powerless that God appears to the world, as Jesus so trenchantly described in the parable of the nations (Matt 25:31-46). Our response to the hungry, thirsty, lonely, naked, sick, and imprisoned is our response to God, for "'whatever you did for one of the least of these brothers of mine, you did for me'" (Matt 25:40). The humblest act of kindness sets off a chain reaction that shakes heaven itself, for whatever is done to the little and least is done to Jesus, and whatever is done to Jesus is done to God!

THE KINGDOM OF GOD IS LARGER
THAN OUR EXPERIENCE OF IT (9:38-41)

Although Mark's Gospel is shorter than Matthew's and Luke's, it is often the case that when the three Synoptics contain a common story Mark's version is the fullest. This is true in the present pericope. Matthew reproduces only the final verse of Mark's account about kindness to disciples of Jesus (Matt 10:42). Luke has a brief two-verse plea for tolerance (Luke 9:49-50). Mark's account, however, contains a complete lesson on discipleship. The issue is a common one to religious communities, especially

10. The negligible value of children is suggested by a comment of R. Dosa ben Harkinas in the Mishnah: "Morning sleep and midday wine and children's talk and sitting in the meeting-houses of ignorant people put a man out of the world" (*m. Avot* 3:11). Moreover, girls under the age of twelve could be sold as slaves by their fathers (*m. Ket.* 3:8).

in their founding stages: What constitutes true membership in the community? The early Hebrews had questioned whether the Spirit of God rested on two men who did not belong to the seventy designated elders of Moses (Num 11:24-30). Early Christian communities debated criteria that would distinguish true prophets from false prophets (1 John 4:2; *Did.* 11:8-12; *Herm. Man.* 11:7-16). The challenge presented itself even within Jesus' apostolic fellowship. Must all disciples belong to the Twelve, or can a genuine follower of Christ exist outside their number? As is true of many religious traditions, so also in this instance, the founder shows himself to be more broad-minded than the sectarian inclinations of his disciples.

38 The story begins with John, the son of Zebedee, reporting, "'Teacher, we saw a man driving out demons in your name and we told him to stop, because he was not one of us.'" It is unusual for Mark to ascribe sayings of this sort to named individuals. Mention of John in this instance is apparently owing to his memorable remark. This is the only instance in Mark where John the apostle is mentioned alone. Elsewhere John is mentioned as the brother of James (1:19, 29; 3:17; 10:35, 41) or as one of Jesus' trusted triumvirate (5:37; 9:2; 13:3; 14:33). Being in Jesus' inner circle had at least some deleterious effects on John — as inner circles often do — for John's elitist attitude toward the unnamed exorcist in v. 38 repeats a similar attitude on his part when he and James desired to call down fire on inhospitable Samaritans (Luke 9:54), and again when he and James asked to sit on Jesus' right and left hands in glory (10:35). The "we" in v. 38 thus probably includes James. In complete disregard of the lesson of the preceding story, John regards his call as a disciple not as a call to service but as an entitlement of privilege and exclusion.

John's report that the independent exorcist "'was not following *us*'" is depressingly ironic.[11] We should expect him to say "'because he was not following *you*.'" It is not a little presumptuous at this stage of discipleship for John to think himself and the other disciples worthy of being followed. This is yet another echo of their inflated self-importance (so 9:34). Gundry rightly notes the absurdity of the Twelve's telling the independent exorcist

---

11. The end of v. 38 is subject to many variations in the Greek manuscript tradition. Of the variations, three principal readings emerge: (1) "and we forbade him, because he was not following us"; (2) "who does not follow us, and we forbade him"; and (3) "who does not follow us, and we forbade him, because he does not follow us." The last reading is a conflation of the first two and thus later. The first reading is preferred because of better manuscript support (א B Δ Θ Ψ) and because the second phrase appears to have been brought into better grammatical conformity with the first part of the sentence. See B. Metzger, *TCGNT,* 101. All the variants read "us" (= disciples) rather than "you" (= Jesus).

to stop doing what they could not do in 9:14-29.[12] Grundmann suggests that the Greek tense of the verb "he was not following us" indicates that the independent exorcist had been invited to join the Twelve but had refused.[13] Neither grammar nor syntax, however, necessitates this conclusion, and we wonder if Jesus would have shown such approval of the unnamed exorcist had he expressly rejected the call to discipleship (e.g., 10:22-23). Luke 9:49 lessens the offense of "not following us" by reading "not following *with* us." John's attitude leaves no doubt of the suspicions that the Twelve harbor toward other followers of Jesus. The mention of Capernaum in v. 33 above prompts the question whether the independent exorcist belonged to a rival cadre of disciples there.[14]

39 Contrary to what John and the disciples expect, Jesus charges them *not* to prohibit the independent exorcist. The present tense of the Greek imperative *kolyete* ("'Do not stop him'") implies that Jesus' counsel is not limited to this particular instance but is valid for all such instances, that is, "'Do not stop such people.'" The reason given is that "'No one who does a miracle in my name can in the next moment say anything bad about me.'" A Jewish proverb (though later than Jesus' day) ran: "A door that is closed is not easily opened."[15] The idea behind the proverb is similar to the saying in v. 39: anyone so acting in Jesus' name is empowered by God, and one so empowered cannot lightly discard or disregard his vocation. "No one who is speaking by the Spirit of God says, 'Jesus be cursed,' and no one can say, 'Jesus is Lord,' except by the Holy Spirit" (1 Cor 12:3). Thus, works and wonders in Christ's name are evidence of the call and commission of Christ, and fellow disciples should be cautioned against thinking ill of those who bear such "fruit" (Matt 7:16).

40 This thought is followed by a pronouncement, "'Whoever is not against us is for us.'" This saying shows the Master to be more inclusive than his disciples. The making known of his name is more important than their distinctions (see Phil 1:12-18). How the saying of v. 40 is to be reconciled with Matt 12:30//Luke 11:23 (and *P.Oxy.* 1224) ("'He who is not with me is against me, and he who does not gather with me scatters'") is

---

12. R. Gundry, *Mark*, 510-11.

13. W. Grundmann, *Das Evangelium nach Markus*, 197.

14. This story does not answer the question, frequently asked, whether morally good people who have not heard of Christ are acceptable to God. The unnamed exorcist was not a stranger to the gospel but acting "in [Jesus'] name," i.e., in his authority and power. The issue raised in this story is whether there can be true followers of Christ who do not share the experience of the Twelve? Or, in a slightly broader context, how should believers regard those who take up the name and mission of Jesus but belong to other traditions?

15. Str-B 2.19.

not immediately apparent. One possible resolution rests on the difference between the plural pronoun in Mark (i.e., Jesus and the disciples) and the singular pronoun in Matthew and Luke (i.e., Jesus alone). Thus, whereas there can be no neutrality with regard to the person of Jesus, the disciples must be tolerant of those who differ from them. Theologically speaking, the church should be unambiguous in its proclamation of Christ but tolerant of those who differ from it. Cranfield draws the following principle: "While the principle of Mk ix. 40 should govern the attitude of the Church toward those without, the principle of Mt. xii. 30 must be part of the Church's preaching both to those without and to those within."[16]

Although the above interpretation is defensible biblically and theologically, it is instructive to ask how this verse functions specifically in Mark 9:40? The answer results in another line of interpretation, namely, that Jesus is not at this point forcing anyone's hand for a decision; and fortunately so, for even the disciples are ignorant and ambivalent. It is not yet the hour for a final decision, which would be premature (Rom 14:4). Only at the cross will the evidence be present for a full verdict, and at that time those who are not for Jesus will be against him. For the present, a season of grace precedes the hour of judgment.

41 This saying preserves a rare occurrence of Jesus calling himself the Christ.[17] This is only conceivable in the wake of Caesarea Philippi, where Peter announced Jesus to be the Christ (8:29). Following that momentous declaration, Jesus now instructs the disciples privately on the meaning of his mission. The concept of Christ is not further elaborated, except to emphasize that the disciples *belong* to him (Rom 14:7-9). Given the misunderstanding and behavior of the disciples, the assurance of Jesus that "you belong to Christ" is not inconsequential.[18]

9:41 concludes with a reminder (see the comment on 9:37) that the humblest act of kindness — even the giving of a cup of cold water — does not go unrewarded by God. What is done to a follower of Jesus is received by Christ as done to himself. "'I tell you the truth, whatever you did for one of the least of these brothers of mine, you did for me'" (Matt 25:40).

16. C. E. B. Cranfield, *The Gospel According to Saint Mark*, 311. Two further discussions that view the sayings as complementary are F. Conti, "Un'analisti di tipo logico-matematico su Mt 12,30 e Mc 9,40," *RevistB* 41 (1993): 73-74; A. de la Fuente Adánez, "A favor o en contra de Jesús. El logion de Mc 9,40 y sus paralelos," *EstBib* 53 (1995): 449-59.

17. Although the NIV reads "in *my* name" (v. 40), the stronger manuscript tradition omits the pronoun. The omission of the pronoun results in acceptable but somewhat unconventional Greek (i.e., *"because* you are Christ's disciples"), which explains why copyists were inclined to add "my." If the pronoun were original, it is hard to imagine why a copyist would omit it.

18. On the function of "Christ" in Mark's Gospel, see J. Kingsbury, *The Christology of Mark's Gospel* (Philadelphia: Fortress Press, 1983), 93-94.

DISCIPLESHIP: COUNTING THE COST (9:42-50)

The sayings in this unit are grouped around a sequence of catchwords: "causes of sin" (vv. 42-47), "fire" (vv. 48-49), and "salt" (vv. 49-50). The catchwords function as mnemonic devices, which suggests that this unit of material may have come to Mark as a unit of oral tradition, all of which is loosely ordered around the theme of discipleship. The printing of this pericope in verse rather than in prose format would throw its parallelism and linking words into greater relief. Several of the sayings appear in different contexts in the other Gospels. The sayings about cutting off one's hand (v. 43) and gouging out one's eye (v. 47) appear not only in the parallel in Matt 18:8-9 but also in variant forms in Matthew's Sermon on the Mount (5:29-30) after Jesus' teaching on adultery. The saying on salt (v. 50) also appears in the Sermon on the Mount (Matt 5:13) as an illustration of the distinctiveness of discipleship, whereas Luke appends it to a section on the cost of discipleship (14:34-35). The various forms and locations of the sayings suggest that Jesus uttered them on difference occasions and/or that they were transmitted without their accompanying contexts by the early church and used according to the editorial designs of each evangelist. The large number of Greek textual variants among the sayings also suggests that they circulated without narrative contexts, for a copyist was more inclined to alter a saying in order to adapt it to a new context than to alter a saying that was anchored to a host narrative. The meaning of vv. 42-48 is clear enough in its present form, but the brevity, terseness, and lack of context of the sayings in vv. 49-50 make a conclusive interpretation more difficult to render.

42 The saying about "'causing one of these little ones . . . to sin'" repeats the thought of v. 41, that whatever is done to a follower of Jesus, whether for good (v. 41) or bad (v. 42), is done to Jesus himself. The "little ones" here does not refer to children, but rather (as in v. 41) to "these little ones *who believe in me*," that is, to disciples.[19] The saying clearly reinforces the supreme value that Jesus places on common and ordinary disciples — "the poor in spirit," to quote the Beatitudes (Matt 5:3). The placement of the saying here applies its truth to the independent exorcist in v. 38 who was put down by John. It becomes an admonition not to discount the faith of another because he or she is not affiliated with an official Chris-

---

19. It is difficult from the Greek manuscript tradition to say for certain whether "believe *in me*" is original. The presence of "in me" is well attested (A B L W Θ Ψ), but the absence of the phrase in other weighty manuscripts (ℵ D Δ) and the possibility of the phrase having been added from Matt 18:6 cast doubt on its originality. See Metzger, *TCGNT*, 101-2. The prominence of Jesus as an object of belief in vv. 37, 40, and 41 argues for its originality, however.

tian circle. Such a Christian may be even more effective, for the exorcist of v. 38 possessed powers beyond those of the disciples (9:18!). Writing to the church in Rome in the 90s of the first century, Clement of Rome quoted v. 42 as an admonition against schism in the church (*1 Clem.* 46:8).

9:42 is a sober warning against inhibiting, injuring, or destroying the faith of simple and ordinary disciples. The Greek word translated "cause to sin" (*skandalizein*) means "to cause to stumble" or "to offend," and in this instance refers to destroying the faith of a fellow believer or causing a believer to fall away from God. The punishment for such an offense is calamitous. "'It would be better for him to be thrown into the sea with a large millstone tied around his neck,'" says Jesus. In the ancient world grain was ground by cylindrical-shaped millstones so large that they could be turned only by the power of beasts of burden. The inimitable imagery of being heaved into the sea with a millstone tied around one's neck is typical of Jesus and argues in favor of the authenticity of the saying. The millstone imagery was doubly dreadful for the Jews, who as a rule feared the sea and regarded drowning as a horrible form of death.[20] The saying also attests to the irrevocability of certain acts (Rev 18:21). Hurling a sinner to a watery grave was a graphic way for Jesus to convey the finality of God's wrath against spiritual pride.

43-48 These verses shift the focus from jeopardizing others to endangering self. The textual confusion in vv. 44 and 46 is apparently owing to a later scribe having inserted v. 48, which is a quotation from Isa 66:24, after vv. 43 and 45 in order to achieve three parallel strophes. The most reliable Greek manuscripts of Mark, however, retain the Isaiah quotation only at v. 48 (so the NIV).[21]

The instruction to hack off body parts that cause one to stumble is an example of metaphoric hyperbole characteristic of Jesus and is not meant to be taken literally. Both masochism and bodily mutilation (with the exception of circumcision) were strictly taboo in Judaism (Deut 14:1; 23:1; 1 Kgs 18:28; Zech 13:6). Both Jesus and early Christianity eschewed a dichotomy characteristic of Greek Platonism that made the body and the material world inferior to mind or spirit. On the contrary, the Gospels and epistles repeatedly affirm that the body (e.g., sexual morality, financial integrity, the treatment of others) is often the manifestation of spiritual reality. Indeed, the giving of a cup of cold water in v. 41 immediately preceding attests to the spiritual and eternal consequences of bodily acts.

---

20. For example, Josephus recounts a story of a group of Galilean rebels who outraged and terrified the nobility by drowning partisans of Herod in the Sea of Galilee (*Ant.* 14.450).

21. See Metzger, *TCGNT,* 102.

The fact that a saying is not meant to be taken literally is not to diminish or discount its importance, however. If anything, the hyperbole enhances the teaching that God is more important than even those things most indispensable to us. It attests to the uncompromising offense of the gospel and of the authority of Jesus, that nothing — not even things we value supremely like eyes, hands, and feet — should stand in the way of eternal life. Justin Martyr (*Apol.* 1.15.2) quotes the reference to gouging out an eye in v. 47 with reference to chastity. In the Talmud (*b. Nid.* 13*b*) the cutting off of one's hand also refers to sexual transgressions. While the metaphor in v. 43 certainly includes lust and sexual offenses, it should not be limited to them alone. The metaphors of eyes, hands, and feet are all-inclusive of what we view, what we do, where we go. Likewise, Xenophon (*Memorabilia* 1.2.54) writes that "a man's dearest friend is himself; yet, even in his lifetime he removes . . . from his body [nails, hair, etc.] whatever is useless and unprofitable." Xenophon's view of life is a polar opposite to Jesus'. Jesus does not counsel the removal of body parts because they are "useless and unprofitable"; rather, he signals the inestimable worth of the kingdom of God, which surpasses things of *incalculable value*. For Jesus a man's dearest friend is *not* himself but the one God who opens to him the possibility of the kingdom of God — for the sake of which nothing — not even life itself (8:36-37) — is comparable. As important as eyes, hands, and feet are to us — or whatever else claims ultimate allegiance — they are not life; the kingdom of God is life, and nothing in this life should be allowed to prevent one from entering the kingdom. The choice is literally between God's kingdom and "the fire that never goes out."

The Greek word for "hell" in vv. 43, 45, and 47 is *Gehenna,* from which the Hinnom Valley, the steep ravine to the southwest of Jerusalem (Josh 15:8) where human sacrifice had been practiced under Ahaz and Manasseh (2 Kgs 16:3; 21:6), derives its name. The detestable practice of human sacrifice was later excoriated by Jeremiah (Jer 7:31; 32:35) and abolished by King Josiah (2 Kgs 23:10), who desecrated the Hinnom Valley by making it a garbage dump. "'To go into hell, where the fire never goes out,'" became a symbol of divine wrath and punishment in subsequent Judaism and Christianity, or of the darkness, pain, and torment resulting from it.[22]

To the image of smoldering putrefaction in the Hinnom Valley,

22. *1 Enoch* 27:1-2; 54:1ff.; 90:26ff.; 4 Ezra 7:36; Ign. *Eph.* 16:2; *2 Clem.* 17:7. On Gehenna, see Str-B 4/2.1,016-1,165. The conclusion of v. 43 is subject to a series of variant readings in the Greek manuscript tradition. The best-attested reading (א A B C K X Θ Π) and the one that best explains the existence of the others is the reading adopted by the NIV. See Metzger, *TCGNT,* 102.

Mark appends a saying that comes from the final verse of Isaiah (66:24): "'Where their worm does not die and the fire is not quenched.'" The imagery of devouring worm and consuming fire, gruesome and grotesque, seems hardly necessary given the already lurid picture of the Hinnom Valley. Its use here conforms in one important respect to its use in Isaiah, where it concludes two chapters of promise and salvation by a final forceful warning of the consequences of rebellion against God. The quotation of this verse in v. 48 serves as the strongest possible warning against misjudging or trivializing the call and commission of discipleship. Who would imagine that in the simple and mundane tasks of either enabling or hindering believers in faith disciples are charting eternal destinies for themselves (Luke 9:23)? But they are. The horrible imagery of these verses is intended as a sober admonition to disciples *now* rather than simply as a prediction of the future. The architectural plans of eternity are being drawn by the behavior of disciples today. 9:48 is a warning against rebellion against God and a summons to faith in the present, and especially to the ridding of whatever hindrances and impediments would prevent one from entering true life in the kingdom.

49-50 9:49 and 50 combine disparate and somewhat opaque sayings based on salt and fire. It appears that the word "fire" at the end of v. 48 prompted Mark to include the saying of v. 49, and that "salt" in v. 49 led in turn to the inclusion of the saying of v. 50. In addition, not only does v. 49 exist in several different forms in the manuscript tradition, but the variant readings suggest attempts at interpreting the puzzling statement that "'Everything will be salted with fire.'"[23] Interpretations of vv. 49-50 are frequently offered on the basis of the properties of fire and salt. Thus fire and salt both test and prove substances, and because of this they are helpful metaphors of discipleship. Again, since the fire in v. 49 is no longer a fire of perdition as in v. 48 but of purification (so Num 31:23; Mal 3:2), disciples are to allow the sacrifices inherent in following Jesus to purify their lives. Likewise, salt is a preservative. In a world without refrigeration, salt preserves foods, and especially meat, from putrefying. Christians, similarly, are a preservative in society, apart from which society will become rotten.

---

23. The saying exists in three principal forms: (1) "For everyone will be salted with fire," (2) "For every sacrifice will be salted with salt," and (3) "For everyone will be salted with fire, and every sacrifice will be salted with salt." The first reading is to be preferred because of its manuscript support and because its difficulty explains the existence of the other two. Reading 2 can be explained as follows: in search of a clue to the meaning of reading 1, a scribe wrote Lev 2:13 in the margin, which in later manuscripts was incorporated into the text itself. Reading 3 can be explained as a conflation of readings 1 and 2. See Metzger, *TCGNT,* 102-3; and Cranfield, *The Gospel According to Saint Mark,* 314-15.

The above interpretations are generally valid, but they fall short of explaining either the presence or meaning of fire and salt at the conclusion of Mark 9. Since v. 49 occurs only here and in no other Gospel, it must hold special significance for Mark. The most promising interpretation of vv. 49-50 is to understand them against the background of temple sacrifice, in which both fire and salt played indispensable roles. Israelite burnt offerings (an unblemished bull, ram, or bird) were required to be wholly consumed by fire in order to be acceptable. Smoke rising from the consuming fire was a pleasing incense to Yahweh (Leviticus 1). Salt, too, was not only a sign of the covenant (Num 18:19), but it was required to accompany all Israelite sacrifices (Lev 2:13).[24]

In the present context fire and salt appear to be symbols of the trials and costs of discipleship. Discipleship to Jesus lays a total claim on one's life; in the language of sacrifice, it must be totally consuming or it is worthless. Rather than consuming believers in frustration and failure, however, trials make their walk holy and acceptable to God. The disciple who takes up the cross of Jesus and follows on the way to Jerusalem (8:34), who nurtures the faith of another believer (v. 42), who willingly forsakes things precious but injurious to the life of faith is himself a holy sacrifice, a "living sacrifice" according to Paul (Rom 12:1).[25]

This helps explain the puzzling phrase "salted with fire" (v. 49). Testing by fire is not simply a painful necessity of discipleship, but an *offering* itself pleasing to God, a seasoning or salting with fire. If fires of trials and adversity beset the faithful (1 Pet 1:7; 4:12), they do so as a consequence of their following the Son of Man who *must* suffer. In costly discipleship to the Son of Man believers become salt and light to the world (Matt 5:13-16). The willingness of disciples to bear shame and hardship for Christ is a reflection of Christ's redemptive sufferings and a harbinger of hope to the world.

---

24. A necessity of life in biblical times (Sir 39:26), salt was also an essential element in offerings and sacrifices. It was prescribed to accompany burnt offerings (Ezek 43:24), cereal offerings, and indeed "all your offerings" (Lev 2:13), and it appears in a list of provisions for the temple (Ezra 6:9). See J. R. Ross, "Salt," *IDB* 4.167; Str-B 2.21-23.

25. See the helpful discussion of C. Link, "Exegetical Study of Mark 9:49," *NotesTrans* 6/4 (1992): 21-35, who paraphrases vv. 49-50 thus: "For — according to Scripture — all of us (you and I) will be made a burnt offering consecrated to God. Your allegiance to me is the most important thing. Be on your guard, don't lose it. Keep this commitment above all else, then you will be at peace with each other." Link makes the further suggestion that this saying was transmitted to Mark by Peter, who, in view of 1 Pet 1:7; 4:12-13, is the one disciple who should remember the saying after Jesus' shocking rebuke following the first passion prediction (8:29-33). So, too, O. Cullmann, *The Christology of the New Testament*, trans. S. Guthrie and C. Hall (London: SCM Press, 1986), 319.

CHAPTER TEN

"On the Way" through Judea

MARK 10:1-52

The material in chap. 10 is set in Jesus' journey through Judea. In addition to bringing Jesus and the disciples to Jerusalem, the journey also symbolizes the theme of discipleship. As Jesus nears Jerusalem, his teaching about his mission and the claims of discipleship becomes increasingly specific. Chap. 10 begins with the call to discipleship in the most fundamental aspects of life — marriage (vv. 1-12), children (vv. 13-16), and possessions (vv. 17-31). For a third time Jesus foretells his death and resurrection; and like his teaching on discipleship itself, the prediction is the most explicit yet (vv. 32-34). For the first time Jesus declares the servant-role of the Son of Man "'not to be served, but to serve, and to give his life as a ransom for many'" (v. 45). Mark concludes the chapter with the healing of Bartimaeus, whose trust in Jesus for the recovery of his sight and following of Jesus "on the way" to Jerusalem represent the quintessence of discipleship (v. 52).

DISCIPLESHIP AND MARRIAGE (10:1-12)

Marriage and divorce were in Jesus' day, as they are in ours, matters of great interest and controversy. In ancient Judaism, marriage was not regarded as a union of equals for the mutual benefit of both husband and wife but rather as an institution whose chief purpose was the establishment and continuance of the family and whose chief enemy was childlessness. Mark's placement of Jesus' teaching on marriage at the beginning of this section signals the importance of the marital union in the kingdom of God. In Judaism the foremost responsibility of an observant

Jewish male was knowledge and mastery of the Torah, under which he was expected to order the necessities of life, among them marriage. Jesus, however, teaches that marriage is not a male-dominated institution but a new creation of God, to which both husband and wife are equally responsible to practice discipleship in lifelong obedience.

1 "Jesus then left that place and went into the region of Judea and across the Jordan." "That place" from which Jesus set out refers to Galilee, and probably Capernaum, which was Mark's last place designation (9:33). The demarcation between Jesus' Galilean and Judean ministries is made even more explicit in the parallel of Matt 19:1, "When Jesus had finished saying these things, he left Galilee and went into the region of Judea." Mark reports that Jesus goes to "the region of Judea and across the Jordan." This destination caused copyists problems, resulting in a very uncertain textual tradition. The chief problem lay with the reference "across the Jordan" or Transjordan (= Perea), for Transjordan is not in the direction of Jerusalem.[1] Although it is impossible to decide for certain which is the best reading, a reasonably strong case can be made for the reading of the NIV that brings Jesus to Judea and Transjordan (i.e., Perea).[2]

The fact that Transjordan is not in the direction of Jerusalem is only an apparent problem, for internal evidence corroborates the reading adopted by the NIV and argues that a sojourn of Jesus in Judea and Perea fits with Mark's narrative purpose. The wording of Mark 10:1 is virtually parallel in Greek *(kai ekeithen anastas erchetai eis ta horia tēs Ioudaias kai peran tou Iordanou)* to the wording of 7:24 that Jesus "left that place and went into the vicinity of Tyre" *(ekeithen de anastas apēlthen eis ta horia Tyrou)*. This parallelism suggests that before going to Jerusalem Jesus

---

1. Of the three principal variants, *dia tou peran Iordanou* ("through Transjordan"), though reasonably well attested (A K X Π), looks like a scribal change to explain that Jesus came into Judea "through Transjordan." A second reading, simply *peran* ("across"), also reasonably well attested (C D W Δ Θ), is possibly an assimilation to Matt 19:1, which identifies Judea as "across the Jordan." This reading also looks like an attempt to place Jesus in Judea rather than in Perea. While Transjordan can technically refer to either side of the Jordan, the great majority of references mean east of the Jordan rather than west, thus arguing against this reading. The preferred reading is *kai peran* ("and across"), which is slightly better attested than the other two readings (ℵ B C L Ψ) and also the most difficult, and thus the most preferred reading. See Metzger, *TCGNT,* 103.

2. For arguments that the phrase in question refers to a region in Perea called "Judea," see W. Grundmann, *Das Evangelium nach Markus,* 270, who quotes a reference to "across the Jordan" in Josephus, *Ant.* 12.228-31, suggesting that the phrase refers to a Jewish settlement established by John Hyrcanus in Transjordan. B. Pixner, *With Jesus Through Galilee,* 108-13, also believes that Batanea in Transjordan was considered Judea (so *War* 5.56). Both of these arguments are strained, however, for Judea was almost universally understood to refer to the region west of the Jordan.

completes ministries in Gentile regions in the north (7:24[, 31]) and Jewish regions in the south (10:1), both beginning from Galilee. These parallel references appear to be counterparts of the earlier reference in 3:8 that Jesus' ministry attracted people from Judea, Jerusalem, Idumea, the regions across the Jordan, and Tyre and Sidon. With the exception of Idumea, every place mentioned in 3:8 is repeated in 7:24(, 31) and 10:1. The effect of these references is to show the *universal significance* of Jesus' ministry, extending throughout all Palestine. Jesus not only received both Gentiles and Jews (so 3:8), but he also went out to both Gentiles (7:24, 31) and Jews (10:1). In addition to setting forth the universal significance of Jesus' ministry, Mark will likewise show the *universal guilt* of humanity for the death of Jesus, who is rejected by both Jews (8:31) and Gentiles (9:31), and likewise condemned to death by the Jewish Sanhedrin (14:53) and by the Gentile Pilate (15:1).

2 In Judea and Perea Jesus taught the crowds, as was his custom. Although Jesus commonly taught in synagogues, there is evidence, here as elsewhere (2:13; 4:1; 6:6, 34), that he also taught crowds in the open air. As he taught, "Some Pharisees came and tested [Jesus] by asking, 'Is it lawful for a man to divorce his wife?'"[3] Mark, as we have noted, seldom records what Jesus taught, and v. 2 is no exception, for it is not the lecture that Mark records but the question-and-answer period afterward.

Mark's record of the question of the Pharisees is surprising since, as was well known, Jewish law permitted divorce. The only question concerned the grounds of divorce, as recorded in the parallel in Matt 19:3, "'Is it lawful for a man to divorce his wife *for any and every reason.*'"[4] This final phrase was the crux of the controversy over divorce in Jesus' day, as is reflected in a celebrated passage in the Mishnah:

> The School of Shammai say: A man may not divorce his wife unless he has found unchastity in her, for it is written, "Because he hath found in her *indecency* in anything." And the School of Hillel say: [He may divorce her] even if she spoiled a dish for him, for it is written, "Because he hath found in her indecency in *anything.*" R. Akiba says: Even if he found another fairer than she, for it is written, "And it shall be if she find no favour in his eyes." (*m. Git.* 9:10)

---

3. The Western text (D) omits mention of the Pharisees in v. 2, reading simply, "And people were asking him." Contra Metzger, *TCGNT,* 103-4, this is probably not the original reading, for textual support for including "the Pharisees" is widespread and impressive. Moreover, the presence of *peirazontes* ("testing"), which elsewhere characterizes the Pharisees but not the crowds (8:11; 12:5), also argues for the inclusion of Pharisees.

4. The difference in Matthean wording again argues for Markan priority, for we can explain why Matthew would alter Mark, but not why Mark would alter Matthew.

As this passage indicates, Jews and Jewish law were agreed that divorce was permissible. The more conservative school of Shammai argued that the sole ground was "indecency," that is, adultery, whereas the liberal school of Hillel argued that divorce could be granted "for any matter" (NIV, "for any and every reason"; Matt 19:3), that is, for many causes beyond adultery. Not even among the Essenes at Qumran, the most conservative faction of Judaism in Jesus' day, was divorce expressly forbidden. The two texts that deal with marriage at Qumran (CD 4:20–5:6; 11QT 17:15-19) are primarily concerned with forbidding polygamy, but the failure of either passage to forbid divorce and remarriage suggests that the latter were at least allowed.[5] Given the universal acceptance of divorce among first-century Jews, it seems reasonable to conclude that "for any matter" is implied in the question of the Pharisees to Jesus in v. 2.[6] That is, first-century Jews would supply the phrase "for any matter" into the question, which had been omitted for convenience, but apart from which the question made no sense. The question to Jesus thus looks like an abbreviated question whose full connotation exceeded its wording in the ears of its hearers, as today, for example, we speak of "the Second Coming *of Jesus*," or "civil rights *of minorities*," or "equal rights *of women*." The sense of the question asked of Jesus seems to have been, "'Is it lawful for a man to divorce his wife *for any grounds other than adultery?*'"

Mark informs us that the motive of the question of the Pharisees was not simple inquiry; it was rather a "test," indeed, an attempt to trap Jesus (8:11; 10:2; 12:15). If Jesus is in Perea, which was under Antipas's jurisdiction, the question may have been put to trap him on the issue of Antipas's marriage to Herodias, over which the Baptist had lost his head (6:18). If that is the context of the question, then Jesus is being asked whether Antipas was justified or not in divorcing the daughter of King Aretas to marry Herodias. But even if the question is not politically motivated, the Pharisees surely suspect Jesus of holding views on the subject of marriage that differ from theirs. They intend to demolish his position by causing him to compromise the authority of the Torah. Their objective is to maintain a permissive divorce policy — and the more permissive the better. Schürer summarizes the Jewish position on divorce thus: "divorce was relatively easy in those days and the Pharisees and rabbis intended to keep it so."[7]

---

5. For a discussion of marriage and divorce at Qumran, see D. Instone-Brewer, "Nomological Exegesis in Qumran 'Divorce' Texts,'" *RevQ* 18 (1998): 561-79.

6. See Instone-Brewer, "Jesus' Old Testament Basis for Monogamy," in *The Old Testament in the New Testament: Essays in Honour of J. L. North*, ed. S. Moyise, JSNT 189 (Sheffield: Sheffield Academic Press, 2000), 89-91.

7. E. Schürer, *History of the Jewish People*, 2.486.

The Pharisees reflect the view that marriage is a disposable contractual arrangement. Twice they inquire about possible grounds of its dissolution (10:2, 4). Their attitude reminds us of a person who has just been granted a bank loan and then asks under what conditions he might be absolved from repaying it. The starting point in Jewish discussions of divorce was Deut 24:1-4, the passage on which *m. Giṭ.* 9:10 (cited above) was based, as well as the question of v. 4.[8] The intent of Deut 24:1-4 was manifold. Most obviously, it discouraged hasty divorces by requiring a man to stipulate a reason for divorce in writing, and also by prohibiting him from remarrying his divorced wife. The certificate of divorce guaranteed the divorcée at least a modicum of dignity and the right to remarry another man if she chose. It thus safeguarded the rights of the woman as much as possible in a patriarchal culture, although divorce did entail a stigma since a priest was forbidden from marrying a divorcée (Lev 21:7), and a second marriage "defiled" (Deut 24:4) a man's first wife, thus making it impossible for him to remarry her. Thus, as originally intended Deut 24:1-4 did not encourage divorce but rather attempted to preserve an equable ruling in the unfortunate event of divorce. In the question of the Pharisees in v. 4, however, the reference to Deut 24:1-4 no longer serves to limit the ill-effects of divorce but rather as a *pretext* for divorce, "if a man finds anything indecent in [his wife]." As we have seen, the pretexts ranged from adultery alone to the most feeble of excuses, including a wife's failure in simple household duties or failure to please her husband as did another woman.

3-5 "'What did Moses command you?'" asks Jesus. He can hardly have been surprised by the appeal to Deut 24:1-4, that "'Moses permitted a man to write a certificate of divorce and send her away.'" Despite the Mosaic authority of Deut 24:1-4, Jesus does not receive it as conclusive for the question of marriage and divorce. Deuteronomy 24 was given "because your hearts were hard," says Jesus. It is, in other words, a text of concession, not a text of intention. You do not learn to fly an airplane by following the instructions for making a crash landing; you will not be successful in war if you train by the rules for beating a retreat. The same is true of marriage and divorce. The exceptional measures necessary when a marriage fails are of no help in discovering the meaning and intention of marriage. Jesus endeavors to recover God's will for marriage, not to argue about possible exceptions to it. His opponents ask what is permissible; he points to what is commanded.[9] Deut 24:1-3, he argues, is

8. See D. Instone-Brewer, "Deuteronomy 24:1-4 and the Origin of the Jewish Divorce Certificate," *JJS* 49 (1998): 230-43.
9. M. Hooker, *The Gospel According to Saint Mark*, 235.

not a pretext for divorce but an attempt to limit its worst consequences for women. The divine intention for marriage cannot be determined from a text about divorce.

6-9 In order to discern the divine will for marriage, Jesus applies *analogia Scriptura*, the principle that Scripture rightly interprets Scripture. He goes behind the authority of the Torah and appeals to a prior and more fundamental authority in the order of creation: "'at the beginning of creation God "made them male and female."'"[10] In this pronouncement Jesus again presumes a divine authority resident in himself, for he does not *deduce* a conclusion from Scripture (as do the scribes), but he *declares* the will of God as set forth in a creation text over against a legal text from Moses.[11] The quotation of Gen 1:27 in 10:6 evinces that Jesus understands marriage to be a God-ordained union between one male and one female.[12] That marriage is a union of male and female is further evinced by the reference to "father and mother" and to the man being "united to his wife" in v. 7.[13] The same verse is cited to the same effect in the DSS (CD 4:21). Twice the Pharisees ask about exceptions to marriage, and twice Jesus declares God's original will for marriage, that "'they are no longer two, but one'" (v. 8), and "'what God has joined together, let man not separate'" (v. 9).

Jesus' teaching on marriage is governed by a new understanding of the roles and responsibilities of both husband and wife in marriage. In Jewish law, power over marriage and divorce lay predominantly in the hands of men. A woman's place in Judaism depended largely on her relationship to a man — as father, husband, or son. Likewise, Jewish texts relating to women typically channel the discussion through male brokerage. A discussion on women's vows in Numbers 30, for example, shows the extent to which male consent was required in order to ratify or nullify a woman's vow. Likewise, nearly one-sixth of the Mishnah is devoted to the subject of women, but the texts on women have little to say about women in their own right. They are chiefly concerned, rather, with fe-

10. Several important Greek manuscripts (א B C L D) omit "God." The quotation of Gen 1:27 clearly intends God as creator of male and female, however.

11. See T. W. Manson, *The Teaching of Jesus* (Cambridge: Cambridge University Press, 1951), 291-93.

12. There is no hint here or elsewhere in Scripture that God-ordained marriage could include same-sex "unions."

13. Although two major manuscripts (א B) omit the last part of v. 7 ("and be united to his wife"), the reading should likely be retained because (1) the manuscript evidence for including it is both widespread and diverse and (2) without the reading "the two will become one flesh" in v. 8 it could be misunderstood to refer to the father and mother rather than to the husband and wife. See Metzger, *TCGNT*, 104-5.

male transitions in life from the allegiance of father to husband, or of husband to son.

Jesus' teaching on marriage, to the contrary, is predicated on a different estimate of women. Quoting Gen 1:27 (10:6), he acknowledges that God created humanity uniquely as male and female. By expressly mentioning the two sexes, Jesus declares that maleness and femaleness are rooted in the creative will of God and are foundational for marriage. As a sovereign creation, woman is not man's subject but his equal. Appealing further to a supplementary creation text from Gen 2:24 in 10:7-8, Jesus declares that a husband's obligation to his wife surpasses his obligation to his own parents. In the Torah the commandment to honor one's parents is one of the Ten Commandments of God and second only to the commandment to honor God (Exod 20:12). But the effect of v. 7 is to declare that a husband's allegiance to his wife in the union of marriage *surpasses* his allegiance to father and mother, making marriage second only to obedience to God in sacredness. The union of male and female in marriage results in "one flesh," a new creation itself, "no longer two, but one."

The greatest difference between Jesus and the rabbis, however, is this: by giving a husband principal control over his wife, the Jewish divorce policy made the man the lord of the marital relationship. According to Jesus, however, it is neither man nor woman who controls marriage, but rather God, who is the lord of marriage: "'what *God* has joined together, let man not separate.'"[14]

10-12 In 10:10 the discourse shifts to a "house," which typically in Mark signifies further explanation of Jesus' teaching delivered to his disciples. "'Anyone who divorces his wife and marries another woman commits adultery against her,'" declares Jesus. This is the first mention of remarriage in the narrative, which has been devoted to marriage and divorce. The word for "adultery" (Gk. *moichan*) occurs twenty-seven times in the NT, always in the restricted sense of immoral sexual activity with a person married to someone else. Mention of remarriage in vv. 11-12 implies that the sin of adultery occurs as a result of remarriage rather than as a result of divorce. This implication is somewhat misleading, however, for in Jewish law remarriage was valid only if the grounds of divorce were valid. If the divorce was invalid, then the individual is still married and a second marriage becomes adulterous. Thus the thrust of Jesus' teaching is not simply to proscribe remarriage after divorce but to deny the Pharisees' presumption for divorce in general.

10:11 is a startling declaration, for in rabbinic understanding a husband's adultery was reckoned against a woman's father or husband, not

---

14. On "the lord of marriage," see Grundmann, *Das Evangelium nach Markus*, 272.

against the woman herself. Jesus' declaration, however, imputes to women the status of sovereign moral agents. In v. 12 Jesus further establishes a woman's moral agency and responsibility by declaring that if she is responsible for initiating divorce and then remarries she must bear full culpability for her action.

It is often supposed that 10:12 could not have been spoken by Jesus since Jewish law did not grant the right of divorce to women (Josephus, *Ant.* 15.259). V. 12 is commonly accepted, even by conservative scholars, as a Markan interpretation for the particular benefit of Gentile women, who did possess the right of divorce in Greco-Roman society. This conclusion is not necessary, however, and is almost certainly mistaken. First, the supposed Hellenizing of the saying is not itself entirely satisfactory, because Gentiles did not consider a woman who divorces her husband and marries another an adulteress, whereas Jesus does.[15] Second, there is scattered evidence suggesting that women did in fact possess the right to divorce their husbands in Judaism. One example is the divorce of Herodias in 6:17, who divorced her first husband Philip in order to marry Antipas (*Ant.* 18.110). The Mishnah also granted a Jewish woman the right of divorce (a) if, on the basis of illness, occupation, impotence, or unwillingness, a husband could not fulfill his conjugal rights, (b) if the husband had coerced the woman to marry him, or (c) if the woman were underage.[16] Again, the Elephantine documents show that some Jewish Egyptian women were able to divorce their husbands as far back as the fifth century B.C.[17] Finally, and most importantly, a recently published second-century Jewish divorce certificate (*Se'elim* 13) substantially confirms that women did possess the right of divorce in Judaism. This legal document, written by a lawyer on behalf of a certain Shelmazion, daughter of Joseph Qebshan of En Gedi, states "that this is from me to you a bill of divorce and release."[18] The foregoing evidence indicates that the right of women to divorce men, although perhaps not as widespread or as accessible to Jewish women as to Jewish men, was neither impossible nor unknown. V. 12 therefore need not be assigned to an exclusively Greco-

---

15. R. Gundry, *Mark*, 534.

16. See Str-B 2.23-24.

17. B. Porten and A. Yardeni, *Textbook of Aramaic Documents from Ancient Egypt* (Jerusalem: Hebrew University Press, 1986-96). Moreover, a passage from Philo (*Spec. Leg.* 3.30) narrates Deut 24:1-4 with the *woman* rather than the husband as the subject, which would suggest that Philo accepted the right of women to divorce their husbands.

18. See D. Instone-Brewer, "Jewish Women Divorcing Their Husbands in Early Judaism: The Background of Papyrus Se'elim 13," *HTR* 92 (1999): 349-57, who argues on the basis of the papyrus in question and supplementary evidence that such divorce certificates were "part of normal practice in some sections of early Judaism."

Roman milieu. Rather, it reflects divorce practices prevalent in at least some segments of Jewish society.

Mark 10:1-12 is a blueprint for an entirely new norm of marriage, as necessary in our day as in Jesus'. According to the plain sense of 10:1-12, Jesus does not allow grounds for divorce. It is of course possible to argue that the categorical denial of divorce should be qualified by the exception of adultery, as understood by Matt 5:32; 19:9, on the ground that adultery was conceded by all Jews to be an acceptable cause for divorce. If so, then the implication of vv. 11-12 would be that there are no grounds for divorce *except adultery*. Although it is possible that the exception of adultery is implied in vv. 11-12, I do not believe that we can say for certain that it is. The same logic does not apply to supplying "except for indecency (= adultery)" in vv. 11-12 as for supplying "for any matter" in v. 2, for v. 2 reflects Jewish opinion whereas v. 12 reflects Jesus' judgment, which differed from Jewish practice on many points.

Whether or not Jesus allowed for divorce on the basis of adultery is therefore not certain; and even in the case of adultery there is no indication that he demanded divorce, as did the rabbis. If the guilty partner repented and ceased from sin and the other partner forgave him or her, the marriage could be redeemed. The adultery clause, at any rate, is not the key to Mark's narrative. The essential thrust of 10:1-12 is the inviolability of the marriage bond as intended and instituted by God. Jesus does not conceive of marriage on the grounds of its dissolution but on the grounds of its architectural design and purpose by God.[19] Human failure does not alter that purpose (Rom 3:4). The intent of Jesus' teaching is not to shackle those who fail in marriage with debilitating guilt. The question is not whether God forgives those who fail in marriage. The answer to that question is assured in 3:28, "'All the sins and blasphemies of men will be forgiven.'" There is, after all, no instance in Scripture of an individual seeking forgiveness and being denied it by God. The question in our day of impermanent commitments and casual divorce is whether we as Christians will hear the unique call of Christ to discipleship in marriage. In marriage, as in other areas to which the call of Christ applies, will we seek relief in what is permitted, or commit ourselves to what is intended by God and commanded by Christ? Will we fall away in trouble and difficulty (4:17), or follow Jesus in the costly journey of discipleship, even in marriage? Will we sunder the divine union of "two become one flesh," or will we honor and nurture marriage as a gift and creation of God?

19. See G. Collier, "Rethinking Jesus on Divorce," *ResQ* 37 (1995): 80-96, who rightly argues that Jesus grounds his teaching not in moral casuistry but in the divine will. In his teaching on marriage, "Jesus himself is crying out, 'Look for the heart of God.'"

DISCIPLESHIP AND CHILDREN (10:13-16)

After discipleship in marriage, Jesus addresses in turn the issue of discipleship regarding children.[20] The modern West regards tenderness to children as a virtue. Relief organizations appeal for support by showing little lives disfigured by hunger and war. Politicians secure votes by holding and kissing infants. Ancient Jewish society, however, did not regard children with the same affection. Children, like women, derived their position in society primarily from their relationship to adult males. Sons, to be sure, were regarded as a blessing from God, but largely because they insured the continuance of the family for another generation — and increased its workforce. Childhood was typically regarded as an unavoidable interim between birth and adulthood, which a boy reached at age 13. One will search Jewish and early Christian literature in vain for sympathy toward the young comparable to that shown by Jesus.

13 "People were bringing little children to Jesus to have him touch them, but the disciples rebuked them." The indefiniteness of who brought the children, where, and for what occasion is vintage Mark, who often blurs contextual details in order to accentuate the word and work of Jesus. The response of the disciples to the children replays their exclusivism and elitism toward the independent exorcist in 9:38, which again indicates that their attitude continues to be formed by societal standards rather than by Jesus. According to Mark, "the disciples rebuked [the children]." The word for "rebuke" is a severe description, used elsewhere in Mark of exorcisms (1:25; 3:12; 9:25), opponents of God's will (4:39; 8:30-33), or of outright censure (10:13, 48). Like Peter, the disciples "do not have in mind the things of God, but the things of men" (8:33).

14 Jesus sharply opposes their behavior. Mark spoke earlier of Jesus' anger at the condition of the leper (1:41), but v. 14 is the only passage in the Gospels where Jesus is said to be "indignant." The word for "indignant" (Gk. *aganaktein*) means "to arouse to anger," that is, to vent oneself in expressed displeasure rather than simply brooding about it. The object of a person's indignation reveals a great deal about that person. Jesus' displeasure here reveals his compassion and defense of the helpless, vulnerable, and powerless. "'Let the little children come to me, . . . for the kingdom of God belongs to such as these.'" Rather than disbarring children, Jesus commends them as the true heirs of the kingdom he inaugurates. This statement again reveals Jesus' unique authority, for he un-

---

20. Gundry, *Mark,* 545, rightly defends the chronology of the story here on the grounds that if Mark (or a pre-Markan redactor) were rearranging materials without regard to chronology, this story would more likely be coupled or conflated with 9:33-37.

ashamedly presumes to correlate the kingdom of God with himself. In coming to Jesus the children are coming to the one in whom God's present reign is made manifest.

15 Jesus repeats this lesson with a dominical pronouncement: "'I tell you the truth, anyone who will not receive the kingdom of God like a little child will never enter it.'" Children — particularly little children — are often praised for their innocence, spontaneity, and humility. It is often assumed that it is because of these qualities that Jesus commends them. It does not appear, however, that this is the reason — or at least the primary reason — why Jesus blesses the children. The emphasis in this brief story falls on the children themselves rather than on their virtues, real or imagined. The latter remain unidentified. The Greek word for "little children" is a diminutive *(paidia)*, meaning "very young," or "infants," or as Luke 18:15 says, "babies." The terminology suggests the children are below the "age of accountability," and hence it is not their virtue but their helplessness that is stressed.[21] If we assume that Jesus commends children because of their innocence, purity, or even spontaneity, then we must conclude that the disciples' acceptability in God's kingdom depends on similar virtues. But, as Mark's depiction of the disciples makes repeatedly clear, that is exactly what they are not, nor are we. We are not innocent and eager, but slow, disbelieving, and cowardly. In this story children are not blessed for their virtues but for what they *lack*: they come only as they are — small, powerless, without sophistication, as the overlooked and dispossessed of society.[22] To receive the kingdom of God as a child is to receive it as one who has no credits, no clout, no claims.[23] A little child has absolutely nothing to bring, and whatever a child receives, he or she receives by grace on the basis of sheer neediness rather than by any merit inherent in him- or herself. Little children are paradigmatic disciples, for only empty hands can be filled.

10:15, especially, has played a significant role in the discussion of infant baptism. The pericope about Jesus and the children, of course, is about blessing children, not baptizing them, but both the blessing of Je-

21. The aspect of helplessness is accentuated in the version of this saying preserved in the *Gospel of Thomas* 22, which identifies the children as nursing infants: "'These little ones being suckled are like those who enter the kingdom.'"

22. The uniqueness of Jesus' behavior and teaching are further appreciated by comparing them to those of *Thomas the Contender* (139.11-12), a gnostic tractate from Nag Hammadi, which cites this same story to the effect that babes are simply like beasts *until* they become perfect!

23. A point made by J. L. Bailey, "Experiencing the Kingdom as a Little Child: A Rereading of Mark 10:13-16," *WordWorld* 15 (1995): 58-67, who sees children as the epitome of vulnerability, in solidarity with whom disciples also experience the kingdom of God.

sus and the wording of the narrative establish a positive context in which to consider the question of infant baptism. Calvin argued that if children were brought to Jesus to receive the kingdom, which is the sum of the blessing sealed through baptism, why should they be denied baptism?[24] Cullmann argues that the language of the pericope has been chosen by Mark in order to answer the question of the propriety of infant baptism.[25] Although Cullmann's point is possible, it seems more probable that the language of early Christian baptism was taken from this passage, for infant baptism was scarcely an issue at the time Mark wrote his Gospel. Nevertheless, the correlations in language between this pericope and later church baptismal liturgies indicate that the church early perceived the significance of this story for the baptism of infants.

16 People wanted Jesus to touch their children (v. 13). Jesus did more than touch them, however. "He took the children in his arms, put his hands on them, and blessed them." What exactly did people hope to receive from the touch and blessing of Jesus? The ritual of **blessings** was well known in Israel. Noah blessed Shem and Japheth (Gen 9:26-27), Isaac blessed Jacob and Esau (Gen 27; 28:1-4), and Jacob blessed his sons and grandsons (Genesis 48–49). Such blessings tended to be officious in nature, related particularly to the passing on of one's name or property. "A father's blessing establishes the houses of his children," declares Sir 3:9.[26] The laying on of hands was also a priestly rite of investiture in Israel, whereby wisdom (Deut 34:9) and the spirit of office (Num 27:18-20) were conferred on the ordinand. This rite was also continued in early Christianity (Acts 6:1-6; 13:1-3).

In his healing of the sick and aid of the needy, Jesus laid hands on more common people and more frequently than did Jewish society in general. His touch brought blessings, but it was also a blessing, a tangible expression of God's unconditional love for the unclean, foreigners, women, and children. Jesus' personal touch of common people became a distinguishing mark of his bearing and ministry. It also became an essential characteristic of the movement he founded, sparing it from the incipi-

24. J. Calvin, *Commentary on a Harmony of the Evangelists*, vol. 2 (Edinburgh: T. & T. Clark, 1945), 390-91.

25. Specifically, Cullmann argues that *mē kōlyete auta* ("do not hinder them," v. 14) is the same wording approving baptisms in the early church (*Baptism in the New Testament*, trans. J. Reid, SBT [London: SCM Press, 1950], 72-78). For a counter view, see G. R. Beasley-Murray, *Baptism in the New Testament* (London: Macmillan, 1962), 320-29.

26. Later Judaism formalized blessings on the Sabbath or holy days, and often in the synagogue. A typical fatherly blessing of a son is that of Gen 48:20, "'May God make you like Ephraim and Manasseh,'" and of a daughter, "'May God make you like Sarah, Rebekah, Rachel, and Leah'" (see Ruth 4:11), followed by the Aaronic benediction (Num 6:24-26). See *EncJud.* 4.1,087.

ent hierarchy and elitism, whether professional or ascetic, so common of religion. "Another gospel would have resulted and not that of Jesus, and another church rather than his church, had children been kept from Jesus and had Christianity been made into something for men alone."[27]

DISCIPLESHIP AND POSSESSIONS (10:17-31)

The call to discipleship involves a cost of discipleship. Fishermen must leave boats and nets (1:16-20), a tax collector his tax table (2:14), and Peter his false conception of the Messiah (8:33). Another disciple will have to leave a bystander's security and literally take up Jesus' cross (15:21). The call to follow Jesus does not constitute an additional obligation in life, but rather judges, replaces, and subordinates all obligations and allegiances to the one who says, "'Follow me.'" Anything, even the obligation to parents (Matt 8:21), is a hazard if it impedes the following of that call.[28]

The rich man in the present story, with his possessions and social status, is a striking contrast to the simple children of the previous story. He receives a clearer picture of the kingdom than anyone so far in Mark's Gospel, and he displays great eagerness in accepting it. His enviable assets, however, prove a greater liability in inheriting eternal life than do the deficits and paucity of the little children in the previous story, for they embody the essence of the kingdom of God, whereas he turns away from it.

17 Jesus is still in Judea, continuing "on his way" to Jerusalem. Matthew identifies the man who approached Jesus as young (19:20), and Luke calls him a ruler (18:18); hence the common name of this story as "the rich young ruler." Mark, however, calls him in Greek simply "one" or "a certain person." Unspecified designations such as this are typical of Mark, and in the present instance the "one" enhances the applicability of the story for all readers. The man "ran up to [Jesus] and fell on his knees before him." His haste and submission suggest his earnestness to become a disciple. "'Good teacher,' he asked, 'what must I do to inherit eternal life?'" No one who heard Jesus teach in Galilee asked a question of such magnitude, nor indeed have Jesus' own disciples. At last Jesus is asked *the* essential question, capable of divulging the meaning of his ministry.

18-19 Ironically, Jesus withholds the anticipated answer. Perhaps he senses that the question of the man's lips is not the question of his

---

27. A. Schlatter, *Die Evangelien nach Markus und Lukas,* 103-4.

28. Billy Graham said of this story: "The young man came with the right question, to the right man, and received the right answer, but he made the wrong decision."

heart. "'Why do you call me good?' Jesus answered. 'No one is good —
except God alone.'"[29] This response is a frequent source of puzzlement,
but given Jesus' servant posture and the fact that he has sought to veil his
messianic identity, it is perhaps not as puzzling as often supposed. It is
not essentially different from the testimony of John 5:19, that "'the Son
can do nothing by himself; he can do only what he sees the Father doing.'"[30] It is helpful to recall that in Judaism only God is characteristically
called "good." Rabbis welcomed any number of titles (e.g., 12:38), but
only rarely was a rabbi addressed as "good teacher," for fear of blasphemy against God, who alone is good. Similarly, the response of Jesus in
v. 18 directs the man unambiguously to God. The "me" in the rhetorical
question is emphatically thrust to the front of the sentence, meaning
"'Why do you call *me* good?'" Likewise, the pronouncement that "'No
one is good — except God alone'" could also read "except the *one* God,"
expressly directing the man to Israel's one true God (Deut 6:4). In addition, Jesus gives the man a digest of the ethical commandments in the
Decalogue in v. 19 (Exod 20:12-16; Deut 5:16-20). To the prohibitions
against murder, adultery, theft, false testimony, and dishonoring of parents, Jesus commands the man not to defraud the poor.[31] This commandment is not found in the Ten Commandments but may have been added
because of its relevance to the rich man, since wealth is often gained at

29. Matthew 19:17 sensed the dishonor inherent in Mark's text and changed
"'Why do you call me good?'" to "'Why do you ask me about what is good?'" This
makes the following statement in Matthew ("'There is only One who is good'") into a
non sequitur. The resultant reading in Matthew is a compelling argument in favor of
Markan priority.

30. 10:18 has been remembered and quoted by Justin Martyr, *Apol.* 1.16.7; and
Hippolytus, *Refut. Om. Haer.* 5.7.25-26. Note George MacDonald's reflection on this
verse: "The Father was all in all to the Son, and the Son no more thought of His own
goodness than an honest man thinks of his honesty. When the good man sees goodness,
he thinks of his own evil: Jesus had no evil to think of, but neither does He think of His
goodness; He delights in his Father's" (C. S. Lewis, *George MacDonald: An Anthology*
[New York: Macmillan, 1978], 25).

31. The commandment "do not defraud" is excluded from v. 19 by several weighty
manuscripts (B K W Δ Π Ψ). It should likely be retained, however, because of its considerable manuscript support (ℵ A B C D X Θ) and because a copyist would be more inclined
to delete a rogue statement than include one in a list of the Ten Commandments. Although the addition is not among the Ten Commandments, it reflects the will of God as
expressed in Exod 20:17; Deut 24:14; Sir 4:1. Lists of the Ten Commandments in early
Christian literature often reveal selectivity, additions, or both. A list in Rom 13:9 includes
only adultery, murder, theft, and covetousness. A list in *Did.* 2:1-3; 6:1-2 includes the
same four plus a dozen additional commandments, including prohibitions against sodomy, abortion, infanticide, and magic. A list in *Barn.* 19:4-8 includes adultery and covetousness and a further eighteen prohibitions, also including abortion, infanticide, and
sodomy.

the expense of the poor.[32] The expressed emphasis on both God's goodness and commandments in Jesus' response to the man suggests that despite his moral zeal (or perhaps because of it) something is lacking in his relationship with God. If "'no one is good — except God alone,'" then the man still lacks something before God, even if he keeps all the commandments. Jesus' unexpected counterquestion intends to move the man beyond confidence in his moral rectitude to the ultimate purpose of his life, which is to know God.

20 The man asks what he should *do* in order to inherit eternal life (v. 17), which suggests that he understands behavior to be the ultimate requirement of religion. Jesus accordingly directs him to the moral law as stated in the second half of the Decalogue (v. 19). The commandments of God lie at the root of right behavior and direct one to God. "'Teacher,' he declared, 'all these I have kept since I was a boy.'" For the second time the man addresses Jesus as "Teacher," and in the second address, as in the first in v. 17, the reader hears the same assurance of the man's remarkable moral record.

Christian readers may be inclined to doubt the sincerity of this announcement. Did not Jesus show that evil *intent* is the same as *deed* (Matt 5:21-48)? With the lone exception of the final commandment against coveting, however, the Ten Commandments speak only of *acts,* and these could indeed be kept — even if one's intent was otherwise. In his pre-Christian days Paul could also announce that "according to righteousness by law I was blameless" (Phil 3:6). In their *magnum opus* on Judaism, Strack and Billerbeck affirm: "That a person possessed the ability without exception to fulfill God's commandments was so firmly rooted in rabbinic teaching, that in all seriousness they spoke of people who had kept the entire Torah from A to Z."[33]

21 Christian readers often assume that the man was hypocritical in bringing his moral report card to Jesus. That would not seem to be the case, however, for Mark says that "Jesus looked at him and loved him." Jesus did not look on hypocrisy with love. Should it be countered that v. 20 reveals arrogance rather than hypocrisy, that, too, may be a misjudgment. Given Jesus' affection for the man, it seems more reasonable to assume that his ready presentation of his goodness was childlike, unreflec-

---

32. Contra W. D. McHardy, "Mark 10:19: A Reference to the Old Testament?" *ExpTim* 107 (1995-96): 143, who argues that the addition of "Do not defraud" is unexplained, and therefore must have been a catchword written by a scribe in the margin of a manuscript, which later became inadvertently included in the text. The reason suggested in the previous footnote better explains the inclusion of the commandment, whereas there is no evidence for McHardy's marginal hypothesis.

33. Str-B 1.814.

tive perhaps, but not arrogant. The word for "looked at" (Gk. *emblepein*) is an intensified compound of the normal word for "look," meaning "to look at intently," "to examine," or "to scrutinize." Jesus is not being deceived by the rich man. He sees inside him and "loved him." The word for "love" (Gk. *agapan*) is the highest form of love in the NT, meaning love that characterizes God and of which God is worthy. There must have been something rare and admirable in the man, for of no one else in the Gospel does Mark say that Jesus "loved him."

It is often further assumed that if one followed the law perfectly one would be assured of eternal life. In this passage Jesus teaches something quite different. We may safely assume that the man has kept the law, for Jesus does not challenge his statement to this effect in v. 20. But even if the law were kept, the most essential thing is still lacking! "'One thing you lack,' [Jesus] said. 'Go, sell everything you have and give to the poor, and you will have treasure in heaven. Then come, follow me'" (also Luke 12:33-34). How profoundly ironic is the kingdom of God. The children in the former story who possess nothing are not told that they lack anything, but rather that the kingdom of God is theirs; yet this man who possesses everything still lacks something! Only when he sells all he has — only when he becomes like a vulnerable child — will he possess everything. To the question what the man must do to inherit life in the future (v. 17), Jesus directs him to the present. He must do something *now*. His full adherence to the moral law, good and necessary as it is, is no substitute for following Jesus.[34] The question about the law, in other words, is answered with reference to a relationship with Jesus! True obedience to the law can be rendered only in discipleship to Jesus, and unless obedience to the law leads to discipleship with Jesus it is incomplete and futile. In following Jesus the man "will have treasure in heaven" (v. 21). Jesus offers himself as a substitute for the man's possessions.

22 "At this the man's face fell. He went away sad, because he had great wealth." What a contrast to his earlier confidence (vv. 17, 20). As long as the man stands on his own merits he is self-assured; but the word of Jesus calls him beyond his safe haven, just as it earlier called disciples to weigh anchor and cast out into the deep where there is no security but

---

34. "Although [Jesus] did not oppose the law, he did indicate that what was most important was accepting him and following him. This could eventually lead to the view that the law was unnecessary, but it appears that Jesus himself did not draw this conclusion, nor does this seem to have been an accusation against him. . . . [H]e regarded his own mission as what really counted. If the most important thing that people could do was to accept him, the importance of other demands was reduced, even though Jesus did not say that those demands were invalid" (E. P. Sanders, *The Historical Figure of Jesus* [London: Penguin Press, 1993], 236-37).

Jesus. Mark describes his reaction with a particularly descriptive word in Greek, *stygnazein*, meaning to be "shocked," "appalled," or "overcast as the sky." "The deceitfulness of wealth . . . chokes the word" (4:19). A person who leads an exemplary life — who even endears himself to the Son of God — can still be an idolater.

What should we deduce about **wealth** and **poverty** from this account? Two things may be said about the scriptural attitude toward possessions. On the one hand, wealth was commonly regarded as a sign of God's blessing (Job 1:10; 42:10; Ps 128:1-2; Isa 3:10). Later rabbinic tradition agreed, considering poverty the severest affliction in the world, outweighing all other adversities combined.[35] On the other hand, however, the OT champions the cause of the sojourner, widow, orphan, fatherless, and poor. Jesus especially sides with this latter tradition. Jesus displayed uncommon solidarity with the poor, needy, and bereft because in compassion God exalts the poor above the rich and powerful (1 Sam 2:1-10; Luke 1:46-55). Jesus does not teach or uphold poverty as an ideal, but he does, as here, regard the awareness of need that results from poverty as a blessing. The greatest enemies to faith and obedience are self-satisfaction and pride, and nothing removes those bulwarks more effectively than poverty.

23-25 The last we hear of the rich man is that "he went away sad" (v. 22). Without saying any more Mark has said everything, for to leave Jesus is to forsake the kingdom of God and the possibility of life. Mark now shifts from the rich man to the disciples, which indicates that the wealth and possessions that prevented one man from following Jesus are also matters of concern for those who do follow Jesus. The relevance of the lesson on possessions for the disciples is implied by the introduction to this verse, which says that "Jesus looked around." The Gk. *periblepesthai* is a key word for Mark, occurring six times in his Gospel and only once elsewhere (Luke 6:10) in the NT. It signifies a commanding survey of the situation, as though Jesus looks to see whether the disciples will follow the rich man's example.[36]

Twice Jesus warns, "'How hard it is for the rich to enter the kingdom of God'" (10:23-24). In v. 22 the Greek word for the man's "wealth" is *ktēmata*, meaning "possessions" or "landed property," that is, real estate. In v. 23 Jesus uses a more general term for "rich" (Gk. *chrēmata*), which rhymes with the former term but generally means "monetary wealth." The change in wording implies that wealth in its manifold and

---

35. Str-B 1.818-26.
36. 3:5, 34; 5:32; 10:23; 11:11. 9:8 is the only use of the word in Mark without Jesus as subject.

more liquid forms is as dangerous to faith as the obvious wealth of great property owners. Again, "'It is easier for a camel to go through the eye of a needle than for a rich man to enter the kingdom of God.'"[37] We should like to see the glint in Jesus' eye as he made this comment. The humor of this saying does not lessen its pungency, of course. Commentators have tried to eviscerate the force of this inimitable saying by suggesting that the original Greek meant "rope" instead of "camel." Not only is there no textual evidence for such a reading, but it is equally impossible for a rope to go through the eye of a needle. Nor is "the eye of the needle" a small city gate through which camels might enter Jerusalem by kneeling — as though the rich may enter the kingdom of God if only they humble themselves. There is no evidence for this legendary gate until the ninth century A.D.

To be sure, wealth is a potential danger to faith. Wealth is not categorically condemned by Jesus, however. Neither the unnamed woman of 14:3-9 nor Joseph of Arimathea (15:43; Matt 27:57) is either questioned or condemned in Mark, although both are wealthy. For *this* man wealth is an actual danger, as it doubtlessly is for most disciples, for it prevented him from doing the one thing necessary for salvation. Wealth can and often does exist in other than material forms.[38] Anything that causes disciples to forget their poverty and childlikeness before God and that prevents them from following Jesus Christ — this, too, is a camel before the eye of a needle.

26-27 The disciples' reaction, interestingly, parallels the rich man's. They, too, are "amazed" (Gk. *thambein*, v. 22) and "even more amazed" (Gk. *perissōs ekplēssesthai*, v. 26). "'Who then can be saved?'" they reply.[39] The word of Jesus comes to them, as to the rich man, not as a

---

37. The Western text (D) arranges the sequence to read vv. 23, 25, 24, 26, presumably to achieve a more consistent narrative sequence. Nevertheless, the normal verse sequence is doubtlessly correct, based on (1) superior textual support and (2) slightly awkward sequence, which argues for its originality. V. 24 displays textual variation as well. A superior number of manuscripts reads "'How hard it is *for those who trust in riches* to enter the kingdom of God.'" The qualification achieved by the additional words, as Metzger notes (*TCGNT*, 106), makes Jesus' statement less rigorous and categorical. Although the manuscript support for the qualified reading is clearly superior, the longer reading is suspect because it compromises a difficult saying of Jesus. The shorter reading is preferable.

38. The Cynic philosopher Diogenes castigated Alexander the Great for concupiscence in a similar regard. "If you wish to become good and upright," said Diogenes, "throw aside the rag you have on your head and come to me. But you certainly cannot, for you are held fast by the thighs of Hephaestion" (*HCNT*, 118).

39. The reading of the NIV, "[They] said *to each other*, 'Who then can be saved?'" is the least-well-attested reading and scarcely original. The strongest reading both textually

314

comfort but as an offense. It surpasses human possibility. It drives them inward, where they discover only weakness and inadequacy. The command of Jesus makes them aware of what they *lack,* as did Jesus' word to the rich man in v. 21. It is the same lack or deficit with which Jesus sent the disciples into mission without provisions, so that they would learn to trust in God (6:7-13). The disciples' sense of inadequacy at the command of Jesus is, in fact, a "severe mercy" (Rom 11:22), a beneficial handicap that is intended to draw them away from trust in their own abilities to the one who would be their saving Lord.

Jesus looks as intently and knowingly at them as he did at the rich man. The Gk. *emblepō* at 10:21 and 27 means to perceive the intent of something or someone. He sees what they do not see. The response, "'Who then can be saved?'" which to the disciples seems to spell futility, is, unbeknown to them, a doorway to hope. This at last is the right question, and this accounts for the fact that Jesus answers their question about discipleship whereas he avoided the rich man's question about salvation in vv. 17-18. The question reveals the utter futility of human efforts before God. The possibility of their truly following Jesus is as hopeless as the father curing his epileptic son in 9:22-23. Jesus, in fact, answers the disciples as he did the father, "'With man this is impossible, but not with God; all things are possible with God.'"[40] Neither the father of the epileptic nor the disciples have within themselves the power to do what Jesus asks. Jesus will himself be cast upon the all-sufficiency of God in Gethsemane, when, before the imminence and terror of the cross, he will confess, "'*Abba*, Father, everything is possible for you'" (14:36). The word of Jesus makes evident within the disciples what it should have made evident within the rich man — their deficiency. But the deficiency that appears as inability, even futility, appears to Jesus as openness to the potential of God.[41] It is not they who will do something for God or accomplish his word, but God who will accomplish his word within them. What God commands, he also gives. There is within this interchange between Jesus

---

and contextually is "[They] said *to themselves . . . ,'*" which was changed in the Alexandrian textual tradition, evidently, to "[They] said *to him.'*" See Metzger, *TCGNT,* 106.

40. Compare Philo's version of Moses' speech to the Israelites trapped at the Red Sea: "'Do not lose heart,' [Moses] said, 'God's way of defense is not as that of men. Why are you quick to trust in the specious and plausible and that only? When God gives help He needs no armament. It is His special property to find a way where no way is. What is impossible to all created beings is possible to Him only, ready to His hand'" (*Moses* 1.174 [LCL, no. 289]).

41. See the discussion of emptiness and fullness in *Ap. Jas.* 1:4:5-22. But whereas the *Apocryphon of James* counsels want of reason and fullness of Spirit, Jesus promises the all-sufficiency of God in the face of human insufficiency.

and the disciples the unmistakable kernel of the doctrine of grace as later expounded by the apostle Paul.

28-30 "Peter said to him, 'We have left everything to follow you!'" If "with man [discipleship] is impossible," of what value are human sacrifices that, although undeniably shy of God's ideal, are still genuine and costly from a human perspective? Do Peter's sacrifices of having left all things to follow Jesus count for anything, or are they ultimately worthless? The plaintive statement of Peter in v. 28 is essentially a plea. The pronoun "we" is emphatic, begging for affirmation in the face of a standard that threatens to reduce not only Peter but all disciples to insignificance.

Jesus responds in 10:29-30 that the sacrifices of Peter and of all disciples in the name of Christ will be rewarded a hundred times as much in this world, and with eternal life in the world to come. The remarkable thing about the list of v. 29 is that our most essential natural network of relationships and allegiances — homes, families, and fields — must be forsaken, for the scandalous call of Christ takes priority over them and requires the severing of old allegiances. One cannot follow Jesus with one's former baggage: one must give up his nets, another his riches. Ironically, however, one will receive a hundred times over what one forsook for Christ's sake (v. 30). Mention of "persecutions" in v. 30 is noteworthy, for it is the only negative term in a list of blessings. Its presence in the list reminds disciples that Christian existence is not utopia, and Christian faith is not an insurance policy against adversity and hardship. Not only is this generally true of discipleship, but the presence of "persecutions" likely held special meaning for Mark's congregation in Rome that suffered so profoundly under Nero's persecutions. Their sufferings — and all suffering that results from faithfulness to the gospel — are not a sign of divine abandonment or disfavor, but an inevitable concomitant of faith. Followers of Jesus must be clear that discipleship is not a "both . . . and," but an "either . . . or." Jesus will have no divided allegiances; he will have all of us or he will not have us at all — so jealous is his love.

But to conceive of discipleship solely in terms of its costs and sacrifices is to conceive of it wrongly — as though in marrying a beautiful bride a young man would think only of what he was giving up. To Peter's plaintive assertion of having left "everything to follow" Jesus, Jesus promises "a hundred times as much." The sacrifices they make in leaving "homes, brothers, sisters, mothers, children and fields"[42] to follow Jesus

---

42. "Father" is omitted from the list (as in 3:35), perhaps because disciples are to have no father but God. *Ap. Jas.* 4:25 includes "villages" in the list, thus adding "society" to the bonds of kinship and occupation.

(v. 29) are nothing compared to the returns they will receive in the community of faith now and in heaven in the life to come (Rom 8:18). Authentic acts of obedience and discipleship are like the five loaves and two fish (6:38) that Jesus receives and multiplies to feed the five thousand. Simple, humble, yet costly acts of discipleship are like the despairing seeds that against all odds yield a harvest a hundred times greater (4:8, 20). From the perspective of a bumper crop one looks back on the labor and risk of sowing in a vastly different light. The miracle and plenty of the harvest verify the inherent rightness of the costly act of sowing; likewise, the reward of eternal life makes the sacrifices of discipleship look insignificant in comparison to the lavish blessing of God.

31 "'Many who are first will be last, and the last first.'" This chiastic saying is preserved in several layers of early church tradition.[43] Its simplicity captures a profound irony of discipleship. The kingdom of God topples our cherished priorities and demands of disciples new ones. It takes from those who follow Jesus things they would keep, and gives to them things they could not imagine. Those who take their stand on their riches — whatever they be — will have nothing to stand on. Those who give up everything — not only possessions but even people and places, indeed their own lives (8:35) — to follow Jesus will not simply be compensated for their sacrifices but surfeited a hundred times over with the same, and in the world to come with eternal life.

THE THIRD PASSION PREDICTION (10:32-34)

For the third and final time (8:31; 9:31) Jesus predicts his death and resurrection. Following the three lessons on discipleship in 10:1-31, the third passion prediction, which is the most explicit of the three, reminds Jesus' followers that discipleship is always and ultimately following Jesus, who goes to Jerusalem to suffer (10:33-34) and "to give his live as a ransom for many" (v. 45). Discipleship is thus not only characterized by identifiable behaviors within marriage (vv. 1-12), with children (vv. 13-16), and with possessions (vv. 17-31), but, as demonstrated by Bartimaeus, by expressly "following Jesus along the road" (v. 52). The centrality of Jesus is further emphasized by Mark, who, in contrast to the third passion prediction recorded in Matt 20:17-19 and Luke 18:31-34, shows Jesus "leading the way" (v. 32) to Jerusalem.

32 Again Mark expressly states that Jesus is "on the way," remind-

43. Matt 19:30; 20:16; Luke 13:30; *Barn.* 6:13; *Gospel of Thomas* 4.

ing his readers that to know Jesus is to follow him, even on the way of suffering. For the first time Mark also identifies the destination: they are "on their way up to Jerusalem." *Up* is the proper word for the journey, for Jerusalem, which is only twenty miles from Jericho (v. 46), is 3,500 feet higher in elevation. *Up* is also symbolic of the suffering that awaits Jesus in Jerusalem and the ardor of discipleship. Despite the grave ascent, Jesus is not lagging behind like a prisoner going to the gallows, but "leading the way," like Isaiah's servant of the Lord who "set [his] face like flint" (Isa 50:7). How revealing of Jesus' self-understanding and how instructive for discipleship that he displays his prominence in humility and willingness to suffer. Nowhere else in Mark, notes Eduard Schweizer, does Mark speak of Jesus leading the way, except in the prophecies of 14:28 and 16:7. "Here he is the Master who goes before his disciples, whose responsibility it is to follow him."[44] When it comes to humility and suffering, Jesus does not only teach: he leads the way.

The disciples, on the other hand, lag behind "astonished" and "afraid." These are not novel reactions. The disciples were also "afraid" (Gk. *phobeisthai*) at the second passion prediction (9:32), and they were "astonished" (Gk. *thambein*) immediately before in v. 24. Peter just avowed, "'We have left everything to follow [Jesus]'" (v. 28), but here he and others follow for reasons other than free and genuine obedience. Our discipleship is never as noble as we imagine it, but Jesus accepts it nevertheless. In that, too, the humility of Jesus is evident.

The Greek of 10:32 is unclear whether Jesus is followed only by the Twelve or by a larger retinue. There appears to be a distinction (although it is more pronounced in the NIV than in the original Greek) between "those who followed" and "the Twelve." V. 32 may be further evidence that Jesus' followers exceeded only the Twelve (15:41). Nevertheless, Mark indicates that Jesus directed his teaching primarily to the latter.

33-34 The fear of the disciples provides an occasion for Jesus to teach "them what was going to happen to him." A measure of anxiety is perhaps necessary in order to learn the way of the Christ. "'We are going up to Jerusalem,'" declares Jesus ominously. The use of "we" immediately after the revelation of what would happen to "him" has sobering implications. Disciples face a moment of truth when they realize that their fate is enmeshed in Jesus' fate. The bell tolls not only for Jesus but for them too.

The three **passion predictions** can be set in parallel columns for comparison.

---

44. E. Schweizer, *Erniedrigung und Erhöhung bei Jesus und seinen Nachfolgern,* ATANT 28 (Zurich: Zwingli Verlag, 1962), 12.

8:31	9:31	10:33-34
the Son of Man	the Son of Man is going to be betrayed into the hands of men.	the Son of Man will be betrayed (14:41)
must suffer many things and be rejected by the elders, chief priests,		to the chief priests (14:53)
and scribes		and scribes. (14:53) They will condemn him to death (14:64) and will hand him over to the Gentiles, (15:1) who will mock him (15:29-30) and spit on him, (14:65; 15:19) flog him (15:15)
and that he must be killed and after three day rise again.	They will kill him, and after three days he will rise again.	and kill him. (15:37) Three days later[45] he will rise again. (16:1-2)

The third prediction is clearly more detailed than the first two. The verses in parentheses in the third prediction refer to their corresponding fulfillment in the passion narrative. The close parallelism between the third prediction and subsequent events in Jerusalem is probably owing to the fact that the church, which handed on this information to Mark, remembered Jesus' words in light of events surrounding his passion.

That is not to suggest, however, that the passion predictions are so-called *vaticinia ex eventu*, that is, retrojections after the fact into the life and ministry of Jesus. It is a curiosity that scholars, who can predict with con-

---

45. The manuscript tradition reveals that Mark's characteristic wording, *meta treis hēmeras* ("after three days"; so ℵ B C D L Δ Ψ) has been wrongly altered to *tē̜ tritē̜ hēmera* ("on the third day"; so A K W X Θ Π) in order to correspond to the more common formula in Matt 20:19; Luke 18:33, etc. See Metzger, *TCGNT*, 107.

siderable accuracy what will happen if they publish certain views, for example, are prone to deny that Jesus could have foreseen his impending fate and to ascribe the three passion predictions to later editorial hands. It is surely fantastic to imagine that the early church, which was careful to distinguish its own teaching from that of Jesus on lesser matters (e.g., Acts 15:28; 1 Cor 7:25), would consider ascribing such an audacious claim to Jesus without historical precedent. Indeed, given the opposition to Jesus, we should be surprised if he had no intimation of his impending death. The apostle Paul had definite intimations of his own death (Acts 20:22-23), and similar examples in more recent history are not unknown.[46] What went on in a Roman prison was no secret to anyone living in the Roman Empire. Jesus knew well the fate of his predecessors (Luke 13:34-35; Psalms 22 and 69; Isaiah 50; 53), and he had no reason to expect to be exempted from it.

Nor does it appear that the passion predictions have been harmonized, whether by the early church or by Mark. A glance at the synopsis of the three passion predications reveals that the second prediction (9:31) is the simplest and least detailed of the three. This argues against an evolutionary process of development in the three predictions. Different agents are responsible for Jesus' death in the three predictions: the whole Sanhedrin is responsible for Jesus' death in the first prediction (8:31), the Gentiles in the second (9:31), and the chief priests, scribes, and Gentiles in the third (10:33). Nor does the sequence of details in the third prediction fully correspond to the sequence of events in the passion narrative.[47] All this suggests that the passion predictions have not been artificially harmonized in accordance with the passion narrative. This is all the more significant given the fact that the rudimentary prediction of Jesus' rejection, death, and resurrection readily lent itself to such harmonization. The differences among the three predictions argue for their originality with Jesus and their faithful preservation in the memory of the church. Jesus will be handed over by the Sanhedrin and killed by the Gentiles. This thrice-repeated fact will make the confession of 15:39 all the more remarkable, for the first human to confess Jesus as God's Son will come from one of the parties responsible for his death!

46. That people have in certain instances foreseen the future in remarkable correspondence to subsequent events is shown by two examples from Holocaust literature. See Corrie ten Boom's vision of her arrest and deportation long before it happened in *The Hiding Place* (Washington Depot: Chosen Books, 1971), esp. 127; and Madame Schächter's vision of Auschwitz in Elie Wiesel's *Night* (New York: Avon Books, 1969).

47. So C. E. B. Cranfield, *The Gospel According to Saint Mark*, 335.

SELF-SERVING SONS OF ZEBEDEE AND
SELF-SACRIFICING SON OF MAN (10:35-45)

Following each of Jesus' passion predictions in 8:31, 9:31, and 10:33-34, the disciples jockey for position and prestige. The request of James and John in v. 37 is the third and most blatant example of human self-centeredness in contrast to Jesus' humility and self-sacrifice. In response to their exclusive request, Jesus instructs the Twelve that the economy of God's kingdom is not based on power and control but on service and giving, for the latter are not only the ethics of the kingdom but the means of redemption.

35-37 For the only time in the Gospel of Mark, James and John, sons of Zebedee, are mentioned apart from the Twelve (1:19-20; 3:19) or from Peter (5:37; 9:2; 13:3; 14:33). (See further on the Zebedee brothers at 9:38.) Their names are anchored to this story because of the audacity of their request. Mark's source for this narrative is most probably Peter, who had reason to remember and relay this story. Peter, James, and John comprised Jesus' earthly inner circle, and the request of the brothers to exclude him from the heavenly circle in glory cannot have been soon forgotten by the chief apostle. "'Teacher,' they said, 'We want you to do for us whatever we ask.'" "Teacher" is the honorific title that suppliants, whether friends or foreigners, normally use in the Synoptics when making requests of Jesus. The aorist tense of the Greek verbs for "ask" and "do" indicates that they have a specific request in mind. The request for an assurance beforehand from Jesus betrays the brothers' misgivings about their request. Their asking Jesus to sign a blank check, as it were, is even more elitist than the statement of the apostle John in 9:38. It is self-serving, callous toward Jesus, and an offense to their comrades.

Jesus asks the brothers, "'What do you want me to do for you?'" The answer to that question, not only in the case of the Zebedee brothers but in ours as well, lays bare our true motives, revealing whether we seek our own glory or the glory of God. This is the same question Jesus will ask of blind Bartimaeus in the following story (10:51). But the response of Bartimaeus will differ greatly from that of the brothers. Bartimaeus asks for faith, James and John ask for fame; Bartimaeus wants to follow Jesus "on the way,"[48] James and John want to sit with him in glory. The Greek

---

48. See S. Schlumberger, "Le récit de la foi de Bartimée (Marc 10/46-52)," *ETR* 68 (1993): 73-81, who rightly argues that the Bartimaeus story is not simply about a healing but more importantly about becoming a disciple and following Jesus on the way to the cross.

wording of the brothers' request to sit with Jesus in glory carries echoes of an original Hebrew question, which likely goes back to their original request.[49] Although Jesus has been clear and consistent about the suffering awaiting him in Jerusalem, the disciples have heard him only selectively. Like the pilgrims in the Psalms of Ascents (Psalms 120–134), they regard the way to Jerusalem as a procession to grandeur. Nevertheless, despite the ill-concealed ambition of the brothers to sit beside Jesus in glory, and despite their continued misjudging of Jesus' mission, v. 37 does in fact reveal that they acknowledge Jesus to be the Messiah, and believe that in Jerusalem he will inherit his messianic kingdom. In Jewish custom the place of highest honor was at the center of the company, followed by the right and left hands, respectively. "Of three walking along, the teacher should walk in the middle, the greater of his disciples to his right, the smaller one at his left, and thus do we find that of the three angels who came to visit Abraham, Michael went in the middle, Gabriel at his right, Raphael at his left," instructs the Talmud (*b. Yoma 37a*).[50] The brothers hope to honor Jesus while honoring themselves. How easily worship and discipleship are blended with self-interest; or worse, self-interest is masked as worship and discipleship.

38 To the request of James and John, Jesus responds that they do not know what they are asking. Even in his refusals of our requests God reveals his humility and grace, for how wretched we should be if God granted every request for which we foolishly prayed. The same is true of Jesus' first disciples. They are quick to claim the benefits of God's kingdom, but slow to hear the costs of participating in it. Jesus speaks about its costs as a "cup" and a "baptism."[51] In the OT, a "cup" usually symbolizes something allotted by God. It can signify joy and prosperity (Pss 16:5; 23:5; 116:13), but more frequently it signifies God's judgment and wrath.[52] In the response of Jesus to James and John it conveys the sense that Jesus' impending suffering and death (10:33-34) are ordained and willed by God. In going to Jerusalem Jesus is not simply electing a course of action but fulfilling a role assigned to him. We cannot say for certain,

---

49. The unusual Greek expression *dos hēmin hina . . . kathisōmen* (lit. "Give to us that we might sit") reflects the proper Hebrew wording, *tenah lanu-lašebet*. Matt 20:21 improves the wording to acceptable Greek, which again argues for Matthew's use of Mark rather than the reverse.

50. Further, see Str-B 1.835.

51. For a review of allusions to "cup" and "baptism" in the Jewish tradition, see J. D. M. Derrett, "Christ's Second Baptism (Lk 12:50; Mk 10:38-40)," *ExpTim* 100 (1988-89): 294-95.

52. Pss 11:6; 16:5; 75:8; Isa 51:17, 22; Jer 25:15-28; 49:12; Hab 2:16; *Mart. Isa.* 5:13; *Mart. Pol.* 14:2; 4QpNah 4:6.

but the idea of "drinking" the cup ordained for him may imply the added sense of God's wrath on human sin that Jesus must "drink." Context attributes a similar sense to "baptism" as to "cup," although this is the first instance of "baptism" being used metaphorically of suffering in our literature.[53] "Baptism" expresses Jesus' solidarity with sinners and his willingness to bear their judgment before God. The cardinal point of v. 38 is that Jesus' question ("'Can you drink the cup . . . ?'") requires a negative answer: despite their claim, the disciples *cannot* drink the cup and undergo the fate that only Jesus must undergo. The reason why becomes apparent in v. 45 when, for the first time in Mark, Jesus reveals the vicarious effects of his self-sacrifice for others.

39 James and John, however, think that they *can* emulate Jesus in matters pertaining to the "cup" and "baptism." (They were not nicknamed "sons of thunder" for nothing [3:17; Luke 9:52-53].) They will indeed drink a cup and undergo a baptism, concedes Jesus, but Jesus invests the metaphors with a slightly different sense when he uses them of the disciples. With reference to himself, "cup" and "baptism" signify the unique way charted for him by God and the means by which his atoning "ransom" (10:45) will be achieved. With reference to the disciples the same imagery refers to the persecutions (v. 30) that they will reap as a consequence of following him.[54] The pronouncement that the brothers will drink the cup that Jesus drinks and be baptized with his baptism is often seen as a prediction of their martyrdom. Although the "cup" will carry the connotation of martyrdom in later Christian tradition,[55] there is no evidence in v. 39 that its sense is so intended. If it were, we might expect a concomitant reference to their glory. Verse 39 seems best read as a reminder and renewed call to discipleship, which ineluctably entails sacrifice and suffering. Disciples of Jesus do not decide to accept or reject hardships on the basis of the future rewards accruing from them. They accept suffering on the sole basis that it is the way of Jesus. "The Son of

53. The parallel in Matt 20:23 omits it. H. Koester argues that baptism as a metaphor for martyrdom and death reflects later Christian usage (e.g., Rom 6:3-11) and thus was a later interpolation in Mark's text (*Ancient Christian Gospels: Their History and Development* [Philadelphia: Trinity Press International, 1992], 278). Luke's similar use of "baptism" in another context (12:50), however, may argue for its originality with Jesus. The OT also speaks symbolically of the waters of calamity that overtake a sinner (Pss 42:7; 69:2; Isa 43:2). Surely it does not place undue strains on our credulity to imagine that Jesus could and did apply this same sense to "baptism."

54. Hippolytus (*Refut. Om. Haer.* 5.8.11-12), the early third-century church father, cites a passage that he attributes to the *Gospel of the Nazarenes*, in which the "cup" refers to Jesus going to the Father, as in John 13:33.

55. "The cup of Christ" in *Mart. Pol.* 14:2 and "the cup that the Lord has mixed" in *Mart. Isa.* 5:13 refer to the impending martyrdoms of Polycarp and Isaiah, respectively.

God suffered unto the death, not that men might not suffer, but that their sufferings might be like His."[56]

40 As for the glory the brothers seek, Jesus defers entirely to God: "'[it] is not for me to grant.'" The "me" is emphatic in Greek, implying that the fulfillment of their request is not within the authority of Jesus. Rather, "'these places belong to those for whom they have been prepared.'" This unduly periphrastic translation of the NIV renders a simple Greek phrase, "but for whom it has been prepared,"[57] which surrenders the whole matter of rewards and glory to the hidden purpose of God. God's name is not mentioned doubtlessly because of the Jewish custom of avoiding the use of the divine name when possible for fear of profaning it. A providential undercurrent is nevertheless unmistakable here.[58] The purpose of God cannot be thwarted, but neither can it be fully deciphered beforehand. The disciples are not to follow Jesus because they know in advance what will happen or because of what they hope to get. The rightness of their way is determined solely by the fact that it is where Jesus leads.

41-42 Not surprisingly, the other apostles "became indignant with James and John." Their indignation may owe to the fact that they harbor similar ambitions, but it also, and more obviously, owes to the fact that the request of the Zebedee brothers excludes them from the closeness of fellowship in glory that they presently enjoy with Jesus.

Jesus seizes the occasion to teach a lesson of supreme importance. The NIV says that he "called them together," but he "summoned them" would be more appropriate, for the Gk. *proskaleomai* occurs on nine occasions in Mark when Jesus gathers the disciples and/or crowds for a decisive lesson. The world, says Jesus, practices leadership from a model of dominance, authority, and the effective uses of power and position. The wording behind the NIV, "those who are regarded (Gk. *hoi dokountes*) as rulers," is curious. This exact phrase occurs elsewhere in the NT only in

---

56. G. MacDonald, *Unspoken Sermons,* First Series, 1867.

57. An interesting textual variant developed in v. 40 owing to the fact that ancient Greek manuscripts printed words together with no spaces between them. The sequence of Greek letters αλλοις was read by several early versions (Italian, Coptic, Ethiopic, Syriac) as ἄλλοις, i.e., "to others." The resultant meaning would be that the kingdom of God was not prepared for the disciples but "for others." Such a reading clearly contradicts Jesus' teaching. The more sensible reading of the same sequence of letters, both grammatically and contextually, is ἀλλ' οἷς, i.e., "but to whom," which is signified in several major Greek manuscripts (A B K Θ Π Y) by the placement of a breather (') in the middle of the sequence of letters.

58. The original hand of Sinaiticus (א) reads, "for whom it has been prepared *by my Father.*" The addition of "by my Father" has doubtlessly been suggested by context and by the parallel in Matt 20:23. The overwhelming weight of the manuscript tradition rightly favors the shorter reading adopted by the NIV.

Gal 2:2, 6, 9, where it refers to the apostles in Jerusalem. Commentators invariably find the expression slightly pejorative, thus relativizing the power of those in authority as those who *appear* or *presume* to rule. But neither Galatians 2 nor 10:42 demands such a nuance. Several uses in classical literature reveal *hoi dokountes* to be a technical term for designated leaders who are visible and prominent.[59] It can carry this meaning in Galatians 2, without the added sense of pretension on the part of the apostles in Jerusalem. Likewise, with reference to v. 42, T. W. Manson rightly notes that the "kings or emperors in the first century A.D. did not *seem* to rule. They *did* rule, and usually with a heavy hand."[60] Moreover, *hoi dokountes* parallels "their high officials" (Gk. *hoi megaloi*) in v. 42, which is certainly not a pejorative designation. Thus, in the use of both terms Jesus appears to be alluding to the actual power that established rulers exercise. And they do so by "'exercis[ing] authority over them.'" "Exercising authority" is the translation of a Greek verb, *katakyrieuein*, meaning "to gain mastery or power over others," "to subdue," "to function as a despot" (also Acts 19:16). A second Greek verb, *katexousiazein*, means essentially the same, "to exercise authority over."[61]

43-44 Jesus rejects this model. "'Not so with you,'" he counters (see also 1 Pet 5:2). The Greek verb in 10:43a (omitted by the NIV) is remarkable in this statement. The best textual evidence suggests that it is the present of the verb "to be" (Gk. *estin*), not the future (Gk. *estai*), that is, "'It is not this way among you,'" as opposed to "'It shall not be this way among you.'"[62] V. 43a is thus not an admonition to behave in a certain way as much as a description of the way things actually are in the kingdom of God, and even among disciples of the kingdom. Thus, to fail in being a servant is not simply to fall short of an ideal condition but to stand outside of an existing condition that corresponds to the kingdom of God.

At no place do the ethics of the kingdom of God clash more vigorously with the ethics of the world than in the matters of power and service. The ideas that Jesus presents regarding rule and service are combined in a way that finds no obvious precedent in either the OT or Jewish tradition.[63] In a decisive reversal of values, Jesus speaks of greatness in

---

59. G. Schunack, *"dokeō," EDNT* 1.341.

60. T. W. Manson, *The Teaching of Jesus: Studies in Its Form and Content* (Cambridge: Cambridge University Press, 1963), 313-15.

61. One recalls Milton's domineering Satan, ". . . whom now transcendent glory raised / Above his fellows, with Monarchal pride / Conscious of highest worth" (*Paradise Lost*, 2.427-29).

62. On the textual variations, see Metzger, *TCGNT*, 108.

63. D. Seeley, "Rulership and Service in Mark 10:41-45," *NovT* 35 (1993): 234-50. Seeley goes on to argue that there is a precedent for such ideas of rulership and service,

service rather than greatness of power, prestige, and authority: "'whoever wants to become great among you must be your servant, and whoever wants to be first must be slave of all'" (see 9:35; Luke 22:24-27). The preeminent virtue of God's kingdom is not power, not even freedom, but service. Ironically, greatness belongs to the one who is not great, the *diakonos,* the ordinary Greek word for waiting on tables (on *diakonos,* see further at 9:35). The preeminence of service in the kingdom of God grows out of Jesus' teaching on love for one's neighbor, for service is love made tangible.

Pursuing the point still further, Jesus declares that "'whoever wants to be first must be a slave of all.'" The pronouncement is, of course, an oxymoron, for a slave (Gk. *doulos*), who was inferior even to a servant (Gk. *diakonos*), was in ancient society the last and least of all. The idea of a slave being first is as absurdly paradoxical as a camel going through the eye of a needle (v. 25) — and it probably likewise induced smiles and shaking heads from Jesus' audience. The desire for power and dominance focuses attention on self and this kills love, for love by nature is focused on others. The implications of *diakonos* and *doulos* for the Twelve, as well as for ministers and leaders in the church of every generation, are inexhaustible. The Christian fellowship does not exist for their sake, but they for it. Nor is the apostle or Christian leader above the congregation, but part of it. The congregation does not belong to him; rather, he belongs to it.

45 What Jesus teaches about service and self-sacrifice is not simply a principle of the kingdom of God but a pattern of his own life that is authoritative for and transferable to disciples (so Rom 15:2-3). The "for" (Gk. *gar*) at the beginning of v. 45 is strongly purposive: disciples should adopt the posture of servants and slaves not on the basis of ethical reasoning but *because* it is the posture of the Son of Man. "'For the Son of Man did not come to be served, but to serve, and to give his life as a ransom for many.'" The life to which the gospel calls believers is not an ethical system but "the way of the Lord" (1:3), of which Jesus is the pattern and incarnation (see Pol. *Phil.* 5.2). This model of ministry cannot come from the secular order, but only from the unique way of Jesus, which defies the logic of this world and its fascination with dominance, control, yields, results, and outcomes. The key to the model both incarnated and commanded by Jesus is in the verbs "to serve" and "to give." The reason

---

however, in some Greco-Roman philosophers, who argue that wise governance consists in serving one's subjects rather than tyrannizing them. While this is true, there is no evidence in the texts Seeley cites for the idea of vicarious ransom on behalf of others that Jesus presents in v. 45.

why a servant is the most preeminent position in the kingdom of God is that the sole function of a servant is to give, and giving is the essence of God.

10:45 is crucial not only for Mark's portrait of Jesus but also as an aperture into Jesus' self-consciousness.[64] It echoes the spirit, if not the exact wording, of Isaiah's Servant of the Lord, whose "life [is] a guilt offering" (Isa 53:10) and who "will justify many, and . . . bear their iniquities" (53:11). Although the reference to ransoming "many" may suggest either preferential or partial treatment, this is scarcely its meaning. In Semitic grammar, "the many" normally stands for totality, all.[65] "The many" is not a select and worthy few; rather, in its five uses in Isaiah 53 the expression refers to the very "transgressors" and "sinful" for whom the Servant pours out his life. In Isa 52:15 it refers expressly to "many nations," that is, the Gentiles, the non-elect outsiders. This is an important affirmation, for the only other hints of vicarious atonement in the Jewish tradition limit it to Israel alone, whereas the "many" of Isaiah's Servant and of Jesus includes *Gentiles* as well as Jews.[66]

The most distinctive role of the Son of Man, however, is his giving "'his life as a *ransom*.'" In the language of the day, ransom referred to bail paid for prisoners of war and slaves, or release from jail. Both the Heb. *kipper* and Gk. *lytron* behind "ransom" mean "to cover over," "atone for," or "expiate."[67] The thought of v. 45 actually exceeds the teaching of Isa-

64. See M. Wilcox, "On the Ransom-Saying in Mark 10:45c, Matt 20:28c," in *Geschichte — Tradition — Reflexion: Festschrift für Martin Hengel zum 70. Geburtstag*, ed. H. Canick, H. Lichtenberger, and P. Schäfer, vol. 3: *Frühes Christentum* (Tübingen: Mohr/Siebeck, 1996), 173-86, who makes a strong case for the originality of the saying with the historical Jesus.

65. 1 Tim 2:6, which closely echoes Mark 10:45, says that Christ was a ransom "for all men." Note also the interchangeability of "many" and "all" in Rom 5:12-21. At Qumran, "the many" refers to the "full assembly" (1QS 6:7-8). See J. Jeremias, *"polloi,"* TDNT 6.536-45; G. Nebe, *"polys,"* EDNT 3.131-33.

66. Despite a long history of scholarly debate, the idea of a Messiah whose suffering and death have atoning significance remains poorly attested in Judaism outside the NT. 2 Macc 7:37-38 and 4 Macc 6:27-29; 17:21-22 appear to have a rudimentary concept of vicarious atonement, although the texts are neither entirely clear nor developed. At any rate, atonement in both 2 Maccabees and 4 Maccabees is made only for Israel (to compensate for unfaithfulness to the law) and not for all humanity. There is virtually no evidence that Isaiah 53 was ever applied to the Messiah; indeed, the *Targum of Jonathan* interprets the sufferings of the Servant of Yahweh as *not* referring to the Messiah. Schürer's conclusion highlights the difference between Judaism and Mark 10:45: "In none of the many works discussed here is there the slightest allusion to an expiatory suffering of the Messiah" (*History of the Jewish People*, 2.547-49).

67. On the meaning of "ransom," see F. Büchsel, *"lytron,"* TDNT 4.341-49; K. Kertelge, *"lytron,"* EDNT 2.364-66; B. Lang, *"kipper,"* TDOT 7.288-303. In a survey of epigraphical evidence related to *"lytron,"* A. Y. Collins, "The Signification of Mark 10:45

327

iah's Servant of the Lord, for Jesus is not a passive (and perhaps unknowing) instrument of Yahweh. The initiative of his atoning work lies within
himself as the Son of Man, who, in stark contrast to the power-mongerers
of v. 42, freely offers his life as the ransom price for all (John 10:11; Rom
8:2-4). As God's own delegate, and through his suffering, death, and resurrection, Jesus freely and obediently offers his life as a substitute *in behalf of* humanity. Jesus is supremely conscious of offering a payment to
God that can be offered by no one else. The ransom Jesus offers in his life
is not contingent on something outside himself. Origen (third century
A.D.) would later develop the theory that the ransom of Jesus was necessitated by and paid to Satan. Satan, however, is not mentioned in v. 45, nor
even in Mark's passion account. Satan was last mentioned in 8:33, and
there he attempts to *avert* Jesus from suffering and death! The death of the
Son of Man on behalf of "the many" is a sacrifice of obedience to God's
will, a full expression of his love, and a full satisfaction of God's justice.

A MODEL DISCIPLE (10:46-52)

The story of the healing of blind Bartimaeus is unique among the healings of the Synoptics for its warmth and interest in the person healed.
Bartimaeus is, in fact, the only person healed in the Synoptic Gospels
whose name is given. A number of details anchor it to a Palestinian context: Jericho, the Aramaic name Bartimaeus, Son of David, and the reverent expression *"Rabbouni."*[68] The story of this blind beggar who ironically
sees Jesus more clearly than those with two good eyes climaxes Mark's
teaching on faith and discipleship. Chap. 10 is full of references to discipleship,[69] but none of the disciples demonstrates the faith, insight, and
discipleship of Bartimaeus. This, the final healing miracle in the Gospel,
reaffirms Jesus' messianic status (vv. 47-48) and introduces a series of epi-

---

among Gentile Christians," *HTR* 90 (1997): 371-82, concludes that the use of the term in
v. 45 corresponds to the use of the term in the Hellenistic and Roman periods, which used
the word with reference "to transactions between human beings and gods in which sins
were forgiven and offenses expiated, and thus not only in the contexts of the manumis-
sion of slaves and the ransoming of captives. The evidence suggests that the notion of the
Son of Man giving his life as a ransom for many (Mark 10:45) belongs to the same complex of ideas as the saying over the cup (Mark 14:24), according to which the blood of Jesus was poured out for many. . . . [B]oth sayings interpret the death of Jesus by describing
it in a metaphorical way as a ritual expiation of the offenses of many."

68. J. Jeremias, *New Testament Theology,* vol. 1, trans. J. Bowden (London: SCM
Press, 1971), 89-90.

69. Verses 10, 13, 23, 24, 27-28, 32, 35-36, 46, 52.

sodes in chaps. 11 and 12 in which both Jesus' status and divine authority run into conflict with those of the religious leaders in Jerusalem.

46 With the exception of a different place name, this story is introduced in the exact wording of 8:22, suggesting that both stories were anchored in oral tradition to the places named. On the final leg of the journey to Jerusalem, Jesus passes through Jericho. Jericho (along with Damascus) lays claim to being one of the oldest continuously inhabited cities on earth. It lies 840 feet below sea level, some twenty torturous miles and 3,500 feet below Jerusalem to the southwest. Jesus is accompanied by the disciples and "a large crowd," which again (v. 32; 15:41) indicates that his retinue exceeds simply the Twelve. On the way out of Jericho a blind beggar calls to Jesus. His Aramaic name, Bartimaeus, means "son of Timaeus," a translation that Mark may have added for the benefit of his Gentile readers.[70] Bartimaeus, a blind beggar, is "sitting by the roadside."[71] He is, in other words, sidelined or marginalized. The difference in his position "beside the road" (Gk. *para tēn hodon*) at the beginning of the story and "on the road" (Gk. *en tę̄ hodǭ*) at the end of the story signifies the difference between being an outsider and an insider, a bystander and a disciple.

47 What Bartimaeus lacks in eyesight he makes up for in insight. There is an air of expectancy as Jesus the Nazarene passes his way. This is only the second time Mark has identified Jesus as the *Nazarene*. The NIV reads "Jesus of Nazareth," but the Greek is not "Nazareth" (*Nazaret*) as in 1:9, which doubtlessly designates a place name (see further at 6:1), but "Nazarene" (*Nazarēnos*; so 1:24; 10:47; 14:67; 16:6; see further at 1:24). At the first (1:24) and last (10:47) healing miracles in the Gospel Mark designates Jesus as "the Nazarene." In both instances the term probably connotes more than Jesus' place of origin. A similar expression is used of Samson in Judg 16:17 (LXX, A text), who is called *naziraios theou*, God's powerfully anointed one. Mark's use of the term "Nazarene" in the healing stories of 1:24 and 10:47 may also carry connotations of Jesus' powerful anointing by God.

70. B. M. F. van Iersel and J. Nuchelmans, "De zoon van Timeüs en den zoon von David. Marcus 10,46-52 gelezen door een grieks-romeinse bril," *Tijd. Theol.* 35 (1995): 107-24, advance the intriguing though speculative thesis that "son of *Timaeus*" recalls the name of the principal speaker in the then best-known dialogue of Plato — *Timaeus*; and that Mark's use of the term symbolizes the conversion and discipleship of the Greco-Roman world to Jesus.

71. The NIV follows a majority of Greek manuscripts in reading, "[Bartimaeus] was sitting by the roadside begging." The reading of a smaller but weightier group of manuscripts (א B L Δ Ψ), *prosaitēs ekathēto para tēn hodon* ("[Bartimaeus] was a beggar sitting beside the road") is preferable, however, not only because of manuscript support but because it better explains the existence of the other readings. See Metzger, *TCGNT*, 108.

Hearing of Jesus, Bartimaeus cries out, "'Jesus, Son of David, have mercy on me!'" Ever since the promise of 2 Sam 7:11-14 that God would raise up an offspring to David and "establish the throne of his kingdom forever," pious Israelites had awaited a Davidic descendant as Messiah.[72] The actual title "Son of David" first appears in the middle of the first century B.C. in *Pss. Sol.* 17:21. There, however, it refers to a warrior king who will punish sinners, whereas here it refers to one who will have mercy on them. Bartimaeus's determined hailing of Jesus as "Son of David" carries explicit messianic overtones and shows that he looks to him as the Messiah who can bring healing and wholeness.[73]

48-50 For the first time in Mark the crowd (rather than Jesus) tries to silence someone. But the motive of the crowd is quite different from Jesus' injunctions to silence: Jesus wants to prevent people from premature and false confessions, whereas the crowd wants to prevent people from coming to Jesus (cf. 10:13). But nothing can silence Bartimaeus; indeed, opposition only fans the flame of his persistence. The kingdom of heaven, it has been said, is not for the well-meaning but for the desperate. Bartimaeus is desperate, and his desperation is a doorway to faith. He shouts louder, "'Son of David, have mercy on me!'" "Jesus stopped. . . ." On those words hangs the fate of Bartimaeus. The original Greek reads, "And Jesus stood (still)." How remarkable that the Son of Man allows the cries of a poor and powerless person to stop him in his tracks. He stands for Bartimaeus as he will later stand for Stephen (Acts 7:56). Bartimaeus throws off his cloak, jumps to his feet, and comes to Jesus. "Cloak" translates the Gk. *himation,* the outer robe that ancients wore over an inner nightshirt-like garment called a *chitōn.* The crowd may silence Bartimaeus, the townsfolk may begrudge him a place to beg, but faith such as this goes not unrewarded.

51-52 "'What do you want me to do for you?'" asks Jesus. This is the same question he asked of the sons of Zebedee (v. 36), but Bartimaeus responds differently; whereas the Sons of Thunder asked for extraordinary glory, Bartimaeus asks only for ordinary health. Surely Bartimaeus's need should be obvious to Jesus. The most practical response would be for Jesus to heal him and be on his way. But for Jesus, Bartimaeus is not a problem to be dealt with. Jesus will not do something to him, but something *with* him. He responds to the blind man not as an "It" but as a "Thou," to use the language of Buber, by asking him a question, thus al-

---

72. Further messianic texts include Isa 11:1, 10; Jer 23:5; 33:15; Ps 89:4-5; *Pss. Sol.* 17:21-40; 4 Ezra 12:32; 1QFlor 1:11-13.

73. On "Son of David," see E. Lohse, *"huios Dauid," TDNT* 8.482-92; O. Hofius, "Ist Jesus der Messias? Thesen," *JBTh* 8 (1993, *Der Messias*): 107.

lowing him to express himself as a person rather than apologizing for himself as a social problem or victim.

According to the NIV, Bartimaeus says, "'Rabbi, I want to see.'" The Greek, however, uses a more reverent epithet, "'*Rabbouni*'" (so also John 20:16). In extant Jewish literature *rabbouni* is seldom used with reference to humanity, and practically never as a form of address. It is frequently used as an address to God in prayer, however. Its use here suggests Bartimaeus's — and Mark's — estimation of Jesus.[74] In humble trust Bartimaeus asks not for wealth, power, or success, but only for sight; he asks not to be superhuman, but simply human. For the well, normalcy may seem the bare minimum, but for the ill and troubled normalcy is God's greatest gift. Jesus declares, "'Go, your faith has healed you.'"[75] The word for "healed" (Gk. *sōzō*) also means "saved," combining both physical and spiritual dimensions. In Bartimaeus's case the word is doubly appropriate, for "he received his sight" and "followed Jesus along the road." The latter description designates the model disciple for Mark.[76] Jesus has transformed Bartimaeus from a beggar beside the road (v. 46) to a disciple on the road (v. 52). Faith that does not lead to discipleship is not saving faith. Whoever asks of Jesus must be willing to follow Jesus . . . even on the uphill road to the cross.

74. See Str-B 2.25.

75. In the apocryphal *Acts Pil.* 6:4 Bartimaeus appears, along with others whom Jesus has healed, as a personal witness for Jesus at his trial before Pilate! "And another Jew hastened forward and said: 'I was born blind; I heard any man's voice, but did not see his face. And as Jesus passed by I cried with a loud voice: *Have mercy on me, Son of David.* And he took pity on me and put his hands on my eyes and I saw immediately.'"

76. See H.-J. Eckstein, "Markus 10,46-52 als Schlüsseltext des Markusevangeliums," *ZNW* 87 (1996): 33-50, who sees 10:46-52 as the theological center of the Gospel of Mark. While I believe that the theological center of the Gospel is not this pericope but rather 15:33-39, the healing of Bartimaeus is surely the sum and center of all that Mark desires to convey about faith and discipleship.

CHAPTER ELEVEN

The Barren Temple

MARK 11:1-26

Mark places the passion narrative of chaps. 11–16 in the context of Easter week. This means that fully one-third of Mark's Gospel (and nearly one-half of John's, chaps. 12–21) is set during the last seven days of Jesus' life. The disproportionate emphasis on this brief time period signals the importance of the final week in Jerusalem for an understanding of Jesus' mission and purpose. The passion narration in chaps. 11–16 resumes the fast pace of the first three chapters of the Gospel. Once Jesus arrives in Jerusalem, to which he has been "on the way" since 8:27, events quickly transpire to complete his mission and revelation as the Son of God.

It is not impossible that Mark has compressed events that took place perhaps over as long as several months into chaps. 11–16. While this cannot be proven, several observations and data scattered throughout these chapters point in this direction. The description in the Mishnah of the celebration of the fall harvest festival known as the Feast of Tabernacles, for instance, which included waving branches of palm, willow, myrtle, or citrus, and shouting "Hosanna" (*m. Suk.* 3:3-9), is closer to the description of Jesus' entry into Jerusalem (11:8-10) than is anything associated with the spring Passover celebration. Sporadic references in the passion narrative also suggest a lengthier ministry in Jerusalem (e.g., "When evening came, they went out of the city," 11:19; "'Every day I was with you, teaching in the temple courts, and you did not arrest me,'" 14:49). The composite character of chap. 13 (as we shall argue) also suggests a longer period of time. Most importantly, there seem to be too many events recorded in Mark 11–16 to have occurred in a single week. Mark follows a daily chronology that stops at day three at 11:20.[1] That means that the events of

---

1. 10:46–11:11 = Sunday; 11:12–11:19 = Monday; 11:20-? = Tuesday.

11:27–14:11 would all fall into a day and a half (Wednesday and Thursday morning) of Easter week, which seems nearly impossible.

The Gospel of John may present a more reasonable time frame of Jesus' passion in Jerusalem. According to the Fourth Gospel, Jesus was in Jerusalem for the Feast of Dedication (10:22), which occurred in mid-December, after which he retired across the Jordan into Perea (10:40; 11:54). The Fourth Gospel, in other words, places Jesus in Judea and Jerusalem at least four months or longer before his crucifixion. The problems we noted in Mark's passion narrative can certainly be resolved against the longer time period suggested by John, especially if it includes the Feast of Tabernacles in the fall.

It may be that Mark, whom Papias says arranged material according to his own design, telescopes a longer historical process into Passover week. At least two reasons can be advanced for his doing so. First, a one-week passion narrative served catechetical and liturgical purposes by reducing more than a third of the Gospel and the all-important events of Jesus' passion in Jerusalem into a block of material that could be read and celebrated during Easter week. But second and more important, the material in the passion narrative is oriented around the focal point of the temple, and has been gathered and presented in order to show that Jesus supersedes the temple as the *locus Dei.* All the material in chaps. 11–13 is either set in the temple or directly related to it. Like the prophets before him (e.g., 2 Kgs 22:15-20; 23:26-27; Isa 51:17-23), Jesus pronounces God's judgment on Zion. Jesus is not a reformer of the temple, for neither his teachings nor his ministry institutes a program of change and improvement. He is rather its fulfillment and replacement, for his death on the cross — and not the powerful temple cult — is the perfect atonement for sin. At Golgotha the temple curtain is torn asunder (15:38) and Jesus is confessed as the Son of God, the object of saving faith (15:39).[2]

JESUS ENTERS JERUSALEM (11:1-11)

Mark 11 begins a unit of thought that extends through chap. 13. The theme of this unit is Jesus' conflict with and rejection of the temple in Jerusalem, including the religious system and leadership centered there. From his initial visit to the temple in 11:1-11, the breach between Jesus

---

2. See W. R. Telford, *Mark,* NTG (Sheffield: Academic Press, 1997), 137-38; J. P. Heil, "The Narrative Strategy and Pragmatics of the Temple Theme in Mark," *CBQ* 59 (1997): 76-100.

and the temple is evident. He enters Jerusalem triumphantly, but he is not received in the temple triumphantly (as, e.g., in Matt 21:10-11). The indifference with which he is initially received (v. 11) quickly turns to opposition (11:28), and eventually to his condemnation to death (14:63-64).

1 The story begins on the eastern approach to Jerusalem. Mark reports that Jesus and the disciples "approached Jerusalem and came to Bethphage and Bethany." The sequence of place names will puzzle those familiar with the modern road from Bethany through Bethphage to Jerusalem, because today one encounters the towns in the opposite order from which Mark mentions them. Mark's sequence of Jerusalem — Bethphage — Bethany is not so problematic as is sometimes supposed, however, for the ancient Roman road that Jesus followed did not follow the course of the modern road, but lay north of it. From Jericho the Roman road ran southwest along what is today Wadi Umm esh Shid, and then directly up to the summit of the Mount of Olives, which was near if not at Bethphage ("house of unripe figs"). En route the traveler passed between Bahurim immediately to the north (2 Sam 3:16; 16:5; 17:18; Josephus, *Ant.* 7.225) and Bethany further to the south.[3] A steep road ran down from Bethphage to Bethany, a kilometer south on the eastern side of the Mount of Olives. The object of 11:1 is to bring Jesus and the disciples to the top of the Mount Olives, from which the disciples are dispatched to fetch a donkey for Jesus to ride into Jerusalem. Mark mentions Bethany in v. 1 not because it is on the route from Jericho to Jerusalem but in order to identify the place where Jesus will spend nights while he is in Jerusalem (11:11). The meaning of v. 1 is thus: "And on their way to Jerusalem they came to Bethphage (near Bethany) on the Mount of Olives."

The **Mount of Olives** rises over 2,600 feet above sea level (some 300 feet higher than Jerusalem) and runs north to south on the eastern side of the Holy City. Already before David's time the Mount of Olives had been a place of worship (2 Sam 15:32). At the fall of Jerusalem in 586 B.C. Ezekiel had a vision of the glory of the Lord departing from Jerusalem and settling on the Mount of Olives (Ezek 11:23). According to Zech 14:4 the Mount of Olives would be the site of final judgment, and the rabbis and Josephus (*Ant.* 20.169) associated it with the coming of the Messiah. Mark, who sel-

---

3. R. Beuvery, "La Route Romaine de Jérusalem a Jéricho," *RB* 66 (1957): 72-101; B. Pixner, *Wege des Messias und Stätten der Urkirche,* Studien zur Biblischen Archäologie und Zeitgeschichte, Band 2, Herausgegeben R. Riesner und C. Thiede (Giessen: Brunnen Verlag, 1991), 372-75. C. E. B. Cranfield, *The Gospel According to Saint Mark,* 348, seems to be thinking in terms of the modern road rather than the old Roman road in saying that "Bethany would be reached before Bethphage." Likewise, E. Schweizer, *The Good News According to Mark,* 227, is needlessly dismissive in saying, "It is clear that Mark, writing at a later date, is not acquainted with these places."

dom mentions place names, may mention the Mount of Olives here in order to associate its messianic significance with Jesus' entry into Jerusalem.

2-6 From the summit of the Mount of Olives Jesus sends two unidentified disciples to fetch a colt for him to ride. According to the NIV, Jesus directs the disciples "'to the village *ahead of* you,'" but the Gk. *katenanti* means "opposite," which could imply Bethphage or perhaps Bahurim or Bethany. Mark is as vague about the identity of the village as he is about the two disciples. The "colt" (Gk. *pōlos*) can mean either the young of a horse or donkey (although the second was more common in Palestine). We are not told how Jesus knows about the colt. Jesus knew the area well, however, for he crossed the Mount of Olives each morning and evening en route from Bethany to Jerusalem and back (11:11; Luke 10:38), and he bivouacked at the foot of the Mount of Olives near the Kidron brook (14:32; Luke 21:37; 22:39; John 18:2). His knowledge of the colt and its owners indicates acquaintance with both prior to this story, which again argues for a sojourn in Jerusalem in excess of one week (see the introduction to this chapter). If the disciples are questioned about taking the colt, they are to say that "'The Lord needs it and will send it back here shortly.'"[4] Who "Lord" refers to is a matter of debate. The Gk. *kyrios*, like the German "Herr" or the English "lord," can mean either "Lord" or "sir," depending on the context. Mark calls God "Lord" not infrequently (1:3; 11:19; 12:11, 29, 30, 36), but the word scarcely refers to God in this instance. Mark also uses *kyrios* once as "master" or "owner" (12:9). If the animal's owner were in Jesus' retinue, then Jesus' reference to him and the promise to return the donkey would assure bystanders that the beast is not being stolen. But we have no hint that the owner is with Jesus; moreover, it is not the owner but Jesus who needs it. The most obvious referent of *kyrios*, therefore, is Jesus. On occasion in Mark Jesus refers to himself as "Lord" or uses the term in relation to himself (2:28; 5:19; 12:36, 37), and it appears that he does so here again. His hearers, of course, may have understood the term in the sense of "master," but the use of *kyrios* rather than "I" or even "Son of Man" appears to be another instance of Jesus' *exousia*, that is, his presumption to divine authority.

---

4. The latter half of the message in v. 3 ("'and [he] will send it back here shortly'") is considerably less clear in the original Greek than in the NIV translation. The manuscript tradition is divided regarding the word order of the phrase, and the best manuscripts (א B A C D K X Θ Δ) put the verb in the present tense rather than in the future (W Π Ψ; NIV), i.e., "'and [he] sends it immediately here again.'" It is thus not clear whether the phrase is part of the message to send the colt quickly or a promise that Jesus will return it shortly. The presence of *palin* ("back" or "again"), as well as the assurance of the bystanders in v. 6, however, argues that the phrase should be understood as a promise that Jesus will return the animal shortly (so Matt 21:3). See B. Metzger, *TCGNT*, 108-9.

The first six verses of our narrative are devoted to preparation for the entry into Jerusalem and are narrated so as to demonstrate Jesus' precise foreknowledge and sovereignty over subsequent events. Subtle details in the story carry messianic connotations. The colt is identified in the OT as the mount of the Messiah (Zech 9:9; Gen 49:11). The commandeering of a beast of burden was the prerogative of a king in ancient times, and this, too, suggests Jesus' kingly role.[5] An unbroken beast of burden was regarded as sacred (so Num 19:2; Deut 21:3), which made it appropriate for a king, since according to the Mishnah (*m. Sanh.* 2:5) no one else may ride a king's horse. The entry — and its inconclusive end (v. 11) — accord exactly with Jesus' foreknowledge and authority. Jesus thus does not enter Jerusalem as an unknowing victim, but with the same foreknowledge and sovereignty with which he traveled "on the way."

7-10 Unlike Matt 21:5 and John 12:15, Mark does not overtly identify Jesus' entry into Jerusalem with the messianic quotation from Zech 9:9, with which we readily associate the triumphal entry:

> Rejoice greatly, O Daughter of Zion!
>> Shout, daughter of Jerusalem!
> See, your king comes to you
>> righteous and having salvation,
>> gentle and riding on a donkey,
>> on a colt, the foal of a donkey.

In keeping with his servant and secrecy motif, Mark prefers subtle messianic imagery to open proclamation. The spreading of cloaks and branches before Jesus is, of course, suggestive of the ceremonious welcome of a king, as in the inauguration of Jehu: "They hurried and took their cloaks and spread them under him on the bare steps. Then they blew the trumpet and shouted, 'Jehu is king!'" (2 Kgs 9:13).[6] The shout of "Hosanna" is a transliterated Hebrew word meaning, literally, "Save, I pray." "'Blessed is he who comes in the name of the LORD'" (Ps 118:25-26) referred not to the Messiah but to pilgrims entering the temple sanctuary, meaning that the pilgrim is blessed in God's name.[7] The acclamations of vv. 9-10 were thus probably less specific than later Christian readers have

---

5. See M. Hooker, *The Gospel According to St Mark*, 258.

6. Plutarch records that when Cato retired from military service the soldiers honored him by "casting their mantles down for him to walk upon" (*Lives*, "Life of Cato the Younger," 12 [*Plutarch's Lives*, LCL, vol. 8]).

7. The quotation of Ps 118:25 in *Did.* 10:12 also refers to traveling missionaries, not to the Lord. On the meaning of the Ps 118:25-26 quotation, see M. H. Pope, "Hosanna: What It Really Means," *BRev* 4/2 (1988): 16-25.

tended to understand them; they could have intended a pilgrim greeting as much as a messianic acclamation. The acclamation in v. 10, "'Blessed is the coming kingdom of our father David!'" is not part of Psalm 118 or of any psalm. The reference to the coming kingdom is certainly eschatological, but the reference to "our father David," which is not elsewhere found in Judaism,[8] is not necessarily messianic, as "son of David" would be. At any rate, Jesus preached about the kingdom of God, not "the coming kingdom of our father David," and the ascription of the latter to him reveals a confusion on the part of the crowd about his true mission.[9] The summary effect of the quotation in vv. 9-10 is thus not overtly messianic. Indeed, had the crowd intended the acclamations of vv. 9-10 to refer to a specific messianic fulfillment in Jesus we should be surprised that Jesus was not promptly arrested by Roman authorities (see Acts 5:37; 21:38), or that charges to that effect were not raised at his trial (14:55-58). There are of course subtle messianic undertones in Jesus' riding a colt into Jerusalem as the gentle and peaceable Messiah of Zechariah 9, but it is doubtful whether the crowd or authorities grasped their full significance.[10] Like that of countless other Passover pilgrims to Jerusalem, Jesus' entry was apparently regarded by the masses as a pilgrimage rather than as a messianic triumph.

11 The object of Jesus' triumphal procession is not Jerusalem in general but specifically the temple. Jesus makes a commanding survey (Gk. *periblepesthai;* see further on the term at 10:23) of the temple operation. The long trek "on the way" from Galilee (8:29) and the ride from the Mount of Olives have brought Jesus to his point of destination, indeed, of destiny. It appears to be the moment for him to receive the messianic kingdom. But, ironically, nothing happens. The clamoring crowds mysteriously vanish. In a complete anticlimax, Mark reports that the hour was late and that Jesus departed with the Twelve for Bethany.

8. Schweizer, *The Good News According to Mark,* 229.

9. D. Lührmann, *Das Markusevangelium,* 189.

10. Attempts to liken Jesus' entry into Jerusalem to the entry of conquering kings (e.g., P. B. Duff, "The March of the Divine Warrior and the Advent of the Greco-Roman King: Mark's Account of Jesus' Entry into Jerusalem," *JBL* 111 [1992]: 55-71) and to the typology of Zechariah 14 are not as pronounced or compelling as their advocates suppose. The similarities of Jesus' entry into Jerusalem with warrior/ruler processions stop at the superficial level of the citizenry meeting the warrior/ruler at the gates and escorting him into the city with hymns of acclamation. In Jesus' case there is no mention of his royal dress, no retinue of slaves, no speech from him, no feast in the city, and no sacrifice in the temple to the gods, all of which typify official warrior/ruler processions. In contrast to Jesus' humble entry into Jerusalem, note the pomp and panoply of Julius Caesar's procession into Rome when he became dictator. See C. Maier, *Caesar,* trans. D. McLintock (London: Fontana Books, 1996), 442-47.

This text is traditionally called the Triumphal Entry. That is an appropriate designation for Matt 21:1-11 and John 12:12-19, but scarcely for Mark. Matthew says, "The whole city was stirred and asked, 'Who is this?'" (21:10). Luke reports that the city was so electrified that the stones were ready to cry out (19:40). Mark's account is noteworthy for what does *not* happen. The whole scene comes to nothing. Like the seed in the parable of the sower that receives the word with joy but has no root and lasts but a short time (4:6, 16-17), the crowd disperses as mysteriously as it assembled. Mark is warning against mistaking enthusiasm for faith and popularity for discipleship. Jesus is not confessed in pomp and circumstance but only at the cross (15:39). The most expressed messianic symbol in Jesus' entry — the riding on a colt in allusion to the humble Messiah of Zech 9:9 — is either short lived in the minds of the crowd or missed altogether. Jesus enters the temple alone, and having sized it up, he leaves for Bethany with the disciples. This is the first of Mark's clues that the temple is not the habitation of God's Son. Jesus is indeed the Messiah, but he is veiled and unrecognized. Even when he stands at the center of Israel's faith, he stands alone.

THE BARREN TEMPLE (11:12-25)

The cursing of the fig tree is the only miracle of destruction in the canonical Gospels. The history of interpretation of this controversial episode begins in the Synoptic tradition itself, for Matt 21:12-22 alters Mark's sandwich construction (A^1 — cursing of the fig tree, vv. 12-14; B — clearing the temple, vv. 15-19; A^2 — withering of the fig tree, vv. 20-21)[11] to a simple sequence of clearing the temple (Matt 21:12-17) and cursing the tree (21:18-20). Luke 13:6-9 replaces the episode with a parable, and John omits the curse of the tree and places the clearing of the temple at the beginning of his Gospel.[12] The moral difficulties posed by the curse of an in-

11. The interrelation between the cursing of the fig tree and clearing of the temple is established at several points. Most obviously, all the material from 11:1–13:37 is oriented around the temple, which invites a connection between the fig tree and the temple. There is also a parallel between "his disciples heard him" (v. 14) and "the chief priests and the teachers of the law heard this" (v. 18). Finally, in the OT the fig tree is often used as a symbol for Israel, and more than once Israel is judged under this symbol.

12. The Synoptics are doubtlessly correct historically in placing the temple clearing at the end of Jesus' ministry, for the accusation of the Sanhedrin in the following story (Mark 11:28) presupposes the temple clearing. John, who often uses historical data for theological purposes, apparently places the event near the beginning of his Gospel in order to show Jesus' early and irrevocable break with official Judaism.

nocent tree have especially vexed scholars in the post-Enlightenment era, and have given rise to diverse and inventive interpretations.[13] Bertrand Russell accused Jesus of "vindictive fury" for blaming the tree for not producing figs out of season. The whole episode tarnished the character of Jesus in Russell's opinion, who wrote, "I cannot myself feel that either in the matter of wisdom or in the matter of virtue Christ stands quite as high as some other people known to history."[14] Even scholars more friendly to the Christian faith than Russell find the episode offensive. For T. W. Manson the story is out of character for Jesus. "It is a tale of miraculous power wasted in the service of ill-temper (for the supernatural energy employed to blast the unfortunate tree might have been more usefully expended in forcing a crop of figs out of season); as it stands it is simply incredible."[15]

The earliest commentary on the Gospel of Mark by Victor of Antioch in the fifth century already understood the event as an *enacted parable*, in which the cursing of the fig tree symbolized the judgment to befall Jerusalem. Mark's sandwich technique demonstrates that Victor of Antioch surmised correctly. Mark's placement of the cursing of the fig tree and Jesus' action in the temple in an A^1-B-A^2 sandwich pattern signifies that he intends readers to see in the fate of the unfruitful fig tree the judgment of God on the unfruitful temple.

12-14 The sandwich complex begins on the road from Bethany, which John 11:18 identifies as "fifteen stadia" (slightly less than two miles) from Jerusalem. Jesus is hungry, and seeing from a distance a fig tree in leaf he approaches it in hopes of finding something to eat. In disappointment at finding no figs, and in earshot of the disciples, he condemns the tree.

After the fig harvest from mid-August to mid-October, the branches of fig trees sprout buds that remain undeveloped throughout the winter. These buds swell into small green knops known in Hebrew as *paggim* in March-April, followed shortly by the sprouting of leaf buds on the same branches, usually in April. The fig tree thus produces fig knops before it produces leaves. Once a fig tree is in leaf one therefore expects to find branches loaded with *paggim* in various stages of maturation. This is implied in 11:13, where Jesus, seeing a fig tree in full foliage, turns aside in hopes of finding something edible. In the spring of the year the *paggim*

---

13. See W. R. Telford, *The Barren Temple and the Withered Tree: A Redaction-Critical Analysis of the Cursing of the Fig-Tree Pericope in Mark's Gospel and Its Relation to the Cleansing of the Temple Tradition*, JSNTSup 1 (Sheffield: JSOT Press, 1980), 1-38.

14. Bertrand Russell, *Why I Am Not a Christian, and Other Essays on Religion and Related Subjects* (New York: Clarion Books, Simon and Schuster, 1957), 17-19.

15. "The Cleansing of the Temple," *BJRL* 33 (1951): 279.

are of course not yet ripened into mature summer figs, but they can be eaten, and often are by natives (Hos 9:10; Cant 2:13). The tree in v. 13, however, turns out to be deceptive, for it is green in foliage, but when Jesus inspects it he finds no *paggim;* it is a tree with the signs of fruit but with no fruit.[16]

The most puzzling part of the brief narrative of the cursing of the fig tree is the end of 11:13, "because it was not the season of figs." This phrase is usually understood to exonerate the tree for not producing fruit since it was not yet the season. Understood as such, the phrase makes Jesus' curse vindictive and irrational, as Bertrand Russell deduced. But this is neither the only nor the best way to understand the phrase. It is better simply to distinguish between mature figs (Gk. *sykē;* Heb. *te'enim*) and early or unripe figs (Heb. *paggim*). The end of v. 13 might be paraphrased, "It was, of course, not the season for figs, but it was for *paggim.*"[17]

In narrating the episode of Jesus and the fig tree Mark exploits its symbolic import, seeing in the curse of the tree the fate of Jerusalem and the temple. The prophets had often used the fig tree as a symbol of judgment (Isa 34:4; Jer 29:17; Hos 2:12; 9:10; Joel 1:7; Mic 7:1). In a scathing denunciation of Judah, Jeremiah says, "There will be no figs on the tree, and their leaves will wither" (8:13). Jesus, according to Luke (13:6-9), had in fact told a parable with the same image and point. Like the prophets who had on occasion dramatized a particularly trenchant message by action (Isa 20:1-6; Jer 13:1-11; 19:1-13; Ezek 4:1-13), Jesus dramatizes the end of the temple by an enacted parable. The leafy fig tree, with all its promise of fruit, is as deceptive as the temple, which, despite its religious commerce and activity, is really an outlaws' hideout (v. 17). The curse of the fig tree is a symbol of God's judgment of the temple.[18]

15-16 Mark now turns to the central part of the sandwich in 11:15-18, the clearing of the temple. Jesus enters Jerusalem, but the focus is again on the **temple** rather than the city itself (v. 11). Herod's temple, Israel's third temple (following the temples of Solomon and Zerubbabel), was still under construction in Jesus' day (13:1), having been begun in 20

---

16. See Telford, *The Barren Temple and the Withered Tree,* 28; C.-H. Hunzinger, "*sykē,*" *TDNT* 7.751-57; Str-B 1.856-57; F. F. Bruce, *The New Testament Documents: Are They Reliable?* (Downers Grove: InterVarsity Press, 1973), 73-74; J. C. Trevor, "Fig Tree," *IDB* 2.267.

17. So, too, G. Dalman, *Arbeit und Sitte in Palästina,* Band 1/2 (Hildesheim: Georg Olms Verlagsbuchhandlung, 1964), 378-81.

18. See the material gathered in Telford, *Barren Temple and Withered Tree,* 132-37, and his conclusion: "Enough has now been said about the fig-tree's use in image and symbol to justify the conclusion that Mark's readers, steeped in the Old Testament tradition, would readily have understood Jesus' cursing of the barren fig-tree as at the very least a judgment upon Israel."

B.C. The temple consisted of four divisions and was of immense and grandiose proportions. The first and largest division was the Court of the Gentiles, an open-air quadrangle measuring some 500 yards long by 325 yards wide (= thirty-five acres), and enclosed by a portico supported by rows of columns. According to Josephus (*Ant.* 15.391-425), the columns were thirty feet high and so massive that it took three persons with hands joined together to surround one of them at the base. The columns were crowned with Corinthian capitals, and the ceiling of the porticoes was ornamented with wood carvings. In the area enclosed by this massive perimeter of porticoes merchants sold sheep and doves for sacrifice and exchanged foreign currency into the Tyrian shekel, the closest available currency (of pure metal, and with no image) to the Hebrew shekel commanded in Exod 30:13-16. The temple precincts were overseen by the Sadducees, and the immense volume of trade and exchange in the Court of the Gentiles was crucial not only for the maintenance of proper worship but also for the financial gain of the Sadducees and Sanhedrin. The volume of trade that went on in the Court of the Gentiles was conducted on a scale commensurate with the grandeur of Herod's temple itself.[19] Emil Schürer writes that "this huge quantity [of animals], so great as to be almost unbelievable, gave the Temple cults its peculiar stamp. Day after day, masses of victims were slaughtered there and burnt, and in spite of the thousands of priests, when one of the great festivals came round the multitude of sacrifices was so great that they could hardly cope with them."[20] The enormity of the temple industry may be further appreciated by a comment from Josephus (*War* 6.422-27) that in A.D. 66, the year the temple was completed, 255,600 lambs were sacrificed for Passover!

The other three divisions of the temple — the Court of the Women, the Court of Israel (only for circumcised Jewish males), and the Holy of Holies — belonged within the sanctuary, a freestanding and sublime edifice of 150 yards long by 100 wide that commanded the center of the Court of the Gentiles and faced east. The sanctuary was separated from the Court of the Gentiles by a wall, called *Soreq*, on which the following warning was posted at intervals in Greek, Latin, and Aramaic: "No foreigner may enter within the railing and enclosure that surround the Temple. Anyone apprehended shall have himself to blame for his consequent death."[21]

19. H. D. Betz, "Jesus and the Purity of the Temple (Mark 11:15-18): A Comparative Religion Approach," *JBL* 116 (1997): 464, describes Herod's temple "as a gigantic votive gift for Herod's kingship," and maintains that the offerings and sacrifices were planned on a commensurate scale.

20. *History of the Jewish People,* 2.308.

21. Knowledge of Herod's temple depends on three ancient sources, Josephus

Given the size of the Court of the Gentiles, it is unlikely that Jesus brought the whole operation to a standstill. Had he done so he surely would have provoked a response from the temple police or Roman garrison in the Antonia Fortress adjacent to the temple, or elicited an accusation to that effect at his trial. Nevertheless, Mark leaves no doubt that Jesus lodged a protest in physical terms against the temple bazaar, and that the protest caught the attention of the Sanhedrin (11:27-28).

The Court of the Gentiles was a virtual stock market of animal dealers and money changers, all of whom were necessary to ensure proper sacrifices and offerings for the many pilgrims, especially at festivals, to the temple. In righteous indignation Jesus drives the animal dealers from the temple and overturns the tables of the money changers.[22] The reference in 11:16 that Jesus "would not allow anyone to carry merchandise through the temple courts" is enigmatic. The common interpretation that Jesus was forbidding the Court of the Gentiles to be used as a thoroughfare of traffic and commerce is reasonable, but it claims no definite scriptural support.[23] Likewise, the suggestion that Jesus was commandeering sacred vessels brought into the temple in accordance with Zech 14:21 is not only strained but out of context with the temple clearing.[24] The best conjecture about the meaning of v. 16 relates to the word "merchandise" (Gk. *skeuos*). More than one-third of the uses of *skeuos* in the LXX refer to sacred cult objects related to the tabernacle, altar, or temple. Josephus uses the term likewise (*Ant.* 18.85; *War* 1.39). If the term is used similarly here, then v. 16 refers to Jesus' stopping the flow of sacrifices and thus im-

---

(*Ant.* 15.391-425), the Mishnah (*m. Middot*), and the *Temple Scroll* (11QT) in the DSS. For comprehensive reconstructions of Herod's temple, see J. Patrich, "Reconstructing the Magnificent Temple Herod Built," *BRev* 4/5 (October 1988): 16-29; and Kathleen and Leen Ritmeyer, "Reconstructing Herod's Temple Mount in Jerusalem," *BARev* 15/6 (November-December 1989): 23-42.

22. J. Marcus, *The Way of the Lord: Christological Exegesis of the Old Testament in the Gospel of Mark* (Edinburgh: T. & T. Clark, 1992), 11, sees a connection between Mark 11:1-18 and Josephus, *War* 4.574-78, in which Simon entered into Jerusalem during the Jewish revolt of A.D. 66-70 and attacked the forces of John of Gischala and the Zealots in the temple. In my judgment, the correspondence between Josephus and Mark at this point is of a quite general nature, and certainly coincidental rather than intentional.

23. Attempts to support this interpretation on the basis of *m. Ber.* 9:5 and Josephus, *Ag. Ap.* 2.106 are strained. The latter passage is not about making a shortcut through the Court of the Gentiles, but about forbidding additional vessels to be added to the temple furnishings besides the altar, table, censer, and lampstand stipulated by the Torah. Likewise, the prohibition in *m. Ber.* 9:5 to bring staff, sandal, wallet, or dust on one's feet into the temple is concerned with defilement of the holy place, not with its use as a thoroughfare.

24. Contra C. Roth, "The Cleansing of the Temple and Zechariah xiv 21," *NovT* 4 (1960): 177-78.

peding the temple sacrificial cult in yet another way, which is entirely consistent with the context of vv. 15-18.[25]

17-19 The Messiah was popularly expected to purge Jerusalem and the temple of Gentiles, aliens, and foreigners (see *Pss. Sol.* 17:22-30). Jesus' action, however, is exactly the reverse. He does not clear the temple of Gentiles, but *for* them. One of the effects of interrupting the sacrificial system is to enhance the position of Gentiles in the temple, for the Court of the Gentiles was the only place available to non-Jews for worship. The appeal to Scripture ("'Is it not written?'"; see further at 1:2) attributes the authority of God's will to Jesus' attack on the sacrificial system: "'My house will be called a house of prayer for all nations.' But you have made it a 'den of robbers.'" The reference to the "house of prayer for all nations" comes from Isa 56:7. Isaiah 56 speaks of the extension of God's salvation to people who formerly were excluded from it: foreigners, eunuchs, exiles, and Gentiles. The passage that Jesus quotes in the temple, in other words, *includes* the very people that the Messiah, according to *Psalms of Solomon* 17, would *exclude*! In itself, this reveals that Jesus is a very different kind of Messiah than the one epitomized in Jewish expectation. The temple and covenant are not reserved exclusively for Israel but include *"all nations"* — eunuchs, foreigners, and Gentiles (13:10). The temple is not the sole property of Israel but a witness to the nations, the place where anyone who "loves the name of the LORD [may] worship him" (Isa 56:6), a place where God "will gather still others" (Isa 56:8).

That, at least, was the *purpose* of the temple, had it not been perverted into "'a den of robbers.'" Those words from Jer 7:11 are a stern denunciation of the temple operation,[26] even more so in light of 7:12, which describes the destruction of the Israelite cult site at Shiloh (see 1 Sam 3:11-14).[27] "Robbers" (Gk. *lēstēs*, 11:17; 14:48; 15:27) emphasizes the financial rapacity and extortion inherent in the temple cult. In assaulting the money changers and animal sellers and calling the Sanhedrin a club of thieves Jesus attacks not the spiritual corruption of the temple (which was typical of the OT prophets, for example), but its commercialism and financial misappropriation. Likewise, the image of a *"den* of robbers" localizes the castigation to the temple. Mark does not say that Jesus pronounces judgment on the Jews. The judgment is against the temple, and, as the following story indicates (11:27-33), against the religious authorities who superintended it. To conclude that the judgment was against the

---

25. W. R. Telford, *Barren Temple and the Withered Tree,* 93.

26. Once the temple was destroyed in A.D. 70, early Christianity applied the import of v. 17 to Christians, e.g., "If we do not do God's will, we shall be like the saying, 'My house became a den of robbers'" (*2 Clem.* 14:1; similarly, Justin Martyr, *Dial. Trypho* 17.3).

27. J. Frankovic, "Remember Shiloh," *JerusalemPersp* 46-47 (1994): 24-31.

Jewish people as a whole would deny God's relationship with his covenant people, and to deny God's sovereignty over historic Israel is inevitably to deny his sovereignty over the process of redemption. Jesus is
rather repeating an ancient prophetic refrain: "Ephraim is blighted, their
root is withered, they yield no fruit" (Hos 9:16). As was true in chap. 7,
the accent falls on a distortion — in this case of the temple — that eclipses
its purpose in God's will.[28] The clearing of the temple thus cannot be
taken as a global attack of Jesus on Judaism or on Jews or even on the
Pharisees; it is rather a specific censure of the Sanhedrin ("the chief
priests and the teachers of the law," v. 18) and the temple as the organ of
religious exploitation. The combined effect of the quotations from Isa 56:7
and Jer 7:31 is to assert that Gentiles (also 13:10) have access to God's self-
revelation to Israel on the basis of sincerity of heart rather than by legal
and cultic purity. The clearing of the temple thus enacts the principle earlier enunciated in 2:23–3:6.

Mark assures readers that the chief priests and scribes "heard" (Gk.
akouein, v. 18) the message of the clearing of the temple, just as the disciples had "heard" (Gk. *akouein*, v. 14) about the curse of the fig tree. Both
groups, in other words, understood and perceived Jesus' intent. As a consequence, the Sanhedrin "began looking for a way to kill him," that is, to
plot his death (3:6).[29] The Greek word translated "looking for" (*zētein*) always in Mark connotes the attempt to control Jesus (see further on the
term at 1:37). The plot of the Sanhedrin is rooted in fear. The Greek verb
phobeisthai ("to fear") occurs a dozen times in Mark, and always of fear
that separates people from Jesus. In the present instance the fear of the
Sanhedrin, as the following story will evince (11:32), is due to invidiousness of the crowd's amazement at Jesus' teaching. The amazement of the
crowd in v. 18 is expressed in identical wording to the amazement of the
synagogue in 1:22. The effect of this repetition is to convey that Jesus' authority supersedes that of the religious leaders in both the temple and the
synagogue, that is, at both the heart and periphery of Israel. The synagogue and the temple were the two places in Judaism where the teaching

28. See Betz, "Jesus and the Purity of the Temple (Mark 11:15-18): A Comparative
Religion Approach," *JBL* 116 (1997): 455-72, who argues that Jesus was not opposed in
principle either to the temple or to sacrifices, but rather to the increasing commercialism
of the temple, particularly in the wake of Herod's Hellenizing influences, which subverted the temple's original purpose.

29. The theme of Jesus' betrayal or handing over occurs as early as 1:14, where
John's arrest foreshadows Jesus'. It continues in 2:20 with the passing reference to the
taking away of the bridegroom; in 3:6 with the plot of the Pharisees and Herodians; in
3:19 with the hint of Judas's betrayal; in 3:20-21 with the alienation of Jesus' friends; in
6:3-4 with the alienation of his family and hometown; and above all in the three ominous
passion predictions (8:31; 9:31; 10:33-34).

of God was revealed and practiced. In the same two places the teaching of Jesus supersedes the Torah and temple cult, holding the crowds in amazement.

The B-component of the Markan sandwich concludes with the note that Jesus and the disciples went "out of the city" at night.[30] The wording of the verse (Gk. *hotan* = "when[ever]," *exeporeuonto* [imperfect] = "they were going out") may suggest a habitual practice rather than a single episode and thus support the theory of a longer stay in Jerusalem than one week (see the introduction to this chapter). At any rate, that Jesus "went out of the city" should be granted its full symbolic force that he has parted ways with the temple cult. On his second night in Jerusalem, according to Mark's chronology, Jesus again (v. 11) separates himself from the Holy City.

20-21 Mark completes the fig tree–temple sandwich with the note that on the following day the fig tree had "withered from the roots." That expression recalls the seeds in the parable of the sower that sprouted quickly but had no depth of soil and "withered because they had no root" (4:6). The Greek words for "wither" (*xērainein*) and "root" (*rhiza*) likewise recur in the parable of the sower. The repetition of this graphic imagery in v. 20 is a further reminder to readers that there will be no harvest from the temple. Mention of Peter in v. 21 once again suggests that Mark's source for the fig tree–temple episode is Peter's memory of the episode (so, too, 14:72).

Although vv. 15-19 are commonly known as the "cleansing of the temple," Jesus' action does not have the character of a "cleansing," that is, the removing of impurities and restoration to a rightful function. A cleansing act is clearly the thought of Isa 55:1-8 and *Pss. Sol.* 17:32ff. Quoting the latter:

> He [Messiah] shall purge Jerusalem, making it holy as of old:
> So that nations shall come from the ends of the earth to see his glory.

What Jesus does in the temple goes beyond a purging or corrective act, however. It attacks the very commerce upon which the temple cult depended, laying an ax at the root of the temple as an institution.[31] Together

---

30. The textual tradition is divided whether "he" (= Jesus; ℵ C D X Θ) or "they" (= Jesus and disciples; A B K Δ Π Ψ W) left the city. The singular pronoun agrees with the subject of the parallel statement in v. 11 and the singular subject of Jesus in vv. 15b-18; whereas the plural pronoun agrees with the plural subject of v. 15a and the verb in the following verse. Neither reading is thus more difficult than the other. On the basis of slightly superior manuscript evidence, the plural reading is preferable.

31. The dismissal of the clearing of the temple as a mere fiction of Mark by

with the subsequent events of Holy Week, Mark portrays the clearing of the temple not as its restoration but as its dissolution. Like the fig tree, its function is "withered from the roots" (v. 20). "'Not one stone [of the temple] will be left on another,'" says Jesus in his final temple discourse in Mark, "'every one will be thrown down'" (13:2). In his own body (14:22) the temple is broken down and in himself, "as a ransom for many" (10:45), it is being raised anew in three days, a temple not made with human hands (14:58). Not the blood of animals slaughtered by the high priest on the Day of Atonement, but his *own* blood, the "blood of the covenant" (14:24), will make Israel right with God. Indeed, at the moment of his death, the great curtain that divides the Holy of Holies from the Court of Israel is torn in two (15:38), dramatizing the dissolution of the temple as the means of approach to God. In his sacrificial death on the cross, Jesus alone is the access to God. The fig tree thus symbolizes the temple: as the means of approach to God, the temple is fundamentally — "from the roots" — replaced by Jesus as the center of Israel.[32]

23-25 Mark concludes the fig tree–temple episode with sayings on faith, the power of prayer, and the necessity of forgiveness. The withered fig tree is an object lesson to the disciples to "'Have faith in God.'"[33] The earnestness of the command to believe in God is reinforced by the asseveration, "'I tell you the truth.'" Jesus illustrates the power of faith with

---

B. Mack, *A Myth of Innocence: Mark and Christian Origins* (Philadelphia: Fortress Press, 1991), 292, and D. Seeley, "Jesus' Temple Act," *CBQ* 55 (1993): 263-83 is both baffling and groundless. Mack maintains that the act cannot be historical because there is no evidence of an anti-temple attitude in Jesus. This curious assertion is contradicted by repeated evidence in Mark that the scribes (see the discussion of the term at 1:22) and the religious authorities from Jerusalem (e.g., 3:6, 22!) challenged and opposed Jesus from early in his ministry. See the necessary corrective of E. P. Sanders, *Jesus and Judaism* (Philadelphia: Fortress Press, 1985), 75: "Jesus predicted (or threatened) the destruction of the temple and carried out an action symbolic of its destruction by demonstrating against the performance of the sacrifices. He did not wish to purify the temple, either of dishonest trading or of trading in contrast to 'pure' worship. Nor was he opposed to the temple sacrifices which God commanded to Israel. He intended, rather, to indicate that the end was at hand and that the temple would be destroyed, so that the new and perfect temple might arise."

32. See Telford, *The Barren Temple and Withered Tree*, 238-39; J. R. Edwards, "Markan Sandwiches: The Significance of Interpolations in Markan Narratives," *NovT* 31 (1989): 206-8; E. Weir, "Fruitless Fig Tree — Futile Worship," *ExpTim* 106 (1995): 330.

33. A small but weighty group of manuscripts reads *ei echete* ("if you have faith"; ℵ D Θ), but a much stronger collection of uncial manuscripts (A B C K L W X Δ Π Ψ), plus a variety of minuscule manuscripts and early versions, reads *echete*, the imperative to "have faith." The latter reading (adopted by the NIV) is the more probable reading. Metzger, *TCGNT*, 109, corroborates this judgment by noting that *Amēn legō hymin* ("I tell you the truth") is always introductory, and not preceded by a protasis, such as "If you have faith in God. . . ."

Hebraic hyperbole about the moving of a mountain. The symbol of a mountain may have been suggested by the horizon to the south of Jerusalem that is dominated by a peak in the shape of a volcano, which comes into view as one reaches the crest of the Mount of Olives from the village of Bethany. This peak is actually the fortress of Herodion, one of many citadels built by Herod the Great for refuge in case of war or rebellion. Herod had literally removed an adjacent hill, the base of which is still visible today, in order to surround the citadel of Herodion with a rounded earthwork "in the form of a breast," to quote Josephus.[34] Herod's architectural ambitions had changed the face of Judea, yet whoever believes in God, says Jesus, can move greater mountains than Herodion — indeed, cast them into the sea![35]

Mark's following the fig tree–temple sandwich with a call to faith signifies that Jesus, and not the temple, is the object of faith. Faith is the opposite of "doubting in one's heart" (v. 23). Faith is also the opposite of fear (4:40; 5:36; 6:50). It is a choice to trust in Jesus despite everything to the contrary, and to expect from him what cannot be expected from anything else in the world. There is thus an inevitable connection between faith and prayer, with which Mark ends this section (vv. 24-25). V. 24 resembles several statements in the Gospel of John (14:13-14; 15:7, 16; 16:23) and attests that true prayer is making requests of God in faith. Faith believes enough to ask, and asking is rooted in the conviction that God intends that his "will be done on earth as it is in heaven" (Matt 6:10). Faith is more certain of God's steadfastness than of human inabilities and vicissitudes. Therefore, "'whatever you ask for in prayer, believe that you have received it, and it will be yours.'"[36] This expression reflects Semitic thought in which the certainty of a future act, based on the trustworthiness of God, can be referred to in the past tense. Both faith and prayer stand in continuity with God's character and in conformity with his will.

---

34. Josephus, *War* 1.419-20. Also, A. Negev, *Archaeological Encyclopedia of the Holy Land* (Jerusalem: SBS Publishing Inc., 1980), 143-44; J. Murphy-O'Connor, *The Holy Land: An Archaeological Guide from Earliest Times to 1700*[4] (New York: Oxford University Press, 1998), 281-85.

35. The *Gospel of Thomas* 48 applies the saying about moving mountains in a different and ambiguous context: "Jesus says, 'If two make peace with one another in one and the same house, (then) they will say to the mountain, "Move away," and it will move away.'"

36. The Greek aorist tense *elabete* ("you have received it") echoes a prophetic perfect in Semitic usage, i.e., a future event that is so assured that it can be spoken of as already completed. The boldness of expression, which claims strong manuscript support (א B C K L W X Δ Π Ψ), was subsequently altered to the present *lambanete* ("you are receiving it"; A K X Π), or the future *lēmpsesthe* ("you will receive it"; D Θ). See Metzger, *TCGNT*, 109-10.

The final instruction in v. 25 is about forgiveness of sins, which is the feature of faith that most perfectly epitomizes God's nature. The reference to standing in prayer reflects the customary prayer posture in Judaism. V. 25 is an unmistakable echo of the forgiveness petition in the Lord's Prayer, and its interpretation immediately following (see Matt 6:12, 14).[37] V. 26 is absent from the earliest and most important manuscript tradition and was not part of Mark's original text. Its appearance in the later manuscript tradition is best explained as an insertion by copyists in imitation of Matt 6:15.[38]

37. The tradition that Mark utilizes was, at this point at least, familiar with the so-called Q tradition.

38. See Metzger, *TCGNT*, 110.

CHAPTER TWELVE

Jesus and the Sanhedrin

MARK 11:27–12:44

This section continues and contributes to the larger theme of Mark 11–13 that is defined by Jesus' opposition to and rejection of the temple. Mark 11:1-26 adumbrated the end of the temple system, which, in the person and work of Jesus, was "withered from the roots" (11:20). Beginning in 11:27, Mark presents a series of seven conflict stories between Jesus and the religious leaders. These conflicts extend to the end of chap. 12 and resemble the conflict stories of 2:1–3:6. As in the earlier Galilean controversies, in the Jerusalem controversies Jesus acts with incomparable authority, providing both hearers and readers with glimpses of his messianic and filial consciousness; but unlike the Galilean controversies, the Jerusalem controversies are all set in the temple and in opposition to the powerful religious authorities housed there. In the present section Mark moves from Jesus' opposition to the temple complex to the religious leaders themselves. The religious authority that Jesus opposes is centered in the Sanhedrin, the influential judiciary of seventy-one leaders that dominated Jewish religious and even political life to some degree. The Sanhedrin is presupposed in the controversy in 11:17-33 and in the parable in 12:1-12. Three subsequent stories are targeted to Pharisees (12:13-17), Sadducees (12:18-27), and scribes (12:28-40), the three groups that comprised the Sanhedrin. Traps are laid and snares are set to catch the Galilean teacher. Even more remarkable than their cleverness are Jesus' responses. He does not mount a counterstrategy of evasion and escape. Rather, he joins the field in a final attempt to reveal himself rather than defend himself to those who would judge him rather than understand him. The section concludes with a story of a powerless and penniless widow in 12:41-44 whose faith moved her to give her whole life, an ironic but crowning contrast to the powerful but faithless religious authorities.

349

THE AUTHORITY OF THE SON (11:27-33)

The temple in Jerusalem, in all its Herodian immensity and grandeur, with its commanding view of Jerusalem and the Mount of Olives and its unrivaled historical and theological significance, becomes the inevitable stage for the challenge to Jesus' authority. The characteristic of Jesus that left the most lasting impression on his followers and caused the greatest offense to his opponents was his *exousia*, his sovereign freedom and magisterial **authority**. In his first public appearance in Mark, Jesus astounds the synagogue congregation by his supremacy over both Torah experts and the demonic world (1:21-28). Both effects — his teaching and his exorcisms — derive from his divine authority. The authority of Jesus emerges as the foundation and impulse of his subsequent ministry and exhibits itself by his laying claim to prerogatives that otherwise belong only to God. Jesus binds Satan, "the strong man" (3:27); he presumes to forgive sins (2:10); he claims supremacy over the Torah and the Sabbath (2:23–3:6); and he replaces the temple in Jerusalem as the *locus Dei*, the place where God meets humanity (15:38-39). His speech to and about God is unique among Jewish rabbis: his frequent prefacing of statements with *Amēn* ("Truly I say to you") presumes to speak with the authority of God; his reference to God as *Abba* (14:36) exhibits a filial closeness to God unparalleled in Judaism; and his suggestive use of *egō eimi* ("I am," 6:50; 14:62) repeats God's self-revelation to Moses (Exod 3:14).[1] Until 11:27-33, however, Mark has not divulged the source of Jesus' *exousia*. Now for the first time, in the temple and before the Sanhedrin, that is, in the most authoritative place and before the most authoritative body in Israel, Jesus opens a window of understanding into his own authority.

27-28 "They arrived again in Jerusalem" refers to Jesus' third day in Jerusalem according to Mark's chronology, that is, Tuesday of Holy Week. Once again Jesus' destination is not Jerusalem per se but the temple. "While Jesus was walking in the temple courts, the chief priests, the teachers of the law and the elders came to him. 'By what authority are you doing these things?' they asked." The "chief priests, scribes, and elders" were the three groups that comprised the **Sanhedrin**, although in this instance they represent a delegation from the Sanhedrin rather than the entire council. The Sanhedrin, a buffer organization between Rome and the Jewish nation, was composed of seventy-one members who held near complete freedom in religious matters and restricted power in political matters. This is the only instance in Mark in which the Sanhedrin ap-

---

1. See J. R. Edwards, "The Authority of Jesus in the Gospel of Mark," *JETS* 37 (1994): 220-25.

proaches Jesus (apart from his trial in 14:55). Both the approach and question of the Sanhedrin attest that the issue of Jesus' authority was a matter of concern at the pinnacle of the Jewish religious establishment.

What the Sanhedrin means by "these things" is not entirely obvious, although it ostensibly points to the preceding clearing of the temple (11:15-19).[2] The overturning of tax tables and scattering of livestock were in themselves grounds for the opposition of the Sanhedrin. The temple episode, however, was only the most recent incident in a history of such provocations, which included Jesus' presumption to forgive sins (2:5), accept sinners (2:15), call tax collectors into fellowship (2:13), redefine the Sabbath (2:28), and lay an ax to the root of the oral tradition (7:1-13), the temple (11:12-20), and now the Sanhedrin. The clearing of the temple, in other words, was not a momentary aberration of Jesus but a characteristic expression of his authority.

The question, "'By what authority?'" indicates that for the Sanhedrin the issue is not simply what Jesus did, but his *right* to do it. The stakes in Jesus' answer were not negligible. The Mishnah would later prescribe that appeal to a false authority in religious matters was grounds for capital punishment.[3] Although the Mishnah was not codified until a century and a half after Jesus, many of its prescriptions date to Jesus' day and earlier. This one was in effect in Jesus' day, as the accusation of the chief priest in 14:63 attests. The question of the Sanhedrin also reveals that Jesus' adversaries recognize his unique empowerment, which on an earlier occasion had been attributed to the demonic (3:22). A second and related question, "'Who gave you authority to do this?'" acknowledges that no one possesses authority on his own to do what Jesus does. Such authority, presumably, could derive only from God, and yet for Jesus to attribute his authority to God could lead to the charge of blasphemy (14:63). Thus, similar to the question of 2:7 ("'Who can forgive sins but God alone?'"), Jesus' presumption to speak and act in place of God is again at center stage.

29-30 Jewish rabbis often answered a question by posing a counterquestion, as does Jesus in this instance. Remarkably, everything that needs to be known about Jesus can be summed up in "one word,"[4] or, more precisely, one event — the baptism of John. Was John's baptism "'from heaven, or from men?'" asks Jesus. Out of reverence for God Jews

2. John 2:13-22 preserves an independent witness linking the question of the religious authorities to Jesus' clearing of the temple.

3. "The false prophet and he that prophesies in the name of a strange god" were to be strangled (*m. Sanh.* 11:1).

4. The "one word" (*hena logon,* v. 29) appears to correspond to the "one Son" (*hena huion,* 12:6) in the following story.

avoided using the divine name, and Jesus follows the custom here, substituting "heaven" in its place. The categories chosen by Jesus are noteworthy. He does not appeal to the great rabbinic schools of Hillel or Shammai, nor even to the Torah or the temple. The categories necessary to comprehend Jesus and his mission surpass these. Nothing shy of "heaven and man," God and humanity, will suffice to answer the Sanhedrin. As on the earlier question of Sabbath observance (2:23–3:6), the counterquestion of Jesus required the Sanhedrin to make a judgment that lay beyond their control. What Jesus now asks of them cannot be answered from their power base in the Torah, the temple, or Roman authority. Thus, the question of Jesus implies that he stands not under the Sanhedrin but over it.[5] His counterquestion is evidence of the very authority about which he is questioned.

The question about John the Baptist seems at first glance to be either irrelevant or evasive. What does John's baptism have to do with Jesus' authority? Jesus' counterquestion about John often strikes readers as a diversionary tactic, like a raccoon jumping into a stream to shake the hounds from its scent. Ironically, the counterquestion contains the seeds of the truth the Sanhedrin hopes to learn, for it was at the baptism by John that the heavens were parted, the Spirit of power descended into Jesus (Gk. *eis auton*, 1:10), and the voice from heaven declared him God's Son. The baptism of Jesus, in other words, was the event that inaugurated his *exousia*, his conscious oneness with the Father, and his sovereign freedom and empowerment for ministry. If the Sanhedrin wants to know whence Jesus received authority to do "these things," it must reconsider John's baptism. A decision about John is a decision about Jesus. If John's baptism were solely "from men," that is, fully explainable by empirical science, then the Sanhedrin may be justified in its accusation of Jesus. But if John's baptism was "from heaven," that is, divinely inspired — as the crowds believed and as the Sanhedrin evidently feared — then Jesus' authority exceeds mere human authority and must be explained by the authority of God.

31-33 "[The Sanhedrin] discussed it among themselves." Already in this ostensibly neutral description Mark hints at the Sanhedrin's equivocation and compromise.[6] The Greek word for "discussed," *dialogizesthai*,

---

5. "All [Jesus'] actions and words are connected with John and go back to the spirit of God's descent on him after he had accepted baptism at John's hand. Jesus has the right to act the way he does because of what the voice from heaven said to him. He, more than the authorities, is at home in the temple, because God has called him his dear son" (B. M. F. van Iersel, *Reading Mark* [Edinburgh: T. and T. Clark, 1989], 148).

6. The calculation of the Sanhedrin would be further stressed if the variant reading offered by D and Θ were original, *legontes, ti eipōmen* ("saying, 'What might we say?' "). The

appears seven times in Mark, always in contexts of people trying to evade the force of Jesus' word or claim on them.[7] The term suggests that the Sanhedrin shifts to mere strategy and expediency. The revelatory potential of Jesus' question is thus reduced to a calculated dilemma: a decision for John will appear to support the cause of Jesus, whereas a decision against John will alienate the crowds, for whom John was popularly regarded as a prophet. And so they answer, "'We don't know.'" That, of course, is not entirely true. They certainly have some suspicions about who Jesus is, and they might learn more if they enter into honest dialogue with him. In reality, they are *unwilling* to know. The judgment of the Sanhedrin is again (11:18) clouded by fear of popular opinion, for "everyone held that John really was a prophet" (v. 32).[8] To those unwilling to commit themselves, Jesus refuses to commit himself. "'Neither will I tell you by what authority I am doing these things.'" Those who cannot be honest with themselves cannot be honest about Jesus.

Unwillingness to make a judgment about God's first acts eliminates the possibility of knowing the last act in Jesus. The Sanhedrin opts for "suspended judgment," or "keeping an open mind," as we say today. In reality, it shuffles among the options of skepticism, unbelief, and cowardice. If there is faith even as small as a mustard seed, Jesus responds, "'Truly I tell you'" (Gk. *Amēn legō hymin*); but in the face of calculated unbelief he responds, "'Neither will I tell you'" (Gk. *Oude egō legō hymin*, v. 33).

The failure of the delegation of the Sanhedrin to come to a proper understanding of Jesus is often attributed to the fact that the Sanhedrin failed to receive John's preaching of repentance. Had the temple authorities and emissaries received John's baptism of repentance (1:4-5), it is suggested, they would have found no offense in Jesus. While this is partially true, it fails adequately to explain the breach between the Sanhedrin and Jesus in the temple interrogation. The crux of the Sanhedrin's error is not the issue of repentance, for in Mark repentance is a penultimate and secondary feature of John's proclamation. The primary function of John

---

shorter reading (*legontes*, "said" [omitting the following interrogative]) claims far stronger manuscript support, however, and is to be preferred, especially in light of the fact that Western (D) and Caesarean (Θ) text types tend to expand and paraphrase readings. See B. Metzger, *TCGNT*, 110.

7. It occurs three times in 2:6, 8 (2 times) of the inner turmoil and resistance of the scribes to Jesus; twice of the questions and confusion among the disciples in 8:16-17; again of the argument among the disciples about who was greatest in 9:33, and finally of the consternation of the Sanhedrin in 11:31.

8. Three important Greek manuscripts read that "everyone *knew* that John was really a prophet" (*ēdeisan*; D W Θ), but the more idiomatic *eichon* ("held") claims superior manuscript support.

was announcing and preparing for the Coming One (1:7-8).[9] Mark alludes to this function in v. 32 by noting that all the people — and the Greek emphasizes *all* — held John not to be a preacher of repentance or moral reformer, but a "prophet." According to Mark, in other words, John's function was first and last to introduce Jesus. Concomitant to that announcement, as the theme of chaps. 11–13 shows, is that institutional religion, even its pinnacle in the powerful and prestigious Sanhedrin, is vacuous unless it is centered in the "Stronger One," declared to be God's Son at the baptism of John. John's significance for Jesus — and in this instance for the Sanhedrin — is as a herald of Jesus' divine Sonship, with which Mark begins (1:1, 11) and ends (15:39) his Gospel. The "these things" of which the Sanhedrin inquires can be understood only if they are seen as consequences of the authority *(exousia)* of Jesus as the Son of God, which John's baptism inaugurated. What Jesus does as God's servant has meaning only because of who he is as God's Son. The *exousia* of Jesus is in fact the *exousia* of God.

THE SENDING OF THE SON (12:1-12)

This is the only major parable outside chap. 4 in the Gospel of Mark. The unique placement of the parable should alert us to its significance. It is a story of Israel's relationship to the Son of God, depicted in terms of tenant farming and recast in OT imagery (Matt 23:34).[10] The parable de-

9. See K. Huber, "Zur Frage nach christologischen Implikationen in den 'Jerusalemer Streitgesprächen' bei Markus," SNT(SU) 21 (1996), 13: "In my judgment, with the reference to John the Baptizer, Jesus lays claim to its content for himself and signifies indirectly that in his own person the announced 'Stronger One' has become reality, i.e., that he himself is this Messianic figure."

10. The authenticity of the parable of the vineyard has frequently been doubted on the grounds of a presumed incompatibility in the parable between the allusion to Isa 5:1-7 and the practice of tenant farming in Galilee. For a recent review of the problem, see J. Kloppenborg Verbin, "Isaiah 5:1-7, the Parable of the Tenants and Vineyard Leases on Papyrus," in *Text and Artifact in the Religions of Mediteranean Antiquity: Essays in Honour of Peter Richardson,* Studies in Christianity and Judaism, No. 9, ed. S. Wilson and M. Desjardins (Wilfrid Laurier University Press, 2000), 111-34, who concludes "that Mark's version of the parable is fundamentally incoherent" (130). Kloppenborg Verbin's negative judgment rests, first, on the assumption that the allusion to Isaiah 5 robs the parable of being "read realistically" and transforms it into an allegory. This criticism is unsustainable on at least two grounds. First, the parable is not intended, as Kloppenborg Verbin seems to assume, to be a manual on viticulture in first-century Galilee but rather to retell the story of Israel by means of a custom familiar to all hearers. Because of its familiarity, the custom needed only be alluded to, not fully rehearsed. Second, the assump-

scribes "the kind of thing that went on in Galilee during the half century preceding the general revolt of A.D. 66."[11] Secular records of the day as well as rabbinic literature depict a widespread system of absentee land-owners who employed middle men to supervise tenant farmers.[12] Such practices became the raw data for illustrative stories and morals well be-yond the circle of Jesus. A rabbinic commentary dating nearly a century after Jesus developed the following parable on the theme, "the Lord's portion is his people" (Deut 32:9):

> This is like a king who owned a field that he leased to tenants. They be-gan to appropriate it as their own and steal. Thereupon the king took the field from them and gave it to their sons who behaved even worse. When a son was born to the king, the king said to the tenants, "You

---

tion that a parable cannot contain allegorical elements goes back to Jülicher's narrow and inadequate judgment of parables. Like all narrative images, parables can seldom be re-duced to a single point. The two most famous parables in the OT, Nathan's rebuke of Da-vid (2 Sam 12:1-6) and Isaiah's parable of the vineyard (Isa 5:1-7), both contain allegorical elements. That Jesus' parables did not contain allegorical elements on occasion is an un-justified *a priori* assumption (see the discussion of 4:13-20). Kloppenborg Verbin's second judgment against the authenticity of Mark 12:1-12 rests on the assumption that "Mark clearly speaks of a newly planted vineyard" (129), which makes the owner's request of the tenants unreasonable, since vineyards produced grapes only the fifth year after planting. The parable, however, does not say that the owner sought produce the first year, but *tō kairō* (12:2, "at harvest season"), i.e., when a crop appeared. Neither of Kloppenborg Verbin's judgments therefore impugns the authenticity of the parable as it stands. The history of Israel's response to God is, after all, the dominant motif of the OT prophets (e.g., Jer 7:25-26; Hos 11:1-11). It should hardly be surprising if in a parable Jesus should rehearse that history in relation to himself. For a comprehensive scholarly de-fense of the essential authenticity of the parable of the vineyard, see K. Snodgrass, *The Parable of the Wicked Tenants: An Inquiry into Parable Interpretation* (Tübingen: J. C. B. Mohr [Paul Siebeck], 1983).

11. C. H. Dodd, *The Parables of the Kingdom* (Collins: Fontana Books, 1961), 94. Fur-ther, J. Jeremias, *Die Gleichnisse Jesu* (Göttingen: Vandenhoeck & Ruprecht, 1965), 67ff.

12. A report dating from 257 B.C. discovered in the Zeno papyri documents an agent who traveled to Galilee to inspect his finance minister's property. Much like our parable, the document includes reports on the production of the vineyard, cisterns, and living spaces. See M. Hengel, "Das Gleichnis von den Weingärtnern Mc 12:1-12 im Lichte der Zenonpapyri und der rabbinischen Gleichnisse," *ZNW* 59 (1968): 12-15, who con-cludes: "The analogies to our parable are obvious. We encounter a considerable eco-nomic domain in Galilee, carried on according to capitalistic methods, which produced large quantities of wine. The system consisted of absentee landowners who employed agents to supervise their property." For complementary assessments, see C. A. Evans, "Jesus' Parable of the Tenant Farmers in Light of Lease Agreements in Antiquity," *JSP* 14 (1996): 65-83; and R. MacMullan, *Roman Social Relations, 50 B.C. to A.D. 284* (New Haven and London: Yale University Press, 1974), 1-27, who further documents "the vulnerabil-ity of property when its owner was away, [and] the invitation to violence, . . . beatings, maulings, and murder."

must leave my property, it is no longer possible for you to remain; render to me my due portion." (*Sifre Deut* 32:9)[13]

1 As in all Jesus' parables, the basic theme of this parable is drawn from the soil and the experience of everyday life in Palestine. According to Mark's account, Jesus takes the farm crisis of his day[14] — enhanced by several prophetic allusions — and tells Israel's story in the form of a parable. Prophetic imagery in the parable includes the themes of conspiracy (Gen 37:18-20), the sending of servants (Amos 3:7; Zech 1:4-6), and Israel as God's inheritance (Ps 2:8). The dominant biblical allusion, however, is Isaiah's famous metaphor of Israel as the vineyard of Yahweh.

My loved one had a vineyard
   on a fertile hillside.
He dug it up and cleared it of stones
   and planted it with the choicest vines.
He built a watchtower in it
   and cut a winepress as well.[15]
Then he looked for a crop of good grapes,
   but it yielded only bad fruit. (Isa 5:1-2)[16]

Isaiah's judgment was an oft-repeated theme in the OT, and was certainly familiar to Jesus' contemporaries. A similar gavel of judgment was sounded by Jeremiah:

13. Cited in Str-B 1.874.
14. "Vineyard leases represented a particular type of agricultural lease. Unlike the lease of farmland on which the tenant might plant one of several possible annual crops, the lease of a vineyard involved the care of a perennial crop representing significant capital investment. Vines normally took five years to become productive and required constant irrigation. They could suffer damage through neglect, and the proper operation of a vineyard regularly involved care for an adjoining reed plantation, from which supports for the vines were obtained, periodic manuring of the vines and maintenance of water installations" (Kloppenborg Verbin [see n. 10 above], 125).
15. There is a fragmentary allusion to the winepress of Isa 5:1-2 in 4Q500 of the DSS.
16. J. Jeremias, *The Parables of Jesus,* rev. ed. (London: SCM Press, 1963), 71, maintains that *periethēken phragmon* ("he put a wall around it") is a mistranslation of the Heb. text of Isa 5:2, *yezzeqehu* ("he dug it up"), and thus evidence that Mark 12:1 is quoted from the LXX and "must therefore be due to secondary editorial activity." The Hebrew word in question, however, can also be translated "to surround with a wall, provide with a hedge" (so *HALOT* 2.810). Mark 12:1 is thus arguably a valid translation of the Hebrew. Whether Mark is translating an original Hebrew quotation into Greek or loosely quoting from the LXX is uncertain, but in neither case does the claim of "secondary editorial activity" appear to be justified.

From the time your forefathers left Egypt until now, day by day, again and again I sent to you my servants the prophets. But they did not listen to me or pay attention. They were stiff-necked and did more evil than their forefathers. (7:25-26; see also 25:4-5)

2-5   The practice of absentee land ownership thus becomes the occasion of a prophetic judgment against the "tenant farmers," that is, the Jewish leaders and the temple authorities. A landowner leases property to tenant farmers to work in his absence. At harvest season he sends a hired hand to collect his produce. But the tenants, in the words of C. H. Dodd, "pay their rent in blows."[17] Other hands are sent, receiving the same or worse treatment. As a last resort the landowner sends his son; surely a family member will command respect. But the tenants see it otherwise: if they do away with the heir, they will come by the property. So they kill the son, cast his body to the birds, and seize the property. At this point the landowner intervenes decisively, destroying the tenants and then leasing the property to others more deserving.

Two points are worthy of note so far. First, the landowner takes vengeance not on the vineyard but on the tenants of the vineyard. That is, the parable cannot be interpreted as a blanket judgment on the Jewish people, but rather on their leaders, particularly the Sanhedrin. Second, the heroic party is not the tenant farmers but the landowner, who justly settles accounts. The parable thus cannot be construed as evidence for a vision or program of a popular uprising against oppression on the part of Jesus. Regardless of popular sentiment about absentee land ownership in Jesus' day, it is the tenants who are defiant rebels against a rightful owner. That must surely be understood as Jesus' judgment on the Sanhedrin and Jewish leadership for confiscating the things of God.

6   The climax of the parable comes in 12:6: "'He had one left to send, a son, whom he loved.'" What farmer in his right mind would surrender his son to such tenants? It is a question worth asking, for it suggests the indefatigable love of God. True, according to Jewish law a son possessed legal rights that a slave did not; thus, the son is "the heir."[18] In

---

17. *Parables of the Kingdom*, 93.

18. In Jewish law, a son possessed legal rights denied to a slave. See J. D. M. Derrett, "Fresh Light on the Parable of the Wicked Winedressers," *RIDA* 10 (1963): 31, who writes that in adjudicating disputes with tenants, "formal 'protest' must be made before witnesses, warning the tenants that legal action would commence against them. Slaves, however, could not make this protest, nor could slaves adjure witnesses — a serious handicap in so involved a matter. By that period it had not yet become possible to plead one's cause through an agent — one must actually transfer one's rights to the 'representative.' Therefore, the son had to be sent."

sending the servants the owner appealed to the integrity of the tenants; in sending his son he appeals to the right of law, for the son was the only person, save himself, who possessed legal claim over the vineyard. This is why the owner says, "'They will respect my son.'" The son goes as the father's representative, with the father's authority, to the father's property, to claim the father's due.

The son represents not only the father's legal claim, however, but also his *compassion.* Everything in 12:6-7 underscores this point. The word for "send" (Gk. *apostellein*) carries the sense of a divine commission (3:14; 6:7; Luke 11:49-51; 13:34-35).[19] And the son differs from the slaves in several important respects: they are many, he is unique;[20] they are hirelings, perhaps even themselves property, he is the heir; they are forerunners, he is the last and final word of the father. Above all, the son is "beloved." The word recalls Abraham's love for Isaac (Gen 22:2), Jacob's love for Joseph (Gen 37:3), God's love for Israel (Isa 5:1), and especially the Father's love for "the beloved Son" at the baptism (1:11). The reference to the "beloved son" (Gk. *huion agapēton*) in the parable recalls only one other relationship in the Gospel, that of Jesus and the Father (1:11; 9:7). In the story of the sending of the son Jesus is speaking of his own unprecedented role in the history of Israel.[21]

7-8 The farmers, however, reject the overture of love. The *Gospel of Thomas* 65, which also preserves this parable, is ambiguous about the actual guilt of the tenants, even suggesting that they mistreated the emis-

---

19. A further allusion to Isaiah's vineyard is evident here. After the vineyard proves fruitless, the LXX asks the rhetorical question, "'What more shall I do for my vineyard?'" (Isa 5:4). Jesus gives the answer in this parable: God will send his only Son!

20. The retelling of this parable in the *Shepherd of Hermas* greatly alters the roles of the owner's son and servant (only one). The servant who receives the vineyard from the owner does not rebel against the owner but works the field faithfully and industriously, so much so that on the owner's return the virtuous servant is made coheir of the vineyard with the son (*Herm. Sim.* 5:2:1-8). The *Shepherd* thus empties the parable of its christological emphasis and fashions it into a moral of justification by works.

21. See J. D. Kingsbury, *The Christology of Mark's Gospel* (Philadelphia: Fortress Press, 1989), 114-18. W. Bousset, *Kyrios Christos: A History of the Belief in Christ from the Beginnings of Christianity to Irenaeus,* trans. J. Steely (New York and Nashville: Abingdon Press, 1970), 80, denies that v. 6 is a self-designation of Jesus, maintaining that "nowhere else in his parables did Jesus push his own person into the foreground in such a way as here." Bousset's sweeping generalization is untenable. We have noted throughout the commentary that Jesus intentionally puts his own person into the foreground (see **Authority of Jesus**, Introduction 6.1). There is no reason he cannot do so in a parable intended to depict his role in the history of Israel. "If Jesus spoke of God as his Father, as the evidence of his prayers decisively establishes, it is difficult to see why he could not take the further step of referring to himself as the Son" (I. H. Marshall, "The Divine Sonship of Jesus," *Int* 21 [1967]: 93).

saries because they did not know them. In Mark's account of the parable it is because they *do* know him that they kill him. No longer content with the owner's produce (v. 2), the farmers go for his property as well. "'Come, let's kill him,'" they say. Those are the same words spoken by Jacob's sons when they connived to dispatch the beloved Joseph (Gen 37:20). If the farmers kill the heir, they reason, then they will become the heirs.[22] If humanity can dispense with God, or even kill God, then humanity can become God. "'So they took him and killed him, and threw him out of the vineyard.'"[23] Jesus echoes the prophets: what is the history of Israel if not rebellion against God (Matt 23:34)? What is the sum total of human history if not the attempt to rid the universe of God?

9-11 The vineyard, however, is not a human possession, not even Israel's possession, but God's possession, his work and purpose in history. In the rhetorical question of 12:9, "'What then will the owner of the vineyard do?'" the Greek word for "owner" is *kyrios*, which is doubly appropriate, for it means both "owner" and "God as Lord." God is indeed the "owner of the vineyard" (so Isa 5:3). The judgment that Jesus pronounces against the vineyard echoes a similar judgment in the DSS, "I will tell you what I am going to do with my vineyard: [I will] remove its fence so that it can be used for pasture, destroy its wall so that you trample it. For I will leave it flattened" and a habitation for brambles and thistles (4Q162 [4QpIsa]). "'He will come and kill those tenants and give the vineyard to others,'" says Jesus.[24] By Mark's day, the "others" were cer-

---

22. Some interpreters argue that in the absence of the landowner the tenants might, according to usucaption, expect to acquire ownership by length of tenancy. According to *m. B. Bat.* 3:3, however, "tenants and guardians cannot secure title by usucaption."

23. The parallel verse in Matt 21:39 alters this part of the parable thus: "'So they took him and threw him out of the vineyard and killed him.'" Matthew's sequence of events more closely corresponds to the actual passion events, i.e., Jesus was arrested, taken out of Jerusalem, and crucified (so John 19:17; Heb 13:12). Matthew's alteration again argues for Markan priority, for it is easier to explain why Matthew might alter the Markan sequence to correspond to the historical sequence of the passion than to explain why Mark would corrupt an otherwise historical allusion in Matthew. It is possible (though not very likely, in my judgment) that the difference in sequence reflects the Evangelists' understanding of those responsible for Jesus' death: for Mark, Jesus is killed inside the vineyard and then thrown outside, i.e., both rejected and killed by Jews; whereas for Matthew and Luke, Jesus is thrown outside and killed, i.e., rejected by the Jews but killed by the Romans. At any rate, Mark's unusual sequence argues for its provenance in Jesus rather than in the early church, from which we would expect a sequence like that of Matthew and Luke at v. 8.

24. Matt 21:41 places this statement in the mouth of the hearers. In Mark's version of the parable it is not a conclusion of the hearers, however, but a pronouncement of Jesus, which invests it with greater authority.

tainly understood to mean Gentiles.[25] Yet that is not to suggest that either the verse or its understanding was a product of the later Gentile mission. Mark 7:24–8:10 anchors the inclusion of Gentiles to the essential mission of Jesus, and the quotation of Isa 56:7 in the clearing of the temple, "'My house will be called a house of prayer for all nations,'" reveals that Jesus condemned the temple system for its failure to include Gentiles.

The parable concludes with a quotation from Ps 118:22-23 (vv. 10-11).[26] The reference is to a stone that was rejected in Solomon's Temple, only to become the head of the porch. This quotation played an important role in early Christianity as an explanation for the Jewish rejection of Jesus (Luke 20:17; Acts 4:11; Rom 9:33; 1 Pet 2:6-8; *Acts Pet.* 24:10).[27] Only Mark (and the parallel in Matt 21:42), however, includes the subsequent verse: "the Lord has done this, and it is marvelous in our eyes" (v. 11 = Ps 118:23). This additional verse rings with a strong providential note, that the human rejection of God's "cornerstone" was not only foreseen but used by God for his glory. This additional verse is important for Mark's interpretation of the parable. In the parable of the sower (4:3-9), it will be recalled, the sorry prospects for a crop do not frustrate the ultimate harvest. Likewise in this parable Jesus' present rejection and humiliation are painfully apparent, but God is using the rejection of his Son for a greater

25. The idea of the "vineyard" passing to Gentiles was apparently not only a Christian concept. An interesting letter from the second century by a Mara bar Serapion to his son uses the death of Jesus as an example of justice prevailing over tyranny: "What was the murder of Socrates to the Athenians? Their reward for it was hunger and plague. Or what gain did the inhabitants of Samos receive from the burning of Pythagoras? Their land was suddenly covered with sand, in a single hour. Or the Jews, through the murder of their wise king? For it was precisely from this time on that they lost their kingship. God righteously avenged the rejection of the wisdom of these three. The Athenians died of hunger, the people of Samos were covered by the sea, with no chance to be saved. And the Jews, desolated and driven into exile from their own kingdom, are now dispersed throughout every place. But Socrates is not dead after all — because of Plato, and neither is Pythagoras dead, because of the statue of Juno, and neither is the wise king [of the Jews] dead, because of the new laws which he ordained." Although this letter was possibly written by a Jew ("bar Serapion" = Ar., son of Serapion?), it was probably not authored by a Christian, who doubtlessly would have identified the "wise king" as Jesus and who scarcely would have set him on a par with Socrates and Pythagoras. For the quotation and further analysis, see *HCNT,* 124-25.

26. See the discussion of these verses and their place in Mark's scheme in J. Marcus, *The Way of the Lord: Christological Exegesis of the Old Testament in the Gospel of Mark* (Edinburgh: T. & T. Clark, 1992), 111-29.

27. Also in the *Gospel of Thomas* 66 the saying about the rejected stone is appended to the parable of the vineyard. Within rabbinic Judaism the stone was interpreted metaphorically, sometimes with reference to Abraham, sometimes to David, and even on occasion to the Messiah. In the last instance, the builders were regarded as the scribes and the rejected stone as the Messiah. See Str-B 1.875-76.

purpose that will be "'marvelous in our eyes.'" The Son of God can lay no claim to immunity from the sufferings of the world. That was also the message at Caesarea-Philippi: the Son must suffer, and his vindication, which Mark attests in Spartan simplicity in 16:6 ("he was raised [by God]"), rests solely in the Father's hands.

12 The Greek of v. 12a might be translated, "[The religious leaders] were conniving to seize him, because they knew [Jesus] had spoken the parable against them." "Conniving" (Gk. *zētein*; see further on the term at 1:37) and "seize" (Gk. *kratein*; see further at 3:21) are staple terms in Mark for attempting to throttle Jesus and oppose God's purpose in his ministry. Moreover, for the third time since entering Jerusalem Mark notes that the opposition of the religious authorities to Jesus is rooted in their fear of the crowds' response to Jesus (11:18, 32; 12:12). The delegation of the Sanhedrin is beginning to act like the tenants in the parable!

The parable of the vineyard and tenants is permeated with a sense of God's indomitable providence. True, it looks as though the schemes of the rebel tenants will wreck the owner's vineyard, but they do not prevail, nor can they. Even the son fulfills his perilous mission in the assurance that the father's purpose is being accomplished through his death and seeming defeat. The father's vineyard is not dispossessed or destroyed, but rather the wicked tenants are judged and others more worthy are found to continue the vineyard. The parable thus echoes the same theme of providence seen in the parable of the sower (4:3-9), in which even lousy farming conditions could not cancel or counteract the inevitable harvest of God. Once again the voice of Jesus is audible in this parable, supremely aware of his role in the Father's economy. There is yet another reminder of his inevitable death (8:31; 9:31; 10:33-34), and yet an equally supreme confidence that his penultimate defeat will not only result in the Father's ultimate purpose, but be the means by which it is accomplished. The parable's testimony to the sure purposes of God conveyed a profound sense of hope to Mark's beleaguered church in Rome, so ravished by Nero's insane persecutions, as it can also in our day, when the church (at least in the West) is often caught in compromise and confusion and decline. The existence of the vineyard is assured not by the self-aggrandizement of the tenants but by the self-sacrifice of the Son.

THE TEST OF THE PHARISEES (12:13-17)

Each of the stories in 11:27–12:44 is set against the backdrop of the opposition of the Sanhedrin. The Sanhedrin consisted of three major groups,

Pharisees, Sadducees, and scribes. Beginning with this story, each of these groups puts Jesus to the test — the Pharisees on the question of taxation (12:13-17), the Sadducees on the question of the resurrection (12:18-27), and the scribes on the question of scriptural interpretation (12:28-44). In each story Jesus is addressed as "Teacher" (12:14, 19, 32), and in each Jesus demonstrates his authority, his *exousia,* which derived from his baptism by John (11:29-30) and which has characterized his ministry from its inception (1:22, 27).

13-14   The question about taxation begins with typical Markan imprecision, "Later they sent some of the Pharisees and Herodians to Jesus." The original Greek omits "later," introducing the pericope in the historical present without any suggestion of time lapse ("And they send to him . . ."). The impression left is one of persistent challenges to Jesus' authority. Who sent the two parties we are not told, but the Sanhedrin is a likely guess. The Greek verb *apostellein,* which means to send with a specific purpose, and the added note that they intended "to catch him in his words," connote that they hope to expose Jesus as a false teacher. The Greek word for "catch," *agreuein,* occurs in the NT only here and connotes violent pursuit. The test thus bears a distinct resemblance to the Pharisees' earlier test in the synagogue in 3:1-6, although the Pharisees are now less restrained and more aggressive. In both instances they share an unlikely alliance with the Herodians (see on the term at 3:6). The coalition of the Herodians and Pharisees, who tended toward legal purity, would appear to be at best an awkward alliance, forged more by a common enemy in Jesus than by any agreement among themselves. The bulk of this story is devoted not to the question of taxation but to the ill-intent of the Pharisees and Herodians, which is a second likeness to 3:1-6 and which is also corroborated by the parallels in Matt 22:23-33 and Luke 20:27-40.

The statement in 12:14 that Jesus is "'a man of integrity'" who is "'not swayed by men,'" but "'teaches the way of God in accordance with the truth'" is full of Semitic character and verbal constructions, doubtlessly reflections of the words of Jesus' interlocutors. The statement is notable on two counts. First, despite the insincerity of the Pharisees and Herodians, it is a true statement. Jesus is indeed such a person. Moreover, a person who is not "'swayed by men, because you pay no attention to who they are,'" is unlikely to be influenced by such flattery. Jesus recognizes the motives of the inquirers for what they are: "But Jesus knew their hypocrisy. 'Why are you trying to trap me?' he asked" (v. 15; cf. John 2:24-25).

Hoping to impale Jesus on the horns of a dilemma, they ask, "'Is it right to pay taxes to Caesar or not?'" The Greek word for "taxes," *kēnson,* is a transliteration of a Latin word, *census,* indicating that the Evangelist writes to a community whose frame of reference is shaped by Latin.[28] A question about paying taxes to Caesar was predictable in Jerusalem, and particularly in the temple, for in Judea money and goods went directly into Roman coffers, whereas in Galilee the same were funneled to Rome through Herod Antipas.[29] The tax referred to is an imperial poll tax, first instituted in A.D. 6.[30] The amount required to satisfy the poll tax was a denarius (v. 15, another Latin loanword), which was the average daily wage in Palestine (Matt 20:2, 9). A denarius was a Roman silver coin bearing the semi-divine bust of Tiberius Caesar (A.D. 14-37) with an abbreviated Latin inscription, *Tiberius Caesar Divi Augusti Filius Augustus* ("Tiberius Caesar Augustus, Son of the Divine Augustus"). The reverse side bore an image of Tiberius's mother Livia and the inscription, *Pontifex Maximus* ("High Priest"). The question of the Pharisees and Herodians is, of course, intended to imperil Jesus in a compromise: support for taxation will discredit him in the eyes of the people, whereas his refusal to pay the tax will bring the Roman Imperium down on him.

15-17 Jesus, however, refuses to be maneuvered into either position.[31] He knows their "hypocrisy" and nefarious intent. The Greek word translated "trap" *(peirazein)* means "to test or tempt" (8:11). Retaining his own authority, Jesus requests a denarius and asks, "'Whose portrait is this?'" There is some irony in the fact that the inquirers possess the requisite coin for the tax, whereas Jesus does not. They apparently share more complicity in the tax system than their question suggests. Since the image and inscription are Caesar's, says Jesus, the coin belongs to Caesar.

By this reply Jesus acknowledges the legitimacy of human government. It distances Jesus from all forms of political anarchy, best exemplified in his day by the Zealots, who believed that the overthrow of the Roman Imperium was the will of God. On the other hand, Jesus' answer cannot be construed to mean that God and government are two separate and exclusive entities independent of one another. God is sovereign over all human affairs, including political affairs. This passage affirms that

28. For a discussion of Latin loanwords in Mark, see V. Taylor, *The Gospel According to St. Mark,* 45.

29. E. P. Sanders, *The Historical Figure of Jesus* (London: Allen Lane, The Penguin Press, 1993), 252.

30. Josephus, *War* 2.117; *Ant.* 18.1-10. As a result of this taxation Judas the Galilean founded a rebel cause that grew into the Zealot movement. In A.D. 66 the Zealots plunged the nation into revolt against Rome, which resulted in the annihilation of both the Jewish rebels and the nation.

31. *Egerton Papyrus* 2 preserves a fragmentary version of this pericope until this point. Rather than concluding with the request and saying about the coin, however, *Eg. Pap.* 2 concludes with Jesus quoting Isa 29:13.

there are duties to governments that do not infringe on ultimate duties to God (Rom 13:1-7; 1 Tim 2:1-6; 1 Pet 2:13-17), while vigorously rejecting that governments may assume total claim over their citizens, "as though the State, over and beyond its special commission, should and could become the single and totalitarian order of human life, thus fulfilling the Church's vocation as well."[32]

Not the least interesting aspect of Jesus' brilliant response is that he does not stop at the question asked of him. Duty to Caesar is surpassed by duty to God. "'Give to Caesar what is Caesar's and to God what is God's'" (so, too, Justin, *Apol.* 1.17.2). This saying, reminiscent of Jesus' reply to Peter in 8:33 ("'You do not have in mind the things of God but the things of man'") declares that ultimate authority in life belongs to God.[33] One cannot consider political and civil duties apart from faith, but only as expressions of the prior and ultimate claims of God.[34] In the saying of v. 17 the unmistakable *exousia* or authority of Jesus again emerges. Caesar and God were ultimate and uncontested authorities in the political and religious climate of Jesus' day, and yet Jesus presumes to speak for both. That ultimate authority resided with God is clearly implied in Jesus' use of the word "image" (v. 16 in Greek), which is the same word used in Gen 1:26 of humanity's creation in God's image. If coins bear Caesar's image, then they belong to Caesar. But humanity, which bears God's image, belongs to God!

THE TEST OF THE SADDUCEES (12:18-27)

A second test of the Sanhedrin comes from the sect of the Sadducees. This is the only story in the Gospel of Mark where Jesus has an exclusive encounter with the **Sadducees**. Of the several parties and sects of Judaism in first-century Palestine, two dominated Jewish life in general and the Sanhedrin in particular. They were the Pharisees (see at 2:18) and Sadducees. Both parties seem to have arisen during the Maccabean revolt against Seleucid tyranny (early second century B.C.). Despite their common ori-

---

32. *The Theological Declaration of Barmen,* art. 5.

33. The *Gospel of Thomas* (100) preserves this saying thus: "They showed Jesus a gold (coin) and said to him: Caesar's agents demand taxes from us. He said to them: Give to Caesar what belongs to Caesar; give to God what belongs to God; and give to me what is mine." This version of the saying expressly differentiates between God and Jesus, whereas Mark's version makes no such differentiation.

34. See D. T. Owen-Ball, "Rabbinic Rhetoric and the Tribute Passage (Mt. 22:15-22; Mk 12:13-17; Lk. 20:20-26)," *NovT* 35 (1993): 1-14.

gin, they differed greatly in outlook. The Pharisees believed in divine sovereignty, while the Sadducees affirmed human free will alone; the Pharisees believed in angels and demons, whereas the Sadducees did not; the Pharisees accepted a broader understanding of Scripture and revelation, which included both written (Torah, Writings, and Prophets) and oral traditions, whereas the Sadducees accepted only the written Torah; and finally, as this story indicates, the Pharisees affirmed the resurrection of the dead, which the Sadducees expressly denied (12:18; Acts 23:8). The Sadducean denial of angels, demons, and the afterlife derived from their exclusive reliance on the Torah, which does not set forth these doctrines.[35] The Sadducees were thus theological conservatives, and the Pharisees theological progressives.

Differences between the two sects did not stop at doctrine, however. The Sadducees further differed from the Pharisees on social and political matters. The Sadducees comprised a clerical and lay aristocracy associated with the priesthood. Already prior to the Maccabean Revolt (167 B.C.) the priesthood had exerted a dominant influence among the Jews, and hence the Sadducees, like the priesthood, belonged to the highest social stratum of Jewish society, marked by "wealth" and "men of rank," to quote Josephus. The association of the Sadducees with the priesthood meant that their influence was focused above all in the temple and in operations associated with it. The priesthood was an important political as well as religious influence. The Sadducees' close alliance with the priesthood thrust them into the political fray, as is evidenced by their receptivity to Hellenism and, during Jesus' day, their collaboration with Roman rule.[36]

18 As in his introduction of the Pharisees in 12:13, Mark introduces the Sadducees with similar haste and without indicating lapse of time; literally, "And the Sadducees come to [Jesus]." Their introduction continues the rapid tempo of events befalling Jesus in Jerusalem. In the current pericope the Sadducees focus their test of Jesus on the subject of the resurrection. They believed that at death the soul perished along with the body, and hence that there were no future rewards or punishments. The **doctrine of the resurrection** is, in fact, only vaguely foreshadowed in the OT (Isa 26:19; Ezekiel 37; Dan 12:2; Ps 73:23). The view that typifies

---

35. E. Main, "Les Sadducéens et la Résurrection des Morts: Comparaison entre Mc 12,18-27 et Lc 20,27-38," *RB* 103 (1996): 411-32, argues that the Sadducean objection to the doctrine of the resurrection of the dead was due not only to the fact that it is not explicitly mentioned in the Torah. The formulation of their question to Jesus on the basis of a positive commandment of the Torah indicates that in their thinking the belief in the doctrine of the resurrection logically contradicts the teaching of the Torah.

36. Josephus, *Ant.* 13.173, 297-98; 18.16-17; *War* 2.164-66. On the Sadducees in general, see E. Schürer, *History of the Jewish People*, 2.404-14.

the OT understanding of the afterlife is not resurrection but Sheol, a netherworld characterized by a pale and joyless existence. By Jesus' day, however, there was a prevalent belief in the resurrection, not only among the Pharisees but among a majority of Jews.[37] "Whoever denies the resurrection of the dead has no share in the world to come," declares the Mishnah (*Sanh.* 10:1). This general belief in resurrection seems to have been extrapolated, at least among the rabbis, from the few OT allusions to it, from reason, and from the precedents of Enoch and Elijah, who were believed not to have died. The Sadducees, however, rejected the majority tradition on this issue, as their test of Jesus indicates.

19-23 In order to discredit the idea of resurrection from the dead — as well as Jesus who had spoken of his own resurrection (8:31; 9:31; 10:34) — the Sadducees devise an ingenious stratagem based on the concept of **levirate marriage** (Gen 38:8; Deut 25:5-6).[38] Levirate marriage was a practice whereby a man was obligated to marry a childless widow of his brother in order to preserve the name and memory of his deceased brother and to ensure the establishment of his deceased brother's property inheritance within the family line. The practice is first mentioned with reference to Onan (Gen 38:8-10), who, in order to annihilate the line of his brother, refused to have a child by Tamar, wife of his deceased brother Er. The OT boasts of two women, Tamar (Genesis 38) and Ruth (Ruth 3–4), who actually violated prescribed sexual morality to ensure the preservation of their genealogy through levirate marriage. In the Apocrypha, the book of Tobit tells the story of a woman who married seven men and remained childless (3:7-15) — a story that may have inspired the fantastic plot proposed by the Sadducees to Jesus.[39] The custom of levirate marriage was not devised (as were, e.g., polygamy and concubinage) for the expressed purpose of allowing a man to have more than one wife, nor to condone sexual promiscuity or immorality. Levirate marriage was, rather, a compensatory social custom designed to prevent intermarriage of Jews and Gentiles and to preserve honor and property within a family line in cases where a woman's husband was deceased.[40]

37. See O. Schwankl, *Die Sadduzäerfrage (Mk 12,18-27 parr): Eine exegetisch-theologische Studie zur Auferstehungserwartung*, BBB 66 (Frankfurt am Main: Athenäum, 1987), chap. 3.

38. 12:19 appears to be a paraphrase or conflation of both Gen 38:3 and Deut 25:5-6, rather than a direct quotation from either text, in either the MT or the LXX.

39. The book of Tobit may have inspired the Sadducees' story, although in Tobit the seven husbands were not brothers, and each was killed by the wicked demon Asmodeus before the marriage was consummated.

40. Str-B 1.885-97. Further, see S. B. Frost, "The Memorial of the Childless Man," *Int* 26 (1972): 437-50.

The Sadducees' question is a brilliant artifice designed to explode what they consider the superstition of life after death. In the minds of the Sadducees, simple wit and common sense are sufficient to reduce the idea of the resurrection to an absurdity. Their question is framed on the Pharisaic and rabbinic assumption that the world to come is essentially an extension of earthly conditions, including the married state, although under more glorious conditions.[41] The question of the Sadducees is based on the assumption of monogamy rather than polygamy as the marriage ideal. The impossibility of a woman's being married to seven men in heaven intends in their minds to render the whole concept of resurrection ridiculous. If Jesus were to accept the assumption that the life to come stands in unbroken continuity with the present, he would either have to argue on technical grounds, perhaps, that the first husband had rights to the woman in heaven, or concede to the Sadducees.

24-25 But Jesus does neither, nor does he follow their logic. Demonstrating the authority about which he was earlier questioned (11:27-33), he takes an independent and sovereign tack, addressing the question of resurrection first according to *manner,* and then to *fact.* As to *manner,* Jesus declares the Sadducees "'in error because you do not know the Scriptures or the power of God.'" The Greek word for "error," *planan* (from which "planet" is derived), means "to wander off track" or "to be led astray." The audacity of Jesus' accusation of the Sadducees would be like claiming that Wall Street knows nothing of finance! Scripture (the Torah) and power (the Sanhedrin) were precisely the Sadducees' stock-in-trade, the two matters in which they majored. In magisterial authority, Jesus asserts that what the Sadducees claim to know best they in fact know least. They are vulnerable not at their weak points but at their strong points. They have gone astray not at the periphery or in the incidentals of their belief system but at the heart and center of their beliefs.

The resurrected life is not a prolonged earthly life but life in an entirely new dimension (1 Cor 15:40-44). Earthly conditions and conventions must yield to heavenly, where "'they will neither marry nor be given in marriage.'" In this pronouncement Jesus cuts against the grain

---

41. The textual condition of the beginning of v. 23 is most uncertain. The reading of the NIV ("'At the resurrection whose wife will she be . . . ?'") reflects the best manuscript witnesses (א B C L Δ Ψ; and C D W with the addition of "therefore"). Other witnesses, however, read, "'At the resurrection, *whenever they are raised,* whose wife will she be . . .'"; A K Π Θ). Despite the poorer manuscript support, the longer redundant reading may well be original, based on the fact that (1) it accords with Mark's style (cf. 13:19), (2) the phrase *whenever they are raised* is not needed and hence would not be added by a scribe, and (3) its omission by copyists can be explained as an effort to eliminate the redundancy. See Metzger, *TCGNT,* 110-11.

of the majority opinion among Jews of his day, who affirmed that married life characterized the resurrected state.[42] For Jesus the taxonomy of earthly realities is insufficient to explain the life to come; an entirely new category, "'like the angels in heaven,'" is necessary to fathom resurrected existence. The idea that resurrected existence would be angelic in nature was not unknown in the first century (*1 Enoch* 15:4; *2 Apoc. Bar.* 51:10). Interestingly, the categories of v. 25 — marital existence and angelic existence — repeat those of Gen 6:1-2, in which the "sons of God" condescended to take human wives.[43] But in v. 25 the order is reversed: whereas Gen 6:1-2 appears to signify for the author of Genesis that the effects of the fall extended even to heaven, Jesus' use of the same categories in v. 25 signify the full redemption of the fallen order, in both its earthly and heavenly manifestations, and the full realization of glorified heavenly existence. God's power to create and restore life bursts the limits of both logic and imagination. The glorious realities of the life to come can no more be accommodated to the pedestrian routines of earthly life than can butterflies be compared to caterpillars. Present earthly experience is entirely insufficient to forecast divine heavenly realities: we can no more imagine heavenly existence than an infant *in utero* can imagine a Beethoven piano concerto or the Grand Canyon at sunset.

26-27 In 12:26-27 Jesus speaks to the *fact* of the resurrection. The method of debate recorded in these two verses reflects vintage rabbinic practice. This reminds us that Jesus' rhetorical repertoire included rabbinic techniques as well as his better-known parables and aphorisms. To evince that resurrection from the death is taught — or at least assumed — in the Torah, Jesus quotes Exod 3:6, which falls *within* the Torah accepted by the Sadducees. "'I am the God of Abraham, the God of Isaac, and the God of Jacob.'" The point of his citing God's declaration to Moses at the burning bush may not at first be apparent or compelling to readers unaccustomed to rabbinic debates. Jesus, who accepted as axiomatic that the patriarchs and prophets were still alive (Matt 8:11; Luke 16:22-25; John 8:56), argues that the promises of God are made not to the dead but to the

42. See Str-B 1.887-89. As far as we know, only one passage from the rabbinic era (Midrash to Psalm 146) argues that sexual intercourse is forbidden in the world to come. Otherwise, on the basis of Ezekiel 37, the rabbis argued for the continuation of earthly circumstances and conditions in the resurrected state, including marriage and sexual intercourse in it.

43. This likeness is even clearer in Luke 20:35-36, where the angels are called *huioi theou* ("sons of God"), as they are in Gen. 6:2. Justin Martyr's quotation of this passage in *Dial. Trypho* 81.4 follows Luke's text. *1 Enoch* 15:7 (and perhaps also *The Pseudo-Titus Epistle* [*NTApoc* 2.55-56, 62-63]) appears to have Gen 6:1-2 in mind when God rebukes the Watchers thus: "'I did not make wives for you, for the dwelling of the spiritual beings of heaven is heaven'" (*OTP* 1.21).

living. If Abraham, Isaac, and Jacob are dead, as the Sadducees believe, then God's promise to them was limited to the duration of their earthly lives, which renders his promises finite and unfulfilled. God's word, however, cannot be bound; it is not an epitaph of human limitations but a promise of divine potential. God would not pledge himself to the dead unless the dead were raised to life. Jesus' argument for the reality of resurrection is based on the assumption that the call of God establishes a relationship with God, and once a relationship with God is established, it bears the promise of God and cannot be ended, even by death. The relationship is the result of the promise and power of God that conquers the last enemy, death itself.

Jesus concludes in 12:27 not only with an affirmation of resurrection but also with a condemnation of the Sadducees' position, "'You are badly mistaken.'" The Greek word for "mistaken" is again *planan*, that is, "'You are way off base.'" If truth is to be asserted, its opposite must be denied. The belief of the Sadducees is contrary to and incompatible with the truth of God, and the only hope of correcting it (if it can be corrected) is not to ignore it but to expose it. The ultimate answer to the Sadducees, however, is not the exegesis or even the authority of Jesus (neither of which they accept), but the *life* of Jesus, for the empty tomb will verify his teaching to the Sadducees (16:6). Jesus does not simply announce the resurrection — he *is* the resurrection (John 11:25).

THE TEST OF THE SCRIBES (12:28-34)

The third group of the Sanhedrin to test Jesus is the scribes. The present question about the greatest commandment does not contain the invective that Jesus otherwise experiences from the scribes; indeed, this is the one story in Mark where a scribe approaches Jesus on amicable terms — and where a scribe is commended by him.[44] The subsequent story about Da-

---

44. W. Grundmann, *Das Evangelium nach Markus,* 335-36, characterizes it as a "Schulgespräch" (lesson) rather than a "Streitgespräch" (controversy). He views Mark's account as irenic, and Matt 22:34-40 and Luke 10:25-28 as polemic, attributing the latter to a later stage of tradition after opposition between synagogue and church hardened. Grundmann exaggerates the differences between Mark and the other two Synoptists, however, for apart from *peirazein* (Matt 22:35; Luke 10:25), which can mean "test" in a neutral sense rather than "tempt," Matthew and Luke are absent of invective. Nor is the argument about later stages of tradition compelling, for Mark, too, displays significant opposition between Jesus and the scribes; indeed, this is the only friendly encounter between the two in his Gospel.

vid's son (12:35-37), however, and especially the denouncing of the scribes in 12:38-40, resumes the controversy motif, indicating the general opposition of the scribal guild to Jesus.

28 The approach of the scribe comes immediately on the heels of the controversy with the Sadducees, again implying that Jesus is engaged in non-stop challenge and debate in the temple. For the first time since arriving in Jerusalem Jesus is approached by an individual rather than a group. The scribe "came . . . heard . . . [and] saw." His personal interaction with Jesus, including the emphasis in the pericope on "hearing" (Gk. *akouein*; vv. 28, 29, 37), testifies to the scribe's sincerity. His sincerity, in turn, helps to account for his positive encounter with Jesus.

Impressed with Jesus' wisdom in answering the Sadducees, the scribe asks, according to the NIV, "'Of all the commandments, which is the most important?'" This is not an entirely accurate translation, however, for according to the Greek text the word "all" (Gk. *pantōn*, either masculine or neuter, genitive plural) does not modify "commandments" (Gk. *entolē*, feminine). The sense of the question is thus not which is the most important commandment, but rather which commandment supersedes *everything* and is incumbent on all humanity — including Gentiles.[45]

The scribes concerned themselves with proper exposition of the law and earned a reputation as experts in its interpretation (see further on the scribes at 1:22). The rabbinic tradition counted 613 commandments in the Torah, 365 prohibitions, and 248 positive commands. Among the commandments, rabbis differentiated between what they called "heavy" and "light" commandments. The latter made less demand on one's will or possessions, whereas heavy or weighty commandments concerned life's uncompromising essentials. Heavy commandments were accorded utmost seriousness and, when broken, were assessed the severest penalties. When Jesus spoke of breaking "one of the least of these commandments" (Matt 5:19), he himself observed the distinction between heavy and light commandments. It was not uncommon to ask reputed teachers, as the scribe does in this instance, to declare themselves on the weightiest of the commandments, or to summarize the Torah in a nutshell. The Mishnah and Talmud preserve a number of answers from famous rabbis to such questions. Twenty years before Jesus, Rabbi Hillel summarized the Torah in a negative version of the Golden Rule: "What you would not want

---

45. See C. I. K. Story, "Marcan Love Commandment: 'The greatest of these is love' (1 Corinthians 13:13)," *Lexington Theological Quarterly* 34/3 (1999): 152, who notes this subtle grammatical distinction and argues, on the basis of 11:15-17 and 12:9, that the question must also include Gentiles.

done to you, do not do to your neighbor. That is the entire Torah, everything else is interpretation." A century after Jesus, in A.D. 135, Rabbi Akiba reduced the Torah to Lev 19:8, "You shall love your neighbor as yourself." A century after Akiba a rabbi quoted Prov 3:6 as the heart of the law, "In all your ways acknowledge God, and he will make your paths straight." Later still in A.D. 260, Rabbi Simlai quoted Hab 2:4, "The righteous will live by his faith."[46]

29-30 Jesus is prepared with his own answer. "'Hear, O Israel, the Lord our God, the Lord is one. Love the Lord your God with all your heart and with all your soul and with all your mind and with all your strength.'" This passage from Deut 6:4-5, known as the *Shema* (Heb. "to hear"), was recited morning and evening by every pious Jews. As a creedal summary it was and is as important to Judaism as is the Lord's Prayer or the Apostles' Creed to Christianity. The *Shema* was the standard by which Josiah, the greatest reformer king in Israel's history, was judged (2 Kgs 23:25). Four times in v. 30 the world "all" is repeated, emphasizing the necessity of a total response of love to the lordship of God. God is the one and only Lord, not only of Israel but of every individual as well. God lays rightful claim to every facet of human personality: heart (= emotions), soul (= spirit), mind (= intelligence), and strength (= will). Each of the four commandments is prefaced by the Greek preposition *ex*, meaning "from the source of," rather than "by means of." Thus, we are commanded to love God not simply *with* our whole heart, but *from* our heart.[47] Both the Hebrew and Greek versions of Deut 6:4-5 describe a threefold response to God — heart, soul, and strength. Mark quotes Jesus adding a fourth response, the love of God with one's whole mind or understanding.[48]

---

46. See Str-B 1.900-908. The custom of asking renowned teachers to declare themselves on seminal commandments was not limited to Jewish rabbis. Questions about what constituted the most virtuous, most beautiful, most difficult, or what produced the greatest good or happiness also abounded in Hellenistic philosophy (see *HCNT*, 129).

47. Story, "Marcan Love Commandment: 'The greatest of these is love' (1 Corinthians 13:13)," *Lexington Theological Quarterly* 34/3 (1999): 155, writes, "In Mark 12:30 the preposition is *ek (ex)*, i.e., 'out of,' occurring four times, indicating *not instrument but source*. Earlier, Jesus has cited the heart as the *source* from which issue all the evils which define a person (Mark 7:21). Now the heart is viewed as the source out of which there may issue the Divinely-inspired love for God."

48. The LXX version of Deut 6:4-5 (according to manuscript B [Vaticanus]) renders the Hebrew word for "heart" *(leb)* by *dianoia* ("mind") rather than by *kardia* ("heart"). The presence of *dianoia*, "mind," in v. 30 may derive from this variant version. If so, this indicates that Mark quotes the *Shema* from a textual tradition represented by the B text of the LXX. But it is also possible that Jesus added a fourth article to the *Shema*, as he earlier added a commandment to the Ten Commandments (10:19). If so, the change from a threefold to fourfold response to God is a further example of Jesus' *exousia*, his sovereign authority, in interpreting the Torah.

31 The scribe asks for only one commandment, but as in the response to the Pharisees and Herodians in the temple earlier (12:17), Jesus goes the second mile in his answer by adding the commandment from Lev 19:18, "'Love your neighbor as yourself.'" In the OT "neighbor" meant only fellow Jews; it did not include non-Israelites and Gentiles. The early Christians, however, clearly believed that Jesus expanded the idea of neighbor. This is evident from Luke 10:25-29, where this saying is prefaced to the parable of the Good Samaritan. For Jesus, the neighbor includes even despised Samaritans![49]

"'There is no commandment greater than these,'" concludes Jesus, thus bringing the commandments to love God and neighbor into a unity. The fact that Jesus adds the commandment from Lev 19:18 to the *Shema* indicates that it takes both commandments to realize the one will of God. The combination of the two commandments has become a commonplace in subsequent Christianity, but it is important to realize the revolutionary achievement of Jesus' answer. Although love of God and love of humanity were occasionally affirmed separately in Israel, there is no evidence that before Jesus they were ever combined.[50] It does not appear that any rabbi before Jesus regarded love of God and neighbor as the center and sum of the law. For Jesus, the requirements of the *Shema* cannot be fulfilled in ritual or sacrifice but in unfeigned love of God, wholly and genuinely. The *Shema* must also be complemented by the love of neighbor. Love of neighbor, moreover, is the chief means of loving God, and is received as love of God; likewise, love of God expresses itself in love of neighbor (1 John 4:20). Jesus' answer avoids the danger of mysticism, which results in a detached and disembodied love of God; as well as the danger of humanism, which acts toward humanity without reference to God and without the understanding that human beings are inviolable creatures of God.

At the same time, the two commandments are not blended into a compromising hybrid. The order in which Jesus declares the commandments implies that love of God is prerequisite to loving one's neighbor.

---

49. Not uncommonly Lev 19:18 is quoted as a rationale for self-esteem or self-love, i.e., "Love your neighbor *as yourself*." It is questionable, however, whether such an interpretation was intended either by Leviticus or by Jesus. In all the Bible there is no command to self-love. The Bible takes for granted that human beings *do* love themselves, i.e., they habitually act in their best interest. The command to love one's neighbor takes the concern that humans naturally exhibit toward themselves and commands them to extend it to *others* as well.

50. For example, love of God is commanded in *T. Iss.* 7:6; *T. Dan* 5:3; and love of neighbor in *T. Zeb.* 5:1-2; *T. Benj.* 3:3; Philo, *Spec. Leg.* 2.62-63; but in none of the passages are the two combined.

The Greek word for "love" in vv. 30-31 is *agapan*, which in the NT is the form of love characteristic of God (1 John 4:7; 1 Corinthians 13). Whoever does not find the source of love in God will fail to exhibit God's unique love to one's neighbor. Love of God is prior to love of neighbor and establishes its possibility. For Jesus, love fulfills the law: love *for* God releases the love *of* God. "Dear friends, since God so loved us, we also ought to love one another. . . . We love because he first loved us. If anyone says, 'I love God,' yet hates his brother, he is a liar" (1 John 4:11, 19-20).[51]

32-33 The scribe is as pleased with this answer as he was with Jesus' earlier answer to the Sadducees. In both instances (vv. 28, 32) he says, according to the Greek, *kalōs*, "'Well said!'" We might expect of the scribe, who was associated with the Sanhedrin and temple, an endorsement of the superiority of priestly sacrifices to all other forms of worship. But not so. The scribe's rejoinder to Jesus reflects a collage of OT texts (Deut 4:35; 6:4; Lev 19:18; 1 Sam 15:22; Isa 45:21; Hos 6:6). His knowledge of Scripture, which is considerable, is not surprising for a scribe. He agrees with Jesus that "burnt offerings and sacrifices" must yield to a right relationship with God and a moral relationship with others. The offerings referred to were the kind that were consumed by fire rather than eaten by worshipers, which meant they were dedicated solely and wholly to God. Even the most sacred duties, in other words, may not take precedent over *agapē* love — and they have no meaning unless they are expressions of it.

The exchange between Jesus and the scribe in this pericope is an important reminder, perhaps even corrective, to Christian misreadings of Jesus and Judaism. Not uncommonly, Christian readers mistakenly assume that Jesus and "the Pharisees" or "the Jews" were without exception locked in intractable opposition at every point, and that Jesus categorically rejected everything Jewish. There is also a small but vocal group of academic scholars who promote the view that Jesus was more like a wandering Cynic iconoclast than a Jewish rabbi, that his message of protest was the essential element of his ministry and that his Judaism was largely incidental. This story, however, along with others,[52] reminds us that Jesus found within the traditional confessional elements of the Torah the dis-

---

51. That the early church learned Jesus' summary of the law is well attested (Matt 25:31-46; Rom 13:8-10; Gal 5:14; Jas 2:8; *2 Clem.* 3:4; *Did.* 1:2; 2:7; *Gospel of Thomas* 25). On Jesus' summary of the law, see Grundmann, *Das Evangelium nach Markus,* 338.

52. Jesus orders the healed leper to show himself to the priest and observe the Jewish rite of cleansing, 1:44; Jesus attends and teaches in synagogues, 1:22; he reinterprets the Torah, but does not abrogate it, 2:27-28; 7:1-23; 10:2-12; he selects twelve disciples in correspondence to the twelve tribes of Israel, 3:13-19; he celebrates Passover in Jerusalem, 14:1; and he locates his essential teaching about God (12:28-34) and himself (12:35-37) within the categories of Jewish Scripture.

tinguishing canons of his own belief and ministry. It further reminds us that Jesus and his Jewish interlocutor — and surely not this scribe alone — found themselves in substantial agreement on the sum and purpose of the law.[53]

34 The encounter closes on a note of irony: the scribe ostensibly has come to pass judgment on Jesus, but it is Jesus who passes judgment on the scribe. The scribe is equipped and authorized to pass judgment on the law, but Jesus possesses a higher authority. In yet another display of sovereign authority, Jesus declares, "'You are not far from the kingdom of God.'" That is a striking remark because the subject of conversation has been the Torah, not the kingdom of God or eternal life. It is hard to imagine an ordinary scribe or rabbi presuming to pronounce judgment on such a matter. The scribe can judge whether or not one is faithful to the Torah; but Jesus, who affirms the essence of the Torah, also supersedes the Torah — as he supersedes every creedal confession and formulation. One draws near to the kingdom of God not by proper theology but by drawing near to Jesus. Jesus exhibits his filial and messianic authority in declaring who is on the threshold of the kingdom of God, which is present not in the Torah but in himself.

THE QUESTION OF THE DAY (12:35-37)

The preceding story ended with the note that "from then on no one dared ask [Jesus] any more questions" (12:34). The wording of v. 34 (particularly in Greek) is strong and unequivocal, signifying that Jesus has prevailed over challenges from the Sanhedrin (11:27-33) and its various constituencies — the Pharisees (12:13-17), Sadducees (12:18-27), and scribes (12:28-34). Jesus has bested the field and debate is closed. Jesus does not quit the field, however, but he takes it. The meaning of his person and the kingdom he proclaims cannot be understood by mere responses to human interrogation — especially when the interrogation is antagonistic. The questions and categories of the Sanhedrin, the supreme authority in Judaism, are not sufficient to reveal and encompass Jesus. And if theirs are not sufficient, no human agenda is sufficient to reveal or obscure, to prove or disprove, the meaning of Jesus. He earlier declared that new wine cannot be poured into old wineskins (2:22). It is now his turn to set the agenda, to determine both wine and wineskins. According to Mark's chronology, the above encounters have occurred on

---

53. M. Hooker, *The Gospel According to Saint Mark,* 289.

a single day. "After a day of questions comes the question of the day," says Ralph Martin.[54]

35 "While Jesus was teaching in the temple courts, he asked, 'How is it that the teachers of the law say that the Christ is the son of David?'" Two things are significant about this question. First, it is set in the temple (the Greek says simply "temple," not "temple courts"). The temple is the religious center of Israel and the seat of the Sanhedrin's authority. Here, where policy is determined and executed, Jesus chooses to test conventional understandings of Messiahship by the larger categories of "Lord" and "Son." Second, the question is posed to the scribes (NIV, "teachers of the law"), the intellectual and religious elite of Judaism. The setting and subject thus recall the parable of the vineyard (12:1-12), in which Jesus also spoke of the Son of God in relation to Israel's rulers.[55] The issue about *identity* that Jesus raised privately with the disciples on the road to Caesarea Philippi (8:27) is now raised publicly in the temple of Jerusalem.

Jesus asks the scribes about their understanding of the Messiah (on Messiah/Christ, see at 1:1; 8:29). He does so by citing Psalm 110, in which he invites the temple audience to reconsider whether "**Son of David**" (see at 10:47) is conceptually adequate to explain the Messiah (see also on the term at 10:47). As early as 2 Sam 7:12 the hope of a Davidic deliverer arose in Israel (see also Isaiah 9, 11; Jer 30:9; Ezek 34:23). The earliest expressed correlation of "son of David" with Messiah, however, does not occur in Jewish literature until *Pss. Sol.* 17:21, which was produced about a century before Jesus: "O Lord, raise up their king, the son of David, that he may reign over Israel thy servant." The idea of a Davidic Messiah was thoroughly current by Jesus' day, as is evidenced by the "Eighteen Benedictions," which formed a standard part of the religious vernacular of the synagogue, "Have mercy, Lord our God, over the kingdom of the house of David, the Messiah of your righteousness" (Ben. 14). That Son of David and Messiah were correlated in the first century is strongly suggested by the fact that every early Christian writer who mentions Psalm 110 interprets it messianically.[56] Jesus' question in v. 36 indeed rests on such an

---

54. *Where the Action Is* (Glendale: Regal Books, 1977), 106.

55. Both Matt 22:41-46 and Luke 20:41-44 omit reference to the temple and scribes. Mark's mention of both accentuates Jesus' authority vis-à-vis Judaism.

56. Not surprisingly, in the centuries after Jesus rabbinic literature avoided correlating "Son of David" and "Messiah." The fact that Psalm 110 was interpreted messianically in the first century A.D., then nonmessianically for nearly two centuries (usually with reference to Abraham rather than to David), and only afterward again messianically, is to be explained by the fact that the Jewish rabbis, in their struggle with emergent Christianity, denied messianic associations of "Son of David" in hopes of undercutting proof texts for Jesus as the Christ. Only after A.D. 250, when the rift between

assumption. Although Jesus and the early church did not accept the military-political connotations normally associated with Messiah, early Christianity certainly affirmed that the Messiah would come from the "house" (Luke 1:69) or "throne" (Luke 1:32) or "seed" (Rom 1:3; 2 Tim 2:8) of David.

36-37 As in the previous questions about the resurrection (12:26-27) and the great commandment (12:28-34), Jesus' question to the scribe again echoes rabbinic exegetical traits. He prefaces the quotation, saying, "'David himself, speaking by the Holy Spirit, declared'" (see 2 Sam 23:2). That is a direct allusion to the divine inspiration of the following quotation.[57] The effect of the preface is to convince his hearers that the proof-text — and the point he draws from it — bears the weight of divine revelation.

The quotation in v. 36 is from Psalm 110, the most frequently quoted OT text in the NT.[58] The point, which hinges on a twist in wording, may escape us without further explanation. The crux is the first line, "'The LORD said to my Lord. . . .'" Psalm 110 was originally a coronation hymn that would have been sung, chanted, or recited at the inauguration of the kings of Judah and Israel. The opening line in Hebrew reads "'The LORD (*Yahweh*) declared to my lord (*adonai*).'" The first Lord refers to God and the second to the king; that is, at his coronation the king of Israel was inducted as God's vicegerent and seated symbolically at God's right hand. The right hand signified honor and closeness to God, and legitimacy to rule with dominion and justice. The Psalm thus originally referred to God and the king of Israel. With the destruction of the monarchy in 586 B.C., Psalm 110 was reappropriated, with the rights of the king frequently being transferred to the Messiah, whose kingdom would not fail as had the Davidic monarchy. It was this subsequent interpretation that is reflected in Jesus' quotation of Ps 110:1 and question in v. 36, where the first Lord refers to God and the second to the Messiah. A comparison of the two interpretations of the Psalm may arouse suspicion or skepticism in us today that the interpretation assumed by Jesus is less valid than its original sense, or even bogus. It surely cannot have seemed so to Jesus. It is more probable that in his day the true and ultimate meaning of Psalm 110 was understood with reference to God and the Messiah, of whom the earthly Israelite monarchy had been a shadow or preparation. Thus, to return to

---

synagogue and church was irreconcilable, did Jewish rabbis again entertain messianic interpretations of Psalm 110. See Str-B 4.452-58.

57. Str-B 1.909.

58. Psalm 110 is quoted or alluded to thirty-three times in the NT, and an additional seven times in early Christian authors. See D. M. Hay, *Glory at the Right Hand: Psalm 110 in Early Christianity* (Nashville/New York: Abingdon Press, 1973), 15, 45-47.

the implication of the Psalm in Jesus' question, if David, who was believed to be the author of the Psalm, said, "'The LORD [= God] said to my Lord [= Messiah]: Sit at my right hand until I put your enemies under your feet,'"[59] then the Messiah is obviously superior to David, and not merely a descendant, as Judaism popularly held.

In Jesus' preceding argument with the Sadducees (12:18-27) he asserted that the resurrection is not simply an extension of earthly existence; here in the question about David's son he argues that the Messiah is not simply an extension of his Davidic precursor. The Messiah will indeed be a recognized descendant of David, but he will surpass David's lineage. "Son of David" may assert certain truths about the Messiah, but it falls short in essential ways of capturing his identity.[60] The quotation from Psalm 110 is used here, as it was later used throughout Christian writings, ultimately not as a description of Jesus' purpose and work, but as a description of his transcendent *status*, sitting at God's honored and authoritative right.[61] That is signaled in Jesus' final cinching question, "'How then can [Messiah] be [David's] son?'" It is the same question Mark poses to his readers. The answer, of course, is that the Messiah is not simply David's son; he is God's Son.[62]

---

59. Mark's quotation of Ps 110:1 follows the LXX verbatim (which in turn renders the MT accurately), with the exception of *hypokatō* ("under"; so B D W Ψ) as opposed to *hypopodion* ("a footstool"; so א A K L X Δ Θ Π). Arguments in favor of the latter reading are (1) stronger manuscript support, and (2) the fact that the quotation otherwise follows the LXX verbatim. Arguments in favor of the first reading are (1) that a scribe would be more likely to replace an alien word in a quotation (*hypokatō*) with the original word in the quotation (*hypopodion*), and (2) in repeating the quotation from memory an "under" seems demanded by the context. The arguments favoring "under" are stronger than those favoring "a footstool" and may suggest that Mark (and Matt 22:44) preserved an oral version of the quotation.

60. Interpretations of this passage often fall prey to an argumental fallacy, i.e., that disproving one point in an argument falsifies an entire argument. Both A. Schlatter (*Die Evangelien nach Markus und Lukas,* 128) and T. W. Manson (*The Teaching of Jesus* [Cambridge: Cambridge University Press, 1963], 266-67) assert that because Jesus questioned the adequacy of the Davidic lineage to explain the concept of Messiah he denied the Davidic lineage altogether. This is not only unwarranted, but it creates a false opposition between Jesus and Israel. Jesus raises the issue of "Son of David" and "Messiah" not to pose a contrast but to argue that a point of derivation (from David) does not fully account for the concept of Messiah. While affirming that the Messiah comes from David, Jesus further maintains that the Messiah surpasses David (so Rom 1:3; 2 Tim 2:8).

61. Hay, *Glory at the Right Hand: Psalm 110 in Early Christianity,* 155.

62. See Kingsbury, *The Christology of Mark's Gospel,* 108-14; and Marcus, *The Way of the Lord: Christological Exegesis of the Old Testament in the Gospel of Mark,* 139-45. Marcus sees in vv. 35-37 a "very lofty picture of Markan christology; Jesus, as a result of his exaltation to God's right hand, seemingly attains a status close to that of God himself." The divine Sonship of Jesus versus his Davidic sonship is supremely manifested in *Barn.*

A WIDOW'S TWO CENTS' WORTH (12:38-44)

In the final episode of Jesus' public teaching ministry, Mark sets the religious pretense of the scribes (vv. 38-44) and the humble faith of a widow (vv. 41-44) in acid contrast. The widow's offering, despite its ostensible insignificance, is for Mark the most fitting response to the subterfuge of the Sanhedrin, for rather than seeking Jesus' life (12:12), she gives her whole life (v. 44).

38-41 Jesus is again teaching in the temple. He observes two types of people: one group is the scribes, commanding and ostentatious; the other is "one poor widow," to translate the Greek of 12:44 literally. Mark records only a snippet of Jesus' (and the early church's) opposition to the scribes (see fuller treatments in Matthew 23; Acts 7:51-53). Mark's brief exposé, however, reveals the scribal penchant for pretense and even rapacity. The scribes (see at 1:22) commanded unrivaled authority in first-century Palestine. Their "flowing robes" were full-length prayer shawls with tassels attached to the four corners, in contrast to the colorful common Jewish dress. Made of wool or linen, these blanket-like mantles, known as *tallits*, distinguished rabbis and scholars as men of wealth and eminence. "The most important seats in the synagogues" refers to the benches along the walls of the synagogues, and especially to the dais at the front of the synagogue, which *faced* the congregation seated on the floor in the middle of the synagogue. These "first seats," as they were called in Greek, were reserved for teachers and persons of rank, and afforded the best position from which to address the congregation. When a scribe walked down the street or passed through a marketplace, everyone (with the exception of laborers) was expected to rise before him. Such position and privilege fostered the desire to make an impression, "to be greeted in the marketplaces . . . and have places of honor at banquets."

In what respect, however, did scribes "devour widows' houses"?[63]

12:10: "See again Jesus, not as son of man, but as Son of God, but manifested in a type in the flesh. Since therefore they are going to say that the Christ is David's son, David himself prophesies, fearing and understanding the error of the sinners, 'The LORD said to my Lord, sit thou on my right hand until I make thy enemies thy footstool.'"

63. Manuscripts D and W add "widows *and orphans*," but the addition of orphans looks like a scribal expansion reflecting the concern for widows and orphans in both Israel (e.g., Exod 22:22; Deut 14:29; Isa 10:2) and early Christianity (Jas 1:27). Had the words been original, there is no reason why they would have been omitted. G. Schwarz, "Die Häuser der Witwen verzehren"? (Markus 12,40/Lk 20,47)," *BN* 88 (1997): 45-46, suggests that "devouring widows' houses" is a Greek mistranslation of an original Aramaic saying which was a euphemism for "sleeping with widows" — i.e., the scribes are being condemned for sexuality immorality rather than for greed. Schwarz's evidence is suggestive rather than conclusive, for (1) doubt necessarily remains about the recon-

Josephus (*Ant.* 18.81-84) tells of a Jewish scoundrel exiled to Rome who affected the ways of a scribe ("he played the part of an interpreter of the Mosaic law and its wisdom") and succeeded in persuading a high-standing woman named Fulvia to make substantial gifts to the temple in Jerusalem. The bequests, however, were embezzled, and Rome — from Emperor Tiberius on to plebs in the street — was outraged. Such incidents may lie behind the charge of "devour[ing] widows' houses." The prophets had railed against "making widows their prey and robbing the fatherless" (Isa 10:2; also Amos 2; Micah 3). The reference to "devour[ing] widows' houses" would have given Mark's Roman readers, to whom the Fulvia scandal was a recent memory, a special frame of reference for the rapacity of the scribes. Unlike the Sadducees, for example, the scribes were not as a rule wealthy. They were largely dependent on gifts of worshipers and benefactors for their livelihood. Then as now, some persons exploited the esteem in which they were held to abuse the generosity shown to them by others.

The judgment of Jesus on those who practice religion for the purpose of self-advancement is blunt and stern: they "'will be severely punished.'" Jesus has immediately before defined the lifeblood of genuine religion to be *love* of God and neighbor (12:29-31). The totality of the law that Jesus summarized in Lev 19:18 is a commandment to help others. Some people, however, harm others rather than help them. The worst of these use religion as both a means and justification of their harm. Trafficking in piety for the purposes of self and greed incurs from Jesus an even sterner rebuke than his rebuke of hypocrisy in 7:1-23.[64] Religious pride and injury of others in the name of religion will be assessed, to quote the Greek literally, "abundant judgment."

41-44 The scene now shifts to the temple treasury, where Jesus observes the crowd.[65] The crowd has played a slightly more positive role in Jerusalem than it did in Galilee, where it often prevented people from ap-

---

structed Aramaic, (2) to show that words *can* carry a euphemistic sense does not mean that they always *do,* and (3) it is doubtful that Mark, a native of Jerusalem (Acts 12:12), would misunderstand such a saying.

64. One recalls Bunyan's exposé of such religiosity in *Pilgrim's Progress*. Mr. By-Ends, a fair-weather Christian, asks if a minister should not use his position "to get the good blessings of this life." Mr. Money-Love readily agrees that it is not only permissible but a *virtue* to use religion to cash in on all possible benefits. Christian condemns such sham piety: "whoever takes up religion for the world will throw religion away for the world" (John Bunyan, *The Pilgrim's Progress* [New York: Signet, 1964], 93-99).

65. Among a plethora of minor textual variations related to Jesus sitting opposite the temple treasury, two manuscripts (W Θ) have him "*standing* opposite the temple treasury," evidently to heighten the reverence of his position, in accordance with the Jewish custom of standing for prayer. The textual evidence for his sitting is far superior.

proaching Jesus. In Jerusalem the crowd has delighted in Jesus' teaching (11:18; 12:37), and its sympathy for Jesus has forced the Sanhedrin to temper the expression of its antagonism (11:32; 12:12). Even in the temple "the crowd [was] putting their money into the temple treasury. Many rich people threw in large amounts."

In addition to worship, one of the most important functions of the **temple** in Jerusalem was as a depository for and the administration of vast amounts of wealth. In this respect the Jewish temple was no different from other temples in the ancient world. Unlike the other tribes of Israel, the tribe of Levi possessed no land. In place of land, the Levites were responsible for superintending the temple, which accrued great quantities of wealth in the form of dues, taxes, and donations of valuable objects and money (2 Kgs 12:4). The vessels used for sacrificial worship were required by the Torah to be made of gold or silver. In addition, there were stocks of priceless curtains and priestly garments, and virtual warehouses of flour, oil, grain, wine, incense, and other valuable products. The temple could and also did function as a repository of the wealth of individuals who deposited money there in the belief that a sacred place was a safe place. Given the financial resources and treasures of the temple, it is not surprising that the officer in charge of its administration, the *gazophylax*, was, according to Josephus, second in importance only to the chief priest.[66]

The "temple treasury" of 12:41 was located in the Court of the Women, the first enclosure of the sanctuary in which Jewish women and children were allowed to worship (Josephus, *Ant.* 19.294). The Mishnah (*m. Sheq.* 6:5) reports that there were thirteen Shofar-chests in the temple, each dedicated to a special offering.[67] These trumpetlike receptacles were, as their name suggests, shaped like a Shofar or ram's horn, and positioned with the tapered end upward in order to prevent theft. Into one of these receptacles (perhaps one of the latter designated for freewill offerings) "a poor widow" deposits "two lepta" (v. 42), the smallest coinage in circulation.[68] The NIV glosses over the fact that Mark converts the sum into the equivalent of a Roman coin, a *quadrans*, for the benefit of his Roman readers. Jesus could have known the amount of the woman's offering in various ways. In cases where a contribution was rendered for

66. On the temple treasury, see Schürer, *History of the Jewish People*, 2.279-87.

67. New Shekel dues, Old Shekel dues, Bird-offerings, Young birds for the whole offering, Wood, Frankincense, Gold for the Mercy-seat, and the remaining six were for Freewill-offerings (*m. Sheq.* 6:5). On the particular purposes of each offering, see Str-B 2.38-40.

68. A denarius was the standard wage for a day's labor (Matt 20:8-10); a lepton was 1/64th of a denarius.

priestly service, the attending priest examined the currency for genuineness, inquired of the purpose of the gift, and verified that the contribution corresponded to the prescribed sacrifice. The priest then directed the worshiper to deposit the amount in the appropriate receptacle. All this was spoken aloud and would have been audible to bystanders. If, however, the gift were a simple freewill offering, perhaps the appearance of the woman betrayed her poverty, or, more likely, the sound of the coin in the treasure chest tolled the size of her gift.[69]

Mark's description of the scene accentuates the poverty and insignificance of the widow and her gift. The scribes are ostentatious and prepossessing, and the crowds are rich and extravagant; but by contrast this "one poor widow" contributes two of the smallest coins in circulation.[70] In purely financial terms, the value of her offering is negligible — and unworthy of compare to the sums of the wealthy donors. But in the divine exchange rate things look differently. That which made no difference in the books of the temple is immortalized in the Book of Life. Jesus prefaces his pronouncement on the widow's gift with solemn authority: He "summoned" (Gk. *proskaleesthai*) the disciples, saying "'I tell you the truth'" (Gk. *Amēn legō hymin*, v. 43), this poor widow has put more into the treasury than all the others, for they gave out of their wealth; but she, out of her poverty, put in everything — all she had to live on.'"[71] How powerfully ironic is the word "more" in Mark's description. Everything about this woman has been described in terms of *less*, particularly in comparison to the scribes and wealthy crowd. And yet, the contrast between her genuine piety and faith and the pretense of the wealthy is beyond compare.

For Jesus, the value of a gift is not the amount given, but the cost to the giver. That point will be repeated in the story of the woman in 14:3-9 who gives an extravagant gift of perfume: the value of her gift is light-years greater than the two lepta of the poor widow here; yet, remarkably, each is equally praised by Jesus for doing what they could. Their generos-

---

69. For a discussion of temple offerings, see Str-B 2.37-46. Some commentators suggest that the widow's offering was originally a parable of Jesus, following *Lev. Rab.* 3:5: "A woman once brought a handful of flour for an offering. The priest rejected the offering and said, 'Look what this woman brings! How can such an offering qualify as a sacrifice or provide a priest enough to live on?' Then the priest was warned in a dream, 'Do not despise her, for she is like a person who has sacrificed her whole life'" (cited in Str-B 2.46). The likeness notwithstanding, there is no further evidence that the widow's offering was originally a parable.

70. On the contrast between the scribes and the widow, see G. Smith, "A Closer Look at the Widow's Offering: Mark 12:41-44," *JETS* 40 (1997): 30-31.

71. Compare the saying of Rabbi Jonathan, "He that fulfills the Law in poverty shall in the end fulfill it in wealth; and he that neglects the Law in wealth shall in the end neglect it in poverty" (*m. Avot* 4:9).

ity and sacrifice, if not their respective amounts, are the same.[72] In the temple, others gave what they could spare, but the poor widow spared nothing. Others gave from their surplus, but she gave from her need, "'all she had to live on.'"

The nameless widow concludes Mark's account of Jesus' public ministry. The sacrifice of "'all she had'" is the keystone in Mark's arch of faith. The initial call of Jesus to the fishermen beside the sea to leave all and "'Come, follow me'" (1:17) is perfectly fulfilled in the giving of two simple lepta, which symbolize an undivided heart. This widow's selfless act is not showcased primarily for its moral value, exposing the gulf between her humble piety and the pretense of the scribes, or to unmask tests and traps of the Sanhedrin, although it does that.[73] Rather, as v. 43 reveals ("Summoning *his disciples*"), the chief purpose of the widow is as a model of discipleship. No gift, whether of money, time, or talent, is too insignificant to give, if it is given to God. And what is truly given to God, regardless how small and insignificant, is transformed into a pearl of great price. What may look like a great gift, conversely, may in reality be little in comparison with what one *could* give. The widow's giving "'all she had'" is a true fulfillment of the call to discipleship to follow Jesus by losing one's life (8:35). The final Greek words of the chapter might be paraphrased, "she lay down her whole life." That is what Jesus will do on Golgotha.

---

72. See Hooker, *The Gospel According to Saint Mark*, 296.

73. Examples can be found in both Judaism (see n. 71 above) and Hellenism praising the piety of the poor over that of the rich. Euripides writes: "Often I see that poor people are more wise than the rich, and with their own hands offer small gifts to the gods and [one sees in them] more piety than those who bring oxen to sacrifice" (*Danae Fragment* 329; cited in *HCNT*, 178). For further examples, see E. Klostermann, *Das Markusevangelium*, 130).

CHAPTER THIRTEEN

Watchfulness in Tribulation and Triumph

MARK 13:1-37

Chapter 13 is the longest block of teaching in the Gospel of Mark. It is cast in the form of a final discourse of Jesus, not unlike the farewell discourses of major biblical figures such as Jacob (Genesis 49), Moses (Deuteronomy 32–33), Joshua (Joshua 23), Samuel (1 Samuel 12), and Paul (Acts 20:17ff.). The subject is eschatology, in which future events, including some as distant as the coming of the Son of Man in final judgment, are prefigured by the destruction of the temple and the fall of Jerusalem. Like chap. 4, chap. 13 is a collection of Jesus' teachings and sayings from various occasions that have been gathered by Mark into the present chapter. This is evident from the fact that some of the teachings preserved in Mark 13 appear in entirely different contexts in other Gospels.[1] The absence of the original contexts of the various sayings and their indefiniteness combine to make this one of the most perplexing chapters in the Bible to understand, for readers and interpreters alike.[2]

---

1. Matthew places the material in Mark 13:9-13 about bearing witness before rulers not at the end of Jesus' ministry but at the beginning, as instructions to the Twelve on their inaugural mission trip (Matt 10:17-22). Luke preserves a portion of the same material in yet a third context (Luke 12:11-12).

2. Major studies of Mark 13 include C. E. B. Cranfield, "St Mark 13," *SJT* 6 (1953): 189-96, 287-303; 7 (1954): 284-303; G. R. Beasley-Murray, *Jesus and the Future* (London: Macmillan, 1954); L. Hartman, *Prophecy Interpreted: The Formation of Some Jewish Apocalyptic Texts and of the Eschatological Discourse Mark 13 par.*, ConBNT 1 (Lund: C. W. K. Gleerup, 1966); R. Pesch, *Naherwartungen. Tradition und Redaktion in Mk 13* (Düsseldorf: Patmos-Verlag, 1968); D. Wenham, *The Rediscovery of Jesus' Eschatological Discourse*, Gospel Perspectives 4 (Sheffield: JSOT Press, 1984); and T. J. Geddert, *Watchwords: Mark 13 in*

The most important hermeneutical key to the chapter is the placement of the discourse at the conclusion of the temple material in Mark 11–13.[3] The chapter is introduced by Jesus leaving the temple (v. 1) and going to the Mount of Olives, where, "sitting opposite the temple" (v. 3), he pronounces its destruction. Mark has chosen to set the entire discourse, in other words, in the context of the destruction of the temple. The closest thing approximating a "sign" requested by the disciples (v. 4) is "'the abomination that causes desolation'" in v. 14. Mark flags this event with his most pronounced editorial admonition in the Gospel, "'let the reader understand'" (v. 14), reminding readers that events surrounding the destruction of the temple and fall of Jerusalem are a type and foreshadowing of a final sacrilege before the eschaton. This admonition, as well as the concluding admonitions in the chapter to "watch" (vv. 33-37), indicates that the purpose of the eschatological discourse in Mark 13 is not primarily to provide a timetable or blueprint for the future so much as to exhort readers to faithful discipleship in the present.

Mark 13 is frequently interpreted in relative detachment from the rest of the Gospel, often as an apocalypse. **Apocalyptic**, meaning "unveiling," is a broad and rather ill-defined term for a type, or perhaps theme, of Jewish literature that concerns final events before the end of time, including visions (often in bizarre imagery) of the defeat of chaos and the restoration of creation, and of the coming of the Son of Man to judge the wicked and establish a kingdom of righteousness. Only in limited aspects, however, does Mark 13 resemble apocalyptic (e.g., in the coming of the Son of Man and in references to the end of time). Otherwise, three chief features of Christian apocalyptic are absent: the pairing of this age with the age to come; the pairing of heaven and earth; and the pairing of those who belong to the church and those who do not.[4] Other features characteristic of Jewish apocalyptic are also absent: there are no visions or bizarre imagery, no resurrection, no final judgment and punishment of Satan and his minions, and no description of the idyllic messianic epoch following the Parousia. Mark's style is also uncharacteristic of apocalyp-

---

Markan Eschatology, JSNTSup 26 (Sheffield: JSOT Press, 1989). Beasley-Murray and Pesch offer thorough reviews of the history of interpretation of Mark 13.

3. Mark 13 is linked to the foregoing temple motif by the common admonition to "Watch out" (*blepete;* 12:38; 13:5, 9, 23, 33) and by the parallel statements that Jesus was sitting opposite the treasury (*kathisas katenanti tou gazophylakiou,* 12:41) and sitting opposite the temple (*kathēmenou autou . . . katenanti tou hierou,* 13:3).

4. W. A. Meeks, "Social Functions of Apocalyptic Language in Pauline Christianity," in *Apocalypticism in the Mediterranean World and the Near East: Proceedings of the International Colloquium on Apocalypticism, August 12-17, 1979,* ed. D. Hellholm (Tübingen: Mohr [Siebeck], 1983), 689.

tic. Jewish apocalypses generally relate visions in the first person singular, whereas chap. 13 is woven on the warp of second person plural imperatives. These imperatives are more hortatory than revelatory (as is the purpose of first person apocalyptic narrative), exhorting readers to waiting and watchfulness, in confident trust in the outworking of God's sovereign purpose in history.

Although Mark 13 contains some apocalyptic features, it is not an apocalypse in any ordinary sense of the term. Consequently, the use of "apocalyptic" to characterize the chapter is an obstruction rather than an aid to understanding it.[5] Nor is it an excursus independent of the remainder of the Gospel. It is most reasonably and fruitfully seen as the culmination of Mark's polemic against the temple begun in chap. 11. The events of the future are connected to the fall of the temple by the question of the disciples in 13:4, "'Tell us when these things (Gk. *tauta*) will happen? And what will be the sign that they (Gk. *tauta panta*) are about to be fulfilled?'" In the context of chap. 13, Mark employs "these things" (Gk. *tauta*) or "all these things" (Gk. *tauta panta*) with reference to the destruction of the temple, not to the end of the age. (Translations of the Greek terms vary in the NIV and English translations.) The scheme begins in 13:2 with Jesus declaring the destruction of "these" (Gk. *tautas*) great temple buildings. The question of the disciples in 13:4 when "these things" (Gk. *tauta/tauta panta*) will happen refers back to that destruction, as does the reference to "these (Gk. *panta*) birth pangs" in v. 8. Two further uses of the terminology occur in v. 29 (Gk. *tauta*) and v. 30 (Gk. *tauta panta*), indicating that the generation that will not pass away until "all these things have happened" is the generation of the fall of Jerusalem. This linguistic pattern is a clue that Mark intends readers to understand vv. 1-13 and 28-31 with reference to the destruction of the temple in Jerusalem.

Two other blocks of material in the chapter are held in close connection with the destruction of the temple. They are vv. 14-27, the description of the tribulation and subsequent coming of the Son of Man; and vv. 32-36, the reminder of the unknown day and hour of the return of the Son of Man and the consequent reminder to present watchfulness. These two sections are designated by the expression "those days" (vv. 17, 19, 20, 24; or "that day," v. 32). "Those days" is a stereotype for the eschaton in the prophets (Jer 3:16, 18; 31:29; 33:15; Joel 3:1), and it appears likewise in Mark 13. Chap. 13 is thus constructed according to a twofold scheme of

---

5. See M. Hooker, *The Gospel According to Saint Mark*, 298-99; W. Grundmann, *Das Evangelium nach Markus*, 349; C. E. B. Cranfield, *The Gospel According to St Mark*, 388; L. Morris, *Apocalyptic* (Grand Rapids: Eerdmans, 1972), 74-77; L. Gaston, *No Stone on Another: Studies in the Significance of the Fall of Jerusalem in the Synoptic Gospels* (Leiden: E. J. Brill, 1970), 50ff.

tension and paradox, alternating between the immediate future (related to "these things") and the end of time (related to "those days"), in which the destruction of the temple and fall of Jerusalem function as a prefigurement and paradigm for the Parousia.[6]

- A[1] 1-13 End of the temple and fall of Jerusalem
- B[1] 14-27 Tribulation and Parousia
- A[2] 28-31 End of the temple and fall of Jerusalem
- B[2] 32-37 Parousia and watchfulness

Most importantly, Mark 13 admonishes readers against attempts at constructing timetables and deciphering signs of the Parousia. Disciples are admonished to be alert and watchful (vv. 5, 9, 23, 33, 35, 37), reminded that they do not know the time of the end (vv. 33, 35), and warned not to be led astray by even the most obvious signs (vv. 5, 6, 21, 22), for the end is not yet (vv. 7, 13). No one is either encouraged or commended for attempting to be an eschatological code-cracker. That is folly, for even the Son of Man is ignorant of the End (v. 32). The premium of discipleship is placed not on predicting the future but on *faithfulness in the present*, especially in trials, adversity, and suffering.

THE DESTRUCTION OF THE TEMPLE (13:1-2)

"As [Jesus] was leaving the temple." This is more than a physical description. Rather, it symbolizes Jesus' final and definitive break from the temple. He has thrice predicted his death at the hands of Jewish and Gentile leaders (8:31; 9:31; 10:33-34); he has countermanded the authority of the Sanhedrin (11:27-33), which was located in the temple; and he has challenged each group comprising the Sanhedrin — the Pharisees (12:13-17), Sadducees (12:18-27), and scribes (12:35-40). The temple has been judged and condemned as a "den of robbers" (11:17), symbolized by an accursed and withered fig tree (11:12-22). Jesus' judgment of the temple was well enough known to his adversaries to play a significant role in his death sentence (14:58; 15:29-30). In v. 1, his footsteps obey his will: Jesus leaves the temple, never to return.

---

6. For a discussion of the twofold alternation between immediate and ultimate future in Mark 13, see P. Müller, "Zeitvorstellungen in Markus 13," *NovT* 40 (1998): 216-21. Müller makes no reference, however, to the distinction between "these things" and "those days."

As Jesus leaves, "one of his disciples said to him, 'Look, Teacher! What massive stones! What magnificent buildings!'" It is not unusual for Mark to leave individuals in the Gospel unnamed; indeed, it is the rule for him to do so. It is curious, however, why the disciple who points to the stupendous construction site is unnamed, whereas Peter, James, John, and Andrew in the next verse are identified. Perhaps the unnamed disciple is Judas, who elsewhere is identified by his materialism (14:10-11; John 12:4-6; 13:29). The infamy of his betrayal may have caused his name to be discreetly omitted, as it is in the Last Supper discourse (14:20-21).

In Jesus' day the **temple** had already been under construction fifty years, and was still unfinished. At no place was Herod the Great's obsession with grandeur and permanence more apparent than in the Jerusalem temple (see further at 11:15 and 12:41). Herod enlarged Solomon's temple to an esplanade measuring some 325 meters wide by 500 meters long, with a circumference of nearly a mile. The immense thirty-five-acre enclosure could accommodate twelve football fields. The southeast corner of the retaining wall hung some fifteen stories above the ground that sloped down to the Kidron Valley. The blocks of stone used in construction were enormous; Josephus (*War* 5.189) reports that some were forty cubits (approximately sixty feet) in length. No block that size has been found in the existing foundation, but stones north of Wilson's Arch measure forty-two feet long, eleven feet high, fourteen feet deep, and weigh over a million pounds. The magnitude of the temple mount and the stones used to construct it exceed in size any other temple in the ancient world.

And this was merely the retaining wall. Above, on the south end of the esplanade, perched the gleaming Royal Portico, "a striking spectacle," to quote Josephus. The portico was forty-five feet wide and consisted of three aisles supported by four rows of columns. The columns were crowned with Corinthian capitals and rose to a height of forty feet, supporting a cedar-paneled ceiling above. "The thickness of each column was such that it would take three men with outstretched arms touching one another to envelop it," reports Josephus (*Ant.* 15.413). In the center of the esplanade stood the sanctuary, which, as ancient writers noted, was shaped like a lion, broader in the front (fifty meters) and narrower in back (thirty meters). It rose to a height of fifty meters and was a visual collage of gold and silver, crimson and purple, radiating the rising sun like a snow-clad mountain. The figures Josephus gives for the blocks of stone in the sanctuary exceed in size even those of the foundation (*War* 5.222-24). A vast and stupendous complex it was. No wonder the disciples were overwhelmed![7]

7. Three ancient sources describe the Jerusalem temple: Josephus, the Mishnah

As remarkable as the proportions of the temple is Jesus' attitude toward it. "'Do you see all these great buildings? Not one stone here will be left on another; every one will be thrown down.'"[8] Earlier Jesus spoke of "the fig tree withered from the roots" (11:20). The fig tree, as we saw, symbolized the temple. In Jesus' final judgment of the temple the symbolism is dropped and its destruction is pronounced in concrete terms — stone by stone.[9] The disciples drop their jaws over building blocks, but Jesus dismisses them as stumbling blocks. Herod, the disciples, and Josephus might marvel at the temple (as do modern archaeologists and tourists), but Jesus declares it an abortive endeavor. Jesus' judgment is, to be sure, directed to the perversion of the temple's God-ordained purpose, but it is worth considering the wider ramifications of his judgment. How much of our nationalism, culture, and civilization itself could (or should) withstand the judgment of God?[10] Like a system of cells that has become malignant, the temple has forsaken its intended purpose and must be eradicated. Josephus's lamentation over the destruction of "that splendid city of world-wide renown" forty years later attests to the fulfillment of Jesus' judgment: "Caesar ordered the whole city and the temple to be razed to

---

tractate *Middot,* and the *Temple Scroll* in the DSS. Of these, Josephus provides the most complete and accurate description, especially in *War* 5. Further, see E. P. Sanders, *Judaism: Practice and Belief, 63 BCE–66 CE* (London: SCM Press/Philadelphia: Trinity Press International, 1992), 51-102; J. Patrick, "Reconstructing the Magnificent Temple Herod Built," *BRev* 4/5 (1988): 16ff.; K. and L. Ritmeyer, "Reconstructing Herod's Temple Mount in Jerusalem," *BARev* 15/6 (1989): 23ff.; D. Bahat, "Jerusalem Down Under: Tunneling along Herod's Temple Mount Wall," *BARev* 21/6 (1995): 31ff.

8. Two uncial manuscripts (A K) read *lithos epi lithō* rather than *lithos epi lithon,* which is attested by the vast majority of manuscripts. The first reading (and Luke 21:6) is probably owing to scribal improvement since it is grammatically superior to the majority text. The second reading, however, is firmly preferred.

9. Jesus' prediction of the temple's destruction stands in line with a chorus of similar Jewish predictions, not only in the OT (Ps 74:4-7; Jer 7:14; 9:11; 26:6; Mic 3:9-12) and Apocrypha (2 Macc 14:33) but also in extracanonical Jewish literature, including *T. Jud.* 23:1-5; *T. Levi* 10:3; 14; 15:3; *1 Enoch* 90:28-29; 91:11-13; *Sib. Or.* 3:665; 11QT 30:1-4; *Lives of the Prophets* 12:11. As far as we know, all the foregoing texts antedate A.D. 70. Added to those who foresaw the temple's destruction are Josephus himself (*War* 3.351-52; 6.311), and at least two rabbis, Yohanan ben Zakkai and Zadok. The corruption of the Herodian temple was widespread and widely recognized. There is every reason to believe that Jesus could — and did — predict the temple's destruction. On the subject, see C. A. Evans, "Predictions of the Destruction of the Herodian Temple in the Pseudepigrapha, Qumran Scrolls, and Related Texts," *JSP* 10 (1992): 89-147. M. Hengel, *Studies in the Gospel of Mark,* trans. J. Bowden (London: SCM Press, 1985), 14-16, also gathers significant information to show that "Mark or his tradents [could have] imagined a future destruction of the temple in a similar way." I should like to suggest that Jesus could have foreseen the same destruction — and did.

10. A question deftly raised by Cranfield, "St. Mark 13," *SJT* 6 (1953): 192-93.

the ground. . . . All the rest of the wall encompassing the city was so completely leveled to the ground as to leave future visitors to the spot no ground for believing that it had ever been inhabited" (*War* 7.3).

STANDING FIRM DESPITE INFIRMITIES (13:3-13)

In this section Mark directs the teaching of Jesus to events leading up to the destruction of the temple. Jesus' teaching falls into two parts, each prefaced by an admonition in Greek, *blepete* (translated by the NIV as "'Watch out'" in v. 5, and "'be on your guard'" in v. 9). The first admonition concerns false Messiahs and natural and political disasters (vv. 5-8); the second concerns persecutions of Christian believers, with particular emphasis on their "handing over" (Gk. *paradidomi*), a word that carries double connotations of "betrayal" and "being handed over to the purposes of God." In both admonitions Jesus warns that the "signs" do *not* portend the end!

3 The Mount of Olives rises three hundred feet above Jerusalem and is separated from it by the Kidron Valley. From this vantage point Jesus and the disciples have a commanding view of the eastern expanse of the temple mount, and, on top of it, the glimmering facade of the sanctuary. According to the Mishnah, someone "standing on top of the Mount of Olives should be able to look directly into the entrance of the Sanctuary" (*m. Mid.* 2.4). The summit of the Mount of Olives had earlier been the place from which Jesus began his triumphal entry into Jerusalem (11:1). The description of the Mount of Olives as "opposite the temple" (v. 3) is, in this instance, highly symbolic: just as Jesus immediately before had pronounced judgment on the scribes while sitting "opposite the [temple treasury]" (12:41), now he delivers his final judgment "opposite the temple." Moreover, he is "sitting," with the posture of an authoritative teacher.[11] Equally significant is that the Mount of Olives, according to Zech 14:1-8, is the place from which God declares the capture, sacking, and devastation of Jerusalem. Once again Jesus consciously positions himself to assume the role of God.

4-5 Peter, James, John, and Andrew ask Jesus privately, "'Tell us, when will these things happen? And what will be the sign that they are all about to be fulfilled?'" (v. 4). These four disciples, the first to be called by Jesus at the Sea of Galilee (1:16-20), are now the audience for his final speech. The first half of the question refers back to the destruction of the

11. C. Schneider, *"kathēmai,"* TDNT 3.443-44.

temple in v. 2, where "'no stone will be left on another.'" The second half of the question about the "'sign that they (Gk. *tauta*) are all about to be fulfilled'" has an eschatological ring to it (Dan 12:6-7). The repetition of *tauta* ("these things") shows that this question also refers to the destruction of the temple, but the use of the Greek verb *syntelein* (NIV, "fulfilled"; so, too, Dan 12:6 LXX), which is often a technical term for the end time,[12] hints that the destruction of the temple is a paradigm of something greater. A connection between the fall of Jerusalem and the arrival of the kingdom of God was thus apparent to Jesus' disciples, and certainly to Mark's audience, who lived in close proximity to the momentous events here predicted. The connection between the two events was not unique to Jesus and the disciples, but widely accepted by the Zealots and undoubtedly others up to the time of the destruction of Jerusalem. Josephus, who wrote extensively about the Jewish Revolt in A.D. 66, leaves no doubt that Jewish defense strategies were motivated by religious considerations, in hopes that Messiah would come in the heat of battle over the temple.

The word for "sign" (Gk. *sēmeion*) is one of the most important words in chap. 13. Thrice in 8:11-12 Jesus was asked by the Pharisees for a sign. He steadfastly refused the request, intimating that it was itself a sign of disbelief rather than faith. The same word is used equally pejoratively here and in v. 22. The NIV reads, "Jesus said to them," but the Greek reads, "Jesus *began* to speak to them," which is not only a Semitism but a solemn preface indicating the importance of the following admonition. Jesus warns that signs deceive and lead astray (Gk. *planan*, the same word used of the error of the Sadducees in 12:24, 27). Moreover, the "signs" mentioned in vv. 6-13 indicate the opposite of what one would expect — that the end is *not yet*. The disciples — and believers since — want to know the future, but Jesus directs them unflinchingly to the present: "'Watch out that no one deceives you.'"[13] Beginning in v. 5 and continuing throughout the chapter, there is a running admonition against future speculation at the expense of present obedience.

6 Threats to discipleship will come from many quarters. Contrary to what might be expected, the greatest threats are not external dangers but those inside the household of faith. Deceivers will arise claiming, "'I am he.'" These will not be only sporadic and occasional appearances; there will be many who appear in messianic guise, and they will lead

---

12. E. Lohmeyer, *Das Evangelium des Markus,* 269.

13. A near verbatim parallel admonition is found in the *Gospel of Mary* when the Blessed One greets Mary in the annunciation: "Beware that no one lead you astray *(planan)."* See *NTApoc* 392.

many astray. In the years preceding the Jewish Revolt in A.D. 66 several messianic pretenders arose. In the mid-forties Theudas (Acts 5:36) boasted of various signs (including the ability to part the Jordan River) that, according to Josephus, "led many astray" (*Ant.* 20.97-98). Josephus adds another account about an Egyptian who claimed to be a "prophet" (Gk. *goēs,* "magician"), who likewise succeeded in deceiving the populace (*War* 2.261-63).[14] The Greek of v. 6 reads simply, "I am," which is the name for God in the OT (Exod 3:14). "I am" is the same claim Jesus has made of himself (6:50; 14:62). There is thus no material difference between Jesus' claim and that of impostor claimants. Believers must be alert to how the claim is used: Does it represent God, or does it merely use God and the articles of orthodoxy for ulterior purposes? Impostors will even come "in my name," that is, with more than words. Their powers and credentials will give the impression that they are Christ, and they will have no small affect.[15] The spate of gnostic literature contained in both the Nag Hammadi corpus and the NT Apocrypha testifies to the proliferation of Jewish and especially gnostic sects in the latter half of the first century that raised an alien message in the name of Jesus of Nazareth. In the second Jewish revolt (A.D. 132-35), Bar Kokhba made claim to being the Messiah, and his claim swept many devout Jews into the revolt.

7-8 Other threats will come from international affairs, wars, and natural calamities that will befall non-believers as well as believers. The litany of woes in these verses could summarize every age perhaps, but they fit the first generation of Christians particularly well. There were fears of war in A.D. 40 when Caligula (Roman emperor, A.D. 37-41) attempted to erect a statue to himself in the temple of Jerusalem. Josephus uses a phrase very similar to 13:7 to describe the rumors of war circulating in Caligula's day.[16] The rumors of Caligula's day turned out to be only that, but twenty-five years later total war broke out in A.D. 66 when the Zealot revolt plunged Palestine into a catastrophic defeat by Rome. There were famines during the reign of Claudius (Roman emperor, A.D. 41-54; see Acts 11:28). Earthquakes struck Phrygia in A.D. 61 and leveled Pompey in A.D. 63. The language of vv. 7-8 finds striking parallels in Tacitus's description particularly of the last years of Nero's megalomania

14. For discussions of these and other messianic pretenders, see A. Y. Collins, "The Apocalyptic Rhetoric of Mark 13 in Historical Context," *BR* 41 (1996): 14-18.

15. M. Hooker's suggestion in *The Gospel According to Saint Mark*, 306-7 that "'I am he'" refers to false claims that the Parousia is at hand (or has occurred) is strained. That is clearly an issue in 2 Thess 2:1-2, but the implication in v. 6 is of false Messiahs who will lead the faithful astray.

16. Cf. *akoas polemōn* ("reports of wars") in v. 7 with *tou polemou phēmais* ("reports of war") in *War* 2.187.

and the civil wars that followed his suicide in A.D. 68.[17] Not surprisingly, toward the end of the first century Revelation 6 contains a similar list of wars, famine, earthquakes, and persecutions.[18]

The purpose of the litany of woes in 13:8 is *not* to lure believers into speculations about the end, but to anchor them to watchfulness and faithfulness in the present. All "these (things)" (v. 8), which culminate in the destruction of Jerusalem referred to in v. 2, are only "'the beginning of birth pains.'" Believers ought not to be alarmed, for "'the end is not yet'" (v. 7). Remarkably, the calamities of these verses do not interrupt or impede the kingdom. The adversities and downsizing of the church described in vv. 9-11 will, in fact, provide unprecedented opportunity for witness to the nations. The Book of Acts is a commentary on these verses, for in tribulations (many of which parallel vv. 7-13), the numbers and faith of believers in the early church actually grew. The metaphor of "birth pains" is also instructive, for in Judaism motherhood was the ultimate validation of a woman's worth, and birth pains ended the disgrace

---

17. Tacitus commences his *Histories* in A.D. 68 with this prologue: "The history on which I am entering is that of a period rich in disasters, terrible in battles, torn by civil struggles, horrible even in peace. Four emperors fell by the sword; there were three civil wars, more foreign wars, and often both at the same time. There was success in the East [referring to the Vespasian-Titus victory in Judea], misfortune in the West. Illyricum was disturbed, the Gallic provinces wavering, Britain subdued and immediately let go. The Sarmatae and Suebi rose against us . . . even the Parthians were almost aroused to arms through the trickery of a pretended Nero. Moreover, Italy was distressed by disasters unknown before or returning after the lapse of ages. Cities on the rich fertile shores of Campania were swallowed up or overwhelmed; Rome was devastated by conflagrations, in which her most ancient shrines were consumed and the very Capitol fired by citizens' hands. Sacred rites were defiled; there were adulteries in high places. The sea was filled with exiles, its cliffs made foul with the bodies of the dead. In Rome there was more awful cruelty. . . . Informers were no less hateful than their crimes; for some, gaining priesthoods and consulships as spoils, others obtaining positions as imperial agents and secret influence at court, made havoc and turmoil everywhere, inspiring hatred and terror. Slaves were corrupted against their masters, freedmen against their patrons; and those who had no enemy were crushed by friends" (*Hist.* 1.2 [LCL]). For a discussion of the various wars and uprisings in the 40s and 50s of the first century, see N. H. Taylor, "Palestinian Christianity and the Caligula Crisis, Part II: The Markan Eschatological Discourse," *JSNT* 62 (1996): 27-29.

18. The NIV reads only "famines" in v. 8, but an impressive number and diversity of manuscripts read "famines *and tumults*" (*limoi kai tarachai;* A K X Θ Δ Π Σ W). Although it is possible that the addition *"and tumults"* is owing to the tendency of scribes to add rather than delete words (so B. Metzger, *TCGNT,* 112), it seems equally if not more probable that *tarachai* was omitted because its final letters closely resemble those of *archē* ("beginning") that follow. Moreover, "famines" is preceded by three sets of doublets in v. 8, which suggests that the final set may also have been a mnemonic doublet, "famines and troubles." For a close parallel to v. 8, see 4 Ezra 13:31.

of childlessness. Likewise, the church's "birth pains" in tribulation will validate rather than annihilate its existence.

9-10   Threats to faith will also come through persecution of believers. The NIV perhaps overtranslates the Greek phrase *blepete de hymeis heatous* as "'You must be on guard.'" A more fitting translation would be, "You must be clear in your own minds" — with emphasis on "you." The point is to rid believers of utopian fantasies and remind them that adversity and persecution are not aberrations of the Christian life but rather the *norm*. Without saying who will betray them, Mark says that believers will be haled before "local councils[19] and synagogues" and "rulers and kings." Believers, in other words, will be persecuted by Jews and Gentiles, by religious and secular authorities. They will be betrayed, beaten, and arraigned before legitimate authorities for Jesus' sake and as a witness to said authorities (8:35; Matt 8:4). But their sufferings will not be without purpose. Suffering and persecution will afford believers unprecedented opportunities to declare their faith before kings, authorities, and rulers (Acts 12:1-3; 23:33; 25:6, 19ff.). Rather than abandoning them in the hour of crisis, God will empower them to witness to the nations.

The statement in v. 10 that "'the gospel must first be preached to all nations'" is often suspected of being a Markan insertion since it is absent from the parallel passages Matthew 10 and Luke 21, and occurs in a different context in Matt 24:14. It is not impossible that the saying has been taken from a different context and included here by Mark, but it does not interrupt the train of thought, as is sometimes supposed. Indeed, it forms a parallel to 1:14-15, where John the Baptizer's arrest provided the context for the proclamation of the gospel by Jesus. Here, too, the persecution of believers (v. 9) provides the context for the proclamation of the gospel to all nations (v. 10). Once again the sufferings and persecutions of believers are not signs of the end, but signs that attend authentic preaching of the gospel!

11   The inevitability of persecution ought not produce anxiety and fear but rather the assurance of God's presence in the Holy Spirit. Disciples are again reminded that faithfulness does not consist in forecasting the future and determining preemptive responses, but rather in trusting that God will give them grace to complete their service in his name, and indeed will even speak through them in their deepest need. In their first mission the disciples spoke for God (6:7-12), but in their sufferings God will speak through them by the Holy Spirit!

12-13   Persecution will even break up families. Siblings will turn

19. The original Greek word is "sanhedrins," which in the plural refers to local Jewish councils or courts rather than to the Great Sanhedrin in Jerusalem (*m. Sanh.* 1:6).

against one another, parents against children, and children against parents, as foretold by the prophet Micah (7:6). In the Jewish world it was the household more than the individual that determined identity and bore witness to God: "'But as for me and my household, we will serve the LORD'" (Josh 24:15). The breakup of families thus attacks and jeopardizes life and faith at the most intimate and formative level. It is not impossible that the family betrayals referred to in v. 12 allude not simply to natural families but specifically to Christian families (so 3:33-35), that is, to Christians informing on one another under interrogation. V. 12 does not explicitly designate the family members as Christians, but the fact that the verse is set within the context of the persecution of believers in vv. 9-13 could imply that. Describing the Neronian persecution of A.D. 64, Tacitus writes that those who confessed that they were Christians were first arrested, and then *on their disclosures,* many Christians were further arrested (*Ann.* 15:44). A generation later, sometime after A.D. 110, Pliny the Younger testifies to the same method of interrogating Christians "who have been denounced" — presumably by fellow Christians (*Letter to the Emperor Trajan* 10.96). If v. 12 does include betrayals of Christians by fellow Christians, then the statement in the following verse that "'all men will hate you'" includes even those *within* the church: fallible and false believers within the community of faith will conspire with the world to persecute true disciples. If believers experience the tragic betrayal (Gk. *paradidomi*) of fellow believers, then they will share the very experience of Jesus, who was betrayed (Gk. *paradidomi*) by Judas, one of the family of the Twelve (3:19).[20]

Loyalty to Christ will be odious and loathsome to the world, and believers will be hated (13:13). One again recalls Tacitus's comment about the Neronian persecution, that Christians were "a class hated for their abominations" (*Ann.* 15.44; cf. John 15:19). Not even the claims of kinship, however, can be allowed to take precedence over Jesus Christ. "'But the one who has endured to the end will be saved'" (similarly 4 Ezra 6:25). This promise is a supreme comfort in the midst of trials. Believers are not expected to do what they cannot do (i.e., to prevail over all adversities), but to do the one thing they can do in every crisis — to endure and be steadfast. When they do, they will be saved.[21]

20. The idea that v. 12 refers to inner-church betrayals has been advanced by T. Radcliffe, "'The Coming of the Son of Man': Mark's Gospel and the Subversion of the Apocalyptic Imagination," in *Language, Meaning and God: Essays in Honour of Herbert McCabe O.P.,* ed. B. Davies (London: Chapman, 1987), 167-89; and B. M. F. van Iersel, "Failed Followers in Mark: Mark 13:12 as a Key for the Identification of the Intended Readers," *CBQ* 58 (1996): 244-63.

21. There is a parallel to v. 13 in 4 Ezra 6:25, "'It shall be that whoever remains after all that I have foretold to you shall be saved and shall see my salvation and the end of my

Mark 13:6-13 describes the experience of the church following the ascension of Jesus. The Book of Acts, as we noted, provides a commentary on nearly every verse in this section. That commentary, of course, is not limited to Acts, for the phenomena herein are descriptive in varying degrees of every epoch of church history. However long it lasts, the period of time here depicted is an interim prior to the Parousia. Mark does not give believers a blueprint for the future, but rather confidence in God's purpose and presence in the interim of the church. The present warnings repeat and extend Jesus' call to discipleship in 8:34, "'If anyone would come after me, he must deny himself and take up his cross and follow me.'" The word for "betray" (Gk. *paradidomi*), which is used repeatedly of Jesus in Mark (3:19; 9:31; 10:33; and ten times in chaps. 14–15), is now applied to believers (13:9, 11, 12). The hour has come for believers to bear the cross of which Jesus spoke. They bear his cross by standing "'firm to the end'" (v. 13; Dan 12:12). The life of faith is not an exemption from adversity but a reliance on the promise of God to bear witness to the gospel in adversity, and to be saved for eternal life through it.

THE TRIBULATION (13:14-18)

13:14 introduces a particular disaster, "'"the abomination that causes desolation,"'" that will precipitate suffering of indescribable magnitude. The verse is doubly difficult to interpret because of Mark's explicit admonition to understand ("'let the reader understand'") something that is so enigmatic — and that has until now defied certain explanation. What is the meaning of this most difficult and debated text?

14-18 Verse 14 should be paired with v. 7: what the disciples formerly *heard* ("'when you hear,'" v. 7), they will now *see* ("'when you see,'" v. 14). The "'"abomination that causes desolation"'" is a phrase taken from three cryptic references in Dan 9:27; 11:31; 12:11 to a scandal

---

world.'" Compare God's commendation of Abdiel, who single-handedly opposed Satan's rebellion, in *Paradise Lost* 6:29-37:

> Servant of God, well done, well hast thou fought
> The better fight, who single hast maintaind
> Against revolted multitudes the Cause
> Of Truth, in word mightier than they in Armes
> And for the testimonie of Truth hast born
> Universal reproach, far worse to beare
> Than violence; for this was all thy care
> To stand approv'd in sight of God.

that would defile and profane the Jerusalem temple. The same phrase is used in 1 Macc 1:54 to describe Antiochus IV (Epiphanes), the Syrian general who outraged the Jews in 168 B.C. by erecting an altar to Zeus on the altar of burnt offering in the temple and sacrificing a sow on it.[22] The sacrilege of Antiochus in the Jerusalem temple became the dramatic provocation for the Maccabean Revolt, which against all odds earned Jews their only century of political self-rule between the fall of Jerusalem to Nebuchadnezzar in 586 B.C. and the formation of the State of Israel in 1948.

In its original context, "'"the abomination that causes desolation"'" thus referred to the abomination wrought by Antiochus IV against the temple and Judaism in the second century B.C. This event is recalled in 13:14 as a prefigurement or symbol of something equally outrageous and cataclysmic to occur in the future. Mark's "aside" to "'let the reader understand'" is nearly as baffling as the abomination itself. Although it occurs in the mouth of Jesus, it can scarcely have been spoken by him since Jesus is speaking, not writing.[23] It is the most explicit editorial comment that Mark has made so far (3:21b, 30; 7:3-4, 19c; 16:8c).[24]

What event does Mark desire us to understand? There are three major possibilities. One was the egomaniacal attempt of Caligula, Roman emperor from A.D. 37-41, who attempted to erect statues of himself in the temple of Jerusalem and have them worshiped as god (Josephus, *War* 2.184-203). The reference to the "'"abomination that causes desolation" *standing*[25] where it does not belong'" could be taken as a reference to Caligula's mad ambition.[26] Despite the suitability of Caligula's statue

22. The presence of this unique phrase in Daniel is one of several reasons why many scholars believe that Daniel was composed at the time of the Maccabean Revolt, and that its narrative of Nebuchadnezzar's invasion of Jerusalem three centuries earlier is a cloak for events surrounding Antiochus IV's assault on Jerusalem and the temple (see Dan 11:31).

23. The suggestion that Jesus was referring to reading the book of Daniel is forced.

24. "'Let the reader understand,'" it has been suggested, may have been a scribal gloss in the margin of an early manuscript that was subsequently incorporated into the text of the Gospel. That Mark nowhere else interjects himself so explicitly into the text makes this an intriguing suggestion. However, since there is no manuscript evidence that the phrase was ever absent from Mark's text, we have no alternative but to consider it Markan.

25. The Greek participle *hestēkota* is a masculine singular accusative, referring to a man (or something masculine) standing.

26. For a recent proposal of this thesis, see N. H. Taylor, "Palestinian Christianity and the Caligula Crisis, Part I: Social and Historical Reconstruction," *JSNT* 61 (1996): 101-24; the same author, "Palestinian Christianity and the Caligula Crisis, Part II: The Markan Eschatological Discourse," *JSNT* 62 (1996): 13-41, who follows the general thesis of Gaston, *No Stone on Another*. Taylor's thesis is not implausible, but its speculations substantially exceed our limited knowledge of events surrounding the Caligula crisis.

standing as the abomination of desolation, it differs in two significant respects from 13:14-17. First, during the Caligula debacle the Jews did not "'flee to the mountain'" (v. 14), but rather "presented themselves, their wives and their children, ready for the slaughter" (Josephus, *War* 2.197). Their behavior, in other words, was the opposite of that enjoined in vv. 14-16. Second, and more important, the Caligula statues were never erected — thanks to the refusal of Petronius, the general in charge of operations, and Caligula's subsequent assassination. Hence there was no need to flee Jerusalem, which, as we noted, they refused to do anyway. The Caligula crisis thus fails in several important respects to parallel vv. 14-17.

A second possibility is to see 13:14 fulfilled in the destruction of the temple by Titus. This is the most common explanation of the passage. Already in the Synoptic tradition this correspondence is made by Matt 24:15, which not only expressly identifies "'"the abomination that causes desolation"'" as coming from "'the prophet Daniel,'" but also its standing "'in the holy place.'" Luke 21:20 and 19:43, likewise, describe armies and an encirclement of Jerusalem. The reference to "'standing in the holy place'" in Matt 24:15 could be a reference to Titus's entry of the temple in September of A.D. 70 (Josephus, *War* 6.260); and Luke's references clearly describe the *circumvallatio,* the defense perimeter erected by the Roman Tenth Legion under Titus in the siege of Jerusalem, unforgettably described by Josephus in *The Jewish War.*[27] Allusions to the siege of Titus and the destruction of Jerusalem appear in other literature as well.[28]

The correlation of Mark 13:14 with the destruction of the temple is much less apparent, however, at least as that event is recorded by Josephus. Certainly, vv. 14-18 portend a disaster in *Palestine.* People on their flat-roofed Palestinian houses must flee by the outside staircase without going inside (v. 15; see the discussion of Palestinian houses at 1:29 and 2:1), and the field worker will have no time to fetch his outer cloak (v. 16). Worst of all will be the fate of pregnant women and nursing mothers (v. 17; see Luke 23:29-31), and anyone fleeing in winter when the wadis — the ravines and gorges — are swollen and impossible to cross (v. 18).

In other respects, however, Mark 13:14 departs substantially from events surrounding the destruction of the temple by Titus.[29] Mark does not locate "'"the abomination that causes desolation"'" in the temple (as

27. A similar *circumvallatio* can still be seen today surrounding Masada.

28. Two second-century gnostic texts, *2 Apoc. Jas.* 5:4 and *Testim. Truth* 9:3, allude to Titus's siege and destruction of Jerusalem. Likewise, *2 Apoc. Bar.* 7:1–8:5; 48:34-47; 4 Ezra 10:21-24, stemming from the late first century; and *m. Sot.* 9:15 allude to the fall of Jerusalem (cited in *HCNT,* 133-35).

29. See Hengel, *Studies in the Gospel of Mark,* 16-18: "The reference to the inhabitants does not fit into any authentic historical situation known to us."

does Matt 24:15), but rather "'where it does not belong.'" This enigmatic description is possibly a Jewish circumlocution for the temple, similar perhaps to the frequent references to Jerusalem in Deuteronomy as "the place where God will make his name known," but we cannot be sure. Otherwise, v. 14 says that *when* "'"the abomination that causes desolation"'" is in place, *then* the inhabitants should flee to the hills. Josephus, however, describes refugees fleeing *into* Jerusalem before the war with Rome, not out of it. Moreover, once Titus was in the temple, indeed once the *circumvallatio* had been erected, flight did not spell safety but certain death — either by the Romans or the rebel bandits, who were equally murderous (*War* 6.366). Even Eusebius, who *does* equate the destruction of Titus with "'"the abomination that causes desolation"'" (*Hist. Eccl.* 3.5.4), makes no attempt to reconcile v. 14 with historical circumstances attending the fall of Jerusalem, for he records the flight of Christians from Jerusalem long *before* the invasion of Titus — and then not to the hills but to Pella in Transjordan (*Hist. Eccl.* 3.5.3). Again, v. 18 speaks of flight in winter, whereas Titus's siege of Jerusalem happened in summer (July-September, A.D. 70). Josephus shows no interest in Titus standing in the temple (see *War* 6.260), but rather repeatedly emphasizes the fire and conflagration that destroyed the temple, of which there is no mention in Mark.[30] Objectively speaking, a correlation of v. 14 with the destruction of the temple is only approximate, at best.[31]

A third possibility is that "'"the abomination that causes desolation"'" refers to "the man of lawlessness" as conceived in 2 Thess 2:3-4, who will exalt himself in the temple as God (or as "a Son of God," according to *Did.* 16:4). The agreements of 2 Thessalonians 2 with v. 14 are much closer. The "man of lawlessness" corresponds to the man *standing* (masculine participle) in v. 14; and the description of him parodying God in the temple correlates with "'"the abomination that causes desolation" standing where he *does not belong.*'" Both texts depict a blasphemous Antichrist who will do a scandalous deed that will trigger the return of the Lord.[32] Both texts also warn disciples against mistaken eschatological assumptions, especially against being deceived by signs and wonders.[33]

---

30. A reference to the destruction of the temple by fire in the *Gospel of Peter* 26 is an obvious attempt to correlate the abomination of desolation with the siege of Titus.

31. The Phanni incident, recounted by Josephus, *War* 4.155, is even less likely. After seizing the temple in A.D. 66, the Zealots conscripted a clown named Phanni to make a mockery of the high priest and his sacrifice. Although Josephus calls the incident a "monstrous impiety," it pales in comparison to the disaster described in Mark 13:14-18, and can thus scarcely be the same event.

32. See Wenham, *The Rediscovery of Jesus' Eschatological Discourse*, 176-80.

33. Mark 13:14 and 2 Thess 2:1-2 find a third parallel in *Didache* 16, which also

To sum up the discussion of 13:14. First, its wording argues strongly for a pre–70 A.D. composition of the Gospel of Mark, for we should expect greater correspondence with the cataclysmic collapse of Jerusalem, as is particularly the case with Luke, if Mark were writing after A.D. 70. Second, v. 14 looks to be a genuine prediction of Jesus and not a so-called *vaticinium ex eventu* (a prediction retrojected back onto his lips), for had it been composed after either Caligula or Titus we should again expect greater correspondence to the circumstances of those events.[34] The ambiguity of v. 14, which eludes exact interpretation, is its strongest claim to authenticity. Finally, and most importantly, v. 14, like 2 Thessalonians 2, indicates that Jesus foresaw the rise of a terrible antagonist, an Antichrist, who at some future time will unleash a severe tribulation on the people of God, which in turn will usher in the return of the Lord. Mark relates this abominable event only cryptically and suggestively to the destruction of the temple.[35] In so doing he imputes both historical and eschatological value to the same event. V. 14 is thus the hinge of Mark 13 that links "these things," relating to the destruction of Jerusalem in A.D. 70, with "those days" of the End. The "'"abomination that causes desolation"'" alludes to the destruction of the temple in A.D. 70, but it is not exhausted by it. The "abomination" is a mysterious (2 Thess 2:7!) double referent, a historical medium that anticipates an ultimate fulfillment in the advent of the Antichrist and the final tribulation before the return of the Son of Man. Titus's destruction of Jerusalem is like a scouting film: it gives an authentic picture of one's future opponent; but there is, of course, a great deal of difference between clashing with players in the stadium as opposed to simply watching them on film.

We thus do not have a foolproof "sign" in "'"the abomination that causes desolation."'" Like the disciples, the church throughout the ages has sought for infallible proofs of the End. That is perhaps inevitable, for

---

speaks of apostasy leading up to a world deceiver as Son of God, followed by a great tribulation, and then the coming of the Lord.

34. Note Wenham's conclusion in *The Rediscovery of Jesus' Eschatological Discourse*, 373: "It must be admitted that if this pre-synoptic tradition [i.e., the one shared by 2 Thess 2 and Mark 13:14] was well-known by the early 50s, and if the teaching in it was known by Paul and all the evangelists as the authoritative teaching of Jesus, the onus of proof must be on those who deny the teaching to Jesus, not on those who affirm it."

35. The correlation between v. 14 and the destruction of the temple is implied (1) by the reference to "Judea," which localizes the abomination in Palestine; (2) by the fact that 2 Thess 2:4 alludes to Dan 11:36-37, and thus itself echoes "'the abomination that causes desolation'"; and (3) by the fact that the reference to Daniel's "'abomination that causes desolation'" (i.e., the temple sacrilege and destruction by Nebuchadnezzar/ Antiochus IV) generally parallels Titus's destruction of the Jerusalem temple.

certain knowledge relieves us of the responsibilities of waiting and watching. But "'"the abomination that causes desolation"'" is no such sign. It requires scrutiny and watchfulness. The salvation brought by Jesus is not a salvation of knowledge. The salvation of Jesus is rather a *way* — of following, of faithfulness, of standing guard at our posts, for "'"no one knows about that day or hour"'" (13:32). It is not a way of dispensing with mystery but of living *in* mystery.

THE TRIBULATION (13:19-23)

The catastrophe that befell Jerusalem in the Jewish War of A.D. 66-70 was a prolepsis, a paradigm in history of the woes that would transpire at the end of history before the return of the Son of Man. We noted in the introduction to this chapter that Mark 13 is orchestrated by antiphonal time frames, alternating between an immediate future ("these things," leading up to the fall of Jerusalem) and the ultimate future ("those days" of the great tribulation and the Parousia). The hinge between the two futures occurs in "'"the abomination that causes desolation"'" in v. 14. Events between v. 14 and v. 27 anticipate the ultimate eschatological future, signified by "those days" (vv. 17, 19, 20, 24), a semitechnical term in Jewish eschatology for the final reckoning at the end of time (e.g., *1 Enoch* 80:1; *4 Ezra* 4:51).

19-20   The reference to the great tribulation is patterned after Dan 12:1, in which the archangel Michael warns the elect what will befall them at the end time. The "tribulation" (vv. 19, 24; Gk. *thlipsis;* NIV, "distress") that accompanies "those days" is also a semitechnical term in Jewish literature for the woes of the end time (Dan 12:1; Joel 22:2; 1 Macc 9:27; *As. Mos.* 8:1). The original Greek of v. 19 is prolix and redundant, presumably in an attempt to express that nothing like "those days" has ever happened before or since.[36] Circumstances will be so dire that unless God intervened to curtail them, "'no one would survive'" (v. 20). The particular phrase "cut short those days" occurs in apocalyptic literature with refer-

---

36. Josephus resorts to such language and categories in describing the destruction of Jerusalem: "no other city ever endured such miseries, nor since the world began has there been a generation more prolific in crime" (*War* 5.422). Likewise, in describing the enigmatic war between the sons of light and lot of darkness, the *War Scroll* of Qumran says, "Of all their sufferings, none will be like this, hastening till eternal redemption is fulfilled" (1QM 1:12). Note a similar parallel to v. 17 in *Sib. Or.* 2:190: "Alas, for as many as are found bearing in the womb on that day, for as many as suckle infant children, . . . alas, for as many as will see *that day.*"

ence to the final eschaton (*Barn.* 4:3).[37] Again, the reference to the "elect" (Gk. *eklektos*), which occurs in Mark only in this section (vv. 20, 22, 27), is used exclusively in the Synoptic Gospels of eschatological relationships.[38] A situation is depicted that has no parallel in human history; apart from God's gracious intervention and assistance it will be humanly unsurvivable. God will spare the elect, if not from suffering, at least from annihilation. The cataclysm described here obviously exceeds in horror any known human event, although the fall of Jerusalem is a prototype.

21-22 The language and motifs of vv. 21-22 recall vv. 5-8.[39] But the purpose has now changed, for the earlier warnings referred to messianic pretenders at the fall of Jerusalem as a sign that the end was not yet, whereas here the appearance of false Christs and prophets is a sign that the end is at hand (see 2 Thess 2:2-4; *Gospel of Thomas* 113). The true Messiah is reluctant to perform signs and wonders so as not to coerce people's allegiance; false prophets, by contrast, exploit every means to gain a following (v. 22), as they have since the founding of Israel (Deut 13:1-5).[40] Ironically, the message and signs of the false Christs will be believed — they will lead many astray (v. 6), even of the "elect" (v. 22); on the other hand, the message of the true Christ has not been believed (8:14-21).

23 "'So be on your guard,'" says Jesus. The original Greek is a direct imperative, that is, "'Pay attention!'" "'Keep watch!'" The mark of faithfulness is watchfulness; not foretelling the future but obedience in the present. When Christ returns he will fulfill the many OT prophecies about the End. But second, despite imminent signs, believers cannot calculate when, where, or how the End will come. When it comes, no one will miss it; until it comes, no one should be misled. On his own authority ("'I have told you everything ahead of time'") Jesus warns his disciples and the church not to be distracted or diverted from obedience to the suffering Son of Man, neither by ingenious speculations nor by signs and wonders.

---

37. *Apoc. Ab.* 29:13; *2 Bar.* 20:1; *4 Ezra* 4:26; *1 Enoch* 38:2; 39:6-7; 80:2. See Str-B 1.953; to the contrary, Hooker, *The Gospel According to Saint Mark,* 316.

38. G. Schrenk, *"eklektos," TDNT* 4.186-189; J. Eckert, *"eklektos," EDNT* 1.417.

39. There will be an "arising" (*egerthēsontai,* vv. 8, 22) of messianic pretenders ("'I am he,'" v. 6; false Christs and false prophets, vv. 21-22); and believers will be deceived (*planēsousin,* v. 6; *apoplanan,* v. 22) by signs and wonders (vv. 7-8, 22).

40. There is a discrepancy in the manuscript tradition of v. 22 whether false prophets will "give" (*dōsousin*) signs and wonders, or whether they will "do" them (*poiēsousin;* D K Θ; NIV, "perform"). The first reading is preferable on two counts: (1) it claims much stronger manuscript support, and (2) "give" is a Semitic idiom, which likely goes back to Jesus, whereas "do" can be explained as a scribal harmonization with more acceptable Greek usage.

401

THE RETURN OF THE SON OF MAN IN GLORY (13:24-27)

The mischief caused by the misuse of eschatology — not least in contemporary America — has resulted in a virtual eclipse of eschatology in the life of the church. This unfortunate set of circumstances — both its abuse and its subsequent neglect — has weakened the church rather than strengthened it. If we dispense with eschatology, then the purpose and destiny of history fall into the hands of humanity alone. No one, I think, Christian or not, takes solace in that prospect. Unless human history, in all its greatness and potential as well as its propensity to evil and destructiveness, can be *redeemed*, human life is a futile and sordid endeavor. The longing that things *ought not to be* as they are, and *cannot be allowed* to remain as they are, is essentially an eschatological longing. The grand finale of the gospel preached by Jesus is that there is a sure hope for the future. It is grounded not in history or logic or intuition, but in the word of Jesus, in the asseveration that "in those days" humanity will no longer usurp history but relinquish it to its Lord and Maker, who will return in glory and justice to condemn evil, end suffering, and gather his own to himself.

24-27 Tribulation, suffering, evil, and death are not a full stop to the sentence of history. "'In those days, following that distress,'" the Son of Man will return. More than any other section in Mark 13, this one is a tapestry of Jewish apocalyptic that depicts a cosmic cataclysm of the darkening of the sun and moon, the fall of the stars from heaven, and the sundering of the heavenly bodies.[41] Obviously, this is not a description of the fall of Jerusalem or any other historical cataclysm, but a metahistorical event that includes history but subsumes and supersedes history.[42] It is these upheavals, not bogus reports of pseudo-Messiahs (vv.

---

41. Isa 13:10; 34:4; Ezek 32:7-8; Joel 2:10; 3:4, 15; 4:15; Rev 6:12-14; 8:12; 4 Ezra 5:1-2; *As. Mos.* 10:5; *1 Enoch* 80:2; *Sib. Or.* 3:796-97; *2 Apoc. Bar.* 25. For a full discussion of the signs attending the coming of the Messiah, see Str-B 4/2.977-1,015.

42. Some scholars attempt to argue that the cosmic portents of vv. 24-27 are simply Hebraic metaphors describing divine judgment against pagan gods. In this view, vv. 24-27 do not depict the Parousia but rather the fall of Jerusalem. See R. T. France, *Jesus and the Old Testament* (London: Tyndale Press, 1971), 231-33; T. R. Hatina, "The Focus of Mark 13:24-27: The Parousia, or the Destruction of the Temple?" *Bulletin for Biblical Research* 6 (1996): 43-66; B. M. F. van Iersel, "The Sun, Moon, and Stars of Mark 13,24-25 in a Greco-Roman Reading," *Bib* 77 (1996): 84-92. This view is extremely doubtful. Although the sun, moon, and stars can occasionally function as symbols for pagan deities, it is highly unlikely that they do so in vv. 24-27. The plain sense of the verses is eschatological (e.g., *Barn.* 4:3), and this is confirmed by the reference to "those days" and the shaking of powers "in heaven," both of which are eschatological stereotypes. France recognizes that *hē hēmera ekeinē* ("that day") refers to the final day of judgment in v. 32, but he fails to note

21-23), that will signal the coming of the Son of Man. Schlatter notes that "The description of the Parousia consists almost entirely of quotations from Scripture. Jesus did not create his own imagery for the event in which, in the glory of God, he would reveal himself to the world. He grounded the hope of the disciples solely in the prophetic words, in the same way that he strengthened himself for the cross with the assurance that suffering and the divine will were united in Scripture."[43] This is yet another indication that Jesus saw himself as the fulfillment of Israel's history and that the definitive testimony to his mission was a matter of record in Israel's Scriptures (Luke 24:27!).

In Mark's day (and for some in ours) stars were thought to be heavenly powers that influenced human affairs. At the end of time all such powers, real and imagined, will be obliterated. The picture is one of total cosmic collapse. Darkness and chaos will envelop everything, just as before time (Gen 1:2). Mark will again describe a condition of "darkness over the whole earth" at the crucifixion scene (15:33), as though the primal forces of chaos make a final desperate attempt to engulf God's Son. But that cannot happen. Something happens on a cosmic scale that happened between Jesus and the leper in 1:42: the "divine contagion" overcomes everything unclean and dark and evil. The death of Christ spells the doom of the dark side, not its victory. Thus, the specter of annihilation in vv. 24-27 instills not dread and horror, but confidence and hope! The destruction of the world cannot eclipse the return of Christ, and when he returns, he will "gather his elect" (1 Thess 4:15-18).

"'The Son of Man coming in clouds'" (v. 26) is taken from the vision of Dan 7:13.[44] What remarkable irony this is, coming from a man who has predicted his humiliation and death (8:31; 9:31; 10:33-34) and who even now is preparing for his shameful treatment at the hands of Jews and Romans alike. He who will be crucified as a common criminal (Phil 2:8) will come "'with great power and glory.'" In the OT, "clouds" often symbolize the presence and glory of God.[45] When Jesus returns "in clouds," it

---

that the same designation (albeit in the plural) appears in vv. 17, 18, 20, and 24. Moreover, it is not clear why Mark should be interested in the fall of the Greco-Roman pantheon in the present context. The coming of the Son of Man in v. 27 carries the same sense that it does in 14:62, i.e., to the Parousia.

43. *Der Evangelist Matthäus,* 710. Also cited in Cranfield, *The Gospel According to St Mark,* 406.

44. Modern scholars often interpret the "Son of Man" of Dan 7:13 as a collective of Israel. See, however, the material gathered in Str-B 1.956 in opposition to this view, and the conclusion: "Dan 7:13f is never understood in early Judaism as a collective expression for 'the people of the Holy One' (= Dan 7:27), but always as the individual Messiah."

45. Exod 16:10; 19:9; 24:15-16; 33:9; Lev 16:2; Num 11:25.

can only mean that God is no longer present in the temple but in Jesus, the Son of Man.

The preeminence of the Son of Man is also manifested in 13:27. The OT often speaks of the gathering of exiles and captives to Jerusalem on the Day of the Lord. But here they are gathered to *Jesus*, "'from the ends of the earth to the ends of the heavens.'" This awkward phrase, a combination of Deut 30:4; 13:8 and Zech 2:10,[46] means simply "from everywhere," and graphically emphasizes Christ's universal significance. There is a striking contrast between the vast cosmic array and the particularity of the Son of Man: the elect are as widespread and diverse as all creation, but they converge at a single point: the Son of Man. Jesus is the focal point of divine redemption.

It is equally important to note what this glorious vision of the future does *not* affirm. There is no mention of a millennium, no new Jerusalem, no rebuilt temple, no restoration of Israel or the State of Israel, no battle of Armageddon, and no hints how and when Christ will return. About all these things the text is silent. All these incidentals yield to the preeminent truth of the power and glory of Jesus' future coming and the promise that his elect will be gathered to him. This preview of the future ought not lure us to calculate *when* Christ will return, nor to fear *what* will happen, but to know *that* he will come to claim his own. His coming is his promise, and the gathering of believers to him is our hope.

THE LESSON OF THE FIG TREE (13:28-31)

This section returns to the subject of the fall of Jerusalem of vv. 5-13, as signified by "these things" of vv. 29-30, which refer back to the same terminology earlier. In v. 2 Jesus announced the destruction of "'all these great buildings.'" The disciples ask, "'When these things will happen?'" (v. 4), and Jesus says of the woes at the fall of Jerusalem, "'These are the beginning of birth pains'" (v. 8). "These things" in the present section resumes the same terminology, alerting us that Mark is referring of the fall of Jerusalem and not to the end of the world in the previous section (vv. 14-27). "These things" in vv. 29-30 can scarcely refer to the eschatological events of vv. 24-27, which are not signs of the end, but rather *the* end.

28-29 The almond tree blossoms early in Palestine, often before winter is past. Olives, oaks, terebinths, and evergreens do not drop their leaves or needles in winter, and hence they cannot announce the change

---

46. Further, see Str-B 1.959-60.

of seasons. But the fig tree is different. It loses its leaves in winter, and only late in spring, when winter is past and warm weather is at hand, does its branch grow tender with buds. Jesus saw in the fig a suitable metaphor of the nearness of the end. Just as summer comes each year without human effort, so God fulfills his kingdom in his own time. The fig tree signals the "nearness" (vv. 28, 29) of summer but not its immediacy, that is, *that* summer is coming, if not exactly *when.*

The original Greek of v. 28 speaks of a "parable," but the illustration of the fig tree is not a full-fledged parable, at least in the normal sense of Jesus' parables. It is an analogy or "lesson" (so the NIV). In chap. 11 Jesus applied the image of the fig tree to the destruction of the temple. The same image functions similarly here, signifying an imminent cataclysm that Jesus' contemporaries would witness.[47] Ironically, Jesus uses the figure of the fig tree and the cataclysm following it not as a warning but as an exhortation. When "'its leaves come out, you know that summer is near . . . right at the door.'" "Summer" (Gk. *theros*) and "door" (Gk. *thyra*) form an alliteration in Greek and are positive images. "'When you see *these things* (Gk. *tauta*) happening'" refers to "these (Gk. *tauta*) birth pains" of v. 8, that is, to the events leading up to the fall of Jerusalem in vv. 5-13.

30-31 The fall of Jerusalem once again functions as a mysterious paradigm of the end of the world. The solemn pronouncements accompanying it ("'know the time,'" v. 28; "'Even so, when you see,'" v. 29; "'I tell you the truth,'" v. 30) emphasize exactly how paradigmatic the destruction of the temple is for the eschaton. The "'generation [that will not] pass away until all these things have happened'" (v. 30) has stirred no little controversy in NT theology. According to our interpretation, the generation under discussion is not that of the Second Coming,[48] but the generation contemporary to Jesus that lived to witness the destruction of the temple and fall of Jerusalem.

Beyond the cataclysm, however, stands Jesus himself. "'Heaven and earth will pass away, but my words will never pass away.'" For Jesus to assert that his words will outlive heaven and earth is a remarkable claim of authority. The only being who could reasonably make such a claim is God (so Isa 51:6). Here is an important key to the eschatological predictions of Mark 13, for if Jesus' words will outlive the cosmos, then the world to come is already present in them. The Word made flesh is

---

47. Similarly, the *Apocalypse of Peter* 2 sees in the image of the fig tree the destruction of the house of Israel, which is also a symbol of the final eschaton.

48. Against Bultmann (among others), who asserted that "Jesus' expectation of the near end of the world turned out to be an illusion" (*Theology of the New Testament*, trans. K. Grobel [New York: Scribner's, 1951/1955], 1.22).

thus inextricably related to the Son of Man who comes on the clouds of heaven. If in Mark 13 the events associated with the Incarnation are blended mysteriously with those of the Parousia — events which to our way of thinking are entirely separate — it may help to remember that in God's saving plan the Incarnation, crucifixion, resurrection, ascension, and Parousia are all facets of *one* event — rather like the way several separate mountain ranges blend together as a single range of mountains when viewed through a telescope (2 Pet 3:8). The first and second comings of God's Son comprise one event in the divine plan. Cranfield captures their unity thus: "It was, and still is, true to say that the Parousia is at hand. . . . Ever since the Incarnation men have been living in the last days."[49]

EXPECTANCY AND VIGILANCE (13:32-37)

The Olivet discourse concludes on a note of mystery. When one reviews chap. 13 as a whole, this may seem disappointing, for the discourse began with a request for a sign (v. 4), that is, for special insight into the future. But we learn in conclusion that knowledge of the End exceeds knowability: not only human and angelic knowability but even the knowability of the Son of God. Its sudden consummation is hidden solely in the mystery of God. All the signs that have been given add up to one conclusion: the End *cannot* be prepared for. That is because the End is ultimately not a "then" but a mysteriously present *now*. The sole preparation for the End is watchfulness and faithfulness in the present.

32 The final section of the Olivet discourse begins with a declaration of Jesus, "'No one knows about that day or hour.'" The original Greek begins with an explicit adversative that is not translated in the NIV: "'But concerning that day. . . .'" This sets v. 32 in contrast to the preceding subject of "these things," that is, the fall of Jerusalem. "Day" and "hour" are often charged with eschatological meaning in the Bible.[50] "That day" is coordinate to "those days" of vv. 17, 19, 20, and 24, and thus reintroduces the theme of the Parousia of vv. 14-27. The end, however, is

---

49. Cranfield, *The Gospel According to St Mark,* 408. On the oneness of all aspects of the Christ-event in the divine economy, see same author, "St. Mark 13," *SJT* 7 (1954): 288; and especially K. Barth, *Church Dogmatics: The Doctrine of Creation,* 3/2, ed. G. Bromiley and T. Torrance (Edinburgh: T. & T. Clark, 1960), 485-511.

50. "Day," Isa 2:12; Amos 5:18; Mark 14:25; Luke 21:34; 2 Thess 1:10; 2 Tim 1:12, 18; 4:8; "hour," John 5:25-28; Rev 18:10. See Lohmeyer, *Das Evangelium des Markus,* 283.

shrouded in mystery, for "'not even the angels in heaven, nor the Son, but only the Father'" knows the Parousia.[51]

13:32 has been a stumbling block in the church since at least the second century.[52] Conservatives have either questioned or rejected its authenticity because it ascribes ignorance to Jesus; and liberals have done the same because it attests to Jesus' consciousness of his divine Sonship.[53] The fact remains, however, that the early church is scarcely likely to have attributed a saying to Jesus that ascribes ignorance to him.[54] The saying lays the highest possible claim to have come from Jesus and to represent his mind.[55] The "Son" is properly understood as Son of God rather than Son of Man since the latter does not occur in the Gospels in an absolute sense (i.e., "the Son"), whereas "Son of God" is used absolutely (e.g., Matt 11:27//Luke 10:22).[56] "The Son," which stands correlative to "Father," means "the Father's Son," or the Son of God.

This verse contains an amazing paradox. Here the bold assertion of divine Sonship is yoked to the unlikely limitation of ignorance. In this the only passage in the Gospel of Mark where Jesus explicitly calls himself "the Son," he admits to what he does *not* know and *cannot* do. This irony is, to be sure, very much in accord with Mark's portrayal of Jesus as the Son, for Jesus does not claim the prerogatives of divine Sonship apart from complete obedience to the Father's will but rather forsakes claims and calculations in favor of humble confidence in the Father's will.

51. The idea that the time of the eschaton is known only to God is typical of Jewish apocalyptic. "'Concerning the signs about which you ask me, I can tell you in part; but I was not sent to tell you concerning your life, for I do not know'" (4 Ezra 4:52). See also 4 Ezra 6:11-28; Zech 14:7; *Pss. Sol.* 17:23; *2 Bar.* 21:8; *Tg. Ket. Qoh.* 7:24.

52. 13:32 was frequently discussed by the church fathers of the third and fourth centuries because the Arians cited it in support of their contention that the Son was subordinate to the Father. See the discussion in M.-J. Lagrange, *Évangile selon Saint Marc*, 349-51.

53. Mark 13:32 and Matt 11:27//Luke 10:22 are the only two passages in the NT where Jesus explicitly calls himself "the Son (of God)."

54. "Its offence seals its genuineness" (V. Taylor, *The Gospel According to St. Mark*, 522).

55. For a discussion and defense of authenticity, see B. M. F. van Iersel, *"Der Sohn" in den synoptischen Jesusworten*[2] (Leiden: E. J. Brill, 1964), 117-20.

56. Contra J. Jeremias, *New Testament Theology, Part One: The Proclamation of Jesus*, trans. J. Bowden (London: SCM Press, 1971), 131, who states, "In Mark 13.32, at least, the words *oude ho huios* are secondary because of the absolute use of *ho huios*, which is alien to Palestine; on the other hand, the absolute use of *ho patēr* is assured as a rendering of *'Abba*." The assertion that the absolute use of "the Son" is foreign to Palestine is simply unsustainable. In the Johannine corpus Jesus is called "the Son" twenty times, and in Hebrews, which was written to a Jewish audience, six times. Jesus frequently referred to God as "Father," and it should scarcely surprise us that he also referred to himself on occasion as "the Son," especially in a passage where Father and Son are correlatives.

Equally ironic is the fact that the Son, unlike the disciples, relinquishes all claims concerning the future into the Father's plan. The disciples want an "It" — a sign; Jesus wants a "Thou" — the Father. In these two ironies — Jesus' acceptance of his human limitation and his full relinquishment of the future into the Father's hand — the divine Sonship is not something that sets Jesus apart from humanity but binds him to humanity as an example to follow.[57] The effect of v. 32 thus directs attention exclusively to the Father, for "only the Father knows about that day or hour" (Acts 1:7). In the midst of calamity and destruction, tribulation and persecution, when even the sun, moon, and stars are shaken (vv. 24-25), the believer may rest assured that God is still *Father*, and as Father he remains steadfast in his just will, compassion, and purpose.

33-37 Temptations come in many forms. False prophets raise false hopes; mistaken signs raise fears and anxiety; the delay of the Parousia induces complacency and neglect; lack of knowledge induces resignation and defeat. These and other factors tempt disciples to forsake their vocation. Christian vocation is grounded in a fact twice repeated: "'You do not know when that time will come'" (13:34, 35). But the same vocation is grounded in a consequent imperative: "'Be on guard! Be alert!'" (v. 33). The day and hour will come suddenly (v. 36), when those who are confident of their own calculations are sleeping. Five times — and in three different words — Jesus warns the disciples to watch, to be alert.[58] The mini-parable in v. 34 about the householder away on business who may return at any moment underscores this point.[59] The parable focuses on the doorkeeper, who has but one "charge." The Greek word behind "charge" is *exousia*, the same word used of Jesus' divine authority. Here it connotes the responsibility that legitimates the doorkeeper's position, which is to *watch*. Living faithfully in the present, being attentive to the signs, and being ready at any hour for the return of the master is not one job among others; it is the doorkeeper's *only* job. Disciples are like doorkeepers; their single vocation is "'Therefore keep watch'" (v. 35), whether "'in the eve-

---

57. See Schlatter, *Der Evangelist Matthäus*, 713-14.

58. *Blepete* ("take care," v. 33); *agrypneite* ("be alert," v. 33); *grēgoreite* ("be watchful," vv. 34, 35, 37). The first word implies discernment, the second wakefulness, and the third vigilance. In v. 33 a majority of ancient manuscripts reads "'watch *and pray*.'" Despite substantial manuscript support for this reading, there is reason to doubt its originality since (1) copyists would naturally add prayer to the admonition (perhaps in conformity with 14:38; Metzger, *TCGNT*, 112); (2) the admonition in vv. 33-37 is to watchfulness rather than prayer; and (3) prayer is relatively infrequent in Mark (ten times), and in the imperative only once (14:38).

59. The Teacher of Righteousness at Qumran made a similar point: "the final age . . . might delay, [but] wait for it; it definitely has to come and will not delay" (1QpHab 7:7-10).

ning, or at midnight, or when the rooster crows, or at dawn'" (v. 35). Mark includes the four Roman watches of the night rather than the three Jewish watches for the benefit of his Gentile readers. In the passion narrative, three of the four watches will be mentioned again (14:17; 14:72; 15:1), but the disciples will fail to watch in the first two, and in Gethsemane they will be reprimanded five times for failure to watch (14:34, 37, 38, 40, 41).[60]

"'Watch!'" is the final and most important word of the Olivet discourse. The point of Mark 13 is not so much to inform as to admonish; not to provide knowledge of arcane matters but to instill obedience in believers. "'What I say to you, I say to everyone: "Watch"'" (v. 37). *To everyone* designates a wider audience than the Twelve. This is the word of Jesus to the Twelve, the word of Mark to his readers, and the word of the Spirit to believers in every age. The End is unknown and will come suddenly: live in constant readiness.

---

60. See Hooker, *The Gospel According to St Mark*, 324.

CHAPTER FOURTEEN

The Abandonment of Jesus

MARK 14:1-72

Mark 14 and 15 describe the betrayal, arrest, trial, and crucifixion of Jesus, commonly known as the "passion" (from the Latin word for "suffer"). These chapters correspond more closely, particularly in sequence of events, to the passion narratives of Matthew and Luke, indicating that the passion narrative had been shaped into a structural unit before Mark received it. Nevertheless, the presence of three sandwich conventions in chap. 14 and one in chap. 15 are evidence that Mark is not simply transmitting tradition but also interpreting it for his purposes.

The general theme of chap. 14, the longest in the Gospel, is the abandonment of Jesus. The chapter opens with Jesus and the disciples in Jerusalem, where he is teaching and debating with the religious leaders. Everything, in other words, is as it has been in the Gospel so far. But following the Lord's Supper a rapid and total defection follows, leaving Jesus alone and abandoned. Chapter 14 rehearses in sorry detail how the earlier opposition of the Pharisees (3:6; 11:18; 12:12) metastasizes among the ruling council of the Jews, the Roman rulers, and the populace. The dam breaks within the ranks of his disciples as well, and they all — from Judas to Peter — flee. At the cross Jesus dies utterly alone, condemned by Rome and abandoned by the nation, his people, his followers, and even the Father (15:34). The fate of Jesus poignantly fulfills what Isaiah said of the Servant of Yahweh, all "have gone astray." Accused, assailed, scorned, Jesus suffers as silently "as a sheep before her shearers is dumb" (Isa 53:4-9).

THE SACRIFICE OF FAITH (14:1-11)

The defection from Jesus begins with Judas's plot (14:1-2, 10-11), into which Mark inserts the story of a woman who anoints Jesus' body for burial (vv. 3-9). This is a classic Markan sandwich, in which Mark succeeds in making an all-important third point without uttering a word. As in each sandwich technique, the middle story provides the key to understanding the whole. The bracketing of the devotion of the woman, who remains an unnamed outsider, by the betrayal plot of an intimate insider, creates an acid contrast between faith and treachery. The costly unguent of the woman is an exemplary sacrifice of faith, whereas the plot of Judas to betray his master for a sum of money is a sacrifice of faith in the opposite and worst sense of the term.

1-2 14:1 begins a "new page" of the narrative. The announcement of "the **Passover and the Feast of Unleavened Bread**" is not connected to chap. 13, nor to the temple motif of the preceding three chapters. Rather, it launches a chain of events that leads inexorably to the crucifixion. The Passover celebration, which goes back to the account of the exodus (Exodus 12), was one of the great pilgrimage festivals for which Jews gathered annually in Jerusalem. A year-old unblemished male lamb or goat (Exod 12:5) was ritually sacrificed in the temple on the afternoon of 14 Nisan (March/April), and eaten after sunset (i.e., on 15 Nisan) in family gatherings in private houses (Exod 12:6-20; Num 9:2-14; Deut 16:1-8). The Passover commenced the weeklong Feast of Unleavened Bread (Exod 12:15-20; 23:15; 34:18; Deut 16:1-8), commemorating the hasty departure of the Israelites from Egypt when there was no time to allow dough to rise. The Feast of Unleavened Bread required Israelites to rid themselves of foods but also of yeast. Because of its connection with the Feast of Unleavened Bread, the Passover can refer either to the sacrifice of the lamb and the meal on 14-15 Nisan, or to the entire seven-day observance. Mark distinguishes between the two events in 14:1, which indicates that the two-day time reference refers to Passover.[1]

The reference to the Passover as "two days away" should probably be understood according to the inclusive reckoning of time among the Jews, meaning "the day after" (so, too, 8:31). Mark dates the crucifixion on the day before Sabbath (i.e., Friday, 15:42), and the Last Supper on the night before (i.e., Thursday). The day before Passover would be Wednesday, on which Judas conspired with the religious leaders to betray Jesus.

The betrayal plot originates with Judas entering into collusion with

---

1. Str-B 4.41-76; H. Patsch, *"pascha,"* EDNT 3.50-51; J. C. Rylaarsdam, "Passover," *IDB* 3.663-68.

the religious leaders to betray his master. In other words, the betrayal originates within Jesus' inner circle. The note that Judas was "one of the Twelve" (14:10, 20; 3:19) warns Mark's readers that proximity to Jesus does not guarantee faithfulness. Indeed, greater intimacy with Jesus requires greater watchfulness (13:33-36). As an insider, Judas knows Jesus better than others do, and his knowledge and familiarity provide him means of justifying a deed for which there is no justification. His betrayal, as a consequence, is more grievous (14:19) and heinous (14:21).

Mark identifies the culprits in the plot as "the chief priests and teachers of the law," that is, the leaders of the Sanhedrin. He does not mention "the Jews," or the people, or even the Pharisees.[2] The resolution to kill Jesus is an official decision as opposed to a popular decision, which, according to Mark, is linked to Jesus' attack on the temple (11:18). The description of the plot oozes with intrigue: "The chief priests and the teachers of the law were looking for some sly way to arrest Jesus and kill him." The word for "looking for" (Gk. *zētein*) carries the connotation of seeking to gain power over or control (see further on the term at 1:37). The word for "arrest" (Gk. *kratein*) carries connotations of seizing or repressing (see further on the term at 3:21). The word translated "sly" (Gk. *dolos*) carries the sense of guile and deception; and "kill" (Gk. *apokteinein*) identifies the cold and ultimate objective of the plot. Already in the description of the plot against Jesus a connection with the Passover is discernible, for the language about death, which necessarily described the Passover lamb, is applied to Jesus. The redemption that will be wrought at the cross, no less than that at the Red Sea, will be won at the cost of the death of the Firstborn.

Jerusalem was the only place where the Passover could be celebrated, and the festival drew huge crowds, greatly increasing not only the population of the city but also the threat of a Jewish uprising. The Romans, as a consequence, took massive security precautions during festivals. This helps explain why the Jewish authorities hoped to dispatch Jesus without provoking a confrontation with his Galilean sympathizers (v. 2).

3 Into the plot against Jesus, Mark inserts the story of a woman who anoints Jesus with a costly unguent. Her tenderness and compassion stand in striking contrast to the treachery of Judas and the Jewish authorities. Bethany, a village about two miles from Jerusalem on the eastern side of the Mount of Olives, has been Jesus' base camp since arriving in Jerusalem (11:1, 11, 12). Simon the Leper was presumably known to

---

2. Although the scribes were generally Pharisees, e.g., "the teachers of the law who were Pharisees" (2:16).

Mark's readers, but he is unknown to us. His hosting the gathering indicates that he was a *former* leper since active leprosy would exclude one from all social occasions. It is probable that Mark's narrative relates in somewhat different form the same event of John 12:1-8.[3] If so, Mark's unnamed woman is Mary, sister of Martha and Lazarus, and Simon could be the father of the three.[4]

As a rule, it was a breach of etiquette for a Jewish male fellowship to be interrupted by women unless they were serving food. Mark has often reminded us, however, that societal and even Jewish values are not necessarily to be equated with Jesus' values. In this instance, the woman's intrusion is commended as a demonstration of faith (so 5:34). Mark stumbles over himself in Greek to convey the value of the nard, an expensive aromatic oil extracted from the root of an Indian herb of the same name (see Cant 1:12; 4:13-14). The guests present are understandably shocked by the anointing, estimating the vial of nard to be worth more than three hundred denarii (v. 5).[5] A denarius was a normal day's wage in Palestine (Matt 20:2). Three hundred denarii were thus equivalent to a year's earnings. Women were by and large excluded from careers that afforded the possibility of earning such wages or procuring objects of such value. The nard was very probably a family heirloom, in which case it possessed a

3. Matthew 26:6-13 follows Mark 14:3-9 unusually closely, but the relationship of Luke 7:36-50 and John 12:1-8 to Mark's account is ambiguous. Luke 7:36-50 is likely a different story altogether, for it is set in Galilee, not Judea; the Simon of the Luke account is a Pharisee, not a leper; the woman is a "sinner" who anoints Jesus' feet rather than his head; the objection is to her immorality, not to her extravagance; and the outcome is forgiveness, not anointing for burial. Tatian, moreover, omits the Lukan account from his *Diatessaron;* and it is scarcely conceivable that the Mary of John 12 and the immoral woman of Luke 7 are the same person. John 12:1-8, however, looks to be a variant account of Mark 14:3-9. John agrees in the main with Mark, though setting the story with Mary, Martha, and Lazarus six days before the Passover rather than two days before as in Mark, and identifying the chief objector as Judas. The unusual description of the nard as *myrou nardou pistikēs polytelou[s]* ("pure nard, an expensive perfume") is verbatim in Mark 14:3 and John 12:3, which raises the question whether John was not familiar with the written form of Mark's Gospel. The conflation of Luke's immoral woman with Mark's unnamed woman led the fourth-century Syrian church father Ephraem (and many since) mistakenly to identify the woman as Mary Magdalene — a conclusion for which there is no biblical support. On this final point, see J. Shaberg, "How Mary Magdalene Became a Whore," *BRev* 8/5 (1992): 30ff.

4. See the discussion of Simon's identity in H. B. Swete, *The Gospel According to St Mark*, 321. According to Swete, the suggestion that Simon the Leper was the father of Mary, Martha, and Lazarus goes back to Theophylact, an eleventh-century Byzantine archbishop.

5. Although Origen and the Syriac and Georgian versions omit "more than" (probably to harmonize with John 12:5), the overwhelming majority of manuscripts rightly includes the addition.

sentimental value in addition to its monetary value. Mark reports that she did not pour out the unguent but smashed the jar itself, which means the vessel could never be used again, thus symbolizing the totality of the gift.

The identification of the town and house, which is unusual for Mark, repeats and establishes Mark's "insider-outsider" motif. Bethany lay *outside* Jerusalem. The reference to Simon as *the leper* continues the outsider motif, for in Jewish society a leper was an outsider *par excellence*. If, on the other hand, the woman who anoints Jesus is Mary (John 12:3), her status as an outsider is enhanced if she remains unnamed. Thus, the naming of Bethany and Simon the Leper and the leaving of the woman unnamed all underscore the outsider motif, that is, that this place, this house, and this woman are those from which we should *least* expect an act of exemplary discipleship. But from this most unexpected quarter comes an act of sacrificial generosity that supersedes anything reported of Jesus' inner circle of disciples. The nature of the act itself seems to be what Mark desires us to see. The anonymity of the woman forces us to contemplate the act and nature of discipleship (v. 9) rather than the specific identity of disciples (so, too, 3:33-35; 9:38-41; 12:41-44).

4-5 Not surprisingly, the company is scandalized by the wastefulness of the act, especially in light of the needs of the poor. Their displeasure is not muffled. They were earlier "indignant" (Gk. *aganaktein*) at the presumption of James and John to request special seating in the kingdom of God (10:41); here the same word describes their anger at the woman's extravagance.[6] We cannot know whether their indignation is owing to genuine concern for the poor, or whether, as is often the case, the poor are simply used as a pretext for other motives. Whatever their motives, they regard the costly devotion of the woman as a "waste." Their condemnation obviously demeans the woman and her gift. In asserting that there could be a better use for the money, however, they demean Jesus as well, whom they regard as unworthy of such extravagance. The world has never had a problem with religion in moderation. It has no problem with

---

6. The textual tradition shows a propensity to expand the opening of v. 4. The reading of D and Θ, *hoi de mathētai autou dieponounto kai elegon* ("But his disciples were disturbed and were saying") can be rejected (1) because *dieponounto* is non-Markan (so B. Metzger, *TCGNT,* 112), (2) because of weaker manuscript support, and (3) because "disciples" is probably the result of the scribal tendency to make indefinite words (*tines;* "some") more definite. A series of other variants add the word "saying" (A C K X W Δ Π; followed by the NIV). Despite the strong manuscript of the longer reading, the shorter reading, *ēsan de tines aganaktountes pros heautous* ("But there were some indignant among themselves"), is preferred (1) because of strong manuscript support (א B C L Ψ) and (2) because it better explains the origin of the other readings.

too much wealth or power or sex or influence, but it has a problem with too much religion. That is evident here. The unnamed woman deems Jesus worthy of her sacrifice, whereas the disciples do not. "They rebuked her harshly." The Greek word behind this phrase, *embrimaesthai*, is unusually vehement, meaning "to flare the nostrils [in anger]."

6-7   Jesus does not enter into a debate with the disciples about the virtues of charitable giving. Rather, he defends a person whom they are willing to demean in the name of a theoretical good. "'Let her alone.'" The disciples judge by appearances; Jesus judges by motive. By their standards she has done a wasteful thing; by his she has done "'a beautiful thing.'" Jesus' standard of judgment is that she did what she was *able* to do: "'She did what she could'" (also 2 Cor 8:3). In nearly the same words Jesus earlier affirmed a woman whose gift was a pair of the smallest coins in circulation (12:44). How vastly different that woman's gift from this woman's, yet from Jesus they receive the same commendation! Faith and discipleship are not ideal realms, what we might like to be and do; they are absolute realities, who we are and what we are *able* to give. In Jesus' sight an act has value according to its motive and intent, and that — not its material value — is what makes it serviceable in the kingdom of God. When one acts thus, no gift, not even a mere two lepta (12:41-44), is meaningless; and no gift, even a year's salary, is wasted.

Jesus' statement in 14:7, "'the poor you will always have with you. . . . But you will not always have me,'" should not be taken as indifference to the poor. The OT is full of admonitions to show mercy to the poor, for Israel itself had been a slave people in Egypt. That Jesus taught and practiced mercy to the poor is attested in every stratum of Christian tradition. The essential issue in v. 7 is not the poor, however, but the woman in their midst, and not even the highest social good can be used to justify the injury done to her. Once again Jesus puts forward his own person in scandalous prominence. "'You can help the poor any time you want. But you do not always have me.'" We can, perhaps, justify such a statement from the mouth of God, but it is hard to imagine a justification for such a statement from a mere mortal. In placing himself above the poor Jesus places himself above the great commandment to "love your neighbor as yourself" (12:31). But with unassuming pretentiousness Jesus asserts his priority to all other goods. The value of a gift signals the value of the person to whom it is given. The extravagance of the woman shows that she alone understands Jesus' incommensurable worth.

8-9   The disciples have been forewarned of Jesus' impending death (8:31-33; 9:31-32; 10:32-34). But no overture commemorating his death has been forthcoming from them. What they fail to do, and perhaps even to understand, an unnamed woman understands and does. Anticipating the violent death of one "numbered with transgressors" (Isa 53:12), Jesus knew that his body would be thrown to dogs or cast into a common grave. He accepts the woman's anointing as a preparation for his burial, sparing him the indignity of a criminal's death.

It is often supposed that the woman's anointing of Jesus is a secret and long overdue messianic anointing.[7] Evidence for this suggestion is conspicuously lacking, however. Regal anointing in the OT required the use of oil (1 Sam 10:1; 2 Kgs 9:1-13); here, however, the woman anoints Jesus not with oil but with nard, a completely different substance.[8] If Mark had in mind a messianic anointing we should expect the use of the Greek verb *chriein* (from which *Christos* is derived), but that word is absent; instead, Mark uses a rare word, *katacheein*. The concept of Messiah is much less important than Son of God in Mark's portrayal of Jesus. Mark uses the word *Christos* only eight times in the Gospel, and in all the NT only Titus, James, 1-2 John, and Jude employ it less frequently. Mark's blue chip designation of Jesus is "Son of God," to which he was inaugurally anointed at his baptism in the Jordan by John (1:9-11). There seems to be no reason for a clandestine messianic anointing at this point in the Gospel. The combined evidence suggests that this is not a messianic anointing but an unction in preparation for Jesus' death: "'She poured perfume on my body beforehand to prepare for my burial'" (v. 8).

Jesus concludes with a pronouncement that matches the intensity of the disciples' earlier anger. "'I tell you the truth, wherever the gospel is preached throughout the world, what she has done will also be told, in memory of her.'" What exactly has she done to be worthy of such commemoration? She has of course expended a lavish gift on Jesus, but she also appears to be the first person to perceive that the gospel is realized only in suffering.[9] 14:9 is the last time "gospel" appears in Jesus' mouth in Mark, and as in its first use by Jesus (1:14), it appears in the context of proclamation (Gk. *kēryssein*). The gospel . . . Jesus' passion — these two things cannot be separated, and they must be proclaimed "'throughout the world.'" The woman's deed — if not her name — cannot be forgotten, for she perceives that the mystery of the gospel is revealed in Jesus' death.

7. For example, M. Dibelius, *Jesus,* trans. S. B. Hedrick and F. Grant (London: SCM Press, 1963), 88-89; T. W. Manson, *The Servant-Messiah* (Cambridge: Cambridge University Press, 1953), 84-85.

8. Nor was anointing the head with oil exclusive of royal anointing. It was frequently used as a symbol of honor or for cosmetic purposes, as in the rabbinic story of the woman who scooped a few drops of oil from the ground and placed it on her head to signal the recovery of her honor after a false accusation (*m. B. Qam.* 8:6).

9. Whenever "gospel" is used in Mark, it appears in contexts of suffering (1:1, 14, 15; 8:35; 10:29; 13:10; 14:9).

Excursus: Women in the Gospel of Mark

Women play especially important roles in the Gospel of Mark (1:1–16:8). Not only are they mentioned frequently, but the highest acclaim of Jesus in the Second Gospel goes to women. Mark mentions fifteen different women a total of twenty-two times in the Gospel, not counting the mention of Jesus' sisters (6:3), the "many other women" who followed Jesus from Galilee (15:41), and the mention of the right of women to divorce their husbands (10:12). Of this number, five women are named (Mary, Jesus' mother [6:3], Herodias [6:17], Mary Magdalene [15:40, 47; 16:1], Mary mother of James [15:40, 47; 16:1], and Salome [15:40; 16:1]). To be sure, some women appear in negative roles, such as the mother of Jesus who twice obstructs Jesus (3:31-32; 6:3), and Jesus' sisters once (6:3). The servant girl in the courtyard who questions Peter plays an ambivalent role (14:69ff.), as do Mary Magdalene, Mary the mother of James, and Salome, who bravely visit the tomb of Jesus but fail to declare his resurrection (16:1, 8). The worst roles fall to Herodias (6:17ff.) and her daughter (6:22ff.) for their responsibility in the death of John the Baptist.

Fifteen of the twenty-two mentions of women, however, appear in unusually positive contexts. The value and dignity of women — and girls — are signified by the fact that Jesus heals them (1:30-31; 5:25-34; 5:23, 41-42; 7:25). In their following and serving of Jesus and the Christian fellowship women are models of discipleship (1:30-31; 15:40, 47; 16:1). In special instances they play prominent roles, even preeminent roles, receiving the highest praise that Jesus gives in the Gospel. On two occasions women appear in the heart of the sandwich technique as the ideal of faith (5:21-43) and devotion (14:1-11). The woman with a hemorrhage is a model of faith for Jairus, the synagogue president (5:25-34); and the Syrophoenician women is a model of faith for all "outsiders" (7:25ff.). The widow in the temple is praised for giving more than everyone else, "her whole life" (12:42). And above all, the anointing at Bethany is so exemplary that the proclamation of the gospel in the world is a commemoration of her act (14:9).[10]

10-11 Mark closes the plot against Jesus with Judas's agreement to betray his master (vv. 10-11).[11] Luke 22:3 and John 13:2, 27 say that Satan caused Judas to betray Jesus, but Mark does not lay at Satan's feet the

---

10. On the significance of the woman's anointing for Mark's overall purpose, see S. C. Barton, "Mark as Narrative: The Story of the Anointing Woman (Mk 14:3-9)," *ExpTim* 102 (1991): 230-34.

11. For discussion of both the textual variant and the term "Iscariot," see at 3:19.

moral failure of Jesus' followers. Indeed, Judas's betrayal is a prototype of the defection of the other apostles as well (14:50). According to Mark, his betrayal is more reprehensible only because it was premeditated, and more final only because he foreclosed on the possibility of forgiveness by committing suicide. That money played a part in Judas's decision is probable, for according to the Gospel of John he was the treasurer of the Twelve, and a thief (John 12:6; 13:29). Also according to Mark, the transaction of money accompanied the plot (v. 11). The best way to detect the source of evil in practically any matter is to ask who profits from it financially, and Judas profited from the betrayal. More ideological or even idealistic motives may also have played a role. It has been suggested, for example, that Judas acted as a spy of the Sanhedrin; or that he was a closet Zealot disillusioned with Jesus' political passivity, hoping by the plot to force Jesus' hand to act. What truth there might be in such suggestions we cannot say, for our texts are silent about Judas's motives.[12]

Despite its economy, Mark's account implies that Judas was fully responsible for his betrayal of Jesus. It is he who goes to the chief priests, not they to him; and in one of the bitterest lines in the Gospel, his treachery causes them *joy* (14:11). The account closes with no Hamlet-like soliloquy lamenting a tragic decision, but with Judas's icy resolve to his complete his insidious plan: "So he watched (Gk. *zētein*) for an opportunity to hand him over." Judas is thus not a victim of circumstances or a pawn dominated by greater forces. He is a sovereign moral agent who freely chooses evil in "handing Jesus over" (Gk. *paradidomi*). That word, the final part of the sandwich in vv. 1-11, combines the two essential truths of Jesus' passion: the freely chosen evil of humanity, and the overarching providence of God. Divine grace uses even human evil for its saving purposes.

PREPARATION FOR THE PASSOVER (14:12-16)

The description of the Passover preparation is strongly reminiscent of the preparations for the entry into Jerusalem (11:1-6). In both passages Jesus

---

12. Speculations about Judas proliferated in the apocryphal literature from the second century onward. In general, Judas is a negative example for the fate of the wicked. As a dire warning against apostasy, Papias, Bishop of Hierapolis in the early second century, writes that Judas's body swelled to larger than the size of a wagon and fouled the land with stench. Other traditions tried to explain why Judas betrayed Jesus. A fragment from a series of Coptic texts that claim a relationship to the apostle Bartholomew relates how Judas was induced to treachery not by the devil but (you guessed it) by his wife! See *NTApoc* 1.24; 2.555.

sends two disciples on covert errands that must be completed if events are to proceed. Both errands entail mysterious meetings, and both transpire exactly as Jesus predicts. Both accounts also share a string of eleven consecutive words in common (14:13; 11:1-2). The effect of both stories is to show Jesus' knowledge and complete governance of events as his "hour" (14:35) of death approaches. Jesus is not a tragic hero caught in events beyond his control. There is no hint of desperation, fear, anger, or futility on his part. Jesus does not cower or retreat as plots are hatched against him. He displays, as he has throughout the Gospel, a sovereign freedom and authority to follow a course he has freely chosen in accordance with God's plan. Judas and others may act against him, but they do not act *upon* him.

12 By Jewish reckoning "the first day of the Feast of Unleavened Bread" technically began at sundown (i.e., 15 Nisan) when the Passover, which began at sunset and lasted until midnight, was celebrated. In v. 12, however, Mark appears to place the beginning of the Passover on Thursday afternoon of 14 Nisan when the Passover lambs were slaughtered (NIV, "the sacrifice of the Passover lamb"). Some commentators suggest that Mark may be reckoning time according to the Hellenistic practice of beginning the new day at dawn, which would put both the slaughter of the lambs and the eating of the Passover meal on the same day. This suggestion is not necessary to account for the time references in v. 12, however. Even though Exod 12:6 stipulated the sacrifice of the Passover lamb on the afternoon of 14 Nisan, there is some rabbinic evidence that Passover lambs were regularly sacrificed earlier.[13] Such latitude in sacrifice is hardly surprising given the vast numbers of pilgrims serviced by the temple at Passover. The wording of v. 12 thus reflects a practice evidently accepted by many Jewish pilgrims.

According to Deut 16:5-8, Passover could be celebrated only within the walls of Jerusalem. This produced a great influx of pilgrims into Jerusalem each spring, causing the population to swell to many times its normal size. Josephus reports that at Passover in A.D. 66, the year the temple was completed, 255,600 lambs were slaughtered in the temple. Allowing an average of ten diners per lamb, Josephus calculates that two and a half million people were present in Jerusalem — not counting pilgrims who

---

13. "If a Passover-offering was slaughtered on the morning [instead of the afternoon] of the 14th [of Nisan] under some other name, R. Joshua declares it valid, as though it had been slaughtered on the 13th" (*m. Zev.* 1:3). The ruling of Rabbi Joshua [ben Hananiah], a pre–70 A.D. Jerusalem rabbi, indicates that sacrifice during "twilight" (= afternoon; so Exod 12:6) was more important than the date of the sacrifice. See M. Casey, "The Date of the Passover Sacrifices and Mark 14:12," *TynBul* 48 (1997): 245-47, who argues that sacrifice on 13th Nisan was "accepted practice."

for various reasons were unclean and could not partake (*War* 6.420-27). This is a staggering figure — and probably an exaggeration, for it is inconceivable that so many people could be accommodated by the city limits of Jerusalem in the first century. Josephus's description certainly conveys the crowding and congestion that befell Jerusalem at Passover, however. The mood of expectancy and urgency that characterized all Passover pilgrims pervades Jesus' band of followers as well. Three times in vv. 12-16 (in Greek) the word "preparation" occurs as the disciples inquire where they should prepare the Passover "'for *you* to eat.'" The singular pronoun not only establishes Jesus as the presiding head of the meal, but it anticipates the words of institution in v. 22, "'this is my body.'" Jesus not only presides at the feast; he *is* the feast (1 Cor 5:7).

13-14 Jesus sent the disciples two-by-two into mission (6:7). He sent two disciples to fetch the colt for the entry into Jerusalem (11:1), and he now sends two disciples from Bethany to make Passover preparations in the city (Luke 22:8 identifies them as Peter and John). They are given undercover instructions: "'a man carrying a jar of water'" will meet them and take them to a householder, who will show them their quarters.[14] The reference to a jar of water may locate the meeting in the vicinity of the pool of Siloam on Mt. Zion, to which water was diverted by Hezekiah's tunnel from Jerusalem's only water source, the Gihon spring. A male water carrier would have caught their eye, for carrying water was normally the labor of women or slaves. In order to avoid his own arrest (14:1; John 11:57), Jesus may have arranged the covert meeting in advance.[15] Even so, the instructions of v. 13 hint at divine foreknowledge, for even a man carrying a water jug would have been hard to spot and

---

14. B. Pixner, *Wege des Messias und Stätten der Urkirche,* Herausgegeben von R. Riesner (Giesen/Basel: Brunnen Verlag, 1991), 219-21, reasons that since carrying water was customarily women's work, and the Essene community did not permit women members, the man carrying water was necessarily an Essene. Pixner further argues that the site of the Last Supper was in the Essene Quarter in the southwest corner of Jerusalem (1) because the disciples (being non-Essenes) could not enter the Essene compound (hence the instructions to inquire of "the owner of the house" in v. 14), and (2) because the Essenes, who were known for hospitality (Josephus, *War* 2.124), could be expected to have a guest room. Pixner's chain of reasoning is somewhat speculative, but his thesis is neither impossible nor improbable, for the traditional site of the Last Supper, which has received considerable archaeological attention, neighbors the reputed Essene Quarter.

15. B. Pixner, *Mit Jesus in Jerusalem,* 88, suggests that the secrecy of the instructions was intended to prevent Judas, the betrayer, from knowing the Passover site. According to Pixner, as treasurer Judas should have made the arrangements assigned to the two disciples. This suggestion is quite improbable. Nowhere does the NT hint that Jesus tried to deceive Judas. Judas was well informed about Jesus' whereabouts (John 18:2), and the introduction to the Last Supper presupposes that Judas must be present (vv. 18-21), not excluded.

follow among the huge Passover throng. The instructions for the preparation of the Passover, like those for the entry into Jerusalem (11:1-6), are presented as instances of Jesus' ability to predict and control the events of passion week.

Jewish residents of Jerusalem were expected to make available spare rooms in their houses for Passover pilgrims. The "guest room" (v. 14; Gk. *kataluma*) requested by Jesus was evidently such a room. Mark describes it as "a large upper room, furnished and ready." "Furnished" (Gk. *stronnymi*) should not be understood primarily as "furniture." The Greek word means the "spreading out" of rugs and carpets on which to recline; thus "a well laid out" banquet room. Such a lodging belonged to a person of means and was perhaps located on Mt. Zion, where a number of upscale dwellings have been excavated.[16] The hall so described resembles the meeting place of the early church described in Acts 1:13 and 12:12. If it is the same dwelling, then it belonged to Mary the mother of John Mark, the probable author of the Second Gospel. The suggestion that John Mark was the carrier of the water jar is possible, but without evidence.

The careful and deliberate preparations for the Passover are a clue that in this foundational event Jesus sees the proper context for his own self-revelation. The sacrifice of the paschal lamb will both interpret and be fulfilled in his impending death that will inaugurate a new covenant in his own blood, "'poured out for many'" (14:24).

OBLATION AND OBDURACY (14:17-31)

The Last Supper is set within another of Mark's sandwich constructions, the flanking halves of which consist of the disciples' betrayal and defection. The complex falls into:

> A[1] Betrayal of disciples (vv. 17-21)
> B Last Supper (vv. 22-26)
> A[2] Defection of disciples (vv. 27-31).

16. The Cenacle is identified for modern tourists to Jerusalem as the site of the Last Supper. The present structure, a mosque remodeled from a fourteenth-century church, obviously dates from a much later period, but the site was attested in the fourth century by Cyril of Jerusalem and the Pilgrim of Bordeaux, and in the sixth century by the Madaba map. According to Epiphanius, the emperor Hadrian identified the same site as the place of the Upper Room in A.D. 135. See O. Sellers, "Upper Room," *IDB* 4.735; and, most recently, B. Pixner, "Church of the Apostles Found on Mt. Zion," *BARev* 16/3 (1990): 16ff.

In Mark's sandwich convention the B-part provides the key to understanding the whole. In the present construction the self-sacrifice of Jesus in the Last Supper contrasts dramatically with the infidelity of the disciples. It is, in other words, not the worthy for whom Jesus lays down his life, but precisely for the unworthy — even cowardly and unfaithful followers. The sandwich illustrates the truth of Rom 5:8, "God demonstrates his own love for us in this: While we were still sinners, Christ died for us." The sandwich is also placed in striking apposition to the preceding sandwich of 14:1-11. There the flanking halves concerned the betrayal of Judas; here they concern the betrayal of all the disciples. The central B-part of both sandwiches is also parallel, focusing on the body of Jesus. At Bethany the woman anoints Jesus' body (Gk. *to sōma mou,* 14:8) for burial; at the Last Supper Jesus gives his body (Gk. *to sōma mou,* 14:22) for sinners.

17 Exodus 12:3-4 instructs a man to gather his household at table — and his neighbor's as well if his family is too small — to consume a whole Passover lamb. That the meal Jesus shares with the disciples is a Passover meal is clear from the statements in 14:1-2 and 12, and the description of the preparation for the Passover in vv. 13-16 immediately preceding.[17] The Passover was a family celebration, which means that women and children were a normal and necessary part of the meal. In the course of the meal the youngest boy present asked prescribed questions that the householder answered by retelling the story of the Exodus and by explaining its meaning as symbolized in the Passover meal. Mark's account of the Last Supper is selective, focusing only on Jesus' betrayal and his impending death as the fulfillment of the Passover sacrifice. That Mark does not record the entire Passover ceremony or mention the presence of women (and perhaps children) does not imply that the meal was not a Passover meal or that there were no women present. Mark counts on his readers to know what a Passover meal was like, but he relates only those portions significant for Jesus' self-revelation. As far as the women are concerned, there are several clues in chaps. 14–15 suggesting their presence at the Last Supper.[18]

"When evening came, Jesus arrived with the Twelve." Thus begins

17. On the Last Supper as a Passover celebration, see M. Casey, "No Cannibals at Passover!" *Theology* 96 (1993): 199-205.

18. In 15:41 we are told that "many women" accompanied Jesus from Galilee to Jerusalem. It is hard to imagine that women who had followed Jesus thus far would be excluded from a ceremony at which they were a constituent part. Again, a "large room" (14:15) would not have been necessary if only thirteen people were present for Passover. Finally, the clarification that the betrayer was "one of the Twelve" (14:20) would be unnecessary if only the Twelve were gathered for the Passover.

the description of Jesus' final gathering with the Twelve in his earthly ministry. Jews reckoned the new day beginning at sunset, and "evening" signaled 15 Nisan, the time for the Passover meal. The holiest festival of the Jewish year, Passover commemorated the deliverance from Egypt when the angel of death "passed over" the firstborn in Jewish homes with lambs' blood on the door frames (Exodus 12). As the eldest male interpreted the feast, accents fell on *remembering* their past deliverance from Egypt and on *anticipating* the future redemption of the Messiah. According to the Mishnah tractate *Pesahim* 10, a Passover liturgy consisted of the recitation of the Hallel Psalms (Psalms 113–18). The actual meal was divided into four parts, each concluding with the drinking of a cup of wine. A blessing was first pronounced by the family head over the gathering. Then, in response to a child's question, "'Why is this night different from other nights?'" the father recounted the deliverance from Egypt according to Deut 26:5-9. Third, the father pronounced a benediction over the various foods that symbolized the bitter captivity in Egypt and both the hardships and blessings of the Exodus: unleavened bread, bitter herbs, greens, stewed fruit, and roast lamb. Family and guests were then invited to partake of the meal. Near midnight the feast concluded with the singing of Psalms 116–18 and the drinking of the fourth cup of wine.

18-20 The opening reference to the Last Supper in 14:18 comes several hours into the Passover meal. The group is "reclining," which was the customary position in the ancient world for eating feasts and formal meals, if not all meals. The reference to "eating" (v. 18) signals the third phase of the meal. In the midst of the meal Jesus solemnly announces , "'I tell you the truth, one of you will betray me.'" The celebration of Holy Communion is the purest and holiest moment of the church's life, symbolized by polished chalices and linen altar cloths. What bitter irony to recall that this feast, reminiscent of victory and joy, began with an announcement of treachery! The account of the Last Supper begins on the note of betrayal, and all other elements of the meal acquiesce to it. "'One who is eating with me'" does not limit the field of suspects but *expands* it, for everyone present eats with Jesus. The saying is framed according to Ps 41:9, where a righteous man is betrayed by a friend. Jesus does not mention Judas. His word does not provide relief by identifying the culprit, but its ambiguity provokes soul-searching in each disciple. The announcement evokes grief and protests. The word for "grief" (Gk. *lypein*) is used only twice in Mark (10:22; 14:19), both times of those who fail Jesus. There is joy in following Jesus on the way (10:52), but grief in failing him, as Peter will discover (14:72). "One by one" — a Semitism in Greek — each protests, "'Surely not I?'" The betrayer, continues Jesus, is "'one of the Twelve, one who dips bread in the bowl with me.'" This clarification limits the culprits to the Twelve and exonerates the other members at the Passover meal. The likely suspects, in other words, are dismissed, and all the intimate companions — they whose very hands have been in Jesus' bowl — are suspect.[19] There may have been only one traitor in the formal sense, but by dawn all the disciples will betray Jesus, if not from greed (vv. 10-11), then from weakness (vv. 37-42), fear (vv. 50-52), or cowardice (vv. 66-72). "'Surely not I?'" How that protest echoes down the centuries!

21 This verse is one of the most suggestive verses in Scripture on the relationship between divine causality and human responsibility. It also gives us a rare insight into the mind of Jesus. That the saying represents the mind of Jesus is evinced by the presence of "Son of Man" (see further at 2:10; 8:31), a title used only by Jesus of himself and not by the early church of Jesus. Of special interest is the statement that "'the Son of Man will go just as it has been written about him.'" The phrase "it is written" (see further at 1:2) carries the sense of divine purpose or fore-ordination. There is no place in the pre-Christian tradition, however, where the Son of Man is destined to suffer. The figure who is destined to suffer is rather the Servant of the Lord (Isa 53:6, 10). The idea that the Son of Man must be betrayed and suffer is meaningful only if Jesus, as the Son of Man, identifies himself with the suffering Servant of the Lord,[20] and sees in his passion the fulfillment of the vicarious atonement of others (Isa 53:4, 12).

14:21 further adumbrates the paradox of the crucifixion and atonement as represented in Jesus' words at the Last Supper. The betrayer was one of Jesus' chosen disciples. His betrayal was a grave evil, but it also seemed necessary for the fulfillment of God's plan (Acts 3:17-18; 4:27-28). Thus Jesus goes in accordance with God's predetermined will, but the betrayer is not thereby exonerated of guilt. Neither Jesus nor Judas is an instrument of blind fate or a pawn of divine strategy. "'Woe to that man who betrays the Son of Man! It would be better for him if he had not been born'" (also 1 Clem. 46:8; Herm. Vis. 4:2:6). Divine providence neither cancels human freedom nor relieves responsibility for moral choices. Both currents of divine foreordination and human free will intersect in the Greek verb *paradidomi* (vv. 18, 21), meaning "to deliver up" or "hand over" (NIV, "betrayed"). In one act, Jesus is employed in God's holy and necessary purpose and betrayed by Judas to his enemies.

19. Three important ancient codices (B C Θ) heighten the treachery by reading, "into the *same* bowl with me" *(met' emou eis to hen tryblion)*. Fitting though it is to the sense of the meaning, the emphatic *same* is not present in the majority of manuscripts, and has been rightly omitted by the NIV.

20. V. Taylor, *The Gospel According to St. Mark*, 541-42.

22 Into the context of the infidelity and defection of the disciples Mark places the Last Supper as the central part of his sandwich construction. In comparison to the elaborate arrangements for the Passover in vv. 12-16, the Last Supper is narrated with thrift and brevity in vv. 22-26. The rich and symbolic elements of the Passover have become subsumed in Jesus' simple but momentous words of institution. Already before Mark the Lord's Supper had achieved liturgical form in the early church, although slight variations in the NT are still evident. The words of institution are shortest in Mark 14:22 and Matt 26:26, "'This is my body.'" Paul adds "'which is for you'" (1 Cor 11:24), and Luke, evidently in dependence on both Mark and Paul, adds "'given'" (22:19). In contrast to Mark and Matthew, Paul and Luke also contain a command to repeat the observance. From earliest times the Last Supper has been regarded by the church as the truest representation of its fellowship with Christ.[21]

"While they were eating, Jesus took bread, gave thanks, and broke it, and gave it to his disciples." The words of institution occur after the Passover meal is in progress, probably between the drinking of the second and third cups of wine. If Jesus followed the normal Passover rite, the blessing or thanksgiving as he broke the bread (v. 22) and distributed the wine (v. 23) would have been, "Blessed art thou, O Lord our God, king of the world, who brings forth bread from the earth." According to the Torah, the bread of presentation that was placed on the golden table in the tabernacle Sabbath by Sabbath was called "bread of remembrance" (Lev 24:7). There are seven transitive Greek verbs in v. 22 (eat, take, bless, break, give, say, take), signifying the gracious *activity* of Jesus on behalf of the disciples. When Jesus said, "'This is my body,'" the Aramaic (Jesus' native tongue) behind "body" likely meant "my person," "my whole being," "my self." Likewise, the Greek word behind "body" is not *sarx* (flesh), but *sōma*, "body" or perhaps "being." All the activity signified by the verbs thus results in the gift of Jesus *himself*, wholly and without reserve, in his self-offering for the disciples. They may feed on him by faith whenever they gather for table fellowship in his name. The verb "is" has been the subject of debate and the cause of much division in the history of the church. The actual Aramaic would have been, "'This, my body,'" with "is" implied. When supplied, "is" suggests a too formal, even mathematical, equation between Jesus and the bread; on the other hand, a paraphrase such as "represents" weakens the relationship between Jesus and the bread to a figurative or symbolic likeness.

---

21. *Did.* 9:1-5; Epiphanius, *Pan.* 30.22.4-5; Justin Martyr, *Apol.* 1.66.3; *Dial. Trypho* 111.3.

The verb is ideally understood as a metaphor, "The bread *means* or *conveys* my body."

23-24   Taking the third cup, Jesus gives it to the disciples. Between the offerings of the bread (14:22) and cup (v. 23) lay an interval of time required to eat the meal. The theory that Jesus' words alter the substance of the bread and wine according to the medieval doctrine of transubstantiation overinterprets the sense of our Eucharistic texts. It is unlikely that Jesus' words connote a change in substance in Mark, for he declares "'This is my blood'" *after* the disciples have drunk the cup (v. 23).[22] Furthermore, the near demonstrative pronoun "'*This* is my blood/body'" in vv. 22 and 24 is neuter (Gk. *touto*). If it were meant to designate either the bread or wine, it would need to be masculine (Gk. *houtos*) to agree with both antecedents. The neuter form of "this" points rather to the body of Jesus and away from either bread or wine.[23] Finally, the phrase "'poured out for many,'" although it is symbolized in the pouring of the wine, becomes reality not in the wine of the Upper Room but in Jesus' death on Golgotha.[24] Obviously, neither baptism nor any other rite is a prerequisite for the meal; the only prerequisite at this meal is *need*. Mark is the only Gospel writer who adds, "and they all drank from it."[25] The "all" echoes throughout the remainder of the chapter, recalling both the grace of Jesus and the failure of the disciples: they "all drank" (v. 23), they "all [swear allegiance to Jesus]" (v. 31); but they "all fall away" (v. 27), and they "all fled" (v. 50). The original Last Supper is attended by traitors (v. 18) and cowards (v. 50); it a table not of merit but of grace!

The climax of the meal occurs in the declaration, "'This is my blood of the covenant, which is poured out for many.'"[26] In Hebrew thought the life of a creature resided in its blood; Jesus' reference to the cup as "'my blood'" thus implies his very life. Jewish rabbis spoke of "the blood of the covenant" only with reference to circumcision,[27] but Jesus' use of the expression is obviously vastly different. The "blood of the covenant" cannot be understood apart from the first covenant that Moses instituted by throwing blood on the people (Exod 24:3-8). That covenant was sealed by

22. E. Schweizer, *The Good News According to Mark,* 303-4.

23. A. Schlatter, *Der Evangelist Matthäus,* 742.

24. See L. C. Boughton, "'Being Shed for You/Many': Time-Sense and Consequences in the Synoptic Cup Citations," *TynBul* 48 (1997): 249-70.

25. Although Matt 26:27 commands, "'Drink from it, all of you.'"

26. For a study tracing this statement to the historical Jesus on the basis of multiple attestation, dissimilarity, and coherence, see K. Backhaus, "Hat Jesus vom Gottesbund gesprochen?" *TGl* 86 (1996): 343-56. Contra J.-M. van Cangh, "Le déroulement primitif de la Cène (Mc 14,18-26 et par.)," *RB* 102 (1995): 193-225, who regards v. 24 as a liturgical addition of the Hellenistic community.

27. Str-B 1.991.

necessity with the blood of a surrogate sacrificial animal. The new covenant here instituted (Jer 31:31-34) must be sealed by Jesus' blood; it is not simply thrown *on* the community as in Exod 24:8, but imbibed *into* believers. "'My blood of the covenant'"[28] implies that the blood of Jesus is the only true and efficacious blood of the covenant, of which the blood of animals was merely proleptic. Moreover, the blood of Jesus "'is poured out for many.'" In 10:45 Jesus spoke of the purpose of the Son of Man "'to give his life as a ransom for many.'" At the Last Supper that purpose becomes reality.[29] "Many" does not mean a limited, select group, as it did at Qumran, for example, where "the many" repeatedly designates community members only (e.g., 1QS 6). Rather, "many" alludes to Isaiah's suffering servant, who "bore the sins of many and made intercession for the transgressors" (Isa 53:12).[30] It links Jesus' death to the idea of vicarious sacrifice for the lawless, sinners, and transgressors.[31]

25-26 14:25 falls at the drinking of the final cup of the Passover.[32] This saying shifts the focus of the celebration from the origin of the blood covenant in Exodus 24 to its fulfillment "anew in the kingdom of God." "Until that day" resumes the eschatological motif of chap. 13 (vv. 17, 19, 20, 24, and 32), when God's kingdom will be fully realized. As the sounds of his words die out, his final mission begins. The gathering sings a song, probably the final Hallel Psalms (115–18), then unobtrusively leaves the city, crosses the Kidron Valley to the east, and heads up the Mount of Olives.

27-28 Mark now closes the sandwich construction with a conversation between Jesus and Peter. Peter acts as spokesman for the disciples

---

28. Several Greek manuscripts read, "'This is my blood of the *new* covenant'" (A K P Δ Π X), but "new" is probably a later harmonization of Mark's text with 1 Cor 11:25 and Luke 22:20.

29. See A. Y. Collins, "The Signification of Mark 10:45 among Gentile Christians," *HTR* 90 (1997): 382.

30. J. H. Moulton, *Grammar of New Testament Greek,* 3 vols. (Edinburgh: T. & T. Clark, 1908-63), 26, notes that in the NT "many" often designates a group in its entirety. For further discussion of "many," see at 10:45.

31. The concept of vicarious suffering on the part of the Servant of the Lord in Isaiah 53, here applied to the death of Jesus, is unique in the OT. Judaism had no concept of a ransom for the people as a whole, nor of a Messiah whose death would have saving significance. See W. Grundmann, *Das Evangelium nach Markus,* 391-92.

32. Two sets of textual variants surround the phrase "'I will not drink again'" (v. 25). One set includes adding the word *prostithēmi* ("intend"; D Θ 565). Although *prostithēmi* could reflect the Semitic *hosip,* it is too poorly attested to be considered original. The other variant is the omission of *ouketi* ("not again") in א C L W. The term should probably be retained (1) because of its stronger manuscript support, and (2) because its omission may be the result of scribal assimilation to the parallel in Matt 26:29. See Metzger, *TCGNT,* 113-14.

in vv. 27-31, and his bravado and subsequent defection typify those of the Twelve. The conversation forms a continuation and counterpart to the conversation of vv. 17-21. Prior to the Passover meal Jesus informed the disciples, "'one of you will betray me'" (v. 18); now he informs them, "'you will all fall away.'" Both the self-oblation of Jesus in the Passover meal and his verbal admonitions before and after bring the disciples face to face with the imminence of their own infidelity. Luke reports that Satan asked to "'sift [Peter] like wheat'" (22:31-32), accentuating even more starkly the spiritual danger of the hour. According to Papias (d. A.D. 135), Peter was an important source of information for Mark's Gospel. Papias's testimony in this respect seems trustworthy, for here as many times elsewhere in the Gospel Peter commends himself as an obvious source of this story and for much of what follows in Mark 14.

Reflecting on the effect his death will have upon the flock, Jesus speaks in turbulent imagery, "'You will all fall away.'" The Greek word for "fall away" *(skandalizein)* means "to cause to stumble" or "to fall." It carries a passive sense, that is, it does not mean that the disciples will willfully defect but that external factors will act upon them and cause them to do so. It is, in other words, a lapse rather than an egregious rebellion. *Skandalizein* is the failure to do what Jesus commanded of the disciples in chap. 13 — to be watchful and stalwart. *Skandalizein* is the undermining of the trust and commitment that Jesus endeavored to teach the disciples "on the way."[33] Jesus warns the disciples to guard against the kind of sinfulness of which most of us are most guilty: sins of weakness and irresoluteness rather than sins of intention. We do not plan on sinning, but neither do we hold the fort when we ought.

Jesus follows and fortifies his admonition with a quotation, "'for it is written, "I will strike the shepherd, and the sheep will be scattered"'" (Zech 13:7).[34] The reference to "written" (see on the term at 1:2) and the Scripture citation lend divine authority to Jesus' admonition. In its original context, Zech 13:7 referred to the martyrdom of the eschatological good shepherd.[35] The first person singular, "'I will strike,'" means that

33. See G. Stählin, *"skandalon," TDNT* 7.349-52; Grundmann, *Das Evangelium nach Markus,* 394.

34. The MT and the LXX read, "Strike the shepherd [LXX: shepherds] . . . ," a second person plural imperative instead of the first person singular future here recorded. The textual apparatuses of both the MT and the LXX reveal uncertainty about the person of the verb, however. The MT offers a conjectural emendation of an infinitive absolute, "I will strike" *(hakkah akkeh)* to fit with the poetic meter. Moreover, if the passage were recalled from memory, the change to the first person singular could have been facilitated by the second half of Zech 13:7, "and *I* will turn my hand against the little ones."

35. H. Gese, "Anfang und Ende der Apokalyptik, dargestellt am Sacharjabuch," *ZTK* 70 (1973): 46-48.

God will strike Jesus as the shepherd — or allow him to be struck — in fulfillment of his will.[36] This quotation thus repeats the paradox of 14:21, where evil is used by God to fulfill his greater purpose. The quotation of Zech 13:7 also provides a further glimpse into Jesus' understanding of his passion: that his suffering is ordained by God; in the words of the Servant of the Lord, "It was the LORD's will to crush him and cause him to suffer" (Isa 53:10). Finally, the quotation contains a warning to the disciples, who will be scattered; and beyond the warning a consolation, for Jesus shows compassion on sheep without a shepherd (Matt 9:36).

The consolation continues in 14:28 with the prediction of Jesus' resurrection from the dead (so 8:31; 9:31; 10:34). "'But after I have risen, I will go ahead of you to Galilee.'" This promise bears a curious resemblance to Zech 13:7b, which speaks of God's gathering of his renewed flock as the people of God. Beyond the passion, and in accordance with the Scripture, Jesus sees a renewal and completion of the call to discipleship. The kingdom of God that Jesus brings and embodies cannot be scuttled by human failure. He who first called the apostolic band at the Sea of Galilee (1:16) will again call and reestablish them at the Sea of Galilee (16:7). It is there — not in Jerusalem or in the temple — that Jesus will reconstitute his followers. Like the prophets who foresaw Yahweh leading Israel back to the wilderness and again betrothing her to him (Hosea 2), the resurrected Lord will return and reclaim the fallen disciples in Galilee.

29-31 Whenever Jesus predicts his passion in Mark, the disciples respond with self-assertion and conceit rather than with humility (8:31-32; 9:31-34; 10:33-37). A similar pattern reemerges in Peter's bluster that he will not fall away. His rejoinder in v. 29 is only slightly less rude than his rebuke of Jesus after the first passion prediction (8:32), and its insinuation is even more insulting of the other disciples. "'Even if all fall away'" suggests that Peter is not surprised at the thought of the defection of the other disciples. Perhaps he even expects it of them. At any rate, he does not defend their cause. What he staunchly defends is *his* cause, "'I will not.'" Peter thinks of himself as the exception to the rule; where others fall, he will stand! Jesus interrupts Peter's mock heroics — or attempts to — with the ether of reality: "'today — yes tonight — before the rooster crows twice you yourself will disown me three times.'" The statement is both colorful and emphatic, for in Greek the word "disown" (*aparneesthai*; "deny") is held to the very end of the long chain of assertions preceding it. A threefold denial is not a momentary slip of weakness. "Three times" hammers into Peter — and us as readers — how quickly the most noble

---

36. See S. L. Cook, "The Metamorphosis of a Shepherd: The Tradition History of Zechariah 11:17 + 13:7-9," *CBQ* 55 (1993): 453-66.

convictions can wilt before a serious onslaught.[37] It is of no use to protest that we have not committed the sins we self-righteously condemn in others. The question is not what sins we have committed as much as what sins we *would* commit were we faced with serious pressure, temptation, opportunity, and threat. Alone of the Gospel writers, Mark records two cockcrows (v. 30).[38] Is the first a warning that there is yet time to be strong?[39]

Peter raises his protest another octave, "'Even if I have to die with you, I will never disown you'" (v. 31). Such claims are more easily made in ease and safety than in the crucible of temptation and opposition. In Peter's case the claim will be put to shame a short while later in the presence of a servant girl (14:66-72). He is not alone in the boast, however, for "all the others said the same" (John 11:16). When time comes for bravado, each of the disciples manages to speak for himself. This is a clue that for Mark there is no "guilt by association" or "corporate victimization." They all drank of the cup (14:23), they all confess their allegiance (v. 31), . . . and they all flee (14:50)!

In placing the Last Supper between the betrayal and defection of the disciples Mark vividly conveys that "the many" for whom Jesus pours out his life include his own companions around the table. The sin that necessitates the sending of God's Son is not someone else's sin — the sin of Caligula or Nero or the legion of tyrants ever since — but the sin of the tenants of his own vineyard, of his own disciples — of Peter and James, of you and me. The essential evil in the world and the essential atonement

37. One is reminded of Luther's polemic in *The Bondage of the Will,* that human will and human knowledge, though the most noble of characteristics, are ultimately fickle and blind and inclined to evil (*Martin Luther's Basic Theological Writings,* ed. D. Lull [Minneapolis: Fortress Press, 1989], 185-86).

38. Mark's double cockcrow is not textually certain. Several strong manuscripts (C ℵ D W) omit "twice," but the omission is probably owing to assimilation with Matt 26:34; Luke 22:34; and John 13:38, all of which omit the second cockcrow. The textual support for the two cockcrows is stronger and more diverse than that for its omission. See M. Öhler, "Der zweimalige Hahnschrei der Markuspassion. Zur Textüberlieferung von Mk 14,30.68.72," *ZNW* 85 (1994): 145-50.

39. There is some question whether "cockcrow" should be understood literally. Certain rabbinic passages (e.g., *m. B. Qam.* 7:7) forbade keeping chickens in Jerusalem because their scratching uncovered unclean things. This has led to the suggestion that "cockcrow" was a metaphor for the *gallicinium,* the Roman morning bugle call, or the trumpet blast in the temple at the same hour (*m. Suk.* 5:4). It is hard to imagine animals as useful and ubiquitous as chickens being entirely eliminated from Jerusalem, however. In this ruling as in other rabbinic rulings, exceptions were made, especially if there was a garden or dung heap for chickens to scratch in. "Cockcrow" should be understood literally. See J. Jeremias, *Jerusalem in the Time of Jesus,* trans. F. H. and C. H. Cave (Philadelphia: Fortress Press, 1979), 47-48; Str-B 1.992.

for the evil of the world are present at the table of the Lord's Supper — whenever it is celebrated.[40] Jesus' self-sacrifice cannot be understood except as the consummation of the blood covenant first adumbrated in Exodus. In this respect, the Last Supper is, in the words of Paul, a "remembrance" (1 Cor 11:24; although Mark does not use the word), in which the oblation of Jesus effects the final fulfillment of what the earlier blood sacrifices dealt with only provisionally and proleptically (Heb 7:27; 9:28). At the same time, the Last Supper points beyond itself to the future, "'until that day when I drink it anew in the kingdom of God.'" How crucial is the word "until." Despite the cowardice and treachery of the disciples, despite Jesus' impending agony of the cross, the final word of the Last Supper is the expectation of the coming kingdom of God. Those who partake of the Lord's Supper do so only as grateful sinners who stand "between the times" — between the once-for-all offering of Jesus for "the many" and its universal realization in the coming kingdom of God "in that day."

GETHSEMANE: PRELUDE TO THE CROSS (14:32-42)

In the Last Supper Jesus spoke of the bread and wine as representations of his body and blood, "poured out for many" (14:22-24). The relinquishment of Jesus' body on Golgotha, however, depends on the prior surrender of his will to the Father. That surrender takes place not on a hill outside Jerusalem but in a valley beneath it. According to Mark, the decision to submit to the Father's will causes Jesus greater internal suffering than the physical crucifixion on Golgotha. The cross (8:34) is a matter of the heart before it is a matter of the hand, a matter of the will before it is an empirical reality.

32-35 Jesus and the disciples enter an olive grove called Gethsemane.[41] Gethsemane is derived from the Hebrew, meaning "olive press." It lay east of the Kidron brook at the foot of the Mount of Olives and was a familiar place for Jesus and his followers to gather (Luke 22:39;

---

40. On the theme of the forgiveness of sins in the Last Supper, see O. Hofius, "'Für Euch gegeben zur Vergebung der Sünden.' Vom Sinn des Heiligen Abendmals," *ZTK* 95 (1998): 313-37.

41. J. Murphy-O'Connor, "What Really Happened at Gethsemane," *BRev* 14/2 (1998): 28ff., attempts on the basis of "structural doublets" to argue that Mark has combined two separate accounts in 14:32-42. The alleged doublets strike me as being farfetched, however, nor are they capable of explaining Murphy-O'Connor thesis, which is more assumed than demonstrated.

John 18:1-2). Jesus commands the disciples, "'Sit here while I pray.'" Only twice before has Mark recorded Jesus praying alone (1:35; 6:46; on prayer, see further on those passages and at 9:29). The prayers of Jesus in Mark are all set in times of decision and crises, this being the most traumatic. Separating himself from the Twelve, Jesus takes Peter, James, and John (v. 33) to be alone with him. These three disciples form an inner circle among the disciples and figure prominently in Mark on previous special occasions (5:37; 9:2; 13:3). All three have earlier crowed of their mettle (Peter, 14:29-31; James and John, 10:38-39; 14:31); they should be exactly the companions Jesus needs in the crisis before him.

In Gethsemane Jesus is besieged with intense spiritual affliction. The range and number of expressions describing his sorrow rival the lamentable description of the demoniac in 5:2-5. Jesus "began to be deeply distressed and troubled." "Distressed" (Gk. *ekthambein*) and "troubled" (Gk. *adēmonein*) are rare words in the NT. The first occurs only in Mark (9:15; 14:33; 16:5, 6) and carries the sense of "alarm"; the second occurs only in Matt 26:37//Mark 14:33 and Phil 2:26 and means "to be troubled or distressed." "'My soul is overwhelmed with sorrow to the point of death'" echoes the haunting lament of the downcast and dejected soul of Pss 42:6, 12 and 43:5. The Greek word for "overwhelmed with sorrow" *(perilypos)*, again a rare word, means "burdened with grief," and in the present context "despair unto death." Withdrawing from the three disciples,[42] Jesus collapses on the earth in prayer that the ordeal before him might be avoided (v. 35). Nothing in all the Bible compares to Jesus' agony and anguish in Gethsemane — neither the laments of the Psalms, nor the broken heart of Abraham as he prepared to sacrifice his son Isaac (Gen 22:5), nor David's grief at the death of his son Absalom (2 Sam 18:33). Luke 22:44 even speaks of Jesus' "sweat falling to the ground like drops of blood" (so, too, Justin Martyr, *Dial. Trypho* 103.8). The suffering of Gethsemane left an indelible imprint on the early church (Heb 5:7).

The grim realism of Gethsemane is a guarantee of its historicity. We can scarcely imagine early Christians, and especially Mark, who accentuates Jesus' divine authority, inventing a story of such torment. The very torment provides a sad clue to Jesus' understanding of his impending death. Why, we may ask, is Jesus so assailed by the prospect of his death? Surely we all know individuals who face the prospect of their deaths with greater composure and courage than does Jesus. Did not Socrates

42. A strong cadre of manuscripts reads that Jesus "approached" (*proselthōn;* A C D L ϴ Ψ) the disciples to pray rather than "withdrew" (*proelthōn;* ℵ B K N W) from them to pray. The latter reading is preferable, however, (1) because it agrees with the sense of the narrative, and (2) since *proserchesthe* is much more common in the NT than *proerchesthe,* and therefore a scribe would be inclined to add a *sigma* to the latter word.

greet death as a friend and liberator to a better life (Plato, *Ap.* 29; *Phd.* 67-68)? Did not the Stoics preach serene resignation to fate?[43] Why does Jesus, who has foreseen his death and marched resolutely to Jerusalem to meet it, now quail before it?

The answer must be that Jesus is aware of facing something more than simply his own death. In 10:45 he spoke of the purpose of the Son of Man "'to give his life as a ransom for many.'" That was the objective description of his purpose; now we hear the subjective experience of it. In Gethsemane Jesus must make the first payment of that ransom, to *will* to become the sin-bearer for humanity. Jesus stands before the final consequence of being the Servant of God, "pierced for *our* transgressions, crushed for *our* iniquities" (Isa 53:4-5). It is one thing, fearful as it will be, to answer for our own sins before a holy and almighty God; who can imagine what it would be like to stand before God to answer for every sin and crime and act of malice and injury and cowardice and evil in the world? In acquiescing to the Father's will of bearing "the sin of many, interceding for transgressors" (Isa 53:12), Jesus necessarily experiences an abandonment and darkness of cosmic proportions. The worst prospect of becoming the sin-bearer for humanity is that it spells complete alienation from God, an alienation that will shortly echo above the desolate landscape of Calvary, "'My God, my God, why have you forsaken me?'" (15:34). Not his own mortality, but the specter of identifying with sinners so fully as to become the object of God's wrath against sin — it is this that overwhelms Jesus' soul "'to the point of death'" (v. 34).

36 Another clue to Jesus' understanding of the cross emerges from his reference to his death as "the hour" and "the cup" (vv. 35-36). Taken from the vocabulary of apocalyptic literature, "hour" and "cup" speak of the ultimate purposes of God associated with the end of time (13:32; Dan 11:40, 45). They do not here refer to Jesus' impending arrest but to his messianic destiny as "'the ransom for many'" (10:45) and "'the handing over of the Son of Man to sinners'" (v. 41) in order to redeem sinners.

Only in Mark does Jesus calls God "Abba," a term of intimacy, trust, and affection. The other three Gospels simply record the Greek address *patēr*, "Father." "Abba" recollects Jesus' original Aramaic (Rom 8:15; Gal 4:6), displaying an intimacy, boldness, and simplicity in address to God that was not characteristic of Jewish prayers. Seldom, if ever, did rabbis

43. "Remember that you are an actor in a play, the character of which is determined by the Playwright: if He wishes the play to be short, it is short; if long, it is long; if He wishes you to play the part of a beggar, remember to act even this role adroitly; and so if your role be that of a cripple, an official, or a layman. For this is your business, to play admirably the role assigned you; but the selection of that role is Another's" (Epictetus, *Enchiridion,* 17; see also Arrian, *Epict. Disc.* 3.22.95).

presume such intimacy with God.[44] "Abba" provides crystal clarity into Jesus' consciousness of being God's Son, and of his willingness to drink the bitter cup of suffering as an ineluctable consequence of his complete trust in the Father and obedience to his will. His *exousia*, the divine power and authority that have characterized his life, is now returned to the Father, in trust that the purpose of his life will be consummated in the self-surrender of his death.

Jesus is not the dispassionate actor enjoined by Epictetus, indifferently resigned to the fate decreed for him. Gethsemane, rather, presents us with a uniquely human interplay between the *heart* of the Son and the *will* of the Father. Jesus' prayer is not the result of calm absorption into an all-encompassing divine presence, but an intense struggle with the frightful reality of God's will and what it means fully to submit to it. The fundamental humanness of the prayer is evident in his imploring God in direct address, "'Take this cup from me.'"[45] That is a prayer for God *not* to strike the shepherd (14:27). Is it possible for Jesus to fulfill God's will in all ways but this one, or in some other way? Perhaps, as with Isaac, the sacrifice can be averted even though the arm of Abraham is raised for the dagger's plunge.[46] The plea of Jesus suggests that he is genuinely tempted to forsake the role of the suffering servant.[47] Nevertheless, his will to obey the Father is stronger than his desire to serve himself. Throughout his ministry he has disavowed every exit ramp from the pathway of suffering

44. Evidence in Jewish Palestine is extremely rare of "Abba," or even "my Father," being used in individual address to God. The foremost treatment of the subject remains J. Jeremias, *The Prayers of Jesus*, trans. J. Bowden (Philadelphia: Fortress, 1978), 11-65; also *New Testament Theology*, trans. J. Bowden (New York: Scribner's, 1971), 62-68. Recent critiques of Jeremias (G. Vermes, *Jesus and the World of Judaism* [London, 1983], 39-43; M. R. D'Angelo, "*Abba* and 'Father': Imperial Theology and the Jesus Traditions," *JBL* 111/4 [1992]: 611-30) modify Jeremias's conclusions at isolated points but fail to rebut his central thesis that there are (as yet) no examples of the use of *abba* for God in Jewish texts as early as the Gospels.

45. The imperative "'Take *(parenenke)* this cup from me'" is attested by early and diverse witnesses (B D L W) and is therefore preferable to the first aorist active imperative *parenenkai* read by ℵ A C K Θ Ψ. The latter reading appears to be an attempt to soften the implied clash of wills between Jesus and the Father in Gethsemane.

46. See J. D. M. Derrett, "The Prayer in Gethsemane (Mark 14:35-36)," *Journal of Higher Criticism* 4 (1997): 78-88.

47. The naked vulnerability of Jesus in Gethsemane is something modern readers, on the whole, can "relate to." What attracts us to the Gethsemane story was often seen as offensive to earlier generations of Christians, however. Particularly in the patristic and medieval periods the human weakness of Jesus in Gethsemane was perceived as contrary to orthodox assumptions of his divine aseity and impassibility. See K. Madigan, "Ancient and High-Medieval Interpretations of Jesus in Gethsemane: Some Reflections on Tradition and Continuity in Christian Thought," *HTR* 88 (1995): 157-73.

servanthood, including the temptation to remain with Moses and Elijah in glory (9:2-8). His will conforms to his knowledge of God's will, to undergo the "baptism" (10:38), to accept the "cup" (v. 36), to meet the "hour" (v. 35). In words reminiscent of the prayer he earlier taught the disciples (Matt 6:10), "'Not what I will, but what you will.'"

37-39 The spiritual danger of the hour is not limited to Jesus. There is also danger for the disciples, a lesser and different danger to be sure, but danger nevertheless. The last word of the Olivet discourse was "'Watch, lest [you] be caught sleeping'" (13:36-37). In Gethsemane, the disciples fail that test and fall asleep.[48] Three times Jesus warns them to watch (vv. 34, 37, 38) and "'pray so that you will not fall into temptation'" (v. 38; Matt 6:13).[49] But the crisis before Jesus is cancelled and consumed by their lethargy. Three times Jesus finds them asleep, surely a prelude to Peter's three forthcoming denials (14:30). No wonder Jesus calls the chief apostle "Simon" and not "Peter" (v. 37), for in Gethsemane he has not lived up to his name; he is not a "Rock." The admonition to "'watch and pray,'" for "'the spirit is willing, but the body is weak'" (v. 38), is a necessary reminder that trusting and obeying God are not default responses of disciples of Jesus, but ongoing struggles against temptation and weakness. The church later identified the problem as "sloth" or "accidie," a state of spiritual torpor or indifference that can only be rectified by attentiveness and prayer.[50]

40-42 The events leading up to the Passover and the lateness of the hour have sapped the disciples' energy. That, coupled with the big Passover meal and the wine, cause them to fight with slumber.[51] Their eyes,

---

48. Some scholars assume the Gethsemane story to be a fiction since the solitude of Jesus and sleep of the disciples apparently rule out witnesses of the event (e.g., R. Bultmann, *History of the Synoptic Tradition,* trans. J. Marsh [Oxford: Basil Blackwell, 1963], 267, who regards the account as of "thoroughgoing legendary character"). Such negativism is entirely unwarranted. We are not talking about the disciples staying awake through a Platonic dialogue. The twenty-word prayer recorded by Mark could have been uttered in fifteen seconds and overheard by the disciples before they fell asleep. Nor should other possible witnesses be ruled out, including the mysterious young man of v. 51. See B. Saunderson, "Gethsemane: The Missing Witness," *Bib* 70 (1989): 224-33.

49. The two champion manuscripts of the Alexandrian tradition, ℵ and B, read *elthēte* (NIV, "*fall* into temptation"). Although a greater and more diverse number of manuscripts read *eiselthēte* ("enter"; ℵ[2] A C D L W Θ Ψ), this reading, though very well attested, is likely a scribal harmonization to the parallel accounts in Matt 26:41 and Luke 22:46.

50. Note Paul's struggle between the spirit and the flesh (Gal 5:16-26; Rom 7:15-25). In the second century A.D., Polycarp warned the Philippians against apostasy by citing v. 38, appealing to "the sobering effects of prayer" in the conflict between spirit and flesh (Pol. *Phil.* 7:2).

51. The Mishnah warns the high priest against eating a large meal on the eve of the

435

says Mark, are leaden and weighed down (Gk. *katabarynein*) and they "did not know what to say to [Jesus]" (v. 40), a phrase reminiscent of their bewilderment at the transfiguration (9:6). The third time Jesus finds the disciples sleeping he retorts, "'Enough!'" (v. 41). This translation is simply a guess at the meaning of the original *apechei*, which seems to be an utterance of exasperation, perhaps "'What's the use?'"[52] At the command, "'Rise! Let us go!'" (v. 42), Jesus' resolve to meet his fate brings the disciples to their feet, if not to their senses.

"'The Son of Man is betrayed into the hands of sinners'" (14:41). With that statement the first event of the passion predictions comes to pass (9:31). The last word of the account in Greek is *ēngiken*, "at hand." The prayer in Gethsemane is Jesus' final moment of freedom, for with the arrival of Judas and the soldiers Jesus is swept up into the events he has previously predicted. Certain early witnesses attempt to mitigate the catastrophe at hand by reporting that an angel comforted him in prayer (Luke 22:43; *Gospel of the Nazarenes* 32). But Mark — and the majority tradition — is silent about angelic aid. If Jesus is to fulfill his destiny as God's Son, the only answer to his prayer will resound in the venomous accusations and the hammer blows of Calvary, against which drugged wine will be dull comfort. What profound irony Gethsemane conceals, for when Jesus feels most excluded from God's presence he is in fact closest to God's will! Gethsemane is the prelude to Calvary, for in a valley beneath the city Jesus allows his soul to be crucified; on a hill above the city he relinquishes his body.

THE ARREST: JUDAS AND JESUS (14:43-52)

Compared to the pathos of the Gethsemane prayer, the Gethsemane arrest is narrated in brawny objectivity. Like an ominous drum-roll, the narrative is repeatedly punctuated by the word *seizure* (Gk. *kratein*, vv. 44, 46, 49, 51). Indeed, that word characterizes Gethsemane for Mark: from psychological and spiritual seizure in the preceding prayer to physical seizure in the arrest. The haste and preparedness of the mob testify to its

---

Day of Atonement "since food induces sleep" (*m. Yoma* 1:4, 6-7). See T. Pola, "Die Gethsemane-Perikope Markus 14,32-42 im Lichte des Mischnatraktates Joma (m. Yom 14.6f)," *TBei* 25 (1994): 37-44.

52. See discussions of the expression in C. E. B. Cranfield, *The Gospel According to Saint Mark*, 435-36; M. Hooker, *The Gospel According to Saint Mark*, 349-50. The addition of *apechei to telos* ("the end has arrived") in several Western witnesses (D W Θ) is a later attempt to remove the ambiguity of the expression. See Metzger, *TCGNT*, 114-15.

"hellbent animosity."[53] Jesus is shadowed and apprehended by a relentless bureaucracy in which, then as now, persons and processes are set in motion for which no one seems responsible and which no one is able to stop. The crowd and henchmen are faceless, and even the identities of those who most pique our curiosity — the sword-wielding sympathizer of v. 47 and the streaker of v. 52 — remain anonymous. The only persons named are Judas and Jesus, and the arrest is narrated as a fateful and final meeting between them.

43 Mark describes the arrest squad as "sent from chief priests, teachers of the law, and the elders." These are the three constituent bodies of the Sanhedrin, and this designates the posse "armed with swords and clubs" as authorized by the Sanhedrin. The role of the Sanhedrin in the arrest is further corroborated by v. 49, "'Every day I was with you, teaching in the *temple courts,* and you did not arrest me.'" The instigation for Jesus' arrest appears to rest with the Jewish authorities, the Sanhedrin, and the temple police (Luke 22:52).[54] But there is also evidence of the Roman military in the arrest. The Gospel of John describes Judas heading up a "cohort" (18:3; NIV, "detachment of soldiers") attended by a "tribune" (18:12; NIV, "commander") at the arrest of Jesus. That is Roman military terminology. A cohort (Gk. *speira*) was a tenth of a Roman legion, or about six hundred soldiers (Josephus, *War* 3.67-68; though the number varied); and a tribune was a Roman commander of a thousand soldiers. Mark makes no mention of Romans in the arrest, but that may be because of his desire, as we shall see in the trial before Pilate, to avoid portraying the Romans in an unfavorable light. Nevertheless, the facility with which Jesus' trial is expedited by Pilate in Mark (15:1ff.) suggests prior knowledge of Jesus' arrest on the part of the Roman governor, including perhaps a covert detachment of soldiers.[55] Finally, the size of the arrest squad was an important concern: it needed to be unassuming so as not to raise a commotion at the festival (14:2), but of sufficient muscle to "lead Jesus away securely" (v. 44; NIV, "lead him away under guard").

---

53. So R. Gundry, *Mark,* 858.

54. The Mishnah (*m. Shab.* 6:4) forbids the taking up of "a sword or a bow or a shield or a club or a spear" on the Sabbath and feast days. Some scholars cite this text as evidence that the Last Supper and arrest occurred earlier in the week (so the Gospel of John) and not on Passover night, as Mark records (Grundmann, *Das Evangelium nach Markus,* 405; Pixner, *Mit Jesus in Jerusalem,* 83-84). I am personally unpersuaded by this line of thinking, for we see further infractions of Mishnah regulations at the trial of Jesus. Given the determination of the religious leaders to seize Jesus, it is hardly surprising that the Sanhedrin waives oral tradition in favor of *Realpolitik* — especially if they consider Jesus a blasphemer (14:64), in which case he forfeited legal protection.

55. For further discussion of the issue and reasons for supposing Roman involvement in the arrest, see E. Schweizer, *The Good News According to Mark,* 321-25.

44-45 Judas plays a Faustian role in Jesus' arrest. He is reintroduced as "one of the Twelve" (v. 43). It is unlikely, as some scholars suggest, that this is a blunder on Mark's part, as though he were introducing Judas for the first time (see 3:19; 14:10). References to "the Twelve" or "one of the Twelve" punctuate chap. 14 (vv. 10, 17, 20), reminding readers of the uncomfortable fact that Jesus' betrayal and arrest arise from among his trusted followers. Thus, in v. 43 the antagonist is identified as "Judas, one of the Twelve," but in v. 44 as "the betrayer."[56] As one of Jesus' inner circle, Judas knew of Jesus' daytime movements and where he bivouacked at night (John 18:2). His services were essential for the stealth and success of the conspirators. The sting would be triggered by a "signal" (Gk. *syssēmon*). This word occurs only here in the NT and means a "sign previously agreed on."[57] The particular sign — a betrayal kiss — is somewhat puzzling since nowhere else is Jesus greeted by a disciple with a kiss, nor is it entirely certain, as some commentators maintain, that a kiss was a customary greeting between rabbis and disciples. Kisses of homage and respect were practiced in Israel, however (1 Sam 10:1; 2 Sam 19:40; Luke 7:38; Acts 20:37). When Judas approaches Jesus he kisses him not with modesty and reserve, but lavishly, even passionately, according to the Gk. *kataphilein*. Like Joab's earlier kiss and dagger ruse with Amasa (2 Sam 20:9-10), an act of love is performed for a mission of hate.[58] Whatever else the significance of the betrayal kiss, that gesture, along with the honorific title "Rabbi" (= "my great one"), makes a burlesque of Jesus. The manner of betrayal becomes the first example of the *mockery* of Jesus, which will play a key role in the crucifixion narrative of chap. 15. Judas's derisive plot further scotches theories that he is the victim of superior forces or tragic fate.

46-47 The kiss triggers the sting: Jesus is seized, though in the fracas a flashing sword severs the ear of a servant of the high priest.[59] Later tradition identified Peter as the sword-wielding assailant, but this is not as certain as is often assumed, for Mark attributes the deed not to a disciple but "to one of those standing near."[60] This same phrase will appear in

---

56. "An act of perfidy rather than a pursuit of justice" (Gundry, *Mark*, 858).

57. BAG 802; Str-B 2.50.

58. On the kiss of Judas, see G. Stählin, *"phileō," TDNT* 9.140-41.

59. A comparison of the account of the arrest in the Gospels shows how some details were heightened in the retelling. Mark, the earliest evangelist, says simply that "one of those standing near" drew his sword and cut off the ear of the high priest's servant (14:47). Somewhat later Matt 26:51 sharpens the designation to "one of Jesus' companions." Later still, Luke 22:50 identifies the servant's wound as "the right ear"; and near the close of the first century John 18:10 identifies the swordsman as Peter and gives the servant's name as Malchus!

60. The Greek manuscript tradition preserves the phrase "Then one of those standing near" in several minor variant renderings, none of which refers to a disciple or Peter.

vv. 69-70, where it obviously does not refer to disciples. It is far more likely that the arrest squad, and not the disciples, are armed with swords. Indeed, if the assailant were a disciple we should expect an arrest to follow. But no arrest follows, which at least suggests that the severed ear fell from the misguided valor of a henchman rather than of a disciple or Peter.[61] Peter, of course, figures prominently in the events of chap. 14 and is likely Mark's source for much of it. If Peter were the assailant, it would be surprising for him to conceal his name here and include it in the much more incriminating denial scene. Mark makes nothing further of the sword and severed ear,[62] but it is not impossible that those grisly facts ensured the inclusion of this episode in the passion, for there are not infrequent references to severed ears in gladiatorial shows. The lust for mortal combat in the arena heightened under Claudius (A.D. 41-54) and Nero (A.D. 54-68). Mark appears to be writing at the end of this period, perhaps in A.D. 65, when Nero was exposing Christians to savage spectacles in the arena. Those who stood under Nero's sword may have been offered a modicum of comfort in knowing that Jesus was no stranger to the Roman *gladius*.

48-49 The overkill of arms and security precautions is deflated by Jesus' nonviolent surrender. "How far such defenses are from the will of Jesus, how blind such human intrigues to the thoughts of God," comments Schlatter.[63] The NIV rendering of v. 48, "'Am I leading a rebellion?'" suggests an organized countermovement, perhaps a Zealot uprising. But the Greek word behind "rebellion" (*lēstēs*) does not necessarily connote Zealotism. It often means a common "bandit" or "robber" (11:17; Luke 10:30), as it may in this instance. Jesus is no bandit, and he is angered that the authorities, who have had ample opportunity to judge his character (v. 49; Luke 19:47), impugned him as such.[64] "'The Scriptures

---

61. Gundry, *Mark,* 860.

62. B. T. Viviano, "The High Priest's Servant's Ear: Mark 14:47," *RB* 96 (1989): 71-80, argues from Lev 21:18, and Josephus, *Ant.* 14.365ff.//*War* 1.269ff. that v. 47 refers not to an injury in a melee but to slicing off the earlobe of the deputy of the high priest, thus rendering him unworthy of high office. For Viviano, v. 47 is a theological critique of the temple. Contrary to Father Viviano's assertion, this is *not* "the impression left by the Marcan narrative." The victim is called a servant or slave, not a deputy; and the operation Viviano refers to is a quasi-surgical procedure, hardly the kind of thing accomplished by whacking an opponent with a sword (*spasamenos tēn machairan epaisen ton doulon:* "having drawn his sword he struck the servant").

63. Schlatter, *Die Evangelien nach Markus und Lukas,* 141.

64. The second-century account of the martyrdom of Polycarp is consciously patterned after Jesus' arrest and death. As Jesus was betrayed by "one of the Twelve" (14:43), Polycarp was betrayed by one of his own house (*Mart. Pol.* 6:2). Like Jesus, Polycarp is taken from an "upper room . . . as if they were advancing against a robber,"

[have been] fulfilled'" indeed, for he is "numbered with the transgressors" (Isa 53:12).

50-52 The climax of the arrest comes in v. 50, "Then everyone deserted him and fled." This seemingly innocuous statement carries an incriminating wallop. *All* drank the cup (14:23), *all* pledged to die with him (14:31), . . . and *all* desert! The "all" in v. 50 is made emphatic in Greek by placing it at the end of the sentence: the betrayal of Judas is thus multiplied by the wholesale failure of the disciples; they *all* abandon Jesus and flee. In vv. 51-52 we have the curious reminiscence of the first recorded streaker in history. This reference occurs only in Mark. The indefinite pronoun (Gk. *tis;* "a certain [young man]") looks like a calculated ambiguity; nor are we told how long he has been "following" Jesus. The identity of this naked fugitive has been clothed in much speculation.[65] The few parallels from ancient literature do not further our understanding of the reference.[66] The most common suggestion, now more than a century old, is that the young man is actually Mark, making vv. 51-52 an "anonymous signature" of the author of the Gospel. This is an attractive hypothesis, and not impossible; but if it is Mark, it is a very obscure byline. The other leading line of inquiry, though no more profitable, is to attempt to discover a relationship between this "young man" (Gk. *neaniskos*) and that of the attendant at the empty tomb in 16:5.[67] In light of the meagerness of information, Nineham is right: speculation about the identity of the lad is profitless.[68]

---

and he dies on a Friday (*Mart. Pol.* 7:1). Finally, Polycarp "might fulfil his appointed lot by becoming a partaker of Christ, while they who betrayed him should undergo the same punishment of Judas" (*Mart. Pol.* 6:2).

65. See Saunderson, "Gethsemane: The Missing Witness," *Bib* 70 (1989): 224-33.

66. The flight of Joseph from Potiphar's wife (Gen 39:12) is similar in wording but not in meaning since the young man's flight here is not virtuous but cowardly. The reference in Ahiqar (171/77; 6th/7th century B.C.) appears to moralize on the Joseph story (or situations like it): "If a wicked man grasps the fringes of your garment, leave it in his hand." The bizarre additions to the Gospel of Mark published by Morton Smith (see Epilogue: "The Secret Gospel of Mark") mention the young man of vv. 51-52 with reference to an ostensibly homosexual act of initiation: "and in the evening the young man came to [Jesus], clothed only in a linen cloth upon his naked body. And he remained with him that night; for Jesus was teaching him the mysteries of the Kingdom of God" (*NTApoc* 1.108). These spurious additions in the so-called Secret Gospel of Mark are characteristic of second-century gnostic influence.

67. Both passages use the word *neaniskos* ("young man"), which is not otherwise used in Mark. Still others argue that the cloth in which Jesus is wrapped after the crucifixion (15:46; *sindōn* ["tunic, shirt"], the same Greek word used of the cloth discarded by the young man), signifies Christ taking our sins and failures upon himself. This is an intriguing speculation, but it is uncharacteristically allegorical for Mark and subtle to the point of obscurity.

68. D. Nineham, *The Gospel of St. Mark*, 396.

Mark's leaving him unidentified appears to be intentional and purposeful. The young man represents all who flew in desperation when mayhem broke out at the arrest of Jesus.[69] This particular story speaks for all present. His lack of identity also invites readers to examine their own readiness to abandon Jesus. The prophecy of Amos has come to pass among all of Jesus' followers: "'Even the bravest of warriors will flee naked on that day,' declares the LORD" (2:16; also 1 Macc 10:64).[70] "'There is no one righteous, not even one. . . . All have turned away'" (Rom 3:9-11).

TRUE VERSUS FALSE WITNESS (14:53-72)

For the third time in chap. 14 Mark applies the sandwich technique. The theme of the present sandwich is bearing witness under persecution. Until this point in the Gospel of Mark the theme of witness has played virtually no role (only at 1:44; 6:11; 10:19; 13:9), but now within nine verses the word "witness" occurs seven times in various forms.[71] Even when the word is absent the theme is present. The conspicuous introduction of witnessing in the trial scene reveals that for Mark a true testimony to Jesus, as Jesus has reminded disciples in the passion predictions (8:31; 9:31; 10:33-34), is rendered in the context of suffering, persecution, and the cross. The courage and faithfulness of Jesus within such a context is contrasted to false witness and denial. The disciples are again the foil, but it is no longer Judas (14:1-11) or the disciples in general (14:17-31), but the chief apostle, Peter, whose story in the courtyard of the high priest (vv. 53-54, 66-72) flanks the trial of Jesus before the Sanhedrin (vv. 55-65). As disciples are haled "before councils and kings as witnesses to them" (13:9), the literary juxtaposition of Jesus and Peter in the sandwich creates a sermon without words on the meaning of bearing witness under persecution.

54 The trial scene opens with Peter following Jesus "at a distance" into the courtyard of the high priest (John 18:15). The gap in Peter's discipleship does not comport well with his boast a short while earlier to die with Jesus if necessary (14:31). His distance already foreshadows his de-

---

69. See H. M. Jackson, "Why the Youth Shed His Cloak and Fled Naked: The Meaning and Purpose of Mark 14:51-52," *JBL* 116 (1997): 273-89.

70. See J. M. Ross, "The Young Man Who Fled Naked," *IBS* 13 (1991): 170-74, who maintains that Mark records the event because it happened and because it indicated that the crucifixion was "the Day of the Lord" foretold by Amos 2:16.

71. *Martyria* ("witness, testimony"; vv. 55, 56, 59); *pseudomartyrein* ("to testify falsely"; vv. 56, 57); *katamartyrein* ("to testify against"; v. 60); *martys* ("a witness"; v. 63).

nial, between which Mark sets the story of Jesus' interrogation by the Sanhedrin. How awkward Peter looks in the courtyard of the high priest, trying to mingle with the henchmen who probably arrested Jesus and who will presently mock and beat him (Gk. *hypēretēs*; vv. 54, 65; NIV, "guards"). Peter has forsaken a discipleship of costly following (8:34) for one of safe observation.

53, 55 Between Peter's entrance into the courtyard (v. 54) and his denial (vv. 66-72), Mark narrates the trial of Jesus before the Sanhedrin. Following his arrest, Jesus is taken immediately to the high priest, whom John 18:13-14 identifies as Caiaphas, the high priest who presided over the Sanhedrin from A.D. 18 to 36, and the son-in-law of the powerful high priest, Annas. The customary meeting place of the Sanhedrin was the Chamber of Hewn Stone, north of the temple sanctuary, adjacent to the Court of Israel (*m. Sanh.* 11:2). The hearing recorded by Mark does not take place there, however, but at the villa of the high priest. According to tradition, Caiaphas's house lay a kilometer to the southwest of Gethsemane on the slopes of Mt. Zion. The site is commemorated today by the church of St. Peter in Gallicantu (Cockcrow). Continued excavations have unearthed beneath the church a series of cisterns and grottos that date to the Herodian period (37 B.C.–A.D. 70). These rock-hewn pits would have offered maximum security for the brief internment of prisoners. Early in the fourth century the anonymous Pilgrim of Bordeaux identified the site as "the house of the High Priest Caiaphas, where the pillars to which Jesus was bound and whipped are still evident."[72] The dating of the grottos and the above testimony suggest that St. Peter in Gallicantu commemorates the site where Jesus was interrogated by Caiaphas.

Jesus was arraigned before "the chief priests, elders and teachers of the law" (v. 53), "the whole Sanhedrin" (v. 55), according to Mark. **Jesus' trial before the Sanhedrin** is problematic, for the proceedings described by Mark grossly violate Jewish jurisprudence as stipulated in the Mishnah. The Sanhedrin, the chief governing body of the Jews, consisted of seventy-one members. Since observant Jews refused to honor Gentile Roman hegemony in Palestine, and since Roman administrators were shrewd enough to acknowledge this, a buffer organization of Jewish leaders was established who were willing to cooperate with Rome. This supreme indigenous tribunal mediated between the Jewish populace and Roman occupation, and possessed freedom of jurisdiction in religious matters and partial freedom in political matters, though it is doubtful whether it possessed the right of capital punishment (see John 18:31-32).

According to the Mishnah, twenty-three members of the Sanhedrin

---

72. Cited in Pixner, *Mit Jesus in Jerusalem*, 103.

were necessary to judge capital cases, with reasons for acquittal preceding reasons for conviction. In capital cases, a verdict of guilty required a second sitting the following day. Both sittings had to take place during daytime, and neither on the eve of Sabbath or a festival (*m. Sanh.* 4:1). Witnesses were to be warned against rumor and hearsay (*m. Sanh.* 4:5). A charge of blasphemy could not be sustained unless the accused cursed God's name itself, in which case the punishment prescribed was death by stoning, with the corpse then hung from a tree (*m. Sanh.* 7:5). As mentioned earlier, the chambers of the Sanhedrin were the Hall of Hewn Stones in the Temple (*m. Sanh.* 11:2); there is no evidence that the Sanhedrin ever met formally in the house of the high priest.

Nearly every detail of Jesus' trial violates the rules for capital cases prescribed in the Mishnah. This problem has received lengthy discussion and led to widely differing conclusions among commentators. Certainly the most radical conclusion is that Mark has grossly exaggerated or even falsified the Sanhedrin's role in the death of Jesus in order to exonerate the Romans, whose favor nascent Christianity was trying to court.[73] Another suggestion is that the Mishnah, which was not formally codified until A.D. 200, was either undefined or non-binding on such matters 170 years earlier in Jesus' time.[74]

Much more plausible than either of the above suggestions is that the Sanhedrin short-circuited procedures and contravened the law, egregiously at points, in order to expedite Jesus' execution. Josephus, in fact, records a similar trial in A.D. 62 when the high priest Ananus convened a rump session of the Sanhedrin in order to secure the death of James, brother of the Lord.[75] Mark's description of the trial resembles such a ses-

---

73. This conclusion unjustifiably impugns the historical veracity not only of Mark but of all four Evangelists, who, despite certain differences in reporting the trial of Jesus, agree on the responsibility of the Sanhedrin in delivering Jesus to the Roman governor for execution. The attempt to exonerate the Sanhedrin of its share of responsibility for Jesus' death is often motivated more by the desire to purge the NT of so-called anti-Semitisms than by genuinely historical interests. Regarding "anti-Semitism" in the NT, it must be recalled that the early Christians were themselves mostly Jews, and they appealed to Jews (see Acts 3:17ff.). It cannot be denied that some Christians have historically appealed to the NT as a pretext for perpetrating heinous crimes against Jews. That is not the fault of the NT documents themselves, however, but of a false hermeneutic of collective guilt that holds subsequent generations responsible for the deeds of their ancestors. The goal of interfaith tolerance and respect is not fostered either by altering historical documents or denying historical evidence.

74. Plausible as this suggestion seems, it is not supported at some points where similar evidence can be compared. Sabbath observances, e.g., appear to have been more rigorously upheld in Jesus' day when conservative Sadducean sentiments prevailed than a century later when Pharisaic moderation ruled the day. See Str-B 2.819.

75. Josephus, *Ant.* 20.200-203. Likewise D. Flusser, *Jesus* (Jerusalem: Magnes Press,

sion, for it does not read like a formal sitting of the Sanhedrin but rather a preliminary hearing, like a grand jury driving for an incrimination. The reference to "the whole Sanhedrin" (v. 55) evidently means unanimity among the members gathered, however many there were. Jesus appears already convicted in their eyes; thus, from word one evidence is pressed *against* him (Gk. *kata tou Iēsou*, vv. 55, 56, 57). The Jewish authorities had earlier broken the law by conspiring against Jesus on the Sabbath (3:6; John 9:13ff.); now that Jesus is in their grasp it is hardly surprising that legal formalities are waived. Like Pilate who wrote what he had to (John 19:22), the Sanhedrin does what it must in order to ensure an execution by the governor. It sacrifices its best jurisprudence to the overriding concept of the nation's greater good (John 11:50; what we call "national security" today), resulting in a travesty of justice and the condemnation of an innocent man to death.

56-59 The NIV says that the Sanhedrin was "looking for" evidence against Jesus (v. 55); the Gk. *zētein* always implies negative intent in Mark, and here the intent to condemn Jesus (see on the term at 1:37). The prisoner's record, however, provides no grounds for accusation (v. 55), and the Sanhedrin must resort to false testimony. The "many" false witnesses adduced testify to the determination of the Sanhedrin to dispatch Jesus. Jewish law demanded at least two corroborating witnesses in capital cases (Num 35:30; Deut 17:6; 19:15). But in the hearing before Caiaphas even contrived testimony is unsuccessful, for "their statements did not agree" (v. 56). Mark repeats this observation in v. 59, which suggests that this may be a backhanded testimony to the authority of Jesus: even as a captive — and with well-orchestrated human machinations against him — Jesus cannot be discredited. Attempts to discredit Jesus no doubt characterize every generation — even those like ours that purport to respect all religious beliefs. A false testimony never carries the conviction of truth.

The only charge against Jesus that Mark specifies — again echoed at the crucifixion (15:29) — is that he would destroy and rebuild the temple

---

1997), 146-47, who suggests that the high priest "assembled a sufficient number of judges who were from among his Sadducean friends." Flusser's attempt to exonerate the Sanhedrin of guilt in Jesus' death, however, is unconvincing. He argues that since Jesus "was buried in neither of the two graves reserved for those executed by order of the supreme council" the Sanhedrin was not responsible for his death. We have no idea whether the passage referred to (*m. Sanh.* 6:5) was in effect in A.D. 30; moreover, the passage concerns those who were beheaded, strangled, stoned, or burned, i.e., those executed by Jewish hands and means. Jesus, however, suffered crucifixion at the hands of the Romans, and crucifixion was a defiling form of death. Whether *m. Sanh.* 6:5 applied to victims of Roman execution is questionable.

(14:58). It is a serious charge. As the center of Jewish worship and the seat of the Sanhedrin's power, the temple symbolized the essence and hopes of Judaism. In the Messianic Age to come, the temple, along with the city of Jerusalem, would rival the splendor of the Messiah himself, according to *1 Enoch* 90:28-36. Mark does not actually record Jesus making the claim of destroying the temple (13:1-2?), though it is attested widely in early Christian sources and doubtlessly was uttered by Jesus.[76] Alone of the Evangelists, Mark includes the qualification about the temple being "man-made" (v. 58). This reference signaled not the physical temple but his resurrected body (and was widely understood thus by the early church).[77] For Mark, Jesus has replaced the temple as the place where God meets his people (11:12-21). According to 2 Sam 7:12-14, David's son would build a temple to God's name. This son receives God's promise, "'I will be his father, and he will be my son.'" The builder of God's house, in other words, will be God's Son. In a way truer than his accusers could have imagined, Jesus fulfills 2 Samuel 7, for he will presently confess himself before the high priest as God's Son, and his resurrected body will replace the earthly temple. Whether the high priest understood this subtlety we cannot say, but it is foremost in the mind of Mark, who now shows that the claim to be God's Son provides the conclusive piece of evidence against Jesus.

60-62 Following the chorus of false witnesses, the high priest addresses Jesus personally, "'Are you not going to answer? What is this testimony that these men are bringing against you?'"[78] Throughout his trials before the Sanhedrin and Pilate, Jesus is portrayed by Mark as maintaining *silence*. In the face of the battery of fraudulent charges against him, silence has a strategic value, for any statement Jesus makes will be exploited by the prosecution. Whatever he says in self-defense will result in self-incrimination. His silence is dictated by more than strategic interests,

---

76. Matt 26:61; 27:40; John 2:19-20; Acts 6:13-14; Heb 9:11. Each of these verses speaks of Jesus both destroying and rebuilding the temple, but the *Gospel of Thomas* 71 preserves a saying without rebuilding: "Jesus says, 'I will destroy this house, and no one will be able to build it again.'"

77. John 2:21-22; Acts 4:10-11; 1 Cor 3:11, 16; 1 Pet 2:4-8. A variant reading in the Western text (D) makes the reference to the resurrection explicit, *anastēsō acheiropoiēton* ("I shall *resurrect* a temple not made by human hands").

78. The exact sense of the question is clouded in the Greek manuscripts. According to the NIV (and the majority of manuscript evidence), the high priest wants Jesus to respond to the accusations themselves (*ti*: "what?"). According to a smaller but very impressive group of manuscripts, the high priest wants Jesus to respond to the fact of his accusations (B W Ψ; *hoti* ["that"], i.e., "*for* these men testify against you"). It is difficult to decide which of the two readings is more likely original, but superior textual support tips the scale tentatively in favor of the first reading, followed by the NIV.

however.[79] Mark consciously patterns Jesus' silence in both trials after the suffering servant of Isaiah, whose silence represents his *innocence:*

> He was oppressed and afflicted,
>   yet he did not open his mouth;
> he was led like a lamb to the slaughter,
>   and as a sheep before her shearers is silent,
>   so he did not open his mouth. (Isa 53:7)

The link with the suffering servant is further reinforced by the contemptuous treatment of Jesus following the hearing. The spitting, blindfold mockery, and beating of Jesus with fists (v. 65) recall the mistreatment of the Servant of Yahweh in Isa 50:6.[80]

At only one point does Jesus break silence. The high priest rises to his feet in the middle of the assembly and presses Jesus with the full authority of his office: "'Are you the Christ, the Son of the Blessed One?'" (14:61). In the original Greek the wording is put in the form of a statement with a question implied ("'You are the Christ, the Son of the Blessed One?'"). The "you" is emphatic, and "the Blessed One," a Jewish circumlocution for God's name, means none other than "God's Son." The effect is to put a full christological confession into the mouth of the high priest![81] In vv. 56 and 59 Mark noted that false witnesses could not agree against Jesus; now, in the question of the high priest, his arch-prosecutor confesses his name! How ironic that in the Gospel of Mark the two most complete christological confessions from humans occur in the mouths of those responsible for Jesus' death: the high priest in 14:61, and the centurion at the cross in 15:39!

Throughout Mark, the reader knows that Jesus is God's Son.[82] At least since the parable of the vineyard and tenants (12:1-12), the Sanhedrin is familiar with the claim. In that parable Jesus spoke of the beloved Son as heir of the vineyard, and Mark confirms for his readers that the point was not lost on the "the chief priests, the teachers of the law and the elders" (11:27), the same group before whom Jesus now stands.[83] Until

---

79. The second-century *Gospel of Peter* 10 maintains that Jesus was silent during the passion "as if he felt no pain." Contrary to this gnostic claim, the description of Jesus' suffering in Gethsemane (14:33-36) indicates that he certainly *did* feel pain.

80. See C. Maurer, "Knecht Gottes und Sohn Gottes im Passionsbericht des Markusevangeliums," *ZTK* 59 (1953): 1-38.

81. Both Matt 26:63 and Luke 22:67 make a question of Mark's statement.

82. 1:1, 11, 24; 3:11; 5:7; 9:7; 12:6; 13:32, and other christological clues in 8:29-30; 10:47; 12:35-37.

83. See J. Kingsbury, *The Christology of Mark's Gospel* (Philadelphia: Fortress Press, 1983), 119-22.

the question of the high priest, however, Jesus has steadfastly silenced all proclamations of his divine Sonship. In order truly to understand the meaning of his person something has been missing. The missing element has been the necessity of his suffering. Only in the light of suffering can Jesus openly divulge his identity as God's Son. At the trial the veil is finally removed. The malevolence which the Jewish authorities have harbored since the beginning of Jesus' ministry (3:6) is finally exposed; hence the secret that Jesus has protected since the beginning of his ministry can now be disclosed.

According to Mark, Jesus openly affirms the high priest's question, "'I am!'" (God's Son).[84] In v. 62 Jesus immediately interprets his affirmation with reference to the Son of Man in Dan 7:13 and Ps 110:1. The Son of Man here is a fully divine and exalted figure, "sitting at the right hand of the Mighty One" (Gk. "right hand of [God's] power"; see also *Did.* 16:8). Thus Jesus both affirms his divine Sonship before the high priest and portrays himself as the fulfiller of the eschatological mission of the Son of Man, an affirmation that sets him unambiguously in God's place. Though Jesus is dishonored by the high priest, he will be honored by God; and in place of his present vilification, God will vindicate the Son.[85]

Scholars have often doubted that Jesus would affirm the answer of the high priest on the ground that "Son of God" was not a messianic title in first-century Judaism.[86] They suspect that the conflation of "Messiah" and "God's Son" derived from the early Christian community, or from Mark himself, rather than from Jesus. It is true that "Messiah" and "Son of God" are not synonymous titles: "Messiah" is a less exalted and more functional title than "Son of God." The latter is the fullest title for Jesus in the NT, conveying his filial origin, nature, and purpose with God. But to suppose that the terms were hermetically separated, or that the Messiah

---

84. Matthew's and Luke's wordings are less explicit, but still affirmative. "'You have said so'" (Matt 26:64, literally translated) repeats verbatim in Greek Jesus' rejoinder to Judas's question, "'Is it I, Rabbi?'" (26:25). In both instances a clear "Yes" is implied. Given in response to questioning under oath, "'You have said so'" is understood to affirm the question in Jewish jurisprudence (Str-B 1.1,006). Luke's "'If I tell you, you will not believe me'" (22:67) implies an affirmation as well. See T. de Kruijf, *Der Sohn des lebendigen Gottes. Ein Beitrag zur Christologie des Matthäusevangeliums,* AnBib (Rome: Pontifical Biblical Institute, 1962), 95-97.

85. See J. A. T. Robinson, "The Second Coming — Mark XIV.62," *ExpTim* 67 (1955/56): 339.

86. So G. Dalman, *The Words of Jesus,* trans. D. M. Kay (Edinburgh: T. & T. Clark, 1909), 274, followed by many other scholars. W. Bousset, *Kyrios Christus: A History of the Belief in Christ from the Beginnings of Christianity to Irenaeus,* trans. J. Steely (Nashville: Abingdon, 1970), 95, regards the words as an "utterly impossible addition in the mouth of the high priest."

447

could not have been considered the Son of God, is an error. In addition to the wealth of evidence in the NT itself that relate the two titles, two texts from the DSS now demonstrate that the equation was not unknown in pre-Christian Judaism. Both texts speak of the Messiah as God's Son,[87] thus confirming R. H. Fuller's earlier judgment that "son of God was just coming into use as a Messianic title in pre-Christian Judaism."[88]

63-65 At the response of Jesus "the high priest tore his clothes." The Greek word for "clothes" *(chitōn)* refers to an inner garment like a long nightshirt that was worn next to the skin. The tearing of one's gar-ment was a sign of profound consternation (2 Sam 1:11; 2 Kgs 18:37). The response of Jesus is seized by the high priest as a self-evident blasphemy, the punishment for which was death by stoning.[89] The council concurs that he is "worthy of death," and Jesus is disgraced, mocked, and beat-en.[90] Interestingly, the one specific mockery reported is the taunt for Jesus to "'Prophesy!'" Since the high-priestly clan were Sadducees who denied the existence of angels and spirits (Acts 23:6), it is easy to imagine their desire to discredit anyone like Jesus who was believed to possess the spirit of prophecy.[91] The treatment of Jesus in v. 65 echoes the mockery, spitting on, and beating of the Servant of the Lord in Isa 50:6, and fulfills especially the third passion prediction in 10:33-34.[92]

It is often supposed that Jesus' claim to be the Messiah triggered the explosion from the high priest and his condemnation by the Sanhedrin. This is not the case. It was no crime to call oneself the Messiah, or to be called so by others; for, as Justin Martyr later acknowledged, the Messiah would be only "a man among men" *(Dial. Trypho* 49). A century after Je-sus, Rabbi Akiba openly declared Bar Kokhba, leader of the second revolt

87. The kingdom of the Messiah will be an eternal kingdom, according to 4Q246 2:1, and "He will be called son of God, and they will call him son of the Most High." Again, 4Q174 1:10-11, a series of proof-texts or *Florilegium,* expressly equates the "branch of David" (= Messiah) with the father-son imagery of 2 Sam 7:12-14.

88. *The Foundations of New Testament Christology* (New York: Scribner's, 1965), 32. A. Y. Collins, "Mark and His Readers: The Son of God among Jews," *HTR* 92 (1999): 404, timidly agrees: "The probable use of the expression 'Son of God' by the Qumran commu-nity for the messiah of Israel suggests that such usage was not avoided by all Jews of the late Second Temple period."

89. On blasphemy, see Exod 22:28; Lev 24:16; Num 15:30-31. See Str-B 1.1,016-1,024.

90. The awkward wording at the end of v. 65, *rhapismasin auton elabon,* is a Latinism *(verberibus eum acceperunt;* so BDF, 6), with the general meaning, "they laid blows on him" (rather than "took him and beat him"; so NIV). Further, see Taylor, *The Gospel Ac-cording to St. Mark,* 571.

91. See Flusser, *Jesus,* 190.

92. For spitting as an ultimate form of contempt, see Num 12:14; Deut 25:9; Job 30:10.

against Rome (A.D. 132-135), to be the Messiah, and the mass of people believed it — even after Bar Kokhba's death. The charge of blasphemy was thus not owing to any messianic claim, perhaps not even to the charge that Jesus would destroy the temple (v. 58). Blasphemy was not breaking a holy commandment or even profaning a holy place, but the audacity to ascribe God's honor to oneself, or to equate oneself with God. It was the claim to be God's Son (v. 62), not Messiah, that sealed Jesus' fate before the Sanhedrin.[93] The charge of blasphemy is powerful, if indirect, proof of Jesus' claim to be the Son of God.[94]

Mark's trial scene is profoundly ironic. The Sanhedrin stands on the law and Jesus sits in the dock, but in reality the Sanhedrin breaks the law and Jesus upholds it. The testimony that the Sanhedrin seeks against Jesus is in the end not provided by the false witnesses but by Jesus himself in the claim to be God's Son. Jesus stands on trial before the Sanhedrin, but the Sanhedrin will stand trial before the Son of Man when he returns in glory. The Sanhedrin makes a charade of Jesus' ability to prophesy, but his prophecies all come true. Above all, it is the high priest, not Jesus, who blasphemes, because Jesus *is* God's Son. The irony extends even to the larger framework of chaps. 13 and 14. At the end of chap. 13, amid visions of glory, Jesus anchors his teaching to humiliation and watchfulness; at the end of chap. 14, in utter humiliation, Jesus speaks of his exaltation "'at the Right Hand of Power'"!

66-68 Mark closes the sandwich by returning to Peter, who was left warming himself by the fire at Jesus' hearing (v. 54). The Greek genitive absolute at the beginning of v. 66 (NIV, "While Peter was below . . .") now resumes Peter's story. Typical of Roman villas and larger Mediterranean homes of the time, Caiaphas's courtyard (vv. 54, 66) would have been an open atrium enclosed by the rooms of the surrounding house. The reference to Peter "below" (v. 66) indicates that Jesus' trial took place in a room above the courtyard. "The whole scene is indelibly fixed in the consciousness of the Western world," says one commentator.[95] Remarkably so since the only characters are a servant girl, a few bystanders, and

---

93. See H. Chronis, "The Torn Veil: Cultus and Christology in Mark 15:37-39," *JBL* 101 (1982): 106, who argues "that Mark considers Jesus' divinity to be the real bone of contention at the trial," and thus the reason for the charge of blasphemy. Contra D. Juel, *Messiah and Temple,* SBLDS 31 (Missoula: Scholars Press, 1977), 51, who maintains that the issue at stake was Jesus' Messiahship rather than his divine Sonship, even though Juel correctly notes that "it does not appear that it was blasphemous in Jesus' day to claim to be the Messiah."

94. See O. Hofius, "Ist Jesus der Messias? Thesen," *JBTh (Der Messias)* 8 (1993): 121, who rightly maintains that v. 62 represents Jesus' claim to "einer *wesenhaften* Einheit mit Gott."

95. C. G. Montefiore, *The Synoptic Gospels*[2] (New York: Ktav, 1968), 1.368.

a disciple with second thoughts. Only Peter is identified since it is his story that Mark desires to tell. As in the case of Judas (vv. 43-45), Mark omits Peter's motives and feelings, focusing exclusively on his three denials (vv. 68, 70, 71), which happen exactly as predicted by Jesus (v. 30). Gethsemane, where Peter three times fell asleep as Jesus prayed (vv. 32-42), was thus an omen to his three denials in Caiaphas's courtyard.

But while Jesus was undergoing a formal trial above, a trial of different sorts was taking place below. A servant girl, a portress perhaps, spies Peter and accuses him of being with "the Nazarene" (v. 66). The reference to Jesus as a "Nazarene" is not an especially good omen.[96] It is still cold enough in March/April in Jerusalem to require a fire at night, and the light from the fire (the Greek word for "fire" in v. 54 is *phōs*, "light") allows Peter to be recognized in the dark. Despite Peter's desire to remain inconspicuous, he becomes the center of attention: twice in v. 67 Mark says that the servant girl "sees" Peter (Gk. *blepō* ["see"]; *emblepō* ["see closely"]), and she accuses him emphatically, "'*You* also were with the Nazarene Jesus.'" Peter stumbles over himself to disown the association and retorts with surliness, "'I neither know him nor have any idea what you mean.'" Mark's two Greek verbs for "know" are only an apparent redundancy. The first *(oida)* tends to denote theoretical knowledge, and the second *(epistamai)* practical knowledge; Peter's denial is thus a total denial — in theory and practice! Peter then quits the fire for the forecourt or "entryway" (v. 68).[97] The change of locations puts Peter even further from Jesus.

69-72   But a change of place is no substitute for a change of heart. Like a guilty conscience, the servant girl accuses Peter a second time, and this time she enlists the bystanders in her accusation. "'This fellow is one of *them*'" (v. 69) suggests that the Jesus movement is not unknown among associates of the high priest. Peter must now deny his association with Jesus before more people. The imperfect tense of the Greek verb for "deny"

96. Josephus thinks of Galileans as troublesome and "bellicose from childhood on" (*Life* 45). In Acts 24:5, "Nazarenes" is a term by which Jewish opponents speak of the followers of the "troublemaker" Jesus.

97. Here some early manuscripts add, "and the rooster crowed" (A C D K X Δ Θ Π). A smaller but weightier group of manuscripts omit the phrase (‭א‬ A B L W Ψ). On the one hand, copyists would be inclined to add the phrase to emphasize the fulfillment of Jesus' prophecy. Again, Peter would not have known if the cockcrow was the second if he had not heard the first. On the other hand, copyists would tend to omit the phrase in order to bring Mark into harmony with the other Gospels, who report only *one* cockcrow. Evidence is rather evenly balanced whether the phrase was original or secondary. Logic suggests it was added, for it would seem more likely that a scribe would add the phrase to prepare for the second rooster crow (v. 72) than to delete it if it were original. See Metzger, *TCGNT*, 115-16.

in v. 70 means that Peter "went off," as we say, on an extended denial. The contagion spreads and the bystanders recognize his Galilean dialect.[98] Although Peter hopes to escape notice, he ends up betraying Jesus by what he says, where he stands, and how he says it!

The third accusation is the boldest, and so is Peter's denial. The Greek is coarse and explicit, "He began to curse and swear, 'I do not know this man you speak of'" (v. 71). It may be, as the NIV translation implies, that Peter was not simply being profane but swearing by God's name, which the Gk. *anathematizein* can imply. If that is the meaning, then it is a *worse* profanation. Not surprisingly, Peter cannot bring himself to pronounce Jesus' name, but denies "'this man you're talking about.'" Peter's swearing *against* Jesus is a biting contrast to Jesus' oath *for* his divine Sonship. No amount of protestation can forestall the cockcrow — or the shattering truth of his denial from breaking upon Peter (v. 72). Mark's concluding note is fitting and final: "[Peter] broke down and wept" (v. 72).[99]

The concluding sandwich of chap. 14 sets the bold and revealing confession of Jesus before the high priest in glaring contrast to the denial of Peter before a servant girl. Throughout Mark, the disciples have misunderstood Jesus, and one of them even betrays him secretly. But Peter's renunciation is the first open denial of Jesus in Mark. The fact that it comes from the chief apostle makes it all the more trenchant. Peter does not face a formal trial, nor is he even questioned directly about his faith. He denies Jesus without ever using his name. Peter's example is a warning to disciples — then and now — that faithful witness to Jesus is most important (and most easily betrayed) in simple and ordinary actions and words. It is in everyday matters that disciples are true *martyrs* (the root meaning of which in Greek means "to bear witness"). Mark may have

---

98. A textual variant supported by A Θ and the Majority text reads, "For you are a Galilean and your speech is like [a Galilean]." Although not as well supported textually as the shorter reading preserved in the NIV, this reading may in fact be original, for it explains all the variations in both Mark and Matthew. See M. Holmes, "The Text of the Matthean Divorce Passages: A Comment on the Appeal to Harmonization in Textual Decisions," *JBL* 109 (1990): 652-56. It also makes explicit that the speech of Galileans was distinctive. Note the comment in *t. Berakhot* 32a that "in the school of R. Eliezer [c. A.D. 270] *alefs* were pronounced like *'ayins* and *'ayins* like *alefs*." We do not know that Rabbi Eliezer was a Galilean, but this is further evidence of distinctive speech patterns among some groups of Jews.

99. Two manuscripts read that Peter "began to weep" (D Θ), but the majority of manuscripts offer the more difficult reading *epibalōn eklaien*. The plain sense of *epiballein* is "to cast upon." Although the exact meaning of the phrase is debatable, the most reasonable meaning of v. 72 is that Peter "threw himself upon (the ground) and was weeping."

concluded this section with Peter's story to remind his persecuted congregation in Rome that not even the best Christian or lead apostle is immune to apostasy. Nor (as we shall see) is he beyond the promise of grace! The church can be honest about sin — even the sins of an apostate apostle — because it is so convinced of grace. "Where sin increased, grace increased all the more" (Rom 5:20).

CHAPTER FIFTEEN

The Cross and the Empty Tomb

MARK 15:1–16:8

In chap. 15 the responsibility for the prosecution of Jesus is shifted from the Sanhedrin to Pontius Pilate, the Roman prefect of Judea. As at the trial of the Sanhedrin, Mark portrays Jesus again submitting in silence and acquiescence, this time before the relentless gears of the Roman prosecution beginning with the sentence of Pilate and continuing with the abuse of the soldiers and the crucifixion itself. The crucifixion of Jesus is narrated by Mark, as it is throughout the NT, with utmost restraint and objectivity. There is no intention to exploit the savagery of crucifixion either to sensationalize Jesus' death or to evoke sentimentality from the reader. Especially in Mark the accent on the crucifixion narrative falls not on its brutality and cruelty but on the *shame* and the *mockery* to which Jesus is subjected. As in the prayer of Gethsemane, so, too, at the crucifixion, the inner suffering supersedes the physical horror. The mockery begins in earnest with the soldiers in vv. 16-20. Too weak to bear his own cross (v. 21), Jesus is degraded by punishment befitting a slave or criminal at a disgraceful place (Skull Hill, v. 22), in the company of thieves (v. 27), with a mock accusation (v. 26). Bystanders rail at Jesus (vv. 29-30; see Ps 22:8-9!), and the chief priests taunt him (vv. 31-32). Even those who suffer his same fate reproach him (v. 32). The parade of mockers "shook their heads" (v. 29), which in Judaism signaled scorn and disgust (Isa 37:22; Jer 18:16; Pss 22:8; 44:15; 109:25; Job 16:4). Nevertheless, when Jesus dies, rejected and alone, the most significant event of the Gospel of Mark transpires: the temple curtain is torn in two and the Gentile centurion confesses Jesus as the Son of God. Only at the cross can Jesus be first confessed in faith as the Son of God.

PILATE AND JESUS (15:1-15)

The other three Gospels relate Jesus' trial in greater detail than does Mark. Matthew records the dream of Pilate's wife (27:19) and Pilate's hand washing (27:24); Luke adds the interrogation before Antipas (23:6-12); and John includes a theological discussion between Jesus and Pilate (18:33-38). Mark narrates the trial with greater economy, focusing first on Jesus' silence before Pilate and second on Pilate's unsuccessful attempt to placate the crowd by offering amnesty to Jesus.

Excursus: Pontius Pilate

A balanced assessment of Pilate's role and responsibility in Jesus' death is complicated by the fact that the generally sympathetic portraits of Pilate in the Gospels differ somewhat from reports of him by Josephus and Philo. We do not imagine a ruler bending to the whims of the crowd, as he is portrayed in the Gospels, if he were "inflexible, stubborn, and cruel," in the words of Philo (*Embassy to Gaius* 301-2). A common explanation for this disparate picture of Pilate is that the Gospel writers — and particularly Mark, who writes in Rome under Nero — transfer the responsibility for Jesus' death from the Roman governor to the Jewish authorities in order to avoid offense to Rome.

There may be at least some truth to this view, for Pilate's role in Jesus' arrest and sentence cannot be as negligible as the Evangelists imply. Jesus was crucified, after all, and crucifixion was a Roman execution; hence Roman authority was ultimately responsible for Jesus' death. Likewise, John 18:3, 12 reports that Roman soldiers attended the arrest of Jesus. That Pilate's role exceeded reluctantly rubber stamping the Sanhedrin's death sentence is practically certain, for had there been no collusion between the Sanhedrin and the governor the pace and efficiency of Jesus' crucifixion are hard to explain. Moreover, the charge that Jesus is "King of the Jews" — a title that carried obvious political connotations — is mentioned a half-dozen times in chap. 15 (vv. 2, 9, 12, 18, 26, and 32). This suggests that the Roman authorities were neither uninformed nor unwilling accomplices in Jesus' arrest and death sentence.

The Gospel of Mark was probably written in the middle 60s during Nero's reign. The Roman Empire, in contrast to the earlier Republic, was a totalitarian state, and at no time more so than under Nero. Discretion, if not loyalty, dictated that Rome be portrayed in the best possible light in Mark's Gospel. Mark desired to encourage Christians in Rome, who were themselves victims of persecution, by Jesus' faithful example before Pilate. At the same time he wanted to avoid making claims that could be regarded treasonous, lest his Gospel become cause of further trouble for Christians in the Empire. The delicate task before Mark in chap. 15 is how to report the crucifixion without causing unnecessary offense to the Romans who crucified him. Mark needed to exercise sensitivity in the crucifixion narrative because the tyranny of Pilate paled in comparison to the tyranny of Nero, under whom the recipients of the Gospel were living. This is not to suggest, however, that Mark is embellishing the portrait of Pilate, for we should scarcely expect Mark, who has just shown that bearing faithful witness under persecution is a mark of true discipleship (14:53-72), to deny his own lesson by misrepresenting Pilate in order to avert the possible consequences of suffering for the sake of the gospel. We have, in other words, good reasons for trusting the reliability of Mark's description of Jesus' trial before Pilate. Let us therefore briefly revisit what we know of Pilate to see if we can make sense of the evidence about him presented by Mark, Josephus, and Philo.

The fifth Roman governor of Palestine, Pontius Pilate bore the official title "Prefect," and his residence was at Caesarea Maritima.[1] At Jewish festivals, and especially at the Passover when pilgrims streamed to the temple and religious fervor ran high, the presence of the governor was required in Jerusalem. There Pilate presumably lodged at Herod's Palace on the western wall of the city. Jesus' appearance can be imagined there, since the Praetorium (15:16) was probably located in Herod's Palace.[2]

Pilate's tenure as prefect extended from A.D. 26 to 37, making it the longest tenure of any of the fourteen Roman governors of Judea. He was not an incompetent ruler, but he tended toward intractability, for which he was eventually banished under the emperor Gaius (Caligula). On one occasion, Pilate showed his disdain of Jewish customs by introducing into Jerusalem military standards bearing the emperor's bust, thus violating the Jewish ban on images. The offended Jews proceeded *en masse* to Caesarea, nearly seventy miles away, and staged a nonviolent protest at Pilate's residence for five days! Pilate was initially intransigent and gave orders for his soldiers to slay the protesters in the stadium, but when "they bared their throats, welcoming death rather than transgression of their law," Pilate relented and withdrew the images from Jerusa-

---

1. Various titles were used of Roman governors. Josephus, writing in Greek, uses *hēgemōn* ("ruler"), *epitropos* ("guardian/governor"), and *eparchos* ("prefect"). The NT uses only the first term of Pilate, and Philo the second. Tacitus, writing in Latin, uses *procurator*. A Latin inscription discovered in Caesarea Maritima in 1961 refers to Pilate specifically as *praefectus*, "prefect," and this seems to have been the proper title of pre-Claudian governors. See D. Schwartz, "Pontius Pilate," *ABD* 5.397.

2. On the location of the Praetorium, see the discussion at 15:16.

lem (*Ant.* 18.55-59; *War* 2.169-71; Philo, *Embassy to Gaius* 299-304). On another occasion Pilate spent money from the temple treasury for the construction of a twenty-three-mile-long aqueduct to bring water into Jerusalem. He was again beset by protests from Jewish loyalists, who objected to the use of temple funds for public works. This time Pilate exchanged blows for protests, and in the ensuing melee large numbers were slain by soldiers whose brutality exceeded Pilate's orders, and still others were trampled to death in attempted flight (*Ant.* 18.60-62; *War* 2.175-77). A third episode from Pilate's tenure comes from the NT, which records an outrage in which Pilate, having slain a number of Galileans who had brought offerings to Jerusalem, mixed their blood with their sacrifices (Luke 13:1). A final episode concerns a nondescript Samaritan uprising that Pilate again violently subdued, which led to his removal from office (*Ant.* 18.85-88).

On the whole, Pilate's political record was characterized by insensitive beginnings followed by stubborn responses. Both Josephus and Philo describe his Jewish subjects as equally stubborn and defiant. In exasperation, Pilate on occasion vented his spleen rather than applying either wit or wisdom. He was not wantonly brutal, however, at least not on the scale of a Caligula or a Nero. When he resorted to force he directed it against parties responsible rather than to the general citizenry. Nor was he overly corrupt by the standards of the day. He was capable of constructive endeavors, as testified by the well-intended though ill-funded aqueduct project. His removal of the insignia from Jerusalem indicates that he was not always or entirely intransigent. One of his most notorious demerits was the result of police brutality rather than official decree. Pilate appears to have been a rather typical appointee of the emperor Tiberius, and the dogged qualities that procured the governorship for him in the first place were the same ones that eventuated in his losing it.

In light of this profile it is not too difficult to account for Pilate's treatment of Jesus as described by Mark. Pilate's political instincts tell him that Jesus is a figure to be watched but not necessarily dispatched, at least for the moment. Pilate runs aground, however, when an initial plea on behalf of Jesus elicits protests rather than approval from the crowd. Pilate is no stranger to Jewish protests, which, as much as he detests them, he has learned to respect. In the case of Jesus he responds with a combination of instinct and calculation typical of his office. Judging Jesus to be unworthy either of a stand on principle or of a show of force, Pilate opts to stand down, thus consigning Jesus to a routine crucifixion.[3]

---

3. D. Flusser, *Jesus* (Jerusalem: Magnes Press, 1997), 156, agrees "that Pilate's behavior in the Gospels is not very different from what is reported about him in the other

1 Mark's editorial signature is evident in the transition to the Roman proceeding against Jesus in 15:1.[4] Roman legal proceedings began at daybreak,[5] for by mid-morning Roman patricians and noblemen embarked on pursuits of leisure. The Sanhedrin therefore presents Jesus to Pilate "very early in the morning." The wording of v. 1 is often taken to imply a second meeting of the Sanhedrin, but this does not appear to be the meaning of the Gk. *symboulion poiēsantes*.[6] The phrase recalls the similar description of the Pharisees and Herodians in 3:6 and indicates the completion of the plot against Jesus; hence, the justification of the NIV translation: "[The Sanhedrin] reached a decision" to "hand Jesus over to Pilate." If, as John 18:31 maintains, the Sanhedrin did not have jurisdiction over capital punishment, then Pilate was a crucial link in securing Jesus' execution.[7] But there were other reasons for delivering Jesus to Pilate. The authority of the governor would be important in quelling any popular outcry that might arise on Jesus' behalf. Moreover, a verdict of Rome against Jesus — and especially the shame of death by crucifixion — would severely damage attempts on the part of Jesus' followers to reha-

---

sources." Flusser sees Pilate's cruelty as a compensation for his basic weakness, which could influence him to abandon his designs on occasion (160). Flusser concludes: "It would seem, therefore, that Jesus' tragic end was preceded by no verdict of any earthly judiciary. It was the outcome of a grisly interplay of naked spheres of interest in the shadow of brutal antagonisms" (166). See also H. Bond, *Pontius Pilate in History and Interpretation*, SNTSMS 100 (Cambridge: Cambridge University Press, 1998), 203-7.

4. "Immediately," "taking counsel," "the whole Sanhedrin," and listing the three offices of the Sanhedrin are typically Markan.

5. Seneca, *On Anger* 2.7.

6. *Symboulion poiēsantes* ("marking [or doing] a council") is a Latinism (*consilium capere*; see BDF, 5-6), the more usual wording of which is *symboulion lambanein* (so Matt 12:14; 22:15; 27:1, 7; 28:12). The wording of Mark's Latinism has been subjected to two changes in the Greek manuscript tradition. The first is to improve the style of the sentence by substituting a finite verb, *epoiēsan*, for the participle and adding *kai* ("and") before *dēsantes* ("bound"; so D Θ: "they took counsel . . . and bound Jesus"). The second is to try to alleviate the ambiguity of *symboulion poiēsantes* by substituting *hetoimasantes* (ℵ C L; *hetoimasantes* = "prepare") for *poiēsantes*. The resultant sense would be "to take counsel" or "to make a plan" to ensure that readers understand that the council had already been convened. Despite these changes, the first reading above claims the strongest textual support (see B. Metzger, *TCGNT*, 117).

7. Whether the Sanhedrin possessed the legal right over capital punishment is unclear. John 18:31 implies that it did not, but it is a fact that the Jews not infrequently executed people without Roman authority (despite the note of John 18:31 to the contrary). According to Josephus (*War* 6.124-26; *Ant.* 15.417; see also Philo, *Embassy to Gaius* 307) Jews could execute Gentiles who attempted to enter the temple sanctuary; there is a report of the execution of a priest's daughter in *m. Sanh.* 7:2; Stephen was stoned to death by the Sanhedrin (Acts 6:12-15; 7:57-59); and James, the brother of Jesus, was stoned to death by the Sanhedrin in A.D. 62 (Josephus, *Ant.* 20.200-203).

bilitate him.[8] The vocabulary of v. 1 (the whole Sanhedrin consulted, bound, brought, delivered) reflects a politically conscious *modus operandi*. The bureaucratic redundancy of the Sanhedrin rivals the military overkill at Jesus' arrest (14:43, 48). The play on words in "handed over" is again significant, as it was in chap. 14 (vv. 10, 11, 18, 21, 41, 42, and 44). The word combines two important meanings appropriate to the verse: it portrays Jesus as the victim (betrayed by human wickedness) and as the means of redemption (delivered up according to God's purpose).

2-5 Pilate, the Roman prefect, asks Jesus, "'Are you the king of the Jews?'" The wording of the question in Greek is exactly the same as was the high priest's question in 14:61, that is, it is a statement with a question implied (lit. "'You are the king of the Jews?'"). As in the case of the high priest, Mark's wording makes Pilate an unknowing confessor.[9] Again, even the mouths of Jesus' enemies unwittingly confess him. Before the Jewish authorities Jesus had been charged with threats against the temple (14:57-58) and blasphemy (14:64). These were questions of a religious nature that, in themselves, were of little concern to Pilate. But pretension to Messiahship was a different matter. As we have seen, the claim to be Messiah was not a crime in Judaism, but when translated into its political equivalent, "King of the Jews," it became a more material concern to the governor. The political charge against Jesus is even clearer in Luke 23:2: "'This man subverts our nation, opposes payment of taxes to Caesar and claims to be Christ, a king.'" There is nothing in the NT or extracanonical literature that suggests that Jesus had Zealot leanings, and there is much to suggest otherwise. It is also, however, false to assume that Jesus' message and ministry were devoid of social, economic, and political consequences. In both his teaching and ministry Jesus departed significantly from both Jewish and Roman customs, and his message demanded the same of his followers. The Roman world did not separate religion from politics as does the post-Enlightenment West. True, Rome did not require Jews, as it required other subjugated peoples, to adopt Roman religion and emperor worship, but that did not mean that Rome was indifferent to Jewish religion, especially when devotees of it claimed or were called "King of the Jews." Grundmann asserts that the title is neither messianic nor political but rather an expression of mockery and disdain in the mouth of Pilate.[10] That is a naïve judgment, particularly in light of the Zealot revolt thirty years later. Rome did not arrest and crucify victims

---

8. See W. Grundmann, *Das Evangelium nach Markus*, 422.

9. This, of course, does not imply that either Pilate or the high priest was a believer. The stories in the *Acts of Pilate* (*NTApoc* 1.501-36) that make Pilate into a believer who valiantly but vainly lobbies for Jesus' release belong to later fanciful legends.

10. *Das Evangelium nach Markus*, 423.

who were not at least *perceived* as political threats. Throughout its lengthy evolution, Messiah increased in military and political connotations, particularly following Pompey's subjugation of Palestine in 63 B.C., after which the Messiah was perceived as a divine guerrilla fighter against Roman oppression (on Messiah, see further at 1:1; 8:29).

In reply to Pilate's question, Jesus responds, "'You say so,'" with emphasis on *You*. It is not a direct affirmation, or else Pilate would have immediate grounds for execution. But neither is it a denial. The reply is suggestive, as if to say, "You would do well to consider the question!"

The chief priests also accuse Jesus, but Mark does not specify their charges (15:3). According to John 18:33-38, Jesus and Pilate talk about the nature of political authority. But in Mark, Pilate's solicitations are useless. Jesus remains silent, and his silence in the face of hatred, abuse, and cruelty dominates Mark's portrayal of the passion from here onward.[11] It is not a silence of defeat, but a silence of surrender to God's sovereignty in the passion (Justin, *Dial. Trypho* 102.5).[12] Like the Servant of the Lord,

> He was oppressed and afflicted,
>   yet he opened not his mouth;
> he was led like a lamb to the slaughter,
>   and as a sheep before her shearers is silent,
>   so he did not open his mouth. (Isa 53:7)

11. Several rather late uncial manuscripts (N W Δ Θ Ψ) add to the end of v. 3 that "[Jesus] said not a word to [Pilate]." This is almost certainly a later addition intending to accentuate Jesus' silence before Pilate.

12. Note the insight of J. Guillet, *The Consciousness of Jesus,* trans. E. Bonin (New York: Newman Press, 1972), 209, on the silence of Jesus: "[Jesus] most certainly does not cut himself off from men: during the whole passion, we shall not find in him a single word of condemnation, a single gesture of aloofness, a single movement of withdrawal; and this attitude, at once so natural and so incomprehensible, says more eloquently than 'Father, forgive them' (Lk 23:24) how vast is the forgiveness that fills his heart. But what he has done is stop speaking to men, since he no longer has anything to tell them. Now he is turned toward God — but no longer needing to bear witness to him or asking to be championed before men. This is very different from prophets and martyrs: they die to give testimony, they invoke him for whose name they suffer, they proclaim his excellence and grandeur. Jesus no longer speaks about God, but to him. And a painful dialogue it is; all we know of it, till his last breath, is the anguished supplications in Gethsemane and the cry that rose from the cross into the void. But it is also a dialogue in which the Son truly reveals himself. For Jesus to cleave to God amid this horror and emptiness, and keep his eyes fixed on him though he deprives him of all defense, all protection and all joy, there has to exist between God and Jesus a bond invulnerable to any attack, an unshakeable trust, a certitude stronger than death. Now, at the end, exhausted and crushed, Jesus does not need to turn toward God, for he has never left him: he is the Son."

459

Even in silence Jesus bears witness, for Mark notes that Pilate is "amazed" (Gk. *thaumazein*). Mark twice notes Pilate's amazement (Gk. *thaumazein*); in both instances, ironically, it is evoked by what Jesus does *not* say — by his silence (v. 5) and death (v. 44). Mark often notes the amazement and astonishment, particularly of the crowds, at Jesus' words and deeds. Amazement is not the same thing as faith, although it may become the first step to faith. In this instance, Pilate's amazement may signal a change of mind to seek Jesus' release from the crowd, for Josephus records the same reaction (Gk. *thaumazein*) of Pilate when the crowds protested so valiantly in Caesarea, after which he removed the offending images from Jerusalem (*Ant.* 18.59).

6-7 According to 15:6-15, Pilate decides to scuttle the case against Jesus and even attempts through the proposal of a prisoner release to use Jesus to gain political favor with the crowd. The plan misfires, and Pilate finds the crowd ranged in protest against him, all of which is reminiscent of protests against him recorded by Josephus and Philo. As one reads Josephus and Philo, one is struck with the virulence of the crowd's opposition to Pilate. The description of the vehemence of the protest at the building of the aqueduct[13] is particularly similar to the description of the crowd in vv. 13-14.

The pretext that Pilate uses in order to release Jesus is "the custom at the Feast to release a prisoner whom the people requested" (v. 6). Matthew 27:15, Mark 15:6, and John 18:39 mention this custom specifically, and Luke 23:18 implies it. There is, however, no explicit evidence outside the Gospels for a Passover amnesty as described here, although there is a fair amount of evidence that rulers did release prisoners from time to time (often for the duration of a festival) in both Jewish and pagan societies.[14] As prefect, Pilate possessed authority to commute or pardon the sentence of any criminal he chose. In v. 17 the criminal pardoned is identified as one of "the insurrectionists," a man who had committed murder "in the uprising" (v. 7).[15] We know nothing of the incident mentioned, but

13. "Tens of thousands of men assembled and cried out against him. . . . Some too even hurled insults and abuse of the sort that a throng will commonly engage in. . . . the Jews were in full torrent of abuse" (*Ant.* 18.60-61).

14. See E. Lohmeyer, *Das Evangelium des Markus,* 336-37; and R. Merritt, "Jesus Barabbas and the Paschal Pardon," *JBL* 104 (1985): 57-68.

15. We cannot say for certain whether or not Barabbas was part of the Jewish freedom movement (whether of the Zealots or Sicarii or some other faction). M. Hengel, *The Zealots,* trans. D. Smith (Edinburgh: T. & T. Clark, 1989), 340-41, thinks it likely that he was, on the grounds that Pilate would not have released an ordinary murderer in place of Jesus. I suspect the opposite is more probable, i.e., that Pilate would release an ordinary murderer before he would release an enemy of the state. Mark calls Barabbas a "murderer" (*phonos*), a term, I suspect, that he would not use of a political insurrectionist.

Mark's reference to it as *"the* uprising" indicates that it was known to his readers — and thus testimony to yet another trouble besetting Pilate. The crowd clamors for a known killer over Jesus. The criminal's name, Barabbas (v. 7), in Hebrew means "son of the *abba* [father]." Along with several church fathers, Jerome believed the name meant "son of the teacher," which is not impossible since rabbis were often called *"abba."*[16] Matthew 27:16-17 adds that his given name was "Jesus," which heightens the drama of Pilate's question, "'Which Jesus do you want: the son of *abba*, or the would-be Messiah?'"[17] Mark's wording may actually corroborate Matthew's, for Mark's curious introduction of the prisoner as "a man called Barabbas" (Gk. *ho legomenos*) seems to differentiate this Barabbas from the true "Son of the Father," Jesus. There is a tragic irony in Pilate's amnesty, for a convicted murderer is set free, and in his place the innocent Son of the Father is condemned to death. It is not difficult to see in this prisoner exchange a reflection of the substitutionary understanding of atonement: "While we were still sinners, Christ died for us" (Rom 5:8); "Christ died for sins, the righteous for the unrighteous" (1 Pet 3:18).

8-11 Mark mentions in passing that "The crowd came up and asked Pilate." Later copyists changed the reading to one that seemed more appropriate, "The crowd *cried out* and asked Pilate."[18] Nevertheless, "came up" is probability the original reading and a clue to the location of the Praetorium (see on the term at v. 16). According to John 19:13, Jesus was tried by Pilate at a place called the "Stone Pavement," the Aramaic word for which, "Gabbatha," means "high point." Herod's Palace was situated on the prominent western hill of Jerusalem to which crowds would have to "come up" before Pilate. The crowds went up, according to the NIV, requesting "Pilate to do for them what he usually did." That is a rather interpretive translation of an obscure Greek original, "as he did to them" (v. 8). Evidently the crowd appeals to Pilate to release a prisoner at Passover according to his custom.[19]

16. "Barabbas . . . is interpreted in the so-called Gospel according to the Hebrews as 'son of their teacher'" (*Comm. on Matt* 27:16; cited in *NTApoc* 1.162).

17. See Metzger, *TCGNT*, 67-68; M. Wilkins, "Barabbas," *ABD* 1.607.

18. Although *anaboēsas ho ochlos* ("the crowd cried out") is attested by a majority of manuscripts (א^b A C K W X Δ Θ Π Ψ, plus many minuscules), it is less likely to be the original reading than *anabas ho ochlos* ("the crowd went up"; א B) because there are no other occurrences of *anaboan* in Mark, whereas *anabainein* occurs nine times. See Metzger, *TCGNT,* 117. Moreover, the reading "cry out" is more easily explained: missing the point of the crowd *going up* to the Praetorium, the scribes substituted the more obvious "cry out."

19. Two textual variants attempt to make more explicit what Mark apparently suggests. Three uncials (A C D) read, "what he always was doing," the sense of which is fol-

Pilate, accordingly, asks if the crowd wishes the release of "the King of the Jews." Mark adds editorially that Pilate knew that the arrest of Jesus was incited by envy. This is the only occurrence of envy (Gk. *phthonos*) in the Gospels (with the exception of the parallel in Matt 27:18). Envy is grief or anger caused by another's success.[20] It is another reverse testimony to Jesus' exalted status and integrity, which causes the high priest envy and provokes the arrest of Jesus and his deliverance to Pilate. In the trial before Pilate, opposition to Jesus is fomented and spearheaded by the "the chief priests."[21] According to Mark, opposition to Jesus in Galilee came largely from the scribes and Pharisees; and once in Jerusalem, from the Sanhedrin. The actual arrest and trial of Jesus, however, as vv. 10-11 clarify, were the peculiar responsibility of the high priest.[22] As wealthy Sadducees who knew how to collaborate with Rome, the high priests were scarcely representative of Pharisaic Judaism, not to mention the overwhelming majority of normal Jews, "people of the land." Interestingly, the Jewish historian Josephus several times refers to Pilate's protestors as "the Jews," but Mark is more specific and objective: the prime mover in Jesus' trial and arrest is the high priest, who "stirred up" (v. 11) or incites the crowd to demand the release of Barabbas.

---

lowed by the NIV, "what he *usually* did." The ninth-century Koridethi (Θ) fully explains Mark's implication, "as it was [Pilate's] custom to release for them a prisoner." Both variants are doubtlessly later changes intended to clarify obscure wording.

20. See A. C. Hagedorn and J. H. Neyrey, "'It was out of envy that they handed Jesus over' (Mark 15:10): The Anatomy of Envy and the Gospel of Mark," *JSNT* 69 (1998): 39-40.

21. There are twenty-one references to the chief priest in the Gospel of Mark, all but five of them in chaps. 14–15, and each in explicit opposition to Jesus. There are a comparable number of references (nineteen) to scribes in Mark, but only six occur in chaps. 14–15. This statistic shows that responsibility for Jesus' arrest and trial lay particularly in the court of the chief priest. The Gospels regularly refer to the chief priests in the plural, whereas there was only one ruling high priest at a time, elected annually. The plural is accounted for by the fact that former high priests retained the title and authority of the high-priestly office. Especially influential was Annas (Luke 3:2; John 18:13, 24), high priest from A.D. 6 to 15, who had *five* sons who later became high priests (Josephus, *Ant.* 20.198). Between the high priesthood of Annas and the high priesthood Caiaphas, his son-in-law (John 18:13), who was high priest at the time of Jesus' death (A.D. 18-36), there were three other high priests (Ismael, Eleazar, and Simon). Thus the term "chief priests" could include a half-dozen high priests, plus their influential family members, thus comprising a very considerable power bloc. For a discussion of the role of Caiaphas in Jesus' execution, see Flusser, *Jesus*, 195-206. For a discussion of chief priests in general, see J. Jeremias, *Jerusalem in the Time of Jesus*, trans. F. H. and C. H. Cave (London: SCM Press, 1969), 147-81.

22. The reference to "the chief priests" is absent in Vaticanus (B), but this is probably owing to attempted stylistic improvement on the part of a later copyist since the expression occurs immediately afterward at the beginning of v. 11 (see Matt 27:18). The reference to "the chief priests" in v. 10 is almost certain, and in v. 11 entirely certain.

12-14 Three times Pilate lobbies for Jesus (15:9, 12, and 14).[23] The suggestion that Mark is "reinventing" Pilate so as to exonerate the Roman ruler and vilify Jews is overly simplistic and shows a lack of historical perspective.[24] The commander of the Roman occupation in obstreperous Judea faced political realities that were more subtle and volatile than is often appreciated. Certainly Pilate possessed the power to find for Jesus, but whether, from a political standpoint, it was wise to do so was another question. By and large Pilate disdained his Jewish subjects, but even dictators cannot completely disregard the will of their subjects.[25] We cannot know Pilate's mind, but Mark — and he is followed here by the other three Evangelists — indicates that Pilate harbored doubts about the necessity of Jesus' execution (vv. 10 and 14). Nevertheless, Pilate seems to have concluded that Jesus might still have some *political* value. His "wanting to satisfy the crowd" (v. 15) indicates his underlying *Realpolitik*, that is, his willingness to sacrifice an innocent prisoner for political expediency and security. Whatever Pilate's strategy, the Roman governor becomes the second party implicated in Jesus' death. The chief priests instigated the plot against Jesus, but the Roman prefect bears responsibility for executing it.[26]

23. The textual condition of Pilate's question in v. 12 is particularly uncertain. A majority of manuscripts include "'What *do you wish [that]* I shall do?'" in the first part of the verse. Its omission is supported by a smaller but weightier group of manuscripts (א B C W Δ Ψ). In the latter half of v. 12 "the one you call" is again questionable, being omitted by A D W Θ. For a discussion of the variants, see Metzger, *TCGNT*, 117-18. Both additions deflect responsibility away from Pilate and onto the Jews, which could argue for their secondary nature, since later tradition tended to incriminate Jews as the party responsible for Jesus' death.

24. It is scarcely possible, as some suggest, that Pilate appealed for Jesus' release simply to aggravate the Jews whom he despised. If you find yourself locked in a cage with a lion, you do not want to aggravate it. Pilate managed to aggravate the Jews unintentionally; he had no need to do so intentionally. Even further from the truth is the groundless suggestion that Jesus' trial before Pilate is a fiction. Jesus' execution at the hands of Pilate is attested in all four Gospels, in multiple and various strata of early Christian tradition, and in the Apostles' Creed. It is also attested by the Roman historian Tacitus (*Ann.* 15.44) and by the Jewish historian Josephus, who places his famous testimony to Jesus in the midst of his discussion of Pilate (*Ant.* 18.63-64).

25. A further development perhaps played a role in Pilate's decision. Tiberius had earlier followed the anti-Jewish policy of Sejanus, his influential minister, who was also Pilate's protégé. When Sejanus died in A.D. 31 Tiberius shifted to a much more favorable Jewish policy (Philo, *Embassy to Gaius* 159-60). If Jesus was crucified after Sejanus's death, it would have been in Pilate's political interest to placate the Jews if he were to remain in Tiberius's favor. Pilate's "'Stalinist' devotion to Tiberius" (so D. Flusser, *Jesus*, 160-62) ensured that Pilate would adopt and defend the policies of Tiberius (John 19:12!).

26. Bond, *Pilate in History and Interpretation*, 94-119, objects to the claim that Pilate was a weak governor acquiescing to public pressure. She sees him as a "skillful politi-

In the trial scene, as elsewhere in Mark's Gospel, ineluctable ironies confront us. Pilate, who begins by seeking amnesty for Jesus, ends by seeking it for himself. The Jewish subjects, on the other hand, whose duty it is to obey, assert their will and win the day. The governor is thus strangely governed. The free sovereign (note the first person pronouns in vv. 9 and 12) loses his freedom to forces he presumes to control, whereas Jesus, the silent prisoner who has no control, remains true to his divinely ordained purpose, and thus alone remains truly free. The description of Jesus' trial before Pilate recalls the description of John's beheading by Herod Antipas (6:14-29): Antipas and Pilate are both impotent potentates; Herodias and the chief priests are both *agents provocateurs*; John and Jesus are both silent and defenseless.

15 The "crowd," which plays a major role in Mark (see further on the term at 2:2), plays a further role at the crucifixion. Unlike Jesus who serves the crowd but is not determined by it, Pilate in the end succumbs to the crowd. "Wanting to satisfy the crowd,[27] Pilate released Barabbas to them. He had Jesus flogged, and handed him over to be crucified." **Flogging** was a cruel and merciless preparation for crucifixion. The NT shows no inclination to sensationalize the passion of Jesus by recounting its horrors. Its restraint and discretion, however, may leave modern readers ignorant of the savagery that preceded and attended a Roman crucifixion. As a prelude to crucifixion, Josephus (*War* 2.306) says the prisoner was stripped and bound to a post and beaten with a leather whip woven with bits of bone or metal.[28] No maximum number of strokes was prescribed. The scourging lacerated and stripped the flesh, often exposing bones and entrails. One of its purposes was to shorten the duration of crucifixion, but scourging was so brutal that some prisoners died before reaching the cross. Women were exempted from either suffering or witnessing the *flagellum*, which, according to Suetonius (*Domitian* 11), even horrified the emperor Domitian. It was this terrifying *verberatio*, flagellation, to which Jesus is delivered in v. 15.[29] Again, Mark says that Jesus was "handed

---

cian, manipulating the crowd to avoid a potentially difficult situation, and a strong representative of imperial interests" (117). This seems to be a good description of the way Pilate saw himself, but it does not describe his effect at the trial of Jesus, where he provoked rather than ameliorated the crowd, once again finding himself embroiled in a situation in which he had to react to the crowd.

27. The Gk. *to hikanon poiēsai* ("to satisfy") is another Latinism *(satisfacere)*. See BDF, 6.

28. Suetonius, *Lives of the Caesars*, "Gaius Caligula," 4.26, describes a flogging thus: "[Caligula] flogged the quaestor, who was charged with conspiracy, stripping off the man's clothes and spreading them under the soldiers' feet, to give them a firm footing as they beat him."

29. See C. Schneider, *"mastigoō," TDNT* 4.515-19.

over," that is, what was done from wickedness was still done "by God's set purpose and foreknowledge" (Acts 2:23).

SCOURGE AND SCORN (15:16-20a)

The final passion prediction (10:33-34) is the most specific of the three with respect to details of Jesus' sufferings. The first half of the prediction speaks of the Sanhedrin's role in Jesus' "handing over" (10:33), events that are related and fulfilled in 14:53-65. The second part of the prediction speaks in even greater detail of the role of the "Gentiles." Each detail — the "handing over" (10:33/15:15), "mockery" (10:34/15:20), "spitting" (10:34/15:19), and "flogging" (10:34/15:15) — is fulfilled in the trial before Pilate and the flogging by the Roman soldiers. Both Jewish leaders and Roman soldiers beat Jesus (14:65; 15:19), but in neither instance does the emphasis fall on physical suffering. Rather, the emphasis falls on the derision and mockery of Jesus, although with this difference: before the Sanhedrin it was Jesus' divine status that was lampooned ("'Prophesy . . . ,'" 14:65), whereas before the Romans it is his royal status and political profile that are ridiculed ("'Hail, King of the Jews,'" v. 18).[30] Mark's bitter irony persists: the soldiers, despite their intention, acknowledge in both word (v. 18) and deed (v. 19) Jesus' true identity. Even in rebellion against God humanity still bears witness to God!

16 Once delivered to the soldiers, Jesus is led to the Praetorium and maltreated by "the whole company of soldiers." The word for "whole company" (Gk. *speira*) is a Greek military term for the Latin *cohors*, which was one-tenth of a Roman legion, or some six hundred soldiers. The **Praetorium** refers first to the elite soldiers who were the personal guard of the prefect, and then to the place where they were housed. The location of the latter is much debated. Visitors to Jerusalem today are usually shown the *Lithostratos*, the "Pavement," under the Sisters of Zion Convent on the traditional Via Dolorosa (Way of Sorrows). The worn stone pavement, in which ancient etchings are still visible, is commonly said to be the floor of the Praetorium in the Antonia Fortress where Jesus was mocked and beaten by Roman soldiers. The site is indeed old, but it probably does not date before Hadrian (Roman emperor, A.D. 117-38), or Herod Agrippa I (A.D. 41-44) at the earliest, and is thus not the "pavement" (John 19:13) of Jesus' trial. It is even doubtful that the Praetorium was located in the Antonia Fortress. The Roman governor normally re-

---

30. L. Hurtado, *Mark*, NIBC (Peabody, Mass.: Hendrickson Publishers, 1983), 261-62.

sided at Caesarea Maritima, but his presence was required in Jerusalem at festivals (particularly Passover) when pilgrims flooded the city with prayers — and sometimes plans — for liberation from Rome. There is no evidence that Herod the Great or the Roman prefects who succeeded him ever stayed at the Antonia Fortress when they were in Jerusalem. They resided, rather, in the Herodian palace, which was begun by Herod in 23 B.C. and was both larger and more luxurious than the Antonia. Josephus cannot find words adequate to describe the splendor of Herod's large and lavish palace, "with enough bedchambers for one-hundred guests" (*War* 5.177-83; *Ant.* 15.318). Both Philo and Josephus locate the Roman governors there.[31] The Gospel of John (19:13) notes that the trial before Pilate occurred at "Gabbatha," which in Aramaic means "high point." Herod's Palace was situated on the prominent western hill of Jerusalem (where the Jaffa Gate is today), which may explain Mark's reference to the crowd as "coming up" (15:8) to Pilate. Moreover, the Gk. *aulē* (v. 16), meaning "courtyard" (NIV, "palace"), is not used of the Antonia Fortress, but regularly of the royal atrium of Herod's Palace. The courtyard of Herod's Palace is the most probable site of the flagellation of Jesus.

17-18 In macabre sport, the soldiers drape Jesus with a purple robe and crown him with a wreath of thorns. Purple, the most expensive and prestigious of ancient dyes, symbolized royalty.[32] The crown, normally made of gold leaf, signified royalty or military valor. Jesus' crown is a painful burlesque woven from the spiny stems of the acanthus plant common to the Mediterranean region. The salute, "'Hail, King of the Jews,'" is a parody of Caesar's salute, "Ave Caesar, victor, imperator." The parody is foremost a mockery of Jesus, but in a lesser sense it also

---

31. Philo specifically locates Pilate in Herod's Palace (*Embassy to Gaius* 299), and Josephus describes Florus, the last governor before the Jewish revolt (A.D. 64-66), both residing in the Palace and holding trials there similar to Pilate's trial of Jesus (*War* 2.301; 2.328; also *Ant.* 17.222). See Str-B 1.1,035; J. Murphy-O'Connor, "The Geography of Faith: Tracing the Via Dolorosa," *BRev* 12/6 (1996): 34; E. Schürer, *History of the Jewish People,* 1.361-62. Against Herod's Palace, Bargil Pixner argues on the basis of ancient Christian tradition that the Praetorium was in the old Hasmonean palace that lay midway between Herod's Palace and the Antonia on the slope of the Tyropoeon Valley opposite the southern end of the temple mount. See B. Pixner, "Praetorium," *ABD* 5.447-48; R. Riesner, "Das Praetorium des Pilatus," *BibLeb* 41 (1986): 34-37. The fact that Christian tradition does not identify Herod's Palace as the Praetorium is the major reason why Pixner rejects it. Given the fact that the Roman legion occupied the palace after the defeat of Jerusalem in A.D. 70, we should not be surprised that Christian tradition settled on an accessible site (i.e., the Hasmonean palace) at which to commemorate the flagellation. The combined witness of Philo and Josephus argues in favor of Herod's Palace, as opposed to Pixner's view.

32. The suggestion that Jesus was draped with a red Roman soldier's cloak is not supported by the wording of the text. Mark specifies a purple cloak (*porphyra*), not red (*chlamys kokkinē*).

mocks the Jews. Before the physical scourge of Jesus Mark notes the scorn of the soldiers toward him.[33]

19-20 The possession of power carries with it the inevitable temptation to its misuse. The empowerment of the soldiers and the impairment of Jesus incite the soldiers to proceed from mockery to violence. Jesus is hit on the head with a "staff," or *kalamos* in Greek, a generic word for "reed." The marshes along the Jordan and west shore of the Dead Sea produce a harvest of papyrus reeds, which resemble young bamboo stalks. If this is the meaning of the term, a stick or pole is in view. In Classical Greek *kalamos* can mean the shaft of an arrow, which, given the setting, may be the meaning of the term here. The brutality and banality of the soldiers replay the treatment of Jesus earlier by the Sanhedrin (14:65).[34]

The blows, spitting, and mock prostrations (v. 19) are prelude to the more horrible crucifixion to follow. A Roman execution squad consisted of four soldiers and was overseen by a centurion, a commander of a hundred soldiers. Such a squad marches Jesus to the site of crucifixion (v. 20). Bespattered with blood and ridicule, the figure of Jesus again recalls Isaiah's suffering servant:

> I offered my back to those who beat me,
> > my cheeks to those who pulled out my beard;
> I hid not my face
> > from mocking and spitting. (Isa 50:6)

CRUCIFIXION (15:20b-32)

In reflecting on the crucifixion of Jesus, the earliest Christians found in the suffering righteous man, particularly as depicted in Psalms 22 and 69, Isaiah 53, and Wisdom 2, the supreme prefiguration of Jesus' fate. The drugged wine offered to Jesus before the crucifixion (v. 23) echoes Ps 69:21, "They put gall in my food and gave me vinegar for my thirst." The dividing of Jesus' clothes (v. 24) fulfilled Ps 22:18, "They divide my gar-

---

33. Philo, *Flaccus* 36–39, relates the story of a lunatic who was mocked by the crowd by draping him in a rug for a royal robe, setting a mock crown on his head, and placing a papyrus stalk in his hand as a scepter. Others joined the theatrical farce by saluting him and calling him "lord."

34. The *Gospel of Peter* 6–9 follows closely the scourge and scorn of Jesus in Mark, with the added exception that Jesus is mocked as the Son of God as well as the King of the Jews. Note also Plato's description of the fate of the just individual in *The Republic* 2.5 (4th cent. B.C.), "the just man will have to endure the lash, the rack, chains, the branding-iron in his eyes, and finally, after every extremity of suffering, he will be crucified."

ments among them and cast lots for my clothing." The shaking of heads in scorn (v. 27) fulfilled Ps 22:7, "All who see me mock me; they hurl insults, shaking their heads: 'He trusts in the LORD; let the LORD rescue him'" (see also Ps 109:25; Lam 2:15). Above all, the mockery to "'come down now from the cross that we may see and believe'" (v. 32) paralleled the mockery of the suffering righteous man in Wis 2:17-18: "Let us see if his words are true, and let us put his life to the test; for if the righteous one is God's Son, God will help him and save him from the hand of his adversaries." These passages and others like them influenced the way the early church understood Jesus' death, as well as the details that were remembered and the language in which his death was presented.

20b "Then they led him away to crucify him." With utter objectivity and with no trace of playing on the reader's emotions Mark announces the **crucifixion**, the "most cruel and horrifying punishment," in the words of Cicero.[35] Every totalitarian regime needs a terror apparatus, and crucifixion was Rome's terror apparatus *ad horrendum*, infamous alike for its infliction of pain and ignominy on the victim. "Whenever we crucify the guilty, the most crowded roads are chosen, where the most people can see and be moved by this fear," approved Quintilian (*Declamationes* 274). Crucifixion was a punishment reserved for non-Roman citizens in which excessive cruelty was unleashed on the lowest and most defenseless classes of society — slaves, violent criminals, and prisoners of war. At the defeat of the slave rebellion under Spartacus in 71 B.C. Crassus had more than six thousand slaves crucified along the Via Appia between Capua and Rome. To enhance both the shame (Heb 12:2) and deterrent effect of crucifixion, victims were executed as public spectacles, and men were normally crucified naked, as the gambling for Jesus' clothes attests (although Jewish sensitivities may have prescribed a loincloth).[36] Nor was crucifixion inflicted on men alone; women, particularly slave women and women of the lower classes, could also suffer the horrors of crucifixion.[37] In the art and jewelry of the West the cross has become a fixed symbol, but according to Josephus (*War* 5.449-51), during the siege of Jerusalem the Romans crucified captives before the walls of Jerusalem in different postures and in different ways according to their

35. *Verrine Orations* 2.5.165. For this and other diatribes against crucifixion by ancient authors, see M. Hengel, *Crucifixion in the Ancient World and the Folly of the Message of the Cross,* trans. J. Bowden (Philadelphia: Fortress, 1977), 7-10.

36. On the shame of crucifixion, note Cicero's words: "the very word 'cross' should be far removed not only from the person of a Roman citizen but from his thoughts" (*In Defense of Rabirius* 5.15-16 [cited in HCNT, 157]).

37. K. Corley, "Women and the Crucifixion of Jesus," *Forum* (new series) 1 (1998): 189.

sadistic ingenuity. In 1968 a team of Israeli archaeologists discovered a tomb in Jerusalem revealing the first authenticated evidence of a crucifixion in antiquity. In this particular instance it appears that the arms of the condemned man were tied rather than nailed to the *patibulum* (crossbeam), and that the victim's legs straddled the *stipes* (vertical post), one leg on each side, with a nail penetrating each heel bone laterally.[38]

Depending on the severity of flogging beforehand, some victims survived on crosses several days. Since no major arteries were severed, death came not by blood loss, but from hypovolemic shock or exhaustion asphyxia or heart failure, or a combination of the above.[39] Crucifixion was a ghastly form of death: excruciatingly painful, prolonged, and socially degrading. The thought that God's Messiah could suffer "a cross of shame" (Heb 12:2) was so scandalous that some twenty-five years later Paul confessed that the preaching of a crucified Messiah was "a stumbling block to Jews and foolishness to Gentiles" (1 Cor 1:23). In the second century A.D. the gnostic Basilides was so aghast at the idea of a crucified Messiah that he invented the notion that Simon of Cyrene — and not Jesus — died on the cross![40] Later apocryphal Gospels tend to insulate Jesus from the horrible ordeal of crucifixion.[41] Mark, however, admits its terrible reality, but without sensationalism or sentimentality. His purpose is to emphasize what the crucifixion of Jesus *accomplished*, and *how*, which are well summarized by Martin Hengel: "in the death of Jesus of Nazareth God identified himself with the extreme of human wretchedness, which Jesus endured as a representative of us all, in order to bring us to the freedom of the children of God:

'He who did not spare his own Son,
but gave him up for us all,
will he not also give us all things with him?' (Romans 8:32)."[42]

---

38. J. Zias and E. Sekeles, "The Crucified Man from Giv'at ha-Mivtar: A Reappraisal," *IEJ* 35/1 (1985): 22-27; H. Shanks, "New Analysis of the Crucified Man," *BARev* 11/6 (1985): 20-21.

39. W. Edwards, W. Gabel, and F. Hosmer, "On the Physical Death of Jesus Christ," *JAMA* 255/11 (March 21, 1986): 1,455-63; F. Zugibe, "Two Questions About Crucifixion: Does the Victim Die of Asphyxiation? Would Nails in the Hand Hold the Weight of the Body?" *BRev* 5/2 (1989): 35-43. For the subject of crucifixion in general, see G. G. O'Collins, "Crucifixion," *ABD* 1.1,207-10.

40. Irenaeus, *Adv. Haer.* 1.24.4. The same idea appears in *Treatise of Seth* 55–56 and *Apocalypse of Peter* 81, where Jesus stands by laughing as Simon dies in his stead on the cross!

41. The *Gospel of Peter* 10, e.g., says that Jesus was silent on the cross because he felt no pain.

42. *Crucifixion in the Ancient World and the Folly of the Message of the Cross*, 89.

21 Immediately following the mention of crucifixion in 15:20b, Mark mentions a certain Simon of Cyrene who is forced to carry Jesus' cross. The Greek word for "force," *angareuō*, was commonly used of co-ercing slaves and animals in work. The drafting of Simon was an example of the hated compulsory service that Rome imposed on subjugated Palestine. A condemned man normally carried his own *patibulum*, the heavy crossbeam, to the site of crucifixion; "every criminal condemned to death bears his cross on his back," declared Plutarch (*Moralia* 554 A/B). At the place of execution, the *patibulum* was lashed or nailed to the *stipes*, the upright post. Perhaps because of weakness and blood loss during the flagellation, Jesus was unable to carry the *patibulum*; hence the drafting of Simon. Cyrene, on the north coast of Africa, may indicate that Simon was a man of color. Simon's name is preserved in the parallel traditions of Matt 27:32 and Luke 23:26, but Mark includes two other names in connection with Simon. The mention of three personal names in one verse is extremely unusual for Mark. The names are presented as though Simon is unknown to Mark's readers, but that Alexander and Rufus are known to them. Of Alexander we know nothing further, but a Rufus was a member of the church in Rome in the mid-fifties (Rom 16:13) who is probably the same Rufus mentioned here. It is very conceivable that Mark added the phrase "the father of Alexander and Rufus" into the tradition he received because of the happy coincidence that the two sons were members of the church in Rome. This is yet a further indication that Mark writes to Romans. We are not told whether Simon is a Jew or Gentile, only that he "carried the cross." The mention of Simon immediately following the mention of crucifixion in v. 20b reinforces the most indispensable and distinguishing mark of discipleship for Mark — taking up one's cross and following Jesus (8:34). Simon of Cyrene becomes the first person in Mark literally to fulfill that command.[43] For Mark, discipleship is not a symbolic gesture, but concretely following Jesus. It is worth considering, as Schlatter observes, whether Simon's faithfulness in carrying the cross of Jesus resulted in his sons' participation in the faith and in the church.[44]

22-23 It was both Jewish and Roman custom to execute victims outside the city limits (Lev 24:14; Num 15:35-36; Heb 13:12). Jesus is brought to a place called Golgotha (Aram. *gulgoltah*), meaning "skull." ("Calvary" comes from the Latin *calvus*, meaning "scalp," or "bald head.")[45] The reference to Golgotha as a "place" and the translation of the

43. So E. Schweizer, *The Good News According to Mark*, 345.
44. A. Schlatter, *Die Evangelien nach Markus und Lukas*, 145.
45. A reference in *T. Sol.* 12:3 (*OTP* 1.973) speaks of the "Place of the Skull" where "he (Christ) will dwell publicly on the cross." Although the *Testament of Solomon* is difficult to date (first cent. A.D.?), the reference corroborates the place identified by Mark.

name indicate that Mark's readers are unfamiliar with the site and Hebrew name, which makes sense if he is writing to Romans. In the nineteenth century Otto Thenius of Dresden proposed as Golgotha a hill with a distinct skull appearance outside the present city walls. This site can be seen today overlooking the Arab bus station in Jerusalem. Thenius's proposal was accepted and popularized by General Charles Gordon in 1885, who also discovered what today is known as the Garden Tomb near the outcropping. "Gordon's Calvary" is an attractive hypothesis for Golgotha, not least because of the tranquility and beauty of the nearby Garden Tomb. But from a historical perspective, the Church of the Holy Sepulchre has much greater claim to be the actual site of the crucifixion. From the earliest days of Christianity the natural rock outcropping that in Jesus' day lay outside the walls of Jerusalem, on which the Church of the Holy Sepulchre was already erected in A.D. 335, has been venerated as the site of Jesus' crucifixion. Excavations from 1961 to 1980 under the Church of the Holy Sepulchre have added further support to the site as the Golgotha of the Gospels.[46]

"Wine mixed with myrrh," an allusion to the suffering of the righteous man graphically described in Ps 69:21, was a primitive narcotic offered to deaden the pain of crucifixion victims. Administering it may have been a charitable service rendered by women of Jerusalem (Luke 23:28), as suggested by Prov 31:6, Ps 69:21, and the Talmud.[47] Jesus refused it, perhaps in fulfillment of his vow at the Passover meal not to drink again until his reception in the kingdom of God (14:25). He does not rely on a narcotic to render his final act of obedience, but accepts God's will in a fully conscious state.

24-27 "And they crucified him" (15:24).[48] The simple indicative of

---

46. J. Murphy-O'Connor, *The Holy Land: An Archaeological Guide from Earliest Times to 1700*[4] (New York: Oxford, 1986), 45-55; V. Corbo, "Golgotha," *ABD* 2.1,071-73; R. Riesner, "Golgota und die Archaeologie," *BibKir* 40 (1985): 21-26. An alternative view propounded by Grundmann (*Das Evangelium nach Markus,* 431) and Schlatter (*Der Evangelist Matthäus,* 779) holds that "Place of the Skull" refers to a place of uncleanness, not to the shape of a hill. In this view, Jesus dies for unclean sinners at an unclean location.

47. "When one is led out to execution, he is given a goblet of wine containing a grain of frankincense, in order to benumb his senses, for it is written, *Give strong drink unto him who is ready to perish, and wine unto the bitter in soul.* And it has also been taught: The noble women in Jerusalem used to donate and bring it" (*b. Sanh.* 43a)

48. Codex Vaticanus (B; also [L] Y) read simply *staurousin auton* ("they crucify him"), whereas a stronger and more diverse group of manuscripts (ℵ A C D Θ, plus the Byzantine tradition) reads *staurōsantes auton* ("and when they had crucified him"). Whereas the textual support for the second reading is clearly superior, the first may be original (1) because the simple present is typically Markan, and (2) because a scribe would be inclined to change the simple first reading to the more grammatically felicitous second reading.

the verb and the utter austerity of the statement ground the central act of redemption in a historical fact. A quotation from Ps 22:18 (see also *Gospel of Peter* 12) about dividing garments identifies the fate of Jesus at the cross with that of the suffering righteous man of Psalm 22, thus indicating that the shameful death of Jesus fulfills the prototype of the suffering righteous man. Jews reckoned time beginning with sunrise at 6 A.M.; hence the "third hour" puts the crucifixion at 9 A.M.[49] Both Roman and Jewish custom required the cause of crucifixion to be affixed to the cross, which in Jesus' case reflects the accusation of Pilate (vv. 2, 9, 12, and 18), "King of the Jews."

With Jesus are crucified two robbers (v. 27). Exactly who the two were we do not know.[50] The word for "robber" (Gk. *lēstēs*) is often used by Josephus of Zealots; but it is just as frequently used of common thieves. What, if any, their relationship was to Barabbas is uncertain.[51] Earlier, James and John had asked to sit at Jesus' right and left hands in glory (10:37). Such positions, Jesus reminded them, entail trials and ordeals, a "cup" and a "baptism," in his words. Jesus' ordeal, much greater than his disciples must undergo, places him between two criminals (*Gospel of Peter* 10; *Epistula Apostolorum* 9). The wording about being at the right and left hands of Jesus in 10:40 is remarkably similar to that of v. 27: in a mysterious way, the two criminals occupy the places requested by James and John. Their presence at the crucifixion is viewed as a fulfillment of Isa 53:12, "he was numbered with transgressors."[52]

There are several clues in chap. 15 that Mark intends the trial and crucifixion to be understood as a royal enthronement of Jesus as the Messiah. These clues include the references to Jesus as "'The King of the Jews'" (15:2, 9, 12, 26), the references to royalty in the flagellation scene

---

49. A ninth-century uncial manuscript (Koridethi, Θ) reads "sixth hour" (= 12:00 noon), but this is almost certainly an attempt to reconcile Mark's timing with John's (19:14), who places Jesus' crucifixion at noon on Thursday rather than at 9 A.M. on Friday. John's date and time probably reflect theological interests, i.e., to make Jesus' crucifixion coincide with the slaughter of Passover lambs in the temple.

50. Later tradition supplies them various names: Titus and Dumachus, according to an Arabic infancy Gospel (*HS* 1.408); elsewhere Zoathan and Chammata, or Dyamas and Gestas, or Joatas and Maggatras (see Grundmann, *Das Evangelium nach Markus*, 433, n. 27.

51. On Barabbas, see n. 15 above. On the use of "robbers" in Greek literature and in Josephus, see Hengel, *The Zealots*, 24-46.

52. A reference to Isa 53:12 is present as v. 28 in several later manuscripts (K L P Δ Θ Π). It has only a slight chance of being original, however, for it is omitted by a strong and diverse chorus of manuscripts (א A B C D X Ψ). The addition was undoubtedly taken from Luke 22:37 in order to make explicit that on the cross Jesus fulfills the role of the Servant of the Lord.

(purple robe, crown of thorns, "'Hail, King of the Jews'"), and the mockery of the bystanders that Jesus is "'The King of Israel'" (v. 32).[53] The same motif is suggested by the two criminals flanking Jesus at the crucifixion, who, as we saw above, parallel the sons of Zebedee who asked to sit at Jesus' right and left hands "'in your glory'" (10:37). Nevertheless, the royal-messianic theme must not be overestimated. The concept of Messiah, as we have noted (see at 8:29 and 14:61-62), is a subsidiary concept in the Second Gospel and not Mark's major christological designation. Mark's preeminent title for Jesus is "Son of God," not "Messiah." Messiah, a functional concept, is hinted at in chap. 15; but Son of God, an ontological concept conveying Jesus' divinity, is expressly declared at the climax of the entire Gospel in 15:39.[54]

29-32 At only one point does Mark depart from the reserve and restraint of his narrative of the crucifixion, and that is to emphasize the *mockery* to which Jesus is subjected. In the trial scene Jesus' opponents were limited to chief priests, Pilate, and the soldiers, but at the crucifixion these voices merge in a larger chorus of scorn. Nondescript bystanders shake their heads and ridicule Jesus about his predictions regarding the temple (v. 29; see 14:58). In this, too, Jesus fulfills the prototype of the suffering righteous man whose righteousness is the cause of ridicule (Pss 22:7; 109:25; Lam 2:15). The "hurled insults" of v. 29 (so the NIV) are called "blasphemy" in the original Greek. *Blasphēmia* is used almost exclusively in both Greek and biblical literature of evil speech against God; by implication, the derision hurled at Jesus is blasphemy against God — making the chief priests and scribes guilty of the very thing Jesus was condemned for by the Sanhedrin (14:64)!

"In the same way the chief priests and the teachers of the law mocked him" (15:31). Like the bystanders, the chief priests and scribes see Jesus' inability to save himself as a refutation of his status as Son of God. "'He saved others,'" they taunt, 'but he can't save himself!'" In both theme and wording the position of the mockers reflects Wis 2:18, "'If the righteous one is really God's Son, [God] will help him and save him from

53. See D. Juel, *Messiah and Temple*, SBLDS 31 (Missoula: Scholars Press, 1977), 49-53; M. Hooker, *The Gospel According to St Mark*, 371-72.

54. Rightly seen by H. Chronis, "The Torn Veil: Cultus and Christology in Mark 15:37-39," *JBL* 101 (1982): 97-114; contra Juel, *Messiah and Temple*, 51, who sees "Son of God" as simply an alternative designation for "Messiah-King." Similarly, the attempt of T. Schmidt, "Mark 15.16-32: The Crucifixion Narrative and the Roman Triumphal Procession," *NTS* 41 (1995): 1-18, to argue that vv. 16-32 are modeled on a Roman triumphal procession is doubtful, primarily because the royal motif is not essential to Mark's presentation of Jesus. Moreover, the emphasis on mockery in vv. 29-32 seems to oppose Schmidt's thesis, as do several particulars (e.g., the linkage of Simon in v. 21 with the sacrificial bull?). For a description of Roman triumphal processions, see at 11:7-10, n. 10.

the hand of his opponents." Like the skeptics of Wis 2:17, the religious leaders will believe only if they *see*, if they have empirical proof. The very demand for a sign is here, as in 8:11-13, evidence of unbelief. Faith is not the result of signs and miracles, but the condition for them. The faith Mark wills for his readers is not compelled by sight, but evoked by the person of Jesus, especially in his sacrifice on the cross. The taunt assumes that salvation of self is the greatest good: the surest vindication of a would-be Messiah is therefore the ability to save himself. Jesus, however, has not taken upon himself the mission of self-help and self-fulfillment. He will be a "'ransom for *others*'" (10:45). The struggle in Gethsemane was about affirming and fulfilling that calling (14:32-42). The mockery at the cross fails to penetrate the vast and awful mystery that Jesus is a ransom for others (10:45). The chorus of scorn includes even those who suffer the same fate as Jesus (v. 32).

The taunt for Jesus to come down from the cross is in essence the same temptation that he faced in Gethsemane, that is, to avoid "the cup" of suffering. At Gethsemane Jesus made the costly decision, which he now fulfills, to do the will of God rather than his own will. In this haunting picture of Jesus, fastened to a cross and assailed in mockery, we see "proof of the amazing difference between God's way and everything which men consider their goal or conceive of as being God's way."[55] There is no self-defense from Jesus, no effort to get even or get in the final word, no attempt to preserve at least a modicum of dignity and pride. Jesus surrenders in total vulnerability to the malevolence and violence of the world.

THE SON OF GOD (15:33-39)

Since the arrest of Jesus Mark has narrated the passion as an antiphony between the witness of Jesus and human responses to it. The first antiphony was Jesus' confession before the Sanhedrin (14:61-62), followed by the mockery and maltreatment of the Sanhedrin (14:63-65) and Peter's denial (14:66-72). The second was Jesus' appearance before Pilate (15:2-5), followed by shouts from the crowd for his death (15:6-15) and the mockery and maltreatment of the soldiers (15:16-20). The third antiphony was the crucifixion of Jesus (15:21-26), followed by mockery from the bystanders (15:27-32). The fourth antiphony in the present section consists of the death of Jesus (15:33-37), followed by the confession of

---

55. See Schweizer, *The Good News According to Mark*, 350-51.

the centurion (15:38-39). In the first three antiphonies the human responses are negative and even hostile to Jesus. But in the final antiphony the human response is positive and faithful. In Jesus' death on the cross a Gentile outsider — a Roman officer in charge of Jesus' execution — becomes the first person to confess Jesus in faith as God's Son, thus fulfilling the purpose of Mark's Gospel. While Jesus is alive, humanity wills his death; only in his death can humanity see him as the way to life. The death of Jesus on the cross is thus not a defeat but the consummation of his mission and the climactic revelation of his identity as the Son of God.

33 During the crucifixion "at the sixth hour darkness came over the whole land until the ninth hour." All three Synoptists accompany the death of Jesus on the cross with several portents, the first of which is darkness from 12:00 noon until 3 P.M. The ancients were familiar with accounts of extraordinary occurrences accompanying the deaths of human luminaries. Rabbinic literature records strange and fantastic accounts of events at the deaths of famous rabbis — including the appearance of stars at midday, the weeping of statues, lightning, thunder, and even the dividing of the Sea of Tiberias.[56] Likewise, at least two Roman writers record that at the death of Julius Caesar a comet shone for seven successive days.[57] These and similar portents were usually regarded as divine eulogies honoring the noble dead. For Mark, however, the darkness at midday is not a divine eulogy but something ominous and evil, like the plague of darkness over Egypt at the hardening of Pharaoh's heart (Exod 10:21-23) or even the darkness of chaos before creation (Gen 1:2).[58] The darkness at the crucifixion cannot be well accounted for by natural phenomena: solar eclipses do not occur when the moon is full at Passover; nor is a dust storm likely during the wet spring season. According to Mark, the darkness at the crucifixion is portrayed as an eschatological judgment of God, as in Amos 8:9, "'In that day,' declares the Sovereign LORD, 'I will make the sun go down at noon and darken the earth in broad daylight.'" The emphasis on darkness covering "the whole land" has universal connotations: the whole earth (*gē* in Greek means "earth" as well as "land") is implicated in Jesus' death, not just the Jews.[59]

---

56. Str-B 1.1,040-42.

57. Suetonius, *Lives of the Caesars,* "The Deified Julius," 88-89; Plutarch, *Lives of the Noble Grecians and Romans,* "Caesar," 69.3-5.

58. Likewise the *Gospel of Peter* 15–21 equates the darkness at the cross with blindness and fear; and the *Gospel of Philip* 68 equates it with destruction.

59. By contrast, the *Gospel of Peter* 15 says that the darkness covered only *Judea,* thus attempting to fix responsibility for Jesus' death specifically on Jews. So, too, the *Gospel of Peter* 17, "And they (= Jews) fulfilled all things and completed the measure of their sins on their head."

34 Before the Sanhedrin and Pilate, Jesus remained silent, except for one brief word in each trial. For the first time since v. 2, Jesus cries out, "'My God, my God, why have you forsaken me?'" (Ps 22:1; Justin Martyr, *Dial. Trypho* 99.1). The original Aramaic quotation, "'*Eloi, Eloi, lama sabachthani,'*" doubtlessly reflects Jesus' actual words, which Mark follows with a Greek translation for the benefit of his Gentile readers.[60] Psalms 22 and 69 reverberate throughout the crucifixion account, and the present quotation from the former identifies Jesus with the righteous one who suffers without cause.[61] Rejected and scorned by Israel, sacrificed as a political pawn by Rome, denied and abandoned by his own followers, Jesus is wholly forsaken and exposed to the horror of humanity's sin. Its horror is so total that in his dying breath he senses his separation from God.

The biblical witness to the suffering Son of God has met great resistance in human history. Later Gnostics, in particular, assuming that human suffering fatally compromises true deity, attempted to spare Jesus from agony on Golgotha. In the apocryphal *Gospel of Peter* 19, for instance, Jesus cries, "'My Power, O Power,'" and is taken into heaven without suffering. Gnostics, who believed that true spirit was insusceptible to the ravages of a transient material world, would later maintain that Jesus only appeared to suffer on the cross.[62] Likewise, a suffering Son of God was seen by Jews as a contradiction in terms,[63] by Greeks as foolishness (1 Cor 1:23), and by dispassionate Stoics as an embarrassment.

35-36 The tendency to spare Jesus suffering is evident even in Mark's account (vv. 35-36). Popular Judaism believed that Elijah had been taken bodily into heaven without dying (2 Kgs 2:11) and that he would return in times of crisis to protect and rescue the righteous.[64] The by-

---

60. Although the textual tradition is divided on the word order of *enkatelipes me* ("you have forsaken me"), the quotation is an Aramaic rendering of the Hebrew rather than the LXX, which reads differently, *ho theos ho theos mou, prosches moi hina ti enkatelipes me* ("My God, my God, give heed to me, why have you forsaken me?")

61. Ps 22:1 = Mark 15:34; Ps 22:7 = Mark 15:29; Ps 22:18 = Mark 15:24; Ps 69:21 = Mark 15:23, 36. For a discussion of Psalms 22 and 69 in Mark 15, see J. Pobee, "The Cry of the Centurion — A Cry of Defeat," *The Trial of Jesus*, ed. E. Bammel, SBT 13 (London: SCM Press, 1970), 91-102. For a discussion of the relationship of the cry of dereliction to the words of the suffering servant of Isaiah 53, see A. M. Schwemer, "Jesu letzte Worte am Kreuz (Mk 15,34; Lk 23,46; Joh 19,28ff)," *TBei* 29 (1998): 5-29.

62. Or, conversely, that Jesus suffered because he was "divided." The apocryphal *Gospel of Philip* 68 compares Jesus' abandonment on the cross to Adam, for whom death did not exist until Eve was separated from him.

63. Compare, e.g., the tradition of the death of Rabbi Akiba preserved in *b. Ber.* 61b in which Akiba is depicted like Socrates at his death — composed, worshipful, accompanied by his disciples, reciting the *Shema*, confident of God's presence.

64. See the material gathered in Str-B 1.1,042; 4/2.769-79. Also *b. Ta'anit* 21a, which recounts a legend of a righteous Jew saved from execution by Elijah.

standers invoke the name of Elijah at Jesus' crucifixion, perhaps because they mistake Jesus' call to God (Aram. *Eloi*) as an appeal to Elijah (Aram. *Eli*). Surely if Jesus is righteous, God will spare him from suffering and death, "because anyone who is hung on a tree is under God's curse" (Deut 21:23). The bystanders then — and some today[65] — fail to see what the centurion first sees and understands — that Jesus fulfills God's plan of redemption precisely in his suffering, by "'giving his life as a ransom for many'" (10:45) and taking the curse of humanity on himself.

Hoping to see a miracle of deliverance at the final moment, someone "filled a sponge with wine vinegar" and gave it to Jesus. The "stick" (Gk. *kalamos*) that extends the sponge to Jesus is the same instrument with which the soldiers beat Jesus in v. 19. It is of no more use to Jesus as an olive branch of comfort than it was as an instrument of pain. The "wine vinegar" offered to Jesus was probably a mixture of sour wine or vinegar with water, known as *posca* in Latin, which was available to soldiers on duty as a stimulant.[66] Perhaps as a gesture of compassion, the drink is offered to Jesus. The drink, however, recalls for Mark the "gall" of Ps 69:21, "They put gall in my food and gave me vinegar for my thirst" (so, too, *Gospel of Peter* 16). It is cruel comfort to the righteous man in distress, symbolizing the bitterness of Jesus' mockery from humanity and his rejection by God.

37-39 The NIV places the death of Jesus in 15:37 into a paragraph by itself. The theology of Mark, however, would place it at the *beginning* of vv. 37-39, for Jesus' death is not a terminus but the cause of two exceptional events: the tearing of the temple curtain (v. 38) and the confession of the centurion (v. 39). These two events signify that the death of the suffering Son of God is not a tragic end but an event of divine fulfillment and revelation.

First, the curtain, which is rich in theological symbolism. There were actually two curtains in the temple in Jerusalem (see Heb 9:1-5), one before the Court of Israel and one before the Holy of Holies. Mark uses the Greek word *naos* to describe the temple rather than his more customary *hieron*, but the terms are used interchangeably in the NT and do not enable us to determine what part of the temple is intended.[67] The Court

---

65. How little things change can be seen from two examples in our own time. During the Nazi period, "German Christians" dismissed a theology of the cross as one of weakness and defeat in favor of a theology of a heroic Aryan Jesus. Likewise, many New Age offshoots today either downplay or deny the need for atonement and the suffering of Jesus in favor of the powerful images associated with "resurrection."

66. See Suetonius, *Lives of the Caesars*, "Vitellius," 12, who mentions the sale of *posca* in Puteoli.

67. O. Michel, "*naos,*" *TDNT* 4.882.

of Israel, also known as the Holy Place, was the main sanctuary where Jewish men worshiped; it contained a seven-branch lampstand, a table with twelve loaves of bread on it, and an altar of incense. The curtain before the Court of Israel was a beautifully embroidered Babylonian tapestry, mystically depicting the earth, sea, and heavens that "typified the universe," according to Josephus (*War* 5.210-14). The second curtain (Exod 26:31-37), which Josephus also mentions but does not describe, hung before the "unapproachable, inviolable, and invisible" Holy of Holies, a cubicle some twenty cubits (= thirty feet) square that the high priest entered once a year on the Day of Atonement (*War* 5.219).

It is unclear which of the two curtains Mark intends in 15:38 (so, too, *Gospel of Peter* 20; *T. Levi* 10:3). The Greek word for curtain in v. 38, *katapetasma*, is used by ancient authors of both curtains, although it is used more frequently of the curtain before the Holy of Holies. The biblical usage of the term confirms this distinction. *Katapetasma* occurs three times in Heb 6:19; 9:3; 10:20(?), each with reference to the curtain before the Holy of Holies. In the LXX, likewise, *katapetasma* is used of the curtain before the Holy of Holies (Exod 26:31-37), whereas a different word (Gk. *kallyma*) is used of the curtain before the Court of Israel (Exod 27:16; Lev 16:2, 12). On linguistic grounds the torn *katapetasma* of v. 38 would appear to be the curtain before the Holy of Holies. If this is the curtain intended, then its destruction signifies that at the death of Jesus the veil between God and humanity is removed. The Holy of Holies, which was believed to contain the very presence of Yahweh, is made accessible not by the high priest's sacrifice on the Day of Atonement, but by the atonement of Jesus on the cross.[68]

Other reasons, however, argue in favor of the main curtain separating the Court of Israel from the Court of Women. The outer curtain (the only one described by Josephus) was the only curtain visible to all people. It appears that *schizein* ("to tear") at v. 38 is intended to refer to this curtain. In Mark's only other use of this word at the baptism, the tearing of heaven revealed Jesus to be the Son of God. Likewise, the tearing of the curtain of the temple enables the centurion to confess Jesus as the Son of God. Both confessions depend on the tearing in two of a veil so that something may be witnessed. The only curtain visible to a Gentile centurion was the outer curtain, not the curtain before the Holy of Holies. Moreover, Josephus describes the outer curtain as a tapestry portraying

---

68. The *Gospel of Philip* 85 understands the rending of the curtain to reveal the Holy of Holies: "Therefore the perfect things have been opened to us, together with the hidden things of truth. The holies of the holies were revealed, and the bridal chamber invited us in."

"a panorama of the heavens" (*War* 5.213). That is a striking parallel to the tearing of heaven in 1:10. Thus, at both uses of *schizein* Mark signifies the rending of the skies — to open heaven to humanity in the baptism of Jesus and to open the temple as the *locus Dei* to humanity at the death of Jesus.[69] At the baptism and death of Jesus the heavenly and earthly dwellings of God are opened to humanity.[70]

39 The second sign attending the crucifixion follows immediately on the tearing of the temple curtain. It is the declaration of the centurion, whom Mark designates with a Latinism (Gk. *kentyriōn*) rather than with the normal Greek designation *(hekatontarchēs)*, probably because the former was more familiar to his readers. Like others since the arrest of Jesus, the centurion is a bystander (Gk. *parestēkōs*; 14:47, 69, 70; 15:35), but rather than milling around he stood *"in front of* Jesus."[71] Unlike the previous bystanders who mock Jesus, the centurion "sees and believes" (so 15:32) what they do not. At the death of Jesus he confesses, "'Surely this man was the Son of God!'" "The Son of God" is Mark's load-bearing christological title, which until this moment has remained unconfessed by any human being. The centurion is the first person in the Gospel to confess Jesus as the Son of God, and the confession is evoked by his passion — his suffering and death on the cross.

The passion of Jesus on the cross is the crucial clue to the centurion's confession, according to Mark. In Matt 27:54 the centurion's confession is evoked by the *signs* that attended Jesus' death — the resurrection of saints, the earthquake, and darkness at midday. In Mark, however, the confession is evoked not by miraculous signs, but by Jesus' very death, when the centurion "heard his cry and saw how he died."[72] The confession "the Son of God" is causally linked to the death of Jesus on the cross (John 8:28). This centurion had doubtlessly seen other men die by

---

69. On the rending of the temple veil, see H. Chronis, "The Torn Veil: Cultus and Christology in Mark 15:37-39," *JBL* 101 (1982): 110-14.

70. The *Gospel of the Nazarenes* 36 (*NTApoc* 1.164) also appears to refer to the Court of Israel in describing the destruction of the lintel at the death of Christ: "at the time of Christ's death the lintel of the temple, of immense size, had split." The *Gospel of the Ebionites* 6 (*NTApoc* 1.170) may also refer to the Court of Israel. Josephus also records portents of the destruction of Jerusalem and the temple (*War* 6.288-315). On Jesus and the cross as replacements of the temple, see K. Bailey, "The Fall of Jerusalem and Mark's Account of the Cross," *ExpTim* 102 (1990-91): 102-5.

71. The reading *ex enantias autou* ("in front of," "opposite") is strongly attested (ℵ A B C K L X Δ Π Ψ) and doubtlessly the correct reading, although W reads *autǭ* ("near him") and D and Θ read *ekei* ("there").

72. A majority of manuscripts include "cry" in one form or another in v. 39, but a weighty minority of manuscripts omits it (ℵ B L Ψ), raising some doubt whether the word was originally part of Mark's text. See B. Metzger, *TCGNT*, 121.

crucifixion. But something in this crucifixion — in the very weakness and suffering of Jesus' death — becomes revelatory.[73] The suffering of Jesus on the cross, which utterly contradicts both Jewish messianic ideals and Hellenistic "divine man" conceptions, becomes, by an act of God, the *window* into the heart and meaning of Jesus, the significance of which is only captured in the confession "the Son of God."

It is sometimes supposed that the centurion did not confess Jesus to be *the* Son of God, but *a* son of God. In the original Greek, "Son of God" *(huios theou)* does not possess the definite article, and suggests to some that the centurion must have meant *a* son of God rather than *the* Son of God, that is, one of the many extraordinary heroes known to the ancient world rather than *the* Son of God in an ontological sense. This conclusion is unsustainable on grammatical grounds, however, for in Koine Greek a definite predicate nominative omits the article when it precedes the verb, as it does in v. 39.[74] Grammatically speaking, Mark's use of "Son of God" in 15:39 is meant in the full Christian sense.

It is also sometimes supposed that the centurion's confession means *a* son of God rather than *the* Son of God since it would be unrealistic or impossible for a Gentile army officer to use the title in its full Christian sense. This view is not ultimately compelling. Exactly how the centurion understood the title we cannot know for sure. But it should not be assumed that the centurion was incapable of employing "Son of God" with a Christian understanding. He was undoubtedly aware that Jesus was accused of being "the King of the Jews" (15:2, 11, 18), and not unlikely aware of Caiaphas's accusation of Jesus as the Son of God (14:61-62). As a Roman he was certainly familiar with the concept of deification of rulers in the emperor cult, some of whom were considered sons of god. It is

73. Contra E. S. Johnson Jr., "Is Mark 15:39 the Key to Mark's Christology?" *JSNT* 31 (1989): 8-14, who maintains that a centurion could not be expected to recognize Jesus as the Son of God. That, of course, is precisely the mystery and irony of faith, which is attested throughout the Second Gospel — that faith comes from unexpected quarters. See the insightful discussion of the centurion's confession in J. D. Kingsbury, *The Christology of Mark's Gospel* (Philadelphia: Fortress Press, 1983), 128-34.

74. E. C. Colwell, "A Definite Rule for the Use of the Article in the Greek New Testament," *JBL* (1933): 12-21; R. Bratcher, "A Note on *Huios Theou* in Mark 15:39," *ExpTim* 80 (1968): 27-28. The attempt of Johnson, "Is Mark 15:39 the Key to Mark's Christology?" *JSNT* 31 (1987): 4-7, to refute Colwell's rule is unsuccessful, for although there are some exceptions to the rule (as there are to any grammatical rule), a high percentage of cases supports Colwell's rule — and *all* uses of "Son of God" in the Gospels support it. Thus, when *huios* ("son") or *huios theou* ("Son of God") precedes the verb it is always anarthrous (Matt 4:3; 8:9; 14:33; 27:40, 43; 27:54; Mark 5:7; 15:39; Luke 1:35; 4:3, 9; 8:28), and when the substantive follows the verb it takes the definite article (Matt 3:17; 11:27; 16:16; 17:5; 21:37; 26:67; Luke 3:22; 4:41; 9:35; 10:22; 20:13; 22:71).

sometimes suggested that the centurion's confession in v. 39 is to be understood against the background of the Hellenistic "divine man" concept, that is, that he saw Jesus as a son of god like or superior to the Roman emperors.[75] The insuperable obstacle to this theory, however, is that suffering — especially the abject and shameful suffering of a crucifixion — was as unknown among "divine men" and in the emperor cult as it was within the Jewish concept of Messiah (see the excursus on **Divine Man** at 3:12). For the ancients, suffering was not a sign of God's presence or a channel of redemption, but a categorical refutation of divine election and agency. Martin Hengel's conclusion is verified by all available evidence: "A crucified messiah, son of God or God must have seemed a contradiction in terms to anyone, Jew, Greek, Roman or barbarian, asked to believe such a claim, and it will certainly have been thought offensive and foolish."[76] The fact that the passion and death of Jesus on the cross evoke the confession of the centurion indicates that he, by divine revelation, has been granted the mystery of faith in Jesus as the Son of God.

Excursus: The Son of God

Sons of God were prominent in the Greco-Roman world, primarily as rulers, philosophers, poets, heroes, or miracle workers. In the Hellenistic

75. T. H. Kim, "The Anarthrous *huios theou* in Mark 15,39 and the Roman Imperial Cult," *Bib* 79 (1998): 221-41, correctly notes the importance of 15:39 for Mark's Christology and argues that it should be understood against the Roman imperial cult. Specifically, maintains Kim, the centurion's confession designates Jesus as the true Son of God rather than Augustus, who also considered himself a son of God. Kim's thesis runs aground at two points. He does not address the important question how, if the centurion were thinking in terms of the emperor cult, he would designate Jesus as the Son of God since suffering played no role whatsoever in deified rulers. Kim's further argument that only Augustus and perhaps Tiberius considered themselves sons of God is surely too restrictive. The terminology used by emperors was varied and fluid (e.g., savior [of the world], [new] god, lord [of the whole world], benefactor, and son of god), but each of the emperors of the first century with the possible exception of Tiberius saw himself as a revealed god and employed corresponding titles more or less equivalent to those used by Augustus (see E. Lohmeyer, *Christuskult und Kaiserkult* [Tübingen: J. C. B. Mohr (Paul Siebeck), 1919], 18-19). In his *Lives of the Caesars*, Suetonius openly refers to Julius, Augustus, Claudius, Vespasian, and Titus as deified. Nero, under whom Mark is likely writing his Gospel, was no exception in claiming to be a son of god. Kim cites one instance himself (235). See P. Bureth, *Les Titulatures impériales dans les papyrus, les ostraca et les inscriptions d'Égypte (30 a.C.–284 p.C.)* (Bruxelles: Fondation Égyptologique Reine Élisabeth, 1964), 23-25, who gives further examples of the infatuation with divine titles among first-century emperors.

76. Hengel, *Crucifixion in the Ancient World and the Folly of the Message of the Cross*, 10.

world the status of son of God, along with numerous other titles, was conferred as a result of superhuman distinction (see the excursus on **Divine Man** at 3:12). In the Judeo-Christian tradition, by contrast, "Son of God" designates a unique filial relationship with God made possible not by human accomplishment but by God's grace. The concept of Son of God first appears in the Judeo-Christian tradition in Exod 4:22-23 when God identifies Israel as "'"my firstborn son."'" From its inception as a people Israel is declared to stand in a unique filial relationship to God. In the subsequent history of OT Israel fails to live up to God's ideal, and the concept of sonship begins to undergo a narrowing process from the people as a whole to the king, who becomes both the people's representative before God and God's vicegerent or deputy for Israel. In a special promise to the king in 2 Sam 7:13-14, God swore that a future descendant of David would stand in a unique Father-Son relationship with him, and that God would "establish the throne of his kingdom forever."

Like the people as a whole, however, the monarchy failed to embody the ideal of sonship, and the concept of divine sonship became further narrowed and transformed, although in different directions. In one current, God becomes the father of the God-fearing and righteous remnant in Israel (Ps 103:13; Mal 3:17). In the intertestamental literature the concept Son of God is narrowed still further from the righteous remnant (*Jub.* 1:24ff.; *Pss. Sol.* 13:8; 17:30; 18:4) to a righteous individual (Wis 2:16ff.). Particularly in Wis 2:12-20; 4:10-14; 5:1-5 and Sir 4:10; 23:1-4 the righteous individual will be vindicated as God's Son in the midst of suffering, which will have an atoning effect on behalf of others, thus fulfilling many motifs of the suffering righteous individual in Psalms 22 and 69 and in the Servant of the Lord passages in Isaiah 42, 49, 50, and 52–53. With regard to the monarchy the concept of divine sonship proceeds in a different direction. As the monarchy declined after David and Solomon, and particularly after its demise at the time of the exile, "Son of God" becomes increasingly associated with messianic expectations, in which the Messiah as God's Son — Israel reduced to one, as it were — becomes the eschatological redeemer of God would both fulfill and surpass the ideals of the king as God's Son (4Q174 1:10-13; 4Q246).[77]

At the beginning of the Gospel (1:1), Mark announced *that* Jesus is

---

77. For further references outside the NT correlating "Messiah" and "Son of God," see 4 Ezra 7:28-29; 13:32, 37, 52; 14:9; *1 Enoch* 105:2; *Adam and Eve* 42:2-5. Although the authenticity of some of these passages is questioned, they, along with the evidence from Qumran, testify to a tendency in pre-Christian Judaism to correlate the two titles. See N. Dahl, "Eschatology and History in Light of the Dead Sea Scrolls," in *The Future of Our Religious Past,* ed. J. Robinson (New York: Harper and Row, 1971), 9-28; Juel, *Messiah and Temple: The Trial of Jesus in the Gospel of Mark,* 108-14.

the Son of God, but it remained to be seen *what kind of* Son of God he is. As the Gospel unfolds, it becomes evident that both of the major OT currents of Son of God — its kingly authority and its righteous and atoning suffering — are fulfilled in the person and ministry of Jesus. "Son of God" is the keystone of Mark's presentation of Jesus and the supreme category in which his person is revealed. Jesus is acknowledged to be the Son of God by the Father (1:11; 9:7) and by demons (1:24; 3:11; 5:9), that is, by both the light and dark sides of the spiritual world. He has given veiled hints of his divine Sonship in a parable (12:6) and in the eschatological discourse (13:32), and even received it from the mouth of the high priest (14:61-62). Throughout his ministry he has taught, ministered, and acted with a sovereign authority that elsewhere in Israel characterize God alone. But until the centurion at the cross, no human — not even his disciples — has understood the meaning of "Son of God." This has not been by accident. Jesus has stifled speculation about his identity because all such announcements were premature. Not until his death on the cross can anyone rightly understand who Jesus is, and what "Son of God" means.[78] As defined at the cross, the Son of God is he who gives his life as a ransom for many (10:45). The Gospel of Mark reaches its climax in the confession of the centurion, "'Surely this man was the Son of God'" (15:39). This profession of faith, ironically, comes not from a disciple, relative, or even a fellow Jew. It is rather a Gentile outsider — the captain of the execution squad, and thus an enemy — who first declares Jesus as God's Son. The cross is the supreme revelation of Jesus as God's Son, and hence this title, which derives from God (1:11; 9:7), surpasses all other titles — whether Messiah, Son of Man, prophet, teacher, or Lord. The cross is also the birthplace of faith, for the centurion's confession is a saving confession of Jesus as God's Son.

The cross is the intersection where God meets humanity. Saving confession is not predicated on prior knowledge, proximity to Jesus, or privilege; it is, rather, an act of faith in a divinely revealed act of atonement. The centurion's confession is the saving proclamation of the church, for it is the convergence point of Mark's two major themes: the meaning of Jesus and the meaning of faith. The Son of God, on whom rests the unique blessing and love of the Father, chooses not to exalt himself but to follow a path of servanthood, indeed of vicarious suffering and death, so that through the cross the world might acknowledge him to be the Son and with him share free and joyful access to the Father.

---

78. This is why Mark does not append "Son of God" to Peter's confession in 8:29, as does Matt 6:16; Peter cannot rightly know Jesus as the Son of God until divine Sonship is defined by the cross.

FAITHFULNESS VERSUS FEARFULNESS (15:40–16:8)

A Markan sandwich concludes the Second Gospel in its oldest ascertainable form (15:40–16:8). Mark follows the climactic confession of the centurion at the cross with a story of several women at the cross who later visit the tomb of Jesus on Easter morning. Into the midst of the account of the women Mark inserts the story of Joseph of Arimathea requesting the body of Jesus from Pilate, the Roman prefect. As in each Markan sandwich, the original story is corrected by the second story inserted into its midst. The pattern of the final sandwich is as follows:

> A[1] The women at the cross (15:40-41)
> B   Joseph of Arimathea before Pilate (15:42-46)
> A[2] The women at the tomb (15:47–16:8)

In the present sandwich, the boldness of Joseph of Arimathea is set in contrast to the fearfulness of the women. At the cross they watch "from a distance" (15:40), and on Easter, anxious about who will roll the stone away from the tomb (16:3), they are distressed (16:5) and fearful (16:8) at the presence of the angel. Rather than announcing the resurrection to the disciples as commanded by the angel, they flee and tell no one (16:8). Unlike the women, Joseph does not merely watch but acts with resolution and boldness. He waits expectantly for the kingdom of God, he courageously approaches Pilate, and he becomes the first individual in the Gospel literally to "take the body of Jesus," as commanded by Jesus at the Last Supper (14:22) — the same body that earlier had been anointed for burial by the woman of 14:8.[79]

40-41 Mark concludes the crucifixion narrative by including the names of several women who "were watching from a distance" (Gk. *apo makrothen*).[80] This is undoubtedly an allusion to the lament in Ps 38:11, where the righteous suffering individual mourns his friends and neighbors who "stay far away" (LXX, *apo makrothen*). The Greek word for "watch" *(theōrein)*, which is used again of the women in v. 47 and 16:4, is instructive. In the temple discourse (13:32-37) and in Gethsemane (14:34, 38) Jesus commanded "watching" as a virtue of discipleship (see the description of terms at those passages). The word Mark uses for "watching" here is different, however. Apart from its description of the women in

---

79. On the Markan sandwich, see J. R. Edwards, "Markan Sandwiches: The Significance of Interpolations in Markan Narratives," *NovT* 31 (1989): 213.

80. In the apocryphal *Epistula Apostolorum* 9 the names of the women appear as "Sarah, Martha, and Mary Magdalene."

15:40, 47; 16:4, it occurs four times previously in Mark, and in each instance it depicts spectating or detached observation as opposed to seeing that leads to perception and conviction.[81] The watching of the women is not the kind of seeing that, in the case of the centurion in v. 39, leads to faith; or, in the case of Joseph, leads to action.

The women are identified as "Mary Magdalene, Mary the mother of James the younger and of Joses, and Salome." Mary Magdalene's name appears in all the Gospels as the first witness of the resurrection.[82] The Greek could allow the mother of Joses to be a separate woman, but the NIV is probably correct in regarding Mary as the mother of the two sons.[83] It is difficult to say for certain if this Mary is Jesus' mother, who in 6:3 is also identified as the mother of James and Joses. The fact that, unlike 6:3, 15:40 designates James as "the younger," and that the other brothers of Jesus (Judas and Simon) are unmentioned, arouses at least some suspicion that this is a different Mary. It is possible, however, that "James the younger" is meant to differentiate him from James the son of Zebedee and brother of John, whose mother Salome is also mentioned in v. 40 (Matt 27:56).[84] Likewise, the omission of Jesus' other two brothers, Judas and Simon (6:3), could be explained by the fact that they were not known, as were James and Joses, to the church in Rome. It is sometimes further objected that if Mark intended Jesus' mother he would have written "Jesus' mother" or "his mother" (e.g., John 19:25), and hence that this Mary is another woman. In itself this is a reasonable suggestion, but in the context of Mark's Gospel it is somewhat less persuasive, for Mark's two references to Mary in 3:31 and 6:3 place a calculated distance between her and Jesus. The reference to Mary in v. 40 is also, literally, "from a distance" and not out of character with Mark's otherwise infrequent

81. In 3:11 it refers to the demons who see Jesus' mighty works; in 5:15 to the crowds (who will promptly drive Jesus from their territory) who see the healed demoniac; in 5:35 to Jesus' seeing the commotion in the room of Jairus's daughter; and in 12:41 to the crowd watching people put money in the treasury.

82. The name "Magdalene" is ostensibly derived from Magdala on the west shore of the Sea of Galilee. Mary Magdalene is popularly though mistakenly thought to have been a prostitute. There is no evidence of such in the Gospels. The only reference to her former life is that Jesus had expelled seven demons from her (Luke 8:2; Mark 16:9), but her demon possession is never linked with harlotry. See J. Shaberg, "How Mary Magdalene Became a Whore," *BRev* 8/5 (1992): 30ff.

83. The enclosure of the names of the two boys between the definite article *(hē)* and "mother" *(mētēr)* implies they are her sons: *Maria hē Iakōbou tou mikrou kai Iōsētos mētēr.*

84. On Salome in the Bible and early Christian tradition, see R. Bauckham, "Salome the Sister of Jesus, Salome the Disciple of Jesus, and the Secret Gospel of Mark," *NovT* 33 (1991): 245-75, who corrects several assertions about Salome made by M. Smith, *Clement of Alexandria and a Secret Gospel of Mark* (Cambridge, Mass.: Harvard University Press, 1973), 189-92.

and rather impersonal depictions of the mother of Jesus (see the excursus on **Women in Mark** at 14:9).[85] Given the fact that Mary, James, and Joses have been mentioned earlier in Mark (6:3), and also that Mark, in accordance with v. 41, mentions them in connection with Jesus' Galilean ministry (3:31), it may be supposed, if not proven, that the Mary, James, and Joses mentioned in v. 40 are family members of Jesus.

The personal names in 15:40 are unusual in Mark. Their appearance at this point is significant in order to establish on the evidence of eyewitnesses the death and burial place of Jesus, which will be important for certifying the resurrection (16:1-8). But they are also important because of the description in v. 41. Not chosen disciples (of whom we have heard much), but heretofore unmentioned *women* remain to the bitter end. True, they "were watching from a distance," but even distance is better than absence. Their "following and ministering to [Jesus]" from "Galilee . . . to Jerusalem" encompasses the duration of his ministry. The imperfect tenses of both verbs in Greek indicate not occasional or sporadic accompaniment and service, but the continued presence and service of Jesus throughout his ministry. These and "many other women" have done what Mark throughout his Gospel has defined as discipleship: following and serving Jesus. Only angels (1:13) and women (15:41) are said to have ministered to Jesus in Mark. Faith and followers come from unlikely quarters. A Roman centurion makes the first Christian confession, and women, although not Jesus' most notable followers, have been among his most faithful.

42-43 Into the register of women Mark inserts the story of Joseph of Arimathea, who appeals to Pilate for the body of Jesus (also *Gospel of Peter* 3).[86] "As evening approached" puts events on late Friday afternoon

85. Roman Catholic and Orthodox exegetes traditionally interpret the Mary of v. 40 to refer to someone other than the mother of Jesus since, in dependence on ancient creeds, they hold Mary to be "ever virgin." See J. Fitzmyer, *BRev* 7/5 (1991): 43. Some Protestant scholars follow suit, although for different reasons. For example, V. Taylor, *The Gospel According to St. Mark,* 598, states categorically: "They are clearly not the brothers of Jesus (vi. 3), for Mark would not have designated Mary the Virgin in this roundabout manner." Taylor's reference to "the Virgin" infers that Mark's reverence for Mary parallels John's (19:25-27), but that is not the case. Both of Mark's previous references to Mary in 3:35 and 6:3 are quite "roundabout."

86. J. D. Crossan, *The Historical Jesus: The Life of a Mediterranean Jewish Peasant* (San Francisco: HarperCollins, 1991), 391-94, argues that Joseph of Arimathea is a fiction of Mark. Crossan believes that the *Gospel of Peter,* which omits reference to Joseph, preserves a more reputable historical record. Crossan's need to dispense with Joseph is necessitated by his belief that Jesus' body was thrown to dogs rather than buried in a tomb. His reliance on the *Gospel of Peter* is fancifully ironic, since the latter differs from the canonical Gospels in presenting a far more supernatural account of the burial and resurrection, which Crossan rejects. If Mark were inventing the Joseph figure, he would scarcely have

before sunset. The burial of Jesus requires haste since the following day was the Sabbath and thus another holy day on which work was forbidden. Mark describes Friday by its normal nomenclature, "Preparation Day," although in this instance Friday is Passover and itself a holy day. He further describes it as "the day before the Sabbath." Such descriptions are further indications that Mark is writing for Gentiles since they would be superfluous to Jewish readers.

Crucifixion played a central role in Rome's terror apparatus. It was Roman custom to allow crucified criminals to hang on crosses until they decayed, as a warning to would-be miscreants or rebellious slaves. If requested, however, their corpses might be handed over to relatives or friends for proper burial.[87] The Jews, on the other hand, considered burial of the dead — including even the dead of their enemies — a ritual piety (2 Sam 21:12-14). According to Deut 21:23, a criminal executed for a capital offense (usually by stoning) whose body was hung on a tree in disgrace deserved to be removed and buried before sunset. The Jews took this commandment seriously. Recounting a slaughter in Jerusalem, Josephus testifies that "[The Idumeans] actually went so far in their impiety as to cast out the corpses without burial, although the Jews are so careful about funeral rites that even malefactors who have been sentenced to crucifixion are taken down and buried before sunset" (*War* 4.316-17). Joseph's behavior in the case of Jesus squares perfectly with Jewish custom (John 19:31).[88] Hasty interments, of course, ran the risk of burying someone who had swooned or only appeared dead; Jewish custom safeguarded against this possibility by prescribing periodic visits to the tomb following death.[89]

As a reputable council member, Joseph guarantees that Jesus receives a proper Jewish burial. His retrieving the body from Pilate spares Jesus further indignities at the hand of the Romans. Otherwise a stranger to us, Joseph is said to be from Arimathea, which is likely a variant of Ramah (also known as Ramathaim-zophim), some twenty miles north-

made him a member of the heretofore wholly antagonistic Sanhedrin! See the critique of Crossan's thesis by G. G. O'Collins and D. Kendall, "Did Joseph of Arimathea Exist?" *Bib* 75 (1994): 235-41.

87. See the material gathered in R. Gundry, *Mark*, 982. So, too, Hengel, *Crucifixion in the Ancient World and the Folly of the Message of the Cross,* 47-48.

88. The burial description of 15:42-47 effectively rebuts J. D. Crossan's conjecture (*Jesus: A Revolutionary Biography* [San Francisco: HarperSanFrancisco, 1994], 128-29) that Jesus' body was thrown to dogs ("devoured by scavengers or buried in a common/mass grave," according to M. Borg [Internet posting on "Jesus 2000@info.harpercollins.com," 25 March 1996). There is no evidence at all in the NT or in surviving early Christian literature for Crossan's and Borg's assertions in this regard.

89. Str-B 1.1,047-48.

west of Jerusalem.[90] Joseph was "a prominent member of the council." The Greek word for "prominent" *(euschēmōn)* means honorable and reputable as well as powerful. The council of which he was a member (the Gk. *bouleutēs* means "counselor") must mean the Jewish Sanhedrin.

Joseph's presence in Mark's sandwich convention is owing to more than his virtue as a member of the Sanhedrin, however. Three statements about him in 15:43 distinguish him as a model disciple. First, Joseph is "waiting for the kingdom of God." This surely means more than that he was a pious Jew awaiting fulfillment of the messianic hope. Matthew 27:57 and John 19:38 describe Joseph as a covert disciple. Mark's reference suggests the same. Similar to Luke's description of Simon faithfully awaiting the redemption of Israel (Luke 2:38), Mark emphasizes in Greek Joseph's expectation of the kingdom of God, which in this its last occurrence in the Gospel is fulfilled in Jesus. Joseph also "went boldly to Pilate and asked for Jesus' body." It took courage to request from the governor the body of a man executed as an enemy of Rome. Joseph's unexpected advocacy is yet another twist of Markan irony, for a member of the heretofore antagonistic Sanhedrin appears as a protagonist of Jesus. This is an important reminder that not all Jewish religious authorities opposed Jesus. Like the friendly scribe of 12:34, Joseph of Arimathea does not share the antagonism to Jesus characteristic of his colleagues. Rather, he performs a duty of devotion to Jesus that parallels, in courage if not in cost, the woman's anointing of Jesus' body in 14:8, for she prepares his body for burial and Joseph procures his body for burial (so, too, *Gospel of Peter* 23).[91] Joseph's courageous visit to Pilate thus fulfills the role of a faithful disciple. The present sandwich bears a strong resemblance to that of 14:53-72: both Jesus and Joseph bear brave witness before the authorities, while both Peter and the women shrink back in uncertainty and fear. Finally, one cannot discount the probability that Mark sets Joseph, a leader of the Jews, in conjunction with the centurion, a commander of the Roman army. The behavior of the one and the confession of the other indicate that Jesus is the savior of both Jews and Gentiles.[92]

90. The identification is suggested by 1 Sam 15:34, where the Heb. "Ramah" is translated by the LXX as "Armathaim" (see also Josephus, *Ant.* 13.127). The same identification was made in the early church by Eusebius and Jerome. Further, see J. Pattengale, "Arimathea," *ABD* 1.378.

91. Note the repetition of *to sōma mou* ("my body") at the anointing of Jesus' body in 14:8, in the words of the Last Supper in 14:22, and in Joseph's request for Jesus' body *(to sōma tou Iēsou;* "the body of Jesus") in 15:43.

92. The foregoing paragraph argues against Hooker, *The Gospel According to Saint Mark*, 381; and R. Brown, "The Burial of Jesus (Mark 15:42-47)," *CBQ* 50 (1988): 233-45,

44-45   The description of the release of Jesus' body may reflect Pilate's actual orders.[93] Pilate's release of the body could possibly mean that the governor did not consider Jesus an ordinary criminal. A further gesture of exoneration is also suggested by Joseph's burial of Jesus in a family tomb (presumably), for the Mishnah prohibited those who died ignominious deaths from being buried with their fathers in ancestral tombs (*m. Sanh.* 6:5). The testimony of the centurion before Pilate and the subsequent burial description assure readers that Jesus truly died. Exegetes have occasionally suggested that Jesus did not actually die but only swooned on the cross and later revived in the cool tomb. Mark's account renders such a hypothesis dead wrong. Three witnesses — Joseph (v. 43), Pilate (v. 44), and the centurion (v. 45) — testify that Jesus was dead, two of whom (Joseph and the centurion) had actual contact with the corpse. The body is also referred to brusquely as a "corpse" (v. 45, Gk. *to ptōma*; NIV, "body"). It is further worth recalling that the Romans crucified hundreds of thousands of individuals during their centuries in power, not one of whom is recorded as surviving the cross. This grim fact is proof positive that chap. 16 is not about resuscitation, but about resurrection from the dead.

46   Having obtained permission from the governor, Joseph wraps the corpse in linen sheets with which he has lowered it from the cross, and "placed it in a tomb cut out of rock" (15:46; Acts 13:29).[94] Ordinarily, the body would have been anointed with spices, but the lateness of the hour necessitated postponing anointing until after the Sabbath (16:1). In the original Greek Mark refers to the body of Jesus in the masculine gender, even though both of its antecedents ("body," *sōma;* "corpse," *ptōma*) are neuter. This grammatical incongruity may be owing to Mark's unwillingness, perhaps from reverence, to refer to the body of Jesus impersonally. But it could also be a tacit testimony to the resurrection, that is, that the one who conquered death can never be referred to as a some*thing* rather than as a some*one*. Jewish law prohibited corpses from being bur-

who posit that Joseph buried Jesus not out of devotion but simply out of piety and Torah loyalty, especially to avoid the curse on the land spelled out in Deut 21:23. V. 43 indicates that Joseph is motivated by allegiance to Jesus and the message preached by him. See the critique of Brown's position by G. W. Shea, "On the Burial of Jesus in Mark 15:42-47," *Faith & Reason* 17 (1991): 87-108.

93. The stylized diction of Roman orders is present in "summoning" *(proskalein)* in v. 44, the Latinized word for "centurion" *(kentyrion* rather than the normal Gk. *hekatontarkēs),* and especially "bestowed *(dōreomai* rather than *didomi)* the corpse" in v. 45 (NIV, "gave the body").

94. Some commentators question whether Joseph could have purchased material on the Passover (v. 46). Rabbinic tradition, however, made provision for such emergencies on holy days (e.g., *m. Shab.* 23:1). See Hooker, *The Gospel According to Saint Mark,* 381.

ied inside Jerusalem; rather, they had to be buried at least fifty cubits (c. 75 feet) outside the walls (*m. B. Bat.* 2:9).[95]

Unlike our modern **burial custom** of sealing a corpse in a coffin and lowering it into the ground, Jews cut burial tombs (or enlarged natural caves) in the limestone hillsides of Palestine. The Mishnah specifies a burial vault six by nine feet, with shelflike niches on which bodies could be placed (*m. B. Bat.* 6:8). Nearly a thousand such "kokhim" (Heb.; "niche") tombs have been discovered in and around Jerusalem, some of which have body-shaped depressions carved in their flat upper surfaces. After the flesh of the corpse decomposed, the bones were removed and deposited in ossuaries hewn out beneath the niches, freeing the niche above for repeated use. The OT refers to depositing the bones in ossuaries as being "gathered to their fathers" (e.g., 2 Kgs 22:20). Burial caves were sealed by large, disk-shaped stones that were rolled in channels in front of the opening, sealing ritual impurities within the tomb and keeping animals and grave robbers out.[96]

A visit to the Garden Tomb in Jerusalem reveals a tomb very much like the one Jesus would have been placed in. It is almost certainly not the actual tomb, but that is not so important in Jesus' case since, as Mark assures us, his tomb was anything but a final resting place.

15:47–16:1 Mark now completes the sandwich begun in 15:40 by returning to the story of the women. Two of the women mentioned at the cross are present to watch Joseph bury Jesus. They are Mary Magdalene and "Mary the mother of Joses."[97] Mary appears in the following verse as

95. The *Gospel of Peter* 24 refers to the body being buried in a sepulchre called "Joseph's Garden," reflecting presumably the influence of John 19:41.

96. A. Kloner, "Did a Rolling Stone Close Jesus' Tomb?" *BARev* 25/5 (1999): 22ff., argues that the stone blocking Jesus' tomb would have been a square block rather than a round disk. He bases his argument (1) on the fact that 98% of burial caves in the Jerusalem area (= 900 tombs) used square blocks, and (2) on the claim that the Gk. *kyliein* ("to roll") can mean "dislodge" rather than "roll." Regarding (1), although normal tombs may have used blocks, the tombs of the wealthy (as in the case of tombs of the Herodian family and the families of the Sanhedrin) used rolling disks. Joseph of Arimathea, a prosperous and distinguished council member, can be expected to belong to the latter category. With regard to (2), neither BAGD 457 nor LSJ 1,008 gives any definition for *kyliein* except "to roll." All the Gospels speak of the stone being rolled away (Matt 27:60; 28:2; Mark 15:46; 16:3; Luke 24:2), as do the *Gospel of Peter* 36 and *Epistula Apostolorum* 9. The evidence and arguments of Kloner are insufficient to nullify the unanimous witness of early Christian tradition that the tomb offered by Joseph of Arimathea was sealed by a rolling disk.

97. Two uncial manuscripts, D and Θ, substitute the name of James for Joses in v. 47. That is a later alteration explained by the fact that James was the older of the two brothers and better known in the later church. The reading of Joses alone is supported by the majority of manuscripts, and as the more difficult reading is to be preferred.

the mother of James. This is doubtlessly the same Mary mentioned in 15:40; the mention of one son in 15:47 and of the other in 16:1 is evidently an abbreviation of convenience, assuring readers that the same woman was present at both the burial and the empty tomb. Mark again notes that the women "saw" where Jesus was buried. The word for "saw" is the same as that for "watch" in v. 40 (Gk. *theōrein*), that is, guarded observation.

A Greek genitive absolute in 16:1 connects the narrative consciously to the preceding verse in 15:47. "When the Sabbath was over" indicates that the resurrection narrative is not an isolated event, but specifically related to the death and burial of Jesus. The one who is resurrected is the one who was crucified. The Sabbath was the concluding day of the week for the Jews. The next day (Sunday) was designated as the first day of the new week, or "the first day of the Sabbath" (v. 2), as Mark says in Greek. This specifies Sunday as the day of Jesus' resurrection.[98] The Jews anointed corpses with oil mixed with myrrh and aloes (John 19:39). These "spices" were evidently purchased by the women after sunset on Sabbath in preparation for the anointing of Jesus' body early the next morning.[99] The purpose of anointing was not to embalm, that is, to prevent bodily decay (as was the custom in Egypt) but to perfume the decaying corpse as an act of devotion. Normally, the dead were anointed at the time of interment (according to John 19:39, this was done). According to Mark, however, the lateness of the hour on the day of preparation (15:42) necessitated postponing the anointing of Jesus until after the Sabbath. The anointing of the women lends new significance to the earlier anointing in Bethany (14:3-9). "The women fail to do belatedly what was in fact done by another woman prematurely. Her action was a prophetic sign of [Jesus'] death; theirs is made impossible because of his resurrection."[100]

For the third time Mark lists the names of the women attending the cross, burial, and empty tomb of Jesus (15:40, 47; 16:1). The listing of proper names — so unusual for Mark — certifies on the basis of eyewitnesses the veracity of the events described. More remarkable is the repetition of the list, and even more so that they are the names of *women*. Jewish opinion of women, especially in religious matters, was not always posi-

98. The significance of Sunday for Christians was noted by later rabbis, who occasionally referred to it as "the day of the Nazarenes," or "the day of the Christians" (Str-B 1.1,052-53).

99. On the role of women in caring for the dead in both Hellenism and Judaism, see Corley, "Women and the Crucifixion of Jesus," *Forum* 1 (1998): 181-217.

100. Hooker, *The Gospel According to Saint Mark*, 384. Note the corroborating testimony of the *Gospel of Peter* 50, "[Mary Magdalene] had not done at the sepulchre of the Lord what women are wont to do for those beloved of them who die."

tive.[101] Later accounts verify the resurrection by male testimony (Luke 24:24; John 20:3-10). The presence of women's names attests to the relative early dating of Mark's Gospel.[102] It also attests to the veracity of the resurrection narrative, for had early Christians fabricated the resurrection story, the testimony of women (in all four Gospels!) was no way to go about it. Some two centuries after the Gospels were written, the pagan Celsus could still needle Origen on "the gossip of women about the empty tomb" (Origen, *Contra Celsum* 2.55). The witness of Mary the mother of James and Joses, Salome, and especially Mary Magdalene (v. 1), whose name heads the resurrection witnesses in all four Gospels, endows the resurrection narratives with the highest degree of probability. Unless women were actually present at the tomb, the early church would scarcely have placed them there since Judaism did not accept the testimony of women. The testimony of women is, however, entirely "in character" with the divine economy: those whose testimony is discounted in human society are the first to be included in the divine society (1 Cor 1:26-28)!

2-4 "Very early . . . just after sunrise, they were on their way to the tomb." "Very early" usually designates the time between 3 and 6 A.M., but here it is qualified by "just after sunrise." The apocryphal *Gospel of Peter* 50–54 attributes the women's visit in the early morning darkness to fear, lest they be seen by the Jews. Mark makes no mention of fear of the Jews but notes the sunrise perhaps to insure that the women had not mistaken the tomb in the darkness. Alone of the Gospels, Mark records a conversation on the way to the tomb about who would roll the stone away. The anxiety of the women about this significant detail is due, in part, to the fact that all the men were hiding (John 20:19). The women were evidently left to chance at finding workers in the area to help them roll the stone away from the opening of the tomb. Their problem was solved in a manner they had never considered, for when they arrived the stone was already rolled away.[103] Matthew 28:2 attributes the open tomb to the

101. "This is the general rule: any evidence that a woman is not eligible to bring [usurers, dice-players, pigeon-flyers, traffickers in Sabbath year produce, and slaves] are not eligible to bring" (*m. Rosh HaSh.* 1:8). Further: "Sooner let the words of the Law be burned than delivered to women" (*b. Sot.* 19a); "Happy is he whose children are male, but alas for him whose children are female" (*b. Qid.* 82b). Especially indicative is the morning prayer of Jewish men, who blessed God for not making them heathens, slaves, or women!

102. Although I do not share her ambiguity about the historicity of the resurrection, C. Osiek, "The Women at the Tomb: What Are They Doing There?" *Hervormde Teologiese Studies* 53 (1997): 103-18, rightly argues that the presence of women at the empty tomb anchors the narrative to the earliest layer of tradition.

103. In the canonical Gospels the resurrection is announced but not explained. Only in apocryphal accounts is the latter attempted. In the Old Latin codex Bobiensis the

agency of earthquakes and angels, but the implication in Mark is that God rolled the stone away.[104] The removal of the stone suggests that in all respects the resurrection of Jesus is entirely God's work. The human role in the event is that of witness, not worker. For the first time in history, last rites were all wrong.

5-6 Entering the tomb, the women saw "a young man dressed in a white robe." The "white robe" (Rev 7:9, 13), the "young man," which frequently refers to a heavenly being (Luke 24:4; 2 Macc 3:26, 33; *Gospel of Peter* 36; Josephus, *Ant.* 5.277),[105] and the women's response indicate an angelic encounter. The Greek word for "alarmed" (*ekthambeomai*, v. 5), found only in Mark, means both fear and wonder, astonishment and distress; the same word is used in 14:33 of Jesus' intense distress in Gethsemane. It is hard to imagine such a response at a purely human encounter. When the Bible relates divine-human encounters, mortals invariably sense the dread and terror of their position before the Almighty. The alarm and distress of the women also argue against a hallucination, for not only are *group* hallucinations virtually nonexistent, but the announcement of the angel entirely contradicts what the women expect. The position of the angel "on the right side" of the tomb, a detail without apparent significance, is not the kind of thing a fabricator would include and hence witnesses in favor of a historical remembrance. Whether the angel's position is intended to represent Christ, who sits at the right hand of the Father (12:36; 14:62), is uncertain. The Greek word for "angel" literally means "messenger (of God)." That is precisely the young man's role at the empty tomb: he is a mediator between the ineffability of the resurrection and the women.

The first word of the divine messenger addresses the foremost con-

---

following account appears: "But suddenly at the third hour of the day there was darkness over the whole circle of the earth, and angels descended from the heavens and as [the Lord] was rising in the glory of the living God, at the same time they ascended with him" (cited in Metzger, *TCGNT,* 121-22). Likewise, the *Gospel of Peter* 35-40 relates how the guards at the tomb heard a loud voice from heaven and saw two men come down in great brightness to the tomb. The stone rolled away of its own accord, the men entered the tomb, and they emerged "sustaining the other" (followed by the cross), who then went into the highest of heavens. In the *Gospel of Peter* 45 the guards at the tomb are converted and declare Jesus to be God's Son.

104. Both the *Gospel of Peter* 37 and *Epistula Apostolorum* 9 imply that the stone was removed by divine agency.

105. The use of *neaniskos* ("young man") is, to be sure, the same word used in 14:51, but there is no apparent relation between the two terms (see further on the term at 14:51). The theory of S. R. Johnson, "The Identity and Significance of the *Neaniskos* in Mark," *Forum* 8 (1992): 123-39, that the young man is a paradigmatic disciple converted at the resurrection, who is himself the author of the story, is imaginative but quite unfounded exegetically.

cern of the women — their fear ("'Don't be alarmed'"). He further addresses their hope ("'You are looking for Jesus the Nazarene, who was crucified'"). In Mark, the word translated "looking for" (Gk. *zētein*) occurs ten times, all in pejorative contexts of imposing constraints on Jesus (see on the term at 1:37). It appears to have a similar meaning here, and the response of the angel can be taken as a mild rebuke. The women, intent on their funereal errand, are preoccupied with death. They endeavor with their spices and anxieties to bring some kind of closure, however inadequate, to a tragic drama. But all their preparations leave them unprepared for the reality they encounter; what they intend to be a terminal visit is but a commencement. The Jesus they are "looking for" enshrined in a safe place cannot be found. The visit to the tomb is vintage Markan irony: the living are consumed with death, but the Crucified One is consumed with life.

The Crucified One, says the angel, has been raised! The angel invites the women to see the place where they last saw the body of Jesus (15:47).[106] The references to the place of his burial and to Jesus as the crucified one are of crucial importance. The women are not directed to a mystical or spiritual experience or to a numinous encounter. They are directed specifically to Jesus, who died by a crucifixion they witnessed, was buried in a place they witnessed, and now has been resurrected. The verbs in v. 6 refer to both sides of the Easter event. The announcement of the divine emissary establishes an inseparable continuity between the historical Jesus and the resurrected Jesus. The one whom the angel invites them to know is the one whom they have known. The announcement of the angel is literally the *gospel*, good news, and the place from which the gospel is first preached is the empty tomb that both received and gave up the Crucified One. A new order of existence is inaugurated. The NIV reads, "'He has risen!'" but the Greek is more precise, "'He was raised.'" "Risen" could suggest that Jesus arose on his own, but "was raised" rightly implies that he was resurrected by God. At this moment and in this place the women are witnessing "the kingdom of God come with power" (9:1).

The invitation to examine his resting place is unmistakable evidence of an **empty tomb**. The empty tomb does not prove the resurrection of Jesus, of course, and the NT never adduces it as proof of the resurrection. Already in the early church opponents of the resurrection explained the empty tomb on the ground that Jesus' body had been sto-

---

106. For skeptics who suspect that the women have mistaken an empty tomb for Jesus' actual tomb, v. 6 is evidence that they are standing at a place already familiar to them from 15:47.

len (Matt 28:13). The empty tomb is only one of several facts attending the resurrection. It is not the empty tomb that proves the resurrection, but the resurrection that makes the empty tomb meaningful. The empty tomb testifies that the Jesus who died as a bodily being was raised as a bodily being, and it is the historical place and point in time that marks the transition between his two orders of existence. Along with early Christianity as a whole, Mark is interested in faith in the resurrected Jesus, not in proofs of his existence. It is an encounter with the resurrected Lord, not the empty tomb, that produces faith.

7   The angel's final word to the women is, "tell [Jesus'] disciples and Peter, 'He is going ahead of you into Galilee. There you will see him, just as he told you.'" This announcement, a fulfillment of 14:28, is a remarkable word of grace and encouragement. The flight of the disciples, even Peter's pitiful denial, have not been the last word. It is not given to human beings to speak the last word. The last word belongs to the risen Lord, "'I am going before you.'" The first act of Jesus' ministry was the calling of four fishermen into community with himself (1:16-20); and the first word of the resurrected Jesus is the reconvening of the same community of disciples (14:27-28).[107] The announcement of the angel is not one of deserved blame but a promise of gathering and going before them! God completes his plans for the church despite human failure. If the word of grace from the resurrected Lord includes a traitor like Peter, readers of the Gospel may be assured that it includes those of their community who have also failed Christ.

The Gospels are divided on where the resurrection appearances took place. Matthew and Mark speak of Galilee; Luke and John speak of Jerusalem (although John 21:1-25 also includes a Galilee appearance). **Galilee** plays a privileged role in Mark's Gospel. Capernaum in Galilee is Jesus' chosen residence, from which his ministry exerts great influence in the northwest region of the Sea of Galilee and in the Decapolis. Obstructions to his ministry come largely from outside Galilee, from Herod Antipas in Tiberius and from the scribes and Pharisees in Jerusalem. In particular, the temple in Jerusalem and the Sanhedrin located there have been the seat of opposition and resistance to Jesus. It is not surprising that Mark locates the promised meeting of Jesus with the disciples in Galilee to resume and complete their call.

8   The last we saw of the women was their dismay at the opened tomb in 16:4. Vv. 5-7 were devoted to the words of the angel attending the empty tomb. The final verse of the oldest manuscripts of the Gospel of

---

107. On the promise to go before the disciples to Galilee, note the shift from the future tense in 14:28 to the present tense in 15:7.

Mark reports the women's response to the angel's announcement. There are no exclamations, questions, or conversation of any sort. In abrupt objectivity Mark reports that they left and fled from the tomb, seized with fear and bewilderment. They said nothing to anyone, for they were afraid. In one verse Mark includes a battery of seven negative responses on their part. These terms scarcely depict reverential awe at a *mysterium tremendum.* V. 8 clearly implies a response of fear that inhibits faith. The flight of the women is narrated in the same tense of the same verb (Gk. *ephygon*) as the flight of the disciples in 14:50. "Trembling" (Gk. *tromos*) and "bewilderment" (Gk. *ekstasis*) occur only once and twice respectively in Mark and are expressions of consternation. The failure of the women to speak contravenes the command of the angel, and the final reference to "fear" repeats a word that occurs a dozen times in Mark, in ten of which it is clearly negative.[108] It is clear that Mark does not intend v. 8 to imply reverence or faith on the part of the women, but fear and flight.

The resurrection does not magically dispel fear and cowardice, transforming fallible human characters into faithful disciples. Faithful discipleship consists of following Jesus, not contemplating doing so; acting courageously on his behalf, not standing on the sidelines and watching. In the concluding sandwich of the Gospel, Joseph does the former, the women the latter. Throughout the Gospel, Mark has warned that signs, miracles, and portents do not evoke faith (8:11-13). The same note persists at the resurrection, the greatest of all signs: even the visitation of angels at the empty tomb fails to produce faith. Faith comes rather through hearing the gospel and personal encounter with the One who was crucified and is now raised from the dead. Even at the close of the story, the human characters fail the divine will: in his earthly ministry, Jesus commanded people to silence, and they spoke; in his resurrected state, the women are commanded to speak, and they flee in silence![109]

---

108. *Phobeesthai:* 4:41; 5:15, 33, 36; 6:20, 50; 9:32; 10:32; 11:18, 32; 12:12; 16:8. The only possible exceptions to its negative use in Mark are 5:33 and 6:20. On the negative connotation of v. 8 as a whole, see A. Lincoln, "The Promise and the Failure: Mark 16:7, 8," *JBL* 108 (1989): 286-87.

109. The similarity of wording between 1:44 and 16:8 invites this comparison. In the first command to silence in the Gospel, Jesus orders the healed leper, *mēdeni mēden eipēs* ("don't tell this to anyone"), but he goes out and broadcasts the news; in the final command to the women to proclaim the resurrection, they *oudeni ouden eipan* ("they said nothing to anyone") and fled.

CHAPTER SIXTEEN

The Longer Ending of Mark

MARK 16:9-20

It is virtually certain that 16:9-20 is a later addition and not the original ending of the Gospel of Mark. The evidence for this judgment is complex, and it is necessary to discuss the problems in some detail before taking up the secondary ending itself.

Since none of the autograph copies of documents of the NT survives, the Greek text of the NT is constructed from later copies of manuscripts dating from A.D. 135 at the earliest to about A.D. 1200 at the latest. These copies, of which more than five thousand exist, range in size from scraps little larger than postage stamps to complete manuscripts of the Bible. In general, these copies show remarkable agreement among themselves. The most notorious exception to this otherwise happy rule, however, is the ending of Mark, which presents the gravest textual problem in the NT. The two oldest and most important manuscripts of the Bible, codex Vaticanus (B) and codex Sinaiticus (‭א‬), omit 16:9-20, as do several early translations or versions, including the Old Latin, the Sinaitic Syriac manuscript, about one hundred Armenian manuscripts, and the two oldest Georgian manuscripts. Neither Clement of Alexandria nor Origen shows any awareness of the existence of the longer ending, and Eusebius and Jerome attest that vv. 9-20 were absent from the majority of Greek copies of Mark known to them. An ingenious system of cross-referencing parallel passages in the Gospels that was devised by Ammonius in the second century and adopted by Eusebius in the fourth century (hence the name Eusebian Canons) does not include Mark 16:9-20. The apocryphal *Gospel of Peter* does not contain the longer ending, and concludes, as does Mark 16:8, with the fear of the women. Although a majority of ancient witnesses, including Greek uncial and minuscule manuscripts, church fathers, and versions in other languages do include vv. 9-20, this does not compensate for the textual evidence against them. The inclusion of vv. 9-20 in many manuscripts is accounted for rather by the fact that the longer ending, which must have been added quite early, was naturally included in subsequent copies of the Gospel. Many of the ancient manuscripts that do contain the longer ending, however, indicate by scribal notes or various markings that the ending is regarded as a spurious addition to the Gospel. External evidence (manuscript witnesses) thus argues strongly against the originality of the longer ending.[1]

The secondary nature of the longer ending is further corroborated by the application of the techniques of literary criticism to 16:9-20. This is apparent beginning in the first verse of the longer ending, which is a conspicuous non sequitur: whereas the subject of v. 8 is the frightened and fleeing women, v. 9 begins by presupposing the resurrected Jesus, who appears to Mary Magdalene. The latter, moreover, is introduced as a newcomer ("out of whom [Jesus] had driven seven demons," v. 9), although Mark has mentioned her three times immediately before (15:40, 47; 16:1).[2] In vv. 9-20 Jesus is for the first time in Mark referred to as the "Lord Jesus" (v. 19), or simply "the Lord" (v. 20), rather than Mark's custom of calling Jesus by his given name. Such reverential nomenclature likely derives from later Christian worship. Particularly noticeable is the number of new words that appear nowhere else in Mark. In the so-called shorter ending of Mark nine of the thirty-four words are new,[3] and in the longer ending there are an additional eighteen words that otherwise do not appear in Mark,[4] plus several unique word forms and syntactical constructions.[5] Several of Mark's signature stylistic features are likewise absent from the longer ending.[6] The longer ending also includes themes peculiar to itself, some of which contradict Markan themes. The repeated chastise-

1. The evidence against the longer ending of vv. 9-20 also includes the so-called shorter ending of Mark, a thirty-four-word epilogue to the Gospel that is attested by four late uncial manuscripts and several versions of dubious authority (Old Latin, Harclean Syriac, Sahidic, Bohairic, and Ethiopic). The shorter ending usually occurs in the above witnesses between v. 8 and vv. 9-20, and reads as follows: "They announced briefly to those around Peter all the things they had been commanded. And after these things also Jesus himself sent through them from east to west the holy and imperishable proclamation of eternal salvation. Amen." See B. Metzger, *TCGNT,* 122-26.

2. H. B. Swete, *The Gospel According to St Mark,* 399.

3. *Syntomōs, exangellō, anatolē, achri, dysis, exapostellō, aphtartos, kērygma, sōtēria.*

4. *Phainō, pentheō, kakeinos, theaomai, apisteō, heteros, morphē, poreuomai, hysteros, hendeka, parakoloutheō, ophis, thanasimos, blaptō, analambanō, synergeō, bebaioō, ekoloutheō.*

5. For example, the form of *parēngelmena, Hieron* as an adjective, and the following syntactical constructions: *meta tauta, Kyrios Iēsous, meta to lalēsai, tois met' autou genomenois.*

6. Most notably, the absence of the initial *kai* in Mark's sentence structure, the absence of the historic present tense of verbs, and the absence of *euthys.*

498

ment of the disciples for their "disbelief" (Gk. *apistein; apistia;* vv. 11, 14, 16) of the gospel proclamation (Gk. *kērygma;* vv. 11, 13, 14, 15, 16-18, 20) is unique to the longer ending, and the prominence given to charismatic signs in vv. 17-18 stands in stark contrast to the reserve of Jesus in Mark with regard to signs and sensation (cf. 8:11-13).

External and internal evidence thus necessitates the conclusion that 16:9-20 is not the original ending of Mark but rather a later addition to the Gospel. The longer ending is a patchwork of resurrection appearances (or summaries) taken from the other three Gospels,[7] the chief theme of which is the unbelief of the disciples (vv. 11, 13, 14, and 16). Although the longer ending is clearly secondary, it is nevertheless very old. The earliest witnesses to the longer ending come from the *Epistula Apostolorum* 9–10 (c. 145), perhaps Justin Martyr (*Apol.* 1.45; c. 155), Tatian's *Diatessaron* (c. 170), and Irenaeus (*Adv. Haer.* 3.9-12; c. 180). This means that the longer ending "must be dated to the first decades of the second century."[8] Of further interest in this regard is the fact that the resurrection harmony of the longer ending is composed of texts drawn largely from tradition that later became canonical,[9] and not from the plethora of apocryphal Gospels that were beginning to circulate in the second century. This testifies to a collection of the four Gospels no later than early in the second century, and with the collection a recognition of the authority of the four Gospels vis-à-vis other early Christian literature.[10]

Mark 16:9-20 is thus a later and, in several respects, incongruous addition to the Gospel. Whether or not the longer ending was excerpted from an earlier document and added to the end of Mark or composed specifically for Mark is difficult to say. On the one hand, the awkward splice at v. 9 and the theological incongruities of the longer ending might be taken as evidence for its existence in a prior document.[11] Nevertheless,

---

7. V. 9 = Luke 8:2; vv. 9-11 = Matt 28:9-10; Luke 24:9-11; John 20:11-18; vv. 12-13 = Luke 24:13-35; vv. 14-18 = Matt 28:16-20; Luke 24:36-49; John 20:19-23; Acts 1:6-8; vv. 19-20 = Luke 24:50-53; Acts 1:9-11.

8. M. Hengel, *Studies in the Gospel of Mark,* trans. J. Bowden (London: SCM Press, 1985), 167-69. On the dating of the longer ending, see J. Kelhoffer, *Miracle and Mission: The Authentication of Missionaries and Their Message in the Longer Ending of Mark* (Tübingen: Mohr/Siebeck, 2000), 169-244.

9. In the longer ending of Mark there are certain references to texts from Matthew, Luke, and John, and possible references or allusions to texts from Acts, Colossians, 1 Timothy, Hebrews, and James.

10. See again Hengel, *Studies in the Gospel of Mark,* 72; and Kelhoffer, *Miracle and Mission,* 15. The latter argues that "the decision by the LE's [longer ending's] author that the end of Mark was deficient [was] only possible at a time when the four Gospels had been *collected and compared with one another*" (author's emphasis).

11. For example, Metzger, *TCGNT,* 125: "In view of the inconcinnities between

stylistic arguments are not conclusive in this instance since the longer ending makes no attempt to conform to Mark's vocabulary, style, and theology. The concern of the longer ending is with content rather than style, that is, to rectify the omission of a resurrection appearance of Jesus in Mark. This has been accomplished by adding a resurrection harmony composed of texts from the other three Gospels. Since Mark's lack of a resurrection appearance is unique among the Gospels (and this includes the apocryphal Gospels and those from Nag Hammadi), and since we do not possess an extant text similar to the longer ending, it may be that vv. 9-20 were composed especially with the problem of Mark's ending in mind.[12]

The chief remaining question concerns the original conclusion of the Gospel of Mark. There are two possibilities. One is that Mark concluded at 16:8. This is the position held by a majority of recent interpreters of Mark.[13] In this view, Mark intentionally leaves the conclusion "open-ended." For some scholars Mark has given enough clues in the body of the Gospel for readers to supply the resurrection account themselves.[14] For others the inconclusive ending halts readers in their presumption to preempt the conclusion of the story, forcing them to unconventional responses.[15] For others the sober ending demands readers to ponder the cross and discipleship rather than taking refuge in enthusiasm and triumphalism.[16] Still others suggest that since Jesus' "original Jewish disciples didn't get the message," the risen Jesus is to be found in a Gentile gospel for Gentile readers.[17] In these and similar interpretations, the final word of "fear" in v. 8 leaves readers, like the women, in a state requiring a response of faith. A resurrection announcement as opposed to a resurrection appearance is sufficient, in this view, because for

---

verses 1-8 and 9-20, it is unlikely that the long ending was composed *ad hoc* to fill an obvious gap; it is more likely that the section was excerpted from another document." For further discussion favoring the existence of a preexisting document, see Swete, *The Gospel According to St Mark*, 399.

12. For a discussion of the entire issue and a conclusion in favor of the latter view, see J. Kelhoffer, *Miracle and Mission*, 158-69.

13. For a survey of positions favoring an original ending at 16:8, see J. F. Williams, "Literary Approaches to the End of Mark's Gospel," *JETS* 42 (1999): 21-35.

14. J. L. Magness, *Sense and Absence: Structure and Suspension in the Ending of Mark's Gospel*, SBLSS (Atlanta: Scholars Press, 1986), 14: "Mark affirms and communicates a resurrection and [a] post-resurrection reunion without narrating them."

15. For example, M. Trainor, "The Women, the Empty Tomb, and *That* Final Verse," *BibToday* 34 (1996): 177-82.

16. So R. W. Swanson, "'They Said Nothing,'" *Currents in Theology and Mission* 20 (1993): 471-78.

17. So W. R. Telford, *Mark*, NTG (Sheffield: Sheffield Academic Press, 1997), 149.

Mark faith is elicited by hearing rather than by sight. The conclusion to the Gospel of Mark must be supplied, in other words, by each reader's response of faith.

The chief argument in favor of this view is that our earliest and most reliable manuscripts end the Gospel at 16:8. This is a strong argument, and it is held by excellent scholars. In my judgment, however, the argument is not persuasive. The suggestion that Mark left the Gospel "open ended" owes more to modern literary theory, and particularly to reader-response theory,[18] than to the nature of ancient texts, which with very few exceptions show a dogged proclivity to state conclusions, not suggest them.

Several important arguments can be adduced in favor of the view that 16:8 was not the original, or intended, ending of Mark.[19] First and perhaps most important, it is hard to imagine a Gospel that begins with a bold, resounding announcement of divine Sonship (1:1) ending on a note of fear and panic (16:8). The purpose of the centurion's confession in 15:39 is to bring Mark's readers to a confession of faith, whereas a conclusion at 16:8 leaves them in bewilderment. It has often been rightly observed that v. 8 seems to break off in mid-sentence, and this is more apparent in Greek, where the final word is a conjunction (Gk. *ephobounto gar*; "for they were afraid"). Although Greek sentences very occasionally ended in *gar* ("for"), there are only three known examples of Greek books ending in this way.[20] Given the vast Greek literary corpus, which consists of more than sixty million words, it is scarcely compelling evidence to cite three documents ending with *gar* as a precedent for Mark's ending. At any rate, Mark does not end sentences with *gar*, nor does any of the four canonical Evangelists, and this leads us to assume that the sentence is either broken off or incomplete.

Considering the centrality of Jesus in the Gospel of Mark, and especially the promise of his appearance to the disciples in Galilee (14:28; 16:7), it seems incongruous for Mark to conclude with a resurrection an-

18. The inexplicable ending at 16:8 inevitably leads to convoluted attempts to explain it; e.g., A. Lincoln, "The Promise and the Failure: Mark 16:7, 8," *JBL* 108 [1989]: 295-96: "So the argument has been that vv. 7, 8 provide a closure in which the reader discovers that one set of expectations produced by the preceding plot has been reversed but that, on the review that this provokes, there is a coherence with another consistent pattern of plot which gives an explanation for the initial shock."

19. See T. W. Manson, *The Servant-Messiah: A Study of the Public Ministry of Jesus* (Cambridge: Cambridge University Press, 1953), 93-99.

20. Only in Plotinus's *Ennead* (32.5), Musonius Rufus's *Tractatus XII*, and Plato, *Protagoras* 328c; see Lincoln, "The Promise and the Failure: Mark 16:7, 8," *JBL* 108 (1989): 284; P. W. van der Horst, "Can a Book End with *gar*? A Note on Mark 16:8," *JTS* 23 (1972): 121-24.

nouncement rather than with a resurrection appearance. The expectation of a resurrection appearance is further anticipated by the three passion predictions, each of which ends in a resurrection announcement (8:31; 9:31; 10:34), as well as by the example of Elijah in 9:9-13. Again, Mark's Gospel generally conforms to the skeleton of the *kērygma,* an early preaching outline of the life, death, and resurrection of Jesus. It is worth questioning why a Gospel otherwise faithful to the *kērygma* would depart from it at the crucial point of the resurrection when the other Gospels and Paul (1 Cor 15:3-8) include resurrection appearances as indispensable keystones of the *kērygma.*

The abnormality of Mark's ending is made even more apparent when we compare the Gospel of Mark with the plethora of Gospel-like literature from both the NT Apocrypha and Nag Hammadi. Although the Gospel genre varies considerably in these two bodies of literature, all the documents that purport to deal with the life of Jesus include appearances or words of Jesus, or both, to the disciples following the resurrection.[21] The only exceptions to this are *The Protevangelium of James* and *The Infancy Narrative of Thomas,* which contain only apocryphal legends of Jesus' youth; the *Gospel of Truth* and the *Gospel of the Egyptians,* which do not focus on either the words or deeds of the historical Jesus; and the *Gospel of Thomas,* which contains only supposed sayings of Jesus, but no deeds. Even the *Gospel of Peter,* which breaks off with the fear of the women as does Mark 16:8, contains resurrection appearances of Jesus prior to that event. An ending of the Gospel of Mark at 16:8 is thus not only an aberration among the canonical Gospels but also among the diverse and fluid Gospel genres of the early centuries of Christianity.

One must further consider what effect the fear and bewilderment at 16:8 would have had on Mark's Roman readership as it grappled with faith in the midst of persecution. Would an "open ending" at 16:8 or the promised resurrection appearance of Jesus to the disciples better achieve Mark's purpose of presenting Jesus as God's Son? I think not, nor would an open ending be much encouragement to Mark's readers facing the savagery of Nero's persecution. Finally, as was suggested above, the rather existential interpretation of each reader supplying his conclusion by a decision of faith is more suited to modern sensibilities than to ancient literary canons. If such were Mark's purpose, the dogged appendices in vv. 9-20 are surely artless testimony that he failed in his intent. It

---

21. So *Gospel of the Nazarenes, Gospel of the Hebrews, Gospel of Philip, Gospel of Peter, Acts of Pilate, Epistula Apostolorum, Apocryphon of James, 2 Apocalypse of James, Epistle of Peter to Philip, Gospel of Mani, Gospel of Nicodemus,* and the *Questions of Bartimaeus.* In *Thomas the Contender, Dialogue of the Savior,* and the *Gospel of Mary* the tractate consists of a dialogue of the risen Savior with the disciples.

was the custom in antiquity to conclude books with a resolution of major conflicts, not to leave them unresolved.

There is thus considerable reason to doubt that 16:8 was ever the intended conclusion to the Gospel of Mark. My own judgment is that it probably was not. What might have happened to the original ending we shall probably never know. The most plausible suggestion is that it was lost due to wear-and-tear on the last leaf of a codex.[22] Or perhaps Mark was interrupted or died before completing it. The latter suggestion is a distinct possibility if Mark composed his Gospel, as we suspect, in the mid-sixties of the first century. It would not be surprising if Mark's name were among the martyrs of Nero's reign.[23]

How Mark may have ended the Gospel is, of course, unknown, but one tantalizing piece of evidence allows us to make a brief and modest attempt at a suggested ending. We have noted throughout the commentary that Matthew frequently follows Mark quite closely. That is particularly true of Mark 16:6-8, where the report of the women at the tomb in Matt 28:5-8 parallels Mark nearly verbatim. On the basis of this parallelism it seems plausible to suggest that Mark originally ended more or less like Matthew 28, with the exception of the report of the guards at the tomb in 28:11-15.[24] Two pieces of evidence undergird this suggestion. First, Mark leads readers to expect an appearance of Jesus to the disciples in Galilee (14:28; 16:7), just as Matthew reports in 28:9-10. Second, we have noted that the authority (Gk. *exousia*) of Jesus is one of Mark's signature motifs for Jesus' nature and bearing. Every Markan episode of Jesus' filial authority as the Son of God is reproduced in Matthew.[25] The only place where Matthew includes a reference to Jesus' *exousia* that is *not* found in Mark is in the parting commandment of the resurrected Christ that "all

22. We have examples of other ancient codices missing either first or last leaves. The *Muratorian Canon,* which begins with the last line describing the Gospel of Mark, is missing (at least) the first page. Likewise, the final leaf of Mark in Codex Washington (W) contains a puncture hole and a tattered upper corner; and the final leaf of Mark in Codex Beza (D) is written in a different hand, evidently added later to compensate for a lost final leaf.

23. Adolf Schlatter suggests further possible reasons for an incomplete ending: a hindrance that interrupted Mark's work; persecution; the necessity of flight; a pressing call to another work, leaving the uncompleted Gospel in the hands of fellow believers; or possibly that Mark intended a sequel, as did Luke in Acts (*Die Evangelien nach Markus und Lukas,* 151-52).

24. The report of the guard at the tomb (Matt 28:11-15) is a Matthean addition corresponding to Matt 27:62-66. A variant of the view I propose was suggested by A. Farrer, *St. Matthew and St. Mark* (London: Dacre Press, 1954), 144-59.

25. Mark 1:22//Matt 7:29; Mark 1:27//Matt none; Mark 2:10//Matt 9:6; Mark 11:28//Matt 21:23; Mark 11:29//Matt 21:24; Mark 11:33//Matt 21:27. Matthew does not reproduce Mark's second reference to Jesus' *exousia* ("authority") in Matt 1:27, however.

authority (Gk. *exousia*) in heaven on earth has been given to me" (Matt 28:18). It seems plausible to suggest that Matthew also gleaned this reference to Jesus' authority from the original ending of Mark. Thus, two things Mark has led us to expect in a resurrection narrative — an appearance of Jesus to the disciples in Galilee and a transferal of his authority to the disciples — constitute the essence of Matthew's ending in 28:9-10 and 16-20. Those seven verses have as good a claim as any to being the substance of Mark's original ending.

AN EARLY CHRISTIAN RESURRECTION MOSAIC (16:9-20)

The secondary ending is constructed around the theme of calling the disciples from unbelief (vv. 11, 13, 14 [2x], and 16) to belief (vv. 16, 17). In a general way, it parallels the story of the calling of Thomas from unbelief to belief in John 20:24-29. The secondary ending can be divided into four parts: a resurrection appearance to Mary Magdalene (vv. 9-11), an appearance to two travelers (vv. 12-13), an appearance to the eleven (vv. 14-18), and the ascension (vv. 19-20).

9-11 In all four Gospels, Mary Magdalene's name is found among the first witnesses of the resurrection. Although 16:9-11 come from a later time, they indicate that in the memory of the church Mary was counted not only as the first witness to the resurrection of Jesus but also as the first herald of the resurrection to the church. The first person to proclaim the resurrection testimony upon which saving faith derives (1 Cor 15:14) is a woman.[26] The reference to her being exorcised of seven demons in v. 9 comes from Luke 8:2; her report to the mournful disciples in v. 10 reflects John 20:14, 18 (so, too, the *Gospel of Peter* 26); and the disciples' disbelief reflects Luke 24:11. V. 10 records that the grief of Peter (14:72) has now overtaken the entire apostolic company, although, as the following verse indicates, it is not a grief that leads to faith. The disciples, whose later proclamations of the gospel were met with disbelief, cannot have forgotten their own disbelief of the same message from Mary, and hopefully were more understanding and effective heralds because of it.

12-13 The second appearance to the two travelers presupposes and summarizes the story of the resurrected Jesus appearing to two trav-

26. On the significance of the resurrection witness of the women for the mission and life of the church, see L. Schottroff, "Die mutigen Frauen aus Galiläa und der Auferstehungsglaube," *Diakonia* 20 (1989): 221-26.

elers on their way to Emmaus (Luke 24:13-35). The note about appearing "in a different form" explains why Jesus was not recognized in the original story (Luke 24:16) and is thus the earliest extant commentary on the latter passage. The disciples, however, were no more receptive of the report of these messengers than they were of the report of the women in v. 11.

14 In 16:14 Jesus himself appears to the disciples. The longer ending presents three testimonies to the disbelieving disciples in an order of increasing authority: one female witness (vv. 9-11), two male witnesses (vv. 12-13; the Greek pronouns are masculine), and the resurrected Jesus himself (v. 14). Jesus upbraids the disciples for their disbelief of the earlier witnesses, whose testimony he confirms. V. 14 assures readers that the testimony of the church to the resurrection of Jesus is, in fact, the testimony of the risen Lord himself.

The appearance of Jesus to the eleven in 16:14-18 looks like an early Christian catechism on the resurrection. After v. 14 (which reflects Luke 24:36-38 and John 20:19), the Latin church father Jerome (d. 420) included the following conversation between Jesus and the eleven:

> And [the disciples] made excuse, saying: "This age of iniquity and unbelief is under Satan who, through unclean spirits, does not permit the true power of God to be apprehended. Therefore, reveal your righteousness, now."

To which Jesus responded:

> "The limit of the years of the authority of Satan has been fulfilled, but other terrible things are drawing near. And on behalf of those who have sinned, I was delivered to death, in order that they might turn to the truth and sin no more, in order that they might inherit the spiritual and incorruptible glory which in heaven consists in righteousness."[27]

This later addition to the secondary ending is instructive because it reveals that even after Jesus' victorious resurrection from the dead the early church continued to wrestle with the problems of sin and temptation, and that it blamed its disobedience, at least in part, on the devil.

15 16:15 recalls the Great Commission of Matt 28:19.[28] If our hypothetical reconstruction of the original ending of Mark is correct, some form of this staying was likely part of Mark's original ending. The Greek word for "preach" is in the aorist tense, implying proclamation of the

---

27. *Against Pelagius* 2.15; cited in *NTApoc* 1.248-49.
28. Mark 16:15-18 is quoted verbatim in the third(?)-century *Acts of Pilate*.

gospel for an appointed time rather than indefinitely. Of significance in the saying is that the gospel is of universal import: the disciples are sent "into all the world," and the gospel is ordained for "all creation" (Col 1:23). The "all" (Gk. *hapanta*) is emphatic. The gospel is not intended for Jews apart from Gentiles, or Gentiles apart from Jews, but for *all* creation.

16 The formulaic wording of 16:16 reflects the missionary preaching and outreach of the early church that faith and baptism guarantee salvation (Acts 2:38; 8:36-38; 16:30-33). The separation of the saved from the damned in v. 16 recalls John 3:18 and 20:23. The gospel is thus not only of universal significance but also of eternal consequence for salvation or damnation.

17-18 According to these verses the consequence of salvation is not only assurance and peace but also signs of power, including expulsion of demons, speaking in tongues, healing the ill by the laying on of hands, and preservation from harm in handling snakes and drinking poison. Many of these phenomena appear elsewhere in the NT as miraculous activities, but they are now regarded as signs of faith. Thus, the casting out of demons is found in 6:7 (also Matt 10:1, 8; Luke 10:17; Acts 8:7; 16:18; 19:6); speaking in tongues in 1 Cor 12:10, 30; 14:2, 18; surviving poisonous snakebites in Acts 28:3-6 and Luke 10:19; and healing, particularly by the laying on of hands, in 6:13; Matt 9:18; Acts 3:1-7; 14:8-10; Jas 5:14).

Most questionable of these charismatic signs are the handling of snakes and drinking of poison, whose purpose is not serving the community but their own spectacle. The word for "snake" is the Greek word *ophis*, which means a generic snake or serpent, although not necessarily poisonous, as does the Greek word *echidna* (so Acts 28:3-6).[29] Given the reference to poisonous drink immediately following, one would have expected the latter word in v. 18. The word *ophis* is, however, the same word used in Genesis 3 (LXX) of the temptation of the serpent. This raises the question whether the image of "picking up snakes in their hands" cannot be understood metaphorically, that is, that in the age of salvation the curse of the serpent has been overcome.

With regard to drinking "deadly poison," there is no account of drinking poison with immunity in the NT, although Eusebius (*Hist. Eccl.* 3.39.9) speaks of Justus Barsabas (the disciple not chosen in Acts 1:23), who drank poison without harm. It appears, however, that in the late first century a cult related to poisonous drugs was exerting at least some influ-

---

29. Apart from the story in Acts 28:3-6, the only story of a poisonous bite known to me is from the Jewish Tosefta, which embellishes an earlier story of Rabbi Hanina ben Dosa, who, while praying, was bitten by a poisonous lizard. The pious rabbi suffered no harm, although the lizard was found dead at its hole (*t. Ber.* 3:20).

ence in Jewish-Christian circles. This is made apparent by a reference in Josephus's *Antiquities,* which he completed in A.D. 93-94, that "no one should possess magic potions (Gk. *pharmakoi*) or poison (Gk. *thanasimos*) nor any of the harmful things made by Israelites for harmful purposes" (*Ant.* 4.279). Josephus is ostensibly commenting on Exod 22:18 (which makes no mention of "poison" [Gk. *thanasimos*]). The addition of the term, however, suggests that it was a concern in Josephus's day at the close of the first century. Writing about the same time or shortly later, Ignatius warns the Trallians to refrain from foods that heretics foist on the gullible, mixed like deadly poisons (Gk. *thanasimos*) with honeyed wine, which the ignorant drink blissfully to their death (Ign. *Trall.* 6). The text of the passage is partially corrupted, and it is not entirely clear whether Ignatius intends the poisonous drink to be taken literally or symbolically of the unnamed heresy. But even a symbolic meaning indicates that the practice of poisonous drink was known to his readers. Mark's word for poisonous drink in v. 18 is the same Greek word *(thanasimos)* used by Josephus and Ignatius. The reference to drinking deadly poison without harm thus signals to Mark's readers that those who believe and follow the gospel are guaranteed immunity from heresy, including heretical potions to drink.

16:17-18 are often viewed by Western Christians, in particular, with skepticism or dismissed as superstitions unworthy of genuine faith. Certainly the misuse of such signs is unworthy of genuine Christian faith. The proper purpose of signs, however, is articulated in v. 20, that God "confirms his word by the signs that accompany it." The witness of the early church was accompanied by signs and portents that corroborated the missionary gospel. The same is true in many parts of the world today, especially where concomitant signs help convince non-Christians that the Christian God is more real and powerful than local religious beliefs and cults. The reference to signs in vv. 17-18 is a reminder that the Christian faith is not an idea or philosophy, but a way of life that is empowered by God's Spirit. Schlatter's perspective on charismatic signs is helpful: "The vocation of those who proclaim Jesus far exceeds what is visible to the eye; they bring to the world heavenly gifts. These gifts are also undergirded by signs that reveal to everyone that God's protection, help, and gifts are present with his messengers."[30]

19-20 The ascension in 16:19 combines Acts 1:9-11 with Ps 110:1, and may also recall 1 Tim 3:16 and Matt 26:64. The subsequent mission of the disciples reflects Acts 14:3 and Heb 2:3-4 and once again emphasizes the universal appeal and import of the gospel that was "preached everywhere." Thus, the longer ending of Mark presents us with a resurrection

---

30. Schlatter, *Die Evangelien nach Markus und Lukas,* 154.

harmony from an amalgam of NT stories — some of which reflect liturgical and missionary interests — as a later-first-century or early-second-century attempt to compensate for what was regarded as a defective ending of Mark in 16:8.

The ending of the Gospel of Mark invariably disappoints readers — the shorter ending at 16:8 because it is inconclusive, and the longer ending of 16:9-20 because it is incongruous. Three general and concluding comments may perhaps be made in light of this. First, the longer ending testifies that quite early — and certainly no later than the first decades of the second century — the tradition that would later comprise the NT was already known and appealed to as a foundation for preaching, mission, and catechesis (see n. 9 above). When confronted by an ending of Mark that was considered defective, the church appealed to this evangelical tradition, both written and preached, to rectify the deficiency. The longer ending of Mark thus testifies that the early church, as Paul would exhort the Romans, was itself formed by the gospel and tradition it proclaimed (Rom 6:17). The same relationship between evangelical tradition and community of faith defines the life of the church today, which when appealed to in the face of problems and deficiencies can complete the story of our narrative journey as well.

Second, the longer ending of Mark reminds us that the NT is a product of the church as a believing, confessing, and worshiping community. Apart from the witness of the church in the Gospels and epistles we would not know the gospel of Jesus Christ. The longer ending of Mark, despite its incongruities, testifies that the Gospels are not bloodless historical records but the story of the incarnate God that was handed down by communities of faith in trust that the God who transformed their lives would, through their witness, do the same for their readers.

Finally, the inconclusive ending at 16:8 does not jeopardize the early Christian testimony to the resurrection of Jesus from the dead. Although Mark is most likely the earliest of the Gospels, it is not the earliest resurrection account. Writing in 1 Corinthians 15 about a decade before Mark, Paul gives the earliest record of the event that stands at the center of history and gives meaning to it. The announcement of the angel in Mark 16:6 presupposes the resurrection.[31] Despite differences about particular events surrounding the resurrection, the early church presents a single and univocal witness *that* God raised Jesus from the dead. The church declared to its age, as it does to ours, that "'you will see him, just as he told you'" (16:7).

31. See Magness, *Sense and Absence: Structure and Suspension in the Ending of Mark's Gospel*, 14: "Mark affirms and communicates a resurrection and [a] post-resurrection reunion without narrating them."

APPENDIX

The Secret Gospel of Mark

In 1958 Morton Smith announced that he had discovered at the monastery of Mar Saba in the Kidron Valley between Jerusalem and the Dead Sea the extract of a letter written by Clement of Alexandria. According to Smith, the letter in question was found on the final blank pages of the works of Ignatius of Antioch, the latter of which was copied in 1646. The handwriting of the extract is written in a different hand from the works of Ignatius and has been dated to c. 1750, about a century later than the Ignatius works of which it is a part. In the letter published by Smith, Clement replies to a certain Theodore who has been troubled by the teachings of the gnostic Carpocratians, a sect that indulges in illicit sexual practices based upon a variant version of the Gospel of Mark. Clement refutes the Carpocratians by citing two passages from the suspect version of Mark, which Morton Smith calls the *Secret Gospel of Mark*. The first passage allegedly appears after Mark 10:34, and reads:

> And they came to Bethany. And there was a woman there, whose brother was dead. And she came and fell down before Jesus and said to him: Son of David, have mercy on me. But the disciples rebuked her. And in anger Jesus went away with her into the garden where the tomb was; and immediately a loud voice was heard from the tomb; and Jesus went forward and rolled away the stone from the door of the tomb. And immediately he went in where the young man was, stretched out his hand and raised him up, grasping him by the hand. But the young man looked upon him and loved him, and began to entreat him that he might remain with him. And when they had gone out from the tomb, they went into the young man's house; for he was rich. And after six days Jesus commissioned him; and in the evening the young man came

509

to him, clothed only in a linen cloth upon his naked body. And he remained with him that night; for Jesus was teaching him the mysteries of the Kingdom of God. And from there he went away and returned to the other bank of the Jordan.

At this point, according to Smith, Clement says that the text of *Secret Mark* continues with the canonical text of Mark 10:35-45 and the request of James and John to sit on each side of Jesus in glory. But after 10:46, Clement quotes a second passage from *Secret Mark:*

He came to Jericho. And there were there the sisters of the young man whom Jesus loved and his mother and Salome, and Jesus did not receive them.

At this point the text breaks off and the extract produced by Smith ends.[1]

What can be said to this strange extract discovered under equally strange circumstances? Of first importance is that to date the extract has been seen by no Western scholar except for Smith.[2] Until the original is available for scientific examination by other scholars, a conclusive judgment cannot be rendered. Nevertheless, the material evidence of the extract supplied suggests strongly that *Secret Mark* is a later apocryphon and was original neither to canonical Mark nor to the earliest manuscripts of Mark.

Attempts to argue that the *Secret Gospel of Mark* is older than canonical Mark[3] are clearly mistaken, and have been judged so by a majority of scholars.[4] The most important reason for this judgment is that the material alleged by Smith appears in no other church father and in none of the thousands of ancient manuscript witnesses to the Gospel of Mark. Furthermore,

1. See M. Smith, *Clement of Alexandria and a Secret Gospel of Mark* (Cambridge, MA: Harvard University Press, 1973); the same author, *The Secret Gospel: The Discovery and Interpretation of the Secret Gospel According to Mark* (New York: Harper & Row, 1973).

2. In January 1999 I visited Mar Saba and requested to see the manuscript under question. I was told by the monks that the manuscript had been transferred from Mar Saba to the Greek Orthodox Patriarchate in Jerusalem. In Jerusalem my request to see the manuscript was forestalled by the monks, and I have since heard that its whereabouts are unknown.

3. So H. Koester, *Ancient Christian Gospels: Their History and Development* (Philadelphia: Trinity Press International; London: SCM Press, 1992), 293-303; J. M. Robinson, "Jesus: From Easter to Valentinus (or to the Apostles' Creed)," *JBL* 101 (1982): 5-37; J. D. Crossan, *Four Other Gospels: Shadows on the Contours of Canon* (Minneapolis: Winston, 1985).

4. See critiques in R. Gundry, *Mark*, 603-23; J. P. Meier, *A Marginal Jew: Rethinking the Historical Jesus* (New York: Doubleday, 1991), 120-23; J. Wenham, *Redating Matthew, Mark, & Luke* (Downers Grove: InterVarsity Press, 1992), 142-45; H. Merkel, "Appendix: the 'Secret Gospel' of Mark," *NTApoc* 1.106-9.

that *Secret Mark* is a later addition to canonical Mark is virtually proven by the fact that "they came to Bethany" is a glaring anachronism in the text of Mark since Jesus and the disciples have not yet come to Jericho (Mark 10:46), and Bethany lay beyond Jericho. Finally, the Carpocratians mentioned by Theodore to Clement did not arise until the mid-second century, that is, a full century after the composition of Mark. There can be little question that the extract produced by Smith considerably postdates Mark.

On the whole, so-called *Secret Mark* appears to be a forgery, although whether modern or ancient is difficult to say.[5] At least two observations suggest a modern forgery, perhaps by Smith himself. One is that Smith was of the opinion that Jesus was a magician, and the *Secret Gospel of Mark* produced by him is suspiciously suggestive of such a view.[6] A second observation is that the text of *Secret Mark* displays none of the errors typical of manuscript transmission, leading some scholars to conjecture that the Smith extract may be an original composition.[7] Nevertheless, a forgery by Smith might be expected to produce a less fragmentary extract and one even more conducive to his views of Jesus as a magician. It thus may be that *Secret Mark* is an ancient forgery, typical of the additions and adulterations of the canonical Gospels that arose especially during the heyday of Gnosticism in the second century. The text is an obvious conflation of the story of the raising of Lazarus in John 11 with that of the rich ruler from Mark 10:17-22. The subject of the text is reminiscent of the esoteric themes and interests of the plethora of gnostic-related Gospels and documents familiar to us from Nag Hammadi and various NT Apocrypha. The stylizations of the extract exhibit a conscious attempt to ape Markan literary style.[8] The emphasis on the young man's nakedness and love for Jesus, which could suggest a homosexual encounter,[9] is in

5. See B. Metzger, *Reminiscences of an Octogenarian* (Peabody, MA: Hendrickson Publishers, 1997), 128-32.

6. M. Smith, *Jesus the Magician* (San Francisco: Harper & Row, 1978).

7. See C. E. Murgia, *Protocol of the 18th Colloquy of the Center for Hermeneutical Studies*, ed. W. Wuellner (Berkeley: The Center, 1976), 35-40.

8. Merkel, *NTApoc* 1.107, "In Mark itself the Marcan peculiarities of style are nowhere so piled up as in the 'secret Gospel.'" See also E. Best's review of E. J. Pyrke's *Redactional Style in the Marcan Gospel, JSNT* 4 (1979): 71-76.

9. Gundry, *Mark*, 621-23, correctly reminds us that the text does not explicitly mention homosexual relations (or esoteric baptismal practices related to them). In his view it also need not suggest them. According to Gundry, the young man who wears nothing but a linen cloth represents a model disciple who, in contrast to the rich man of 10:17, has sold all he has and follows Jesus to learn the mystery of the kingdom of God. Gundry's interpretation is a valiant attempt to rescue the extract from infamy, but it fails to take the sexual innuendoes of the story as seriously as they are intended. If Gundry were correct, we would expect Clement to commend the story rather than repudiate it.

further agreement with the sexual libertarianism attributed to the Carpocratians. In sum, the *Secret Gospel of Mark* looks to be a later pseudonym that has nothing to do with either Markan provenance or purposes.

Index of Modern Authors

514

INDEX OF MODERN AUTHORS

Index of Subjects

INDEX OF SUBJECTS

Index of Scripture References

Index of Extrabiblical Literature